The East European Gypsies

Regime Change, Marginality, and Ethnopolitics

This book is the first attempt by a social scientist to explain the age-old predicament of Gypsies (or Roma), Eastern Europe's largest ethnic minority, and their relationship to the region's states and societies. Professor Barany comparatively examines the Gypsies' socioeconomic and political marginality and policies toward them through seven centuries and in seven East European states. He illuminates the reasons why the Roma have consistently occupied the bottom of social, economic, and political hierarchies regardless of historical period or geographic location. Barany argues that the current nostalgia of many Gypsies for the socialist period is easy to understand, given the disastrous effect of the postcommunist socioeconomic transformation on the Roma's conditions over the last decade. He explains the impact of Gypsy political mobilization and the activities of international organizations and NGOs on government policies. This pioneering multidisciplinary work will engage political scientists, sociologists, and historians as well as students of ethnic and racial studies.

Zoltan Barany, Associate Professor of Government at the University of Texas, has written extensively on East European politics, military affairs, and ethnic issues. His most recent book, as co-editor, is *Russian Politics: Challenges of Democratization* (Cambridge University Press, 2001).

The East European Gypsies

Regime Change, Marginality, and Ethnopolitics

ZOLTAN BARANY

University of Texas

CAMBRIDGE
UNIVERSITY PRESS

PUBLISHED BY THE PRESS SYNDICATE OF THE UNIVERSITY OF CAMBRIDGE
The Pitt Building, Trumpington Street, Cambridge, United Kingdom

CAMBRIDGE UNIVERSITY PRESS
The Edinburgh Building, Cambridge CB2 2RU, UK
40 West 20th Street, New York, NY 10011-4211, USA
10 Stamford Road, Oakleigh, VIC 3166, Australia
Ruiz de Alarcón 13, 28014 Madrid, Spain
Dock House, The Waterfront, Cape Town 8001, South Africa

http://www.cambridge.org

First published 2002

Printed in the United States of America

Typeface Sabon 10/12 pt.   *System* QuarkXPress [BTS]

A catalog record for this book is available from the British Library.

Library of Congress Cataloging in Publication Data

Barany, Zoltan D.
The East European gypsies: regime change, marginality, and ethnopolitics/Zoltan Barany.
p. cm.
Includes bibliographical references and index.
ISBN 0-521-80410-8 – ISBN 0-521-00910-3 (pbk.)
1. Gypsies – Europe, Eastern – History.   I. Title.
DX145 .B37   2001   2001025594
947'.00491497–dc21

ISBN   0 521 80410 8   hardback
ISBN   0 521 00910 3   paperback

In memory of my father
Bárány István
1930–2000

Contents

Acknowledgments

The decade of the 1990s fairly accurately corresponds to the period in which I devoted a substantial part of my professional life to learning, thinking, and writing about the Roma (Gypsies), ethnic politics, and marginality. This book is the culmination of this endeavor. I have gathered many debts and am happy to acknowledge them.

My interest in the Gypsies and ethnopolitics was sparked by a coincidence. I spent the momentous year of August 1989–August 1990 at the Research Institute of Radio Free Europe in Munich. In the spring of 1990, the Institute's principal publication, the weekly *Report on Eastern Europe*, featured a series of articles analyzing the conditions of the Roma in East European states. Ronald Linden, then Director of Research at RFE, happened to ask me to write the article on the Hungarian Gypsies. As I began to research the article, I became enthralled by its subject; this initial curiosity turned into a long-term interest in marginal groups and ethnopolitics. Thus Ron, albeit inadvertently, is responsible for getting me started.

A couple of years later Sam Nolutshungu of the University of Rochester invited me to join the Social Science Research Council's Working Group on the Security of Marginal Populations. Through that project I came in contact with a number of scholars whose comments and writings made me reevaluate my assumptions and rethink my arguments. But I am most grateful to Sam, who, with unfailing kindness and munificence, encouraged me to think about some of the theoretical issues in this volume. His sudden passing at the age of fifty-two in the summer of 1997 was an enormous loss to many.

From the time of my arrival in my department in 1991, I have been blessed with a friend and colleague who has been interested in my work and generous with his ideas, advice, and time. Gary P. Freeman has patiently – and often on short notice – read versions of my papers, chapters, and grant proposals through the years. His questions, criticisms, and insights have improved the quality of my work. Conversations with Gary about the key issues addressed in this book have prompted me to sort out my thoughts and look at my subject from different perspectives. This book would be very different without his contribution.

In recent years the Roma have become a fashionable subject of research. Regrettably, a number of academics and activists have jealously guarded their sources, blocked access to their internet newsgroups, and made my work more difficult than it ought to have been. Happily, there are many more counterexamples. I could not possibly list all those who assisted my research in a variety of ways, but I want to mention by name Adam Bartosz, András Bíró, Nicoleta Bițu, Nora Costache, Lena Cruceru, Savelina Danova, Nicolae Gheorghe, Alex Grigor'ev-Roinishvili, Ildikó Haraszti, Karel Holomek, Milena Hübschmannová, Dan Ionescu, Vera Klopčič, Elena Marushiakova, Zdeněk Matějka, Marta Miklušáková, Andrzej Mirga, Mirjana Najcevska, Klára Orgov-ánová, Scott Parrish, Dimitrina Petrova, Livia Plaks, Vesselin Popov, Edit Rauh, Michael Shafir, Emilija Simoska, Ilona Tomova, Luan Troxel, Michal Vašečka, Ivan Veselý, Klára Veselá-Samková, and Cătălin and Elena Zamfir. I am especially grateful to three old friends, Dimitrije Buzarovski, Iván Völgyes, and Larry Watts, who went out of their way to ensure that my visits to Macedonia, Hungary, and Romania were productive. Thanks are also due to the politicians, experts, activists, and ordinary people who were willing to be interviewed for this book. Naturally, all of them are acknowledged in the notes, with the exception of those requesting anonymity. The transcripts of these interviews are in my possession.

Nancy Bermeo, Ulf Brunnbauer, Valerie Bunce, Henry Carey, Daniel Chirot, David Crowe, William Crowther, Sheila Fitzpatrick, Ewa Hauser, Donald Horowitz, John Lampe, Paulis Lazda, Andrew Ludanyi, Neil MacFarlane, John Mueller, Jiří Pehe, Duncan Perry, Konstanze Plett, Robin Alison Remington, Albrecht Schnabel, Anna Seleny, Emilija Simoska, and Sharon Wolchik invited me to speak and/or write on the issues addressed here and thereby contributed to the development of the book's themes. I am particularly grateful to a number of colleagues who took the time to read this work as it evolved. Most of all, I thank Daniel Chirot, who, along with Gary Freeman, critically read the entire manuscript and offered continuous encouragement. I am grateful also to David Crowe, Milton Esman, Donald Horowitz, Rasma Karklins, and Livia Plaks, who commented on one or more chapters. The anonymous reviewers of Cambridge University Press provided useful suggestions as well, most of which found their way into the book. I may not have agreed with all of my readers' recommendations, but I do hope that the finished product does not disappoint them.

Throughout the past decade my father, István Bárány, spent many hours and forints hunting down, purchasing, and mailing source materials and coordinating my travel plans. To the denouement of his long illness he maintained a keen interest in the way the manuscript was taking shape, and it saddens me beyond words that he did not live to see its publication. Though they had little direct impact on this book, my family and friends – Lotti Bárány, Marion Fellenzer, Steven and Judith Franden, Valentine and Zsuzsi Lovekin, Mac McIntyre, Lisa Montoya, Doug Phelan, and Joan Yamini – have offered encouragement and/or diversion. I am most grateful to my wife, Patricia Maclachlan, for her support of my work even when it took me away from home for months at a time. She patiently put up with my "Hungarian moods" and kept her good cheer throughout, which is all the more remarkable as she was completing her own book on the Japanese consumer movement while I was working on mine.

The extensive field work that a project of this scope requires could not have been carried out without substantial financial support. I am most indebted to the Ford Foundation, from whom I received Area Studies Research Fellowships in 1995 and 1996 that helped defray the costs of research trips. The Foundation also awarded me a major grant that freed me from administrative and teaching responsibilities for two semesters and funded five months of field research in 1999. I am especially grateful to my program officer, Julius Ihonvbere, for his support and for judging this a project that "had to be done." Thanks are also due to the International Research and Exchanges Board for underwriting research trips in 1994, 1995, and 1996. My home institution was yet another source of financial support. A Faculty Research Assignment in the fall of 1997 enabled me to do field research and work on the book for a semester. Additional travel funds came from the Department of Government and from the Center for Russian, East European, and Eurasian Studies.

Finally, I want to thank my editor, Lewis Bateman, for his interest in this project from the moment I first mentioned it to him and for the care and professionalism with which he has overseen the manuscript's metamorphosis into book form.

Introduction

Since the fall of communism, the Gypsies (or Roma[1]) have become a frequent topic of the news in Eastern Europe and elsewhere. Indeed, European and North American newspapers have featured more articles about them over the past decade than ever before. Regular readers may well have become weary with the coverage, however, since it rarely departs from the routine portrayal of the astonishing poverty of this or that Gypsy settlement and the anti-Roma biases of East European societies. These images are often reinforced by chance encounters between foreign visitors and at times aggressive Gypsy beggars at the railway stations and tourist spots of East European cities – encounters that seldom leave pleasant memories behind in the minds of the uninitiated. Travelers who were familiar with the region during the communist era may be especially perturbed by the fact that the level of Gypsy destitution has actually *increased* over the past decade. What happened to the Roma? And why is it that they seem to exist perennially on the margins of societies?

THE UNIQUENESS OF ROMANI MARGINALITY

All ethnic groups, nationalities, or peoples (whatever one's preferred terminology might be) are, by definition, intrinsically unique because their particular cultures, languages, traditions, and historical experiences distinguish them from others. The Roma in many ways comprise a most unusual ethnic group not only in Eastern Europe but also in the larger,

---

[1] Some Gypsies prefer to be referred to as "Roma" (which means "men" in the Romani language), the singular of which is "Rom," and the adjective is "Romani." Others would rather be called "Gypsies" in the official language of their country of residence. See, for instance, *The Romanies in Central and Eastern Europe: Illusions and Reality* (Princeton: Project on Ethnic Relations, 1992), 13; Viliam Figusch, ed., *Roma People in Slovakia and in Europe* (Bratislava: Information and Documentation Centre on the Council of Europe, 1995), 43; and *Magyar Nemzet*, 1 February 1997. For stylistic reasons I will use "Roma" and "Gypsies" interchangeably.

1

global sense. The uniqueness of the Gypsies lies in the fact that they are a transnational, non-territorially based people who do not have a "home state" to provide a haven or extend protection to them. There are, to be sure, other ethnic groups who share some of these attributes. The Kurds, for instance, are transnational and without a motherland; they do, however, have distinct territorial affiliations. The Jews are also transnational and were non-territorially based until the birth of the modern state of Israel. The situation of the Roma is truly exceptional, a fact that in many respects explains their marginality as well as their relationship to the states and societies of Europe and beyond.

Marginality – the condition of being subordinated to or excluded by others – is the central theme in the Romani experience. Indeed, Romani marginality is far more comprehensive than that of the Jews, Kurds, or other traditionally excluded or disadvantaged groups. Since their arrival in Europe about seven centuries ago, the Gypsies have been politically, socially, culturally, and economically marginalized by the dominant populations of the region. The magnitude of their exclusion has varied at different times and in different states. Still, although political systems and their policies toward the Roma have changed, these variations have had little apparent effect on Gypsy marginality. The seemingly interminable nature of negative social attitudes (to a large extent based on differences in customs, values, behavior, appearance, etc.) to some degree explains the continual marginal status of Eastern Europe's Romani population. At the same time, however, the Roma themselves have cultivated their marginal status by maintaining their distinctive identity and resisting recurrent attempts at assimilation and integration by dominant groups in the area.

In sum, the Gypsies have no homeland, the size of their communities in every state is proportionately small, they do not control any significant resources, and they have little political power. As a result, states have had few compelling incentives to pay close attention to them. If, like Karl Deutsch, one envisions ethnic stratification as a "layer cake," the Roma have been firmly ensconced at the bottom tier throughout their seven-century presence in Europe.[2] Fredrik Barth in his influential work categorized them as a pariah group subjected to widespread and intense societal rejection.[3] In other words, the Gypsies are not just outsiders but despised outsiders.

The collapse of communism in Eastern Europe created numerous expectations for a wide variety of interest groups. The subsequent

---

[2] Karl W. Deutsch, *Nationalism and Its Alternatives* (New York: Knopf, 1969), 45.
[3] Fredrik Barth, "Introduction," in Barth, ed., *Ethnic Groups and Boundaries* (Boston: Allen & Unwin, 1970), 31.

transition and consolidation of democratic rule fulfilled many of those expectations by establishing pluralist political systems and market economies. The shift to democracy also changed the status of individuals from subjects under authoritarian rule to citizens with substantive constitutional rights. Marginal groups that had not been officially recognized (e.g., homosexuals) but had just begun to emerge as a result of the postcommunist transition processes (e.g., the unemployed and the homeless), along with a number of ethnic minorities that had suffered political exclusion in the past, could now seize the opportunity to participate in politics by establishing organizations to articulate and represent their interests.

Like other peripheral ethnic minorities, the Gypsies have embarked on the process of political mobilization, but in other respects their overall conditions have dramatically deteriorated since 1989. A wide array of socioeconomic statistics convincingly demonstrates their miserable conditions in areas ranging from education to employment and from healthcare to housing. Clearly, the period of democratization has signified more hardship and calamity for the Roma than for any other social group.

THE OBJECTIVES OF THIS STUDY

This book proceeds from a single, overwhelming, and troubling fact: For seven centuries, East European Gypsies have languished at the bottom of social, economic, and political hierarchies. Over those seven centuries, empires, authoritarian, and totalitarian states have come and gone, but in all of them the Roma occupied the lowest rung on the social scale. Contrary to expectations, moreover, the currently unfolding democratic era has brought no fundamental shifts in their conditions aside from providing the opportunity for political activism. Explaining this puzzling phenomenon is the primary objective of this book. In essence, I seek to find satisfactory answers to six broad questions as they pertain to the Roma and their relationship to states and societies:

1. Do different regime types – that is, imperial, authoritarian, or democratic political systems – denote different minority policies; that is, do policies change as regimes change?
2. Do individual states of the same regime type pursue different minority policies?
3. How has the Gypsies' status changed over time, and to what extent do state policies have an impact on that status?
4. Are the changes in their conditions related to specific state policies; and, if so, how much difference do those policies make?

5. To what extent have the Gypsies succeeded in changing their own conditions and influencing state policy?
6. How can the marginality of the Roma be alleviated?

I approach these questions via two competing arguments. The first is that the regime type (in other words, the category or class of political system) is the primary determinant of the minority policies of particular states. States within the same regime type, or so the argument goes, should pursue similar policies toward minorities; and when regimes change, those policies will change as well. This explanation privileges structural–institutional variables having to do with the organization and logic of state power and suggests that extraneous factors (such as the size of the given minority or the attitudes of the state's population toward the marginal group) are not important determinants of policy. Thus, democratic states – based on their presumed commitment to civil, human, and minority rights – would be expected to pursue enlightened minority policies, while authoritarian states – given their customary neglect of such rights – would do the opposite.

$$\text{regime type} \xrightarrow{\text{determines}} \text{state policy}$$
$$\xrightarrow{\text{explains}} \text{change in the conditions of the marginal group}$$

I examine four regime types that prevailed in Eastern Europe over the last several centuries: imperial, authoritarian (signifying the interwar period and World War II), state-socialist, and democratic.

The alternative argument assumes that a given regime or political system type does not conclusively explain either the minority policies of the state or a marginal group's conditions. Rather, the specific circumstances of individual countries (such as historical and cultural attitudes toward minorities, economic resources, the size and organizational strength of ethnic minorities and their mobilization experiences, and the state's sensitivity to international criticism) are largely responsible for the policies that states pursue. According to this line of argument, minority policies will vary across states of the same regime type, while variations may persist through regime upheavals or systemic changes. Thus,

$$\text{country-specific conditions} \xrightarrow{\text{determine}} \text{state policy}$$
$$\xrightarrow{\text{explains}} \text{change in the marginal group's condition}$$

I have selected a diverse group of East European states as a testing ground and source of illustration for my arguments. The empirical analysis begins with an examination of two imperial states: the Habsburg and the Ottoman Empires. The balance of the analysis focuses on seven countries – Bulgaria, the Czech Republic, Hungary, Macedonia, Poland,

Romania, and Slovakia – in their guises as authoritarian, state-socialist, and democratic political regimes.

The comparative approach I employ takes advantage of two important empirical attributes: (1) the presence of Romani communities in each of the above-mentioned states; and (2) the fact that all seven countries underwent several regime changes over the past century; moreover, they did so simultaneously. These conditions provide an appealing opportunity to investigate the fate of the Gypsies under different regime types and during periods of regime change. The Romani experience, in turn, enables us to develop theoretically grounded generalizations about the effects of regime change and the policies pursued by individual states on the status of marginal groups, ethnic mobilization, and ethnopolitics.

The study of the Roma has been dominated by anthropologists, ethnologists, historians, and linguists who utilize the conceptual and theoretical arsenals of their disciplines. A large part of the existing body of literature on the Gypsies has engaged such issues as their historical origins and early migrations in Europe, the linguistic peculiarities of the Romani language, and the cultural and ethnographic attributes of diverse Gypsy groups. Since this book is not concerned with these issues, they are discussed only to the extent that they directly impact upon my central questions. I contend that bringing the conceptual and theoretical tools of political science into this field is rewarded by new insights and findings.

As is clear from the structure of the book the attention to individual regime types is distributed unevenly in the analysis. The imperial and authoritarian eras in the empirical analysis are used primarily for the purposes of offering a background to illustrate the arguments and test the propositions of the theoretical chapters. The state-socialist period is scrutinized more extensively, given its chronological proximity and overall relevance to the postcommunist period. The unfolding period of democratic transition and consolidation receives more consideration allowing for more in-depth comparative analysis.

RESEARCH DESIGN

The purpose of this study is to compare the social, economic, and political dimensions of Gypsy marginality in four regime types and in seven states. This type of inquiry necessitates a two-dimensional research design: a longitudinal (diachronic) dimension, which compares several cases across time

Regime A → Regime B → Regime C → Regime D
Imperial   Authoritarian State-Socialist Democratic

and a cross-sectional (synchronic) dimension, which contrasts two to seven states belonging to the same regime type:

Empires: Ottoman and Habsburg Empires – 1500–1918

Authoritarian states: Bulgaria, Hungary, Poland, Romania, Yugoslavia (especially Macedonia), and Czechoslovakia, the only state in this period which was a functioning democracy – 1918–45

Socialist states: Bulgaria, Czechoslovakia, Hungary, Poland, Romania, Yugoslavia (especially Macedonia) – 1945–89

Emerging democracies: Bulgaria, Czech Republic, Hungary, Poland, Romania, Slovakia, Macedonia – 1989–2000

Although there are Romani communities in every East European state, my selection of these countries is justified by their peaceful conditions and the availability of indispensable resources, both of which have permitted on-site research throughout the last decade. In addition, the Gypsy communities in these states are sufficiently diverse (in terms of their proportion of the overall population, the number of distinct Romani subgroups, as well as differences in their marginal conditions) to provide examples of nearly the entire universe of the Gypsy experience in the region. Although I did not conduct field research in Albania and – aside from Macedonia and Slovenia – in the republics of the former Yugoslavia, whenever possible I attempted to include them in the analysis in order to make the coverage more comprehensive.

This book is the result of a decade's worth of studying, thinking, and writing about its central theoretical and empirical issues. I traveled to Eastern (and Western) Europe for the purposes of library and archival work and field research about a dozen times, including lengthy sojourns in 1991, 1994, 1996, 1997, and 1999. I have made extended research trips to every one of the seven states in my inquiry at least three times (and twice to Slovenia). I interviewed hundreds of scholars, politicians, Gypsy activists, ordinary Roma, and non-Roma concerning the questions addressed in this book. Finally, I did my best to gather a representative sample of public opinion and political, social, and economic data.

The Data Problem

It is important to note that information on the Roma is often unreliable. As I discovered first hand, Romani leaders, activists, and state officials frequently present a skewed picture of reality. The objectivity of much of the recent avalanche of "situation reports" published by human rights organizations is just as notoriously suspect (given their stake in portraying the Gypsies' situation as worse than it actually is and their often one-sided methods of data collection[4]) as are the documents published by politicians who benefit from making conditions appear rosier than they actually are.

Whether the issue is the proportion of the Gypsy population that fell victim to the Nazis, the size of the Romani community in a given state or region, or the number of Gypsies fleeing Eastern Europe for the West, one cannot but be baffled by the truly incredible statistical inaccuracies and disparities one perennially encounters when dealing with Gypsy affairs. Many authors consider themselves free from the conventions of scholarly referencing and documentation and are prone to treat even unreliable data as gospel. A case in point is a recent popular book on the Roma by the journalist, Isabel Fonseca.[5] Take the example of contemporary Romania's Gypsy community. Fonseca categorically asserts that their proportion of the total population is 15% and, just as unequivocally, that 2.5 million Roma live in Romania.[6] One can only wonder where these figures come from. According to the 1992 census, Romania's population was 22,760,449, 15% of which would be roughly 3.4 million, not 2.5 million. In the census, however, only 409,723 Roma declared themselves as such.[7] Although the census figure is certainly too low, just as misleading are Fonseca's numbers. Cătălin and Elena Zamfir, on the other hand, sociologists whose estimates are based on rigorous demographic and statistical research, convey a much more accurate picture of reality. According to them, in 1993 Romania's Gypsy population was approximately 1,010,000, or 4.6% of the total population, a figure they revised to 1.5 million in 1999 in response to methodological improvements and the growth of the Romani community.[8]

Since 1989, East European sociologists and statisticians have rushed to embrace often lucrative opportunities to conduct random surveys of the Romani population. Unfortunately, however, the survey method rarely yields reliable results. Critics note that while Gypsies usually accept payment for their cooperation, those who resent the intrusion, misunderstand the questions, or wish to conform with the expectations

---

[4] These issues will be discussed in detail in Chapters 5 and 7.

[5] Isabel Fonseca, *Bury Me Standing: The Gypsies and Their Journey* (New York: Knopf, 1995).

[6] See ibid., 146 and 278 for the 15% figure *and* 179 where she mentions 2.5 million.

[7] See Dorel Abraham, Ilie Badescu, and Septimiu Chelcea, *Interethnic Relations in Romania: Sociological Diagnosis and Evaluation of Tendencies* (Cluj-Napoca: Editura Carpatica, 1995), 49.

[8] See Elena Zamfir and Cătălin Zamfir, *Țigani: Între ignorare și îngrijorare* (Bucharest: Editura Alternative, 1993), 206, and author's interview with the Zamfirs (Bucharest, 3 November 1999).

of the surveyor have been known to provide misleading information.[9] Even surveyors of Romani descent have trouble acquiring credible data because they are sometimes perceived by their subjects as belonging to the "wrong" Romani group. In the words of Vesselin Popov, an eminent Bulgarian ethnographer, representative samples work as well with the Roma as they would with Amazonian Indians; their cultures, world-views, and relationships to the surrounding populations are too different to permit accurate sampling.[10] Although I do draw on some of the more reliable statistical data to illustrate my points in this study, the reader should be aware of their inherent limitations.

Given the dearth of credible analytical, descriptive, or statistical information about the Roma, I have come to rely on in-depth interviews as an important research tool, keeping in mind William Lockwood's observation that "Half a millennium of persecution has given Romani culture ample opportunity to develop means to evade and mislead both the census taker and the would-be Gypsy scholar."[11] Since obtaining dependable information is often unusually difficult, judicious evaluation of the data culled from interviews and personal observation must suffice. In any event, I have interviewed most of the reputable Gypsy and non-Gypsy experts across Eastern Europe and I am confident of the accuracy of the information they provided.

WHO ARE THE GYPSIES? SOME MARKERS OF ROMANI IDENTITY

Though this book is not about Romani culture and traditions, some discussion of these issues is necessary if the reader is to appreciate the Gypsies' predicament. Even a cursory attempt to explain who the Roma are, where they come from, and how they perceive themselves shatters much of the conventional wisdom about this community. Soon after their appearance in Europe about 700 years ago, observers, travelers, and scholars began to write about the Roma, speculating about their origins and describing their customs and behavior. The bulk of this early corpus is made up of superficial portrayals of Gypsy customs and amounts to little more than embellished recapitulations of oral Romani history. Some chroniclers accepted the Gypsies' own accounts of their origins and lineage uncritically, thereby contributing to the spread of such myths as

---

[9] Interviews with Nicolae Gheorghe, Special Advisor to Contact Point on Roma and Sinti Issues of the Organization for Security and Cooperation in Europe (Warsaw, 16 August 1999) and with Elena Marushiakova and Vesselin Popov, eminent Bulgarian ethnographers (Sofia, 13 November 1999).

[10] Interview with Popov (Sofia, 13 November 1999).

[11] William G. Lockwood, review of *The Gypsies of Eastern Europe*, ed. by David Crowe and John Kolsti in *Contemporary Sociology*, 22:1 (January 1993), 50.

that the Roma had descended from Pharaonic peoples and hailed from Egypt (hence the term "Gypsies," which is derived from "Egyptians"). Although research on the Roma often remains vulnerable to charges of subjectivism, poor methodology, and low academic standards even today, by the mid-nineteenth century serious scholarly work had begun to unearth the facts about Gypsy culture, language, traditions, and history.[12]

Homeland, Migration, and Nomadism

The Romani (or Romanes) language was the only "book" the Gypsies carried with them during their travels; it represents their collective memory and provides linguists and historians with important clues about their origins and centuries-long journey to Europe.[13] Linguistic evidence suggests that the Gypsies originated in the Punjab region of north-western India. They left perhaps as early as in the sixth century A.D., probably due to repeated incursions by Islamic warriors. In contrast to the Jews, who maintained identification with their homeland through their religion and traditions, the vast majority of Roma today have no idea where their ancestors come from; and those who do know will tend to reject the homeland idea altogether.[14] The long journey of the Roma to Europe led them through parts of Persia, Armenia, and Byzantium. A Constantinoplean source mentions the Gypsies as early as 1068.[15] In all likelihood, they reached Europe sometime in the thirteenth century; chroniclers commented on their communities in early fourteenth-century Crete (1322). Romani groups moved north from the southern Balkans to present-day Bulgaria, Romania, and Yugoslavia, some settling along the way, others migrating further to Central Europe and beyond. Scattered Romani groups arrived in contemporary East-Central Europe from the mid to late fourteenth century (Transylvania and Hungary), and

---

[12] A fine work on the evolution of Romani studies is Wim Willems, *In Search of the True Gypsy: From Enlightenment to Final Solution* (London: Frank Cass, 1997). For useful bibliographies see József Vekerdi, *A magyarországi cigány kutatások története* (Debrecen: Kossuth Lajos Tudományegyetem, 1982); Reimer Gronemeyer, *Zigeuner in Osteuropa: Eine Bibliographie zu den Ländern Polen, Tschechoslowakei und Ungarn* (München: K. G. Saur, 1983); and Diane Tong, *A Multidisciplinary Annotated Bibliography* (New York: Garland, 1995).

[13] See Nebojša Bato Tomašević and Rajko Djurić, *Gypsies of the World: A Journey Into the Hidden World of Gypsy Life and Culture* (New York: Henry Holt & Co., 1988).

[14] Nicolae Gheorghe in *The Romanies in Central and Eastern Europe*, 11. See also, for instance, János Báthory, "A cigányság a politika tükrében," *Világosság*, 29 (August–September 1988): 617; and Arne B. Mann, "The Formation of the Ethnic Identity of the Romany in Slovakia," in Jana Plichtová, ed., *Minorities in Politics* (Bratislava: Czechoslovak Committee of the European Cultural Foundation, 1992), 262.

[15] Scott L. Malcolmson, "Wanderer Fantasy," *The New Republic*, 27 May 1996, 38.

throughout the fifteenth century (Slovakia and the Czech Lands), and they reached Poland in the early sixteenth century. Their remarkable mobility during these early years is highlighted by Gypsy sightings in places as varied as Bavaria (1418), Paris (1421), Bologna (1422), Barcelona (1425), England (1501), Denmark (1505), and Norway (1544).[16]

This is not to suggest that once they reached these destinations the Roma settled down permanently. To the contrary, their movements continued in response to political and economic circumstances. The Polska Roma, for instance, arrived in Poland during the second half of the sixteenth century to escape persecution in Germany. After the unsuccessful Hungarian War of Independence (1848–9) a large group of Hungarian Roma fearing increased suppression made their way toward Western Europe. Many Roma enslaved in the principalities of Moldavia and Wallachia (in today's Romania) tried to migrate to parts of the Ottoman Empire where discrimination was far less rampant. Following the emancipation of slaves in 1855–6, an estimated 200,000 Gypsies migrated to Hungary, Bulgaria, Russia, and Western Europe.[17] Fear of persecution and the opening of economic opportunities have continued to spur substantial Romani migration, most recently following the demise of European socialism.

One of the most common misconceptions about the Roma is that they are an intrinsically nomadic people. The historical record indicates, however, that they did not always adopt the nomadic way of life by choice. By all accounts, the Roma left India only because of war and economic hardship.[18] It is important to note, moreover, that when the Gypsies arrived in Europe, the continent had not experienced a major influx of immigrants for centuries. Still, settling was easier in the Balkans than in Western Europe owing to the relatively sparse population and the uneven concentration of state power. Even in Eastern Europe, the intrusion of dark-skinned Roma with their curious customs and strange clothing consequently evoked a negative response from the indigenous populations. Persistent persecution combined with the lack of available land for cultivation and other economic opportunities compelled the Gypsies to move on in search of more favorable conditions. The fact that one of the key policy objectives in medieval Central and Western Europe

---

[16] Gerard Chaliand and Jean-Pierre Rageau, *The Penguin Atlas of Diasporas* (New York: Penguin Books, 1997), 96.

[17] Franz Remmel, *Die Roma Rumäniens: Volk ohne Hinterland* (Vienna: Picus, 1993), 43.

[18] See, for instance, Donald Kenrick and Grattan Puxon, *The Destiny of Europe's Gypsies* (New York: Basic Books, 1972), 14; and S. S. Shashi, *Roma: The Gypsy World* (Delhi: Sundeep Prakashan, 1990).

was to expel, banish, or deport the Roma provides yet another clue to their peripatetic ways. It is also worth noting that at the time of the Roma's arrival in Western Europe, commercial nomadism was hardly extraordinary; the Gypsies did not, in other words, have a monopoly on the migratory way of life.[19]

In other parts of the continent, the Roma were confronted with incentives to abandon their nomadic ways. In the Balkans, for example, many Gypsies who had achieved important economic positions had settled down; those who were less fortunate, meanwhile, were often coerced into a more sedentary mode by the policies of princes and kings. From the sixteenth century on – including the socialist period in Eastern Europe – forced settlement was the main state policy toward the Roma. This strategy succeeded to a large extent. The majority of East European Roma – especially in Hungary, Romania, Slovakia, and the former Yugoslavia – have been sedentary for centuries. "The nomadic class is [sic] now become very rare, if not extinct, in Hungary" wrote the British traveler, Richard Bright, in 1818.[20] Indeed, an 1893 census revealed that less than 2% of the Gypsies in Slovakia were nomadic.[21] In contrast, several West European states chose to expel or deport Gypsies to their colonies rather than sedentarize them, while a larger proportion of those who remained maintained their nomadic or semi-nomadic ways (traveling seasonally from fair to fair, harvest to harvest) far longer than in the East.[22]

One of the most important cleavages within the Romani population has been between peripatetic and sedentary groups. Although the diversity of Romani groups precludes easy generalization, many scholars nevertheless argue that nomadic, as opposed to sedentary, Gypsies are more likely to be self-employed, to maintain occupational and cognitive flexibility, and to sustain Romani traditions, customs, and language. They are also less likely to be proficient in the language of the dominant group of their adopted region than are settled Roma, and they are far less susceptible to state control – hence the persistent attempts to

[19] Thomas A. Acton, "Unity in Diversity," *Cigány Néprajzi Tanulmányok*, 2 (Budapest: Mikszáth Kiadó, 1994), 81.

[20] Richard Bright, *Travels from Vienna Through Lower Hungary with Some Remarks on the State of Vienna During the Congress in the Year 1814* (Edinburgh: Archibald Constable, 1818), 527.

[21] Willy Guy, "Ways of Looking at Roms: The Case of Czechoslovakia," in Farnham Rehfisch, ed., *Gypsies, Tinkers and Other Travellers* (London: Academic Press, 1975), 211.

[22] Still, most of the Sinti in Germany settled well over a century ago and in Spain sedentarism was largely accomplished by 1746. Angus Fraser, *The Gypsies* (Oxford: Blackwell, 1995 [2nd ed.]), 164.

sedentarize them.[23] Settled Gypsies, on the other hand, especially those surrounded by *gadje* (non-Roma), are more vulnerable to dominant group influence and state power, and they are more easily marginalized. As might be expected under such circumstances, nomadic and sedentary Gypsies often view each other with suspicion.

Diversity and Traditions

Another common misunderstanding about the Gypsies is that they are a homogeneous people. To the contrary, they are an extremely diverse ethnic group that can be differentiated according to lifestyle (peripatetic or sedentary), tribal affiliation, occupation, language, religion, and country of residence. In the former Yugoslavia alone there are some twenty principal Romani tribes, many of which can be further subdivided.[24] In Macedonia the vast majority of Gypsies do speak Romani (or Romanes), but in Hungary 80% of them speak only Hungarian. While a detailed discussion of the various facets of Romani diversity is beyond the scope of this book, I shall note some general points that are relevant to this study.

In several East European states, such as Bulgaria and Romania, tribal identity – primarily rooted in the traditional economic activity of a group – remains a significant bond. Suffice it to say that even in relatively small regions a dozen distinctive tribes may coexist. As the pressures of industrialization and modernization required increasing economic specialization, many groups emerged within a specific tribal context that in time acquired their own distinctive identities. In Romania, for instance, the spoon makers (*Lingurari*), makers of wooden bowls (*Kopanari*), gold washers (*Aurari*), gold miners (*Baiesi*), coal miners (*Caravlahi*), and spindle makers (*Vretenari*) were originally members of the *Rudari*, a large tribe of wood carvers and gold-washers.[25]

In Hungary and Slovakia, countries that were the destination of several different waves of Romani migration, the approximate time of arrival and the region of origin are more important distinguishing characteristics than in the Balkans. The *Olah* (or Vlach) Roma made their way from Romania to Hungary in the late nineteenth century, and many still speak related dialects of Vlach Romani. The *Beash* have been in

---

[23] On this issue, see Andrzej Mirga, "Roma Territorial Behaviour and State Policy: The Case of the Socialist Countries of East Europe," in Michael J. Casimir and Aparna Rao, eds., *Mobility and Territoriality: Social and Spatial Boundaries among Foragers, Fishers, Pastoralists, and Peripatetics* (Oxford: Berg, 1992), 259–78, especially 260.

[24] Fraser, *The Gypsies*, 293.

[25] Abraham et al., *Interethnic Relations in Romania*, 417–34. See also Gábor Havas, "A cigány közösségek történeti típusairól," *Kultúra és közösség*, no. 4 (August 1989): 3–21.

Hungary for over 200 years and generally speak an archaic form of Romanian in addition to Hungarian. The vast majority of the Gypsy population in Hungary, however, belongs to the long-sedentary and only Hungarian-speaking *Romungro* (Hungarian Roma) group. Similarly, over 90% of Gypsies in Slovakia are Hungarian or Slovak Roma who settled there in the sixteenth to eighteenth centuries. The rest of the Gypsy population (Vlach Roma) reached Slovakia in the second half of the nineteenth century and are assumed to be the descendants of liberated slaves in the Romanian principalities of Moldavia and Wallachia. All of these distinctive populations may be subdivided into numerous groups based on their ancestral occupation.[26]

Changes in social and economic conditions have allowed an ever smaller number of Gypsies to adhere to the exacting standards of ancient Romani culture and traditions. Thus, it is important to note that most East European Gypsies no longer live by the old customs; they are not, as it were, "orthodox Roma." Although there are several exceptions to this rule, the Vlach Gypsies, who are widely distributed in Eastern Europe and beyond, tend to be the most steadfast preservers of Gypsiness or Gypsihood (*Romanipe*). Among the most important features of *Romanipe* are the "dread of the clinging or haunting presence of the disembodied spirit of someone who has died" and the fear of contamination expressed by the purity code.[27] When strictly observed, the purity code determines interaction between male and female Roma on the one hand, and Gypsies and the *gadje* on the other. Certain types of association or communication between these sides are undesirable because they are deemed unclean (*marime*). These taboos primarily concern coming into contact with menstruating women, the lower body in general and particularly genitalia, and close interaction with non-Gypsies. For instance, food prepared by a menstruating woman is viewed as polluted and thus polluting, as are mixed marriages and using the same washbowl to cleanse one's face and feet.[28] Few things are considered more disastrous to an observant Rom than going to prison where protracted living with the *gadje* in close quarters is unavoidable.

Romani communities are often assumed to exist in a state of carefree anarchy devoid of rules in which potential disagreements are settled by

---

[26] For information on the different groups in Bosnia, see Noel Malcolm, *Bosnia: A Short History* (New York: New York University Press, 1994), 116–17; in Slovenia, see Imre Szilágyi, "A romák Szlovéniában," *Regio*, 7:2 (1996): 81–95.

[27] See Fraser, *The Gypsies*, 242–4.

[28] For an excellent examination of Romani traditions, see Judith Okeley, *The Traveller Gypsy* (Cambridge: Cambridge University Press, 1983). For a more general exposition on the same phenomena see Mary Douglas, *Purity and Danger: An Analysis of the Concepts of Pollution and Taboo* (London: ARK, 1983).

fists and knives. In fact, traditional Gypsy society is governed by widely accepted and long-standing regulations and structures.[29] The most important forums of conflict resolution are the *divano* and the *kris*. The former is essentially an informal mediation procedure to rectify minor grievances. The ultimate source of law and order in a traditional Romani community is the *kris*, which solves criminal, moral, civil, and religious disputes through the participation of judges. In contrast with the *divano*, the rulings of the *kris* are final and binding. The Romani saying, "it is better to resolve our differences as friends at the *divano* than as enemies at the *kris*" aptly elucidates the difference between the two. The judges are always male, as are the traditional leaders (*baro*, *voivode*, etc.) of Romani communities. The selection of leaders is usually based on earned respect, but they also need to be of relatively advanced age (i.e., they should have grandchildren) and to command authority in their bailiwick.

Although traditional Romani society is male-dominated, females prior to and after childbearing age associate with their male counterparts more freely. Women are expected to obey men and are ordinarily held in higher esteem the more children they bear. The vast majority of Romani marriages are endogamous. Marrying across tribes is unusual; many Gypsies intermarry with other Romani groups more rarely than with *gadje*.[30] Most Roma are intensely spiritual, although their religiosity may not be manifested by attending church services. In general, they have adopted the religions of the dominant groups in their environment. Thus, most Roma in Croatia are Roman Catholic, in Bosnia they are Muslim, and in Serbia they are Orthodox Christians.

Perhaps the most important factor of Gypsiness is the division of the world into *Roma* and *gadje*, a division that has contributed to the absence of large-scale integration of Roma into mainstream societies. The survival of the Gypsies and their identity in a hostile European environment for seven centuries is a remarkable feat. Adaptability to different surroundings is often mentioned as the most important attribute of the Romani people. They had to be able to exploit whatever opportunities offered themselves, to find the odd loophole and unoccupied niche in this or that social and economic environment, and to integrate elements of foreign cultures and traditions and still remain unmistakably different. Their fragmented social structure and peripatetic ways served

---

[29] See, for instance, Walter Otto Weyrauch and Maureen Anne Bell, "Autonomous Lawmaking: The Case of the 'Gypsies'," *The Yale Law Journal*, 103:2 (November 1993): 323–99.

[30] Péter Szuhay, "Arson on Gypsy Row," *The Hungarian Quarterly*, 36:138 (Winter 1995): 84.

them well because scattered groups of nomadic people were more difficult to persecute – let alone exterminate – than compact communities of settled populations.

Yet it seems that many Gypsy communities lost this widely recognized adaptability in the fast-changing socioeconomic conditions of twentieth-century Eastern Europe. Over the last hundred years the rift between Roma and their neighbors substantially deepened due to their own inability to compete in new labor markets and to the discriminatory attitudes and policies of dominant groups. Even in the lesser developed parts of Europe, socioeconomic realities no longer permit eking out a living from occupations practiced on the go. In this context, the Gypsies could only retain their identity through rigorous self-segregation, which is increasingly difficult to maintain in the modern era.[31] They truly have become pariahs precisely because of their lost capacity to change with the times.

Because of the diversity of the Gypsy people, it is unclear what *the* Romani identity is – especially since many Gypsies do not consider themselves members of a cohesive ethnic group but instead identify with the subgroup to which they belong. Fundamentally, however, all European Roma share to some extent the same origins, language, culture, and historical experiences.[32] In this book, except in cases when subgroup disparities strongly affect my analysis, I shall employ this generalized concept of the Roma.

THE STRUCTURE OF THE BOOK

This book is divided into three parts. The first two chapters are primarily concerned with theoretical questions and conceptual issues pertaining to minorities in general and the Roma in particular. Chapter 1 deals with the state and its policies toward marginal ethnic groups, investigates the relative impact of regime type and country-specific conditions on marginality, and briefly examines the divergent minority policies of imperial, authoritarian, communist, and democratic systems. The empirical chapters (particularly Chapters 3, 4, 8, and 9) in the second and third parts of the book constitute the tests for the two competing propositions.

Chapter 2 approaches the problem of state–ethnic group relations from the perspective of marginality and ethnic mobilization. I begin by

[31] See Raymond Pearson, *National Minorities in Eastern Europe, 1848–1945* (London: Macmillan, 1983), 19.

[32] On this issue, see Konrad J. Huber, "The Roma: Group Identity, Political Activism, and Policy Response in Post-1989 Europe," *Helsinki Monitor: Quarterly on Security and Cooperation in Europe*, 4, no. 3 (1993): 45.

examining the multidimensional concept of marginality and its utiliza-
tion by social scientists. I then explore the roots and causes of the marginal condition, factors that both alleviate and aggravate it, and the
relevance of this complex concept to the study of politics. By exploring
the evolving political relationship between marginal and dominant
groups, I show that the political dimension of marginality can change
through time and space regardless of corresponding changes in social and
economic marginality. I conclude the section on marginality by briefly
explaining why the concept serves as an extraordinary lens through
which to understand the Romani experience.

The second part of Chapter 2 is concerned with the more practical
question of what marginal ethnic groups themselves can do to alleviate
their predicament. Here I seek to make generalizations about the prerequisites for successful ethnic mobilization, paying particular attention
to such "conventional" resources as effective leadership, group cohesion
and identity, action programs, and alliances with other groups in the
polity. I also explore the significance of the ethnic group's relationship to the state and the policies of various state institutions toward the
ethnic group.

At this juncture, the book's focus shifts to the analysis of Romani marginality and its links to East European states and societies. My primary
concern throughout the balance of the book is to apply the theoretical
themes and concepts outlined in the first two chapters in an effort to
better understand Romani marginality in all its manifestations. Chapter
3, for example, is a longitudinal study of the variations in Romani
marginality (political, social, economic) across pre-1945 regime types
(imperial, authoritarian, totalitarian) and the impact of regime changes
on those variations.

Chapter 4 is devoted to a concise analysis of Gypsy marginality under
state-socialism. Just as in other areas, policies toward the Roma were
remarkably consistent across states during the Stalinist period but began
to diverge from the late 1950s in response to both local conditions and
varying levels of ideological orthodoxy. The chapter therefore focuses on
cross-national differences in social policies toward the Roma and their
impact on the various aspects of Gypsy marginality.

The third part of the book seeks to answer two broad questions. First,
how did the recent transitions to democracy affect Gypsy socioeconomic
and political marginality? Second, to what extent have the Roma's
conditions and political mobilization efforts, as well as the activities of
international and nongovernmental organizations, influenced state policy
toward the Roma during the democratic era?

The focus of Chapter 5 is changes in the socioeconomic marginality
of the Roma caused by the political and economic changes of the 1990s.

I argue that for the vast majority of the Gypsies, the regime change has signified deteriorating employment opportunities, falling living standards, and increasing social isolation and animosity. The reasons for this outcome are largely attributable to the economic changes which accompanied the political transition, intensifying anti-Gypsy prejudices, and the Roma's own attitudes toward education and employment.

Chapter 6 concentrates on the one positive result of postcommunist regime change for the Roma: the diminution of their *political* marginality. To some extent, the Gypsies have succeeded in formulating and developing a distinct ethnic identity and establishing cultural and political organizations. At the same time, however, they have been unable to fulfill their potential due to their lack of organizational experience, cultural factors, and a number of related problems such as internal divisiveness, poor leadership, ill-conceived political programs, and openly hostile attitudes toward state authorities. This chapter traces the development of Gypsy political mobilization and analyzes the reasons for its successes and failures across the region.

As an indirect result of the relaxation of border restrictions in the region, Eastern Europe's "Gypsy problem" has effectively become a European problem as tens of thousands of East European Roma travel to Western Europe in search of more attractive economic opportunities and to escape discrimination. Chapter 7 explores this phenomenon and West European policies to combat it. I argue here that the Roma's marginal conditions remain largely unaffected by migration since West European governments and societies are just as inhospitable toward them as those they leave behind. The second portion of this chapter examines the activities and track record of Gypsy and non-Gypsy international organizations and foundations in their efforts to publicize the Roma's plight and to improve their conditions. I contend that by continually monitoring and relentlessly criticizing state policies, international organizations have done an invaluable service for the Roma given that most East European states – all eager to become members of Western international organizations – are quite sensitive to such censure.

In Chapter 8 the spotlight moves to the state as I comparatively analyze the seven East European governments' policies toward the Roma after 1989. First, I contrast political institutions (i.e., presidency, governments, legislatures, etc.) and their different attitudes toward the Gypsies and their plight. Second, I analyze the institutional structures that states have developed specifically to address the Gypsies' predicament. Finally, I briefly consider particular policy areas (e.g., constitutional and legal issues, education, etc.) and investigate the extent to which East European states committed themselves to substantively improve the Roma's conditions until the late 1990s. I argue that although some of these governments made considerable efforts to reduce the Gypsies socioeconomic marginality, they could have undoubtedly done much more. Moreover, positive state actions have been motivated not so much by Romani mobilization but by the continuous pressure of international organizations.

Chapter 9 is also concerned with state policy, but here the emphasis is on the comprehensive programs that five of the seven states have devised to facilitate Gypsy integration. I comparatively examine these programs and the problems regarding their implementation. In this chapter I contend that it is a mistake to substitute excuses (in order to justify watering down or postponing the implementation of their "Romani policies") to committed and long-term action. I argue that the Gypsies conditions will get worse if comprehensive policies designed to bring tangible improvement in them are not introduced now. These policies are going to pose a major financial burden on East European states and societies, but this burden is likely to be much larger if action is delayed. In the last part of this chapter I recommend some policy options that will likely contribute to and accelerate the Gypsies' societal integration. In a brief conclusion I evaluate the merits and demerits of the main arguments of this study and summarize my findings about the relationship between regimes, regime change, and the driving forces behind state policies toward minorities.

CAVEAT EMPTOR

Those who prefer a romanticized version of the Roma will be disappointed by this book. My purpose is to provide a realistic portrait of Eastern Europe's Gypsy communities and the nature of their interactions with states and societies as I understand them. Given the truly pitiful conditions in which the majority of the Roma live, those who study them can easily lose their objectivity and become de facto Gypsy activists.[33] This widespread phenomenon is neither surprising nor undesirable. I do find purportedly unbiased studies that overlook the fundamental principles of scholarly research and presentation quite disturbing, however. These "activist authors" may be motivated by a twisted sense of political correctness insofar as they overemphasize the injuries the Roma have indisputably suffered in the hands of prejudiced majorities while simultaneously ignoring the Gypsies' responsibility for their predicament

---

[33] My thoughts on these issues were elaborated in more detail in Zoltan Barany, "The Poverty of Gypsy Studies," *NewsNet: The Newsletter of the American Association for the Advancement of Slavic Studies*, 40:3 (May 2000): 1–4; and idem., "In Defense of Disciplined Scholarship: A Response," *NewsNet: Newsletter of the American Association for the Advancement of Slavic Studies*, 40:4 (November 2000): 9–12.

and belittling the efforts of states and organizations to assist them. My approach is that of a social scientist and not of a Romanologist or a Gypsy activist. András Bíró, one of the individuals who has done the most for the East European Roma, expressed the view I entirely concur with when he told an interviewer that "Personally I don't especially like Gypsies. Neither do I hate them. . . . What I dislike is when somebody has to suffer for what he is."[34]

I do not intend to trivialize the very real suffering of and discriminatory policies and popular attitudes toward the Roma in Eastern Europe and elsewhere. Indeed, these problems will be closely examined in this volume. At the same time, however, I think that in order to understand and rectify the Romani predicament it is important to ask those often taboo questions that are customarily ignored by Gypsy activists and Romanologists: To what degree are the Roma themselves responsible for their predicament? How can they help themselves emerge from their situation? What measures should we reasonably expect from state and society in their attempts to alleviate Romani marginality?

East European states and societies that want to be considered democratic must improve their policies and attitudes in order to help their Gypsy citizens transcend their marginal existence. At the same time, Romani communities themselves must make a greater effort to reduce their marginality – an effort that in some instances may involve a reappraisal of long-standing Romani traditions. They must candidly address the issue of their own responsibility for their problems and make a concerted effort to become part of the political and socioeconomic fabric of the societies in which they live. Needless to say, I do not suggest assimilation as an alternative; indeed I find it virtually inconceivable given Gypsy traditions, culture, and history. But I firmly believe that the only viable long-term strategy for the Roma in Eastern Europe and elsewhere is social, economic, and political *integration*.

---

[34] Gábor Kereszty and György Simó, "Helping Self-Help: Interview with András Bíró," *The Hungarian Quarterly*, 36:140 (Winter 1995): 75.

PART I

THE ANALYTICAL FRAMEWORK

1

Regimes, States, and Minorities

This chapter is concerned with issues that are essential to understanding the relationship between the state and marginal groups in general and the East European Roma in particular. The focus here is on the state, its different incarnations in various regime types (also referred to as political system types), and its policies toward minorities. The key theoretical issue in this section of the book is the dynamics of state policy toward marginal groups and ethnic minorities. Is state policy primarily driven by the nature of the regime type under which the individual state can be classified, or is there a set of country-specific variables that best solve this puzzle?

One of the main contentions of this book is that regime type provides useful guidelines to predict state minority policies because it demarcates the range of minority policies. Within a regime type, however, the spectrum of probable state minority policies is large enough to permit significant variation. Moreover, regime change – and especially the transition to democracy – does not necessarily entail either more enlightened minority policies or improved socioeconomic conditions for marginal groups. Particularly in the early stages of transition, democratizing regimes may not have much incentive to abandon the discriminatory policies of the *ancien régime*. Therefore, alternative explanations are necessary to better understand state–minority relations in general and the circumstances of the East European Gypsies in particular.

Even if the empirical evidence supports the competing assumption that state-specific conditions drive state policies toward minorities, this would not mean that regime type has no explanatory value. Rather, it would suggest that regime type sets merely the parameters within which state policies and attitudes may be expected to be found. Clearly, some regime types (e.g., unrestrained authoritarian systems) are more likely than others to abuse human and minority rights. The point is that one might reasonably presume that some democracies will be more tolerant than others just as some autocracies will be more repressive than their peers. Because regime type only suggests the range of policies, there might be considerable overlap between the minority policies of states classified under different regime types. For instance, the minority policies of a liberal socialist state, like Yugoslavia in the 1970s, might actually be very similar to or even more progressive than that of a conservative democratizing state like the Czech Republic in the mid-1990s. In a like vein, differences between the minority policies of states belonging to the same regime type (e.g., state-socialist Hungary and Romania in the 1980s) may be very substantial and may then be primarily explained by the specific contextual factors in individual states.

In sum, this chapter poses two general arguments. The first one contends that the regime type (i.e., imperial, authoritarian, democratic) is the primary determinant of the minority policies of particular states. The alternative argument holds that conditions unique to individual countries are largely responsible for the policies states pursue. My aim in this chapter is to elaborate on these arguments. The analytical chapters in the second and third parts of the book constitute the major empirical test for these propositions.

Before proceeding any further, it is necessary to clarify some of the key concepts of this chapter. States that share common fundamental organizing principles belong to the same *regime type*. For the purposes of this book I distinguish between imperial, authoritarian, state-socialist, and democratic regime types. A *state* "is a vertical structure of public authority" – in contrast with the *nation*, which is "essentially a horizontal network of trust and identity."[1] An *ethnic minority*, on the other hand, is a group with a common ethnic and cultural identity that exists as a subgroup of a larger society.[2] Although the following discussion is meant to be general, I will illustrate my points through examples culled mostly from Eastern Europe. I also want to be more precise about what I rate as "enlightened" or "tolerant" policies toward ethnic minorities in contrast to "repressive" ones. As I view them, enlightened or progressive policies target the extension of minority rights in areas such as culture, education, employment, housing, legal matters, and political participation. In order to be effective, such policies should also have a punitive component that serves as a powerful deterrent to potential discrimination. I consider state policies toward ethnic minorities "indiffer-

---

[1] Cynthia Enloe, "The Growth of the State and Ethnic Mobilization: the American Experience," *Ethnic and Racial Studies*, 4:2 (April 1981): 3–4.
[2] For a critical discussion of these concepts and definitions, see Walker Connor, "A Nation Is a Nation, Is a State, Is an Ethnic Group, is a . . .," *Ethnic and Racial Studies*, 1:4 (October 1978): 379–88.

ent" when they fail to endorse ethnic minority rights or there are inconsistencies between various policy areas (i.e., a state might pursue a progressive housing policy for ethnic minorities but might limit their voting rights), but they stop short of stifling them. I use "repressive" in a more narrow sense and regard policies as such when they actively suppress ethnic minority rights.

PART I. REGIMES AND MINORITIES

An exhaustive library research reveals that no systematic treatment of the relationship between regime type and minorities is available. The unspoken assumption is that states associated with certain regime types pursue more tolerant and enlightened policies, whereas states belonging to other regime types are usually more restrictive and repressive in their approach to marginal populations. In other words, particular regime types coincide with predictable state minority policies that affect the conditions of marginal populations.

This argument suggests that the characteristics of regimes have so strong an effect on state policies that they will explain changes in the conditions of ethnic groups. In different regime types the state may be expected to have dissimilar relations to and views of supportive and adversarial political forces, the prevailing economic system, and various segments of society. Regimes can also be distinguished according to whether or not they recognize and protect the rights of minorities, whether or not they support institutional–structural arrangements for the articulation of minority interests, and, ultimately, as Rasma Karklins put it, whether their "established political culture is based on negotiated consensus or control."[3] From our perspective, then, the regime type to which a given state belongs is important to study because political relations with ethnic groups cannot be separated from politics in general. To recognize what regime changes might entail for marginal groups we need first to examine the four regime types under study to ascertain whether or not we can make meaningful generalizations about them. The period of regime change (i.e., the phase of transition between regime types) is frequently characterized by political instability, the absence of unambiguous direction in policies, and even chaos. I set this issue aside for the moment; the discussion here speaks to mature, consolidated polities.

Empires

"An empire is a large composite polity linked to a central power by indirect rule" which may tolerate a significant level of social and economic

---

[3] Rasma Karklins, *Ethnopolitics and Transition to Democracy: The Collapse of the USSR and Latvia* (Baltimore: Johns Hopkins University Press, 1994), 9.

pluralism.[4] The argument is that imperial states generally pursue moderate policies toward marginal groups. An empire that has already consolidated its rule over its territory and subject peoples (such as the Habsburg Empire in the nineteenth century or the Ottoman Empire in the sixteenth century) tends to pursue restrained policies toward marginal groups. Ordinarily one could expect such states not to enforce cultural or religious homogeneity, for instance, given the costs associated with communication, transportation, the maintenance of public order, and other factors. The benefits to be gained from such coercive policies generally are not worth the risk of ethnic upheavals that jeopardize the state's stability. Mature imperial states, therefore, may be expected to follow a relatively temperate approach to ethnic minorities: They may grant cultural and religious rights, and they may even construct alliances with marginal groups (e.g., to ensure the success of a military campaign), but they are usually reluctant to extend political rights. Their main concern typically is to maintain the state's political stability, to conserve and possibly expand its territory, and to maximize tax revenues. Based on this exposition, one would expect the empires' treatment of their Romani minorities to be neglectful, ambivalent, or indifferent.

Empires mainly come about and grow through military conquest (e.g., Ottoman) and/or dynastic/marital politics (e.g., Habsburg). They are formed, as Alexander Motyl writes, by transforming "distinct societies with autonomous institutions and regional elites into politically subordinate civil societies."[5] The domination of the imperial center does not put an end to the uniqueness of the newly conquered societies, but they lose their real or potential political sovereignty. Highly centralized rule is one of the key characteristics of empires. This is true for the entire period of the Ottoman Empire and for the Habsburg Empire even after 1867 when, with the formation of the Dual Monarchy, it had effectively

---

[4] Charles Tilly, "How Empires End," in Karen Barkey and Mark von Hagen, eds., *After Empire: Multiethnic Societies and Nation-Building: The Soviet Union and Russian, Ottoman, and Habsburg Empires* (Boulder, CO: Westview Press, 1997), 3. The rest of Tilly's definition reads: "The central power exercises some military and fiscal control in each major segment of its imperial domain, but tolerates the two major elements of indirect rule: (1) retention or establishment of particular, distinct compacts for the government of each segment; and (2) exercise of power through intermediaries who enjoy considerable autonomy within their own domains in return for the delivery of compliance, tribute, and military collaboration with the center." For another definition, see Joseph Rothschild, *Ethnopolitics: A Conceptual Framework* (New York: Columbia University Press, 1981), 228–9.

[5] Alexander Motyl, "From Imperial Decay to Imperial Collapse: The Fall of the Soviet Empire in Comparative Perspective," in Richard L. Rudolph and David F. Good, eds., *Nationalism and Empire: The Habsburg Monarchy and the Soviet Union* (New York: St. Martin's Press, 1992), 19.

become a state with two capital cities, Vienna and Budapest. Empires are relatively stable entities that may endure for centuries. Through the long life of an empire it is subject to various evolutionary processes dictated by changing internal and external environments. Some empires are flexible enough to respond to challenges (e.g., military threats, political mobilization of ethnic groups, economic progress) while others are resistant to change and manage to uphold their policies. The particular institutional arrangements of empires can be very different as illustrated by the Habsburg and Ottoman empires.

Absolutist rule characterized the Habsburg Empire until about 1867, when outside pressured forced it to institute limited policies of decentralization and pluralism to prevent its own disintegration. These reforms could only stall its fall given the local elites' increasing demand of national self-determination and their growing displeasure with Vienna and especially Budapest. The Habsburgs who acquired their East European lands through marriage or royal succession extended privileges to the local land-owning aristocracy (such as exemption from taxation and military service) and exerted their control through them. The nobility directly controlled the population through its many prerogatives, which included levying taxes and recruiting soldiers, although the central state's authority extended to the entire community.

In the Ottoman Empire the imperial bureaucracy and the professional Ottoman class were politically dependent on and entirely subservient to the sultan. Members of the bureaucracy were recruited from alien elements (from conquered lands) and were – especially during the first stages of the Empire – the sultan's personal slaves.[6] Since the Ottomans acquired their territories through conquest, they did not need to make concessions to the local nobility, who, in most cases, escaped or were killed. Not surprisingly, in the Ottoman lands, in contrast to the Habsburg Empire, assets (including land) could be taken from landlords; and, at least in the first two centuries of Ottoman rule in the Balkans (the fifteenth and sixteenth centuries), property was not hereditary. In the late nineteenth century the Ottomans also introduced belated political–institutional reforms which included, in 1876, the First Ottoman Parliament, a multiethnic and diverse legislature unique among imperial states.[7]

Aside from their institutional structures, there were a number of other profound differences between the Habsburg and Ottoman empires. While the Habsburg Empire performed relatively well in terms of

[6] S. N. Eisenstadt, *The Political System of Empires* (New York: Free Press, 1963), 278, 285.
[7] See Caglar Keyder, "The Ottoman Empire," in Barkey and von Hagen, eds., *After Empire*, 35.

industrial development especially after the mid-nineteenth century, one of the Ottoman Empire's organizational principles was the rigid separation of rulers from producers which thwarted economic progress.[8] Relations between church and state was not as divisive an influence in the Ottoman Empire as it was in the Habsburg lands. In contrast to Ottoman-ruled territories, the vast disparities in historical experiences as well as socioeconomic and political development made the formation of a uniform system all but impossible in the Habsburg Empire.

Such intra-imperial diversity in the Habsburg domain was manifested in a number of areas. The Slavic peoples under Habsburg rule (and, particularly after 1867, even Romanians) tended to be pro-Russian while the Austrians, Germans, and Hungarians of the Empire shared pro-German sympathies in matters of foreign policy. In administrative affairs also, there were important differences (again, particularly after 1867) between the Western and Eastern Habsburg lands, with more centralized rule in the former areas.[9] The aristocracy played a less progressive role in the Eastern Habsburg lands than in the West. In Hungary, for instance, the motor of commercial and industrial development was the Jewry, not the local aristocracy and the middle class as in Bohemia.

The crucial point is that even a cursory examination of the two empires divulges major variations in the empires' policies toward ethnic minorities. Ottoman rule was more tolerant of and less intrusive for ethnic minorities than Habsburg domination. Although one may distinguish several dividing lines among the peoples of the Ottoman lands, the most important was not ethnic, linguistic, religious, or racial but a class-based separation in the Marxist sense. The sultans created a professional class to carry out administrative, political, and military functions. The key distinctions were between this professional Ottoman class and the *reaya* (subject peoples). Religion was an important separator of the privileged Muslims from the *zimmi* (infidels); nevertheless, the Ottoman state did not discriminate by language or race, and conversion to Islam was not a state policy.[10] In fact, the initial success of the Ottoman Empire was mainly due to its moderate taxation and tolerant rule of ethnic and religious minorities.[11] The Ottoman's moderation vis-à-vis ethnic minorities was especially evident in the empire's periphery, where their control was generally less firmly established.

---

[8] See, for instance, Ernest Gellner, *Encounters with Nationalism* (Oxford: Blackwell, 1994), 17–18.

[9] See Robert A. Kann and Zdenek V. David, *The Peoples of the Eastern Habsburg Lands, 1526–1918* (Seattle: University of Washington Press, 1984), 12–13.

[10] See Peter F. Sugar, *Southeastern Europe under Ottoman Rule, 1354–1804* (Seattle: University of Washington Press, 1977), 31–59, 285–8.

[11] See Anthony D. Smith, *Theories of Nationalism* (New York: Harper & Row, 1971), 66.

This relatively liberal minority policy was concomitant with the Ottomans' pragmatic approach to immigration as demonstrated by the sultans' open invitation to tens of thousands of persecuted Jews from Spain (who were followed by their oppressed brethren from Austria, Bohemia, Poland, and elsewhere).[12] The most important institutional expression of Ottoman administration was the millet system aptly described by Donald Horowitz as the paradigm of parallel ethnic structures.[13] The millets were organized along denominational lines in which Muslim, Christian, and Jewish communities, guided by their religious leaders, enjoyed a great deal of autonomy.

In the Habsburg Empire ethnic, linguistic, and religious minorities enjoyed neither the level of autonomy nor the tolerant state attitudes emblematic of Ottoman rule. In the Habsburg lands forced conversion to the state religion, Roman Catholicism, and the selective persecution of especially protestant churches was state policy in certain periods.[14] Discriminatory measures, based not only along religious, but also along ethnic and linguistic lines with some nationalities (Germans, Hungarians) enjoying a privileged status over others (Slavic peoples, Romanians), were widespread. Given the Ottoman Empire's liberal treatment of the Jews, it is particularly noticeable that in the Habsburg Empire their nationality status was fully acknowledged only in Bukovina and Bosnia-Herzegovina, partially recognized in Austria, and not at all in Hungary.[15] At the same time, certain imperial institutions, most prominently the armed forces, were encouraged to and succeeded in achieving a remarkable level of ethnic harmony.[16] Moreover, Habsburg rule could also be relatively mild-mannered when compared to those of other states, a point well illustrated by Vienna's moderate policies pursued in Polish territories against the conspicuous intolerance of Prussia and Russia against their Polish subjects.[17]

---

[12] For an insightful exposition of Jews in the Ottoman territories, see Suna Kili, "The Jews in Turkey: A Question of National or International Identity," in Russell F. Farnen, *Nationalism, Ethnicity, and Identity: Cross National and Comparative Perspectives* (New Brunswick, NJ: Transaction Publishers, 1994), esp. 299–308.

[13] Donald L. Horowitz, "Three Dimensions of Ethnic Politics," *World Politics*, 23:2 (January 1971): 232.

[14] See, for instance, John Breuilly, *Nationalism and the State* (Chicago: University of Chicago Press, 1993), 133–9.

[15] Robert A Kann, *The Multinational Empire: Nationalism and National Reform in the Habsburg Monarchy, 1848–1918*, Vol. 1 *Empire and Nationalities* (New York: Columbia University Press, 1950), 30.

[16] See István Deák, *Beyond Nationalism: A Social and Political History of the Habsburg Officer Corps* (New York: Oxford University Press, 1993).

[17] See Robert A. Kann, *A History of the Habsburg Empire, 1526–1918* (Berkeley: University of California Press, 1974), 249.

After 1867 Austria's minority policies had seen a certain degree of liberalization, although ethnic minorities under Hungarian rule (Croats, Slovaks, Serbs, Romanians, Ruthenes, etc.) had fared considerably worse. Hungary had continued to pursue a vigorously assimilationist policy. As late as in 1918, the legislature in Budapest rejected universal suffrage to be introduced in the Hungarian Kingdom (i.e., the part of the dual monarchy ruled by Hungary).[18] Only its authors considered the Nationalities Act of 1868 as generous. The Act spoke of a "single, indivisible Hungarian nation," although it did acknowledge that the nationalities constituting this "nation" had equal rights.[19] Romanians received perhaps the most appalling treatment from Hungary; in the late nineteenth century one Magyar vote weighed as much as twelve Romanian votes in Transylvania.[20]

A few words should be said about the atypical minority policies of the Russian and Soviet Empires. By the standards of most empires, particularly in the nineteenth century, and especially after the assassination of Tsar Alexander II (1881), Russia's treatment of ethnic minorities was extremely repressive. The underlying goals of the Soviet Union were imperial: to maintain and expand the multiethnic state and to transform its ethnically diverse population into the idealized species of new Soviet men and women. The Soviet Union was a centralized polity where political power was concentrated in Moscow from where it radiated to the internal empire (the USSR proper) and to the external empire (which included Eastern Europe). Nevertheless, in a number of important respects the USSR was different from the Habsburg and Ottoman empires: Its economic system had little in common with the classic imperial model, its interests frequently worked against those of its dominant nationality (Russian), and it was also quite successful in disseminating its supranational ideology.[21]

The foregoing discussion intended to show that although the Habsburg and Ottoman states belong to the same regime type, their specific policies and general approach to ethnic and other minorities diverged significantly. The main reason for this disparity is that ethnic identity was a far more important distinguishing characteristic of individuals in the Habsburg Empire than in the Ottoman state. At the same time, it is also important to note that ethnic minorities are generally better off in

---

[18] R. V. Burks, *East European History: An Ethnic Approach* (Washington, DC: American Historical Association, 1961), 21.

[19] See Andrew C. Janos, *The Politics of Backwardness in Hungary, 1825–1945* (Princeton, NJ: Princeton University Press, 1982), 125–6.

[20] Kann, *A History of the Habsburg Empire*, 355–6.

[21] Victor Zaslavsky, "The Soviet Union," in Barkey and von Hagen, eds., *After Empire*, 91.

empires – especially at the periphery of imperial lands – than in authoritarian states because empires are concerned mainly about imposing political order but they are "rather indifferent to the ethnosocial and ethnocultural heterogeneity of subject populations."[22] After the collapse of East European empires, many ethnic minorities in the region found themselves in multiethnic states where the problem of minority policy had to be tackled anew.

Authoritarian States

An authoritarian state is a polity with limited, not responsible political pluralism with often extensive social and economic pluralism.[23] Although a large variety of states may be called authoritarian, in this book the label refers to the East European countries in the interwar period and during World War II. The argument is that authoritarian states generally pursue more repressive policies toward ethnic minorities than their imperial counterparts, for several reasons.

First, their dominion extends to a far smaller territory than that of empires, and the resources required to establish rigorous control of their domain are generally more available. In other words, the state's coercive potential is enhanced in authoritarian systems. Second, although few if any authoritarian states can be considered homogeneous nation-states, ordinarily they have a smaller number of minorities constituting a smaller proportion of their overall populations which are, therefore, easier to control. Third, given the absence or weakness of democratic processes, authoritarian states can limit or proscribe the representation of minority interests and/or disregard their political and socioeconomic demands. Finally, in such states, considering the relatively small proportion of ethnic minorities and the high coercive potential of the state, minorities do not have the power to threaten state stability. Therefore, the state might implement repressive minority policies (targeting, for instance, the denial or cultural rights, assimilation, and even expulsion) without jeopardizing its own stability.

Some authoritarian states either claim to be nation-states or intend to ethnically "homogenize" their population through a variety of methods. Fascist states, the extreme variety of the authoritarian type, might resort to the most violent forms of coercive exclusion (i.e., genocide) of an

---

[22] Joseph Rothschild, *Return to Diversity: A Political History of East Central Europe Since World War II* (New York: Oxford University Press, 1989), 10.

[23] Juan J. Linz and Alfred Stepan, *Problems of Democratic Transition and Consolidation: Southern Europe, South America, and Post-Communist Europe* (Baltimore: Johns Hopkins University Press, 1996), 44. See also Juan J. Linz, *Totalitarian and Authoritarian Regimes* (Boulder, CO: Lynne Rienner, 2000).

"undesirable" ethnic group. As the case of Nazi Germany shows, such actions may be "justified" by ethnic identity and fear of racial pollution (Jews and Gypsies), political creed (Communists), sexual orientation (homosexuals), or physical disability (the handicapped).

At this point, I need to address a source of potential conceptual misunderstanding. I subscribe to the conventional usage of totalitarianism inasmuch as I consider Nazi Germany and the Soviet Union under Stalin as the ideal types of this regime. Nevertheless, East European states were not totalitarian throughout the communist period (1945–89). There were profound differences between these polities in the 1950s and the 1980s as well as between states like Albania and Poland. To accommodate these disparities, I use the "state-socialist" label, which refers to the entire communist period. The "authoritarian" designation here, then, refers to the East European states between the conclusion of World War I, when they achieved sovereignty, and the end of World War II (i.e., 1918–45). The exception is Czechoslovakia, which may be considered a functioning democracy during the two decades of its independence (1918–38).

Because of their diversity, making anything other than low-level generalizations about authoritarian states is difficult. It may be confidently stated, however, that they are generally characterized by strong centralized rule and limited political pluralism and autonomy for local authorities. A multiparty system is usually in place, although ordinarily parties whose political orientation are most objectionable from the rulers' perspective are either outlawed or allowed only token representation. In mature authoritarian systems, political elites may be inconvenienced by the activities of contending parties, but their rule is seldom seriously challenged by them. Perhaps most importantly, in authoritarian systems the rulers' accountability to the electorate is limited. To the extent that meaningful elections are held at all, they are utilized to demonstrate popular support of the political system rather than to register the electorate's real preferences.

In contrast with totalitarian systems, in authoritarian states there may be a wide range of genuine economic and societal pluralism and a robust civil society might be in place. Similarly, the majority of production and distribution units may be in private hands, although major components of the economy (typically, defense related industries) are often under state ownership or control. Another important difference between totalitarian and authoritarian systems is that the former are guided by a complex ideology (such as fascism or Marxism–Leninism) that permeates most areas of human affairs. Authoritarian regimes, on the other hand, are not dominated by rigid ideologies but rather by an often haphazard amalgam of pragmatic ideas that are supposed to rationalize the rule of elites and establish their legitimacy. A simple way to conceive of the difference between totalitarian and authoritarian states is to recognize that the state controls a far larger spectrum of private and public activities in the former than in the latter.

"Ethnic minorities generally fare better in empires," writes Joseph Rothschild, than in "would-be nation states whose central elites view themselves as the custodians of explicit and specific national cultures that serve them as comprehensive integrationist ideologies and programs."[24] The different conditions in the states of authoritarian Eastern Europe counsel against facile generalizations concerning the treatment of ethnic minorities, although Rothschild's statement is certainly supported by the evidence. Again, while it seems that the authoritarian regime type itself may indicate a certain range of policy, within that range the variation is substantial. In East European authoritarian states, policies toward ethnic minorities were, to a large extent, influenced by the geopolitical situation at the end of World War I. Rather than creating nation-states (which in the East European context would have been extremely difficult, in any case), the Paris peace conferences established states with substantial ethnic minorities. The new states' ethnic policies often hinged primarily on historical experience and were motivated by – in the case of the subject populations of the empires (e.g., Slovaks, Romanians) – revenge for maltreatment suffered in the past. Those states that lost territories (Hungary and Bulgaria) wanted to regain at least some of them along with their own nationals who now lived in foreign states usually hostile to them.

Hungary and Hungarian minorities abroad provide a useful case for understanding the ethnic affairs of interwar Eastern Europe. As noted above, ethnic minorities under Hungarian tutelage (especially Romanians, Ruthenes, Slovaks) suffered even more injustice than those under Austrian rule in the imperial age. It is not terribly surprising that the millions of Hungarians who became citizens of the new Romania and Czechoslovakia in 1918 were also subjected to relatively harsh treatment. But substantial ethnic minority populations existed in all East European states; and policies toward them, generally speaking, were hardly enlightened. In interwar Poland, for instance, Poles comprised only 69% of the population with 14% Ukrainians, 8.5% Jews, 3% Byelorussians, 2.5% Germans and others completing the picture.[25] Hungary's population was the most homogeneous although substantial Jewish and Romani communities remained in the country even after World War I.

---

[24] Rothschild, *Return to Diversity*, 10.
[25] B. Olszewski, *Obraz Polski dzisiejszej: Fakty, cyfry i tablice* (Warsaw: Orbis, 1938), 112.

In the domain of ethnic relations the most important impulse of the newly independent states of Eastern Europe was to promote the "national" elites' culture, ethos, and economy at the expense of the subordinate populations.[26] This policy was quite consistent in some states throughout the period (e.g., Romania), although in others (e.g., Poland) a certain measure of policy fluctuation is observable between "cultural pluralism and peaceful coexistence to open conflict and coercive Polonization."[27] Between the subordinate ethnic minorities and the dominant nationalities another classification may be reserved for those peoples who officially belonged to the latter but, in fact, were politically and economically often exploited by them. The best examples of this category are (a) the Slovaks vis-à-vis the Czechs and (b) the Croats with respect to the Serbs. Embittered by the policies of the dominant ethnic group, Slovaks and Croats had become increasingly disenchanted with the federal arrangement and found themselves on opposing sides in World War II. Notwithstanding their handicapped status, they tended to treat ethnic minorities subordinate to them just as harshly as the state-nation.

Policies toward ethnic minorities associated with a state whose intentions were perceived as threatening (especially ethnic Hungarian minorities) were more repressive than toward those whose home state was considered an ally. Even Czechoslovakia, the region's only democratic state, "pretended to be a nation without ever successfully integrating its numerous ethnic groups," notes Vojtech Mastny, "particularly not its two supposedly ruling nationalities, the Czechs and the Slovaks."[28]

The East European states experienced the totalitarian period and World War II differently. Poland, the Czech lands, Albania, and most of Yugoslavia were occupied throughout the war while Hungary, Romania, Bulgaria, Slovakia actively supported the German war effort from 1941. The territorial changes resulting from the war and Hitler's practice of rewarding allies (Hungary and Bulgaria) with territories they lost after World War I had a particularly injurious effect on ethnic minorities whose conditions were often desperate to begin with. Genocidal policies based on ethnic identity caused the deaths of millions of others, often at the hands of their compatriots. The crucial point is that even in these

---

[26] See, for instance, Irina Livezeanu, *Cultural Politics in Greater Romania: Regionalism, Nation Building, and Ethnic Struggle* (Ithaca, NY: Cornell University Press, 1995).

[27] Andrzej Mirga, "The Effects of State Assimilation Policy on Polish Gypsies," *Journal of the Gypsy Lore Society*, series 5, 3:2 (1993), 69.

[28] Vojtech Mastny, "Eastern Europe and the West in the Perspective of Time," in William E. Griffith, ed., *Central and Eastern Europe: The Opening Curtain?* (Boulder, CO: Westview Press, 1989), 21. See also S. Harrison Thomson, *Czechoslovakia in European History* (Princeton, NJ: Princeton University Press, 1943), 284–305.

years there were significant differences in state policies toward minorities between East European states. For instance, the deportation of Gypsies and Jews to the death camps was pursued willingly in Romania (even though Marshall Antonescu's policies were inconsistent because at times he did protect them), reluctantly in Hungary, and not at all in Bulgaria proper. At the same time, both of the latter countries delivered Jews and Roma in the territories they recovered during the war.[29]

State-Socialist Systems

A socialist state is dominated by a Marxist–Leninist party that permits minimal political, economic, or social pluralism. State-socialist or communist states follow inclusive ethnic policies. Since in this regime type there are even fewer constraints on the state's domestic political control than in authoritarian (although not fascist) systems, communist states may be expected to resort to the use of force in their integration and assimilation policies. The quintessential institutional–structural element of state-socialist systems is the Communist Party. The Party controls not only political life but social organizations, the armed forces and the police, channels of information and communication, and, to the extent possible, the economy. In the ideal type of communist regimes there is no political, social, or economic pluralism. Political power is centralized to the extreme, and only symbolic forms of diversity are allowed (such as the inconsequential fellow traveler parties in some East European states). The ruling elites derive their legitimacy from their knowledge of and allegiance to the official ideology, Marxism–Leninism. Although the rigidity implied by this model began to soften after the mid-1950s in some East European states, the fundamental attributes of communist systems remained unaltered until their collapse.

Given communist elites' commitment to ideology, in order to understand minority–state relations in states of this type the views of the principal proponents of Marxism–Leninism are worth considering. Fundamentally, Marx expected national differences to disappear in time because in his conception class identity (i.e., relation to the means of production) rather than nationality was the decisive line of division between people. Marx and Engels said remarkably little about ethnic minorities and their struggles for self-determination because they did not think such efforts represented a force powerful enough to prevent the proletarian

[29] See, for instance, Mario D. Fenyo, *Hitler, Horthy, and Hungary: German-Hungarian Relations, 1941–1944* (New Haven, CT: Yale University Press, 1972); Nicholas M. Nagy-Talavera, *The Green Shirts and the Others: A History of Fascism in Hungary and Rumania* (Stanford, CA: Hoover Institution Press, 1970); and Marshall Lee Miller, *Bulgaria During the Second World War* (Stanford, CA: Stanford University Press, 1975).

movement from taking its inevitable course.[30] They viewed nationalism on a case-by-case basis: Irish and Polish nationalisms were progressive because they were directed against imperial rule while they opposed the Czech drive for independence (owing to the Czechs' aid to the defeat of the Hungarian War of Independence in 1848–9) as well as pan-Slavism, which they considered a tool of the tsars.[31] In essence, Marxist–Leninist ideology conceived of nations and nationalism as a temporary, albeit unavoidable, evil best viewed in political rather than ethnocultural terms.[32] It assumed that with the establishment of communist rule the ethnic consciousness of people will gradually recede as their new identity, that of *homo sovieticus* (the "New Soviet Man"), awakens and becomes their paramount source of identity.

Issues of ethnicity and nationalism confronted Lenin and Stalin on a day-to-day basis and forced them to develop more pragmatic approaches tailored to political exigencies. Lenin acknowledged the power of nationalism and called for an anti-tsarist coalition of all nationalities in the Russian Empire, promising self-determination to them under Bolshevik rule. Once the nationalism of new states emerging from the Russian Empire posed obstacles to the advance of socialism, however, the Bolsheviks proclaimed it retrogressive, "the ideology of bankrupt capitalist expropriators, unjustly resisting their own expropriation."[33] Stalin, the Bolsheviks' expert on nationalities, proposed a rigid, objectivist definition of nationhood (based on common language, territory, economic life, culture) that allowed subsequent manipulation and political maneuverability.

The Soviet Union was a multinational system that repressed nationalism but encouraged and institutionalized both territorial nationhood and ethnocultural nationality.[34] The Soviet state emphasized the maintenance of the ethnic group's linguistic autonomy (in fact, some Central Asian nationalities were equipped with written languages of their own[35]),

---

[30] Richard Pipes, *The Formation of the Soviet Union: Communism and Nationalism, 1917–1923* (Cambridge, MA: Harvard University Press, 1964), 21–3.

[31] See, for instance, Robert R. King, *Minorities under Communism: Nationalities as a Source of Tension in Balkan Communist States* (Cambridge, MA: Harvard University Press, 1973), 15–24.

[32] Zaslavsky, "The Soviet Union," 86.

[33] Elie Kedourie, *Nationalism* (London: Hutchinson, 1961), 91.

[34] Rogers Brubaker, *Nationalism Reframed: Nationhood and the National Question in the New Europe* (New York: Cambridge University Press, 1996), 7–8. For a superb treatment of the Soviet Union and the national question, see Yuri Slezkine, "The USSR as a Communal Apartment, or How a Socialist State Promoted Ethnic Particularism," *Slavic Review*, 53:2 (Summer 1994): 414–52.

[35] Kenneth Minogue and Beryl Williams, "Ethnic Conflict in the Soviet Union: The Revenge of Particularism," in Alexander J. Motyl, ed., *Thinking Theoretically about Soviet Nationalities* (New York: Columbia University Press, 1992), 226.

its multinational structure was written into the constitution, and several other instruments (such as the nationality rubric in internal passports) actually stimulated rather than stifled the ethnic consciousness of minorities. Still, the extensive control mechanisms of the USSR managed to keep the many diverse ethnic minorities together in what appeared to be a stable multinational state.

After the imposition of communism, East European states had to bring their ethnic policies in line with those of the Soviet Union. Ideologically, nationalism was an anathema to these systems, at least until the mid-1950s when the limited relaxation of Moscow's control allowed them some creative experimentation. There were two distinctive varieties of nationalist policies: one directed against the Soviet Union to indicate the growing gap between the particular East European state and the USSR, the other directed against a national minority within the state. Albania, Poland, and Romania were perhaps the most successful in integrating some of nationalism's elements into the communist doctrine which served these regimes' purposes of demonstrating their political distance from the Soviet Union and achieving a modicum of popular support and legitimacy. The other type of nationalism, when nationalist themes were exploited against ethnic minorities, was evident especially in Poland (Germans and Jews), Romania (Hungarians), and Bulgaria (Turks) at various times during the communist period.

East European constitutions codified the rights of ethnic minorities, but these rights were not taken seriously. Entire ethnic groups, such as the Gypsies, were not only left unmentioned in constitutions and minority laws, but in some states there was no specific category for them even in census forms. As Soviet control loosened, the diversity between East European states increased. Some communist parties initiated liberal policies to the extent permitted by the restrictive framework of the state-socialist system, while others became more dictatorial. The fundamental reasons for this disparity lay in the political orientations of the East European regimes themselves and Soviet policy toward them. More reform-friendly regimes were willing to probe the patience of the Kremlin by introducing less restrictive policies with more (Hungary and, periodically, Poland) or less (Czechoslovakia in 1967–8) success while conservative elites chose to strengthen their control over state and society (Bulgaria, Czechoslovakia, Romania). On the other hand, the Soviet Union allowed strategically less important states (Hungary, Romania, Bulgaria) more elbow room for policy experimentation (although the two Balkan states chose to stick by their hardline policies) than more important ones. The reasons why Poland, a strategically key Warsaw Pact state, had undergone some liberal periods (e.g., most of the 1970s) were the inability of its elites to prevent domestic crises, their unwillingness to repress entire social strata, and

Soviet calculation that a heavy-handed repression of Poland might well be counterproductive.

These differences between liberal and conservative socialist states were also manifested in their minority policies. Once it was possible to depart from Soviet orthodoxy, the political orientation of states and the attributes of their national minorities rather than systemic constraints determined policy. In the conservative states (Bulgaria, Czechoslovakia, Romania) the approach to ethnic minorities had become more repressive as time went on. Their policies included reorganizations of administrative units to minimize minority population, relocation of ethnic groups and settling them in areas dominated by the majority population, discriminatory investment practices, demolition of ancient ethnic villages, selective persecution of minority churches and religious activities, and coercive change of names. Several other states of the region (Albania, East Germany, Poland, and Hungary) had only relatively small communities of national minorities and generally pursued more progressive minority policies.

Democracies

Democracy is nearly impossible to concisely define. Robert Dahl refers to its ideal form when he writes that a democracy is a political system in which the government is continuously and completely – or nearly completely – responsive to the preferences of its citizens who are considered its political equals.[36] In this book the variant of democracy I deal with is the first decade of nascent, developing democracy of postsocialist East European states (1989–2000). My contention is that, of all regime types, liberal democracies pursue policies that are the most favorable for ethnic minorities and other marginal groups. Unlike states in other regime types, a liberal democracy generally enjoys substantial legitimacy and widespread popular support for the fundamental design of the state. Democracies are marked by inclusiveness, the willingess to negotiate and compromise, institutionalized competition for influence, and an extensive array of civil liberties guaranteed by law. By their very nature, liberal democracies are more concerned with human rights and minority rights than are states under other regime types. One can, therefore, expect democratic states not only to allow for the representation

---

[36] Robert A. Dahl, *Polyarchy: Participation and Opposition* (New Haven: Yale University Press, 1971), 1–2. See also 1–9, 231–49. For more recent and insightful reflections on democracy, see Larry Diamond, *Developing Democracy: Toward Consolidation* (Baltimore, MD: Johns Hopkins University Press, 1999), 1–19; and John Mueller, *Capitalism, Democracy, & Ralph's Pretty Good Grocery* (Princeton, NJ: Princeton University Press, 1999), 137–63.

of minority interests but also to make reasonable efforts to accommodate them.

Democracies are political systems primarily characterized by pluralism in political, social, and economic affairs. Democracies are flexible enough to allow the representation of a broad range of political interests and approaches, societal activities and organizations, and economic pursuits without the interference of the state. It is useful also to recall the Jeffersonian axiom that democracy is not a state or condition but a process, a "work in progress," which needs perennial improvement. Much of this book deals with polities that only recently commenced their transition from state-socialism to democracy. Thus it is important to determine the criteria of democratic consolidation. According to Linz and Stepan, democracies are consolidated when civil society is free to develop, political society is autonomous, the rule of law ensures citizens' freedoms and the independence of associational life, economic society is institutionalized, and the state bureaucracy is usable by the democratic government.[37]

One of the major challenges of democracies, as with other types of regimes, is to accommodate marginal groups, particularly ethnic minorities. Few have been as unequivocal in their pessimism as John Stuart Mill, who suggested that "Free institutions are next to impossible in a country made up of different nationalities. Among people without fellow-feeling, especially if they read and speak different languages, the united public opinion necessary to the working of representative government, cannot exist."[38] Still, there can be no doubt that democratic states have been more successful in mediating and resolving ethnic conflicts than have states of any other regime type. The reason is that democracies have been able to devise a number of institutional arrangements (such as power sharing and vote pooling) that dominant and marginal ethnic groups alike can learn to live with.[39]

Democracy does not, of course, denote equality between dominant and marginal ethnic groups. In fact, parties of the ethnic majority may well find it electorally punishing to make concessions to minorities. The conflict-solving power of a mature democracy lies in its framework and inherent flexibility which allow disadvantaged groups to articulate and represent their interests through political mobilization. As John Mueller notes,

[37] Linz and Stepan, *Problems of Democratic Transition and Consolidation*, 7–15.
[38] John Stuart Mill, *Three Essays* (New York: Oxford University Press, 1975), 381–2.
[39] A succinct examination of this issue is Arend Lijphart, "Multiethnic Democracy" in Seymour Martin Lipset et al., eds., *The Encyclopedia of Democracy* (Washington, DC: Congressional Quarterly Press, 1995), 853–65.

The important issue in reconciling minorities to democratic rule . . . is to convince them that . . . their interests can be maintained in a democracy, and that this can come about not because the majority will embrace them with fraternal good will . . . but because democracy leaves the minority free to organize to pursue its interests – and so vastly increase its political weight – on issues that matter most to it.[40]

The notion of incomplete democracies in which the rules of democratic governance apply only to the dominant population (such as segregation in the United States, apartheid in white democracy in South Africa) calls attention to two requirements of resolving ethnic/racial conflicts. First, a large section of society should be committed to democracy "as the most effective safeguard of all their interests and aspirations," and, second, "both the majority and the minority must recognize that democracy is the best solution for their relationship."[41]

As far as ethnic minorities are concerned, the most important attribute of consolidated democracies is tolerance. Democracies recognize ethnic minorities as corporate entities with rights that enable them to maintain their distinct educational, cultural, and linguistic identities. Human rights are essentially nonmajoritarian; "in democratic societies, where the majority is well positioned to care for its own rights and interests, one of the most important functions of human rights is precisely to constrain the majority."[42] Consolidated democracies can accept a range of ethnic political activity that may include protests, demonstrations, and even riots. The more democratic the political environment, the more likely ethnic groups will be to voice their concerns nonviolently.[43]

Although the East European states established democratic institutional structures soon after the fall of communism, the accommodation of ethnic minorities was generally not at the top of their agendas. Even in states that have been relatively quick to create the institutional framework for dealing with minority concerns, many view democracy as majority rule and overlook minority rights. These and other problems "have helped create an environment in which a politics of national identity poses a threat to democratization," especially where the state has

---

[40] John Mueller, "Minorities and the Democratic Image," *East European Politics and Societies*, 9:3 (Fall 1995): 520–1. See also idem., *Capitalism, Democracy, & Ralph's Pretty Good Grocery*, 158–60, 187–9.

[41] George Schöpflin, "Nationalism and National Minorities in East and Central Europe," *Journal of International Affairs*, 45:1 (Summer 1991): 55–6.

[42] Jack Donnelly, "Human Rights in a New World Order: Implications for a New Europe," in David P. Forsythe, ed., *Human Rights in the New Europe: Problems and Progress* (Lincoln, NE: University of Nebraska Press, 1994), 19.

[43] Ted Robert Gurr and Barbara Harff, *Ethnic Conflict in World Politics* (Boulder, CO: Westview, 1994), 85.

been designated as the "national-state" of the dominant ethnic group.[44] In several East European states, democracy is scarcely consolidated or mature.

There are important differences between the progress that individual states have made in their democratization processes.[45] The Czech Republic, Hungary, Poland, and Slovenia are considerably ahead of Slovakia, Romania, Bulgaria, and the other Yugoslav successor states. A closer look at the region reveals, however, that states that have succeeded in consolidating democracy may pursue indifferent minority policies while others where serious problems with democratization remain may have had more positive attitudes toward minorities. The most conspicuous example is the Czech Republic, which is one of the leaders of political and economic transitions yet has lagged behind others in protecting ethnic minorities, particularly the Roma. In contrast, Macedonia's policies toward the Roma have been far more enlightened even as that state has faced a variety of profound political, economic, and ethnic difficulties.

PART II. REGIME TRANSITION AND MINORITIES

Although there are significant variations of minority policy within regime type, one would assume that a change from one regime type to another would make a perceptible difference in state policies. Systemic transition from one regime type to another is usually rooted in interrelated sources such as massive societal change, economic development, and redistribution of political power that may culminate in revolution, civil war, or a negotiated replacement of one elite with another. Even in the case of basically simultaneous regime collapse and subsequent change in several states, such as we have witnessed in Eastern Europe, the transition may well transpire at different speeds resulting in different levels of democratization at any one time. For instance, by 1995 Poland and Slovenia had advanced farther in consolidating democracy than had Romania or Slovakia.[46] Our concern here, however, is the impact that systemic change will have on ethnic minorities. What kind of changes can be determined?

---

[44] See Julie Mostov, "Democracy and the Politics of National Identity," *Studies in East European Thought*, 46:1 (1994): 10.

[45] Two excellent articles that speak to the diversity of the post-socialist experience in Eastern Europe are Valerie Bunce, "The Political Economy of Postsocialism," and M. Steven Fish, "Postcommunist Subversion: Social Science and Democratization in East Europe and Eurasia," both in *Slavic Review*, 58:4 (Winter 1999): 756–93 and 794–823, respectively.

[46] See Zoltan Barany, "The Regional Perspective," in Aurel Braun and Zoltan Barany, eds., *Dilemmas of Transition* (Lanham, MD: Rowman & Littlefield, 1999), 91–111.

One of the key effects of regime change is the change in institutional arrangements it makes possible. For instance, transition from an imperial system to an authoritarian state allows and at times necessitates the creation of new institutions such as independent political parties, ministries, or governmental departments that express the sovereignty of the unitary state. The period of transition is a time marked by struggle and uncertainty. Completed regime change – and the creation of a legal and institutional system that ensures the enforcement of civil and minority rights – may take several years or more (hence the differentiation, for instance, between phases of democratic transition and consolidation), and it may not be apparent early on what sort of political and socioeconomic system will emerge and what regime change will ultimately mean to ethnic minorities.[47]

Transition periods tend to go hand in hand with a decline in the effectiveness of state power and flagging state attention to concerns that are not directly related its survival. As such, they generally create opportunity space for mobilization by disenfranchised or marginal groups. Organizations and informal groups that do not directly aim to defeat the weakening regime usually find that the fluid political situation stimulates a higher degree of state tolerance toward them and thus increased elbow room to pursue their objectives. C. G. Pickvance has noted that urban renewal and environmental protection movements tend to flourish in the phase of collapse of authoritarian regimes and prior to the subsequent formation of political parties. Urban movements in Spain during the last years of the Franco regime, or environmental activism in the late communist period in Hungary and Bulgaria are good examples of this phenomenon.[48] Many Roma and other East Europeans found that the transition period was concomitant with more lenient state attitudes toward black market activities and similar minor commercial infractions.

At the same time, regime transition tends to amplify nationalist and extremist social attitudes and thus denotes special difficulties for ethnic minorities. Changes in the economic system often signify deteriorating living standards for various social strata whose growing insecurity creates a need to find community with others similarly effected.[49] Regime change might evoke nationalist sentiments in the disenchanted masses of

---

[47] On this issue, see for instance Myron Weiner, "Peoples and States in a new Ethnic Order?" *Third World Quarterly*, 13:2 (1992): 317–33.

[48] See C. G. Pickvance, "Where Have Urban Movements Gone?" in Costis Hadjimichalis and David Sadler, eds., *Europe at the Margins: New Mosaics of Inequality* (Chichester, England: John Wiley & Sons, Ltd., 1995), 206.

[49] See Lucian W. Pye, *Politics, Personality, and Nation Building: Burma's Search for Identity* (New Haven: Yale University Press, 1962), 5.

the majority group, particularly if those who seem to profit from the economic transition are members of ethnic minorities. This, in turn, provides an auspicious opportunity for "ethnic entrepreneurs" to forge new social alliances and loyalties and manipulate nationalist themes. In post-communist Eastern Europe, political liberalization and especially the newly gained freedom of expression for a time removed prior limitations from the dissemination of nationalist and racist views and propaganda and encouraged the emergence of nationalist leaders. Still, strong popular support of extremist parties and politicians has proved ephemeral in most of the region.

Until the recent democratic transition, changes in regimes have generally had a negative impact on East European ethnic minorities. The fall of empires promised a new era for repressed peoples, but the initial period of idealism was soon superseded by more albeit new types of ethnic domination in the interwar era and even worse abuse of minorities under fascist rule. The imposition of state-socialism again precluded the autonomous political development of ethnic communities. Finally, the transition to democracy has established minority rights, although not all ethnic minorities have been treated fairly by states, nor have all minorities been equally successful in articulating and representing their interests.

In this book I will argue that the Roma have historically suffered more from regime changes than have other ethnic minorities in the region. One fundamental reason for this is that the positive aspects of regime changes (economic progress, increases in political participation, etc.) have made a smaller impact on the Romani communities than on other peoples.

PART III. THE STATE AND ETHNIC MINORITIES

If we accept the reasoning that a specific regime type or change from one regime type to another does not fully explain changes in state policies toward minorities, we need to look for a competing or complementary explanation that will fit the evidence better. The answer lies in the circumstances and conditions of the given state which clearly affect its minority policies and override the general tendencies of particular regimes. The second general argument which I explore in the book is that the particular conditions of individual countries drive state policies toward marginal and ethnic groups. In other words, the satisfactory explanation we are looking for is unique to the state in question.

What are these "particular conditions" that help explain state minority policies? They range from the government's political orientation, socioeconomic conditions, the ratio of the given marginal group to the dominant group, the presence of other ethnic groups and the threat they might pose to the state, societal attitudes and state efforts to change them, and the willingness of the state to consider and respond to criticisms levelled against its policies by international institutions. The suggestion that these factors shed some light on state policies toward minorities is easy enough to accept; still, it seems useful to spell out a cluster of more specific propositions that isolate the burden of explanation to particular factors. Clearly, none of the following five variables yield a full explication by itself, but altogether they provide an answer that adequately explains impulses, motivations, and concerns on which state policies toward minorities are based.[50]

Political–Institutional Characteristics of the State

A state's political and institutional attributes are determined by numerous factors. The legacies of the past (in newly democratizing states of Eastern Europe the legacy of communism is particularly important) and the given country's political traditions influence the political attitudes of the state and its representatives. So do the traditions of minority relations and past social attitudes toward minority groups. There are a number of more tangible components, however. Although there may be substantial differences from country to country within the democratic regime type, in democracies the constitution and legal instruments pertaining to minorities should demarcate the boundaries of state policies toward minorities. The definition of citizenship and the circle of individuals who benefit from citizenship rights may be a telling illustration of prevailing state and societal attitudes.

A consideration of state policy must distinguish between the political actors who devise, represent, and execute it. The formulation and implementation of policy depends on the relative and actual power of various political actors in the political institutional system. The perspectives of different political institutions on marginal groups can and often do differ. Similarly, the decision-making power of various political institutions also varies in different states. For instance, in some countries, presidents possess a great deal of power to set policy, while in others their power to do so is very limited. One should also appreciate the special importance of the views local authorities take on minorities. In essence, local officials personify the state to minorities since the implementation of governmental policies largely hinges on them. The inclusion or exclusion of

---

[50] As an element of theory the "country-specific conditions" argument is troubling because it is so open-ended. The five propositions below emphasize contextuality simply because there are many variables that influence state behavior. As Milton Esman suggests, "What this seems to demonstrate, once again, is the impossibility of a general theory in the study of ethnic politics." (Letter from Esman to the author, 23 March 1999).

ethnic minorities in policy-making will also likely affect state policy toward them.

The capacity of states to influence or change societal attitudes toward minorities is rarely recognized. The state does have the power to increase society's tolerance and understanding of the marginal population's predicament through the enactment and enforcement of antidiscrimination laws and/or the introduction of affirmative action programs. Although such policies may be met with popular opposition, the key to their success is consistent, long-term, and patient implementation. An important question that is seldom explicated in discussions of minority policy is the financial situation of the state. Education, housing, employment, and other programs devised to assist minorities can be very costly, and a government may not have the financial resources to put them into practice. The political elites of an impoverished state might have the most progressive of intentions toward minorities, but if they do not have the resources to help them the marginal groups' material conditions may not improve at all.

These points capture the salient political and institutional factors that impact upon state policy. The argument, then, is that the political and institutional characteristics of the state strongly affect its policies toward minorities.

Societal Attitudes

Societal perceptions and views of the minority group do make a difference in the types of policies state and government authorities formulate and implement. This is especially true for democratic systems in which elected politicians are accountable to their constituents. If a dominant population is supportive of a marginal group, the state (especially a democratic state) will be more likely to introduce pro-minority policies. A minority that enjoys the backing and sympathy of the majority may expect such support to translate into more favorable treatment from the state. In contrast, unfavorable majority view of a given marginal group may find expression in less liberal and tolerant state policies. One might argue, then, that state policies toward minorities are influenced by societal attitudes.

The Marginal Group's Socioeconomic Conditions

The economic conditions, educational level, employment structure, cultural development, and a number of other socioeconomic factors associated with a given minority have a bearing on state minority policies. A marginal group's demographic attributes (actual size and proportion in the overall population, birth rate, life expectancy, etc.) are also salient variables that could impact on the formulation of state policy. Marginal groups without substantial economic resources – especially if they are not politically organized and enjoy the support of neither society at large nor outside protectors – may be ignored or neglected by the state with impunity.

A minority group whose marginal status is rooted not in its economic exclusion but in its separation from the rest of society or in its political marginality may also attract state attention. In this scenario the benevolent, enlightened state might conceive policies that encourage the societal or political integration of the group. Alternatively, the wealth or perceived wealth of a politically and/or socially marginalized group (such as the Jews in Nazi Germany) might trigger discriminatory state policies aiming at the seizure or redistribution of their property.

It is important to recognize that different conditions in different states lead to different policies. For instance, the desperate poverty of a minority group in a conservative and poor state is unlikely to generate the same policies as the same condition in a liberal and wealthy state. Thus, the argument is that state policies toward a minority group are influenced by the socioeconomic conditions of that minority.

The Minority's Political Mobilization Level

In some regime types, marginal groups enjoy the opportunity to get involved in politics by organizing parties and participating in national and local elections. The political clout that such marginal groups acquire depends on a number of variables (leadership, organizational traditions and culture, number of parties, group cohesion, etc.) and may also be assumed to influence state policies toward the given minority. Especially in liberal democracies, a well-organized, politically active minority group that can effectively represent its interest usually (although not without exceptions) has better chances of inducing favorable state minority policies than do marginal communities with less political efficacy. In other words, the political attributes of a minority affect state minority policies.

International Organizations and Nongovernmental Organizations

Finally, the activities of supranational organizations can also motivate changes in state policy toward minorities. A powerful organization may be able to utilize various tools in influencing state minority policy by publicizing the conditions of a marginal group in the given state, criticizing that state's policy toward its minorities, refusing membership to the state, and so on. In addition, an international organization specifically representing the interests of a certain minority or minorities can also be an effective harbinger of change in state policy.

Changes in state minority policy effected by international organizations or supranational bodies may have negative or positive influence on a marginal group's conditions. For instance, the persistent demands of the Nazi government that Hungary begin the deportation of Jews and Gypsies had a tragic impact on their communities. In the age of democratization, however, East European minority groups, particularly the Roma, have generally benefited from the attention of international organizations and nongovernmental organizations (NGOs).

It is important to note that just like the other factors influencing state policy mentioned above, the efficacy of international organizations and NGOs to a large extent depends on the state's responsiveness to their activities. For instance, international organizations and NGOs regularly condemned the minority policies of East European communist states, but their criticisms at the time fell on deaf ears. Since 1989, however, international organizations have been far more effective in large part owing to the fact that the key foreign policy objective of nearly all of the region's states is integration to Western political, economic, and military alliances. Among the criteria these organizations have set for prospective members are the strict enforcement of minority and civil rights and the alleviation of ethnic conflicts. In short, the argument is that nongovernmental and international organizations, particularly if they have a leverage vis-à-vis a given state, possess the power to influence that state's minority policies.

SUMMING UP

In this chapter I attempted to show that individual regime types do not generate a satisfactory explanation for state minority policies because there is a considerable variation between the policies of states belonging to the same regime type. We saw that imperial systems tended to be tolerant toward ethnic and religious minorities but also noted the substantial disparities between Habsburg and Ottoman approaches to marginal groups. Similarly, the brief analyses of authoritarian, state-socialist, and democratic types suggested that notwithstanding the broad patterns that such regime types indicate concerning minority policies (i.e., repressive, inclusionary, and enlightened, respectively), there is abundant variation in all of these cases.

To understand the sources and nature of minority policies, we need to have more information. We ought to know more about the particular characteristics of states themselves, their institutions and political proclivities, the attitudes of the dominant group or groups they represent toward minorities, and even such matters as their sensitivity to international criticism. Just as importantly, we should know more about the minority group toward which state policy is directed. Clearly, the socio-economic and political attributes of the minority group play a role in determining state policy. The variation between the minority policies of states belonging to the same regime type is explained precisely by these variables.

In the rest of this book I will evaluate these arguments through the experience of East European Gypsy communities in a variety of states, regimes types, and historical periods. But first let us examine two concepts central to this book: the determinants of marginality and political mobilization, the process that marginal groups may utilize to improve their conditions.

2

Marginality and Ethnic Mobilization

In the previous chapter my focus was on the state and its interaction with minority groups. Now the emphasis shifts to the other side of the equation as I concentrate on two phenomena that are crucial to the understanding of the minority experience in general and the Romani existence in particular: marginality and ethnic mobilization. The concept of marginality provides the most appropriate theoretical handle to understanding the Gypsies' centuries-long plight in European societies. Therefore, I want to examine the various dimensions and components of marginality to appraise their utility to my inquiry. As I shall show, marginality is in many cases a multidimensional situation with separable economic, social, and political faces. Although a marginal situation may be reduced through numerous ways, perhaps the most effective method to alleviate political marginality is political mobilization, the second concept to be reviewed in this chapter.

Ethnic political mobilization is a complex process that has become an important dimension in the political lives of postauthoritarian and postcommunist politics. This concept is particularly important for this study because political mobilization has been a significant new element in the lives of Gypsy communities across Eastern Europe in the last decade. Ethnic mobilization does not happen in a vacuum. It has historical, political, social, and economic prerequisites and criteria one ought to be familiar with. The purpose of this discussion is to create a framework in which the Romani political mobilization may be properly considered.

PART I. MARGINALITY

The Concept of Marginality

Boiled down to its essentials, marginality denotes the subordinate position of a subject relative to that of another. Marginality is, by definition, relational; a marginal group is disadvantaged *relative* to a dominant group or groups. Nearly anything can be considered as marginal in the appropriate context. One can speak of a group of individuals whose cultural status is marginal compared to another group, an industry whose importance to the national economy is marginal in relation to that of another, a state whose influence on international affairs is marginal in contrast to that of another, and so on. In this book we are interested in the marginality of an ethnic group, defined here as a group of individuals that is "socially distinguished or set apart by others and/or by itself, primarily on the basis of cultural and nationality characteristics."[1]

"Margin" stems from the Latin *margo* meaning edge, border, frontier. Marginality is an elastic concept that can be interpreted in many ways and may denote a subordinate situation in a plethora of contexts. The early work on marginality was almost entirely dominated by sociologists whose influence on the field has waned little since then. The first American scholars who studied marginality in the 1920s and 1930s followed in the footsteps of German sociologists, especially Georg Simmel.[2] Their focus was squarely on migration and the marginal experiences of immigrants and, to a lesser extent, on racial minorities. According to a classic definition by Chicago sociologist Robert E. Park, who based many of his examples on the experiences of European Jews in America, marginality is a type of personality that arises out of the conflict of races and cultures.[3] In his influential study, *The Marginal Man*, Everett V. Stonequist described his subject as "one who is poised in psychological uncertainty between two (or more) social worlds; reflecting in his soul the discords and harmonies, repulsions and attractions of these worlds, one of which is often 'dominant' over the other."[4] In other words, the marginal person is "one whom fate has condemned to live in two societies and in two not merely different but antagonistic cultures."[5]

In the last fifty years anthropologists, economists, and sociologists have used the concept to analyze ever more diverse fields of scholarly

---

[1] Joe R. Feagin, *Racial and Ethnic Relations* (Englewood Cliffs, NJ: Prentice Hall, 1984; 2nd ed.), 9.

[2] See Georg Simmel, *Soziologie: Untersuchen über die Formen der Vergesellschaftung* (Berlin: Duncker and Humbolt, 1908); idem., "The Stranger," in *On Individuality and Social Forms*, David N. Levine, ed. (Chicago: University of Chicago Press, 1971), 143–9; and H. Kurt Wolff, ed., *The Sociology of Georg Simmel* (Glencoe, IL: The Free Press, 1950).

[3] Robert E. Park, "Human Migration and the Marginal Man," *American Journal of Sociology*, 33:6 (May 1928):881–93; and idem., *Race and Culture* (Glencoe, IL: The Free Press, 1950).

[4] Everett V. Stonequist, *The Marginal Man: A Study in Personality and Culture Conflict* (New York: Charles Scribner's Sons, 1937), 8.

[5] Ibid., xv.

inquiry.[6] Especially since the 1970s, the concept of marginality has become a popular tool among sociologists discussing a wide array of disparate phenomena from homelessness and deviance of all sorts to the study of urban decay and sociospatial inequality while economists have used it to explain black markets, industries reliant on immigrant labor, and third-world economies.[7] Spatial inequality and exclusion have engaged social geographers focusing on urban–rural and suburban–inner-city dichotomies.[8] Historians, too, have found marginality a helpful concept in reflecting on the past. "Marginality and pluralism," wrote William H. McNeill, "were and are the norm of civilized existence" because "civilized societies have nearly always subordinated some human group to others of a different ethnic background."[9] More recently, innovative work in theology has employed marginality as a concept critical to understanding Jesus. According to Jung Young Lee, "The determinants of Jesus' marginality, class, economic, political, social, and ethnic orientations made him the marginal person *par excellence*, so the stories of incarnation ought to be interpreted from the perspective of marginality."[10]

---

[6] For synopses of these diverse approaches, see J. Perlman, *The Myth of Marginality* (Berkeley: University of California Press, 1979); Lesley D. Harman, *The Modern Stranger: On Language and Membership* (Amsterdam: Mouton de Gruyter, 1988); and Antoine Bailly and Eric Weiss-Altaner, "Thinking about the Edge: the Concept of Marginality," in Costis Hadjimichalis and David Sadler, eds., *Europe at the Margins: New Mosaics of Inequality* (Chichester, UK: John Wiley & Sons, 1995), 219–36.

[7] See, for instance, James R. McIntosh, *Perspectives on Marginality* (Boston: Allyn and Bacon, 1974); Charles H. McCaghy, James K. Skipper, Jr., and Mark Lefton, eds., *In Their Own Behalf: Voices from the Margin* (New York: Meredith, 1974; 2nd edition); Thomas McCormick, "Marginal Status and Marginal Personality," *Social Forces* 34 (October 1977): 48–55; Russell Ferguson, et al., *Out There: Marginalization and Contemporary Cultures* (Cambridge: MIT Press, 1990); C. Jacquier, "Le développement social urbain," *Les Temps Modernes*, no. 545–6 (January 1992), pp. 165–79; Doug A. Timmer and D. Stanley Eitzen, "The Root Causes of Urban Homelessness in the United States," *Humanity and Society*, 16:2 (May 1992), 159–75; A. Jazouli, *Les années banlieues* (Paris: Seuil, 1992); George S. Bridges and Martha A. Myers, eds., *Inequality, Crime, and Social Control* (Boulder, CO: Westview, 1994); Dough A. Timmer, D. Stanley Eitzen, and Kathryn D. Talley, *Paths to Homelessness: Extreme Poverty and the Urban Housing Crisis* (Boulder, CO: Westview, 1994).

[8] See, for instance, David Sibley, *Outsiders in Urban Societies* (Oxford: Blackwell, 1981); idem., *Geographies of Exclusion: Society and Difference in the West* (London: Routledge, 1995); and R. Shields, *Places on the Margin: Alternative Geographies of Modernity* (London: Routledge, 1991).

[9] William H. McNeill, *Polyethnicity and National Unity in World History* (Toronto: University of Toronto Press, 1986), 6.

[10] Jung Young Lee, *Marginality: The Key to Multicultural Theology* (Minneapolis: Fortress Press, 1995), 79.

Regardless of the specific context, marginality denotes a subordinate or peripheral position that arises out of a conflict between races, ethnic groups, sexes, cultures, religions, lifestyles, social or economic status, and so on. The flip side of marginality is "centrality," a notion that indicates domination or, at the minimum, a dominant position. Marginality is relative to centrality just as a subordinate position is relative to a dominant one and the identity of a stranger is relative to that of the host. Although the concept of marginality evokes a geometric metaphor of center and periphery, there are many different and interrelated dimensions of marginality (such as socioeconomic marginality) which counsel against a mechanical acceptance of this image.[11]

The classic works of Simmel, Park, Stonequist, and others focused on the marginality of individuals or groups who find themselves in alien social environments. They are habitually referred to as "strangers" whose position is determined by the fact that they are not members of the group from birth but come to it later and, according to Simmel, import "qualities into it, which do not and cannot stem from the group itself."[12] Paul Siu constructed a typology that differentiates between three types of strangers: the marginal man, the sojourner, and the settler. In this conception the marginal man is characterized by a "bicultural complex" whereas "the essential characteristic of the sojourner is that he clings to the culture of his own ethnic group."[13] According to Harman, "Gypsies, drifters, migrant workers" – that is, "those who define themselves as temporarily or permanently homeless," – might be considered sojourners.[14] The Roma may be thought of as fitting in the "sojourners" subcategory but not because they are migrants or drifters since most of them have settled long ago. They are strangers of the sojourner variety, to use Simmel and Siu's terminology, owing to most Gypsies' reluctance to integrate let alone assimilate into the dominant societal group.

Markers of the Marginal Identity

Hardly anyone is in a dominant socioeconomic or political situation in every respect. That is to say, nearly everyone is marginal in one context or another. To take a specific example, the young Franklin Delano Roosevelt, the scion of Hudson Valley aristocracy who belonged to dominant and privileged groups in virtually every category (race, gender,

---

[11] This is especially true for a Marxist approach to the subject. See Bailly and Weiss-Altaner, "Thinking About the Edge," 219–32.

[12] Simmel, "The Stranger," in Wolff, ed., *The Sociology of Georg Simmel*, 402.

[13] Paul C. P. Siu, "The Sojourner," *American Journal of Sociology*, 58:1 (1952): 34.

[14] Harman, *The Modern Stranger*, 29.

education, economic position, social status, etc.), was marginalized at Groton, where his lack of athletic ability relegated him to the role of carrying the school baseball team's bags. Later in life his political identity as a Democrat prompted his ostracism by his Hyde Park neighbors; still later being stricken with polio acquainted him with yet another kind of exclusion.

FDR's case also points to the fact that some aspects of marginality are more significant than others. The particular determinants that "affect the intensity and significance of the marginal experience more than others" often have interdependent relations with other factors of marginality.[15] The list of determinants that are suggestive of more comprehensive than single-factor marginality includes race, gender, economic status, education, and occupation. And yet one ought to remember that marginality is usually contextually determined, and factors that are not decisive in one setting may be so in another. For instance, race is a more important determinant of economic or educational marginality in North America than is religion. In a like vein, religion is not a crucial marker of marginality or centrality for a Protestant in a secular society like the Netherlands in contrast to his fellow believers living in Northern Ireland or Saudi Arabia.

Proximity to the dominant group is an integral factor in designating and maintaining membership in a marginal population. Spatial, social, and cultural distances between dominant and marginal groups are some of the key variables that define the nature and extent of a population's marginal condition.[16] Though the immense variety of marginal groups frustrates attempts to make reliable generalizations, indigenous people, multistate populations who straddle international boundaries, displaced people and refugees, as well as legal and illegal labor migrants are nearly always marginalized.[17] Similarly, the status of women has historically been peripheral to that of men, the status of homosexuals has been peripheral to that of heterosexuals, and the status of blue collar workers has been peripheral to that of bureaucrats, even in socialist systems. Societal groups with high birthrates have generally been associated with substandard income, housing, and education. Although "marginality" usually suggests "minority," the two are certainly not synonymous.[18] Marginal populations may comprise numerical majorities as in the cases

---

[15] Lee, *Marginality*, 32–3.

[16] On this issue, see Harman, *The Modern Stranger*, 12–13.

[17] Sam C. Nolutshungu, "International Security and Marginality," in Sam C. Nolutshungu, ed., *Margins of Insecurity: Minorities and International Security* (Rochester: University of Rochester Press, 1996), 21–2.

[18] See Philip Vuciri Ramaga, "Relativity of the Minority Concept," *Human Rights Quarterly*, 14:3 (August 1992): 409–28.

of South African Blacks and Albanians in Serbia's formerly autonomous region of Kosovo.

Marginality may be a result of exogenous circumstances (i.e., factors outside of one's control) or may be rooted in the marginal person or group itself. Social marginality, for instance, may originate in the prejudices, ostracism, and discriminatory policies leveled against an individual or group by the larger society. A more specific example might be a given trade association's refusal to admit members of a religious or ethnic group. At the same time a group may decide to remain outside of larger society for the sake of maintaining its traditions, language, or culture. If members of a religious sect or ethnic community refuse to enter certain occupations or professions open to them, their marginality stems from an endogenous source. Religious groups like the Quakers, the Mennonites, and the Amish *choose* to remain outside of mainstream society. A group of immigrants may segregate itself and depend on each other for social and emotional support and identity maintenance. Many Gypsies reject social relationships with non-Gypsies in order to safeguard their separate identity, traditions, and language. Similarly, Greenwich Village socialists in the 1910s and contemporary Libertarians, as the work of Susan Herbst shows, remained politically marginal intentionally.[19] These examples all point to a phenomenon that may be called self-marginalization or self-exclusion.

Although there are many types of marginality, for the purposes of this book it seems sufficient to distinguish between three types – economic, social, and political. The ultimate economic marginality is that experienced by the homeless, the poorest of the poor. In general, recent immigrants, migrant workers, and people of little formal education may also be considered excluded in the economic sense.[20] Economic discrimination may be a matter of deliberate public policy or the cumulative result of social practices extended over a long period of time.[21] In most cases, ethnic and racial minorities enjoy less favorable economic conditions than does the dominant ethnic community. In 1991, for instance, 11.3% of whites lived below the federally set poverty line in the United States, in contrast with 28.7% of Latinos and 32.7% of African-Americans. The situation was even more skewed when looking at the racial background

---

[19] See Susan Herbst, *Politics at the Margin: Historical Studies of Public Expression Outside the Mainstream* (New York: Cambridge University Press, 1994).

[20] See, for instance, Enrico Pugliese, "New International Migrations and the 'European Fortress'," in Hadjimichalis and Sadler, eds., *Europe at the Margins*, 51–8.

[21] Ted Robert Gurr and James R. Scarritt, "Minorities at Risk: A Global Survey," *Human Rights Quarterly*, 11:3 (August 1989): 384. Curiously, the authors list only the Gypsies living in Czechoslovakia as suffering from discrimination (400).

of those living at half the poverty rate or lower (3.9%, 9.9%, and 15.8%, respectively).[22]

Social marginality usually entails a condition in which an individual or a group of people is shunned, rejected, or ostracized by another. Social exclusion may be occasioned by any of a number of factors or "causes" such as race, ethnic background, economic status, religion, culture, traditions, appearance, or physical handicap. A Hispanic man may be ostracized by a group of Black men. A Muslim in Bosnia may decline to do business with a person of Orthodox faith for no other reason than religion. The relative poverty of a person may prevent her more affluent colleagues from socializing with her. A high school student who does not wear the clothes preferred by his peers may be shunned by them. Women are still often marginalized in their professional lives for no reason other than their gender.[23] Social marginality is more difficult to alleviate when it has multiple causes. Black women participants of the civil rights movement had suffered not only for their race but also for their gender. A similar situation prevailed for Black feminists. As Bell Hooks notes:

Black women were placed in a double bind; to support women's suffrage would imply that they were allying themselves with white women activists who have publicly revealed their racism, but to support only black male suffrage was to endorse a patriarchal social order that would grant them no political voice.[24]

Marginality is generally a multidimensional condition. Dimensions of marginality are often but not always interrelated. On the individual level, a poor and oppressed male, for instance, is often the central and dominant person in a household, just as a woman belonging to a dominant ethnic group may be a marginal member in her home.[25]

Forms of marginalization (political, social, and economic) may not coincide. There are a number of germane examples in modern history. In the Ottoman Empire many rich merchants were Greeks and Jews, yet they did not enjoy the same political rights as their peers of the Muslim

---

[22] U.S. Census Bureau, "Poverty in the United States: 1991," *Current Population Reports*, Series P-60, No. 181 (Washington, DC: U.S. Government Printing Office, 1992), 17–19. See also, John E. Schwarz and Thomas J. Volgy, *The Forgotten Americans* (New York: W. W. Norton, 1992).

[23] See, for instance, Paul Atkinson and Sara Delamont, "Professions and Powerlessness: Female Marginality in the Learned Occupations," *The Sociological Review*, 38:1 (February 1990): 90–110.

[24] Bell Hooks, *Ain't I a Woman: Black Women and Feminism* (Boston: South End Press, 1981), 3.

[25] For an insightful treatment of this notion, see Lee, *Marginality*, Chapter 2.

faith.[26] An even more complex situation existed in the western districts of the Russian Empire where Russians were "politically dominant, Poles culturally dominant, Jews commercially dominant, with Byelorussians and Ukrainians constituting respective demographic majorities."[27] The phenomenon of economically dominant yet politically marginalized populations is not limited to the past. Some contemporary examples are the situation of ethnic Chinese in Indonesia as well as that of people of Indian ethnic heritage in Trinidad and Tobago.

Ethnic marginality is the type of marginal condition that this study is most concerned with. This marginal situation stems from the dominant ethnic group's exclusion of the subordinate ethnic group based on their different ethnicity. The relationship between marginality and the subordinate ethnic group is central because its ethnic marginality usually determines the socioeconomic and political frameworks in which the ethnic group exists. Ethnic marginality most often occurs when an ethnic community lives outside of the state in which it comprises the dominant population. In its "own" state the ethnic group is rarely marginal: Think of Poles living in Belarus versus those residing in Poland. A small number of ethnic groups defy this logic precisely because they do not constitute the majority or dominant ethnic population in *any* state. Examples of these transnational ethnic communities are the Kurds and the Roma as were the Jews until the creation of the modern state of Israel. Ethnic marginality does not by definition signify forms of political, economic, or social exclusion. In practice one finds, however, that ethnically marginal groups nearly always suffer from multiple types of exclusion.

Altering Marginality

The good news is that marginality is not a static condition; through time and across boundaries the marginal status may change. For instance, Estonians were politically marginalized in their own republic by Russians during the Soviet period, but since gaining independence in 1991 they have become the dominant population and have pursued discriminatory policies against their former oppressors. The marginal condition may be alleviated and even terminated in a number of ways. Members of a marginal ethnic group might be willing to embark on the gradual process of assimilation. Assimilation proceeds through several stages. It begins with a person's segregation within his own group and runs to increasing avoidance of association of any kind with his ethnic

---

[26] See, for instance, S. N. Eisenstadt, *The Political System of Empires* (New York: Free Press, 1963), 348.

[27] Joseph Rothschild, *Ethnopolitics: A Conceptual Framework* (New York: Columbia University Press, 1981), 79.

group in order to accelerate assimilation and gain acceptance by the dominant ethnic group. At the end of the process, the assimilated individual or group integrates elements from many realms of society and culture into a more or less stable identity.[28] The processes of acculturation and assimilation do not proceed with the same speed in different cases, and they may not take place at all.

Interestingly, Robert Park uses the example of the Roma as a case when assimilation between divergent cultures and races does not occur. "The chief obstacle to cultural assimilation of races," Park explains, "is not their different mental, but rather their divergent physical traits." Still, according to Park, in the long run "peoples and races who live together, sharing in the same economy, inevitably interbreed, and in this way" at least relations between them will eventually become social and cultural.[29] One wonders though, what Park meant by "in the long run" since numerous cases show, not the least that of the European Gypsies, that different racial groups have lived side by side for centuries with modest levels of assimilation. A more sensible argument is Kliot's who suggests that the larger the differences between an ethnic minority and the majority group, and the higher the costs of assimilation, the more likely a group is going to preserve and promote its separate identity.[30]

A more customary method of reducing marginal condition is through migration. People who are excluded on the basis of their rural residence far from the educational, economic, and social opportunities offered by an urban center may alleviate their marginality by moving to the city. Similarly, people residing in poorer countries can hope to diminish their economic marginality by moving to more affluent ones. As the example of the millions of Southern European guest workers who moved to Northern and Western Europe in the 1960s and 1970s shows, while migrants usually succeed in reducing their economic disadvantage in their native land they become marginal in both the economic *and* social context in their new homes. Another case of interstate migration is the German exodus from interwar Eastern Europe back to their historic homeland. In-country migration may substantially decrease marginal conditions in states with large regional economic disparities. For instance, Italians from Calabria and Sicily have been migrating to Lombardy for decades. In the early twentieth century, millions of

---

[28] See Daniel Glaser, "Dynamics of Ethnic Identification," *American Sociological Review*, 23:1 (February 1958): 31–40; and Ronald A. Remnick, *Theory of Ethnicity* (Lanham, MD: University Press of America, 1983), 27–30.

[29] Park, *Race and Culture*, 353–4.

[30] See N. Kliot, "Mediterranean Potential for Ethnic Conflict: Some Generalizations," *Tijdschrift voor Econ. en Soc. Geografie*, 80:3 (1989): 147–63.

African-Americans left the South for, in effect, lesser economic, social, and political marginality in the Northeast and the upper Midwest.

From our perspective the effect that regime change has on ethnic marginality is particularly important. Does regime change introduce any major changes into the life of marginal groups or does it leave them unaffected? My argument is that, in general, regime change creates momentous opportunities for the alleviation of the marginal condition only when the emerging new political system is a democracy. Shifts from one authoritarian system to another are scarcely accompanied by the dominant ethnic group's increased regard for persecuted ethnic communities. The process of regime transition nevertheless tends to heighten the sense of common deprivation in marginalized groups who are more likely to organize themselves in transitional societies. It should be noted that research has unearthed no evidence that those experiencing the most deprivation will be most likely to participate in movements.[31] As the recent East European transitions have demonstrated, the chance for marginalized ethnic groups to mobilize might at the same time evoke anti-minority sentiments from the dominant group. Sudden change, as Václav Havel notes, usually "brings new freedom and responsibilities, and many find it difficult to cope with them."[32]

Interaction between Marginal and Dominant Groups

Marginality is always relational: center to periphery, domination to subordination, excluder to excluded. Marginality is explained only in relation to centrality. For social scientists, one of the most intriguing questions is posed by the interaction between the marginal and the dominant groups. How do relations between peripheral and central groups develop? Through what methods do dominant groups ensure the preservation of their privileged position? How can excluded groups be effective in combatting sources of their marginality?

The dominant group defines the marginal group through the lenses of the dominant social norms, religion, ethnic identity, and economic and occupational status. Conversely, as Stonequist suggests, the marginal man learns to see himself from two viewpoints, that of his group and that of the group he aspires to be a member of.[33] Although Park, Stonequist, and others take it as a given that members of marginal groups crave to be parts of the dominant group, it is not necessarily so. Some

[31] See C. G. Pickvance, "Where Have Urban Movements Gone?" in Hadjimichalis and Sadler, eds., *Europe at the Margins*, 197–218.

[32] These are Havel's words quoted by Henry Kamm in *New York Times*, 10 December 1993.

[33] Harman, *The Modern Stranger*, 23.

groups – hippies, counterculture types, members of some religious organizations, and so on – actually might be content with their position on the margin. These groups – and in many ways various ethnic groups including some Gypsy communities can be counted among them – may exclude themselves by maintaining their customs and traditions rather than lose their identities and become members of the dominant social, ethnic, or religious group.

By virtue of its central position the dominant group usually has numerous ways of ensuring and maintaining its position. The dominant position does not have to be supported by military or economic might; instead it may be based on other foundations, such as perceived cultural superiority. Think, for instance, of the favored position of a literate culture in contrast to an illiterate or unwritten one. The culture, history, and identity of illiterate communities might be bent and manipulated by people who possess the ability to read and write. The Yugoslav writer, Ivo Andrić, describes such a situation in his book, *The Bridge on the Drina*:

It was known that he was writing a chronicle of the most important events in the history of the town. Among the citizens this gave him the fame of a learned and exceptional man, for it was considered that by this he held in some way the fate of the town and every individual in it in his hands.[34]

A dominant group is usually able to shape the cultural identity of a marginal group through the educational system. For example, until recently, Hispanics and Blacks had virtually no input in the curricula of American school systems, which imparted little knowledge to minority students about their histories and cultures. Clearly, the topics that are covered and the manner in which they are treated have political implications and may be used to transmit authority to dominant groups.[35] Furthermore, members of the dominant group may exclude children of minorities from educational institutions altogether through quotas or other discriminatory mechanisms. Education is just one of many possible settings – ranging from the judicial system to the housing industry – in which dominant and marginal groups interact. The dominant group's position vis-à-vis the marginal group is often based on or supported by its control of political resources.

Politics and Marginality

Since the 1960s the notion of political marginality has received a measure of scholarly attention (in relation with the civil rights movement, for

---

[34] Ivo Andrić, *The Bridge on the Drina* (London: Allen & Unwin, 1959), 128.
[35] See Pierre Bourdieu and Jean Claude Passeron, *Reproduction of Education, Society, and Culture* (London: Sage, 1977).

instance), but its power to explain or illuminate political phenomena has not been fully utilized. This is partly so because the concept of marginality was mainly used to illuminate the specificities of marginal conditions. Nonetheless, the concept could be much more extensively utilized. It is a valuable tool for studying the political struggles of those groups that have traditionally been positioned outside the mainstream and others that may be in the process of breaking down barriers to their political participation.

In order to understand the political marginality of a community, one must go beyond the analysis of its political behavior. I am interested not merely in the excluded groups' conditions of political marginality but even more in how exogenous political factors might affect their marginality and how marginalized groups themselves can overcome political obstacles. We need to develop a new approach to political marginality that analyzes and explains its roots, causes, and the methods of alleviating them as well as the evolving political relationship between the marginal and the dominant groups. It is important to understand the changes in the political dimension of marginality through time and space and how these changes may occur regardless of corresponding shifts in social and economic marginality.

Marginal condition in the political sense might result from a variety of sources which, in fact, may be rooted not in political but in social or economic marginality. The dominant social or ethnic group usually holds political power and can force the subordinate group into a political marginality justified by the different race, gender, ethnic origin, economic status, or sexual orientation of the latter. For instance, Blacks in South Africa were not allowed to vote until recently. In many Western democracies, women did not enjoy full political rights until the twentieth century, and known homosexuals were politically marginalized in most jurisdictions. Some states, like Bulgaria, still prohibit the founding of political parties based on ethnicity while others, such as Romania, still discriminate against homosexuals. Historically, in most polities political rights were conditioned on a certain level of property ownership and/or social status.

To appreciate the divergent sources of political marginality, I propose a four-part typology that Table 2.1 presents in a more succinct form. This typology suggests four general areas in which political marginality is rooted. First, endogenous or internal political causes refer to the shortcomings (e.g., incompetent leadership, inappropriate political programs) of the marginal group's own political mobilization process. Second, exogenous or external political causes allude to the actions of states or societies that limit the marginal group's political opportunities. Such actions might include banning the marginal group's political activities, or playing rival organizations of the marginal group off against each

Table 2.1. Sources of Political Marginality

Source	Endogenous	Exogenous
Political	Defects in mobilization (e.g., weak leadership, poor organizational work, uncoordinated political campaigns)	State and societal discrimination (e.g., prohibitive laws, attempts to divide ethnic political parties)
Socioeconomic	Absence of strong ethnic identity, lacking ethnic cohesion and solidarity, low levels of education, poverty, etc.	Societal discrimination in culture, education, employment, tensions in interethnic relations, etc.

other. Third, there are endogenous social and/or economic causes such as the absence of ethnic solidarity, low educational attainments, and lack of resources. Finally, exogenous socioeconomic causes have to do with the social and/or economic characteristics of the marginal group's environment that precipitate or cause its political marginality. The most common examples are prejudiced treatment (e.g., in the media or in the education system) or even outright persecution (e.g., by skinhead gangs) of the marginal group by the dominant group that create or contribute to political barriers.

Political marginality may be manifested in a variety of ways: by limitations on political representation and voting rights, denial of cultural rights, exclusion from certain professions, restrictions on housing, refusal of or restrictions on public services, and so on. In contrast, a powerful political position might serve to reduce the group's marginality in other dimensions, such as in the economic realm. There are several examples of previously economically marginalized peoples reversing their exclusion (primarily by converting political mobilization into economic power), like the French in Quebec and the Afrikaner majority among South African whites.[36] Using their political power, Anglos in the nineteenth-century American Southwest managed to push Mexicans into economic marginality. The idea is that if one is politically dominant, one may be able to change the economic rules to reduce one's economic marginality. Political successes do not necessarily produce economic gains, but, in general, time works in favor of those with political clout.

The dominant group's organizations in position to maintain or change the political marginality of the excluded group are the state and its

---

[36] An excellent discussion of this phenomenon is Milton J. Esman, "Ethnic Politics and Economic Power," *Comparative Politics*, 19:4 (July 1987): 395–418.

authorities. The state did not play a major mediating role in society until the economic upheavals of the 1870s when competition for scarce resources among social groups and classes increased precipitously.[37] Until recently, comparative social scientists rarely considered states as organizational structures let alone as potentially autonomous actors.[38] I view the state as an actor that is influenced by society but at the same time possesses the autonomy and power to mold social behavior and to change political and social processes. Furthermore, the state can be instrumental in modifying not only the political but also the social and economic marginality of disadvantaged groups.

Although state policies might prohibit discrimination, marginalization may persist through dominantly accepted views, mores, and customs and as a result of ineffective protective mechanisms for the marginal group. Therefore, the likelihood that prohibitive state legislation will be effective will be higher if it is going to be backed up by the consistent punishment of those who break the law. Certain types of widespread societal prejudices and discriminatory behaviors in time will be associated with negative and costly consequences that might result in changes in societal attitudes. State policies, then, can be effective in reducing marginality by shaping societal attitudes, although this is usually a long-term process. Conversely, marginality may be perpetuated and increased through the persistence of the state's discriminatory policies and laws, which, in turn, might serve to conserve society's exclusionary attitudes.

It is important to differentiate between the various state institutions and their relationship to and interaction with marginal groups. Although momentous decisions pertaining to marginal populations are usually reached in central state institutions like the government, its ministries, or the national legislature, for marginal communities the law is usually personified by local authorities such as law enforcement personnel or aid administrators. The point is that the progressive ideas of central governmental bodies may have little practical value to the excluded community if they are not implemented consistently on the local level.

Properties of Gypsy Marginality

Marginality is the concept that provides the best handle to understanding the Gypsies' centuries-long experience in Eastern Europe and elsewhere. Indeed, they are the marginal ethnic group *extraordinaire*, the

---

[37] On this point, see Herbst, *Politics at the Margin*, 12; and, more generally, Jürgen Habermas, *The Structural Transformation of the Public Sphere: An Inquiry into a Category of Bourgeois Society* (Cambridge, MA: MIT Press, 1989).

[38] Peter B. Evans, Dietrich Rueschemeyer, and Theda Skocpol, eds., *Bringing the State Back In* (New York: Cambridge University Press, 1985), vii.

quintessential strangers, who can be scarcely considered "dominant" or "central" in any context. Perhaps the most important aspect of Romani marginality is that they do not have a homeland (most Roma certainly do not consider India a homeland if they are aware of the India connection at all) and, consequently, a mother state to express concern about them. Does the absence of a homeland make the Roma a diaspora? According to the definitions of John Armstrong and Yossi Shain, it does not because the Gypsies do not regard themselves as belonging to or having a homeland elsewhere, as diasporas, by definition, do.[39]

In every European society the Roma have consistently occupied the lowest rungs of the social, political, and economic ladders. At the same time, the extent and attributes of their marginal conditions have varied considerably through regime types and in different states. The most important factor of Gypsy marginality has been their constant societal exclusion. As we shall see, the Gypsies' economic marginality has changed through the centuries. Before the Industrial Revolution made an impact on East European economies and during the state-socialist era the Roma did have a relatively well-defined although subordinate economic role. The recent advent of democratization has created the prerequisites for their political activism and thus the attenuation of their political marginality. Nevertheless, the societal ill-feeling against the Roma has been a perpetual feature of Gypsy life in all of Europe.

Through the centuries the Roma have been ostracized, persecuted, and stereotyped as lazy, uninhibited, deceitful, dirty, unreliable, and prone to theft and other criminal behavior. "The Gypsies are nearer to the animals than any race known to us in Europe," opined a nineteenth-century British chronicler.[40] In 1911 they were described as "an entire race of criminals, with all the passions and vices common to delinquent types: ignorance, impetuous fury, vanity, love of orgies, and ferocity."[41] Although the Gypsies – like other pastoral and nomadic people – have

---

[39] See John A. Armstrong, "Mobilized and Proletarian Diasporas," *American Political Science Review*, 70:2 (June 1976): 393–408 and Yossi Shain, *The Frontier of Loyalty: Political Exiles in the Age of the Nation-State* (Middletown, CT: Wesleyan University Press, 1989), 51–2. In contrast, Gabriel Sheffer differentiates between stateless (Palestinians, Kurds, Gypsies, etc.) and state-based diasporas as well as between territorially concentrate and dispersed ones. See his "Ethno-National Diasporas and Security," *Survival*, 36:1 (Spring 1994): 61–2. I find the Armstrong–Shain definitions rather more unambiguous.

[40] Cited in David Mayall, *Gypsy-Travellers in Nineteenth Century Society* (Cambridge: Cambridge University Press, 1988), 80.

[41] Cited in Sibley, *Geographies of Exclusion*, 18. For an excellent analysis of more contemporary stereotypes in rural areas, see Peter D. Bell, *Peasants in Socialist Transition: Life in a Collectivized Hungarian Village* (Berkeley: University of California Press, 1984), 283–96.

often been romanticized, they have also been traditionally "held in bad repute and regarded with suspicion."[42] Not surprisingly, in time they had come to prefer as little interaction with non-Gypsies as possible. And yet, communication with the dominant group is usually an important factor in the life of the marginal group. Considering their extensive poverty, the Romani community could scarcely survive without the economic benefits that commercial relations with non-Gypsies could provide.[43]

The Roma have not possessed a distinctive religion or a highly developed written culture. The Romani language (and its numerous dialects) has been unwritten until quite recently, a fact that has contributed to indifference on the part of most Roma about their history. Religion and culture could act as territory substitutes for the Jews, whereas the Gypsies could only rely on a vigorous self-segregation and, with less success, on maintaining their language to preserve their identity.[44] John Berger's distinction between cultures of progress (those that are forward looking and based on a promising and hopeful future) and cultures of survival (which envisage the future as a sequence of acts of survival) is instructive in understanding both Gypsy culture and marginality.[45]

In practical terms the extremely low educational level of most Gypsy communities – the most important reason for their continued marginality in contemporary Europe – can be partly explained by the notion that education requires considerable investment in time, energy, and resources and as such has been conceived by many Roma as a luxury they could not afford. In turn, their lack of education has limited the types of employment available to them. Michael Hechter has called attention to the importance of the specific niche that an ethnic group might fill in the occupational structure and the prestige of that vocation.[46] The Roma could hardly fare worse in this respect: Most of the typical "Gypsy" occupations (such as trash collection, street cleaning, palm reading, livestock trade, prostitution) are held in low esteem.

PART II. ETHNIC MOBILIZATION

Marginal populations are not simply the helpless pawns of dominant groups and state policies. Given favorable circumstances, they may be able to organize and participate in the political process. Unorganized

[42] Anya Peterson Smith, *Ethnic Identity: Strategies of Diversity* (Bloomington: Indiana University Press, 1982), 153.

[43] See, for instance, Sibley, *Outsiders in Urban Societies*, 149.

[44] Raymond Pearson, *National Minorities in Eastern Europe, 1848–1945* (London: Macmillan, 1983), 19.

[45] John Berger, *Pig Earth* (London: Writers and Readers Publishing Cooperative, 1979), 204.

[46] Michael Hechter, "Group Formation and the Cultural Division of Labor," *American Journal of Sociology*, 84:2 (September 1978): 299.

minority groups scarcely get political recognition let alone political influence or strength. Historically, women, African Americans, homosexuals, and other marginal groups found that once they started to organize, the prospects for reducing their political marginality began to brighten. Take the example of the women's movement in America. In the first half of the nineteenth century, women in the United States possessed little political power. Only a decade after the death of Susan B. Anthony (1906), once their political activism had intensified and attracted mass participation, did they start acquiring political clout and, in 1920, the right to vote. The second part of this chapter is concerned with what marginal ethnic groups may be able to do in order to emerge from their predicament. The key to this dilemma is the political mobilization of the ethnic community.

Ethnic Mobilization and Ethnopolitics

In this section I seek to make generalizations pertaining to the conditions necessary and conducive to and the key "ingredients" needed for successful ethnic mobilization. I believe that the importance of conventional factors like identity, leadership, group cohesion, and action program cannot be stressed too much when discussing the prerequisites of ethnic mobilization. Before proceeding further, however, it seems worthwhile to define the key concepts pertinent to the discussion that follows. Milton Esman has defined ethnic identity as "the set of meanings that individuals impute to their membership in an ethnic community, including those attributes that bind them to that collectivity and that distinguishes it from others in their relevant environment."[47] Political mobilization, according to Charles Tilly's definition, is "the process by which a group goes from being a passive collection of individuals to an active participant in public life."[48] Ethnic mobilization is "the process by which groups organize around some feature of ethnic identity (for example, skin color, language, customs) in pursuit of collective ends."[49] Finally, ethnopolitics refers to the political activity of ethnic groups. A slightly different way to think about ethnic politics is that it is defined by collective action directed at maintaining, strengthening, or extending ethnic boundaries.[50]

---

[47] Milton Esman, *Ethnic Politics* (Ithaca: Cornell University Press, 1994), 27. See also the discussion in Saad Z. Nagi, "Ethnic Identification and Nationalist Movements," *Human Organization*, 51:4 (1992): 308.

[48] Charles Tilly, *From Mobilization to Revolution* (New York: Random House, 1978), 69.

[49] Susan Olzak, "Contemporary Ethnic Mobilization," *Annual Review of Sociology*, 9 (1983): 355.

[50] Michael T. Hannan, "The Dynamics of Ethnic Boundaries in Modern States," in John W. Meyer and Michael T. Hannan, eds., *National Development and the World System: Educational, Economic, and Political Change, 1950–1970* (Chicago: University of Chicago Press, 1979), 268.

Political mobilization denotes the deliberate activity of a group of individuals for the realization of political objectives. Mobilization is attitudinal insofar as there is a firm commitment to action and requires "means of translating this commitment into action or observed behavior."[51] These goals generally encompass enhanced interest representation; the cessation of political, social, economic and other types of discrimination; and the improvement of the given collective's conditions and relative standing in society. Mobilization needs to produce and maximize political resources that will amplify the group's influence; these typically include attracting votes, activating sympathetic third parties, building coalitions, and lobbying and may entail political goods like disruptions, protests, and violence, which may be used as bargaining chips.[52] Mobilization may be measured by the active membership of the organizations created, the amount of resources accumulated, the number of programs established, and the number and size of demonstrations and protests organized.

A variety of causes may bring about ethnic mobilization, but conditions of relative deprivation – whether cultural, social economic, or political – are nearly always at its root. Ethnic mobilization may occur even in the absence of such exclusion or marginalization in cases where the mobilizing community intends to improve its circumstances vis-à-vis other ethnic groups in society. Ethnic mobilization may be triggered or stimulated by the complete or partial removal of obstacles in the way of ethnic activism, the emergence of charismatic leader(s), and/or instances of particular distress or injustice suffered by the given ethnic group. The nature of ethnic mobilization may depend on the identity of those blocking it (whether it is the state, a particular political actor, or another ethnic group), the circumstances of the injury suffered by the ethnic group (e.g., violent or nonviolent), and prevailing political, social, and cultural rules, norms, and values affecting political activity. In sum, ethnic mobilization is fueled by people's grievances about their relative deprivation and their determination to pursue their political interests.[53]

Clearly, the chances of marginal populations to acquire political and economic power are increased if they manage to organize themselves in a cohesive way.[54] Ethnopolitics may be thought of as the final stage of a

---

[51] J. P. Nettl, *Political Mobilization: A Sociological Analysis of Methods and Concepts* (New York: Basic Books, 1967), 32–3.

[52] Michael Lipsky, "Protest as Political Resource," *American Political Science Review*, 62:4 (December 1968): 1144–58.

[53] Ted Robert Gurr, *Minorities at Risk: A Global View of Ethnopolitical Conflicts* (Washington, DC: U.S. Institute of Peace, 1993), 123.

[54] See, for instance, Stephen Mennell, "The Formation of We-Images: A Process Theory," in Craig Calhoun, ed., *Social Theory and the Politics of Identity* (Cambridge, MA: Blackwell, 1994), 183.

process that begins with ethnic mobilization.[55] This process may be divided into three distinct phases. The first is the formation and strengthening of ethnic identity, the sharpening of the ethnic group's boundaries vis-à-vis other groups. The second is the securing of the important prerequisites necessary for political action, such as financial resources, leaders, media outlets, and the further enhancement of the group's unique identity through the sharing of symbols and participation in social activities. The third stage is the actual political action taken to promote the interests of the ethnic group through political participation.

From the perspective of my case study it is particularly notable that during the phase of systemic political change (and especially in the transition from authoritarian to democratic regimes), social and political movements – whether urban, ethnic, nationalist, or environmental – seem to flourish.[56] Ethnic political activity, whether institutional or non-institutional, tends to increase during political upheavals because such periods frequently coincide with the breakdown of authority and create favorable circumstances for activism. The end of state-socialist rule in democratizing states permitted the political organization of virtually all marginal populations, including the Roma. In mature democracies where universal suffrage ensures that nearly all citizens enjoy the right to affect political outcomes, marginal groups have been able to gain political recognition.

In the past fifty years many marginal ethnic groups residing in states whose political systems permitted ethnic activism have attempted some sort of political organization. Indeed, a recent study showed that only 27 of 233 communal groups surveyed did not leave any record of political organization since 1945.[57] A successful political mobilization process, one that manages to activate a significant proportion of group membership and to achieve at least some of its political ends, depends on a number variables. We should consider these before we turn to the discussion of ethnic mobilization.

Ethnic Identity and Its Formation

A fundamental requirement of political mobilization is the presence of a clearly formulated identity that members of the marginal group share,

---

[55] See, for instance, Beatrice Drury, "Ethnic Mobilization: Some Theoretical Considerations," in John Rex and Beatrice Drury, eds., *Ethnic Mobilization in a Multicultural Europe* (Aldershot, England: Avebury, 1994), 15. She conceptualizes ethnic mobilization as a four-stage process.

[56] Pickvance, "Where Have Urban Movements Gone," 206. For a substantive discussion see Chapter 2 in Rasma Karklins, *Ethnopolitics and Transition to Democracy: The Collapse of the USSR and Latvia* (Baltimore: Johns Hopkins University Press, 1994), 23–41.

[57] Gurr, *Minorities at Risk*, 7.

accept, and uphold. Ethnic groups embarking on the process of political mobilization must formulate, refine, and strengthen their ethnic identity. Ethnicity, like all identities, is relational; it attests to a consciousness of collective identity woven from several attributes like shared history, traditions, culture, and language.[58] But it is only one of a number of identities a person or a group of persons might strongly embrace. Daniel Bell lists five "macrosocial units," key markers of individual and group identity: national, religious, ethnic, class, and gender.[59] These are obviously significant, but there may be many other identities important in the given context. For a Franciscan monk or a soldier in the Foreign Legion, ethnic identity may be of secondary importance compared to their vocational identities. In a like vein, many young men in contemporary Europe and Latin America may well consider their support for a favorite soccer team a far more notable identifying attribute than the type of work they do. Though the importance of ethnicity among the slices that round out one's entire identity is contextually determined, for most people ethnic belonging tends to be one of the most important – if, indeed, not *the* most momentous – marker of their self, their identity. In the words of Joseph Rothschild, the great advantage of ethnicity over other emblems of personal identity is "its capacity to arouse and to engage the most intense, deep, and private emotional sentiments."[60]

Ethnicity, then, is one of a cluster of identity options whose value is enhanced in some circumstances and denied in others.[61] Ethnic identity should not be confused with national identity. Culture, for instance, is a far more important ingredient of ethnic than of national identity. Assimilation, on the other hand, may be the goal of an ethnic group but not that of a nation.[62] Even more than national identity, ethnic identity needs to be preserved and maintained. Throughout history, many ethnic groups have, in fact, vanished as they were gradually absorbed by other ethnic groups and lost their identity. The preservation of spatial, social, and cultural distance from other ethnic groups, along with the refusal of ethnic

---

[58] On this issue, see Dickson Eyoh, "From the Belly to the Ballot: Ethnicity and Politics in Africa," *Queen's Quarterly*, 102:1 (Spring 1995): 40; and Liah Greenfeld, *Nationalism: Five Roads to Modernity* (Cambridge, MA: Harvard University Press, 1992), 13.

[59] Daniel Bell, *Ethnic Groups and Boundaries: The Social Organization of Culture Differences* (Boston: Little, Brown, 1975), 152–8.

[60] Rothschild, *Ethnopolitics*, 60.

[61] See Sandra Wallman, "Introduction: The Scope of Ethnicity," in Sandra Wallman, ed., *Ethnicity at Work* (London: Macmillan, 1979), 1–16.

[62] See Cynthia H. Enloe, *Ethnic Conflict and Political Development* (Boston: Little, Brown & Co., 1973), 159; and, more generally, Anthony D. Smith, *National Identity* (Reno: University of Nevada Press, 1991).

assimilation and integration, may, in favorable circumstances, ensure the survival of an ethnic group's unique identity.[63]

The presumption that an ethnic group would, by definition, possess a well-formed identity is erroneous, particularly in the cases of populations marked by cultural, social, and linguistic diversity. In order to flourish, ethnic identity must be consciously preserved, sustained, and strengthened.

Ethnic groups contemplating collective action must succeed in developing a heightened group consciousness in which cultural traits which were usually taken for granted are given new meanings and in which these symbols become salient markers in the construction of new (political) identities.[64]

Ethnic identity may be formed and strengthened through a number of methods. These may include the celebration of a historical personality, the commemoration of pivotal past events whether fortunate (e.g., a victorious battle) or cataclysmic (e.g., the Holocaust), and the organization of festivals to conserve the ethnic group's traditions and culture. The chief objective of these endeavors is to endow individuals' ethnic [as opposed to other (e.g., geographic, occupational, gender)] identity with meaning, substance, and depth. Ethnic identity "is developed, displayed, manipulated, or ignored in accordance with the demands of particular situations."[65] Ethnic consciousness, like national consciousness, tends to develop unevenly among various socioeconomic strata and regions of a country.[66] This is all the more so in ethnic groups made up of different tribes or other subgroups.

Historically, ethnic groups have often found it advantageous and even imperative to deny their true ethnic identity and adopt another. As Nelson Kasfir noted, the "identity chosen may be rationally selected by calculating costs and benefits, or it may be conditioned by deeply held values."[67] In a strongly anti-Semitic or anti-Romani environment chances are that, for the sake of self-preservation, fewer Jews or Gypsies would identify themselves as such than in more favorable surroundings. In some cases there may be such social stigma attached to belonging to a certain ethnic community that the denial of identity is nearly complete.

---

[63] See Berger, *Pig Earth*, 195–213, and especially 204.
[64] Drury, "Ethnic Mobilization," 22.
[65] Smith, *Ethnic Identity*, 1.
[66] E. J. Hobsbawm, *Nations and Nationalism Since 1780: Programme, Myth, Reality* (Cambridge: Cambridge University Press, 1990), 12.
[67] Nelson Kasfir, "Explaining Ethnic Political Participation," *World Politics*, 31:3 (April 1979): 372.

The persistence of ethnic identity has much to do with a group's success in coping with the problems of adaptation to outside forces and circumstances.[68] Marginal ethnic groups that maintain nomadic or seminomadic lifestyles, *ceteris paribus*, are usually more effective in preserving their ethnic identity than their settled counterparts, which the dominant population can control with less difficulty. For a heterogeneous ethnic group – one that is marked by geographic, cultural, tribal, or linguistic diversity – the formation and articulation of its identity is more difficult than for more cohesive ethnic groups. Identity is closely connected with collective memory; therefore, literate cultures with written sources chronicling a common past are usually more successful in formulating their identity than preliterate ones.[69]

Whether or not members of an ethnic group are aware of their shared ethnic identity, they do, by definition, have such an identity. The purpose of identity formation, preservation, confirmation, and articulation is precisely to make members of the ethnic group cognizant of their common identity – in other words, to make them appreciate their collective past. "Wherever the memory of the origin of a community . . . remains for some reason alive," wrote Max Weber, "there undoubtedly exists a very specific and often extremely powerful sense of ethnic identity."[70] For Weber, shared political memories constitute a vital component of ethnic identity and, thus, are extremely important for ethnic group membership. While the political mobilization of an ethnic group is extremely difficult without a well-rounded collective identity, the mobilization process itself contributes to the formation of the ethnic group's political identity.[71] Ethnogenesis, a conscious attempt to achieve the status of a cohesive ethnic minority, is, in itself an act of political mobilization.[72] Ultimately though, ethnic mobilization may be considered the politicization of ethnic identity.

---

[68] George Pierre Castile, "On the Tarascannes of the Tarascans and the Indianness of the Indians," in George Pierre Castile and Gilbert Kushner, eds., *Persistent Peoples: Cultural Enclaves in Perspective* (Tucson: University of Arizona Press, 1981), 173.

[69] See Harold Isaacs, *Idols of the Tribe: Group Identity and Political Change* (Cambridge, MA: Harvard University Press, 1989 [originally published in New York: Harper & Row, 1975]), 115–43; David Lowenthal, *The Past Is a Foreign Country* (New York: Cambridge University Press, 1985); and James Fentress and Chris Wickham, *Social Memory* (Oxford: Blackwell, 1992).

[70] Max Weber, *Economy and Society: An Outline of Interpretive Sociology* (Berkeley: University of California Press, 1978), 390.

[71] For an unorthodox treatment of this notion, see Anne Norton, *Reflections on Political Identity* (Baltimore: Johns Hopkins University Press, 1988).

[72] See Slawomir Kapralski, "Identity Building and the Holocaust: Roma Political Nationalism," *Nationalities Papers*, 25:2 (1997): 269.

Other Prerequisites of Ethnic Mobilization

A highly developed and strong ethnic identity is necessary but not sufficient for ethnic mobilization. The success of ethnic mobilization efforts depends on several additional criteria. Let us consider the most important of these.

Past Mobilization Experience, Independence, or Autonomy

Ethnic mobilization processes are helped by the ethnic community's prior experience in political activism. Such mobilization background might be drawn on, learned from, and critically examined by the community. Memories of past independence or autonomy may also propel the ethnic group toward political activism (one salient example is the Albanian community in Kosovo in the late 1990s).

Ethnic Solidarity and Social Capital

Ethnic political mobilization is promoted by a population that is cohesive and has developed some degree of ethnic solidarity. This ethnic fellowship may be the result of numerous factors. Prejudicial state policies in housing, welfare, education, taxation, and so on, often foment mobilization processes. In many developing societies where labor markets are segregated by ethnicity, ethnic solidarity increases, and along with it the propensity of disadvantaged ethnic groups to mobilize.[73] A less tangible "ingredient" beneficial to mobilization is what might be described as social capital.[74] That is, it helps if members of the mobilizing community trust each other, have confidence in their neighbors, live by commonly accepted social norms and values, and engage in coordinated collective activities. Ordinarily, groups that do not possess such resources will find organizing collective action more difficult.

Leadership

An indispensable part of the "standard equipment" that ethnic groups need to make credible political claims is the availability of a pool of potential leaders who enjoy some measure of authority in the ethnic community, who are capable to lead to furnish the group with some

---

[73] See Charles C. Ragin, "Ethnic Political Mobilization: The Welsh Case," *American Sociological Review*, 44:4 (August 1979): 619–35; Susan Olzak, "Contemporary Ethnic Mobilization," *Annual Review of Sociology*, 9 (1983): 358–63; Francois Nielsen, "Toward a Theory of Ethnic Solidarity in Modern Societies," *American Sociological Review*, 50:2 (April 1985): 133–49; Juan Diez Medrano, "The Effects of Ethnic Segregation and Ethnic Competition on Political Mobilization in the Basque Country, 1988," *American Sociological Review*, 59:6 (December 1994): 873–89.

[74] See Robert D. Putnam, *Making Democracy Work: Civic Traditions in Modern Italy* (Princeton: Princeton University Press, 1993), 163–85.

organizational form. Ordinarily the individuals who are qualified for leadership come from the ranks of the intelligentsia; therefore, it is helpful if the overall educational level of the ethnic community allows the formation of a critical mass of educated individuals who can take on leadership roles.

The importance of the leader(s) is paramount because those in leadership positions may determine the success or failure of the organization or movement. Individuals dominating the ethnic movement might be "natural" leaders whose academic qualifications, economic position, social standing, and political background may predestine them for leadership. Alternatively, leaders may emerge by way of a deliberate selection mechanism that might adopt criteria such as the capacity to successfully interact with the given ethnic group as well as with other (particularly the dominant) ethnic group(s), politicians, or business leaders.

If the group is divided by disagreements, leaders need to negotiate compromises and achieve a consensus on at least the fundamental goals and tactics of the mobilization process. Competition and rifts within ethnic elites generally impede while cooperation fosters the ethnic group's chances for mobilization.[75] One of the key tasks of the leader is to forge links with the population hitherto uninvolved in politics.[76] The individual leader's success in enrolling the participation of the population to a large extent depends on the level of support (s)he receives and the number of rivals who challenge him/her.

Organizations

The institutional form through which mobilization itself is expressed is one of the most significant aspects of ethnic mobilization. Once it is decided to create an organization, a number of issues need to be deliberated. Would an exclusive, elite-type organization serve the group's objectives better, or do circumstances require a mass party or movement? What would be the main profile of the organization: political, economic, or cultural? A principal condition of any ethnic group's political effectiveness is raising the communal consciousness of its members.[77] The mobilizing groups must also identify the people (e.g., businessmen, intellectuals, women) who the group wants to attract to the organization and the method of their recruitment.

---

[75] Paul R. Brass, *Ethnicity and Nationalism: Theory and Comparison* (New Delhi: Sage, 1991), 25–30.

[76] John Breuilly, *Nationalism and the State* (Chicago: University of Chicago Press, 1993), 19.

[77] Enloe, *Ethnic Conflict and Political Development*, 160.

Ethnic parties do not exist in all multiethnic political systems. Nonetheless, in many ethnically divided societies, parties tend to organize along ethnic lines.[78] A decisive organizational question of the ethnic group's political representation is the number of its institutions. It would appear logical that a single organization that acts as the sole representative of the ethnic group would increase cohesion in the community. In fact, Paul Brass has argued that it is critically important "that one political organization be dominant in representing the demands of the ethnic group against its rivals."[79] Still, some ethnic communities are so deeply split along occupational, tribal, or other lines that it would be a mistake to expect one organization to articulate their diverse interests. Conversely, a relatively homogeneous ethnic population might create a large number of organizations owing to rivalries within its leadership or dissimilar political views among its members. Under what conditions is a single organization able to assert itself and what circumstances foster organizational fraction? The answers to these questions may depend on numerous related variables such as leadership competition, generational disputes, interfamilial and clan tensions, ideological cleavages, and class differences.

If more than one party represents an ethnic group, they might find it beneficial to cooperate, particularly come election time. The establishment of an umbrella organization or electoral coalition aiming to represent the entire ethnic community can be very effective in increasing the ethnic group's political voice. Alternatively, an ethnic party may need the political and organizational assistance of mainstream parties. Alliance structures are often governed by the political conditions of the moment, but might yield increased political representation, stability, support, and strength for the ethnic party.[80]

Organizations evolve and develop according to their internal dynamics created by their leaders and members, their internal rules, and endogenous hierarchies and structures, and of course they are affected by their socioeconomic and political environments. Highly developed organizations are characterized by adaptability, complexity, autonomy, and cohesion.[81] In contrast, organizations that are marked by rigidity, simplicity, subordination, and disunity are usually incapable of achieving their goals and rarely survive for long.

---

[78] See Donald L. Horowitz, *Ethnic Groups in Conflict* (Berkeley: University of California Press, 1985), 291–7.

[79] Brass, *Ethnicity and Nationalism*, 49.

[80] Hanspeter Kriesi, et al., *New Social Movements in Western Europe: A Comparative Perspective* (Minneapolis: University of Minnesota Press, 1995), 53.

[81] See the "criteria of political institutionalization" in Samuel P. Huntington, *Political Order in Changing Societies* (New Haven, CT: Yale University Press, 1968), pp. 12–24.

Ideology, Profile, Program

As Esman notes, "ethnic mobilization is facilitated by and indeed usually requires an ideology, a coherent set of articulated beliefs" about collective identity, interests, and aspirations the reasons that justify collective action.[82] Although such a group credo is useful in shaping the movement and encourages cohesiveness, successful ethnic mobilization can occur in its absence. More important is the decision a mobilizing ethnic group must make about the profile of its activities. It might choose to concern itself primarily with cultural (e.g., familiarizing its members and the larger society with its traditions), economic (e.g., reducing rates of unemployment), political (e.g., placing representatives in the legislature), or other issues. Mobilization also requires the identification of a shared objective(s) that the collective desires to achieve. Such aims might be general (e.g., the improvement of the group's economic conditions) and/or specific (e.g., the halting of discriminatory practices against members of the group in a given school district). Consensus about certain goals can be expected to increase an ethnic group's ability to take joint action.[83]

Ordinarily, gauging the effectiveness of the movement's activities is more difficult the more general the goal to be realized. Identifying sensible, realistic goals is crucial for the success of ethnic mobilization and for the accomplishment of these aims. What is a reasonable objective is primarily determined by situational factors. In exceptional cases, setting unrealistic goals or exploiting the appeal of an archaic, mythical past could be essential to mobilization and might even be more effective than the identification of a more practical goal.[84]

Political Opportunity

If the authorities representing the dominant group do not grant marginal groups the chance to pursue their political mobilization, even the ethnic group possessing all mobilizational criteria will fail to succeed. Doug McAdam, Herbert Kitschelt, Sidney Tarrow, and others associated with the political opportunity structure approach have called attention to the critical importance of the external environment (broadly speaking, the state and the political system) to social movements.[85] The state's perception of the ethnic group's capacity to mobilize, the potential threat

---

[82] Esman, *Ethnic Politics*, 34.

[83] Enloe, *Ethnic Conflict and Political Development*, 183.

[84] See Norman Cohn, *The Pursuit of Millennium: Revolutionary Millenarians and Mystical Anarchists of the Middle Ages* (New York: Oxford University Press, 1970); and Murray Edelman, *The Symbolic Uses of Politics* (Urbana, IL: University of Illinois Press, 1985).

[85] See, for instance, Doug McAdam, *Political Process and the Development of Black Insurgency, 1930–1979* (Chicago: University of Chicago Press, 1982) and Dough McAcam, John D. McCarthy, and Mayer N. Zald, eds., *Comparative Perspectives of Social*

the group might pose to the state's stability, and the resources the group might marshal to support or oppose state policies are always important to ethnic movements. Nonetheless, political opportunity is not a single variable but a cluster of several, such as the presence or absence of influential allies and realignments in the party system.[86]

Political opportunities are sometimes extended by the state to specific communities, while at other times the entire population may benefit from them. Kitschelt has noted that social movement organizations (and, by extension, ethnic-based organizations) are most influential in open and strong political systems as opposed to closed and weak ones.[87] The provision of new mobilization opportunities might signal a weakening state that is forced to make compromises or systemic crisis and transition. Such was the case in most East European countries after 1989. The reality of "political opportunities," writes Tarrow, "provides the major incentives for transforming mobilization potentials into action."[88] In the final analysis, however, it is more the changing consciousness of the marginal group than the attitudes of the dominant population that will create and define the field for ethnic political activism.[89]

Financial Resources

Mobilizing ethnic groups are rarely rich in resources; in many cases the reason for their mobilization is to reverse their economic deprivation. Publicizing activities, printing newspapers and campaign materials, maintaining offices and lines of communication, and paying salaried employees takes money. No active organization can exist without financial support, and determining where the required funds will come from [state or foundation patronage, private donations, membership fees, or external resources (such as an emigré community)] is a dilemma that is better tackled early on.

Communications

The mobilizing group must get its message out to the community, and this requirement presupposes a number of factors. In order to be receptive, the population in question should have high literacy rates and share

Movements: Political Opportunities, Mobilizing Structures, and Cultural Framings (New York: Cambridge University Press, 1996).

[86] Sidney Tarrow, "Social Movements in Contentious Politics: A Review Article," *American Political Science Review*, 90:4 (December 1996), 880.

[87] Herbert Kitschelt, "Political Opportunity Structures and Political Protest: Anti-Nuclear Movements in Four Democracies," *British Journal of Political Science*, 16:1 (January 1986): 63–7.

[88] Sidney Tarrow, *Power in Movement: Social Movements, Collective Action, and Politics* (New York: Cambridge University Press, 1994), 99.

[89] Rothschild, *Ethnopolitics*, 68.

a common language.[90] Given that the dominant group usually supervises the media which is often prejudiced toward ethnic minorities, it is particularly important that the group control (and, preferably, own) media outlets (newspapers, radio, and television stations) or at the very least maintain connections to sympathetic media agencies. Needless to say, the group should also enjoy certain minimum living standards that would allow it to have access to radios, television sets, books, and newspapers.

Symbols

The mobilizing group is assisted by shared symbols that are widely recognized and surrounded by the affection and loyalty of the community.[91] The flag, monuments and public spaces endowed with historical meaning, poems, anthems, cherished songs, and the anniversaries of historical events can all be meaningful tokens of the community's commitment to collective action. When there is no such symbol or tradition readily available to the ethnic group (because, for instance, they have not been preserved in popular memory or in written or pictoral form) it must be "invented," that is, it has to be created afresh.[92] In some cases, as recent work on Latvia shows, a community might find strength and identity not so much in shared history but in other, unexpected sources such as nature and the surrounding physical environment.[93]

The relative weight of these prerequisites is difficult to determine because it hinges on the given context. Still, in general, variables like political opportunity and financial resources are more important than the availability of symbols or a large pool of potential leaders. In sum, the most prominent factors necessary for successful mobilization include political opportunity and a legal framework that allows for the expansion of the ethnic group's political role, cohesive leadership, viable organizations, past mobilizational experience, a realistic political program, adequate financial resources, and positive media coverage.

---

[90] See Donald R. Browne, Charles M. Firestone, and Ellen Mickiewicz, *Television/Radio News & Minorities* (Washington, DC: The Aspen Institute, 1994); Remnick, *Theory of Ethnicity*, 34–7; and Tarrow, *Power in Movement*, 125–7.

[91] For recent work on the importance of symbols in political movements, see Jan Kubik, *The Power of Symbols against the Symbols of Power: The Rise of Solidarity and the Fall of State Socialism in Poland* (University Park: Pennsylvania State University Press, 1994); and Ulf Hedetoft, ed., *Political Symbols, Symbolic Politics: European Identities in Transformation* (Brookfield, VT: Ashgate, 1998).

[92] On this issue, see Eric Hobsbawm and Terence Ranger, eds., *The Invention of Tradition* (Cambridge: Cambridge University Press, 1983).

[93] See E. V. Bunkše, "God, Thine Earth Is Burning: Nature Attitudes and the Latvian Drive for Independence," *GeoJournal*, 26:2 (1992): 203–9. One might also recall Lowenthal's argument in his *The Past Is a Foreign Country* that people have lost their connection to the past.

Attributes of Romani Political Mobilization

A substantial part of this study is devoted to the examination of Gypsy political mobilization. The point I want to make here is that the Roma's preparation for collective political action is extremely poor by virtually all criteria of successful ethnic mobilization discussed above.

Romani Identity

Gypsy ethnic identity is weak. According to Michael Stewart, "with the exception of Gypsy intellectuals who run the Rom(ani) political parties, the Rom(a) do not have an ethnic identity" at all.[94] I disagree. The Gypsies certainly do have a distinctive identity, but it is difficult to define owing to the diversity of the Romani population. Fundamentally, all Roma to some extent share the same origins, language, culture, and historical experiences in Europe. The problem is that many Roma do not consider themselves part of a cohesive ethnic group but identify themselves with a tribe or other subgroup to which they belong.

Past Mobilization Experience

The Roma can draw on few past mobilization activities and accumulated political resources. In the nineteenth century and between the two world wars, Gypsy mobilization did occur on a very limited scale, but once the state found Romani political activism inconvenient, it put an end to it without much difficulty. Romani organizations of the socialist era were controlled by the state and therefore their value for postcommunist political activism is limited.

Language and Communication

The Gypsies do not share a common language. There is no one Romani language but rather several major and dozens of minor dialects. More importantly, a large proportion of East European Gypsies speak no dialect of Romani whatsoever. Although languages can and do disappear the loss of language is not an irreversible process.[95] As Prime Minister David Ben Gurion noted in the late 1950s, "Only a hundred years ago there was not a single Jew in the world whose mother tongue was Hebrew; today it is the spoken language of hundreds of thousands."[96]

---

[94] Michael Stewart, *The Time of the Gypsies* (Boulder, CO: Westview, 1997), 28.
[95] Livonian (spoken by a handful of people in Estonia and Latvia) is a recent example. See *The New York Times*, 4 December 1997.
[96] Cited in Rupert Emerson, *From Empire to Nation: The Rise to Self-Assertion of Asian and African Peoples* (Boston: Beacon Pres, 1962), 139.

Ethnic Solidarity and Social Capital

There is little ethnic solidarity between the Roma although group cohesion and trust among those belonging to the same subgroup may be very strong.[97] Benedict Anderson writes about "imagined community," the personal and cultural feelings of belonging to a nation.[98] This sentiment is precisely what most Gypsies do not share at the present time.

Symbols

The absence, until recently, of a written Romani tradition has cheated the Gypsies out of some symbols that could have aided their mobilization process. Still, there is a Romani flag, a Romani anthem, and an incredibly rich oral tradition; the trouble is that many Gypsies are unaware of it.

Financial Resources

The Roma constitute the economically most disadvantaged population in Europe. Mobilization is costly, which, in the case of a poor community, means that financial support – aside from the potential contributions from the thin stratum of affluent Roma – must come from outside sources.

Leadership and Organization

Some Gypsy activists are bona fide activists, but, just like in mainstream political life, many enter politics for personal gain. Consequently, there are legitimate questions concerning their claims that they provide genuine representation for their communities. The vast majority of the Roma have remained politically passive either due to lack of interest or confidence in their power to influence political outcomes. The greatest obstacle to the authentic representation of Romani interests, however, has been the internal dissension within and between their communities and the subsequent proliferation of their organizations. The attempts of Gypsy parties to form electoral coalitions have met with modest success in part because mainstream parties usually consider alliance with the unpopular Roma a political liability.

---

[97] See, for instance, Zsolt Csalog, "Jegyzetek a cigányság támogatásának kérdéséről," *Szociálpolitikai Értesítí*, 2 (1984): 39; Jerzy Ficowski, *The Gypsies in Poland: History and Customs* (Warsaw: Interpress, 1985), 56; and Elena Marushiakova and Vesselin Popov, "Political Socialization of Gypsies in Bulgaria," presented at the "Ethnic Issues in Bulgaria" conference (Munich, 13 September 1992).

[98] Benedict Anderson, *Imagined Communities: Reflections on the Origin and Spread of Nationalism* (London: Verso, rev. ed., 1991).

Profile and Programs

The programs of Romani parties are often determined by the aspirations of individuals; thus, there is often little consensus at the elite level, and it is often difficult to determine which of the many leaders represent which goal. Still, the general aims of these organizations are similar across the region and much like those of other marginalized ethnic minorities (e.g., guaranteed minority rights and civil rights, affirmative action programs, broadcast time in state-owned media, etc.).

Political Opportunity

In the postcommunist period communities the Gypsies received the chance to organize and gain representation in the political system. Although the state has not been averse to manipulating ethnic political organizations, the Roma are free to participate in political competition.

SUMMARY

This chapter examined two concepts – marginality and ethnic mobilization – that, together with regime types, regime change, and state-minority relations, round out the analytical framework of this study. I argued that marginality was a useful tool for understanding the Romani experience because it so clearly captures critical notions central to that experience: their peripherality vis-à-vis the political, economic, and social centers; the variegated subordination to dominant groups; and the skewed interaction between marginal and dominant populations. I explained the components and determinants of social and economic exclusion, emphasized the dynamics of political marginality which has traditionally received little attention in the scholarly literature, and underscored the ways in which marginal conditions may change.

The section on the political mobilization of ethnic communities illuminated the complexity of this process and examined the most important "ingredients" necessary for its success. I explained the importance of a strong ethnic identity, past mobilizational experience, competent leadership and organizations, the cohesiveness of the ethnic group, financial resources, and other criteria. Finally, I noted the problematic nature of the Gypsies' preparation, background, and current position in view of the prerequisites of political activism.

The balance of this book is going to elaborate on these themes through the experiences of Eastern Europe's Gypsy communities. Anchored in the empirical analysis of the Roma and their relations with East European societies, I will argue the following:

1. Their marginal conditions, rather than remaining stagnant, have actually gone through subtle but important changes explained partly by changes in regimes, state policies, economic conditions, societal attitudes, political mobilization, and so on.
2. Their marginal conditions are the result of exclusionary dynamics in three different and isolable dimensions – political, social, and economic – as well as of the specific Romani traditions and history.
3. The various dimensions of their marginal conditions in certain historical periods have changed independently of each other and, at times, in opposite directions (e.g., their political conditions have improved, but their socioeconomic situation has deteriorated in the emerging postcommunist democracies).
4. For a number of both endogenous and exogenous reasons, the Roma have been unable to capitalize on their chances for ethnic mobilization and achieving political representation approximating their proportionate size in East European societies.
5. In order to alleviate their marginal conditions the Roma must embark on a road of socioeconomic and political integration.

PART II

NONDEMOCRATIC SYSTEMS AND GYPSY MARGINALITY

3

The Gypsies in Imperial and Authoritarian States

It is important to put the Romani experience in the proper historical and socioeconomic context, which is to a large extent determined by the geographic focus of this book. Quite simply, Eastern Europe has been the less developed and less progressive part of Europe. The region's comparative backwardness has been a long-standing phenomenon rooted in its geographic situation as well as in historical, political, economic, and social developments and trends dating from the Middle Ages.[1] Suffice it to say that by the time the Roma arrived in the Balkans in the thirteenth century, that part of Europe in many respects was already manifestly behind Western Europe.

This chapter is divided into three sections. The first and second parts analyze the Roma's conditions and relationships to state and society in the imperial era and the interwar decades, respectively. The third section addresses the persecution and survival of the Gypsies during World War II. The conclusion summarizes the impact of regime change on the shifts in Romani marginality and changing state policies from the Middle Ages to the mid-twentieth century.

PART I. THE GYPSIES IN THE IMPERIAL AGE

The objective of this section is to show the differences in Romani marginality in the two major East European empires. The disparate philosophies and organizing principles of these states that belong to the same

---

[1] See Daniel Chirot, ed., *The Origins of Backwardness in Eastern Europe: Economics & Politics from the Middle Ages until the Early Twentieth Century* (Berkeley: University of California Press, 1989). For shorter expositions, see idem., "The Rise of the West," *American Sociological Review*, 50:2 (April 1985): 181–95; Andrew C. Janos, "The Politics of Backwardness in Continental Europe, 1780–1945," *World Politics*, 41:3 (April 1989): 325–59; and George Schöpflin, "The Political Traditions of Eastern Europe," *Daedalus*, 119:1 (Winter 1990): 55–90.

regime type created dissimilar conditions for the Roma, as well as for other ethnic groups.

Social Marginality

Throughout most of the imperial period the majority of East European Roma lived in lands directly ruled by the Ottoman Empire or its vassal states (such as the Romanian principalities). "For nearly half a millennium," Braude and Lewis write, "the Ottomans ruled an empire as diverse as any in history. Remarkably, this polyethnic and multireligious society worked."[2] One of the crucial foundations of this uncommonly stable state was the millet system – the self-administration of different religious communities – often cited as an important precedent and model for minority rights.[3] By the standards of the age, the Ottoman Turks devised a sociopolitical system that was humane and tolerant. The legal traditions and practices of religious groups were recognized and protected and, while their relations with the Muslims were firmly regulated, Christian and Jewish millets were free to run their internal affairs.[4] In essence, for minority groups the Ottoman Empire was the embodiment of relatively harmonious and enduring ethnic coexistence.

Though their social position was decidedly subordinate and marginal to other groups, most Gypsies fared considerably better in the Ottoman Empire than in other regions. The Roma occupied the lowest tier of the social scale together with "other people with no visible permanent professional affiliation,"[5] but they had a definite place in society. In areas where the number of settled Roma was substantial, cities and towns had Gypsy quarters [Sliven (Bulgaria), for instance, had a 1,074-strong Romani community in 1874]; elsewhere they slept in huts and tents erected beyond town lines and were required to pay for the use of the municipality's pastures. Local administrators made recurrent attempts to settle wandering Roma in order to turn them into reliable taxpayers. Tax evaders faced jail and, in exceptional cases, the slave markets.

Even in the Ottoman Empire the Roma were subjected to widespread societal prejudice and contempt, though they were rarely physically per-

---

[2] Benjamin Braude and Bernard Lewis, "Introduction," in Braude and Lewis, eds., *Christians and Jews in the Ottoman Empire: The Functioning of a Plural Society* (New York: Holmes and Meir, 1982), 1.

[3] See, for instance, Patrick Thornberry, *International Law and the Rights of Minorities* (Oxford: Oxford University Press, 1991), 29.

[4] Will Kymlicka, *Multicultural Citizenship* (New York: Oxford University Press, 1995), 156.

[5] Peter F. Sugar, *Southern Europe under Ottoman Rule, 1354–1804* (Seattle: University of Washington Press, 1977), 77.

secuted. The Turks despised them not because of their ethnicity – after all the empire was a mélange of races and religions – but because they viewed them as less reliable and trustworthy than other peoples.[6] Dominant groups considered unsettled Roma to be useless parasites because they did not have stable occupations. Muslim Roma were taxed higher than other Muslims based on the rationale that they did not follow the rules of Islam and did not live Muslim lifestyles (most Gypsy women, for instance, refused to wear a veil); in essence, their behavior was inconsistent with the religion. At the end of the seventeenth century the hardening of Ottoman attitudes against the Roma had been manifested by a state campaign that accused them of widespread pimping and prostitution and by steeply increased taxes.[7] The Gypsies also acquired a reputation for thievery and for habitually committing other (usually petty) crimes that contributed to the deepening of negative social biases.[8]

And yet, for those hundreds of thousands of Roma who were for centuries enslaved in the Romanian principalities of Moldavia and Wallachia the Ottoman Empire became the promised land.[9] It is difficult to say exactly when slavery was established in the two principalities, but there are sources dating back to 1348 that mention bequests of Gypsy slaves. By the late fourteenth century, slavery seems to have been firmly in place and it proved to be an enduring institution. The common historical explanation for the Gypsies' bondage is that in these backward, poverty-stricken regions where skilled labor was scarce, the migration-prone Roma were enslaved in order to keep them in place and to minimize the cost of their labor. This interpretation is only partly convincing owing to the fact that a substantial proportion of Gypsy slaves performed menial agricultural work or domestic chores at the residences of the royal family, at the homes of the landowners (*boyars*), and at monasteries. The treatment of the slaves depended largely on individual owners, but they could be and occasionally were killed by their masters without consequences. In time, *tsigan* (Gypsy) and

---

[6] Interview with Ilona Tomova, presidential adviser on ethnic and religious issues (Sofia, 8 March 1995).

[7] Noel Malcolm, *Bosnia: A Short History* (New York: New York University Press, 1994), 116. See also Maria Todorova, *Imagining the Balkans* (New York: Oxford University Press, 1997), 70.

[8] See, for instance, Péter Szuhay and Antónia Baráti, eds, *Pictures of the History of Gypsies in Hungary in the 20th Century* (Budapest: Néprajzi Múzeum, 1993), 216–25.

[9] Vera Mutafchieva, "The Turk, the Jew, and the Gypsy," in Antonina Zhelyazkova, ed., *Relations of Compatibility and Incompatibility Between Christians and Muslims in Bulgaria* (Sofia: International Centre for Minority Studies and Intercultural Relations, 1995), 53.

rob (slave) became juridically and culturally synonymous terms in the Romanian principalities.[10]

Although their slave status was affirmed in 1749, subsequent legislation prohibited the sale of Roma separately from their families. Urban intellectuals had called for the abolition of slavery in the 1830s, but only after the reformist statesman Mihail Kogălniceanu started his campaign for emancipation in 1844 did it seem achievable. Slave owners were finally ordered to free the Roma in 1855–6, and emancipation was fully realized by 1864. It should be mentioned that politicians in Bucharest were strongly influenced by French criticisms of Romanian slavery, especially because they looked to Paris for inspiration in developing a modern state.[11] Thus, Western pressures had played a positive role in hastening social progress in Eastern Europe already in the mid-nineteenth century.

In independent Hungary (prior to 1526) the Roma were tolerated, although they did not enjoy the same freedoms as in the Ottoman Empire. Initially, most Roma migrated through Hungary; but owing to the intense persecution and expulsion orders in Western Europe, by the fifteenth and sixteenth centuries a growing number of Gypsy groups had come to regard Hungary a destination country. Some Roma received letters of safe conduct from Hungarian King (and Holy Roman Emperor) Zsigmond (or Sigismund, 1387–1437) and other sovereigns. These documents lost their effectiveness, however, because anti-Roma attitudes had strengthened and because the Gypsies became quite apt at forging them.[12] A fair number of Roma were widely respected as prized gunsmiths under the reign of King Mátyás (or Matthias, 1458–90). Still, the plea of György Thurzó, the imperial governor of "Royal Hungary" (that remained under Habsburg tutelage after the Turks had overrun the rest of the country in 1526), for understanding the Gypsies' plight and encouraging authorities to let them settle was an uncharacteristic act of benevolence.[13]

In the Habsburg Empire the Gypsies encountered far more overt persecution, and their coexistence with the dominant populations was considerably more fraught with contention than that in Ottoman-ruled lands. They did not possess equal rights with the other subjects of the empire and were merely tolerated by them. The majority of Roma lived

---

[10] Nicolae Gheorghe, "Roma-Gypsy Ethnicity in Eastern Europe," *Social Research*, 58:4 (Winter 1991): 834.

[11] Angus Fraser, *The Gypsies* (Oxford: Blackwell, 1995, 2nd ed.), 224.

[12] See József Antall, "Tanulmány-vázlat a cigányokról, (1957)," *Közös út-Kethano Drom*, 1:1 (January 1993): 43 (incidentally, the author was Hungary's first post-communist prime minister).

[13] Fraser, *The Gypsies*, 155.

outside of villages and led lives separate from the dominant groups, although commercial and social contacts assured them a place in society. Anti-Gypsy prejudices were generally deep-seated and frequently culminated in well-publicized trials on absurd grounds. In 1782, for instance, an entire Romani community in northern Hungary was charged with cannibalism, then tortured into confessions resulting in the execution of 41 before an inquiry ordered by Emperor Joseph II revealed that the presumed casualties were alive.[14]

The wave of Romanticism that swept parts of Eastern Europe following the French Revolution evoked considerable interest in the Gypsies – especially in their rich traditions, myths, and mysticism – and a small measure of paternalistic compassion toward them.[15] "The mustache," a poem by the nineteenth-century Hungarian poet, János Arany – contrasting the cunning and happy-go-lucky Gypsies with the vain and stingy Magyar landowner – exemplifies well this jovially condescending attitude.[16] A substantial number of Roma fought on the Hungarian side in the 1848–9 War of Independence, many of them provided music for the soldiers, thereby cementing the reputation and "acceptability" of Gypsy musicianship. Hungarian nobility often employed Romani musicians and, in most exceptional cases, even married Gypsy virtuosos.[17] The rise of the musicians and, to a lesser extent, skilled craftsmen in contrast to the growing impoverishment of nomadic and/or unskilled Gypsies points to the increasing stratification within the Romani population which began in the nineteenth century.

After Bulgarian independence from Ottoman rule (1878) the Roma's social position declined further. About 80% of them were adherents of Islam, which now became the minority religion associated with the former oppressors. As the wave of industrialization reached Bulgaria, more and more Romani craftsmen were ruined economically. Some still supplied services to the rural population and in agricultural areas continued to retain a well defined place in society. Similarly, following emancipation, the growing anti-Gypsyism of peasants, rooted partly in their own miserable conditions and in the exaggerated and generalized reputation of the Roma as common criminals, strongly affected Romanian Gypsies.

---

[14] H. M. G. Grellmann, *Dissertation on the Gypsies* (London: Ballantine, 1807, 2nd. ed.), cited by Isabel Fonseca, *Bury Me Standing: The Gypsies and Their Journey* (New York: Knopf, 1995), 88.

[15] See, for instance, Lech Mróz, "The Cursed Nation: Daniłowicz's View of the Gypsies," a foreword to Ignacy Daniłowicz, *O cyganach wiadomość historyczna* (Oświęcim: Biblioteczka Cyganologii Polskiej, 1993), xxix.

[16] János Arany, "A bajusz," in *Arany János költeményei* (Budapest: Helikon, 1983): 242–7.

[17] Péter Szuhay, "A cigány bandáról," *Amaro Drom*, 5:2 (February 1995): 18–20.

The widespread Romani perspective that considers institutionalized education a waste of time and energy was clearly reflected in their educational attainment already in the imperial age. Churches played a crucial role in public education throughout this period, but they did not concern themselves with Gypsy children until the late eighteenth–early nineteenth century. The system of state-supported public schools, wherever it existed, had little effect on most Roma; it was fortunate to reach the children of peasants. One of the imperial era's few reliable and detailed surveys, conducted in Hungary in 1893, revealed that 70% of Gypsy children never attended school and 90% of the entire Romani population and 98% of those maintaining nomadic lifestyles were illiterate.[18] Bulgaria was the first East European state to establish schools for the Roma, but in 1910 their literacy rate was a mere 3% and it increased only to 8% after World War I.[19] The growing social stratification of Gypsy society was signaled by the drastically different educational standards of a small minority, particularly musicians, who emphasized the importance of schooling (especially in music) to their offspring.[20]

Economic Conditions

Although the Roma were at the bottom of the imperial era's economic and occupational scales, they had a well-defined position in imperial economies and played useful and valuable economic roles. In general, the more backward and less developed a region, the more important was the Gypsies' economic contribution. In essence, traditional Romani skills were appropriate to pre-industrial economies, but industrialization resulted in their gradual economic displacement and increasing marginalization. In Western Europe, where urbanization and industrial development commenced long before the east, the economic role of the Gypsies declined earlier than in the Habsburg and Ottoman empires. As waves of industrialization reached the states of Eastern Europe, so diminished the relevance of the Roma to their economic lives. The majority of the Gypsies under Habsburg rule lived in Hungary and Slovakia – that is, the less developed parts of the empire. In these primarily rural, agricultural-based economies they played a consequential economic role longer than in, say, Austria or the Czech Lands. Because the Ottoman Empire was considerably less industrialized than the Habsburg domain

---

[18] See Archduke József and Henrik Wlislocki. *A cigányokról* (Budapest: Pallas, 1895), 10.

[19] David M. Crowe, "The Roma (Gypsies) of Bulgaria and Romania: An Historical Perspective," read at the conference on "Ethnic Conflict in Bulgaria and Romania," Duke University (Durham, NC; September 1996), 7.

[20] See, for instance, Arne B. Mann, "Rroma (Gypsies) in Municipalities," report to the Council of Europe, Strasbourg, 7 December 1995, 5.

and there was a virtual absence of state-supported economic development under Turkish rule, the Roma remained a valued economic contributor for a longer period of time.

When the Roma arrived in Europe, many were palm readers and pretended to be religious pilgrims, undertakings that were well-suited to the zealous religiosity and deep-seated superstitiousness of the time. By the fifteenth century, some settled Gypsies had acquired reputations as talented craftsmen, particularly in various types of metallurgical work (especially smithery) as well as in shoemaking and cobbling. As time went on, the range of "typical" Gypsy occupations had expanded to include chimney sweeping and broom-making and in the eighteenth century the shearing, clipping, and training of domestic animals.[21] Some Gypsies not only were talented artisans and craftsmen but also controlled entire trades in certain areas. In the Romanian principalities, for instance, they enjoyed a virtual monopoly on smithing.[22] The Roma had also gained fame as superb entertainers. Gypsy bands – generally playing the dominant group's traditional music rather than their own – had become sought after at carnivals and public events and as court musicians. Romani dancers, bear tamers, palm readers, and fortune tellers had also been in demand and became the indispensable part of fairs and markets, major social events of rural society at the time. Most settled Gypsies, however, adopted "unconventional" trades. Although they ordinarily enjoyed far better material conditions than their peripatetic brethren, the economic integration of settled Roma with more mainstream occupations was thwarted by the refusal of trade guilds to accept them into their membership.

For logical reasons, many occupations common among the Roma were practiced on the road and required the use of minimal equipment. Their reputation as thieves, beggars, and prostitutes contributed to expulsion and persecution that went hand in hand with the prohibition of settling and of land ownership. Thus, their traditional propensity to keep moving and engage in occupations – peddling, wood carving, bear-taming, tinkering, basket-weaving – that afforded a certain amount of personal independence and liberty and could be exercised while traveling was reinforced. In their travels the Roma had ample opportunity to learn about the medicinal qualities of herbs and plants and the necessity to try and cure their ailments. As a result of this accumulated knowledge

---

[21] See György Rostás-Farkas and Ervin Karsai, *ősi cigány mesterségek és foglalkozások* (Budapest: OMIKK, 1991).

[22] David M. Crowe, "The Gypsy Historical Experience in Romania," in David M. Crowe and John Kolsti, eds. *The Gypsies of Eastern Europe* (Armonk, NY: M. E. Sharpe, 1991), 63.

and skill a number of Roma (mostly women) became well known as healers, herbalists, and persons apt at resetting broken bones.[23]

Although some sources suggest that the Roma were hard workers, the vast majority of chroniclers have little flattering to say about their work ethic. The Roma did participate in seasonal farm work as hired hands, but they were "seldom industrious" in such endeavors.[24] Archduke Joseph was a noted Romanologist who corresponded with his daughter in Romani and was perhaps the most important supporter the Gypsies had in nineteenth-century Hungary. Even he writes, however, that the Roma were simply not cut out for agricultural work because they were liable to leave their jobs for long periods of time without explanation.[25] The fact that they were "universally reluctant to become regimented wage earners" did nothing to endear them to their neighbors.[26]

An important and somewhat underappreciated element of the Gypsies' occupational history is their involvement in military endeavors. Roma were not only master gunsmiths but also respected soldiers in some European states. In the Ottoman Empire a considerable number of Gypsies provided services to the Turkish administration, especially to the military. Those who specialized in the manufacture and maintenance of weapons and ammunition of all sorts enjoyed a particularly good livelihood and, as Fraser writes, gained little from the Habsburg recovery of territories from the Ottomans in the late-seventeenth century.[27] In the sixteenth to eighteenth centuries the finest messengers and scouts as well as the most effective spies of Transylvanian princes were Roma.[28] Many Gypsy men were forced into military service across Europe, others volunteered in order to escape poverty and persecution.

The belated arrival of the Industrial Revolution in Eastern Europe, however, dealt a major blow to the Romani way of life, one from which they have yet to recover. Large-scale industrial production led to falling prices of consumer products and reduced demand for goods traditionally manufactured and/or mended by the Roma. Ultimately, economic progress jeopardized the Gypsies' established productive status in these societies. Equally important is the fact that the vast majority of the

---

[23] See, for instance, Ilona Tomova, *The Gypsies in the Transition Period* (Sofia: International Center for Minority Studies and Intercultural Relations, 1995), 18.

[24] Richard Bright, *Travels from Vienna Through Lower Hungary with Some Remarks on the State of Vienna During the Congress in the Year 1814* (Edinburgh: Archibald Constable, 1818), 526.

[25] Archduke József and Wlislocki. *A cigányokról*, 7–9.

[26] Isabel Fonseca, "Of No Fixed Abode," *Times Literary Supplement*, 29 January 1993, 7.

[27] Fraser, *The Gypsies*, 176.

[28] Tamás Bihari, "Cigány bánat, magyar bánat," *A világ*, 24 April 1991.

Gypsies – as a result of their traditional attitudes toward institutional-ized education, their poverty, and the majority population's discrimina-tory policies – could not adapt to the emerging economic conditions that required specialized training and education.

Imperial Policies Toward the Gypsies

As I suggested in Chapter 1, the two major East European empires con-ducted quite different policies toward the Roma. In the Habsburg Empire, where state building developed further and economic and social progress received more emphasis, the state pursued more intrusive and discriminative minority policies. In contrast, the Ottoman state did not accept "the idea of minority–majority or developed a political sense of nationality." Had they done so, "it could easily have liquidated the patchwork of races and religions under its rule, transforming them into one homogeneous Muslim or Turkish group."[29] Instead, the Ottomans viewed the conquered lands as tax farms under Muslim rule and main-tained a *laissez faire* perspective vis-à-vis their subject peoples as long as dues were collected and social peace persisted.

For the Gypsies and other ethnic minorities the Ottoman conquest of their lands rarely signified a worsening in their conditions. To the con-trary, the Turks often eliminated the local aristocracy because they were the source of potential opposition to the new rulers and owing to the notion that they were expendable as far as the Ottomans were concerned. The new governors – in some cases, such as Albania, ethnically indige-nous but always Muslim – generally did not interfere with local affairs. Their most important functions were to guarantee law and order and the timely and full payment of levies. Ethnic Turks, for the most part, were administrators, soldiers, and members of the judiciary. The Ottomans were actually dependent on the ethnic minorities – Armenians, Bulgari-ans, Greeks, Serbs, and so on – for the execution of a wide array of com-mercial, industrial, and agricultural tasks. The Sultan's invitation and welcome of the Jews fleeing from the Spanish inquisition in the late fif-teenth century was as much a gesture of magnanimity as it was a recog-nition of the empire's economic interests.[30]

[29] Kemal Karpat, *An Inquiry into the Social Foundations of Nationalism in the Ottoman State*, Research Monograph No. 39 of the Center for International studies of the Woodrow Wilson School of Public and International Affairs, Princeton University (1973), 39.

[30] See A. Schmuelevitz, *The Jews of the Ottoman Empire in the Late Fifteenth and Six-teenth Centuries* (Leiden, Netherlands: Brill, 1984); and Suna Kili, "The Jews of Turkey: A Question of National and International Identity," in Russell F. Farnen, ed., *Nation-alism, Ethnicity, and Identity: Cross-National and Comparative Perspectives* (New Brunswick, NJ: Transaction, 1994), 299–317.

The Ottoman Empire, with the marked absence of systematically repressive policies and legislation characteristic of the rest of Europe, was a haven for the Roma. The state accepted or, put differently, did not care about their customs and religious identities. Although some suggest that the Ottoman state did not discriminate against the Roma at all, but that instead the Roma suffered from the preexisting prejudices of other ethnic groups, clearly this was not the case.[31] Muslim Gypsies were not exempt from some taxes that other Muslims (like the Bulgarian-speaking Pomaks) were, and could move up in the Ottoman hierarchy with much more difficulty than others. The Ottomans also subjected the Roma to forced settlement policies – in order to transform them into reliable and reachable taxpayers – although these efforts were less coercive and more haphazard and inconsistent than elsewhere in Europe.

When the Roma arrived in Central and Western Europe in the early fifteenth century, they initially encountered populations that were often sympathetic to their alleged religious pilgrimage and respectful of the letters requesting safe passage they carried. This tolerance proved to be ephemeral as the Gypsies' poverty increasingly turned them to begging and thieving. The ensuing widely chronicled brutal persecution the Roma experienced on a massive scale in Medieval Western Europe remained unsurpassed until World War II. In pre-Habsburg East-Central Europe the Roma were also victims of intense persecution with the partial exception of Medieval Hungary. Already in the late fifteenth century the laws of deportation were enacted in the Holy Roman Empire. By one partial tally, as many as 133 anti-Gypsy laws were written there in 1551–1774.[32] In Moravia the expulsion of the Gypsies was decreed as early as 1538, while in Bohemia the first anti-Roma legislation was passed in 1541, following the outbreak of fires in Prague, supposedly set by Roma.[33] In Poland, too, the Sejm (legislature) passed repressive laws but some moderation (or, possibly, pragmatism) was demonstrated by Polish kings who, in the sixteenth century, allowed the Gypsies to select their own leaders in order to simplify tax collection.[34] In the mid-seventeenth century the Polish monarchs nominated or confirmed the "King of the Gypsies" who were initially Gypsies but later came from the Polish gentry.

---

[31] Interview with Dincho Krastev, Director of the Library of the Bulgarian Academy of Sciences (Sofia, 7 March 1995).

[32] R. A. Scott Macfie, "Gypsy Persecutions," *Journal of the Gypsy Lore Society*, series 3, vol. 22 (1943): 71–3, cited by Fraser, *The Gypsies*, 149.

[33] *Struggling for Ethnic Identity: Czechoslovakia's Endangered Gypsies* (New York: Human Rights Watch, 1992), 5.

[34] Rajko Djurić, Jörg Becken, and A. Bertolt Bengsch, *Ohne Heim-Ohne Grab: Die Geschichte der Roma und Sinti* (Berlin: Aufbau-Verlag, 1996), 177.

Once they established their East European empire, Habsburg monarchs showed little interest in understanding the Gypsies' plight. Charles VI (1711–40), frustrated by the Roma's resistance to conform to imperial laws and norms, was the most brutal among them. He ordered the extermination of all Roma in his domain, a command that was not taken seriously by those who were supposed to implement it. Perhaps motivated by Charles' heavy-handed approach, his immediate successors, his daughter Maria Theresa (1740–80) and her son Joseph II (1780–90), became the two Habsburg emperors most keen on improving (according to their own definitions) the Gypsies' conditions. At a time when several European powers, especially Britain and Portugal, sought to rid themselves of their "Gypsy problem" by deporting them to their colonies, Maria Theresa and Joseph – along with the Bourbons of Spain – were the only European monarchs attempting to find more rational solutions. It bears noting, though, that unlike Spain, the Habsburg Empire possessed no faraway colonies. Maria Theresa and Joseph fancied themselves enlightened rulers who wanted to elevate the Roma into the ranks of "civilized" and "useful" citizens. The tens of thousands of nomadic Gypsies roaming around the empire free of any state control did not suit their ideals of absolute monarchy.

The policies of Maria Theresa and her son comprise a textbook example of forcible assimilation. The Empress' four major "Gypsy decrees" illustrate this strategy.[35] The first edict (1758) ordered all Gypsies to settle, pay taxes, and do mandatory service to churches and landowners, and it prohibited Romani ownership of horses and wagons and also prohibited their leaving the villages to which they were assigned without permission. The second decree (1761) mandated compulsory military service for Gypsies. The third (1767) eliminated the authority of Romani leaders over their communities, banned traditional Gypsy dress and the usage of Romani language, and instructed villages to register the Roma in their jurisdiction. Maria Theresa's last major decree concerning the Roma (1773) forbade marriages between Gypsies and ordered Roma children over age five to be taken away to state schools and foster homes, resulting in the virtual kidnapping of approximately 18,000 Gypsy children from their parents. The intention behind this edict was to dilute Romani bloodlines and to speed up their assimilation. Joseph II continued and expanded his mother's assimilationist policies by extending them to Transylvania, confirming previous restrictions and adding new ones, such as ordering monthly reports on Gypsy lifestyles from local authorities, permitting the Roma to visit fairs only in special

---

[35] This discussion draws on Bright, *Travels from Vienna*, 539–40; and Fraser, *The Gypsies*, 156–7.

circumstances, and banning nomadism and traditional Gypsy occupations (such as smithery).[36] Joseph also emphasized improvements in Gypsy education and health and directed the Roma to attend religious (Roman Catholic) services weekly.

Most of these policies did not bring the intended results. The enforcement of the imperial decrees and the attached punitive sanctions by local authorities was decidedly lackadaisical. They were concerned with the disruptions in the lives of rural society caused by the coerced insettlement of the Roma, they needed the Gypsies' economic contribution, and military commanders were rarely enthusiastic about the forced conscription of Gypsies. In fact, only a few counties, especially in the western part of Hungary, interpreted the imperial instructions in full seriousness.[37] By the early nineteenth century the failure of Habsburg Gypsy policy had become apparent. Nearly all Gypsy children soon escaped from their virtual captivity back to their parents. Under the reign of Joseph II, unwanted Gypsies were shuffled between villages equally opposed to the settlement of the "undesirables." Considering the brutal pragmatism and coerciveness of Habsburg policies, one is perplexed by the remark of Emil Sčuka, a prominent Czech Gypsy leader, that "since Maria Theresa no one has done anything *for* my people."[38] It is certainly true, however, that following the failure of these eighteenth century policies there were no further major imperial attempts to address the Gypsies' living conditions. In the last decades of the Habsburg Empire the Romani issue became a police question dominated by the repressive regulations of local authorities. The fact that the judicial system did not consider the Gypsies equal citizens is demonstrated by the legion of discriminatory laws and decrees enacted in this period.[39]

The two Habsburg emperors' policies toward the Gypsies should be viewed as an early and rather crude attempt at social engineering driven by pragmatic considerations. Chapter 4 will illuminate the similarity of these policies to those of the East European socialist states two centuries later. An important pattern can be identified in the approaches of eighteenth-century European states toward the Gypsies. In more developed Western Europe, where the Gypsies' economic role had declined faster, expulsion and deportation to colonies was a common strategy; but the further East one looks, the settlement policies are more preva-

---

[36] See a detailed list of Joseph's decrees in Bright, *Travels from Vienna*, 540–2.

[37] See Konrad Bercovici, *The Story of the Gypsies* (London: Jonathan Cape, 1929), 92–117.

[38] "Schwerpunkt Roma," *Der Standard* (Vienna), 21 October 1993.

[39] See, for instance, László Pomogyi, *Cigánykérdés és cigányügyi igazgatás a polgári Magyarországon* (Budapest: Osiris-Századvég, 1995).

lent. The most extreme manifestation of forced sedentarization – in large part driven by the Gypsies' still valuable economic contribution – was the enslavement of the Roma in the Romanian principalities. Moreover, intriguing parallels may be pointed out between the two late eighteenth-century Habsburg rulers and their counterpart in Spain, a state that had increasingly found itself in Europe's socioeconomic periphery. In Spain, too, particularly under the reign of Charles III (1759–88), settlement policies were preferred to expulsion or deportation. Maria Theresa prohibited the use of the term "Gypsy" and decreed that they should be referred to as "New Peasants" (*Neubauern*) or "New Hungarians"; so did the King of Spain, who banned the term *Gitano* in 1772 in favor of "New Castilians."

Traditionally, there has been little ethnic solidarity between disparate Romani groups. Speaking in the late nineteenth century, a Spanish Rom noted that "those who are rich keep aloof from the rest, will not speak Calo, and will have no dealing but with the Busne [non-Gypsies]," a situation that cheated the Roma of their "natural" protectors and supporters.[40] Nonetheless, it is important to note the first signs of Gypsy mobilization dating from the late imperial period. In 1879, the Roma organized a conference in Hungary focusing on the political and civil rights of European Gypsies. In 1906, Bulgarian Gypsies sent a petition to the parliament in Sofia demanding equal rights.[41] The 1913 memorial service Gypsies held in honor of Kogălniceanu in Romania served to strengthen ethnic identity and solidarity.[42] Although these endeavors were predictably ridiculed in contemporary newspapers, they should be appreciated as early efforts at ethnic organization. Thousands of Roma served in the Austro-Hungarian armed forces in World War I, although information about their performance is scant and often unreliable.

PART II. THE GYPSIES IN THE INTERWAR PERIOD

The peace settlements in the wake of World War I signified the conclusion of the imperial age and heralded a radical transmutation of the East European state system. As a result of the redrawing of the map, all new states included substantial ethnic minorities. The attention of political elites was generally limited to their countries' nationals living in neighboring states; by and large, the Roma held an inconsequential place in their political programs.

---

[40] George Borrow, *The Zincali: An Account of the Gypsies of Spain* (London: John Murray, 1893), 134.
[41] David Crowe, "The Roma (Gypsies) of Bulgaria and Romania," 6.
[42] Crowe, "The Gypsy Historical Experience in Romania," 68.

Changes in Socioeconomic Marginality

The regime change from the imperial system to what were soon to become authoritarian states had negatively affected the material conditions of the Gypsies. The Romani population was beset by a number of social problems (lack of education, extensive poverty) and plagued by their inability to adapt to the region's slowly modernizing economies. Most East European Roma tried to cling to their old ways of life in the interwar period, a strategy that was made feasible by state neglect. Their educational attainments remained vastly inferior to both those of dominant populations and other ethnic minorities.[43] Aside from a few exceptions (especially in Czechoslovakia) the state did not establish schools specifically catering to the Gypsies' educational needs, and those Roma who did attend were likely to fall through the cracks because they were given minimal attention in their schooling. Although the constitutions of several interwar states prescribed education in the native languages of ethnic minorities, these regulations failed to make a positive impact for the Roma for several reasons. First, in most areas, Gypsy communities were proportionately too small to justify special schools. Second, the dearth of qualified Romani-language teachers frustrated effective education. Third, Gypsy students were characterized by low attendance rates explained in large part by lack of parental encouragement, poverty, and discriminatory behavior from peers and teachers alike.

The Roma had become increasingly uncompetitive in the labor markets of interwar Eastern Europe. They either insisted on the continued practice of their traditional occupations, took on unskilled manual labor, or became unemployed. Only an insignificant number of Gypsies had acquired modern trades. The typical Romani occupations had remained essentially the same as in the imperial era. Those who engaged in wage labor generally got jobs – street cleaners, garbage collectors, and so on – that few others would accept. Most Gypsies continued to reside in rural areas and, if there was a demand for their services, provided seasonal help to local peasants. Although the land redistribution schemes that followed the break-up of large estates did benefit a small number of Gypsies (especially in Romania and Yugoslavia), most of them had lacked the experience and know-how necessary to run their farms and soon lost them. In sum, the vast majority of Roma could not respond to the challenge posed by the region's belated industrialization process.

---

[43] See, for instance, Anna Krasteva, "Ethnocultural Panorama of Bulgaria," *Balkan Forum*, 3:3 (1995): 238–40.

The interwar period, then, was synonymous with increasing Gypsy impoverishment and socioeconomic marginalization.[44] A growing proportion of the Roma lived in Gypsy ghettos marked by incredible filth, heaps of garbage, the absence of adequate drinking water, and basic sanitary facilities that were the hotbeds of contagious diseases. Even in Czechoslovakia, indisputably the most prosperous East European state at the time, many Roma were so poor that their conditions were improved by imprisonment, especially in winter, because jails at least provided food and shelter.[45] Not surprisingly, the proportion of criminal acts – the overwhelming majority of which had continued to be subsistence theft – had increased though certainly did not justify the widespread popular view of Roma as criminally inclined. According to 1935 data from Hungary's Zala county, for instance, the Gypsies comprised 0.77% of the county's population and were responsible for 2.04% of all crimes committed.[46]

In the interwar era the growing economic exclusion of the Roma was concomitant with their increasing social marginalization. A number of differences should be noted between the conditions of those living in urban and rural areas. The Roma generally got on much better with their neighbors in the villages than in cities and towns. In Bulgaria and Slovakia, for example, the Roma were relatively well integrated into village societies, and in rare cases well-to-do Gypsies even employed *gadje* (non-Roma).[47] In the Czech Lands, however, the Roma's situation remained more precarious. Part of the reason for this difference was that Slovaks, unlike Czechs, had a long experience of coexistence with the Roma. In the Czech Lands, where Gypsies remained largely nomadic, they were widely considered unproductive parasites. In Slovakia, however, their economic contribution was valued and they were historically permitted, encouraged, and at times forced to settle.[48] A group of

---

[44] See, for instance, István Kemény, *Beszámoló a magyarországi cigányok helyzetével foglalkozó 1971-ben végzett kutatásról* (Budapest: MTA, 1976), 50.

[45] Josef Kalvoda, "The Gypsies of Czechoslovakia," in Crowe and Kolsti, eds., *The Gypsies of Eastern Europe*, 95.

[46] Author's calculations from data in Béla Balogh, "A cigánykérdésről," *Csendörségi Lapok*, 14 March 1937, 181; cited in László Karsai, *A cigánykérdés Magyarországon, 1919–1945: Út a cigány Holocausthoz* (Budapest: Cserépfalvi, 1992), 23.

[47] Milena Hübschmannová, "Economic Stratification and Interaction: Roma, an Ethnic Jati in East Slovakia," in Diane Tong, ed., *Gypsies: An Interdisciplinary Reader* (New York: Garland, 1998), 236; and interviews with Ilona Tomova (Sofia, 8 March 1995) and Nikolai Gentchev, a Professor of History at the University of Sofia (Sofia, 7 March 1995).

[48] Willy Guy, "Ways of Looking at Roms: The Case of Czechoslovakia," in Farnham Rehfisch, ed., *Gypsies, Tinkers, and Other Travellers* (London: Academic Press, 1975), 204.

Slovak intellectuals even founded an organization in 1930, the League for the Cultural Uplifting of the Gypsies (which later turned into the Society for the Study and Solution of the Gypsy Question), which aimed to understand the Roma better.[49]

Although anti-Roma prejudices ran deep in East European societies, they were not nearly as strong as anti-Semitism, perhaps because the Roma were not feared or envied but, rather, were regarded with contempt. In stark contrast with the Roma's social marginality in the Czech Lands, dominant groups in the Yugoslav republics of Serbia and especially Macedonia (where a substantial number of sedentary Roma had lived in relative harmony for several centuries) accepted them.[50] Perhaps owing to the area's slow socioeconomic development, the Gypsy community had been considered a productive component of Macedonian society.

The interwar period was particularly trying for Eastern Europe's rural population. The collapse of the world grain market in 1926–7 and the subsequent depression had an especially devastating socioeconomic effect on the region because its economies were still based primarily on agriculture. Though the Gypsies were unquestionably the poorest societal group, in some especially backward areas the economic conditions of landless peasants were not much better. In impoverished rural regions, social tensions had increased and were manifested by fierce competition for the few available jobs that required no skills. Gypsy communities often became the target of hostilities because Roma would often work for even less than peasants. Not suprisingly, the Roma, who were protected by no one, were easy prey for the local population. In some cases, unchecked anti-Gypsy sentiments erupted and led to persecution or show trials. In 1928 in the Slovak village of Pobedim, six Roma fell victim to a pogrom occasioned by their alleged theft of some crops from nearby fields. A year later, Gypsies were accused of cannibalism in Košice (Slovakia). Though they were acquitted, the affair reinforced the population's anti-Gypsy prejudices and in several cases led to the expulsion of long-settled Roma from Slovak towns.[51]

The Interwar States and Their "Gypsy Policies"

The enactment of progressive constitutions and the creation of pluralist polities that indicated an auspicious beginning for post–World War I

---

[49] David J. Kostelancik, "The Gypsies of Czechoslovakia: Political and Ideological Considerations in the Development of Policy," *Studies in Comparative Communism*, 22:4 (Winter 1989): 308–9.

[50] Zoltan Barany, "The Roma in Macedonia: Ethnic Politics and the Marginal Condition in a Balkan State," *Ethnic and Racial Studies*, 18:3 (July 1995): 515–31.

[51] Mann, "Rroma (Gypsies) in Municipalities," 2–3.

state building were followed by the East European polities' decline into authoritarianism within a decade. The exception was Czechoslovakia, which remained fundamentally democratic. Generally speaking, state minority policies were inconsistent and depended on the ethnic minority in question.[52]

Although there were notable variations in the actual treatment of the Roma, in this period Gypsy policies across Eastern Europe were broadly similar. The state typically ignored them because they were not considered to pose a pressing problem, possessed minimal political and economic resources, and did not enjoy the backing of any important group or foreign government. To the extent that coherent policies were formulated at all, their aim was to settle the remaining nomadic Roma by limiting their mobility through the confiscation of their vehicles, the issuance of special identity cards, registration, fingerprinting, and occasional police raids. Government policies bore decidedly mixed results because, in the absence of serious governmental concern with the "Gypsy question," their implementation hinged largely on the vigor of local authorities. The lack of proper supervision and accountability allowed many a local council or police force to overstep their boundaries.

The interwar Polish state paid no attention to its relatively small Gypsy minority.[53] Although the Czechoslovak Republic granted the status of national minority to the Roma in 1921, it also sustained many of the Habsburg period's anti-Gypsy laws and decrees. New discriminatory measures were implemented already in the 1920s when all Gypsies had to be fingerprinted and registered. Law 117 of 1927 condemned the Roma as asocial citizens, limited their personal liberty, introduced Gypsy identity cards, and decreed that Romani children under 18 be placed in special institutions.[54] Following the establishment of the independent Slovak state, a 1939 statute classified the Roma into those who were settled and employed and "others"; the latter could not receive citizenship.

---

[52] See, for instance, C. A. Macartney, *National States and National Minorities* (London: Oxford University Press, 1934); Hugh Seton-Watson, *Eastern Europe Between the Wars* (Hamden, CT: Archon Books, 1962); and Joseph Rothschild, *East Central Europe Between the Two World Wars* (Seattle: University of Washington Press, 1974).

[53] Andrzej Mirga, "The Effects of State Assimilation Policy on Polish Gypsies," *Journal of the Gypsy Lore Society*, series 5, 3:2 (1993): 69.

[54] Ignacy-Marek Kaminski, *The State of Ambiguity: Studies of Gypsy Refugees* (Gothenburg: University of Gothenburg Press, 1980), 161; and Vladimír Gecelovský, "Právne normy týkajúce sa Rómov a ich aplikácia v Gemeri (1918–1938)," in Arne B. Mann, ed., *Neznámi Rómovia: Zo života a kultúry Cigánov-Rómov na Slovensku* (Bratislava: Ister Science Press, 1992), 79–90.

The Hungarian government devised no consistent policy toward the Gypsies. They were treated differently from other minorities to the extent that minority policies were formulated vis-à-vis the ethnic Germans and Slovaks but not toward the Roma. This neglect of the Gypsies had also been evident in the authorities' willingness to overlook a number of adverse phenomena affecting the Roma from their abysmal health standards to the widespread absenteeism of Gypsy pupils. Like other East European governments, Hungarian authorities either ignored them or enacted laws and regulations to make them more susceptible to social and political control. A 1928 law ordained semiannual Gypsy police raids in order to weed out the criminal and parasitic elements from the Romani communities. As in Czechoslovakia, special regulations required the fingerprinting and registration of all Roma.[55]

In concert with a number of international agreements as well as its 1923 Constitution, Romania recognized minority rights. Actual government policies, however, amounted to little more than the gradual Romanianization of ethnic minorities, including the Gypsies.[56] For the most part, though, the state did not take notice of the Roma, which is shown by the fact that from 1856 to 1933 no specific "Gypsy laws" were introduced in spite of the existence of large nomadic Romani groups.[57] The radicalization of Romanian politics in the mid- to late 1930s, on the other hand, produced numerous anti-Gypsy legislations.

Dominant groups in Bulgaria viewed the Roma as one of the country's traditional ethnic minorities, but, for the most part, they fell outside the purview of the Sofia government; only local authorities paid attention to them and nearly always in a negative context. Profound ethnic problems had plagued Yugoslavia (until 1929 the Kingdom of Serbs, Croats, and Slovenes) from its inception, and, not surprisingly, the Roma signified only a minor issue to politicians in Belgrade. At the same time, Yugoslav Gypsies – most of whom had lived in Serbia and Macedonia – had enjoyed more extensive minority rights than elsewhere in Eastern Europe.

Romani Mobilization

Notwithstanding the unfavorable sociopolitical environment, the Roma had made noteworthy efforts at political mobilization in some East European states in the interwar era. Although these endeavors were doomed by the increasingly extremist political environment of the 1930s,

---

[55] See János Bársony, "Der Zigeunerholocaust in Ungarn," ms (1994), 3–4.
[56] See David M. Crowe, *A History of the Gypsies of Eastern Europe and Russia* (London: I. B. Tauris, 1995), 127–8.
[57] Franz Remmel, *Die Roma Rumäniens: Volk ohne Hinterland* (Vienna: Picus, 1993), 45.

they represent an important attempt by the Gypsies to reduce their political marginality. Small as these achievements may seem, they do suggest that, wherever possible, the Roma were willing and able to make a dent in their centuries-long political exclusion. Trond Gilberg noted that Gypsy political and socioeconomic consciousness was particularly low in interwar Eastern Europe.[58] He is certainly correct when one compares them with other ethnic minorities. Doing so, however, misses the point because at no time – prior to 1989 – have the Gypsies achieved more success in organizing themselves than in this period.

Bulgarian Gypsies began to affirm their ethnic identity with increasing ardor in the 1920s by organizing a number of cultural and educational groups. Some Muslim Roma participated in local elections, much to the chagrin of ethnic Turks.[59] The Gypsies established numerous cultural organizations among which the two most important were the "Egypt Society" (1919) and "Future" (*Badashte*) (1929). As elsewhere in the region, the increasing extremism of the political environment brought an end to Gypsy organizations and activism. By the mid-1930s the Roma were no longer permitted to engage in civic activities. Romani mobilization attempts were less successful in Czechoslovakia and Hungary owing both to the lack of pivotal leaders and material resources and due to the anticipated resistance of local authorities. In Serbia and Macedonia, however, several Romani organizations and newspapers were called to life in the early 1930s, although the shortage of funds did not permit their survival for long.[60] In both regions the comparative tolerance of Gypsies had allowed for a wider range and larger number of cultural activities than elsewhere in Eastern Europe.

The most impressive gains in Gypsy ethnic mobilization had taken place in Romania, the country that became home to the largest Romani population in the world after 1918.[61] Lazar Naftanaila, a wealthy peasant of Gypsy origin, founded the first Romani organization, the "Society of New Peasant Brotherhood" (*Societatea Infratirea Neorustica*) in the early 1920s. Naftanaila recognized that in the absence of any appreciable state attention to the Roma's plight, they had to organize themselves. The Society, based in Transylvania, organized lectures, theater visits, and dance nights and helped to elevate the morale and ethnic awareness of the Roma. Its fame spread to as far as Bucharest and

[58] Trond Gilberg, "Influence of State Policy on Ethnic Persistence and Nationality Formation: The Case of Eastern Europe," in Peter F. Sugar, ed., *Ethnic Diversity and Conflict in Eastern Europe* (Santa Barbara: ABC-Clio, 1980), 190.

[59] Crowe, "The Roma (Gypsies) of Bulgaria and Romania," 7–8.

[60] See, for instance, N. B. Jopson, "*Romano Lil (Tsiganske Novine)*," *Journal of the Gypsy Lore Society*, series 3, 15:2 (1936): 86–9.

[61] See Remmel, *Die Roma Rumäniens*, 45–61.

induced the establishment of other organizations that became increasingly interested in political participation. The most important of these were the "General Association of Romanian Gypsies" (*Asociata Generala a Ţiganilor din Romania*) and the "General Union of Romanian Roma" (*Uniunea Generala a Romilor din Romania*), both created in 1934 with the goal to take their message to all Romanian Gypsies. Although the two organizations advocated similar programs (assimilation and an end to nomadism), they quickly became rivals whose main energies were expended in conducting smear campaigns against each other.

With the proclamation of the royal dictatorship in 1938, the Romanian constitution was suspended and political parties were prohibited. Though Romani organizations were never registered as political parties, the establishment of dictatorship effectively halted Gypsy mobilization. The fractiousness, financial mismanagement, and shortsightedness of these early Romani political institutions harmed not only themselves but also the cause of those they purportedly represented. At the same time, these were important beginnings that strengthened the Roma's confidence and encouraged their political ambitions. Gypsies in Romania also published a number of newspapers, such as the *Neamul Ţiganesc, O Rom,* and *Timpul,* which played a role in promoting Romani ethnic identity although their impact was limited due to the widespread illiteracy among their target audience. The Gypsy organizations of interwar Romania also serve as a valuable reminder to students of contemporary Gypsy mobilization that the Roma had faced problems in the 1920s and 1930s similar to the ones they must deal with today: lack of resources, divisiveness, and incompetent leadership.

Traditional Romani leadership forms had won attention in interwar Poland, where the position of the Gypsy king had been known since the Middle Ages. In 1930, Michal Kwiek, an influential member of the Kalderash tribe, emerged from several pretenders as the "King of Polish Gypsies" and established a "royal dynasty" that was to survive until 1961 and continued to enjoy respect among the Roma.[62] The high point in the life of the royal court was the coronation of the last pre–World War II king, Janusz Kwiek, amidst much theatrical pomp and ceremony in 1937. His cousin, Rudolf Kwiek, declared that these formalities were necessary "for Mussolini, who has promised us Abyssinia, will only take us seriously if we are formally organized and have orderly relations with the Polish state."[63] Although the entire royal affair was

---

[62] For a detailed discussion of this point, see Jerzy Ficowski, *The Gypsies in Poland: History and Customs* (Warsaw: Interpress, 1985), 35–8.

[63] Ibid., 37.

considered farcical by many, local state authorities maintained relations with the Gypsy monarchs (who tended to enjoy significant authority in their bailiwick) and were able to collaborate with them on a number of social issues.

PART III. *PORAJMOS*: THE GYPSY HOLOCAUST

The fact that the Gypsy Holocaust, or *Porajmos*, has been one of the less thoroughly researched periods of Romani history begs an explanation. The answer lies in several factors, which include the general lack of interest among scholars in the issue until recently and the difficulty of researching this topic given the absence of reliable demographic data and the deficient accounting of the Nazi administrators. The extermination of the Gypsies was far less meticulously documented by the Nazis and their collaborators than was the murder of the Jews. The Gypsies, wrote Henry Friedlander, "were deemed so marginal that their murder provoked no intra-agency rivalries and thus required no written authorization."[64] Other reasons should be sought in Romani traditions. History has been an alien concept in Romani culture, where the dead are rarely mentioned and seldom become the subjects of commemoration.[65] As Andrzej Mirga and Lech Mróz noted, "it is inappropriate in this culture to commemorate the time of death, both individual and collective, from the period of World War II."[66] Unlike the Jews and other victims of the Holocaust, many of whom were highly educated, Gypsy survivors did not leave behind diaries, did not write memoirs, and did not do subsequent research into this subject.

After the Fascist ascension to power in 1933, the Weimar Republic's low-intensity persecution of the Roma quickly escalated. Initially the campaign focused on the nomadic Roma, but it was soon extended to all Gypsies residing in Germany.[67] In 1939 the state introduced a ban on Romani children attending school, and a host of other discriminatory measures (including the prohibition of their freedom of movement) were implemented. From December 1938 until mid-1939 the "war on the Gypsies" was centralized and included the creation of a new criminal

---

[64] Henry Friedlander, *The Origins of Nazi Genocide: From Euthanasia to the Final Solution* (Chapel Hill: University of North Carolina Press, 1995), 285.

[65] See Andrzej Mirga and Lech Mróz, *Cyganie: Odmienności nietolerancja* (Warsaw: Wydawnictwo Naukowe PWN, 1994), 31–2; and Slawomir Kapralski, "The Roma and the Holocaust: Inventing Tradition as Identity Building Process," conference paper (University of Kent, 7–8 April 1995), 30–1.

[66] Mirga and Mróz, *Cyganie*, 31.

[67] For a summary of Nazi Germany's policies toward the Roma, see Zoltan Barany, "Memory and Experience: Anti-Roma Prejudice in Eastern Europe," Woodrow Wilson Center (Washington, DC), Occasional Paper No. 50 (July 1998), 7–12.

police apparatus, the *Reichszentrale zur Beampfung des Zigeunerwe-sens*.[68] Fascists Germany intended to exterminate all Gypsies because it perceived them as a threat to racial purity and as blood-sucking para-sites on German society. The Nazis set up an intricate system to catego-rize the Roma ("clean race Gypsies," "mixed Gypsies," and "wandering persons after the Gypsy fashion") based on the proportion of Gypsy blood and on the ethnicity of the spouse. This classificatory scheme was the side product of the Nazi era's state-sponsored race-biology research.[69] German scientists also engaged in sociological and anthropological studies of the Roma and drafted various proposals on how to solve "the Gypsy question," which amounted to little more than devising ways of exterminating large numbers of human beings through the most economical methods available.

Justifying the mass extermination of the Gypsies was not a source of apprehension for the Nazis for some of the same reasons that anti-Roma persecution in the past could proceed with impunity in many diverse set-tings. While there were numerous instances of righteous gentiles trying to and actually succeeding in saving Jews, few Roma received such assis-tance and no state or international organization expressed concern with their fate.[70] Most Gypsies from Germany and from German-occupied Europe were sent to concentration camps in eastern Germany and Poland. In Eastern Europe, many did not survive the roundups in places like Bucharest, Budapest, Belgrade, Brno, Kraków, Łódź, Prague, and Zagreb, where they were often shot on the spot. Once in the camps, the Roma – like the other victims – were decimated by epidemics, malnu-trition, brutality, and medical experiments in addition to methodical mass killings. The Roma were considered the lowest cast of prisoners, only above homosexuals.[71]

[68] Michael Zimmermann, *Verfolgt, vertrieben, vernichtet: die nationalsozialistische Ver-nichtungspolitik gegen Sinti und Roma* (Essen: Klartext, 1989), 23–4.

[69] A thoughtful work on this topic is Benno Müller-Hill, *Murderous Science: Elimination by Scientific Selection of Jews, Gypsies, and Others – Germany 1933–1945* (Oxford: Oxford University Press, 1988). See also Wim Willems, *In Search of the True Gypsy: From Enlightenment to Final Solution* (London: Frank Cass, 1997), 196–293.

[70] Some recent examples of the growing literature on rescuers of Jews and others are Carol Ritter and Sondra Myers, eds., *The Courage to Care: Rescuers of Jews during the Holo-caust* (New York: New York University Press, 1986); Gay Block and Malka Drucker, *Rescuers: Portraits of Moral Courage in the Holocaust* (New York: Holmes and Meier, 1992); and Günther B. Ginzel, *Mut zur Menschlichkeit: Hilfe für Verfolgte während der NS-Zeit* (Cologne: Rheinland, 1993).

[71] See Eugen Kogon, *The Theory and Practice of Hell: The German Concentration Camps and the System Behind Them* (New York: Farrar, Straus, & Co., 1949), 39–47. See also Betty Alts and Sylvia Folts. *Weeping Violin: The Gypsy Tragedy in Europe* (Kirksville, MO: Thomas Jefferson University Press, 1996).

There were significant disparities in the East European states' policies toward and the fate of Romani communities. In general, the Gypsy populations in countries under German occupation suffered terribly. Elsewhere the survival of the Roma largely depended on native political elites. In Albania, the *Porajmos* claimed relatively few victims due to the government's inattention to the Roma justified by the relatively small size of the Gypsy population and the fact that their communities were scattered across the country.[72] Dennis Reinhartz had convincingly shown that Croatian Fascists (*Ustashi*) were hardly more merciful in their treatment of the Roma than their German sponsors, claiming that as many as 26,000 Gypsies died in Croatia and in Sardinia where they were deported.[73] In German-occupied Serbia the Roma were subjected to a wide array of repressive laws (e.g., forced to wear yellow *Zigeuner* [Gypsy] armbands) and tens of thousands of them were sent to extermination camps where thousands died. In Yugoslavia and Albania a considerable number of Gypsies joined partisan units at least partly motivated by promises of social and political rights and Romanilanguage schools in postwar Yugoslavia.[74]

Bulgaria was more resolute in opposing German demands to deport and/or exterminate their citizens than any other state in the region. Although the government introduced a number of discriminatory decrees against Jews and Gypsies as early as 1941, Sofia refused to deport them to Nazi deathcamps. According to the German ambassador, the reason for the Bulgarian government's refusal to deliver their "undesirable" minorities to Hitler was the fact that most Bulgarians had grown up with Armenians, Greeks, Jews, and Gypsies and had harbored no innate prejudice against them.[75] At the same time, many Roma and Jews in Macedonia and Thrace – regions acquired by Bulgaria during the war – were rounded up and sent to the gallows. In contrast, no Romani community suffered proportionately more than that of the Nazi-occupied Czech Lands. An intensive settlement campaign began in 1939, and German authorities registered approximately 6,000 Gypsies in 1942

---

[72] John Kolsti, "Albanian Gypsies: The Silent Survivors," in Crowe and Kolsti, eds., *The Gypsies of Eastern Europe*, 54–5.

[73] See Dennis Reinhartz, "Damnation of the Outsider: The Gypsies of Croatia and Serbia in the Balkan Holocaust, 1941–1945," in Crowe and Kolsti, eds., *The Gypsies of Eastern Europe*, 85.

[74] Kolsti, "Albanian Gypsies," 56–7.

[75] Cited by Frederick B. Chary, *The Bulgarian Jews and the Final Solution, 1940–1944* (Pittsburgh: University of Pittsburgh Press, 1972), 153–4. On this issue see also Elena Marushiakova and Vesselin Popov, "The Bulgarian Romanies During the Second World War," in Donald Kenrick, ed., *In the Shadow of the Swastika: The Gypsies During the Second World War* (Hertfordshire: University of Hertfordshire Press, 1999), 89–94.

(5,000 of these led nomadic lifestyles). Nearly all Czech Roma were sent to concentration camps and perished there.[76]

Although Hungarian governments introduced a number of discriminatory laws, there was no institutionalized Gypsy persecution (let alone a centrally formulated Gypsy policy) prior to the supplanting of Admiral Horthy's authoritarian regime by the Fascist Arrow Cross party in the fall of 1944. The Roma's mobility was curtailed, a 1941 law prohibited sexual contact and marriages between Roma and Hungarians (an ironic twist of history, considering that Maria Theresa forbade endogamous Gypsy nuptials in 1773), and local authorities continued to harass them. In the fall of 1944 many Roma, particularly from the western part of the country, were deported to concentration camps and at least several thousand were murdered there. Poland, whose minority population had suffered perhaps more from World War II than that of any other, was occupied by Germany beginning with fall 1939. Roma who could not evade the authorities were rounded up in major cities and sent to the camps where more than 20,000 were killed.[77] According to the Romani activist, Andrzej Mirga, who emphasizes the absence of reliable data, there were approximately 50,000 Gypsies in Poland prior to the war and roughly 15,000 in the mid-1950s.[78]

The brutality of Romanian state policies toward the Gypsies were equaled by only those of Croatia and Serbia. Thousands of Roma perished as a result of pogroms and mass killings in Romania proper, while others were deported to and exterminated in Transnistria.[79] According to David Crowe, approximately 36,000–39,000 Romanian Gypsies had died during the *Porajmos*.[80] The new Slovak state established several Gypsy labor camps and introduced a number of laws that banned Roma from public transport, allowed them to enter towns and villages only on a limited basis, and stipulated that Gypsy dwellings had to be removed from the proximity of public roads.[81] A 1940 decree barred the Roma from the military, and in the following year they were forced to sell their caravans

[76] See Ctibor Necas, "Osudy československých Cikanu za nemecke okupace a nadvlady," *Středny Evropa*, 7 (1992): 117–29; and Markus Pape, *Nikdo vam nebude verit: Dokument o koncentracim tabore Lety u Pišku* (Prague: G + G, 1997).

[77] Jerzy Ficowski, *Wieviel Trauer und Wege: Zigeuner in Polen* (Frankfurt am Main: Peter Lang, 1992), 62–80, especially 80.

[78] Interview with Mirga (Kraków, 29 July 1996).

[79] See Michelle Kelso, "Gypsy Deportations to Transnistria: Romania 1942–1944," in Donald Kenrick, ed., *In the Shadow of the Swastika: The Gypsies During the Second World War* (Hertfordshire: University of Hertfordshire Press, 1999), 95–129.

[80] Crowe, "The Gypsy Historical Experience in Romania," 70.

[81] See Klára Orgovánová, "The Roma in Slovakia," *The East & Central Europe Program Bulletin* (New School for Social Research), 4:4 (May 1994): 3; and *Die Presse* (Vienna), 11 January 1993.

and return to the place where they were registered. Still, Slovakia had no policy to exterminate the Roma. Although after the country was occupied by Germany, several pogroms and mass killings did take place, the number of Gypsy casualties of the *Porajmos* is estimated at no more than 1,000.[82]

How Many Victims?

When reading accounts of the *Porajmos*, one is soon reminded of the statistical inconsistencies and impossibilities so characteristic of Gypsy studies. At the core of the "numbers problem" is the insufficient and unreliable census information pertaining to the Gypsies. This is particularly true for the pre–World War II period when in several countries censuses simply did not include the category "Gypsy"; therefore the Roma were accounted for under a different rubric (usually under the "others" heading). Some Gypsies habitually denied their ethnic identity while others with no permanent address – and before World War II this group comprised the majority of Roma in several European states – were simply not counted. Mirga notes that not only were the Roma uncounted by censuses but they often did not possess any sort of identification papers, which made figures all the more suspect.[83] Henry Huttenbach, a Holocaust historian, believes that Europe's Gypsy population in 1939 may be estimated at 885,000, although figures several times higher have also been published.[84] From a scholarly point of view, short of solid quantitative information – usually yielded by years of painstaking archival research – there is simply no way to safely estimate the number of the Holocaust's Romani victims.[85]

In spite of these profound methodological difficulties, many of those writing on the Roma feel compelled to pepper their accounts of the *Porajmos* with numerical figures. Indeed, it is refreshing to read Angus Fraser (whose book, in my view, is the best available general history of the Roma), who prudently says that "it is impossible to be categorical about numbers of casualties; but precise figures are perhaps not important."[86]

---

[82] Interview with Milena Hübschmannová, Professor of Romistics at Charles University (Prague, 12 June 1995).

[83] Interview with Mirga (Kraków, 29 July 1996).

[84] Henry R. Huttenbach, "The Romani Porajmos: The Nazi Genocide of Gypsies in Germany and Eastern Europe," in Crowe and Kolsti, eds., *The Gypsies of Eastern Europe*, 45.

[85] Incidentally, the number of Armenians massacred in the Ottoman Empire in 1915 is an analogous case to the extent that no reliable census data are available to assist in calculating their number. Thus, one finds estimates of 1.5 million Armenians killed (usually by Armenians) as well as 500,000 casualties (by Turkish sources). I am indebted to Henry Huttenbach for this point.

[86] Fraser, *The Gypsies*, 268.

In his fine recent study on the subject, Guenter Lewy also notes that the estimates he reports – 196,000 by Donald Kenrick in 1989 and "at least 90,000 killed in the territories controlled by the Nazis" by Michael Zimmermann in 1997 – "will have to remain more or less firm estimates and no exact count will ever be attainable."[87]

Authors who do provide "exact" numbers often base their figures on second- or third-hand sources, hearsay, and unreliable estimates. For instance, in their classic work, published in 1972, Kenrick and Puxon freely admit that their data on the deportation of Hungarian Roma came from "personal conversations" yet they feel confident to publish "precise" numbers.[88] In 1994, Kenrick conceded that "In fact at each revision the figure goes down, not up. This is a reason for relief – the number of Gypsies killed was lower than at first thought."[89] A 1995 Reuter's dispatch states that "Romania sent as many as 500,000 Gypsies to death in concentration camp," a curious figure in light of the fact that in the early 1940s Romania's Romani community was estimated at 300,000.[90]

Even more surprising is the denunciation of serious historians by careless journalists, presumably for coming up with unexpectedly low estimates of Romani victims. Thus, the informed reader cannot but be baffled at Fonseca's entirely unsupported and misleading condemnation of " 'revisionist historians' such as László Karsai," who claims "absurdly that no more than a few hundred [Hungarian] Gypsies 'vanished'."[91] First of all, Karsai writes that "a most careful analysis of archival sources" yielded the figure of 5,000 Hungarian Gypsies who were killed or persecuted though as many as 10,000 may have been murdered.[92] Second, he had followed a rigorous methodology and conducted years of archival research permitting him to come closer than anyone to a credible assessment of the Hungarian Romani community's losses.[93] Finally, some activists seem to have a propensity to provide ever greater numbers of Roma victims. In his 1987 book, Ian Hancock estimated 600,000 Roma victims. By 1988, he revised his figure to 1 million to 1.5 million

---

[87] Guenter Lewy, *The Nazi Persecution of the Gypsies* (New York: Oxford University Press, 2000), 222. According to a recent authoritative study of the Auschwitz concentration camp, an estimated 23,000 Roma were killed there. See Ralph Blumenthal, "Auschwitz Revisited: The Fullest Picture Yet," *New York Times*, 28 January 2001.

[88] See Donald Kenrick and Grattan Puxon, *The Destiny of Europe's Gypsies* (London: Chatto, 1972), 125.

[89] Donald Kenrick, "Romanies in the Nazi Period," *Cigány Néprajzi Tanulmányok*, 2 (Budapest: Mikszáth Kiadó, 1994), 70.

[90] Reuter (Bucharest), 2 May 1995; and Remmel, *Die Roma Rumäniens*, 62.

[91] Fonseca, *Bury Me Standing*, 253.

[92] Karsai, *A cigánykérdés Magyarországon*, 12.

[93] Ibid., 7.

Table 3.1. Range of Estimates of Gypsy
Holocaust Victims

Author	Estimate
1. Kenrick, Donald (1998)[a]	200,000
2. Kenrick and Puxon (1972)[b]	219,700
3. Gilbert, Martin (1985)[c]	250,000
4. Kenrick, Donald (1994)[d]	250,000
5. Vossen, Rüdiger (1983)[e]	275,200
6. Liégeois, Jean-Pierre (1994)[f]	400,000–500,000
7. Fonseca, Isabel (1995)[g]	500,000
8. Stewart, Michael (1997)[h]	500,000
9. Hancock, Ian (1987)[i]	600,000
10. Ulč, Otto (1988)[j]	1,000,000
11. Hancock, Ian (1988)[k]	1,000,000–1,500,000
12. Hancock, Ian (1998)[l]	1,500,000

[a] According to Kenrick, "Some 200,000 deaths have been documented and the International Romani Union estimates that as many as half a million Gypsies may have perished . . ."; see Kenrick, "How Many Roads," *Index on Censorship*, 27:4 (July–August 1998): 57.
[b] Kenrick and Puxon, *The Destiny of Europe's Gypsies*, 184.
[c] Gilbert, *The Holocaust* (New York: Holt, Rinehart, and Winston, 1985), 824.
[d] Kenrick, "Romanies in the Nazi Period," 70.
[e] Vossen, *Zigeuner* (Frankfurt am Main: Ullstein, 1983), 85–6.
[f] Liégeois, *Roma, Gypsies, Travellers*, 134.
[g] Fonseca, *Bury Me Standing*, 243.
[h] Stewart, *The Time of the Gypsies* (Boulder, CO: Westview, 1997), 5.
[i] Hancock, *The Pariah Syndrome: An Account of Gypsy Slavery and Persecution* (Ann Arbor: Karoma, 1987), 81.
[j] Ulč, "Gypsies in Czechoslovakia: A Case of Unfinished Integration," *Eastern European Politics and Societies*, 2:2 (Spring 1988): 306.
[k] Hancock, "'Uniqueness' of the Victims," 55.
[l] Hancock cited in Chris Witwer, "Austinites Who Make a Difference," *Austin Monthly*, November 1998, 6.

(and at a Congressional hearing in 1994 testified that "between 75% and 85% of the European Roma were systematically murdered").[94] In a 1998 interview, however, Hancock mentioned only the number 1.5 million. Since none of these figures are supported by satisfactory documentation or referencing, one is left to wonder about where any of these

[94] *Human Rights Abuses of the Roma (Gypsies)*, Hearing before the Subcommittee on International Security, International Organizations and Human Rights of the

numbers come from let alone the body of new evidence or notable research that led Hancock to raise his earlier estimates by 150%.[95]

I shall emulate Fraser's example and give no "precise" figure of my own. It is noteworthy, however, that of the estimates included in Table 3.1, 1–5 are at least partially documented and attempt to explain the methodology yielding the figure while 6–12 marshal no such evidence. Naturally, in my view the first group of figures deserves more credibility. Most important of all, however, it is clear that many tens of thousands of human beings were murdered for no other reason than being Gypsies.

SUMMING UP: REGIME CHANGE AND ROMANI MARGINALITY

In this chapter I establish three important claims. First, various states of the same regime type had pursued different policies toward their ethnic minorities especially as far as the Roma are concerned. In the imperial age, the Ottoman Empire's respect of minority traditions, languages, and religious identity contrasted sharply with the intrusive policies of Habsburg rule. In the interwar period, on the other hand, the Gypsy policies of authoritarian East European states were more similar than under any other regime type to the extent that, by and large, they were characterized by the utter disregard of the Roma's plight and the view that the "Gypsy problem" was essentially a police problem. Even in this era, however, there were important disparities between the actual rights the Roma enjoyed in Yugoslavia in contrast with the institutionalized discrimination of Czech Lands. Finally, in the authoritarian and Fascist states of World War II, there were significant differences in state policies toward the Gypsies in, say, Albania and Bulgaria on the one hand and Croatia and Romania on the other.

Second, since the general tendencies of particular regimes such as the presumed comparative tolerance of ethnic minorities by imperial states did not account sufficiently for minority policies, it is important to identify the other sources of state policy toward the Roma. Regardless of regime type, states pursue common objectives, such as self-preservation, prosperity, security, social tranquility, and, particularly in nondemocra-

---

Committee of Foreign Affairs, House of Representatives (103rd Congress, Second Session, 14 April 1994) (Washington, DC: U.S. Government Printing Office, 1994), 34.

[95] In a 1988 article Hancock refers to a "study undertaken" by Stephen Castles indicating "that Romani losses may be as high as one and a half million." See Ian F. Hancock, " 'Uniqueness' of the Victims: Gypsies, Jews, and the Holocaust,' *Without Prejudice*, 1:2 (1988): 55. In fact, Castles' 259-page book mentions the Gypsies (using the lowercase "g") only twice in passing, and merely says, without any reference or notation, that "6 million Jews, 1.5 million gypsies . . . were murdered." See Stephen Castles, *Here for Good: Western Europe's New Ethnic Minorities* (London: Pluto, 1984), 197.

tic states, control. It is these fundamental aims that provided the most elementary stimulants for policies toward the Roma, a people who seemed indifferent to state control and were perceived to threaten social tranquility. State-specific factors played only subordinate roles in shaping state policy toward the Gypsies. In both periods, negative societal views of the Gypsies seem to have influenced state policy only marginally (with the partial exception of the Habsburg Empire) because these predemocratic states were not particularly concerned with what ordinary people might have thought. Similarly, state policies in both imperial and authoritarian systems were hardly affected by the Roma's socioeconomic situation, although one might argue that their position as society's outcasts was a motivating force behind the assimilationist policies of eighteenth-century Habsburg rulers. In addition, state policies were not influenced by the Roma's political power because they had none. At the same time, the international environment did effect policies toward the Gypsies. This was clearly the case in the Romanian push to abolish slavery. Far more important, however, was the influence of Nazi Germany which kindled the anti-Gypsy policies in Bulgaria, Hungary, Slovakia, and Yugoslavia, although, to be sure, to different degrees.

The third point is that the character of Romani marginality was evolving independently of political regime transition in Eastern Europe. The most important shift took place in the economic conditions of the Roma. As we have seen, once general economic progress began in the region, the Roma gradually lost ground and an increasing number of them became impoverished. This deterioration of their economic status went hand in hand with the worsening of their social situation given that dominant groups increasingly viewed them less as contributors to society and more as parasites. At the same time, the early steps toward ethnic solidarity and strengthening of ethnic identity witnessed in the late imperial age and in the interwar period represent a positive change.

4

The Roma under State-Socialism

The end of World War II found the East European countries physically, politically, socially, and economically exhausted and devastated. Along with the Jews and Gypsies, a large proportion of whom were systematically exterminated, millions of others had died in death camps, on battlefields, and in their own cities and towns. Even before the conclusion of the carnage it became clear that the independence that East European states had gained at the end of World War I would not be restored to them. Instead, for the next four and a half decades the region fell under the Soviet Union's control. Albania and Yugoslavia, two countries that preserved their independence, were also ruled by communists and suffered similar fates.

Unlike any other regime type, communist or socialist systems were defined by their real or professed adherence to Marxism–Leninism, a holistic ideology that supposedly held the answer to all social, economic, and political issues of consequence to the state and its subjects. With the passing of time it became increasingly clear that Marxism–Leninism could not offer suitable solutions to practical problems, but ruling elites – whose fleeting legitimacy was vested in their knowledge of and allegiance to the state ideology – had continued to pay homage to it even as the ruinous effects of their policies were becoming increasingly apparent. Classical Marxism has remarkably little to say about ethnic minorities and nationalism simply because the latter was expected to disappear and the former to matter little in communist societies where class membership was to be the key to one's identity. The rapid emergence of problems pertaining to ethnic groups and nationalities soon made communist elites recognize that potential solutions lay in pragmatic policies and not in ideological canon.

Edward Friedman writes that for "a minority to be pro-socialist would be to play the fool or to be a traitor, the enemy of one's own community."[1] This is both an exaggeration and oversimplification. The impact of state-socialist policies on ethnic minorities was far from uniformly negative. Rather, in this period the situation of many ethnic groups improved in some respects and deteriorated in others. Ethnic minorities that had previously suffered from extensive persecution (e.g., Jews) or were stranded at a low economic developmental level (e.g., Central Asian nationalities) could actually benefit from socialist rule. In this chapter I will show that in some ways the socialist state had substantially reduced the socioeconomic marginality of the East European Roma. Their political situation was overshadowed by the state's obsession with social and political control (which equally affected members of other ethnic groups), but in some ways the change even in this respect was somewhat positive.

This chapter is divided into three parts. Part I analyzes the main objectives and means of state policies toward the Roma focusing on the different approaches of East European states. Part II examines the changes in and the impact of state policies on the Gypsies' socioeconomic marginality during the communist era. In the final section I will show that notwithstanding the state's control of organized activities, this period was not entirely "down time" for Gypsy mobilization.

PART I: THE SOCIALIST STATES' POLICIES TOWARD THE ROMA

The state had more of an impact on the Roma's conditions in socialist (and totalitarian) systems than in any other regime type. East European policies regarding what socialist elites conceived of as their "Gypsy problem" evolved differently from state to state. As in other policy domains, approaches toward the Roma were similar in the Stalinist period given that powerful Soviet control over the region's states (with the exception of Albania and Yugoslavia) did not allow for much straying from Moscow's line. Beginning with the 1960s, however, diminishing direct Soviet supervision allowed the gradual emergence of different approaches.

Policy Objectives

The last time a comprehensive "Gypsy policy" was developed in Eastern Europe prior to communist rule was under the Habsburg emperors of the late eighteenth century. Even more than in the imperial age, the basic goal of communist systems was to dominate the entire spectrum of

---

[1] Edward Friedman, "Ethnic Identity and the De-Nationalization and Democratization of Leninist States," in Crawford Young, ed., *The Rising Tide of Cultural Pluralism: The Nation-State at Bay?* (Madison: University of Wisconsin Press, 1993), 226.

socioeconomic and political activities. Unlike imperial rulers of old, however, East European communist elites were able to concentrate more intensive and extensive control in their hands bolstered as they were by a tremendous coercive apparatus, a rigid hierarchical organizational structure, relatively modern technology, and an effectively suppressed populace. Soviet leaders, de facto superiors of East European elites at least until the mid-1950s, envisioned a homogenized new society composed of socialist men and women to which the Roma, with their "deviant" lifestyles, posed a potential obstacle. Therefore, the fundamental goal was to assimilate them and to transform them into productive, cooperative, and supportive socialist citizens. Initially, at least, the communist regimes' notion of assimilation appeared to be as simple as the application of the formula: (Gypsy) + (socialist wage-labor) + (housing) = (socialist worker) + (Gypsy folklore).[2] The party-state pursued several policies to ensure speedy Romani assimilation: dispersal of compact Romani communities, resettlement, mandatory education, and compulsory wage labor. These policies received firm ideological support from Lenin, who viewed assimilation as an inevitable historical process and condoned actions to accelerate it with the exception of "coercive" operations (a point at times forgotten by his disciples).[3]

The communist party rather than the state bureaucracy served as the primary institutional locus for making "Gypsy policy." Politburo (PB) members decided on the basic approach toward the Roma, but actual policy was usually devised and elaborated in the Central Committee (CC) and its secretariats and departments (especially those dealing with domestic policy). State institutions – particularly councils of nationalities, ministries (especially labor, education and culture, social affairs, and interior), and county, city, and municipal councils – and lower-level party committees were ordinarily responsible for policy implementation. As a general rule, policy making and implementation occurred entirely without the participation of Roma, save for the few token party officials of Gypsy lineage.

One of the basic political questions pertaining to the Roma was the issue of what type of administrative status should be granted to them. By Stalin's criteria of national minorities the Gypsies fell short on several counts.[4] They did not possess a common language let alone a territorial

---

[2] This formula is from Michael Stewart, adopted here with a minor change. See Stewart, "Gypsies, Work, and Civil Society," *The Journal of Communist Studies*, 6:2 (June 1990): 142.

[3] See Walker Connor, *The National Question in Marxist–Leninist Theory and Strategy* (Princeton, NJ: Princeton University Press, 1984), 480.

[4] See I. V. Stalin, *Marksizm i natsional'nyi vopros* (Moscow: Politizdat, 1950).

base, were usually unaware of their history, and did not have a uniform culture. Since the Roma did not "measure up," there was no need to endow them with "national minority" status such as given to Hungarians in Czechoslovakia or Germans in Romania. Consequently, there was no ideological justification for granting them the type of social and cultural institutions (e.g., schools with instruction in their mother tongue, sociocultural organizations, etc.) that national minorities – who typically comprised much smaller populations – ordinarily received. Still, East European states conferred different administrative statuses to their Romani communities.

The 1971 Bulgarian Constitution, unlike its predecessor promulgated in 1947, made no specific references to ethnic minorities but referred to "citizens of non-Bulgarian origins."[5] The authorities in Sofia went as far as denying the very existence of a Gypsy minority (they were absent from censuses after the 1950s) to promote the regime's assimilationist policies. Nevertheless, the Roma were officially referred to as a "minority" until 1974 when they disappeared from all statistical data and were seldom mentioned officially afterwards.[6] In 1948 Czechoslovakia repealed the "nationality" status Gypsies enjoyed in the interwar era. Experts loyal to the regime, like Jaroslav Sus, took pains to explain on "scientific grounds" why the Gypsies were not and would never become a nationality and that the only "correct" policy was to assimilate them.[7] In censuses the Roma were compelled to declare themselves as members of a constitutionally recognized ethnic collective (in the 1980 census 75% declared Slovak, 15% Hungarian, and 10% Czech nationality).[8] In statistics and documents the Gypsies ordinarily appeared under the rubric of "other and nonstated nationalities." Polish official documents customarily referred to the Roma as a "population of Gypsy origin," thus avoiding the formulation of a precise status.[9] Romania's Gypsy minority was tabulated under the residual category of "other nationalities." Although the 1965 Constitution went farther (at least in theory) than the 1947 basic law in guaranteeing special educational and cultural minority rights, the Roma were not included in these changes.

[5] See Hugh Poulton, *The Balkans: Minorities and States in Conflict* (London: Minority Rights Group, 1993, 2nd ed.), 119.
[6] Elena Marushiakova and Vesselin Popov, *Gypsies (Roma) in Bulgaria* (Frankfurt: Peter Lang Verlag, 1997), 40.
[7] See, for instance, Jaroslav Sus, *Cikánská otázka v ČSSR* (Prague: SNPL, 1963), 97–100.
[8] Otto Ulč, "Gypsies in Czechoslovakia: A Case of Unfinished Integration," *Eastern European Politics and Societies*, 2:2 (Spring 1988): 323.
[9] Andrzej Mirga, "The Effects of State Assimilation Policy on Polish Gypsies," *Journal of the Gypsy Lore Society*, series 5, 3:2 (1993): 71.

The Hungarian Roma's administrative status had evolved gradually in concert with the liberalization of the state. In the 1950s, minority experts insisted time and again that the Gypsies did not comprise a nationality and therefore could not be granted national minority status. Champions of the assimilationist policy defended it in the same terms as in Czechoslovakia: "The Gypsies are not a nationality, the solution to their problem is complete assimilation," opined one.[10] A 1961 resolution of the Central Committee of the Hungarian Socialist Workers' Party (HSWP) contended that although the Romani population was not a nationality, it had to enjoy the same "developmental and constitutional privileges" because of its size. After an extensive debate, in 1984 the authorities in Budapest "decided" that the Gypsies did comprise a unique ethnic group, and in 1988 the Politburo of the HSWP granted nationality status to them.[11] In many respects the most generous East European state toward the Roma was Tito's Yugoslavia. According to the 1974 Yugoslav Constitution, all nationalities, including the Gypsies, were equal but republican constitutions did not include references to them.[12] In 1981 the federal state bestowed nationality status to the Roma, although only Bosnia-Herzegovina and Montenegro conferred the attendant privileges.[13] Other republics continued to view the Gypsies as an "ethnic group," the lowest in the three-tier system of "nations" (Croats, Serbs, Macedonians, etc.), "nationalities" (Albanians, Hungarians, etc.), and "other nationalities and ethnic groups" (Vlachs, Jews, etc.).[14]

This brief analysis of the Roma's administrative status hints at the differences between the East European states' policies toward them. Although some of the disparities may seem subtle, they signified substantial divergences in political strategy which, in turn, reflected the increasingly dissimilar paths of the region's states. Generally speaking, the Roma received little political attention until the 1950s as communist elites had to concentrate their efforts on consolidating their power and leading the postwar reconstruction efforts. By the mid-1950s, "what to do with the troublesome Gypsies" became an important issue across the region. The fundamental goal (assimilation) was the same; the means were different. These differences justify extended discussion.

---

[10] See Károly Túróczi, "A cigányság társadalmi beilleszkedéséről," *Valóság*, 5:6 (June 1962): 72–81.

[11] See Gábor Sánta, "Sokan vagyunk és semmink sincs: Beszélgetés Osztojkán Bélával II.," *Beszélő*, 10 August 1991, 18–19.

[12] "Jugoslawiens Zigeuner als politischer Faktor," *Neue Zürcher Zeitung*, 22 October 1982.

[13] Hugh Poulton, *Who Are the Macedonians?* (London: Hurst, 1995), 139–40.

[14] Poulton, *The Balkans*, 5.

Pattern I: Consistent Coercion (Czechoslovakia, Bulgaria)

The year 1958 was a turning point in the destiny of Gypsies in several East European countries. In that year, the CC of the Czechoslovak Communist Party (CSCP) decided in favor of a rapid and comprehensive campaign to settle and assimilate the Roma throughout the country. The resultant legal instrument (Law 74/1958) deprived "nomads" of the right to travel and forced them to find regular employment. This law was tantamount to an administrative attempt to define Roma as a social group (it specified a way of life and did not mention the word "Gypsy").[15] The Prague government established the National Council for Questions of the Gypsy Population in 1965 to coordinate Gypsy policy. In the same year, Slovak authorities recommended to local administrators that no community should include more than 5% Roma. The only period of progressive minority policy coincided with the Prague Spring and its aftermath (1968–9). In the early 1970s, government resolutions in the Czech Lands (1972/231) and Slovakia (1972/94) subjected the Roma to displacement from their settlements to communal apartments in urban areas.[16] Schools punished the use of the Romani language even during breaks between classes.[17] Assimilationist pressures subsided little in the 1970s and 1980s as full employment and the elimination of Romani crime remained key priorities (as witnessed by the government resolution 1974/29).

One of the most controversial policies toward the Roma in all of Eastern Europe was the sterilization of Gypsy women in Czechoslovakia. The program commenced in 1966, offering women (the applicant had to be at least 35 years old and must have had a minimum of three children) the possibility of sterilization. In 1986, regulations were modified to allow women as young as 18 years of age to have themselves sterilized even if they had no children. To make it attractive, the authorities paid those who underwent the procedure up to 25,000 crowns (about ten months' good salary).[18] The sterilization policy intended primarily to slow the rapid growth of the Romani population, though the two major pertinent decrees of the Ministry of Health and Social Affairs of the Czech Socialist Republic in 1972 and 1988 did not explicitly

---

[15] Willy Guy, "Ways of Looking at Roms: The Case of Czechoslovakia," in Farnham Rehfisch, ed., *Gypsies, Tinkers, and Other Travellers* (London: Academic Press, 1975), 222.

[16] Vladimír Šedivý and Viktor Maroši, *Position of National Minorities and Ethnic Groups in the Slovak Republic* (Bratislava: Minority Rights Group, 1996), 21.

[17] See Eva Davidová, *Romano Drom: Česty Romu, 1945–1990* (Olomuc: Vydatelstvi Univerzity Palackého, 1995), 122.

[18] "Alle hassen die Zigeuner," *Der Spiegel*, no. 36 (3 September 1990), 50.

mention them.[19] In fact, the number of sterilized women as well as the proportion of Roma among them had increased from 500 a year in the early 1980s to 2,000 in 1988; and from 36% in 1987 to nearly 50% in 1989 (though the Gypsies constituted only about 2.5% of the population), respectively.[20] According to one source, doctors often sterilized Romani women without their consent, following abortions or cesarean sections.[21]

Bulgaria's assimilation campaign began in 1953–4. Local authorities, particularly in the northern plain where many of the nomadic tribes lived, started to enforce a strict sedentarization policy that received additional impetus in 1956 when the USSR ordered that all nomadic groups be settled as soon as possible.[22] A 1958 Bulgarian government decree (#258) prohibited Gypsy travel, and in the following year the Bulgarian Communist Party (BCP) CC directed local authorities to ensure full Romani employment.[23] In 1962, minority experts decided to create a segregated Gypsy school system because education in integrated settings did not produce the anticipated results quickly enough. The principal aim was to unify Bulgarian society, which meant the rejection of the basic minority rights of Turks, Gypsies, and Pomaks (Bulgarian-speaking Muslims). The regime's methods in service of this objective included changing Muslim names to Slavic ones, forced emigration (to Turkey), and religious persecution. A series of government decrees and party resolutions prescribed measures for "reforming" Romani lifestyle and "developing" their culture. After 1984 the Gypsies were prohibited from speaking Romani, dancing, and playing unique Romani musical instruments in public, and in 1987 the state halted the publication of (Bulgarian language) Gypsy newspapers and closed down the Romani theater. Bulgaria's assimilationist policies were consistent. They succeeded in raising the Gypsies' living standards and educational attainments and continued to deny their right to preserve their language, religion, and culture.[24]

[19] These documents are reproduced in *Struggling for Ethnic Identity: Czechoslovakia's Endangered Gypsies* (New York: Human Rights Watch, 1992): 139–46.

[20] Sharon Fisher, "Romanies in Slovakia," *RFE/RL Research Report*, 2:42 (22 October 1993): 55; and Carol Silverman, "Persecution and Politicization: Roma (Gypsies) of Eastern Europe," *Cultural Survival Quarterly*, 19:2 (Summer 1995): 44.

[21] Paul Hockenos, *Free to Hate: The Rise of the Right in Post-Communist Eastern Europe* (New York: Routledge, 1993), 220.

[22] Interview with Ilona Tomova, presidential adviser on ethnic and religious issues (Sofia, 8 March 1995).

[23] The document is reproduced in *Destroying Ethnic Identity: The Gypsies of Bulgaria* (New York: Human Rights Watch, 1991), 61–6.

[24] Poulton, *The Balkans*, 113; and interview with Tomova (Sofia, 8 March 1995).

Bulgaria and Czechoslovakia actively discouraged objective scholarly research on Romani life, culture, and language in order to erode Gypsy identity. The writings of Milena Hübschmannová and of the few other independent Romanologists of the region were heavily censored. In Bulgaria only two dissertations (both supporting the party line) were completed on the Roma throughout the entire communist period. One of them argued that all foreign organizations engaged in studying the Gypsies "were formed with the purpose of creating a 'fifth column of imperialism' in Bulgaria."[25]

Pattern II: Erratic Intrusion (Poland, Romania)

In the early 1950s Poland became the first East European state to try to integrate nomadic Gypsies by offering them housing and employment. A 1952 government decree established an Office for Gypsy Affairs under the aegis of the Ministry of Internal Affairs' Department of Social Administration which remained the institutional locus of Romani policy until 1989. The offer was accompanied by minimal coercion and the majority of peripatetic Roma refused to settle. A 1960 meeting of the Polish United Workers' Party's (PUWP) Central Committee recognized the meager results borne by this approach and decided to apply more direct pressure on the Roma, drawing on the experiences of Czechoslovakia.[26] In 1964 a more forceful assimilation campaign commenced which included the registration of Roma by local authorities, restrictions on travel and gatherings, and control of Gypsy cultural organizations.[27] The new tactic brought results in a short time. Within a few years, 80% of formerly nomadic children were registered in schools and dispersal policies proved reasonably effective.[28] Still, a larger proportion of Roma (both male and female) were able to remain self-employed, and Gypsy educational standards stayed lower (due to high absenteeism) than in any other East European state.

After the mid-1960s no special legislation was aimed at the Gypsies in Poland and the militia enforced various laws (e.g., on forest maintenance and highway movement) only randomly. Roman Kwiatkowski, a Polish Gypsy leader, remembers habitually traveling with his family caravan in the 1960s and 1970s with militamen either ignoring them or

[25] *Destroying Ethnic Identity: The Gypsies of Bulgaria*, 13.
[26] Mirga, "The Effects of State Assimilation Policy," 72–3.
[27] Adam Bartosz, "The Social and Political Status of the Roma in Poland," *Roma*, no. 40 (January 1994): 16–17; and interview with Roman Kwiatkowski, President of the Association of Polish Roma (Oświęcim, 19 August 1999).
[28] Angus Fraser, *The Gypsies* (Oxford: Blackwell, 1995, 2nd ed.), 275. See also Josefat Zywert, "Problemy mlodżeży cyganskiek w szkole podstawowej," *Kwartalnik Pedagogiczny*, 1 (1968): 103–9.

directing them to a different town. "In Czechoslovakia," he says, "we would have been put in jail."[29] Owing to the lack of comprehensive legislation and the uniform enforcement of existing regulations, Polish Roma were more successful in resisting assimilationist pressures than were Gypsies elsewhere in Eastern Europe.

Romania was the first state that intended to sedentarize nomadic Gypsies by confiscating their horses and wagons as early as 1946 and dispersing compact communities in 1951.[30] By the early 1950s the majority of nomadic Roma were settled. As elsewhere in the region, full Romani employment was a key government objective (reluctant Gypsies were often sentenced to forced labor under the provisions of Decree 153/1970), but this policy was not pursued as vigorously as in Czechoslovakia, for instance. A 1977 Romanian Communist Party (RCP) CC report admitted the half-hearted implementation of the government decree 1976/25 that called for increases in regular Romani employment and education standards. The party's renewed assimilationist campaign included the prohibition of traditional meetings, confiscation of the gold coins that were often the Roma's only valuable possessions, and the assignment of more Gypsies to factory work.[31] According to a 1983 RCP CC document, the results remained mixed and depended largely on the zeal of local jurisdictions.

Actually, after the mid-1970s (and especially following the only partially effective renewal of the RCP's dispersal and education campaign), state attention to the "Gypsy problem" had considerably diminished. In any case, the demand that local authorities demonstrate more vigilance directly contradicted the RCP's 1972 declaration that it had solved the country's ethnic problems. Officials even told a foreign filmmaker planning a documentary on the Gypsies that "there are no more Romanie [sic] in our country."[32] A 1980 RCP CC position broke with the regime's strong pronatalist policy and decided not to encourage couples with more than five children to have more unless one of the parents was employed in a "useful social activity" and all school-age children regularly attended school.[33] The clear target of this policy change was the Gypsy community because many Roma shunned work

---

[29] Interview with Kwiatkowski (Oświęcim, 19 August 1999).
[30] This discussion draws on *Destroying Ethnic Identity: The Gypsies of Romania* (New York: Helsinki Watch, 1991), 17–19.
[31] Franz Remmel, *Die Roma Rumäniens: Volk ohne Hinterland* (Vienna: Picus, 1993), 74–5.
[32] Viliam Figusch, ed., *Roma People in Slovakia and in Europe* (Bratislava: Information and Documentation Centre on the Council of Europe, 1995), 16.
[33] Interview with Cătălin Zamfir, a former Romanian Minister of Social Welfare (Bucharest, 1 June 1996).

in favor of living on per-child subsidies and did not pressure their children to go to school.

Pattern III: Decreasing Pressures (Hungary)

In stark contrast to its sister party to the north, a 1958 Hungarian Socialist Workers' Party Politburo resolution endorsed a policy of active support for Gypsy culture and education and stressed the importance of each minority's national organizations in these efforts.[34] The party resolution of 1961 – which officially recognized, for the first time, the abject poverty and profound socioeconomic marginality of the Roma – was a turning point that began the process of forceful assimilation. In 1964 and 1968, HSWP Central Committee documents deplored the lackluster results of the party's educational, employment, and resettlement policies and acknowledged that bridging the gap between the Roma and the rest of society might well take decades of painstaking work and a large amount of resources. Unlike other East European states, however, Hungarian authorities sponsored Gypsy research that yielded several fine sociological studies that were to become the foundations of changed policies.[35] For instance, the 1974 decision of the HSWP CC's Agitation and Propaganda (Agitprop) Committee ran directly counter to the 1961 resolution by encouraging the formation of Romani clubs, ensembles, and other sociocultural organizations, supporting Gypsy intellectuals, and calling for the establishment of a Gypsy newspaper and even for bilingual education (in areas where Romani children were in a majority). To ensure serious scholarly work on the Roma, in 1982 the HSWP and the Ministry of Education established the Scientific Council for the Coordination of Gypsy Research within the Academy of Science's Institute of Social Sciences.

By the early 1970s the HSWP had realized that its policies should take into account the Gypsies' unique ethnic identity and specific socioeconomic problems. In 1977 a Ministry of Education position paper was the first open break with the assimilationist policy, and it was followed by several important HSWP resolutions.[36] Most significant of these was the 1979 HSWP PB resolution that called for expanding the political

---

[34] David Crowe, "The Gypsies in Hungary," in David Crowe and John Kolsti, eds., *The Gypsies of Eastern Europe* (Armonk, NY: M. E. Sharpe, 1991), 120.

[35] Perhaps the most important product of this crop was István Kemény, *Beszámoló a magyarországi cigányok helyzetével foglalkozó 1971 – ben végzett kutatásról* (Budapest: MTA Szociológiai Intézet, 1976). An abbreviated version of this now classic study was published as István Kemény, "A magyarországi cigánylakosság," *Valóság*, 17:1 (January 1974): 63–72.

[36] János Báthory, "A cigányság a politika tükrében," *Világosság*, 29 (August–September 1988): 619.

presence of "deserving" Roma. The 1984 report and resolution of the HSWP CC Agitprop Committee signaled the end of the assimilationist approach by declaring that the Roma could freely choose between alternative methods of social integration: through preserving its culture, traditions, and ethnic identity or by voluntary assimilation.[37] In many respects (primary education, employment, culture) the resultant policies improved on the Roma's situation although in several regards (such as higher education) they were rather more superficial. Notwithstanding the HSWP's propaganda efforts, Gypsies did not receive their proportionate share of state resources; and, in 1984, two-thirds of them still lived below the official poverty line.[38] There is no doubt, however, that Hungary's Gypsy policies were more successful in integrating the Roma than were the Gypsy policies of other East European states, with the notable exception of Yugoslavia.

Pattern IV: Constructive Interference (Yugoslavia)

The cornerstone of Yugoslav nationality and minority policy was to establish and, if necessary, enforce ethnic harmony in the multinational state. After World War II, Yugoslav communists viewed the Roma favorably and Tito even considered, albeit briefly, the establishment of a "Gypsy autonomous area" in Macedonia to compensate for the Roma's "fanatical commitment to the partisan cause."[39] In contrast to other East European states, the government and the League of Communists of Yugoslavia (LCY) clearly preferred integration to assimilation. In general, the Roma enjoyed a more secure social status and benefited from a more tolerant state, particularly in the last decade of Tito's rule, than elsewhere in Eastern Europe.[40] Especially after 1974 (the year of the new constitution that enlarged the autonomy of republics), the federal government had increased the political visibility of smaller ethnic minorities and the Roma were well served by these policies. In contrast to the other countries of the region, Yugoslav Gypsies were allowed to have a large number of cultural and social organizations relatively free of state control. Another important difference was that many Roma could take advantage of the LCY's land distribution schemes and became owners

---

[37] Gerhard Seewann, "Zigeuner in Ungarn," *Südost-Europa*, 36:1 (January 1987): 27.

[38] L. J. Macfarlane, *Human Rights: Realities and Possibilities* (New York: St. Martin's Press, 1990), 217.

[39] David M. Crowe, *A History of the Gypsies of Eastern Europe and Russia* (London: I. B. Tauris, 1995), 222.

[40] See Carol J. Williams, "Eastern Europe Upheaval Means Even Bleaker Times for Gypsies," *Los Angeles Times*, 20 December 1991; and Zoltan Barany, "Democratic Changes Bring Mixed Blessings for Gypsies," *RFE/RL Research Report*, 1:20 (15 May 1992): 42.

of small farms (particularly in Serbia).[41] At the same time, their situation remained a "serious basic social issue." According to a 1978 government report, the integration of Roma into Yugoslav society lagged far behind the regime's expectations, particularly in terms of their educational attainments and living standards.[42]

Even after Tito's death (1980), the state attempted to accelerate Romani integration, particularly in the field of education. In areas with large Gypsy communities a growing number of schools offered Romani as the language of instruction in the first grade to ease the pupils' transition into the educational system. Overtly discriminatory policies toward the Roma were pursued by republic-level authorities that, along with traditions and history, go far in explaining the substantial differences of the Gypsies' conditions in various republics. For instance, local authorities in Slovenia – the most advanced republic and home to only a small Romani population – followed a policy of territorial segregation and forced socioeconomic integration whereas officials in Macedonia and Serbia tended to adopt far more relaxed attitudes toward the Roma. Within the East European context, Macedonia became the most hospitable place for the Roma. After the 1963 earthquake, city and republic authorities in Skopje poured large sums of money into building up Shuto Orizari (a suburb of the capital), which had quickly grown into the largest Romani community in the world, with a population of approximately 40,000 people in the 1980s. Gypsies there could elect their town council and delegate a member into the Macedonian legislature.

The Reasons for Policy Disparities

Czechoslovakia and Bulgaria were singular among the East European states for their consistent and rigorous pursuit of Romani assimilation from the early 1950s until 1989. In the case of Czechoslovakia the Prague Spring and its immediate aftermath brought a brief respite from intolerant state policies; but with the beginning of "normalization," all reforms were reversed by the new political leadership. As Hübschman-nová recalls, "in Czechoslovakia activists and Roma experts considered Hungary and Yugoslavia the examples of how communist parties could actually have acceptable, progressive policies toward the Roma."[43]

[41] Hugh Poulton, "The Roma in Macedonia: A Balkan Success Story?" *RFE/RL Research Report*, 2:19 (7 May 1993): 43.

[42] See the 1978 report of the Yugoslav Federal Executive Council, cited by Crowe, *A History*, 227.

[43] Interview with Milena Hübschmannová, Professor of Romistics at Charles University (Prague, 27 August 1999).

Throughout the four decades of their rule, Czechoslovak and Bulgarian communists perceived the Gypsies as a major problem that hindered their social engineering efforts. They considered Romani assimilation the only answer to this dilemma.

It is important to note that Czechoslovak authorities treated the other large ethnic minority, Hungarians, relatively well (particularly after the late 1940s) whereas policies toward Bulgaria's large Turkish minority were just as discriminatory as they were toward the Roma. There were many complex reasons for this situation, but two go far in yielding a satisfactory explanation. First, ethnic Hungarians were far better integrated into Czechoslovak society than the Roma in both states or the Turks in Bulgaria. Second, fraternal relations with neighboring Hungary were important to politicians in Prague whereas Bulgaria did not concern itself much with antagonizing Turkey until 1989.

Romania and Poland seem like unlikely prospects to fall under the erratic intrusion pattern. After all, Romania was one of the most repressive dictatorships in the region whereas Poland was one of the most liberal states. A further major difference is that Poland had the smallest Romani population whereas Romania had the largest. Nonetheless, both states' policies toward the Gypsies were inconsistent, albeit for different reasons. In the Polish case the Roma constituted roughly 0.1% of the population; and even if they did not conform to Warsaw's expectations, they did not constitute a major threat to building socialism. In any case, the early efforts of assimilation brought mediocre results and the state ended up not pressing the issue although this was unlikely to have been the outcome of a conscious decision. In many ways the state essentially viewed the Roma in an ethnographic context. For the increasingly nationalist Romanian regime, on the other hand, the Roma comprised a relatively small problem compared to the more cohesive and larger Hungarian minority. Though Bulgaria, Czechoslovakia, and Romania were conservative communist states until 1989, the Gypsy question in Romania simply did not receive the same attention as in the other two countries.

Starting with the early 1960s, Hungary had become the most liberal communist state in the Soviet Bloc. Minority policies were partially motivated by Budapest's concern with the fate of ethnic Hungarians in neighboring countries and its efforts to create state-minority relations that it hoped these states would emulate. The most important implication of this comparatively tolerant approach to the Gypsies was the party-state's willingness to reevaluate its own policies and its efforts to understand the magnitude and attributes of the Romani predicament. Although the party's growing preference for integration versus forced assimilation, promotion of objective research on the Gypsies, and other initiatives did not alter the basic character of its policies, the evolution-ary change in Hungary's approach had been indisputably advantageous to the Roma. After the late 1940s, socialist Yugoslavia's policies were not affected by Soviet expectations. In this multinational state, nation-ality policies received far more concern than elsewhere in Eastern Europe, and the coercive assimilation of ethnic minorities was not a state policy. More than anywhere else in the region, Yugoslavia's Gypsy poli-cies were marked by tolerance and the intention to foster Romani integration.

PART II: SOCIOECONOMIC MARGINALITY

The main purpose of this section is to illustrate the magnitude of changes in the social and economic conditions of the East European Gypsies between the mid-1940s and late 1980s. I will concentrate on four areas in which substantial shifts had taken place mainly as a result of state policy: demography, education, employment, and interethnic relations.

Demography, Health, and Settlement Patterns

It is nearly impossible to precisely establish the size of the East European countries' Gypsy communities in the communist era for reasons addressed earlier (inadequate census figures, lack of data, intentional underestimation or omission). The Roma comprised the largest (Hungary) or the second largest (Bulgaria, Czechoslovakia, Romania) ethnic minority in several states. The most remarkable pattern valid for the entire region was the rapid growth of the Gypsy population during this period. Table 4.1 illustrates this trend. These numbers are based on census data and official state figures (e.g., from ministries of interior). The last column presents what I consider to be reasonable estimates for the late 1980s. In the case of Bulgaria I made an exception and included two separate lines, one for census and other official data and the other for the estimates of eminent ethnographers Elena Marushiakova and Ves-selin Popov. Alas, no such scholarly estimates are available for the other countries.

Although the gross underestimation of the real size of Gypsy com-munities is apparent in nearly every case, some of the most glaring incon-sistencies require some clarification. In the 1960s, Bulgarian communist leader Todor Zhivkov and his Romanian colleague, Nicolae Ceauşescu, followed Nikita Khrushchev's lead and declared the nationality problem "solved" in their respective countries. The reason for the precipitous diminution of the Bulgarian official figures is that the "Gypsy" category

Table 4.1. Eastern European Romani Communities in the Communist Era

Country	1940s	1950s	1960s	1970s	1980s	RealE
Albania[a]			10,000 (1961)	50,000 (1970)		90,000
Bulgaria[b] (off.)		197,865 (1956)	148,874 (1965)	18,323 (1975)		
Bulgaria[c] (est.)	170,000 (1947)	214,167 (1959)		373,200 (1976)	576,927 (1989)	575,000
Czechoslovakia[d]	101,190 (1947)		221,525 (1966)	219,554 (1970)	288,440 (1980)	600,000
Czech Lands	16,572 (1947)		56,519 (1966)	60,279 (1970)	88,587 (1980)	200,000
Slovakia	84,400 (1947)		165,006 (1966)	159,275 (1970)	199,853 (1980)	400,000
Hungary[e]	110,000 (1941)		220,000 (1962)	320,000 (1971)	380,000 (1984)	500,000
Poland[f]			17,000 (1965)	52,000 (1970)	35,000 (1994)	30,000
Romania[g]		104,000 (1956)	76,000 (1966)	229,986 (1977)	760,000 (1987)	1,000,000
Yugoslavia[h]				78,486 (1971)	168,197 (1981)	850,000
Croatia[i]	405 (1948)	1,261 (1953)	313 (1961)	1,257 (1971)	3,858 (1981)	30,000
Macedonia[j]	19,500 (1948)	20,462 (1953)	20,606 (1961)	24,505 (1971)	43,125 (1981)	60,000
Slovenia[k]			282 (1961)	1,284 (1971)	1,435 (1981)	7,500

[a] 1961, census figure cited in Vladimir Ortakovski, "The Posititon of the Minorities in the Balkans," *Balkan Forum*, 5:1 (March 1997): 112. 1970: Grattan Puxon, *Rom: Europe's Gypsies* (London: Report #14 of Minority Rights Group, 1973), 23.

[b] Census data cited by Anna Krasteva, "Ethnocultural Panorama of Bulgaria," *Balkan Forum*, 5:3 (September 1995): 249.

[c] All data, unless otherwise noted, come from Elena Marushiakova and Vesselin Popov, *Gypsies (Roma) in Bulgaria*, 40–4. It should be noted, though, that according to the 1975 census there were only 18,323 Roma in Bulgaria. Interview with Tomova (Sofia, 8 March 1995).

[d] The data for 1947 is cited by Anna Jurová, "Cigányok-romák Szlovákiában 1945 után," *Regio*, 7:2 (1996): 35–6; those for 1966, 1970, and 1980 are Czechoslovak census figures in József Gyönyör, *Államalkotó nemzetiségek* (Bratislava: Madách, 1989), 138.

[e] The data from 1941, 1962, 1971, and 1984 come from Zoltan Barany, "Hungary's Gypsies," *Report on Eastern Europe*, 1:29 (20 July 199): 27.

[f] 1965: David Halberstam, "Gypsies in Poland Confound Regime," *New York Times*, 31 October 1965. 1970: Puxon, *Rom: Europe's Gypsies*, 23. 1994: Andrzej Mirga cited in Helga Hirsch, "Ein polnischer Zigeuner," *Die Zeit*, 9 September 1994.

simply disappeared from censuses after 1956 even though Bulgaria was home to the world's proportionately largest Romani population (6.45% in 1989). In Romania – the country with the most Gypsies in the world – as well as in most of the other states of the region the deficiencies of census-taking were compounded by the fact that many Roma registered themselves as members of other ethnic groups owing to coercion or fear of discrimination.

Special circumstances explain some of the figures in Table 4.1. In the Czech Lands, for instance, there were hardly more than 600–700 surviving Gypsies at the end of World War II yet the census enumerated over 16,000 two years later, a figure that was most probably too low. Such phenomenal growth is explained by the policy of resettling Roma from Slovakia to the Czech Lands, where there was a strong demand for cheap labor. What explains the large increase in the number of Macedonian Roma between the 1970s and the 1980s? The distinguished demographer, Dusan Bubevski, points out that thousands of Muslim Roma moved to Macedonia from other parts of Yugoslavia in the 1970s well aware that the Ankara government allowed ethnic Turks from Macedonia to move to Turkey. These Muslim and Turkish-speaking Roma took a chance, but eventually most were not allowed to enter Turkey.[44] The reason for the exaggerated number of Polish Roma in 1970 is simply flawed data collection.

Romani reproduction rate has been surpassed only by that of ethnic Albanians in Eastern Europe. For instance, in 1980 the average Romani woman in Slovakia gave birth 6.2 times compared to the Czechoslovak

Notes to Table 4.1 *(continued)*

[g] 1956: Cited in Harry Schleicher, "Eine ungeliebte Volksgruppe," *Frankfurter Rundschau*, 27 September 1993. 1966: 1966 census figure quoted in "Gypsies in Eastern Europe and the Soviet Union," 5. 1977: census figure quoted in Smaranda Enache, "Die Minderheit der Roma in Rumänien," *Glaube in der 2. Welt*, 20:4 (1992): 20. 1987: Cited in *Destroying Ethnic Identity: The Persecution of the Gypsies in Romania*, 5.

[h] Figures for 1971 and 1981 come from Stankovic, "Gypsies to Get Their Own Television Program," 19.

[i] The source of all Croatian data is Imre Szilágyi, "A horvátországi romák helyzete," *Regio*, 7:3 (1996): 69.

[j] All data pertaining to Macedonia come from Dusan Bubevski, "Nekoi aspekti na natsionalniot sostav na naselenieto vo SR Makedonija vo periodot 1948–1981 godina," *Problemi na demografskiot razvoj vo SR Makedonija* (Skopje: Macedonian Academy of Sciences, 1985), 536.

[k] The source of Slovenian data is Imre Szilágyi, "A romák Szlovéniában," *Regio*, 7:2 (1996): 83.

[44] Interview with Dusan Bubevski, a demographer at the Institute for Sociological, Political, and Juridical Research (Skopje, 14 March 1994).

average of 2.27.[45] In Hungary the Gypsy birthrate has been over twice as high as that of Hungarians, and the Romani population has doubled every 20 to 30 years. This high birthrate is primarily explained by the Gypsies' low socioeconomic status, which was manifested in, among other things, their ignorance about or reluctance to use birth control methods and the fact that for many a Romani family the only source of regular income was the state-provided per-child subsidy (which, in effect, gave them an economic incentive to have more children).

The high reproduction rate of the Roma exacerbated other problems. Many Gypsy children were born to underage mothers and/or were the product of incestuous sexual relationships.[46] Considering their poor health standards and the minimal prenatal care available to or used by Gypsy women, the unusually high infant mortality rate (generally more than double of the rest of the population) and the high incidence of physical or mental impairment among Gypsy infants were hardly surprising.[47] Although the health indicators of East Europeans were (and are) inferior to those of most industrialized nations, health problems among the Gypsies were more acute than among their fellow citizens. Ignorance, superstition, and, most of all, poverty played an important role in this. Many accounts describe the Roma's refusal to allow doctors making house calls into their homes, tubercular Gypsies fleeing from sanatoria and infecting family members, and the high incidence of alcoholism and malnourishment among them.[48]

As a result of past and present assimilation attempts, long-term coexistence, and more frequent interaction with non-Roma, an ever-shrinking number of East European Gypsies could speak or understand any dialect of the Romani language. In the communist period, Romani was the mother tongue of about 20% of the Gypsies in Hungary, 55–60% in Czechoslovakia, 65–70% in Romania, and about 80% in Macedonia.[49]

[45] Vladimír Srb, "Zmeny v reprodukci československých Romu, 1970–1980," *Demografie*, 30:7 (1988): 305–8. See also idem., "Některé demografické, ekonomické a kulturní charakteristiky cikánského obyvatelstva v ČSSR 1980," *Demografie*, 26:2 (1984): 161–72.

[46] Ulč, "Gypsies in Czechoslovakia," 307. See also Werner Cohn, *The Gypsies* (Reading, MA: Addison-Wesley, 1973), 53–60.

[47] See, for instance, Cohn, *The Gypsies*, 53–60; and *Smena* (Bratislava), 27 May 1987. According to a popular magazine article, in 1986 20% of all Roma born in Czechoslovakia were mentally retarded. See "Prague Against Gypsies," *Time*, 15 September 1986, 40.

[48] See, for instance, László Levendel, "A cigányság gondja – mindannyiunk gondja," *Valóság*, 31:12 (December 1988): 30–2.

[49] See "Gypsies in Eastern Europe and the Soviet Union," *Radio Free Europe Research*, RAD Background Report/72, (12 April 1978), 1–7.

Table 4.2. Percentage of Roma Residing in Urban Areas in Selected Countries

Bulgaria[a]	<20 (1945)	37 (1960)	50.9 (1972)	
Czechoslovakia[b]			52.5 (1980)	
Czech Lands			80.8 (1980)	
Hungary[c]		21.8 (1971)		39.5 (1994)
Romania[d]		28 (1966)	30.5 (1977)	

[a] Marushiakova and Popov, *Gypsies (Roma) in Bulgaria*, 98–9; and *Népszabadság*, 18 August 1997.
[b] Ulč, "The Gypsies in Czechoslovakia," 318–19.
[c] Havas et al., "The Statistics of Deprivation," 68.
[d] 1966: "Gypsies in Eastern Europe and the Soviet Union," 5. 1977: *Destroying Ethnic Identity: The Gypsies in Romania*, 5.

The majority of East European Roma were long sedentary by the beginning of the communist rule, particularly in Bulgaria, Hungary, Slovakia, and Yugoslavia. Nevertheless, tens of thousands (especially among certain groups like the Kalderash and Lovara) maintained their nomadic lifestyles across the region, but primarily in Romania and Poland. In spite of sedentarization policies, and in 1949 75% and in 1964 approximately 60% of the Roma in Poland, in 1973 5% in Yugoslavia, and in 1977 30% in Romania still held on to a nomadic or seminomadic way of life.[50] As a result of state policies supporting permanent settlement, industrialization, and urbanization, the proportion of nomadic Gypsies had diminished while that of those residing in urban areas had increased sharply throughout the communist period as indicated by Table 4.2.[51] Given the housing shortage in industrial areas, many Roma and others (especially men) had become weekly commuters from village to city, a lifestyle that negatively affected their families.

The socialist policy to purchase and then demolish shanties in rural Gypsy settlements and provide their residents with housing in cities was

[50] See Jerzy Ficowski, "Polish Gypsies Today," *Journal of the Gypsy Lore Society*, (4) 29:3 (1950): 92–102; idem., *The Gypsies in Poland: History and Customs* (Warsaw: Interpress, 1985), 49; Mirga, "The Effects of State Assimilation Policy," 73; *Destroying Ethnic Identity: The Persecution of the Gypsies in Romania*, 7.
[51] On this issue, see György Konrád and Iván Szelényi, "Social Conflicts of Urbanization," in Michael Harloe, ed., *Captive Cities* (London: John Wiley & Sons, 1977), 157–86.

a further reason for the Roma's increasing urban location. Nonetheless, the numbers are not quite as impressive as they seem because many rapidly growing villages and towns received the upgraded administrative status of towns and cities in the state-socialist period, thus their residents had statistically become urban dwellers without moving. The bulldozed Gypsy huts were usually built of whatever materials could be found or pilfered (corrugated metal sheets, cardboard, odd pieces of wood and glass), lacked running water and electricity, and did not include sewage treatment or garbage removal services. Many were partially dug in the ground, were infested with rodents and insects, and constituted a significant health hazard to the Roma and their environment. At the same time, living in close quarters with other Gypsies nurtured Romani traditions and communal life. Consequently, the elimination of Gypsy slums was all the more pressing for the state because it viewed the existence of socially autonomous Romani communities as a threat to social stability.

State authorities had destroyed tens of thousands of shanties across the region, although thousands still remained at the end of the communist period. In 1972–81 alone, 4,850 Gypsy families were removed from ghettos and given housing in Slovakia, though in 1983 there were still 400 Romani settlements (with 3,018 shanties for 21,622 people).[52] In Hungary two-thirds of the Roma were slum dwellers in 1971, but this ratio fell to 13.7% by the end of the communist era despite major increases in the Gypsy population.[53] Beginning with the late 1940s the traditional segregation of Roma from non-Roma had quickly decreased owing to the policy of dispersing compact Gypsy communities and resettling them next to members of the dominant population. Neither side was pleased with this arrangement. Many already prejudiced *gadje* (non-Roma) found living in close proximity to the Roma, who were unaccustomed to the confining aura of apartment living, unpleasant. The fact that thousands of Gypsy families acquired apartments on favorable terms quickly (18,600 families in 1965–81 in Hungary alone[54]) while non-Roma ordinarily had to wait for years generated much interethnic acrimony. At the same time, the Roma resented the breakup of their close-knit communities and the concomitant loss of their tradition and culture.

In general, the Gypsies received apartments in the cramped and shoddily constructed urban housing projects. Many local officials assigned

---

[52] See, for instance, Ágnes Diósi, "Legyen világosság!" *Kritika*, no. 1 (1993), 3–5; and Fisher, "Romanies in Slovakia," 55.

[53] Gábor Havas, Gábor Kertesi, and István Kemény, "The Statistics of Deprivation: The Roma in Hungary," *The Hungarian Quarterly*, 36:138 (Summer 1995): 71–5.

[54] (Mrs.) Istvánné Kozák, "A cigány lakosság beilleszkedése társadalmunkba," *Társadalmi Szemle*, 37:8–9 (August–September 1982): 64.

them to flats with fewer comforts [designated as "CS" (*csökkentett értékü* – reduced value) in Hungary, or Category IV in Czechoslovakia] than those allocated to *gadje*, knowing that the Roma would not dare to complain and expecting them to destroy the available amenities in any case.[55] It is a well-known fact that Gypsies had wrecked many apartments across the region (particularly in Hungary and Czechoslovakia, where they obtained more new housing than elsewhere in Eastern Europe) although undoubtedly far fewer than the resultant social indignation indicated.[56] City planners and local authorities did not take Romani taboos and traditions into consideration (e.g., a woman should not live above a man, the need for unisex toilets, bathrooms cannot be next to the kitchen) when resettling Gypsies, although given meager state resources it would have been virtually impossible to accommodate them.[57]

In many cases the Roma responded to the resettlement policy by selling their apartments and rebuilding their shanties in the original sites. In some instances Romani families who were moved into the houses of ethnic Germans expelled from Czechoslovakia and Romania after World War II hawked removable objects and moved back to the ghetto.[58] After the July 1963 earthquake that leveled much of Skopje, the Macedonian capital, including the Gypsy slum of Topana, authorities provided homeless Roma with good-quality housing in other sections of the city. Many of the recipients promptly sold their apartments and returned to Topana.[59] As a result of the mixed success of the resettlement policy, the rate of diminution in residential segregation had decelerated. By the late 1960s segregation was again on the increase, although new forms of separation had come about. The Roma began to converge in certain, usually

---

[55] See, for instance, Márta Gyenei, "A létminimum alatt – Jajhalom (II)," *Statisztikai Szemle*, 71:2 (February 1993): 130–9; and Davidová, *Romano Drom*.

[56] See, for instance, Josef Kalvoda, "The Gypsies of Czechoslovakia," in David Crowe and John Kolsti, eds., *The Gypsies of Eastern Europe* (Armonk, NY: M. E. Sharpe, 1991), 98–9; and Arne B. Mann, "Rroma (Gypsies) in Municipalities," Council of Europe Hearing report (Košice, 9 December 1995): 6.

[57] Other states have encountered similar difficulties in the construction of housing that allowed the implementation of the formerly peripatetic population's socio-cultural needs. The most germane example is Israel's repeated attempts to settle the Bedouin in the Negev. See Yehuda Gradus and Eliahu Stern, "From Pre-Conceived to Responsive Planning: Cases of Settlement Design in Arid Environments," in Yehuda Gradus, ed., *Desert Development: Man and Technology in Sparselands* (Dordrecht: D. Reidel, 1995), 41–59.

[58] William O. McCagg, "Cigánypolitika Magyarországon és Csehszlovákiában, 1945–1989," *Világosság*, 32:7/8 (July–August 1991): 550.

[59] Interview with Ilja Atseski, Professor of Urban Sociology at the Sts. Cyril and Method University (Skopje, 14 March 1994).

run-down, areas of cities and towns attracted by the concentration of their brethren and the relative absence of *gadje*.[60] In time all-Gypsy villages had developed because many non-Roma responded to the in-settlement of Roma by fleeing from their villages.[61]

Education

One of the few advantages bestowed on East European societies by their communist rulers was the increased access to education for previously marginalized social groups. In every state, education became mandatory for all citizens under the age of 16. The result was the virtual elimination of illiteracy, the completion of eight years of basic schooling by most, and enormous increases in the numbers of secondary and post-secondary school graduates. In many respects the source of Romani marginality has been their lack of adequate formal education. One of the most important goals of the communist states' assimilation policy was to bridge or at least diminish the profound differences between the educational attainments of Roma and other ethnic groups. Laws held parents who did not send their children to school responsible, at least in theory. At the end of the state-socialist era the Gypsies were still firmly ensconced at the very bottom of all educational statistics, but the educational campaign did produce substantial results by reducing Romani illiteracy and increasing the educational attainments of most Gypsies. The statistical indicators from this period suggest a population whose scholastic preparation was wholly inadequate for the socioeconomic challenges of the late twentieth century. Therefore, it is important to remember that the majority of East European Roma prior to World War II had no formal education whatsoever. Viewed from this angle, their educational achievements are bound to seem more respectable.

Table 4.3 includes the most reliable numbers I was able to collect. Though there are some inconsistencies and many missing figures, the table does convey the two most important points about Romani education levels: that they had risen dramatically in the communist era and that they still remained very low.

Romani education was affected by several major problems. Most Gypsies did not put a high value on formal instruction; indeed, many

---

[60] See, for instance, János Ladányi, "A lakásrendszer változásai és a cigány népesség térbeni elhelyezkedésének átalakulása Budapesten," *Valóság*, 32:8 (August 1989): 73–90; and idem., "Patterns of Residential Segregation and the Gypsy Minority in Budapest," *International Journal of Urban and Regional Research*, 17:1 (March 1993): 30–41.

[61] See, for instance, Marushiakova and Popov, *Gypsies (Roma) in Bulgaria*, 125.

even considered learning to read and write "a waste of time."[62] As a result of the low priority given to education, many Gypsy families elected to spend the resources necessary for schooling even in a free education system on other things. The long years of schooling necessary for securing high-paying employment (even that of a skilled worker) could be put to better use. In any event, Gypsy children were often ostracized by their peers and discriminated against by teachers. Not surprisingly, in every East European state, Romani school attendance rates were far below and failing rates much above those of other pupils. The humiliating experience of being years older than other students in the classroom drove many Gypsies out of school. Children whose native language was Romani often did not properly speak or understand the language of instruction and thus were at an inherent disadvantage. The shortage of highly educated Roma also meant that there were few teachers (and role models) available to educate Gypsy children in their native tongue. The relatively high occurrence of mental impairment among Romani children served as a convenient excuse for prejudiced school administrators to put difficult but normal children into special schools for the mentally handicapped. Finally, aside from a few exceptions, there were no Romani language textbooks and the assigned readers totally ignored the Roma, their culture, and their history, offering little that Gypsy pupils could identify with.

Many Roma who completed primary school were apparently pushed through by teachers and administrators whose premiums and bonuses depended on graduation rates. The fact that a considerable number of Romani elementary school graduates were functional illiterates was often only realized when they began compulsory military service or started to work. Though the proportion of Roma completing the basic eight-year primary school had increased, the number of Gypsies advancing to secondary school remained small. In fact, in several states the proportion of Roma participating in secondary and postsecondary education began to stagnate from the 1970s on, and it had actually decreased in Hungary by the early 1980s.[63] Only a handful of Roma attended colleges and universities – most benefitting from affirmative action programs. In 1970, for example, 39 Roma were enrolled at Czechoslovak postsecondary institutions, a figure that increased to 191 (97 of them women)

---

[62] Stanisław Stankiewicz, a former Vice President of the International Romani Union cited in Linnet Myers, "Circling the Wagons: With Gypsies' New Freedom Comes More Persecution," *Chicago Tribune*, 28 December 1992. See also Katalin Balogh, "'Minek az iskola?'," *Kultúra és közösség*, no. 4 (August 1989): 58–77; and interview with Andrzej Mirga, President of the Roma Association of Poland (Kraków, 14 June 1994).

[63] See Kertesi Gábor, "Cigány gyerekek az iskolában, cigány felnőttek a munkaerőpiacon," *Közgazdasági Szemle*, 42:1 (January 1995): 30–65.

Table 4.3. Romani Educational Statistics (%)

Country	Illiteracy	Attendance	Eight Years Completed	In Special School	Attends Kindergarten	Postsecondary School
Bulgaria	81.0 (1946)[a]	95.0 (1991)[b]	12.5 (1962)[c] 30.0 (1978)[d]			12.5 (1975)[e]
Czechoslovakia	15.0 (1970)[f] 10.0 (1980)[g]	75.1 (1980–5)[b]	13.0 (1967)[i] 16.6 (1971) 28.7 (1981)[j]	17.1 (1980) 27.6 (1985)[k]		
Czech Lands				17.0 (1970)[l] 22.8 (1980)[m]		
Slovakia			66.0 (1984)[n]	53.0 (1984)[o]	10.0 (1972) 66.0 (1982)[p]	4.0 (1984)[q]
Hungary	40.0 (1961)[r]	~55.0 (1960s)[s] ~95.0 (1987)[t]	2.5 (1961)[u] 26.5 (1971)[v] 77.5 (1985)[w]	28.5 (1980)[x]	22.5 (1972) 75.0 (1989)[y]	
Poland		25.0 (1950–60) 82.0 (1970) 82.6 (1983)[z]				
Romania	37.7 (1956)[aa]		20 (1983)[bb]			
Yugoslavia Serbia	22.5 (1986)[cc]					

[a] Ilona Tomova, *The Gypsies in the Transition Period* (Sofia: International Centre for Minority Studies and Intercultural Relations, 1995), 57.
[b] *Destroying Ethnic Identity: The Gypsies of Bulgaria*, 34.
[c] Interview with Tomova (Sofia, 8 March 1995).
[d] Document 1978/850 of the Central Committee Secretariat of the Bulgarian Communist Party (27 Sept 1978).
[e] Of those who finished primary school. See *Destroying Ethnic Identity: The Gypsies of Bulgaria*, 32.

f "Gypsies in Eastern Europe and the Soviet Union," 3.

g Sharon Wolchik, *Czechoslovakia in Transition: Politics, Economics, & Society* (London: Pinter, 1991), 183.

h Kalvoda, "The Gypsies of Czechoslovakia," 107.

i Puxon, *Rom: Europe's Gypsies*, 18.

j Kostelancik, "The Gypsies of Czechoslovakia," 315.

k Kalvoda, "The Gypsies of Czechoslovakia," 107.

l McCagg, "Cigánypolitika Magyarországon," 555.

m Ibid., 555.

n Ulč, "Gypsies in Czechoslovakia," 320.

o McCagg, "Cigánypolitika Magyarországon," 555.

p Ibid., 320.

q Ulč, Otto. "Gypsies in Czechoslovakia," 320.

r Ibid., 552.

s Interview with János Báthory, an official at the Office for National and Ethnic Minorities (Budapest, 9 June 1994).

t Ibid.

u McCagg, "Cigánypolitika Magyarországon," 552.

v Havas et al., "The Statistics of Deprivation," 69.

w Of these 27.5% completed elementary school during their military service or in evening classes. See *A magyarországi cigányság helyzetének történeti áttekintése napjainkig* (Budapest: Nemzeti és Etnikai Kisebbségi Hivatal, Cigányügyi Főosztály, 1994), 5.

x Crowe, "The Gypsies in Hungary," 124–5.

y *A magyarországi cigányság helyzetének történeti áttekintése napjainkig*, 5.

z Mirga, "The Effects of State Assimilation," 73.

aa Of age 8 and over. Trond Gilberg, "Ethnic Minorities in Romania under Socialism," *East European Quarterly* 7:4 (January 1974): 448.

bb Fraser, *The Gypsies*, 281.

cc Stankovic, "Gypsies to Get Their Own Television Program," 2.

by 1981.[64] Still, only 0.3% of Romani females and 0.2% of males went to university in 1983–4.[65] In 1973 there were fewer than a dozen Romani college students in Serbia, although somewhat more in Macedonia, while in Bulgaria about 700 Roma had completed college during the entire the communist era.[66] In the same period, Poland's higher educational system produced only four Gypsy university graduates.[67] Small as these numbers are, it is important to recognize that prior to the state-socialist era there were only a few college-educated Gypsies in the entire region. The newly degreed Roma were to form the nucleus of the emerging Romani intelligentsia, some of whom were to play key roles in ethnic mobilization.

The Roma's lackluster performance in the school system spurred a variety of educational projects across the region. Starting in 1969, Bulgaria's Ministry of Lower Education established several types of "Gypsy schools" for elementary education and technical training. Within the next two decades, the state created approximately 100 of these schools. Most of them were located in or near Romani settlements, and Gypsies comprised virtually their entire student bodies.[68] In Yugoslavia, Romani language classes were introduced in a number of primary schools (especially in Kosovo and Macedonia) in 1983.[69] To ease the transitional difficulty of Gypsy pupils into the school system, in Slovakia special preschool classes (also called "0-grade") were established.[70] Hungary's Ministry of Education experimented with different types of schools – some segregated, others not, some using Romani as the language of instruction, while others did not – in order to find a winning combination.[71] In several countries, universities set aside places for prospective Gypsy students, although most often they could not be filled owing to the dearth of qualified applicants.

[64] David J. Kostelancik, "The Gypsies of Czechoslovakia: Political and Ideological Considerations in the Development of Policy," *Studies in Comparative Communism*, 22:4 (Winter 1989): 315.

[65] Ulč, "Gypsies in Czechoslovakia," 320.

[66] Grattan Puxon, *Rom: Europe's Gypsies* (London: Report #14 Minority Rights Group, 1973), 18; and Marushiakova and Popov, *Gypsies (Roma) in Bulgaria*, 41.

[67] Helga Hirsch, "Ein polnischer Zigeuner," *Die Zeit*, 9 September 1994.

[68] Elena Marushiakova and Vesselin Popov, "'Gypsy Schools' in Bulgaria," *Objektiv: Newsletter of the Bulgarian Helsinki Committee*, July–September 1994, 8.

[69] Poulton, *Who Are the Macedonians?*, 140.

[70] Arne B. Mann, "Motivation: The Inevitable Condition of Successful Education of Romany Children," Training Course for Teachers, Council of Europe (Špišská Nová Veš, Slovakia, 14–17 September 1994), 1.

[71] See, for instance, Thomas Acton, "Using the Gypsies' Own Language: Two Contrasting Approaches in Hungarian Schools," in Diane Tong, ed., *Gypsies: An Interdisciplinary Reader* (New York: Garland, 1998), 135–40.

Employment and Living Standards

Along with sedentarization and compulsory education, mandatory employment was the third cornerstone of the East European states' assimilationist/integrationist approach to the Roma. The industrialization program demanded a rapidly expanding labor pool, and the state required all able-bodied citizens to work. Within a few years, the proportion of Roma engaged in agricultural work had plummeted along with that of the overall population. The fact that the Gypsies received no land in the postwar land distribution programs (except in Yugoslavia in the 1950s) drove them toward industrial employment even more decisively than members of other ethnic groups. Paradoxically, in some areas, particularly in the Czech Lands, Gypsies were frequently barred from joining agricultural cooperatives because they had no land to contribute.[72] In 1980 only 0.5% of employed Roma in Czechoslovakia were members of collective farms, in contrast with 7.5% of the overall population.[73]

With the formation of cooperatives and state farms and the mechanization of agriculture, many opportunities for seasonal work that in the past had sustained the Roma vanished. Industrialization and collectivization policies destroyed old Gypsy professions (basket weaving, gold washing, herbal–medicinal art, etc.) and, consequently, components of traditional Romani life.[74] A 1972 study by the Social Services Administration in Prague researched the vocational skills of Roma respondents as well as those of their grandfathers and fathers. It found that in the grandparents' generation 90% of men had a traditional Romani trade, a negligible proportion in the parents' generation, and among the respondents themselves almost no one.[75] Nevertheless, a few Gypsy trades did remain in demand. For instance, the Roma maintained their reputation as superb musicians not only as entertainers in restaurants but also, increasingly, as musicians in popular and philharmonic ensembles. In Poland many Roma could continue some of their traditional crafts on-the-go until nomadism was curtailed by state intervention in 1964.

---

[72] Judit Hamberger, "A csehországi romák helyzete," *Regio*, 7:2 (1997): 58.

[73] Vladimír Srb, "Některé demografické, ekonomické a kulturní charakteristiky cikánského obyvatelstva v ČSSR 1980," *Demografie*, 26:2 (1984): 168.

[74] See, for instance, Elena Zamfir and Cătălin Zamfir, *The Romany Population* (Bucharest: Centre of Economic Information ad Documentation, 1993), 11; and Rajko Djurić, Jörg Becken, and A. Bertolt Bengsch, *Ohne Heim-Ohne Grab: Die Geschichte der Roma und Sinti* (Berlin: Aufbau-Verlag, 1996), 178.

[75] Pável Bratinka, *Report on the Situation of the Romani Community in the Czech Republic* (Prague, 1997), Part I, 4. This is an internal report by the deputy foreign minister to the Government of the Czech Republic on the Roma.

Poland's comparatively large private sector and relatively tolerant state policies enabled the Roma to move more freely and earn their living in more "unconventional" ways than elsewhere in the region. In Bulgaria, too, a fair number of Roma were able to utilize their traditional expertise even after the forced sedentarization of the 1950s, the difference being that they were allowed to travel only short distances and only with their immediate families.[76]

Socialist states used various strategies to involve Roma in standard wage labor. In Poland, for instance, where virtually all coppersmiths and tinsmiths were Gypsies, the state first made the practice of these trades illegal in order to weed out nomadism, then it was legalized again, and finally all practitioners were forced into cooperatives directed and controlled by non-Roma. Gypsies could usually fill their weekly quotas in a few days and then, as a matter of course, took off for days straining the patience of their supervisors.[77] In Romania, Gypsy coppersmiths and tinsmiths needed police authorization to pursue their trades, but they were seldom harassed by the authorities. Many Hungarian Roma could engage in commercial activities such as dealing in horses.[78] Gypsies were also active in black market activities across the region. Begging, a traditional Romani occupation, nearly disappeared in the highly regulated societies of the 1950s and 1960s, although with the downturn of the region's economic prospects and the partial relaxation of police control it began to reemerge in the late-communist period.

The majority of Gypsy men found employment as unskilled factory workers especially in heavy industry and at construction projects where the pay was generally higher and work was not quite so monotonous as elsewhere. For instance, in the 1950s scouts from large industrial enterprises recruited many Roma – with promises of above-average pay – to help build the enormous Nowa Huta steel works in southern Poland.[79] In 1983, 83.4% of Romani men in Slovakia worked in the construction industry.[80] Czechoslovakia and Hungary were the most successful in proletarianizing the Roma. In the early 1980s, 83.9% of the Roma in Czechoslovakia were industrial workers as opposed to 33.4% of the entire working population. In Yugoslavia, where unemployment was already a recognized problem in the 1970s, a disproportionate number of Roma ended up in this category because they lacked specialized skills.

---

[76] Vesselin Popov, "Gypsy Nomads in Bulgaria: Traditions and Contemporary Dimension," unpublished manuscript, 1994, 5.

[77] Mirga, "The Effects of State Assimilation Policy," 70–1.

[78] See, for instance, Michael Stewart, "Játék a lovakkal avagy a cigány keresekedők és a szerencse," *Kultúra és közösség*, no. 4 (August 1989): 21–40.

[79] Interview with Mirga (Kraków, 29 July 1996).

[80] Kalvoda, "The Gypsies of Czechoslovakia," 107.

In sum, the employment indicators of East European Gypsies were similar to those of a poorly educated labor force anywhere. Communist propaganda organizations struggled to uphold the ideal of the reliable and industrious Gypsy worker to the Romani population. In reality, however, employers were seldom happy with their Romani employees. According to many observers, the Gypsies were far more likely to change jobs, and their frequency of absenteeism and drunkenness at work was considerably higher and their work discipline significantly lower than that of other ethnic groups.[81]

All in all, the mandatory employment policies of socialist states were relatively successful in integrating the Roma into the work force. A surprisingly large part of the Gypsy population became active participants in the mainstream economy. By the late 1980s the disparity between non-Roma and Roma employment rates had almost disappeared in several East European states. In Hungary, for instance, 87.7% of the entire population and over 90% of all men were active earners in contrast with 85.2% of Romani men (Table 4.4).[82] Their economic integration was concomitant with the loss of many Romani traditions, yet most Gypsies acknowledged wage labor as the source of the fundamental improvement in their living standards.[83]

By all objective measures the material conditions of the East European Roma had improved substantially under communist rule. The vast majority had acquired better housing, universal healthcare, steady incomes, and pension benefits. Their economic marginality in absolute terms had been alleviated, but they still remained the most disadvantaged ethnic group. A large proportion of Gypsies relied on various forms of social assistance (about three-fourths in Czechoslovakia in 1978, for instance[84]). In the more prosperous countries, like Czechoslovakia and Hungary, the generous state support for children had served as an unintended source of motivation for Roma to have more children and live off the child benefits. "The more children, the less expensive is life," was an oft-cited Gypsy saying in Czechoslovakia where many Romani

[81] For an excellent account see Michael Stewart, "Gypsies, Work and Civil Society," *Journal of Communist Studies*, 6:2 (June 1990): 140–62. Stewart talks of "devastatingly intense job-hopping" (147). See also, Ervin Tamás and Tamás Révész, *Búcsú a cigányteleptöl* (Budapest: Kossuth, 1977); János Bársony, *Fövárosi cigány dolgozók az építöiparban* (Budapest: Népművelési Intézet, 1981); Ulč, "Gypsies in Czechoslovakia," 321–2; Zsolt Csalog, *Fel a kezekkel!* (Budapest: Maecenas, 1989); and Michael Stewart, *The Time of the Gypsies* (Boulder, CO: Westview, 1998), 26, 98–101, 123.

[82] Havas et al., "Statistics of Deprivation," 73.

[83] Stewart, *The Time of the Gypsies*, 98.

[84] CTK (Czechoslovak News Service), 11 March 1978 cited in "Gypsies in Eastern Europe and the Soviet Union," 3.

Table 4.4. Romani Employment

Country	All Roma	Men	Women	Industrial	Agricultural	Other
Bulgaria (1983)[a]	85					
Czechoslovakia						
(1970)[b]		66.3	41.2			
(1980)[c]	75	87.7	54.9	83.9	10.2	5.9
Slovakia (1980)			76.6	19.2	4.2	
Hungary						
(1958)[d]		65	30			
(1985)[e]		85.2				
Poland (1968)	34[f]					
Yugoslavia						
(1985)				50[g]	20	30

[a] Interview with Tomova (Sofia, 8 March 1995).
[b] Kalvoda, "The Gypsies of Czechoslovakia," 106.
[c] Ulč, "Gypsies in Czechoslovakia," 321 and Vladimír Srb, "Koncentráce a urbanizáce Cykánu v Československu," *Česky Lid*, 73:2 (1986): 82–92.
[d] McCagg, "Cigánypolitika Magyarországon," 552.
[e] Havas et al., "The Statistics of Deprivation," 73.
[f] Andrzej Mirga, "Roma Territorial Behaviour and State Policy: The Case of the Socialist Countries of East Europe," in Michael J. Casimir and Aparna Rao, eds., *Mobility and Territoriality: Social and Spatial Boundaries among Foragers, Fishers, Pastoralists, and Peripatetics* (Oxford: Berg, 1992), 263.
[g] Poulton, "The Roma in Macedonia: A Balkan Success Story?" *RFE/RL Research Report*, 2:19 (7 May 1993): 43.

families had seven to twelve children.[85] Karel Holomek, a thoughtful Czech Gypsy leader, blames these payments for the fact that many Roma became dependent on state handouts and lost their desire and initiative to help themselves.[86]

Social Relations and Migration

During the communist period the social position of the Gypsy population at large had also improved. Granted, this is not saying much after the widespread persecution of the interwar era, let alone the horror of

[85] Stafanie Pišariková in *Rolnické noviny*, 20 November 1969, cited by Ulč, "Gypsies in Czechoslovakia," 316; and Márta Gyenei, "A létminimum alatt – Jajhalom (I.)," *Statisztikai Szemle*, 71:1 (January 1993): 25.
[86] Interview with Karel Holomek (Brno, 1 September 1999); and Karel Holomek, "Roma in the Former Czechoslovakia," *Helsinki Citizens' Assembly – Roma Section Newsletter*, no. 4 (June 1998): 3.

the *Porajmos*. Societal prejudices survived but physical attacks on the Gypsies were prohibited and some, albeit often inconsistent, state policies even attempted to induce interethnic harmony. The Roma persisted as a unique ethnic group, far more averse to assimilation than other nationalities and ethnic minorities. In order to reduce the socioeconomic gap between the Roma and others, nearly all East European states had introduced some form of positive discrimination policies – such as accelerated housing and preferential training programs – which invoked some, though mostly muted (since few could openly protest with impunity), social resentment.

The disproportionately high incidence of criminal behavior among the Roma exacerbated acrimonious interethnic relations. The Gypsies made up only about 4% of Slovakia's population in 1980, yet they committed 20% of all crimes there.[87] In some Romanian counties as many as 40% of the Roma had criminal records.[88] Widely publicized felonies of some prominent Gypsies deepened anti-Roma biases. In 1987, for instance, Kyril Rashkov, son of the famous Gypsy king Gogo and the chief of a band of Bulgarian Romani robbers, received a 15-year prison sentence for having stolen gold jewelry worth DM 4.1 million.[89] The theft of state property became almost acceptable in the socialist period given that many people of all ethnic backgrounds lifted what was supposedly theirs (emboldened by the communist slogan: "The factory is yours, you build it for yourself"). More troubling was the growing frequency of violent crime among the Roma.

Conventional wisdom held that subsistence theft constituted the largest part of Gypsy crimes. Reliable statistics had shown, however, that the structure of Romani crime tended to deviate from that of other ethnic groups to the extent that the proportion of violent crimes – and of crimes committed by groups, youths, and women among the Gypsies – was considerably higher. In Hungary, for instance, more than 50% of crimes committed by the Roma were violent in 1981.[90] Although Gypsy crime was widely and often unfairly publicized (the police kept separate statistics on Romani crime, and in media reports only the Gypsies' ethnic identity was noted), the socioeconomic circumstances that propelled many Roma toward criminal behavior received much less attention.

---

[87] Kalvoda, "The Gypsies of Czechoslovakia," 106.
[88] *Destroying Ethnic Identity: The Persecution of Gypsies in Romania*, 110.
[89] See *Rabotnichesko Delo* (Sofia), 9 November 1987.
[90] "Előítéletesek," *Köztársaság*, 10 July 1992, 40–1. See also Csalog, *Fel a kezekkel!*; and György Moldova, *Szabadíts meg a gonosztól! Riport a börtönökről* (Budapest: Pannon, 1990).

Gypsy crime, high birthrates, low hygienic standards, lackluster work performance, and positive discrimination programs all contributed to the negative societal attitudes toward the Roma. In a 1978 poll, 28% of Hungarians viewed Gypsy behavior as immoral or illegal and 21% felt that they abused the social welfare system.[91] A decade later, 70% considered the Roma parasites, 79.2% lazy, and 72.3% uneducated.[92] Anti-Roma feelings were especially strong in Romania, where many falsely believed that they received favorable treatment because Nicolae Ceauşescu himself was of Romani heritage.[93] In many places, restaurant managers terrified of the Gypsies' rowdiness refused to admit them, although non-Roma were often not allowed in or would not dare to enter Gypsy taverns either.[94] Parents customarily warned their children to bypass areas where the Roma congregated and tried to avoid sending them to schools where Gypsy children attended. Interethnic tolerance in Macedonia had a relatively long tradition, and anti-Roma prejudices there were not as deep as elsewhere in the region.

In spite of the regimes' efforts, few Gypsies became assimilated in the communist period. Within the thin stratum of educated Roma, many had lost their identity, adopted *gadje* traditions and culture, and married non-Gypsies. A far larger group, however, did not succeed in gaining genuine acceptance from non-Roma society. They became the "strangers" Georg Simmel talked about, not fitting into either social group.

The resettlement of tens of thousands of Roma across the region heavily contributed to the intensity of anti-Gypsy attitudes. In areas where the Roma had been settled for a long time, interethnic tensions were relatively mild because people had time to get used to each other and establish mutually acceptable behavioral norms. Newly arrived Gypsies, however, often encountered overt popular resentment. It is scarcely a coincidence that a disproportionately large number of attacks and other types of violence against the Roma in the 1990s occurred in places like Ostrava and Ústí nad Labem in the Czech Republic, and Hadareni in Romania, where Gypsies had been present only since the communist period.[95] In Slovakia, for instance, where the Roma had lived

---

[91] Cited in Crowe, "The Gypsies in Hungary," 125.

[92] Koos Postma, "Csökken a cigányokkal szembeni előítélet," *Magyar Hírlap*, 23 February 1993.

[93] See Remmel, *Die Roma Rumäniens*, 76–8; Dan Pavel, "Wanderers," *The New Republic*, 4 March 1991, 13; Dan Ionescu, "The Gypsies Organize," *Report on Eastern Europe*, 1:26 (29 June 1990): 41; and János Kenedi, "Why Is the Gypsy the Scapegoat and Not the Jew?" *East European Reporter*, 2:1 (1986): 11–14.

[94] Ulč, "Gypsies in Czechoslovakia," 327.

[95] See Adrian Bridge, "Romanians Vent Old Hatreds Against Gypsies," *The Independent*, 19 October 1993.

for centuries, there have been many fewer disturbances, notwithstanding their significantly higher absolute and relative number there than in the Czech Lands.

A substantial group of East European Roma migrated across international boundaries during the communist period. After Yugoslavia opened its borders in 1963 and allowed its citizens to take up employment in Western Europe, thousands of Gypsies took advantage of this opportunity. By 1984, 13,292 Yugoslav Roma worked abroad, especially in Germany.[96] Even more unusual was the unofficial Romanian policy that encouraged Gypsies to leave the country by instructing border guards to look the other way when Romani families were illegally crossing the frontier.[97] The Roma needed little motivation. Many Romanian Gypsies left illegally for the West during the communist period, by purchasing documents and visas and paying guides (typically ethnic Germans). "For the Gypsies," Dumitru Tranca, a Gypsy patriarch from Bucharest, said, "there was no iron curtain."[98]

PART III: PROGRESS IN ROMANI IDENTITY-BUILDING AND MOBILIZATION

Given communist regimes' obsession with control, it would seem reasonable to assume that no advances could be made in strengthening Romani identity, let alone in creating autonomous Gypsy organizations during the state-socialist period. Although the assumption would not be entirely erroneous, the empirical evidence shows that even within the strict institutional confines of socialist states – and partly as a direct or indirect result of their policies – the Roma managed to gain some advantages useful for their future organizational development. Indeed, to some extent the foundations of the unprecedented Romani mobilization process of the postcommunist era were built in the state socialist period.

From Traditional to Modern Leaders

The turmoil attendant to the introduction of centrally planned economies and state efforts to disperse hard-to-control compact Gypsy communities led to the loss of Romani traditions and culture in the state-socialist period. Many traditional Gypsy leaders fell victim to this process

---

[96] Slobodan Stankovic, "Gypsies to Get Their Own Television Program," Stankovic, Slobodan. "Gypsies to Get Their Own Television Program," *Radio Free Europe Research*, Yugoslav Situation Report No. 2 (11 February 1986): 20.

[97] Dan Ionescu, "Migration from Romania," *Report on Eastern Europe*, Special issue (1 December 1989): 19.

[98] Cited by John Tagliabue, "Romanian Gypsies Search for Safety and Stability in Changing Europe," *New York Times*, 27 November 1991.

and, given that they were generally uneducated in the formal sense, they were seldom able to effectively deal with the *gadje* and their complex bureaucracies. As a result, the influence wielded by traditional Romani leaders declined everywhere in Eastern Europe, though not to the same degree. In areas where nomadism and established lifestyles survived longer, conventional Gypsy leaders were better equipped to maintain their authority in their bailiwick. The state devised different ways to deal with them. In Hungary and Romania, for instance, local officials and the police encouraged them to report on their own people, call the authorities in emergencies, and assist state policies through exercising their personal influence.[99] Local authorities across the region customarily blamed uncooperative Gypsy chiefs for unsuccessful policies, and they accused them of preserving their power, keeping the "naive" Roma under their influence, and actively resisting resettlement and dispersal. In Poland, on the other hand, the more *laissez faire* attitude of the authorities, the cohesion of some Gypsy communities, and the strong influence that traditional leaders had historically enjoyed allowed them to maintain their elevated position in Romani society.

The emergence of a small but critically important Romani intelligentsia was a development corresponding to the waning influence of traditional Gypsy leaders. Some of those who did acquire postsecondary education became active in politics as well as in organizing Gypsy cultural projects. An interesting facet of this issue is that those Roma who studied humanities and social sciences were more likely to become participants in political activities than those who studied natural sciences.[100] Many of the latter – probably due to more attractive employment opportunities and personal considerations – attempted to assimilate and shake off, as it were, their Gypsiness. It is difficult to estimate the size of the East European Romani intelligentsia, but it seems fair to say that by 1989 it comprised approximately two to three thousand people. Among their ranks were dozens of eminent sociologists, writers, painters, poets, teachers and, of course, musicians.

In order to hasten Romani integration, all East European communist parties actively recruited Gypsy members. The party tried to present them in the media as role models to be emulated by their fellow Roma. A Bulgarian Communist Party Central Committee document reveals that 3,500 Roma had joined the party's ranks by 1959 and that thousands

---

[99] See Bihari Tamás, "Cigány bánat, magyar bánat," *A Világ*, 24 April 1991; and interview with Vasile Burtea at the Romanian Ministry of Labor (Bucharest, 15 March 1995).

[100] Interview with András Bíró, President of the Autonómia Foundation (Budapest, 26 July 1996).

more were members of its youth organization.[101] There were probably as many as 10,000 to 12,000 Romani communist party members in Eastern Europe in the mid-1970s who constituted an important support base for the socialist states. None rose to higher prominence than Emil Rigo, a member of the Czechoslovak Communist Party Politburo in 1968 and keen supporter of its assimilationist policies. Another eminent Gypsy leader, Slobodan Berberski, was a member of the Yugoslav communist party's Central Committee as well as an important figure in the international Romani movement. In the late 1940s Shakir Pashov, along with several other Roma, gained seats in the national legislature in Sofia while Gospodin Kolev became a BCP CC member three decades later. Faik Abdi, an economist by training, served as a member of the Macedonian Republican Assembly in 1969–74 while Bekir Arif was for 12 years the elected president of Shuto Orizari's municipal council. Many hundreds of Roma across the region were also employed in various capacities (usually at lower levels) as state and party officials and administrators. For instance, in 1965 Roma held 46 seats in district councils of Baranya County, Hungary, while in 1983, 433 Gypsies served as council deputies in Czechoslovakia.[102]

Although the authorities strictly controlled office-holders (whether Roma or not), the political participation of hundreds of Gypsies was an important benefit to the entire Romani population. Those who held positions in the bureaucracy gained valuable experience and acquired organizational and administrative skills that could be useful resources once the postcommunist transition removed obstacles to ethnic mobilization. At the same time, the diminishing role of traditional leaders and the growing authority of intellectuals had created deep cleavages within the Romani communities, fissures that were to have a damaging impact on Gypsy mobilization.

State Controlled Gypsy Organizations

Although a number of Romani organizations existed in the communist period, they either were entirely controlled by the authorities or enjoyed minimal independence. Most were the toadies of communists and served to bolster the regimes' hollow claim of wide-based social legitimacy and support. As in most other respects, in this area, too, there were major differences between East European states. Generally speaking, the states where communist rule was more liberal (Hungary, Poland, and Yugoslavia) tended to enable Romani organizations to gradually

---

[101] See *Destroying Ethnic Identity: The Gypsies of Bulgaria*, 63.
[102] Puxon, *Rom: Europe's Gypsies*, 16; and Kostelancik, "The Gypsies of Czechoslovakia," 319.

secure increasing autonomy. In contrast, more conservative communist regimes (Bulgaria, Czechoslovakia, Romania) either did not permit the formation of any Gypsy organizations or subjected them to stifling control.

In 1948 and 1957 Czechoslovak party officials refused the requests of Romani spokesmen to establish their own association (one similar to that of other ethnic minorities). In early 1968 the rapidly improving political milieu leading to the Prague Spring allowed for the formation of the Union of Czechoslovak Gypsies, under the aegis of the National Front [a nonparty but party-controlled umbrella organization, similar to the Fatherland Front in Bulgaria or the Patriotic People's Front (PPF) in Hungary]. The Union had separate organizations in the Czech Lands and in Slovakia. The two branches were divided on the issue of the officially recognized "nationality" status that Czech Gypsy leaders, especially Miroslav Holomek, campaigned for but their colleagues in Slovakia played down, focusing instead on improving the Roma's social status and housing conditions. The Union organized festivals promoting Romani culture, published a magazine, and pursued antidefamation activities.[103]

The Union was relatively independent of state control and, as such, it obviously was not suitable for the "normalization" policy. In 1973 the authorities disbanded it in part because it "failed to fulfill its integrative function." There was another important reason for the organization's breakup which is usually ignored in the literature. Both the Czech and the Slovak branch organizations compiled a record of serious financial mismanagement. As one of its leaders, Bartolomej Daniel, told me, the Czech organization was unable to account for 7.5 million crowns and, at a Prague audience with state administrators, Union officials were given the chance to go to prison or cease operations.[104]

Taking advantage of the political instability in the immediate postwar period, Bulgarian Roma founded the Cultural Enlightenment Organization of the Gypsy Minority in Bulgaria in 1946, which soon mushroomed into a federation with over 200 local chapters.[105] In 1947, however, Bulgaria began to implement assimilationist policies that included (a) terminating the Gypsy Cultural and Educational Society, which replaced the

---

[103] See Kalvoda, "The Gypsies of Czechoslovakia," 102–3;

[104] Interview with the Romani historian, Bartolomej Daniel (Brno, 2 September 1999). See also Anna Jurová, *Vyvoj romskej problematiky na Slovensku po roku 1945* (Bratislava: Goldpress Publishers, 1993); and Michal Vašečka, "Roma and the 1998 Parliamentary Elections," in Martin Bútora et al., eds., *The 1998 Parliamentary Elections and Democratic Rebirth in Slovakia* (Bratislava: Institute for Public Affairs), 256.

[105] Crowe, *A History*, 21.

two interwar era organizations (Egypt Society and Future) in 1953, and (b) sending Shakir Pashov, the country's most prominent Romani leader, to a concentration camp in 1954.[106]

The evolutionary nature of socialist Hungary's Gypsy policies is quite well traceable through the country's Romani organizations. In 1961 the Cultural Association of Hungarian Gypsies, organized only four year earlier, was dissolved in concert with the party's assimilationist policies. In 1974, reflecting the changing direction of policy, the HSWP approved the formation of the Gypsy Federation. The leadership of the PPF, which supervised this new organization, usually consisted of the most liberal Hungarian communists. The PPF also actively supported the creation of the National Gypsy Council in 1979 and the Cultural Association of Hungarian Gypsies in 1986. By the mid-1980s, Romani leaders within and without these organizations had become increasingly vocal in demanding the termination of state control which, nonetheless, continued until 1988. Starting with the early 1970s the authorities supported dozens of Gypsy clubs and folklore ensembles that organized art exhibitions, readings by Romani authors, and sport activities. In 1989 approximately 150–200 such groups existed.[107]

In Poland, Roma were allowed to form cultural associations whose activities were overseen by the Ministry of Internal Affairs.[108] The most prominent of these was established in Tarnów in 1963 and has survived the communist period. Other organizations catering to the cultural needs of local Romani communities were formed in Gdańsk, Olsztyn, Andrychow, and elsewhere. The state remained the sole source of financial support for these organizations, providing facilities (usually in houses of culture) and salaries to employees. In many cases the majority of the membership was comprised by interested non-Roma. The state supported but did not control the Federation of Yugoslav Gypsies, which had become a relatively independent representative of Romani interests. In 1986 the International Romani Union and the Yugoslav government organized and financed a large international conference on Romani language and history in Sarajevo. The Roma in Yugoslavia also enjoyed the opportunity to maintain regional associations and cultural organizations. Perhaps the most successful of these was the Romani theater, *Phralipe* ("Brotherhood"),

---

[106] Interview with Krassimir Kanev of the Helsinki Watch Group (Sofia, 6 March 1995).

[107] Erzsébet Ágoston, *A cigány munkanélküli réteg válságkezelésének helyzete* (Budapest: Ministry of Labor, 1994), 6.

[108] Bartosz, "The Social and Political Status," 17–18.

established in Skopje in 1971, which gained international awards and popular acclaim (from all Macedonians) for its staging of contemporary plays.[109] At the other end of the spectrum was Romania, where Gypsy mobilization was the most active in interwar Eastern Europe. Although the General Union of Romanian Roma was resuscitated in 1946, the RCP abolished it eight years later. Afterwards the state allowed no formal Gypsy organizations.[110]

Some East European states (e.g., Hungary, Yugoslavia) published a few magazines for the Roma and an even smaller number of radio and television programs catered to Gypsy audiences. The "Gypsy" media was financed entirely by the state. Especially in the more conservative countries the undisguised aim of these media outlets was to hasten assimilation, though in more liberal states Roma could actually make independent and relatively uncensored contributions to publications and programming. In every case, however, their involvement in the media endowed the Gypsies with experiences and skills that became especially valuable after 1989.

Independent Efforts

One of the quintessential attributes of communist states is their hostility to an independent civil society. Under the assimilationist policies of socialist states, building Romani identity – that is, nurturing Romani traditions and language – was difficult in Eastern Europe, with the partial exception of Yugoslavia.[111] Still, the Roma had proved time and again that they possessed a strong desire to preserve their culture and create independent organizations though most of their initiatives had failed due to state opposition.

In orthodox communist systems even such seemingly innocuous activities as putting together sport teams could not survive for long without state intrusion. A fitting example is the soccer team organized in the mid-1960s by a group of Roma in the Bulgarian town of Lom. The authorities objected to the club's Gypsy name and all-Romani roster. Team members broke up the squad rather than to give in to the officials' demand of including at least five ethnic Bulgarians. In Brno, Czechoslovakia, a group of Romani activists started a Gypsy museum in 1969, but

---

[109] See "Jugoslawiens Zigeuner als politischer Faktor," *Neue Zürcher Zeitung*, 22 October 1982; and interview with Emilija Simoska and Mirjana Najcevska, scholars at the Center for Ethnic Relations at the Institute for Sociological, Political, and Juridical Research (Skopje, 9 March 1994).

[110] Dan Ionescu, "Romania," *Soviet/East European Report*, 7:39 (1 August 1990): 1; and interview with Burtea (Bucharest, 15 March 1995).

[111] See, for instance, András T. Hegedűs, "A cigány identitás változásának problémái," *Kultúra és közösség*, no. 4 (August 1989): 104–12.

the state terminated their activities and put the collection in storage four years later.[112] Still, a 1972 law allowed the Roma to organize state-supervised folklore groups that could serve the unintended purpose of informal political discussions. In Sokolov (northwestern Bohemia) Emil Ščuka founded the Theater "Romen" in 1983, based on the already existing folklore group and inspired by the Romani theater of the same name in Moscow.[113] (Taking the name of the Soviet ensemble ensured that Ščuka's troupe was politically sanctified.) In the same year, Romanian Gypsies created an unofficial association in Sibiu that was never acknowledged by the authorities and ultimately disappeared. In essence, the only autonomous Romani formations that existed in the communist period were the loosely knit informal organizations of the drastically diminished number of traveling or seminomadic Roma (particularly in Poland and Romania) who were able to maintain their traditional ways despite official interference.

It should not be forgotten that Gypsies took an active part in the uprisings of the socialist period. In 1956, hundreds of Roma – among them the colorful character Gábor Dilinkó, a.k.a. "Bizsu," and his men – fought courageously against the Soviet forces in Budapest and elsewhere.[114] During the invasion of Czechoslovakia by Warsaw Pact forces in August 1968, "Gypsy youths went into battle against the tanks" and expressed their solidarity with their fellow citizens.[115] Twenty years later a large number of Roma again proved their valor fighting against communist forces in Romania. Unfortunately, few in Eastern Europe are aware of the Gypsy contribution to their struggles against tyranny.

Dissident organizations did not ignore the Roma. From its birth, Czechoslovakia's Charter 77 group called attention to the Gypsies' plight and discriminatory state policies. In December 1978 an important *samizdat* study by Charter signatory and one-time spokesman, Jozef Vohryžek, analyzed the Gypsies' situation and the state's lacking

---

[112] Burton Bollag, "A Museum Devoted to the Largest Minority Group in Europe – the Gypsies – Gets a Home of Its Own," *The Chronicle of Higher Education*, 26 June 1996, A36; Eva Davidová, "K výstavní prezentaci romského tématu v Československu a v České republice (1962–1997)," *Bulletin Muzea Romské Kultury*, no. 6 (1997): 24–8; and interview with Ilona Lázničková, Director of the Roma Museum (Brno, 2 September 1999).

[113] Interviews with Hübschmannová (Prague, 27 August 1999) and Karel Holomek (Brno, 1 September 1999). See also Ulč, "Gypsies in Czechoslovakia," 325; and Alaina Lemon, "Roma (Gypsies) in the Soviet Union and the Moscow Teatr 'Romen'," *Nationalities Papers*, 19:3 (Winter 1991): 359–72.

[114] Patrin/Üzenet (a television program for and about the Gypsies), Magyar Televízió 1, 2 PM, 27 October 1997.

[115] Ulč, "Gypsies in Czechoslovakia," 310.

comprehension of their predicament.[116] In two additional documents (23/1979 and 3/1990) the group scathingly criticized the government's sterilization program.[117] A prominent dissident and Charter leader, Václav Havel, became a vocal champion of Romani rights in his capacity of Czechoslovak and later Czech president in the 1990s. The main purposes of one of the first Hungarian dissident groups, SZETA (*Szegényeket Támogató Alap* [Fund for Aiding the Poor], established in 1980), was to publicize the growth of the country's underclass and to castigate the communist state for not intervening more energetically to alleviate the Roma's poverty.

In the late 1980s, taking advantage of the erosion of the communist party's power, Hungarian Gypsies started a number of independent organizations.[118] The first of these was the Democratic Federation of Hungarian Gypsies that sprang to life in 1988 with the backing of, but independent from, the Patriotic People's Front. The Federation supported the PPF's liberal policies and received the HSWP's blessing. A far more important development was the funding of the Phralipe Independent Gypsy Organization by Roma and non-Roma intellectuals and activists in April 1989. In many ways, Phralipe originated in the well-organized and successful resistance of its founders – most importantly the Romani school teacher and activist Aladár Horváth – to the erection of a Gypsy ghetto on the periphery of Miskolc, in order to provide the provincial city's elite with choice apartments in 1988.[119] From its inception, Phralipe opposed socialist Gypsy policies and the state-created and sponsored Gypsy federations. For a short time at least, Phralipe managed to link Romani and *gadje* intellectuals with "ordinary" Roma. In Belgrade, Gypsies disappointed by the lack of adequate political representation established the Yugoslav Romany Association (YRA) in July 1989. Its leader, Sait Balić (who was also the president of the World Romani Congress), suggested that the founding of YRA would signify an initial step toward wider Romani emancipation.[120]

---

[116] Jozef Vohryžek, "O postaveni cikánu-romu v Československu," *Charta 77, 1977–1989: Od moralni k demokratické revoluci* (Bratislava: Archa, 1990), 217–25. See also H. Gordon Skilling, *Charter 77 and Human Rights in Czechoslovakia* (London: Allen & Unwin, 1981), 81.

[117] See Ruben Pellar, " 'Sterilization with Grant' of Gypsies in Czechoslovakia," unpublished manuscript (Prague, 28 August 1991), 2.

[118] "Nyerőviszonyok: Roma politikatörténet," *Beszélő*, 11 May 1995, 23.

[119] See János Ladányi, "A miskolci gettóügy," *Valóság*, 34:4 (April 1991): 45–54; and interview with Aladár Horváth (Austin, 31 March 1995).

[120] "Yugoslav Romany Association Established," Tanjug (Yugoslav telegraph agency), Belgrade, 29 July 1989.

The creation of the International Gypsy Committee in 1965 was a momentous development that brought the activities of the international Romani movement into a legitimate institutional framework. Faik Abdi, who participated in the first World Romani Congress (London, 1971), came away with the conclusion that the Roma were not an inherently apolitical people and that cooperation and organizational activities in the international realm might make a substantial contribution to improving their lot.[121] Yugoslav Roma managed to gain several top positions in the International Romani Union in large part because Yugoslavia had a large and relatively dynamic Romani community whose activities were not hindered by the state to the same extent as elsewhere in Eastern Europe. Yugoslavia and Hungary sent official representatives to the gatherings of the international Romani movement though at times Gypsies from Bulgaria, Czechoslovakia, and Romania were able to attend as tourists. The vast majority of East European Roma, however, remained entirely unaware of the existence of an international Gypsy organization.[122]

SUMMARY

In the communist era a fundamentally inclusive approach replaced the preceding period's strategy of often brutal exclusion. Communist elites did their best to assimilate the Roma and bring them under state control. Nonetheless, state-socialist policies had dissimilar effects on the different dimensions of Gypsy marginality. They translated into substantial socioeconomic gains for the Roma and a considerable diminution in their marginality. At the same time, these policies hardly ever brought the magnitude of changes anticipated by the states as can be gleaned from the many party resolutions and official documents lamenting mediocre results. Although the Roma still remained at the bottom of socioeconomic indicators, full employment, free education and healthcare, state assistance in housing and child-rearing, and a number of positive discrimination programs had considerably improved the objective conditions of most Gypsies. Moreover, as a general rule, the Roma did not have to fear for their physical security because the state seldom tolerated overt ethnic conflict.

No wonder, then, that in contemporary Eastern Europe many Roma have positive memories of socialism. In 1991, following interethnic hostilities in a Romanian village, a journalist encountered Gypsies who

---

[121] Interview with Abdi, chairman of the Party for the Total Emancipation of Macedonian Roma (Skopje, 11 March 1994).
[122] *Destroying Ethnic Identity: The Gypsies of Bulgaria*, 14.

"mourned Ceauşescu, whom some even called Papa."[123] As Alena Gronziková, a Gypsy editor in Prague, succinctly put it, "It was better under communism. The average Gypsy had a job, had welfare subsidies, and he was not beaten up."[124] The cost of Romani integration was extremely high, however, and some of the benefits – an 8- to 10-hour workday, mandatory education, and so on – were not only of nebulous value from the Roma's perspective, but often in conflict with their traditions.

The political situation of Gypsies, on the other hand, had deteriorated when compared to that of the interwar era. Aside from a few isolated exceptions, they were not permitted to pursue mobilization activities. Thus, their political marginality in this period was primarily rooted in exogenous political causes (e.g., obstacles posed by the state to Romani mobilization). Nevertheless, state-controlled Gypsy organizations and the policy to integrate the Roma into state and party hierarchies served as something of an unintended training ground for the Gypsy activists of the future. During our interview in Prague, Ivan Veselý – a Slovak Rom who became a prominent Gypsy activist in the Czech Republic – asked me a rhetorical question: "Do you think I would be sitting here arguing about Marx and Weber if it were not for the communists? I would be in the ghetto in eastern Slovakia!"[125] Paradoxically, through their social (especially educational) policies the socialist regimes contributed to the development of what they feared most: Romani identity and Gypsy activism.

Socialist states were heavily charged with ideology that allowed little deviation from the norm. Therefore, regime type was a far more reliable indicator of state policies than in the case of imperial or authoritarian states. Still, the gradual diminution of Soviet control over the East European states and growing concern with the mixed results of policies guided more or less by ideological considerations led to differences between individual states. Eventually it turned out that even as constrictive a regime type as state-socialism permitted the evolution of substantial disparities in state policies. As in imperial and authoritarian states, under socialism, too, state policies were driven by several considerations in addition to regime type. The more indulgent and tolerant approach of Hungary, Poland, and especially Yugoslavia toward the Roma corresponded to the relative liberalism of these states. Gypsy policies in Macedonia reflected the comparative ethnic tolerance in Macedonian society.

---

[123] Isabel Fonseca, "Arson in Bolintin Deal," *Roma Rights*, Autumn 1997, 6.
[124] Cited by Juan O. Tamayo, "Gypsies among Hardest Hit Victims of Europe's Rising Tide of Racism," *Miami Herald*, 4 May 1993.
[125] Interview with Veselý (Prague, 16 June 1994).

The abysmal socioeconomic situation of the Roma across the region clearly served as a major force in shaping state policy. At the same time, the Roma had basically no political clout and international actors had minimal power to influence state policy. Substantial changes in these factors made postcommunist state–Romani relations all the more interesting.

PART III

THE GYPSIES IN EMERGING DEMOCRACIES

5

The Socioeconomic Impact of Regime Change

Gypsy Marginality in the 1990s

The objective of this chapter is to provide answers to two broad questions: How have the Gypsies' socioeconomic conditions changed in the postcommunist era, and how have interethnic relations between the Roma and dominant populations changed in the same period? These questions correspond to the argument stated in Chapter 1, which contends that state policies toward the Roma are in part determined by societal attitudes and the Roma's own socioeconomic conditions. I argue that in both regards the regime change from state-socialism to the nascent democracies was accompanied by profoundly negative effects for the Roma. This chapter analyzes their situation in the 1990s, putting aside for the moment the changes spurred by Romani political mobilization, the efforts of international and nongovernmental organizations, and state policies. In Chapter 8 I will revisit the Gypsies' socioeconomic circumstances to take into account whatever changes occurred as a result of these factors.

This chapter is divided into three sections. In Part I the focus is on the demographic, educational, and employment situation of the Roma in the 1990s. Part II analyzes the Gypsies' social ills focusing on health problems, poverty, and crime. Finally, Part III examines societal relations between the Roma and the dominant groups and explores the phenomenon of interethnic violence.

PART I: DEMOGRAPHY, EDUCATION AND UNEMPLOYMENT

Demography

In the postcommunist era the estimation of the size of Eastern Europe's Romani population remains a chancy undertaking. Numerous long-standing obstacles to accurate calculation remain. Even though postcommunist states have removed legal constraints from the declaration of one's ethnicity, in many cases Roma refuse to identify themselves as such.

This is clear from the census data included in Table 5.1. In the early 1990s less than one-sixth of Gypsies in Slovakia and less than one-third in Romania registered as Roma. In some Romanian counties, like Hargitha and Covasna, reportedly as many as 70% of the Roma registered as Hungarians in 1992.[1] In the same year, Bulgarian census takers found that the majority of the country's Turkish-speaking Roma declared themselves as Turks.[2] Many Gypsies identify themselves as members of other ethnic groups in order to escape the stigma attached to being a Rom in Eastern Europe. Socioeconomically integrated Roma often aspire to assimilate into the dominant society and classify themselves as one of its members. Some Roma justify their reluctance to identify themselves as Gypsies by having no Romani language facility or nothing in common with other Roma.[3] As research among the Croatian Roma has shown, Gypsies at times are prejudiced against themselves, develop self-hatred, and believe that they are less worthy if they embrace their Romani identity in censuses. A Slovak poll found that only 5.6% of the Gypsy children surveyed wanted to be linked to their ethnic background.[4]

Given the diversity of the Romani populations and the rancor between distinctive Gypsy groups, some Roma do not accept a common identity with others and have created new identities in order to escape being considered, at least officially, Gypsies. In Macedonia, for instance, several thousands Roma around Lake Ohrid declared themselves *Egipcani* (Egyptians) of pharaonic lineage, objecting to the term "Roma" (but not to "Gypsies"!) due to what they perceived the term's pejorative connotations. They successfully campaigned to be so classified in the 1991 census (according to which their number was 3,307) and in a letter requested the support of Egyptian President Hosni Mubarak.[5] In some

---

[1] Rompres (Bucharest), 22 May 1992.

[2] See Alexander Kolev, "Census Taking in a Bulgarian Gypsy Mahala," *Journal of the Gypsy Lore Society*, series 5, 4:1 (1994): 33–46.

[3] See, for instance, András T. Hegedüs, "A cigány identitás változásának problémái," *Kultúra és közösség*, no. 4 (August 1989): 104–12; Sándor Oláh, "Szimbólikus elhatárolódás egy település cigány lakói között," in *Egy más mellett élés: A magyar-román, magyar-cigány kapcsolatokról* (Csikszereda: Pro-Print, 1996), 219; and author's interview with Rumyana Kolarova, Professor of Politics at the University of Sofia (Sofia, 6 March 1995).

[4] *The Romanies in Central and Eastern Europe: Illusions and Reality* (Princeton: Project on Ethnic Relations, 1992), 19. It bears mentioning that only a fraction of Slovak Jews declare their ethnicity in censuses because they "don't want to stick out having experienced the difficulties of being 'others'." Interview with Ágnes Horváthová, Head of Secretariat, Slovak Helsinki Commission (Bratislava, 8 September 1999).

[5] Zoltan Barany, "The Roma in Macedonia: Ethnic Politics and the Marginal Condition in a Balkan State," *Ethnic and Racial Studies*, 18:3 (1995): 517–18; *Basic Statistical Data* (Skopje: Statistical Office of Macedonia, 1992), 12; and author's interview with Cvetko

cases Romani men not only marry non-Roma women but adopt the name of their spouses so that their children will have "white" names and easier lives.[6] Their circumstances have compelled many Roma in Eastern Europe and elsewhere to "negotiate their Gypsiness" in public while preserving it in private.[7] This phenomenon of manipulated ethnic identity has been somewhat offset by a growing number willing to classify themselves as Roma in order to be eligible for social assistance.[8]

The refusal of self-identity calls into question the policy of governments and nongovernmental organizations (NGOs) who insist that ethnic identity should be determined by self-identification. They contend that only people who answer the question "What is your ethnic identity?" with "Roma (Gypsies)" or with "Polish Roma," "Albanian Roma," and so on, or with a more specific delineation of a Gypsy subgroup should be considered Roma.[9] If one follows this rationale, must one then conclude that in the early 1990s there were truly only 76,000 Roma in Slovakia and 142,000 in Hungary? Hungarian sociologists like István Kemény, János Ladányi, Iván Szelényi, and others have debated the virtues of standard methodologies used to define the Roma by pointing to ongoing changes in the Gypsies' environment and lifestyle. The only clear lessons that emerge from this dispute are that there is no single way to determine the size of Romani communities and that the Gypsies do not constitute a population that can be unambiguously demarcated.[10]

Table 5.1 features several estimates for each East European country's Romani population in the 1990s. The first column shows the number of Gypsies in the most recent census of the given state. The second represents the mean of the estimates of Romani activists and politicians. The

---

Šmilevski, Professor of Human Resources Development at the Sts. Cyril and Method University (Skopje, 9 March 1994).

[6] Linnet Myers, "Poverty-Stricken Romanian Gypsies Caught in Battle between Germany, Poland," *Chicago Tribune*, 14 September 1993; and interview with Macedonian political-sociologist Georgi Spasov at the Institute for Sociological, Political, and Juridical Research (Skopje, 9 March 1994).

[7] See Carol Silverman, "Negotiating 'Gypsiness': Strategy in Context," *Journal of American Folklore*, 101:401 (1988): 261–75; and Michael Stewart, "Gypsies, Work and Civil Society," *The Journal of Communist Studies*, 6:2 (1990): 152–3.

[8] Imre Szilágyi, "A horvátországi romák helyzete," *Regio*, 7:3 (1996): 72–3. See also Andre Liebich, "Minorities in Eastern Europe: Obstacles to Reliable Count," *RFE/RL Research Report*, 1:20 (15 May 1992): 32–9; and idem., "The Ethnic Mosaic," *Geopolitique*, 35 (August 1992): 37–40.

[9] See, for instance, Csaba Tabajdi, *Az önazonosság labirintusa: A magyar kül- és kisebbségpolitika rendszerváltása* (Budapest: CP Studio, 1998), 670.

[10] See, for instance, János Ladányi and Iván Szelényi, "Ki a cigány?" *Kritika*, 26:12 (1997): 3–6; and Gábor Havas, István Kemény, and Gábor Kertesi, "A relatív cigány a klasszifikációs küzdőtéren," *Kritika*, 27:3 (1998): 31–5.

Table 5.1. Estimates of Eastern Europe's Romani Population in the 1990s (in thousands)

Country	Last Census	Roma Estimate	High Number	Low Number	Probable Figure	Pop. Total[a]	Percentage of Roma
Albania[b]		120	1,000	5	55	3,339	1.65
Bosnia[c]	7		60		35	3,365	1.04
Bulgaria[d]	313	1,000	1,000	577	700	8,240	8.50
Croatia[e]	7	150	150	35	35	4,671	0.75
Czech Republic[f]	33	350	250	150	200	10,286	1.94
Hungary[g]	142	800	1,000	400	482	10,208	4.72
Macedonia[h]	47	220	220		60	2,075	2.89
Poland[i]		60	750	15	35	38,606	0.09
Romania[j]	409	3,000	6,000	800	1,500	22,760	6.59
Slovakia[k]	76	400	500	26	500	5,269	9.49
Slovenia[l]	2		7	5	7	1,971	0.35
Yugoslavia[m]	112	140			537	11,206	4.79
Total					4,146	121,996	3.40

[a] When census numbers were not readily available, I adopted the estimates found in the *CIA World Factbook 1998*.

[b] Column 2: Gorali Mejdani cited in *o Drom: Magazine for and about Roma and Sinti in Europe*, September 1994; p. 17. Column 3: Carol Silverman, "Persecution and Politicization: Roma (Gypsies) of Eastern Europe," *Cultural Survival Quarterly*, 19:2 (1995): 46. Columns 4 and 5: Fredrik Folkeryd and Ingvar Svanberg, *Gypsies (Roma) in the Post-Totalitarian States* (Stockholm: Olof Palme International Center, 1995), 46.

[c] Column 1: 1991 Census. Column 3: This is the prewar figure cited in the Council of Europe's "Fact-Finding Mission to Bosnia and Herzegovina on the Situation of the Roma/Gypsies," 20 June 1996. Column 5: Georg Brunner, "Minority Problems and Policies in East-Central Europe," in John R. Lampe and Daniel N. Nelson, eds., *East European Security Reconsidered* (Washington: Woodrow Wilson Center Press, 1993), 147.

[d] Columns 2 and 3: Manush Romanov, cited in Poulton, *The Balkans*, 116. Column 4: 1990 official figures cited by Tomova, *The Gypsies*, 27. Column 5: Interviews with Elena Marushiakova and Krassimir Kanev (Sofia, March 1995).

[e] Column 1: 1991 census. Column 2: OMRI DD II, no. 21 (30 January 1996). Columns 3–5: Szilágyi, "A horvátországi romák helyzete," 69.

[f] Column 1: 1991 Census. Column 2: According to the Roma Civic Initiative, 300,000 to 400,000, cited in *Report on Human Rights in the CR in 1998* (Prague: Council on Human Rights, 1999), 28. Column 3: Burton Bollag, "A Museum Devoted to the Largest Minority Group in Europe," *The Chronicle of Higher Education*, 26 January 1996, A36. Column 4: According to a August 1993 government report cited by Hamberger, "A csehországi romák helyzete," 59. Column 5: Mann, "Formation of Ethnic Identity," 261; and interview with Roman Kristof, editor of *Romano Hangoš* (Brno, 2 September 1999).

[g] Column 1: 1990 census. Column 2–4: Bihari, "Cigány bánat, magyar bánat." Column 5: Havas et al., "The Statistics of Deprivation," 67.

[h] Columns 1 and 7: 1994 census. Column 2: Faik Abdi in interview with author (Skopje, 29 November 1999). Column 3: Silverman, "Persecution and Politicization," 46. Column 5: Presentation by Professor Elsie Ivancich Dunin at the International Meeting of the Gypsy Lore Society (Arlington, TX, 27 March 1998).

third and fourth columns feature the highest and lowest figures (not including census data) I have encountered. The fifth column is what I consider the most reasonable figures, usually provided by academic specialists who adopted more or less rigorous methodologies in reaching their estimates. The sixth column shows the total population of the East European states, and the last one shows the percentage of Roma (based on scholarly estimates). Table 5.1 shows that Romania is home to Eastern Europe's biggest Romani community, although the proportion of Roma in the populations of Slovakia and Bulgaria is considerably larger.

The most surprising deduction of this table is that the total number of East European Roma is approximately 4.15 million, or about 3.4% of the region's population. This figure, too, may be somewhat off the mark given the already detailed difficulties of arriving at precise numbers which scholars encounter. It should be noted that the scholarly figure for rump Yugoslavia (537,000) dates from 1991. There are significantly

Notes to Table 5.1 (*continued*)

' Column 2: Rajko Djurić, Jörg Becken, and A. Bertolt Bengsch, *Ohne Heim-Ohne Grab: Die Geschichte der Roma und Sinti* (Berlin: Aufbau-Verlag, 1996), 175. Column 3: International Romani Union estimate, *The New York Times*, 27 September 1992. Column 4: David McQuaid, "The Growing Assertiveness of Minorities," *Report on Eastern Europe*, 2:50 (1991): 23. Column 5: Interviews with Andrzej Mirga (Kraków, 1994) and Adam Bartosz (Tarnów, 9 August 1999).

ʲ Columns 1 and 6: 1992 census. Column 2: Ion Onoriu, President of the Rom Democratic Union, cited in Michel Conrath, "Gypsies Suffer Fallout from the Romanian Revolution," AFP (Bucharest), 8 July 1991; and Iulian Radulescu cited in Reuter report (Bucharest), 12 May 1995; Nicolae Gheorghe cited in "In Romania traiesc cei mai multi romi: 3,5 milioane," *Romania Libera*, 12 August 1993. Column 3: *London Observer*, 29 July 1990. Column 4: Author's interview with Dan Ionescu (Munich, 7 July 1993). Column 5: Cătălin Zamfir and Elena Zamfir, estimate derived from their 1998 study (interview with the Zamfirs, Bucharest, 3 November 1999).

ᵏ Columns 1 and 6: 1991 census. Columns 2 and 4: Klára Orgovánová, "The Roma in Slovakia," *The East & Central Europe Program Bulletin*, 1–3. Column 3: Fisher, "Romanies in Slovakia," 56. Column 5: Dušan Ondrušek cites 480,000–520,000 in his "Scenare optimisticke a pesimisticke," in László Juhász, *Rom známena člověk: Diskusia v Cilistove o palcivom probléme* (Bratislava: Friedrich Ebert Stiftung, 1999), 19; Michal Vašečka cites 420,000–500,000 in his "The Roma," 395.

ˡ Column 1: Winkler, "Roma Ethnic Group in Slovenia," 71 cites the 1991 census and notes that 2,293 people declared themselves as Roma and 2,847 declared Romani as their mother tongue. Columns 3–5: Szilágyi, "A romák Szlovéniában," 83.

ᵐ Yugoslavia denotes Serbia and Montenegro. Columns 1 and 5 contain prewar figures from 1991: it is widely believed that the number in contemporary Serbia is significantly less. Column 1: 1991 census (Serbian and Montenegrin figures). Column 2: Cited by Patrick Moore, "What Lies Behind Serbian Skinhead Violence Against Roma?," End Note, RFE/RL II, no. 149 (30 October 1997); Georg Brunner, "Minority Problems and Policies in East-Central Europe," in John R. Lampe and Daniel N. Nelson, eds., *East European Security Reconsidered* (Washington, DC: Woodrow Wilson Center Press, 1993), 147.

fewer Roma there now (indeed, as column 2 shows, in 1997 Romani leaders themselves thought that their community shrank to 140,000) given their migration to Western Europe and elsewhere. I elected to leave this figure for the sake of consistency, and it may be used to absorb potential undercounting in other cases.

The "guesstimates" bandied about by Romani and human rights activists usually lack any serious effort of methical computation. Rudko Kawczynski, a Gypsy leader in Germany, categorically states that there are 15 million Roma in Europe, three-quarters (i.e., 11.25 million) of whom live in Eastern Europe.[11] The Hungarian Gypsy politician, Flórián Farkas, also adopted this number without any reference to its source.[12] Even reputable activist-scholars, Andrzej Mirga and Nicolae Gheorghe, write that the European Roma's numbers are "estimated at between 6 and 12 million," but they fail to tell their audience by whom were such estimates made.[13] Anna Jurová, an eminent Slovak sociologist, is one of a handful of social scientists with the intellectual courage to write that

materials of the Council of Europe, Western publications dealing with Central- and Eastern Europe . . . such as J. P. Liégeois' book *Roma, Tsiganes, Voyageurs* as well as information transmitted by the media routinely exaggerate the number of Roma.[14]

To be sure, the Gypsies continue to have far higher reproduction rates than the dominant populations surrounding them (with the exception of ethnic Albanians). It is clear that their number is growing considerably faster than that of majority populations, which in most East European countries has actually been declining. Demographers and sociologists point to remarkable increases: Between 1977 and 1992 the number of Romanian Gypsies increased by 80% (versus the 5.6% growth of the overall population); in the 1971–93 period Hungary's Romani population registered an increase in excess of 50%.[15] Today there are almost

---

[11] "Kristallnacht in jedem Dorf," *Die Tageszeitung* (Berlin), 29 August 1992.
[12] Tibor Nagy, "Az Únióbeli tagság feltétele: Javuljon a romák helyzete," *Cigány Hírlap – Romano Zhurnalo*, 2:5 (1996): 1.
[13] Andrzej Mirga and Nicolae Gheorghe, *The Roma in the Twenty-First Century: A Policy Paper* (Princeton: PER, 1997), 5. In a 1991 article Gheorghe "estimated" the East European Romani population at "about 3–5 million." See his "Roma-Gypsy Ethnicity in Eastern Europe," *Social Research*, 58:4 (1991): 829.
[14] See Anna Jurová, "Cigányok-romák Szlovákiában 1945 után," *Regio*, 7:2 (1996): 35–6.
[15] Elena and Cătălin Zamfir, *The Romany Population* (Bucharest: Centre of Economic Information and Documentation, 1993), 7; and Csaba Tabajdi, *Látlelet a magyarországi cigányság helyzetéről* (Budapest: Miniszterelnöki Hivatal, 1996), 9.

Table 5.2. Percentage of Roma Residing in Urban Areas in the 1990s

Country:	Bulgaria	Czech Republic	Hungary	Macedonia	Poland	Slovakia
Percentage[a]	52	80	40	95	75	40

[a] Bulgaria: Tomova, *The Gypsies*, 28; Czech Republic and Slovakia: Ondrej Dostál, "Hot Summer for Romany Minority in Slovakia," 1; Hungary: "A vidéki romák tizede kap mezőgazdasági támogatást," *Népszabadság*, 2 April 1998; Macedonia: Mirjana Najcevska and Natasha Gaber, *Survey Results and Legal Background Regarding Ethnic Issues in the Republic of Macedonia* (Skopje: Sts. Cyril and Methodius University, 1995), 24; Poland: interview with Adam Bartosz (Tarnów, 10 August 1999).

twice as many Romani children under 14 as there are in the Czech population at large.[16] The proportion of Roma among East Europeans is expected to grow further in the foreseeable future. According to Hungarian officials, by 2015 the Roma's share in the population will nearly double to approximately 8%.[17] The situation is nowhere as dramatic as in Slovakia, where Slovak and Hungarian couples have on average 1.51 children, as compared to 4.2 for their Romani counterparts. Experts predict that if prevailing demographic trends persist, the Gypsies will form the majority population by the year 2060.[18]

The residential characteristics of the Gypsy population have also been constantly changing. The trend of increasing urbanization has continued particularly with the loss of employment opportunities in rural areas since 1989. Still, as Table 5.2 indicates, the majority of Gypsies in Hungary and Slovakia reside in rural areas of the least developed regions: northeastern Hungary and eastern Slovakia.[19] Many Roma live in segregated Gypsy colonies because of the relative security, social interaction, and traditional lifestyle they provide or because they cannot afford to move out. There are 547 such settlements in Bulgaria and 591 in Slovakia, with total populations of approximately 600,000 and 124,000,

---

[16] *Romové v České republice* (Prague: Socioklub, 1999), 534.

[17] Author's interview with Éva Orsós, President of the National Ethnic and Minority Office (Budapest, 25 July 1996).

[18] Michal Vašečka, "The Roma," in Gregoríj Mešeznikov, Michal Ivantyšyn, and Tom Nicholson, eds., *Slovakia 1998–1999: A Global Report on the State of Society* (Bratislava: Institute of Public Affairs, 1999), 414; and interview with Vašečka, a specialist focusing on the Roma at the Institute for Public Affairs (Bratislava, 10 September 1999).

[19] See, for instance, László Gáspárovich, "Akik a magyar Malcolm X-ek lehetnek, *Pesti Hírlap*, 17 February 1994; and Otto Ulč, "Integration of the Gypsies in Czechoslovakia," *Ethnic Groups*, 9:2 (1991): 111.

respectively.[20] In several East European cities, such as Sliven and Plovdiv in Bulgaria and the municipality of Shuto Orizari in Macedonia, there is a high concentration of Roma. In contrast, the small Romani population in Poland is widely dispersed, and few colonies there are home to more than 250 inhabitants.

Large-scale Romani migration started as soon as the travel restrictions of the communist regimes were revoked. Tens of thousands of Roma have migrated to cities where jobs have been easier to find, while others have moved from impoverished areas to more prosperous ones. The migration of thousands of Roma from Slovakia to the more affluent Czech Lands prior to the 1993 breakup of Czechoslovakia has been widely noted. Gypsies from Albania and Serbia have also been migrating to Macedonia in search of a better life. Many Roma, especially from the Balkans, left their countries intending to move to Western Europe (this phenomenon will be discussed in detail in Chapter 7). The extent of Romani migration precipitated by the wars in the former Yugoslavia is virtually impossible to ascertain, but the number is surely in the tens of thousands.

Education

At the end of the state-socialist era the Roma's educational level was higher than ever before because hundreds of thousands of them completed the eight-grade primary school. Owing to the strong emphasis that communist regimes put on higher education, a large proportion of dominant ethnic groups succeeded in surpassing the educational attainments of their parents. A logical parallel development was the relative devaluation of eight-grade education and the increasing benefits of higher education. At the same time, the number of Roma graduating from secondary and postsecondary institutions remained abysmally low; consequently, even though their absolute educational levels had improved, their educational standing vis-à-vis non-Roma had deteriorated. Prior to 1989, education was less important insofar as individuals of even minimal schooling could (and, in fact, were forced to) find jobs in socialist states. One of the pillars of the evolving postsocialist market economics is labor rationalization. In the new workplace, educational accomplishments are infinitely more important, which, of course, places those of substandard schooling at a disadvantage. Generally speaking,

---

[20] Elena Marushiakova and Vesselin Popov, *Gypsies (Roma) in Bulgaria* (Frankfurt am Main: Peter Lang Verlag, 1997), 121; interview with Ilona Tomova, a sociologist at the Bulgarian Academy of Science (Sofia, 15 November 1999); and *Strategy of the Government of the Slovak Republic for the Solution of the Problems of the Roma National Minority* (Bratislava: Government Publications, 1999), 17.

the socioeconomic impact of the regime change has dealt an additional blow to the Roma owing to their inferior educational status.

Many related factors hinder Romani education. Throughout the region, tens of thousands of Gypsy children grow up speaking Romani and possess inadequate knowledge of the language of the educational system. Aside from a few exceptions, Romani language is not taught in schools because of minimal demand, the lack of qualified teachers and resources, and political will. In Slovakia, for instance, a 1994 survey found that 33% of the Roma wanted some school subjects to be taught in Romani but 45% preferred no Romani language instruction at all.[21] In Macedonia, Gypsies are even more assertive in their opposition to Romani language classes because they disagree about which dialect should be used and they fear that additional classes would put an extra burden on their children.[22] By the end of the communist period a significant proportion of Romani children attended kindergartens where they could learn the majority's language as well as experience a structured environment. After 1989, their participation in kindergarten-level education had steeply declined owing to the lack of incentives for parents to send their children there (attendance was not compulsory and in many cases kindergartens started to charge money for their services) and because of the dissolution of many nurseries and kindergartens. In Slovakia, for instance, 85–90% of Gypsy children attended kindergartens until 1991, but by 1999 only 0–15% did, depending on the region.[23] The absence of Romani children from preschool activities increases their initial disadvantage in the school system.

Rising economic barriers have decreased the Roma's ability to send their children to school. A number of social benefits associated with schools in the past – such as free food and textbooks – were abolished by postcommunist governments. With the removal or reduction of state subsidies, the costs of education have increased substantially, and a growing number of Gypsy (and non-Gypsy) families can no longer provide their children with adequate clothing, school supplies, and transportation. Most Gypsies also live in crowded housing – often without electricity and heat – where conditions are not conducive for study. Other problems such as early pregnancies and marriages add to many Roma's reluctance to go to school. Furthermore, school curricula even in areas where the Roma constitute a majority usually lack any reference to

[21] Vašečka, "The Roma," 411.
[22] See interview with Emilija Simoska, who was Macedonia's Minister of Education in December 1994–January 1996 (Skopje, 23 November 1999).
[23] *Strategy of the Government for the Solution of the Problems of the Roma National Minority* (Bratislava: Government Publications, 1999), 14.

Table 5.3. What Is Most Important in Life to
Succeed? (Romani Respondents over Age 16)[a]

Money	28.5%
Working hard	23.9%
Luck	14.0%
Skills/qualifications	8.0%
Health	7.3%
School/education	4.1%
Job	3.2%
Help from family	2.8%
Relationships	0.8%
Something else (unspecified)	2.3%
No response	5.1%

[a] Unpublished research project directed by Cătălin and Elena
Zamfir, Department of Sociology, University of Bucharest,
21.

Romani history, culture, and experience, which makes it all the more
difficult for Gypsy children to relate to the material. Many Gypsies
who continue to live by their old traditions still believe that education
represents a danger to their ways.[24]

Some Romani activists, like Andrzej Mirga, admit, however, that the
single most important reason for the educational privation of the Gypsies
is to be found in their traditional lack of interest in schooling.[25] The findings of a 1998 Romanian survey reproduced in Table 5.3 underscore this
point. Experts agree that the overwhelming majority of Roma are apathetic about their children's education.[26] Even Romani magazines feature
reports on the (East) European school systems' "constant battle against
the apathy of the [Gypsy] parents against education."[27] In the commu-

---

[24] See, for instance, Ilona Tomova, "Változások és gondok a bolgár cigányközösségben,"
Regio, 7:3 (1996): 63.

[25] Interview with Mirga, a Gypsy activist in Poland (Kraków, 14 June 1994).

[26] See, for instance, Arne B. Mann, "Motivation: The Inevitable Condition of Successful
Education of Romany Children," paper for the Council of Europe, Špišská Nová Veš,
14–17 September 1994; Arne B. Mann, "Rroma (Gypsies) in Municipalities," paper for
the hearing of the Council of Europe (Košice, 9 December 1995); interviews with Roma
throughout Eastern Europe (1990–2000), János Wolfart, chairman of the National
Ethnic and Minorities Office (Budapest, 9 June 1994); Elena Zamfir, Professor of Social
Work at the University of Bucharest (Bucharest, 13 March 1995); Jurová, "Cigányok-
romák Szlovákiában," 64–5; and Ilona Tomova, *The Gypsies in the Transition Period*
(Sofia: International Centre for Minority Studies and Intercultural Relations, 1995), 60.

[27] *o Drom: Magazine for and about Roma and Sinti in Europe* (Amsterdam), Special Issue
in English, September 1994, 12.

nist period the Roma were obligated to send their children to school and readily used the social benefits allocated for this, but the importance of formal education did not become a part of their value system.[28] Now many contend that since under socialism unskilled workers often earned more money than some college-educated people like teachers, there is no sense in spending time at school. Researchers of Helsinki Watch, a U.S.-based international human rights organization, have found, for instance, that Romani parents often do not know that their children's school is segregated and are not concerned even though their children have not been to school for months.[29] Moreover, many adult Roma are functionally illiterate and cannot help with their children's school work.

Many Roma attend segregated schools, particularly in areas where they constitute the majority population. In other places school administrators set up separate classes for Roma and non-Roma because most parents in the dominant ethnic group do not want their children to study in the same classroom with Gypsies. A high percentage of Gypsy children are enrolled in a system of special or remedial schools, designed in the 1950s and 1960s to meet the needs of mentally handicapped and learning disabled children. Through the last 30 years, remedial schools have become, in effect, a school system to educate the Roma. In Bulgaria almost 30% of Romani pupils attended such schools in 1992, and they made up nearly half of the student body in these institutions in Hungary and comprised over 50% in Czechoslovakia.[30] In fact, in the early 1990s Gypsy children were 20 times more likely to be in special schools than in regular schools in Czechoslovakia and were 28 times more likely to be sent to such schools than other pupils.[31]

In many cases Romani children who are not proficient in the language of the school system or have behavioral problems but show no evidence of mental retardation are routinely transferred to special schools (which are often called "Gypsy schools"). Such decisions are usually based on intelligence and psychological tests in the majority language which do not allow for cultural and behavioral differences. Many teachers complain that Gypsy children – particularly because they did not attend kindergarten – are not socialized to function in a structured environment, are aggressive and disobedient, and constitute a major disciplinary

[28] Tomova, *The Gypsies*, 58.
[29] *Struggling for Ethnic Identity: Czechoslovakia's Endangered Gypsies* (New York: Human Rights Watch, 1992), 42.
[30] Tomova, *The Gypsies*, 58; "Cigány nép-kép," *Hírmondó*, 10 April 1996; and Monika Horáková, "Open Letter to the British Helsinki Human Rights Group," European Roma Rights Center information service, 2 April 1999.
[31] *Romnews*, no. 24 (25 April 1996); and George Jahn, "Gypsies Remain Outcasts," Associated Press (Budapest), 27 March 1998.

problem.[32] In addition, teachers are often prejudiced against the Roma or, owing to bonuses tied to minimum graduation rates, are financially motivated to boot "problem children" out of their classes.

Many teachers do not appreciate the magnitude of obstacles faced by Gypsy pupils, and the number of those educators who know Romani or have training in Romani culture and traditions remains negligible. In addition, in some countries, like the Czech Republic, teaching is one of the least prestigious and worst paid jobs; and, as a result of the shortage of teachers, even a person with nothing more than a high school diploma can, in practice, teach high school classes.[33] In Bulgaria, teachers in "Gypsy schools" have usually lower qualifications than their colleagues in mainstream educational institutions. According to Savelina Danova of the Bulgarian Human Rights Project, many teachers who work in schools catering to the Roma are sent there as a form of punishment.[34] The near-universal negative biases of non-Roma pupils toward Gypsy children contribute to the increasing alienation of the latter from the education system. The curriculum in special schools is designed to impart the bare minimum of knowledge to students who can never catch up with their peers in regular schools. Therefore, official claims that those who do well in special education can transfer back to regular schools is exceedingly hollow. In practice, this hardly ever happens.

Marta Miklušáková, the Secretary of the Czech Republic's Council for Human Rights, contends that because of the rapidly decreasing birthrate of Czechs in recent years, schools have actually fought to keep children, and few have been transferred from a regular school to a special school in the last five years. Further, she notes, the most important problem is that many Gypsy parents, who themselves attended special schools, take their school-age children there prior to any testing or evaluation.[35] A

[32] See, for instance, Dimitrina Mihailova, "Socialization Problems of the Gypsy Child in the Bulgarian Society," in _The Ethnic Situation in Bulgaria_ (Sofia: Club '90 Publishers, 1993), 27–31; Mann, "Motivation," 2; "Roma in Hungary: Views of Several Specialists," Research Directorate, Immigration and Refugee Board, Canada (Ottawa, February 1999), 2–3. In a Bulgarian survey 79% of teachers regarded Romani pupils as "disobedient, authoritarian, irresponsible, very aggressive, and having no conscience." See Ivan P. Ivanov, "Institutionalized Racism and Its Victims," _Ethno Reporter_ (Sofia), no. 3 (September 1998), 33.

[33] Interviews with David Murphy of the Nova Škola Foundation (Prague, 23 August 1999); and Marta Miklušáková, Head of the Secretariat of the Czech government's Council for Human Rights (Prague, 26 August 1999).

[34] Interview with Savelina Danova, Executive Director of the Human Rights Project (Sofia, 11 November 1999).

[35] Interview with Miklušáková (Prague, 26 August 1999). See also Kathleen Knox, "Programs Aim to Improve Education for Romanies," _Prague Post_, 18–24 August 1993; and Tom Gross, "Improving Romany Life Helps All," _Prague Post_, 25–31 August 1993.

recent document by the Project on Ethnic Relations, a U.S.-based NGO, reported cases of Bulgarian Roma enrolling their children in schools for the mentally handicapped in order to obtain the free food distributed there.[36]

Vladimír Adam, Head of the Social and Cultural Section of the Czech city of Brno, suggests that special schools have some frequently overlooked positive features. First, Adam notes, teachers in special schools are better qualified and higher paid than in the rest of the school system. Second, remedial schools typically operate with smaller class sizes (15 as opposed to 30 or more in other schools) affording more attention to children. Finally, children have a good chance to graduate from special schools after which they can find manual jobs or further their training in apprentice schools, but those who drop out of regular schools end up with nothing.[37] Valid as these points may be, I agree with Michal Vašečka, a Slovak expert on the Roma, who insists that – at least in Slovakia – thousands of perfectly normal Gypsy children are transferred to special schools as a matter of course, and this phenomenon has dire future consequences not only for the Romani community but for society as a whole.[38]

Since 1989 the absenteeism and dropout rates of school-age Gypsies have skyrocketed across Eastern Europe. In the socialist era many municipalities employed social workers who grabbed Romani (and other truant) children on the streets or in their residences and took them to school.[39] Few towns can afford such expenditure any more, and there is little pressure on them to do so. In any case, most schools are not keen, to say the least, to boost their Romani enrollment. According to studies conducted in the early 1990s, 51.3% of Gypsy children under 14 attend school more or less regularly in Romania, 47.7% in Bulgaria, and 25% in Slovenia.[40] Even worse, a large number of Romani children give up on school entirely. In Slovakia, Gypsy children are 30 times more likely to drop out of school than others, while half of them in Bulgaria and one-third in Slovenia do not go to school at all.[41] A 1998 Romanian

---

[36] Seminar of the Roma Advisory Council, Project on Ethnic Relations (Sofia, 18–19 October 1996), 20.

[37] Interview with Adam (Brno, 2 September 1999).

[38] Interview with Vašečka (Bratislava, 10 September 1999).

[39] Interviews with Milena Hübschmannová, Professor of Romistics at Charles University (Prague, 17 June 1994), and Cătălin Zamfir, Professor of Social Work at the University of Bucharest and a member of the Council of Europe's Expert Group on the Roma (Bucharest, 1 June 1996).

[40] Rompres (Bucharest), 7 April 1993; Tomova, *The Gypsies*, 60; and Imre Szilágyi, "A romák Szlovéniában," *Regio*, 7:2 (1996): 90.

[41] Jahn, "Gypsies Remain Outcasts;" interview with Tomova (Sofia, 8 March 1994); Jasna Žugel, "Integracija romske skupnosti v slovensko družbo," in *Romi na Slovenskem* (Ljubljana: Institute of Ethnic Studies, 1991), 113–21.

study found that 18.3% of Romani children aged 7–16 had never been to school, and Gypsies made up 82.4% of those who never enrolled in this age group.[42] According to the Bulgarian National Statistical Institute, in 1989–1995 26,000 to 33,000 children had dropped out of school annually (most of them are thought to be Roma); in the mid-1990s there were 50,000 Gypsy children in Bulgarian schools in contrast to 120,000 a decade before, notwithstanding large increases in their number in the same period.[43] Official figures are often misleading, however, because ministries of education only keep statistics of those children who dropped out of school, ignoring the multitudes who never enroll.

Roma pupils who do attend school generally fare poorly. Their failure rates, particularly in the first grade, are far higher than those of other children. The ratio of those who complete primary school varies widely across the region. In Hungary, for instance, 80% of the Roma graduate from elementary school, approximately half do in Macedonia, and only around 5% in Croatia.[44] The majority of those Roma who finish primary school cannot do so in eight years: In Slovakia they are 18 times more likely to repeat grades than non-Gypsies, while in Hungary four-fifths of Romani pupils take more than eight years to finish elementary school.[45] Another major problem is that Gypsy children who complete basic schooling are unlikely to further their education. Many Romani parents discourage their children from higher education in favor of joining the work force. The few children who prevail will ordinarily learn a trade (about 90% in Hungary[46]) – usually specialties for which there is little demand in the labor market – rather than going to high school or *gimnázium*, which provides higher-quality education as well as preparation for college entrance exams. The proportion of Roma who enter high school is under 5% everywhere in the region (2.5% in the Czech Republic, 2.8% in Slovakia, and 3.3% in Hungary) in contrast to approxi-

[42] Interview with Cătălin Zamfir (Bucharest, 8 November 1999). See also Gábor Noszkai, "Romák délkelet-európában: Románia," *Amaro Drom*, March 1995, 12.

[43] Tomova, *The Gypsies*, 59; and the Project on Ethnic Relations' Sofia Seminar (18–19 October 1996), 17.

[44] "Cigány nép-kép;" Péter Molnár and Szilvia Szegő, "Cigányok Magyarországon," *Társadalmi Szemle*, 50:6 (1995): 73; interview with Bekir Arif, President of the Progressive Democratic Party of the Roma (Shuto Orizari, 13 March 1994); and Szilágyi, "A horvátországi romák helyzete," 75.

[45] Jahn, "Gypsies Remain Outcasts;" Imre Vajda, "Zsanav aba te ginav," *Amaro Drom*, August 1994, 30.

[46] "Cigány nép-kép." See also Sándor Vincze, "A cigány gyermekek nevelése, oktatása Jász-Nagykun-Szolnok megyében," *Magyar Közigazgatási Szemle*, no. 7 (June 1993): 419–26.

Table 5.4. Educational Attainments of Roma in Selected East
European Countries

Country	Illiterate	Primary	Middle/Trade	Secondary	Postsecondary
Bulgaria[a]					
Roma	8.5	36.7	46.2	7.8	0.9
Bulgarians	0.2	3.0	22.6	54.0	20.2
Turks	2.3	16.0	55.0	24.6	2.0
Czech				2.5	
Republic[b]					
Hungary[c]	9.4	78.3	10.4	1.5	0.2
Romania[d]	22.0	33.7	42.2	3.9	0.7
Slovakia[e]					
Roma				2.8	
non-Roma				38.0	

[a] *Minority Groups in Bulgaria in a Human Rights Context* (Sofia: Committee for the Defense of Minority Rights, 1994), 22.
[b] Gross, "Improving Romany Life," refers to number of those who enter secondary school.
[c] Havas et al., "The Statistics of Deprivation: The Roma in Hungary," 71. The data refer to Roma in all age groups in their survey. Primary school figure indicates those with 1–7 years of schooling (32.8%) *and* those who completed the 8-year school (45.5%).
[d] Zamfir et al., *Romania '89–'93*, 66.
[e] Anna Koptová and Miroslav Lacko, *Human and Civil Rights of Roma in Slovakia and the Czech Republic*, cited in *Transitions*, 4:4 (1997): 38.

mately 40% of non-Roma.[47] The number of Gypsies who successfully complete their high school studies is considerably smaller (less than 2% in Bulgaria, about 1% in the Czech Republic and Hungary[48]). Needless to say, the number of Roma in post-secondary education is infinitesimal, well below 1% everywhere in Eastern Europe.

Although illiteracy is rare among East Europeans, a substantial proportion of the Gypsies cannot read or write. In the early 1990s, 35.5% of Romani men and 18.7% of women were illiterate in Romania, the ratio of those who could read only with difficulty was 23.9% and 25.6%, respectively; at the same time, 25% of Bulgarian Gypsies were unable

[47] Gross, "Improving Romany;" Anna Koptová and Miroslav Lacko, *Human and Civil Rights of Roma in Slovakia and the Czech Republic* (1993) cited in *Transitions*, 4:4 (1997): 38; and "Cigány nép-kép."
[48] Interviews with Arif (Shuto Orizari, 13 March 1994); Tomova (Sofia, 8 March 1995); Laura Conway, *Report on the Status of Romani Education in the Czech Republic* (Prague: Citizens' Solidarity and Tolerance Movement – HOST, 1996), 37; and Péter Radó, *A kisebbségi oktatás fejlesztése* (Budapest: MKM, 1995), 25.

to read and/or write.[49] According to a 1993–4 study conducted by researchers at the Hungarian Academy of Sciences, Roma "with less than seven-grade education are nearly entirely illiterate: they cannot write beyond signing their names, can only read capital letters and those in a way that they are generally unable to comprehend the text."[50] In general, the higher the educational level, the higher the chances of finding employment and the higher the expected income. Mainly as a result of their inferior educational attainments, the Roma have been clobbered in postcommunist labor markets.

Employment

As a number of scholars ranging from Pierre Bourdieu to William Julius Wilson have pointed out, regular work is important not only because it allows one to sustain oneself and one's family but also because it "constitutes a framework for daily behavior and patterns of interaction because it imposes disciplines and regularities."[51] Wilson goes on to say that

in the absence of regular employment, a person lacks . . . a system of concrete expectations and goals. . . . In the absence of regular employment, life, including family life, becomes less coherent. Persistent unemployment and irregular employment hinder rational planning in daily life, the necessary conditions of adaptation to an industrial economy.[52]

After 1989, thousands of inefficient factories and enterprises were shut down or continued operations with a scaled down labor force in Eastern Europe. The resultant decline in the employment rates of the Roma has had a devastating impact not only on their living standards but also on their societal standing, prospects for the future, and their general outlook on life.

The vast majority of Gypsies in contemporary Eastern Europe do not possess any skills that would be valuable at the workplace that increasingly prizes specialized skills. For example, in Bulgaria 75% and

---

[49] Elena Zamfir, *The Situation of Child and Family in Romania* (Bucharest: Romanian Government 1995), 100–1; and Project on Ethnic Relations, *The Roma in Bulgaria: Collaborative Efforts between Local Authorities and Nongovernmental Organizations* (Princeton: Project on Ethnic Relations, 1998), 12.

[50] István Kemény, Gábor Havas, and Gábor Kertesi, *Beszámoló a magyarországi roma (cigány) népesség helyzetével foglalkozó 1993 októbere és 1994 februárja között végzett kutatásról* (Budapest: MTA Szociológiai Intézet, 1994), 8.

[51] William Julius Wilson, *When Work Disappears: The World of the New Urban Poor* (New York: Knopf, 1996), p. 73. See also Pierre Bourdieu, *Travail et travailleurs en Algérie* (Paris: Editions Mouton, 1965), and Joe R. Feagin, *Subordinating the Poor: Welfare and American Beliefs* (Englewood Cliffs, NJ: Prentice-Hall, 1975).

[52] Wilson, *When Work Disappears*, 73.

in Romania 74.2% (58% of men and 88.8% of women) of the Roma have no training in either modern or traditional trades.[53] In Macedonia, where the Romani unemployment rate in 1999 was 76.4%, 91.6% of the unemployed Gypsies were classified as unskilled.[54] A troubling legacy of the communist period – and, more generally, of industrialization – is that because the need for traditional Romani crafts had largely evaporated, most Roma have no knowledge of them even though they might provide the basis for learning a modern vocation. Therefore, most Gypsies are only equipped to do work that requires no skills, such as street cleaning, ditch digging, and the like. The number of Romani intellectuals and professionals remains small, probably under 1%, although it is worth noting that many Gypsies with advanced education are usually well-integrated or even assimilated and choose not to identify themselves as Roma.

Many Roma worked in regular jobs for two or three decades in the state-socialist era. Although there is considerable variation between official and unofficial unemployment figures, the overwhelming majority of the region's Gypsies lost their jobs soon after 1989, and the proportion of those without work among them is many times higher than that in the dominant population. For instance, the overall unemployment rate in the Czech Republic was 2.9% in 1996 but at least 30–50% among the Roma.[55] In economically more advanced countries, like the Czech Republic, Romani employment rates are much higher than in less industrialized ones such as Bulgaria and Slovakia (76% and 70%, respectively[56]). In urban areas where there are more job opportunities the Gypsies also tend to have higher employment rates. In 1992, for instance, 60% of the Gypsies in Hungary and 76% in Bulgaria were officially unemployed but "only" 10% and 62% in Budapest and Sofia, respectively.[57] Unemployment figures usually do not present an entirely accurate picture, however, because many Gypsies may register as unemployed while working on the side on an occasional or semiregular basis.[58] There is no doubt that in rural areas in backward regions and in places where

---

[53] Tomova, *The Gypsies*, 71; Cătălin Zamfir, Marius Augustin Pop, and Elena Zamfir, *Romania '89–'93: Dynamics of Welfare and Social Protection* (Bucharest: UNICEF-Romania, 1994), 64.

[54] *The Situation of the Roma in the Republic of Macedonia* (Skopje: Ministry of Foreign Affairs, 1999), 3.

[55] *Romnews*, no. 24, 25 April 1996.

[56] Tomova, *The Gypsies*, 71, and Gross, "Improving Romany Life."

[57] "Mégis, ki képviseli a romákat?" *Köztársaság*, 3 July 1992; Tomova, *The Gypsies*, 71; and "Plovdiv: Huts and Satellites," translation of an article in *Népszabadság*, 18 August 1997 in http://www.romapage.c3.hu/engrsk14.htm.

[58] Interviews with György Rostás-Farkas, Chairman of the Gypsy Science and Art Association (Budapest, 7 June 1994); Mirga (Kraków, 14 June 1994); and with Roma across the region throughout the 1990s.

the Gypsies constitute the majority population, Romani unemployment is nearly universal. As it happens, the proportion of the Gypsy population in traditionally underdeveloped regions with few job opportunities is far higher than in more industrialized areas. An additional factor contributing to the acute Romani unemployment in rural areas is that after 1989 when many agricultural cooperatives were dissolved, former landowners and members of the cooperatives acquired the land from compensation and land-redistribution schemes which left most Gypsies without employment or land to cultivate. Many Roma who lost their livelihood and already precarious standing in rural society gravitated toward the cities.

Sociologists, labor economists, and most Gypsy leaders agree that the vast majority of Roma became unemployed because they cannot compete in the labor market. A 1999 study analyzing the employment structure of 240 Hungarian companies concluded that "unskilled labor is not needed."[59] Still, Roma often hold the state responsible for their joblessness because they became used to the universal employment of the past. A Bulgarian survey revealed that 65.7% of the Roma blamed "bad national government," 36.6% blamed ethnic discrimination, and only 15.8% blamed their own low level of education and lack of qualifications when asked why they were unemployed.[60] Undoubtedly after years of unemployment many Roma lost their motivation to work and have become resigned to their situation. In the Hungarian city of Ózd, for instance, a spring 1999 program offered employment to 335 Roma but only 91 participated because the rest acquired medical certificates of questionable origin attesting to their inability to work.[61] Some Gypsies actually quit their jobs after the collapse of communism when having one was no longer compulsory.[62]

At impromptu labor markets in East European cities, one rarely encounters Roma perhaps owing to their expectation that they would not be able to get work due to discrimination.[63] There is no doubt that many Gypsies are affected by the persistent biases of the dominant group. Ethnic prejudices are factored into hiring and firing practices, and discrimination is often difficult to prove.[64] In some instances, employment

---

[59] See "Szakképzetlen munkaerőnem kell," *Népszabadság*, 24 June 1999.

[60] Tomova, *The Gypsies*, 73.

[61] "Ózdon ketyeg az etnikai bomba," *Napi Magyarország*, 18 September 1999. See also Pável Bratinka, *Report on the Situation of the Romani Community in the Czech Republic* (Prague, 1997, mimeo), 24.

[62] Jurová, "Cigányok-romák Szlovákiában," 54.

[63] See, for instance, András Bíró's statement in "Roma in Hungary: Views of Several Specialists," 14–15.

[64] Gábor Kertesi, "Cigányok a munkaerőpiacon," *Közgazdasági Szemle*, 41:11 (1994): 1018–19.

agency workers mark the Roma's files with asterisks or the letter "C" (for *cikáň* or *cigány*) to alert their clients who are unlikely to hire Gypsies because of their reputation for low work morale and lax discipline. There are reported cases of employment agencies promising jobs to Roma based on telephone interviews and rescinding the offers when they show up in person to do the paperwork.[65] Those entrepreneurs who are satisfied with the Roma's performance complain that given their lack of education they can only perform the simplest tasks.[66]

Generally speaking, Romani women have been somewhat less affected by changes in the labor market because prior to 1989 more of them were not officially employed than men. Furthermore, the types of income-generating activities that Gypsy women are often involved in – begging, fortune telling, prostitution – do not show up in statistics. In Macedonia, where hiring Romani women for house cleaning and baby-sitting has been a long-standing custom, many managed to keep their jobs. Thousands of Macedonian Roma had spent years as guest workers in Western Europe where some saved enough to start up businesses upon their return.

The entry into the business world tends to be far more difficult for Roma than for non-Roma because the former usually start from an impoverished background and many have a mentality that they are destined to fail; if they do not succeed at first, most are liable to give up.[67] A small number of East European Gypsies were able to begin commercial activities by taking advantage of new opportunities and capitalizing on legal loopholes during the transition period and establish proper businesses afterwards. From the Balkan states many Roma – often registered as unemployed[68] – travelled regularly to Turkey to purchase goods for resale in the open-air markets of the region. Many Romani entrepreneurs are involved in the used car trade, buying, reconditioning, and reselling automobiles. Reportedly a large number of Bulgarian, Polish, and Romanian Roma used the few weeks in which the East German mark was freely convertible to (West) German marks in the newly united Germany quite profitably.[69] In time, police attention to semilegal and illegal commercial activities increased, resulting in the

---

[65] *Report on Human Rights in the ČR in 1998* (Prague: Council on Human Rights, 1999), 16.

[66] Interviews with Bulgarian businessmen (Dimitrovgrad, 4 March 1995).

[67] Interviews with Roma throughout Eastern Europe.

[68] Interviews with Arif (Skopje, 13 March 1994), Tomova (Sofia, 8 March 1995), and Elena Zamfir (Bucharest, 13 March 1995).

[69] Vera Mutafchieva, "The Turk, the Jew, and the Gypsy," in Antonina Zhelyazkova, ed. *Relations of Compatibility and Incompatibility between Christians and Muslims in Bulgaria* (Sofia: International Centre for Minority Studies and Intercultural Relations, 1995), 60.

ebbing fortunes of many a Romani businessman. In the mid-1990s, peddling and street vending was not only outlawed but regulations began to be strictly enforced in many cities and towns across the region, thereby jeopardizing the livelihood of thousands of Gypsies.[70]

PART II: SOCIAL ILLS: HEALTH PROBLEMS, POVERTY, CRIME

Health and Reproduction

"The horrifying conditions of the Roma's health was one of the most traumatic experiences for the team during this survey" concluded sociologist Ilona Tomova in 1994, after conducting in-depth interviews with 1,844 Roma in Bulgaria.[71] The fact that abortion is the number one contraceptive method among the Gypsies – due to cost (it is cheaper than other methods) and ignorance – and the unhygienic lifestyle contribute to the mass occurrence of gynecological illnesses including various types of cancers. Rates of alcoholism and smoking are far higher among Roma than among non-Roma. It is especially troubling that 26% of Tomova's respondents said that if someone in their family becomes ill, they do not seek medical care.[72] Her findings are broadly applicable to most of Eastern Europe. A large proportion of the Roma live in a stunningly unhygienic environment, and their diet lacks nutritional value and occasionally includes long-dead carcasses causing malnutrition, anemia, dystrophy, and other ailments.[73] Lack of sanitation, identity papers, and health records make the job of physicians treating them extremely difficult. The incidence of physical handicap and mental retardation are several times more common among the Gypsies than among the general population. Rates of infant mortality show a similar pattern. In Romania, for instance, it is 23.4 for non-Roma per 1,000 births as opposed to 63 for Roma; in Slovenia the figure for Gypsies is seven times, in Hungary nearly five times higher than for others.[74] Many children are not vaccinated because of ignorance or carelessness. As a result of these and related problems the life expectancy of Roma is much lower than of the general population: in Hungary it is a decade shorter,

---

[70] Interview with Trajko Petrovski of the Institute of Folklore, Skopje (Arlington, Texas, 27 March 1998).

[71] Tomova, *The Gypsies*, 55.

[72] Ibid., 47–57.

[73] Interview with Orsós; "Poor Diet, Lack of Education Affect Roma Children," Associated Press (Bucharest), 14 June 1998; and Gábor Matúz and Ferenc Sinkovics, "Te is! Te is! Neked is!," *Demokrata*, 2:37 (1998): 21.

[74] Zamfir, *The Situation of Child and Family in Romania*, 53, 102; Szilágyi, "A romák Szlovéniában," 89; and Judith Ingram, "Hungary's Gypsy Women: Scapegoats in a New Democracy," *Ms. Magazine*, September–October 1991, 19.

in Bulgaria they are 4.4 times less likely to reach age 60 than their fellow citizens.[75]

"Development is the best contraceptive," the Indian diplomat Karan Singh is reported to have said.[76] The Gypsies' appalling socioeconomic conditions dependably predict their high birth rates. The Roma traditionally marry much sooner than others and have more children. In Bulgaria Gypsy girls often get married at 13, and in Romania many Romani families arrange marriages for their children as young as 12.[77] The birthrate of non-Gypsy women in Romania is 1.79 as opposed to 4.35 for their Gypsy counterparts.[78] According to a recent report, in the Hungarian town of Hajdúhadház more children are born in the 2,600-strong Romani community than in the ethnic Hungarian population of over 10,000.[79] In a highly publicized case a Romani girl of 11 gave birth to a child fathered by her underage boyfriend in eastern Hungary in 1998; subsequent inquiries showed that Gypsies are disproportionately represented in such situations.[80] In Lom, a Bulgarian city on the Danube with a large Romani community, a Gypsy woman of 38 gave birth to her 22nd child in March 1998, having had one a year since the age of 15. She and her spouse have no jobs, and they live with 17 of their offspring (the other five are in orphanages) in a house with no electricity or running water.[81] Having large families is a logical decision for many Gypsies because with every additional child the family income increases as a result of per-child subsidies. In many cases the Roma's sole aim of having additional children is to receive child benefits from the state.[82] In some states, like the Czech Republic, a couple with several children actually receive more money in welfare and child-benefit payments than they would from low-paying jobs.[83]

[75] "Can Hungary Hug Its Gypsies?" *The Economist*, 20 March 1999, 57; and Tomova, *The Gypsies*, 30.

[76] Cited in Gregg Easterbrook, "Forgotten Benefactor of Humanity," *The Atlantic Monthly*, 279:1 (1997): 77.

[77] Tomova, *The Gypsies*, 38; Barbara Demick, "Anti-Gypsy Pogroms Rampant in Romania," *The Philadelphia Inquirer*, 29 November 1993; and interview with film editor Marius Tabacu (Cluj, 25 October 1999).

[78] Zamfir et al., *Romania '89–'93*, 68.

[79] Matúz and Sinkovics, "Te is! Te is! Neked is!," 20.

[80] József Udvardy, "Elhaltan és boldogan?" *Heti Világgazdaság*, 28 August 1999, 91–3.

[81] "Bulgarian Gypsies Threaten 'Human Torch' Protest," AFP (Sofia), 30 June 1998.

[82] Interviews with Marushiakova and Vesselin Popov (Sofia, 13 November 1999); and Michal Vašečka, "The Romanies in Slovakia," in Luboš Vagač, ed., *National Human Development Report for Slovakia 1998* (Bratislava: United Nations Development Program, 1998), 64.

[83] See interview with Mikluśáková (Prague, 26 August 1999); and Bratinka, *Report on the Situation of the Romani Community*.

The situation of a large proportion of East European Gypsy children has considerably deteriorated since 1989 partly as a result of cutbacks in social services. In the early 1990s thousands of East European children, many of them Roma, were adopted by foreign citizens.[84] Thousands of Gypsy children who are abandoned, for whom their families are unable or unwilling to care and were not fortunate enough to be adopted, live in woefully underfunded state homes that provide minimal supervision. Their numbers are growing: In Romania 80,000 children lived in orphanages and other state-run institutions in 1992, but this number increased by 24,000 three years later.[85] Although conditions in them seem to have improved, the problem is far from being "practically solved" as Prime Minister Radu Vasile contended in 1999.[86] According to estimates, the proportion of Romani residents in orphanages is 60% in the Czech Republic, 80% in Romania, and 90% in Hungary.[87] The thousands of Gypsy children living basically permanently on the street and near railway stations, such as Sofia's Central Terminal, is one of the most troubling sights I encountered year after year in my field research across Eastern Europe.

Poverty

After the relative stability of the state-socialist period many Roma have once again had to adapt to a marginal existence of the most severe kind since 1989. Wages earned for employment in the 1980s have been replaced by unemployment benefits, welfare payments, and social aid – especially per-child subsidies – as the chief source of income for the majority of the region's Roma (50–60% in Bulgaria, 70% in Macedonia, and 74–6% in Slovenia, for instance).[88] The vast majority (in 1991

---

[84] "Update on Romanian Adoptions," *The Romani–Jewish Alliance Newsletter*, April 1992, 2; and "Internet Adoption Scandal in Hungary," Open Media Research Institute Daily Digest, Part II (henceforth: OMRIDD II), no. 116 (14 June 1996).

[85] "Romania Acting to Keep Families Together," *New York Times*, 15 December 1996.

[86] RFE II, 3:203 (18 October 1999); and interview with Dianne C. Barber and Amy Cooley, Baptist missionaries who have toured Romanian orphanages repeatedly in the 1990s (Cluj, 25 October 1999).

[87] Interview with Jarka Balážová, editor of the Romani radio program in Prague (Prague, 14 August 1996); presentation by Simona Farcaş at the Gypsy Lore Society Meeting (Arlington, Texas, 27 March 1998); and Nándor Fehérvári, "A szegénységgel kellett mindig szembenéznem," *Új Magyarország*, 11 April 1996.

[88] Gábor Czene, "Foglyai egy országrésznek," *Népszabadság*, 1 December 1998; *The Roma in Bulgaria: Collaborative Efforts*, 8; interview with Neždet Mustafa, Mayor of Shuto Orizari (Shuto Orizari, 24 November 1999); Szilágyi, "A romák Szlovéniában," 88; and Peter Winkler, "Roma Ethnic Group in Slovenia," in Miran Komac, ed., *Protection of Ethnic Communities in the Republic of Slovenia* (Ljubljana: Institute for Ethnic Studies, 1999), 72.

nearly 80% in Hungary[89]) live under the official assessed poverty line. In Romania, sociologists claim that nearly 63% of the Roma (versus 16% of the total population) live below the minimum subsistence level, which is lower than the "poverty line," and over 75% live under the "social minimum" (versus 33.3% of others).[90] More than half of the Gypsy households have no steady incomes in Hungary and Romania, while 7% and 42.6%, respectively, have no income from official sources at all.[91] A substantial number of Roma are not registered as unemployed because of ignorance or shame and, therefore, do not receive benefits. Theft, prostitution, begging, and other illegal activities are swiftly becoming the only source of livelihood for a growing number of East European Romani families.[92] Experts agree that tens of thousands of Gypsies go hungry across the region.[93]

Especially in rural areas many Roma live in places with no drinking water, sewage system, garbage removal, or accessible medical facilities. More often than not, rural Gypsy dwellings are built without permit. In Stolipinovo, a settlement near Plovdiv with a large Romani population, over 90% of the Gypsies' houses are built illegally on municipal land, but residents refuse to leave their dwellings for want of another place to go.[94] Unlike members of the majority population, Roma are rarely forced to demolish their unauthorized buildings. One exception is Albania, where Gypsies who used to live in huts and tents on the outskirts of cities like Tirana and Gjirokastër were ordered to leave because prenationalization owners lay claim to the land.[95] State-subsidized public housing construction programs for the disadvantaged were terminated for fiscal and political reasons after the fall of communism in most East European countries. In any event, just as in the socialist era, Roma frequently refuse to move to better-quality dwellings (provided by local officials intent on demolishing remaining Gypsy ghettos) away from the slums, preferring to maintain their compact communities.[96]

---

[89] Carol J. Williams, "Eastern Europe Upheaval Means Even Bleaker Times for Gypsies," *Los Angeles Times*, 20 December 1991.

[90] Zamfir et al., *Romania '89–'93*, 65.

[91] "Cigány nép-kép;" and Zamfir et al., *Romania '89–'93*, 13.

[92] Tomova, "Változások és gondok," 61.

[93] Interviews with Orsós (Budapest, 25 July 1996), Arif (Shuto Orizari, 13 March 1994), Vašečka (Bratislava, 15 August 1996), Hübschmannová (Prague, 12 June 1995), and Nicoleta Bițu of Romani CRISS (Bucharest, 10 March 1995).

[94] *The Roma in Bulgaria*, 22–3.

[95] Jetske Mijs, " 'A Child Is Not Born with Teeth': Roma in Albania Must Be Patient," *o Drom*, September 1994, 20.

[96] There are many documented cases. See, for instance, interviews with Spasov (Skopje, 8 March 1994) and Ilija Atseski, Professor of Urban Sociology at the Sts. Cyril and Method University (Skopje, 14 March 1994); "Roma in the Czech Republic: Selected

Because mail delivery is made difficult by the frequent absence of names on mail boxes on the Roma's residences, postal workers in some areas – notably in northern Bohemia – have denied service to them.[97] Given that few Gypsies have telephones, the lack of mail delivery impedes their chances of obtaining employment. Across the region, water and electricity are often shut off in the Roma's homes because they are unable or unwilling to pay for services. Thousands of Roma try to eke out a living working in garbage dumps, which also serve as their place of residence.[98] These facilities often contain dangerous materials like mercury and arsenic unbeknownst to most Gypsies. In 1990, a large group of Romani refugees fleeing Albanian and Serbian persecution in Kosovo were assigned shelter at one of Belgrade's sewage-filled garbage depot where, according to Gypsy activist Rajko Djurić, conditions were "worse than in a concentration camp."[99] In fact, Roma use the "concentration camp" metaphor to describe their housing situation with disturbing frequency.[100]

Crime

Given the massive drop in Romani educational attainments, large increases in unemployment and poverty, and already higher-than-average levels of Gypsy criminality, it is hardly surprising that Romani crime rates escalated in Eastern Europe in the 1990s. The rising criminal statistics of the region are explained not just by Gypsy crime. There are other factors that led to a general crisis of public safety affecting the entire population: increasing poverty and social decay, the flagging social control of the post-communist period, and the declining effectiveness of law enforcement. According to some sociologists and Gypsy leaders, the bulk of Romani criminals come from the most disadvantaged 30–5% of the Romani population; their criminality, in turn, is largely responsible for the way ordinary people view the entire Romani community.[101] Many activists admit that Gypsy crimes have multiplied and the attri-

---

Issues," Research Directorate, Immigration and Refugee Board, Canada (Ottawa, December 1997), 14–15; and "Belgian Experts Criticise Conditions of Slovak Romanies," CTK (Czech News Agency) dispatch (Bratislava), 24 February 1999.

[97] "Czech Post Denies Mail Service to Romani Housing Estate," OMRI DD II, no. 109 (5 June 1996).

[98] Interview with Thomas Keil, Professor of Sociology at the University of Louisville (Bucharest, 2 June 1996); and Boris Kalnoky, "Und täglich wartet Jussif auf ein Wunder," *Die Welt*, 19 June 1993.

[99] "Im Schlachthof für menschliche Seelen," *Frankfurter Rundschau*, 23 November 1990.

[100] See, for instance, Ulrich Glauber, "Sie wollen normale Bürger sein," *Frankfurter Rundschau*, 13 October 1993.

[101] "Kettőn áll a vásár," *Demokrata*, 1:7 (1997): 10.

butes of their criminality have changed for the worse; that is, it has become increasingly violent.[102]

As I noted before, all statistics pertaining to the Roma are suspect because they are often distorted by exaggeration, understatement, and selective interpretation. One must work with the evidence at hand, however, taking care to use figures that are reliable in one's assessment. It should be remembered that statistics usually refer to the number of apprehended offenders rather than to all crimes committed. It is quite likely that – owing to their high visibility, the fact that many have criminal records and thus are known to police, and because they seem to be less skillful in evading detection – proportionately more Gypsy perpetrators are caught than others. Having said all this, it is abundantly clear that the rise of criminality among the Roma has been far higher than among the general population. One-third of the criminals apprehended in Bulgaria in 1992 were Roma, who were said to be responsible for 37% of all solved crimes in the country in 1994.[103] According to some estimates, over 50% of adult Gypsies may have a criminal record in the Czech Republic and in some towns they are responsible for three of every four crimes.[104] In Budapest Roma commit 80% of all burglaries and 95% of pocket pickings.[105]

Rates of theft and robbery are particularly high among the Roma, which some experts explain with the Gypsies' traditionally liberal views pertaining to others' property. In Romani culture

Theft as punishment is an accepted form of getting your own back and teaching a lesson; putting your hand on some of the property of the person you quarreled with offers you some satisfaction. That type of theft should not be confused with the increasingly frequent thieving for subsistence.[106]

In a Bulgarian nationwide survey, 18% of the Roma agreed that "since the state does not take care of us, we have to steal" and 33% said that

---

[102] Gypsy activist Emil Ščuka admits that Romani crime rate was "as much as three times higher" among the Gypsy population than among non-Gypsies. See "Gypsies Concerned over Rising Racist Tensions," Associated Press (Prague), 1 March 1991. Adam Bartosz writes that "there is a growing number of audacious and violent assaults in public places and acts of fraud that usually escape detection by the police." Bartosz, "Social and Political Status of the Roma in Poland," *Roma*, no. 40 (January 1994): 20.

[103] Hugh Poulton, "The Rest of the Balkans," in Hugh Miall, ed., *Minority Rights in Europe: Prospects for a Transnational Regime* (New York: Council of Foreign Relations Press, 1994), 84; and Tomova, *The Gypsies*, 83.

[104] Tom Gross, "Gypsies Fall Victim to Czech Racism," *The Sunday Telegraph*, 24 October 1993; and Rainer Koch, "CSFR-Roma fürchten Trennungsfolgen," *Der Standard*, 12 August 1992.

[105] "The Next Great Trek of the Gypsies," *World Press Review*, November 1990, 43.

[106] Péter Szuhay, "Arson on Gypsy Row," *The Hungarian Quarterly*, 36:138 (1995): 90.

"stealing is pardonable sin if there is no other way to feed our children."[107] What some Romani leaders and activists, like Jan Rušenko and Marcel Courtiade, are worried about is that theft by Gypsies from Gypsies is on the rise despite the stigma attached to it in their culture emblematized by the saying "Why would you steal from another Rom – didn't God create enough *gadje*?"[108] Police claim that since 1989 organized gangs of Gypsy pickpockets have been responsible for the dramatic increases in street theft.[109]

In rural communities the situation is worse. Many reports describe how Roma terrorize entire villages whose residents and leaders are rendered impotent by the lack of effective policing and their fear of retribution.[110] After numerous violent robberies committed by the Gypsies the helpless mayor of the east Slovakian town of Jarovnice could do no better than to advise non-Gypsies to stay off the streets after dark.[111] In several cases Roma – who have, in any event, little to lose – have attacked local policemen.[112] Even in some regions of Bulgaria, where they were relatively well-integrated until 1989, any crime committed by the Roma now leads to their complete isolation. Well-known Gypsies, particularly traditional leaders, are frequently accused and/or convicted of crimes and thereby contribute to popular prejudices and send the message to their brethren that there is nothing wrong with criminal acts.[113]

---

[107] "Plovdiv: Huts and Satellites."
[108] Gypsy activist Marcel Courtiade quoted in Linnet Myers, "Circling the Wagons," *Chicago Tribune*, 28 December 1992.
[109] See, for instance, OMRI DD II, no. 37 (21 February 1996); and Yantra Radilova, "Christian or Muslim: They're of an Ilk," *Demokratsiya '91* (Sofia), 7 November 1991.
[110] See a series of articles by Gábor Matúz: "Fegyverbe!? (1)" *Pesti Hírlap*, 26 January 1994 and "Fegyverbe!? (2)" *Pesti Hírlap*, 27 January, 1994; "A polgármesternö és bandája," *Pesti Hírlap*, 17 February 1994; "Én azt akarom, hogy itt csend, nyugalom, és béke legyen," *Pesti Hírlap*, 18 February 1994; "Lovas rendört, munkát, kenyeret," *Pesti Hírlap*, 23 February 1994; as well as Henry Kamm, "Gypsies and the Czechs," *New York Times*, 8 December 1993; "Vastagh Pál polgármesterek közt," MTI (Orosháza), 26 August 1994; "Pacea arabo-ţiganeasca," *Adevărul*, 23 May 1995; "Mafia ţiganeasca," *Libertatea*, 24 May 1995; and "Gádoros, a szabad préda," *Demokrata*, 1:7 (1997): 34–6.
[111] Susan Greenberg, "The Post-Communist Curse on Slovakia's Gypsies," *The Guardian*, 7 October 1993.
[112] "Háromszor lött a rendör," *Magyar Nemzet*, 16 August 1996; "A bosszú még várat magára," *Mai nap*, 18 August 1996, 20–1; "Man Accused of Provoking Attack on Policemen Arrested," CTK (Novy Jičin/Ostrava) 17 February 1998; "Three Romanies Face Proceedings due to attack on policemen," CTK (Prague), 28 February 1998; and "Policeman on Life Support after Fight with Gypsies in Disco," AP (Bucharest), 13 November 2000.
[113] See, for instance, "Und täglich wartet Jussif auf ein Wunder," *Die Welt*, 19 June 1993; Sharon Fisher, "Romanies in Slovakia," *RFE/RL Research Report*, 2:42 (1993): 56;

The available data strongly suggest that, notwithstanding the assertions of activists, violent crimes among the Roma have also risen precipitously. In Bulgaria, 88% of group rapes in 1994 were committed by Roma and, according to prosecution service statistics, eight out of nine murders and burglaries and 15 out of 16 robberies.[114] In Hungary, researchers found that more than 50% of the Gypsies' felonies are violent.[115] According to one 1992 report, Bulgarian Gypsy pimps ran a prostitution ring of ethnic Bulgarian girls aged 12 to 14 who were abducted, gang raped, and psychologically crushed before they were forced into streetwalking.[116] In August 1994 two Romani youths raped, beat, and impaled a cleaning woman through her genitals and then left her for dead in Hungary.[117] Particularly grisly crimes, such as these, exacerbate interethnic tensions.

The phenomenon of Romani crime ought to be viewed in its proper context. The majority of Gypsies have no regular source of earned income, and they are impoverished and are ostracized by the majority population. Quite simply, many Roma have nothing to lose especially because incarceration in many cases signifies an improvement in their situation. Considering that their conditions include all the major socioeconomic catalysts of criminal behavior in an acute form, one may wonder why Romani crime rates are not higher.

PART III: SOCIAL STRATIFICATION AND INTERETHNIC RELATIONS

Social Developments in the Romani Community

The emerging market economies generated growing gaps between rich and poor in East European societies at large and within Romani communities. A few hundred Roma have become extremely wealthy and a few thousand have become quite affluent, although it bears underscoring that the proportion of well-to-do Gypsies is very small, much smaller than the ratio of prosperous people in other ethnic groups. Distinguishing between Romani upper, middle, and lower classes is unwise not because the differentiation in their socioeconomic situation is not real

---

"Gypsy 'Emperor' Sought in Alleged Romanian Copper Theft," AP (Bucharest), 23 May 1994; and "Gypsy 'Emperor' Arrested in Romania," NCA (Bucharest), 27 May 1994.

[114] Tsvetelina Parvanova, "Rights Aides, Police in Rift on Bulgarian Gypsies," Reuter (Sofia), 12 June 1994; and "Bulgarian Gypsies Threaten 'Human Torch' Protest," Agence France-Presse (Sofia), 30 May 1998.

[115] "Cigánybűnözés?" *Köztársaság*, no. 13 (10 July 1992), 40.

[116] Stojan Grebenarov, "Gypsy-Bashing," *The Insider* (Sofia), no. 1 (1992): 23.

[117] "Karóba húztak egy asszonyt," *Új Magyarország*, 11 August 1994.

but owing to the term "social class," which denotes a large number of people. The small number of prosperous Roma does not justify using the class category. It is more appropriate to think of Gypsy society in terms of a thin layer of wealthy people, usually businessmen and entertainers; a somewhat broader stratum of comfortably off but by no means rich professionals, skilled workers, entertainers, activists, and small business owners; and a large class (in this case the terminology is certainly warranted) of poor, unemployed or underemployed people living for the most part on state assistance.

It should be noted that a few experts, like Elena Marushiakova and Vesselin Popov, insist that the majority of Gypsies, especially in the Balkans, are no worse off than surrounding populations.[118] They suggest that what visitors to Romani settlements see largely depends on the guides who will show whatever is in their interest to present (extremely poor Gypsies to NGOs, rich ones to visitors who despise the Roma's indolence, and so on). These two scholars also note that because many well-to-do Roma have moved out of settlements, the traditional Gypsy colony does not give a fair impression of the overall situation. Nonetheless, most researchers agree that the vast majority of East European Gypsies are considerably poorer than dominant groups and I share this view.

Some of the most conspicuously rich Roma are found in the ranks of traditional leaders. Perhaps the most famous among them was Ion Cioabă, an illiterate Kalderash Romani leader of considerable business acumen from Sibiu, Romania, who already prospered under the state-socialist regime. Cioabă, who died in 1997, presided over the annual fall gathering of the Kalderash where "hundreds of Mercedes and BMWs" testified to the wealth of the participants.[119] He became a "king" after the "coronation ceremony" he arranged in 1992, but his royal status was soon challenged by none other than his cousin, Iulian Radulescu, living across the street from him. Not to be outdone, in 1993 Radulescu became "First Emperor of all Gypsies" after a similarly farcical service complete with a 590-gram 24-carat gold crown set with rubies and diamonds.[120] In Katunica, Bulgaria lives the extended family of Kyril

---

[118] Interview with Marushiakova and Popov (Sofia, 13 November 1999).

[119] Isabel Fonseca, *Bury Me Standing: The Gypsies and Their Journey* (New York: Knopf, 1995), 286–7. See also "Alle hassen die Zigeuner," *Der Spiegel*, no. 36 (3 September 1990), 45; and Chris Stephen, "Gypsy Emperor in Quest to Find Roots," *The Guardian*, 22 February 1993. According to Ian Hancock, Cioabă was an engineer. . . . See Hancock, "The East European Roots of Romani Nationalism," in David Crowe and John Kolsti, eds., *The Gypsies of Eastern Europe* (Armonk, NY: M. E. Sharpe, 1991), 147.

[120] See Stefan Stoian's interview with Radulescu in *Baricada* (Bucharest), 16 February 1993, 8–9; Lucy Hooker, "Gypsy Emperor Gets Crown but Loses Respect,"

Rashkov, a.k.a. "Tsar Kyril," which shares several traits with Cioabă's clan: ostentatious wealth, self-conferred "royal" title, and familiarity with the penal system.[121] Rich Gypsies frequently put their wealth on display, which has occasionally backfired given the jealousy, envy, and prejudices of non-Roma – and, according to some reports, other Roma – who immediately assume that criminal activities are the sole source of the Gypsies' gains.

One of the Roma's traditional talents lies in commercial activities, and many have taken advantage of the new possibilities created by the post-communist transition. A considerable number of the newly wealthy Roma acquired their riches owing to their business sense and because, more than others, they could see the many opportunities on the growing "grey" or black markets produced by ambiguities in the legal system.[122] There are plenty of examples of more conventional and large-scale Romani business ventures around the region. In downtown Skopje a Gypsy entrepreneur built a modern shopping center; one of his Hungarian peers employs 180 Roma through his thriving business that extracts precious metals from rock debris near Ózd, a defunct former industrial and mining center.[123] The mother of Gheorghe Raducanu, the sole Romani member of the Romanian parliament in 1992–6, proudly told reporters during the 1996 electoral campaign that her son was the owner of five houses and five shops and would be well taken care of even if he would not be reelected (he was not).[124] In Albania, Macedonia, and Romania many Gypsies, along with their co-nationals, fell victim to the pyramid funds that bilked thousands of small-time investors of their savings in the early 1990s.[125] This was a particularly heavy blow to the Romani community because these schemes robbed a large proportion of the Gypsies with investment capital of the opportunity to explore entrepreneurial avenues. A positive recent development has been the increasing concern of a few affluent Roma with higher education. For example, some well-to-do Romani families have reportedly

The Guardian, 9 August 1993; "Romania's 'Gypsy Emperor' Crowned and Wed," Rompress (Bucharest), 12 August 1993; Roxana Dascalu, "'Emperor' Iulian Holds Court in Romania," Reuter (Sibiu), 7 June 1994; and John Reed, "Two Men Would Be King of the Gypsies, Counting an Emperor," *Wall Street Journal*, 12 December 1997.

121 See, for instance, "Und täglich wartet Jussif"; and interview with Krassimir Kanev of the Bulgarian Helsinki Watch Group (Sofia, March 1995).

122 See, for instance, Dan Ionescu, "Violence against Gypsies Escalates," *Report on Eastern Europe*, 2:25 (1991): 25; Hooker, "Gypsy Emperor"; Cornel Radu Constantinescu, "Ţigani impanzesc Romania cu castele-cort supraetajate," *Adevărul*, 12 May 1995.

123 Interview with Petrovski (Arlington, TX, 27 March 1998); and György Kerényi, "'Abból, amit a magyar ember kidob'," *Magyar Narancs*, 18 August 1994, 12–13.

124 See the interview in *Adevărul*, 7 October 1996.

125 See, for instance, Karin Popescu, "Romanian Gypsies out to Lynch Pyramid Fund Boss," Reuter (Bucharest), 16 February 1994.

sent their children to foreign universities from the southern Hungarian city of Szeged.[126]

According to some experts, most Gypsies prefer to maintain relative equality in the Romani community; if one gets rich, he is obligated to help the others. These specialists suggest that the growing societal intolerance of the Roma in postcommunist Eastern Europe strengthens their social cohesion regardless of the socioeconomic disparities within it.[127] This view is at variance with the little unity or harmony found in the Romani community by others who contend that the Gypsy population is vertically rather than horizontally differentiated, it is becoming increasingly hierarchical, and groups that do better tend distance themselves from those they leave behind.[128] In fact, most Gypsies who live in town not only evidence little solidarity with Roma in squatter settlements but might even attempt to chase them off prized garbage dumps just as one group of Gypsies in Bulgaria drove the other out of their village in order to get their land.[129] Roma from Bratislava did not even visit the ethnic festival held in their hometown in 1996 because it featured the industrious and well-to-do Gypsy blacksmiths of Dunajska Lužna "who would not even talk to black marketeers and beggars like we are."[130]

András Bíró, winner of the alternative Nobel prize of Stockholm's Right Livelihood Award Foundation for his work for the Roma, lamented the lack of solidarity between wealthy and poor Gypsies recounting the following incident:

A well-to-do Gypsy came to me once, telling me that he wanted to put on a charity concert for the benefit of Ethiopian children. I looked him straight in the eye, and asked why he did not put it on for Gypsy children in Mátészalka [a Hungarian town with a large and impoverished Romani community]. In his eyes it was more respectable to help the Ethiopians than his own people. This is a delicate problem, but unfortunately it's a real one.[131]

---

[126] Miklós Halász, "Felszámolták a putri rendszert," *Magyar Nemzet*, 13 August 1993.

[127] Interview with sociologist János Ladányi, in "Budapesten elkezdődött a gettósodás," *Köztársaság*, no. 13 (3 July 1992): 18.

[128] See, for instance, Tamás Bihari, "Cigány bánat, magyar bánat," *Világ*, 24 April 1991; interview with Wolfart (Budapest, 9 June 1994); and *Romove v Česke republice* (Prague: Socioklub, 1999), 540–1.

[129] Interview with Keil (Bucharest, 2 June 1996); and Marushiakova and Popov, *Gypsies (Roma) in Bulgaria*, 69.

[130] Interviews with Roma and with PER's Samuel Abraham (Bratislava, Dunajska Lužna, and Košice, August 1996). On this issue pertaining to the Roma in Slovenia, see Szilágyi, "A romák Szlovéniában," 91.

[131] Gábor Kereszty and György Simó. "Helping Self-Help: Interview with András Bíró," *The Hungarian Quarterly*, 36:140 (1995): 75.

Evidence suggests that in addition to traditional cleavages the Romani population is increasingly divided not only by the differences in their economic conditions but also by their residency status and view of the majority population. Gypsies often complain about the annoying lifestyles of other Roma who invoke or kindle their neighbors' prejudices directed against the entire Romani community.[132]

Gypsy migration splits the Romani population further yet. For instance, Poland's established, middle-class Roma may sympathize with the plight of Gypsy refugees from the Balkans but consider them an obstacle toward their own social integration. A Polish Gypsy leader noted that "when the Romanian Roma came to Poland, I even considered going on TV and saying that they're not part of us. They dirty Polish territory."[133] According to the Romani sociologist and activist Zsolt Csalog, the Romungro (Hungarian-speaking) Gypsies in Hungary have traditionally based their self-esteem and their regard for their brethren on their assimilation level.[134] Many Roma whose educational and social standing enable them to assimilate do just that. Successful Roma who would be in position to help their less fortunate kin are often "lost as Roma" because they tend to turn their backs on the Gypsy community, which is in dire need of their help.[135]

Although the vast majority of Roma are far from social integration in every East European society, there are important disparities in their levels of integration in various states. Often subtle differences of interethnic dynamics may be registered through field research, interviews, and opinion polls.[136] Therefore, it is possible to compile regionwide ranking of Romani social integration which is, to be sure, rough, generalized, and to some extent subjective. In my view, the level of Romani integration is highest in Poland followed by Macedonia, Hungary, Bulgaria, Romania, Slovakia, and, finally, the Czech Republic.

---

[132] See, for instance, Jane Perlez, "Gypsies in Czech Republic Face Discrimination," *New York Times*, 2 July 1998.

[133] Quoted by Linnet Myers in "Poverty-Stricken Romanian Gypsies Caught in Battle between Germany, Poland," *The Chicago Tribune*, 14 February 1993. See also *Gazeta Wyborcza*, 24 August 1994.

[134] Bihari, "Cigány bánat, magyar bánat."

[135] Nicolae Gheorghe cited in Burton Bollag, "Gypsy Studies on the Move," *The Chronicle of Higher Education*, 3 August 1994, A38. See also Halász, "Felszámolták a putrirendszert."

[136] See, for instance, Mary E. McIntosh, Martha Abele MacIver, Daniel G. Abele, and David B. Nolle, "Minority Rights and Majority Rule: Ethnic Tolerance in Romania and Bulgaria," in Leokadia Drobizheva et al., eds., *Ethnic Conflict in the Post-Soviet World: Case Studies and Analysis* (Armonk, NY: M. E. Sharpe, 1996), 37–66; and Krassimir Kanev, "Dynamics of Inter-Ethnic Tensions in Bulgaria and the Balkans," *Balkan Forum*, 4:2 (1996): 213–54.

Broadly speaking, ethnic integration is enhanced by the extent to which different ethnic groups are similar to each other. Although many factors affect the level of the Roma's social integration in Eastern Europe, the most important ones are the amount of time they have lived (especially in a settled way) in the proximity of the dominant population, the size of the Gypsy community, familiarity with the majority language, the presence of (an)other numerically or politically strong minority, and the history of interethnic relations. The notion that the Roma appear to enjoy the best position (relative to the rest of the population) in Macedonia and Poland is not coincidental.[137] Their proportion in the population of both countries is small (2.89% and 0.09%, respectively). Although in Macedonia the absolute and relative size of the Gypsy community is far larger than in Poland, they represent no political threat to the dominant ethnic group, especially in contrast to the much larger Albanian minority (around 25–30% of the population). In the Czech Republic, however, the Roma constitute a relatively small ethnic minority (1.94%) whose profound socioeconomic problems have presented state and society with major dilemmas.

No doubt, an important piece of the answer has to do with cultural and social history. Suffice it to say that Macedonians have peacefully coexisted with the Roma for centuries whereas Gypsies were settled into Bohemia only in the communist era. Macedonians also have a long tradition of relative interethnic tolerance. For instance, the long-standing and common Macedonian practice of employing Roma as household help would be well-nigh unimaginable in the Czech Republic, Hungary, or Slovakia for fear of theft. It is also noteworthy that the Roma's conditions seem far more irreconcilable with the reality of a relatively well-developed and prosperous industrial state like the Czech Republic and less so in the case of a comparatively poor country such as Macedonia. In a recent paper, Rasma Karklins observed the unusually high level of social integration of the Gypsies in Latvia. She explains this by the fact that the Roma have been sedentary for centuries, they know Latvian, their number is very small (about 8,000 or 0.3% of the overall population), and interethnic relations have historically been cooperative and continue to pay dividends through generating mutual goodwill.[138]

---

[137] See Zoltan Barany "Ethnic Mobilization and the State: The East European Roma," *Ethnic and Racial Studies*, 21:2 (1998): 321–2.

[138] Rasma Karklins, "Ethnopolitics and Language Strategies in Latvia," paper presented at the 1997 Annual Meeting of the American Political Science Association (Washington, 28–31 August 1997), 2, 7.

Dominant Group Attitudes Toward the Roma

There can be no doubt – and a slew of opinion polls support this conclusion – that the majority of people in Eastern Europe, as elsewhere, harbor extremely negative attitudes toward the Roma. This is not surprising for three broad reasons. First, most people's perception of and interaction with the Roma are shaped by negative factors and experiences. They are generally aware of the differences in culture and lifestyle, the Gypsies' low educational attainments and poverty, and their social and economic ills, particularly the high rates of Romani crime. Most ordinary people are not inclined to reflect on the multifarious causes of the Gypsies' predicament, particularly because long-entrenched biases and prejudices – often confirmed by personal experience – have already shaped their views of the Roma. It is also quite possible that many East Europeans think of the Gypsies as an irritant on two separate levels. They despise them for their social problems and inability to help themselves, but also, I believe, many people realize that something must be done to help them; after all you cannot just "forget" millions of marginalized people in the middle of Europe in the twenty-first century. At the same time, most people do not know how to help the Roma or do not care enough to sacrifice state resources to assist them, let alone to do something concrete to ease their predicament.

The second reason is that East Europeans, generally speaking, have little tradition of tolerating "others." These are relatively backward societies – particularly when compared to their Anglo-Saxon or Scandinavian counterparts – traumatized by the political and socioeconomic transition of the 1990s. A recent survey of attitudes toward ethnic minorities in Europe, Canada, and the United States found that East Europeans are the most intolerant among them.[139] Nationalism and ethnic enmity are phenomena with long histories in the region. After the fall of communism, nationalism and right-wing extremism returned to Eastern Europe, or, more precisely, they could once again rise to the surface given the ideological vacuum created by the demise of Marxism–Leninism, new laws permitting free speech and association, the liberalization of the media, and the end of Soviet control. A large number of books and articles soon lamented the region's descent into the nationalist-extremist abyss.[140] Nonetheless, following their disturbingly

---

[139] Krassimir Kanev, "The Image of the 'Other' in the Relations of the Religious Communities in Bulgaria," in Zhelyazkova, ed., *Relations of Compatibility and Incompatibility*, 362.

[140] See, for instance, Joseph Held, ed., *Democracy and Right-Wing Politics in Eastern Europe in the 1990s* (Boulder: East European Monographs, 1993); Paul Hockenos, *Free*

"promising" start, by the mid-1990s extremist forces have been relegated to the political margins in most of Eastern Europe just like in democracies elsewhere. The reason is that while voters in the region might have enjoyed the momentary political spectacle of outrageous speeches, articles, and demonstrations, with a few exceptions they have been far too mature to bestow political power to (left- or right-wing) extremist forces. This is not to say that in some states, particularly in Slovakia and Romania until the mid- to late 1990s, nationalist sentiments have not been exploited by central and local governments in order to acquire legitimacy and popular support and to obfuscate other troublesome issues.

The third reason is that postcommunist transition processes have actually contributed to rising intolerance in the region. In the socialist period the party-state did not tolerante deviation from the norms it set and embraced egalitarianism (at least in theory) as a desirable societal goal. In the postcommunist era the nature of especially economic transition generated competition, perceptions of unfairness, and, therefore, higher levels of intolerance. The first decade of democratization has also been concomitant with sharpening antagonisms between people who supported different political parties. Individuals, who enjoyed no opportunity to express their political–ideological preferences in the state-socialist era, now could openly advocate and defend their convictions. The often glaring intolerance of East European politicians and ordinary people of political views different from their own is at least partly a reflection of their lacking experience in this regard. This intolerance is also evident between those advocating different solutions to the Roma's plight.

The general population's prejudices often receive support and encouragement especially from local politicians and opinion makers across the region, although in some countries, like the Czech Republic and Slovakia, individuals have been more willing to publicly verbalize their biases than elsewhere. Miroslav Sladek's right-wing Czech Republican Party gave a new Alfa Romeo sports car to the police in Jirkov, a north Bohemian town, as a reward for being the Czech town that has rid itself of the most Gypsies.[141] Jozef Pacai, the mayor of the village of Medzev in eastern Slovakia went farther suggesting that selective killing was the only way to deal with the Roma.[142] The distinguished Romanian poet,

---

to Hate: The Rise of the Right in Post-Communist Eastern Europe (New York: Routledge, 1993); Paul Latawski, ed., *Contemporary Nationalism in Eastern Europe* (New York: St. Martin's Press, 1995); and Aleksandar Pavkovic, Halyna Koscharsky, and Adam Czarnota, eds., *Nationalism and Postcommunism* (Brookfield, VT: Dartmouth, 1995).

[141] Gross, "Gypsies Fall Victim to Czech Racism."

[142] Henry Kamm, "In New Eastern Europe, an Old Anti-Gypsy Bias," *New York Times*, 29 November 1993.

Stefan Augustin Doinas, known for his liberal views on relations between Hungarians and Romanians, openly stated "I am not a bit xenophobic. . . . But I do hate Gypsies."[143] Boris Dimovski, a well-known Bulgarian intellectual, publicly stated that Gypsies should be put in a ghetto because they are thieves and criminals.[144]

It is fair to say that the majority of East Europeans are not yet fully aware of the magnitude of the Roma's problems. Many think that they are progressive if they think that the Roma should be left alone and allowed to find their own way in the new postsocialist societies instead of realizing that without significant help from state and society they will not be able to do so.[145] In a letter to the editor of *Libertatea*, a Romanian daily, four intellectuals claimed that the Roma were "inclined at birth to larceny, fraud, robbery, violent crime, and so on" and observed that "the only person who has sensed this social danger was Marshal Antonescu," who deported tens of thousands of them in 1942. Intellectuals in Bucharest asked a baffled *Le Monde* correspondent: "How could one integrate people who do not send their children to school?"[146] Another rhetorical question was posed in the form of a letter to the editor by a Hungarian woman. She was walking with her 10-year old son in downtown Budapest, and she was spat at and called a "filthy whore" by two Romani women aggressively hawking their wares because she chose not to react to them. "I wonder who will be blamed if my son becomes a racist; surely not me," she wrote.[147]

The fact that many young people grow up embracing the prejudices of their parents has distressing implications for the future. This point was made all the more poignant by one Magdalena Babičková, a 17-year-old high school senior and finalist of a Czech beauty contest. When asked of her life's ambition, she told a nationwide television audience that she wanted to become a prosecutor in order to cleanse her home-town of Gypsies. It is more worrisome yet that spontaneous applause greeted her announcement and that no one at the contest objected to her views; moreover, the host responded by calling her "a very brave girl" and telling her: "We need that sort of lawyer."[148] In the Czech Republic and Romania, surveys found that young people have more unfavorable

---

[143] Cited in Dan Ionescu, "The Gypsies Organize," *Report on Eastern Europe*, 1:26 (1990): 40.

[144] Interview with Danova (Sofia, 11 November 1999).

[145] Interview with Cătălin Zamfir (Bucharest, 1 June 1996); and *The Roma in Bulgaria*, 20–1.

[146] These quotes are cited by Ionescu, "The Gypsies Organize," 40.

[147] Erika Tarr, "Rasszista lesz a kisfiam?" *Demokrata*, 1:7 (1997): 45.

[148] Peter S. Green, "Czech Beauty Queen Hopes to Purge Hometown of Gypsies," Reuter (Prague), 6 April 1993; and Gross, "Gypsies Fall Victim to Czech Racism."

views of the Roma than do older ones.[149] Little evidence contradicts the dramatic title of a perceptive 1991 article about the East European Roma in the German weekly *Der Spiegel*, which read: "Everyone hates the Gypsies."[150]

Conflicts frequently occur in areas where non-Roma and Roma live in close proximity to one another. In the vast majority of cases, whatever tensions arise from different lifestyles, disparate hygiene standards, and varying levels of socialization are not resolved through violence, but they often remain unsettled allowing for the simmering of tensions under the surface.[151] People who live near the Roma suggest that their customs and behavior are the primary cause of these conflicts. Citizens in the Bohemian towns of Ústí nad Labem and Plzeň who wanted a wall erected between Roma and non-Roma dwellings justified their intention by arguing several points. The Roma, they and many others in the region complain, use staircases as toilets; incessantly torment them with their loud music and interminable parties; throw garbage out the window; and make passing on the street or in hallways a chancy proposition.[152] Non-Roma have few avenues to remedy their problems because local governments are loathe to help them given national and international pressures. Press coverage and human rights reports rarely examine the actual experience of living next to the Roma, who, in many cases, residents contend, are neighbors from hell. In a recent Slovak survey, 94% of the respondents said that they would not want to have Roma as their neighbors; but few of my interviewees across the region were surprised

---

[149] Dorel Abraham, Ilie Bădescu, and Septimiu Chelcea, *Interethnic Relations in Romania* (Cluj-Napoca: Editura Carpatica, 1995), 111; and Dan Ungureanu, "Tinerii ii antipatizeaza pe ţigani," *Tineretul Liber*, 15 February 1994; Judit Hamberger, "A csehországi romák helyzete," *Regio*, 7:2 (1996): 60; and Tatjana Šišková, "Report on 'Education towards Tolerance and against Racism' project in Prague Schools," Czech Center for Conflict Prevention and Resolution (Prague) February 1998, 17 pp.

[150] "Alle hassen die Zigeuner," *Der Spiegel*, no. 36 (3 September 1990): 34–57.

[151] See, for instance, *Destroying Ethnic Identity: The Gypsies of Bulgaria* (New York: Helsinki Watch, 1991), 21; interviews with Tomova and Nikolai Gentchev, a Professor of History at the University of Sofia (Sofia, 7–8 March 1995).

[152] Many reports across the region make these points. See, for instance, Michael Conrath, "Gypsies Suffer Fall Out from the Romanian Revolution," AFP (Bucharest, 8 July 1991); Adrian Bridge, "Romanians Vent Old Hatreds Against Gypsies," *The Independent*, 19 October 1993; "Tüntetés a 'romakonténer' ellen," *Népszabadság*, 24 November 1997; "Hajléktalanszálló létesítését szervezik," *Új Magyarország*, 28 November 1997; Michelle Legge, "Wall to Divide City," *Prague Post*, 20–6 May 1998; Peter S. Green, "2 Czech Cities to Wall Off Their 'Problematic' Gypsies," *International Herald Tribune*, 28 May 1998; Eva Munk, "Czech Gypsies Protest at Plan to Wall Them in," Reuter (Ústí nad Labem), 2 June 1998; "Tension between Romany, non-Romany Population in Czech Town Decreasing," CTK (Ústí nad Labem), 9 June 1998; and Radio Free Europe/Radio Liberty Newsline, Part II (henceforth: RFE/RL II), 3:103 (27 May 1999).

Table 5.5. East Europeans with Negative Views of the
Roma (%)

Bulgaria[a]	71 (1991)		
Czech Republic[b]	91 (1991)	77 (1994)	68 (1994b)
Hungary[c]	79 (1991)		
Romania[d]	68 (1991)		
Slovakia[e]	66 (1991)		

[a] 1991: Times-Mirror Poll cited in Carol J. Williams, "E.
Europe Upheaval Means Bleaker Times for Gypsies."
[b] 1991 (Czechoslovakia): Times-Mirror Poll cited in Williams,
"E. Europe Upheaval Means Bleaker Times for Gypsies."
1994a: Jeremy Smith, "Right-Wing Groups on the Rise in
Czech Republic," Reuters (Prague), 9 February 1994. 1994b:
RFE/RL Daily Report, no. 233, 12 December 1994.
[c] 1991: Times-Mirror Poll cited in Williams, "E. Europe
Upheaval Means Bleaker Times for Gypsies."
[d] 1991: Cited in Noszkai, "Romák délkelet-európában," 12.
[e] Dostál, "Hot Summer for Romany Minority," 2–3.

by such numbers, saying "who *would* want loud, obnoxious, and dirty
neighbors" regardless of their ethnic background?[153]

Social scientists across the region have conducted innumerable polls
gauging East Europeans' views about the Roma and other minorities
through the years. Different survey methods and often inconsistent data
collection renders longitudinal and regionwide comparisons difficult.
Given the smallness of registered differences, the margin of error, and
the uncontrolled conditions of polling, it is hard to say whether anti-
Roma attitudes had increased or decreased in any given country between
the early and mid-1990s.[154] All of the results – regardless of place, time,
and survey method   indicate that the Gypsies are by far the most dis-
liked East Europeans, there has been no substantial change in the way
people think of them, and with increases in education level the respondents' prejudices diminish considerably. Table 5.5 provides a general
sense of the breadth of negative perceptions of the Roma in the region,

[153] László Juhász, ed., *Rom známena človek: Diskusia v Cilistove o palcivom probléme*
(Bratislava: Friedrich Ebert Stiftung, 1999), 43. See, for instance, interview with
Ventzislav Ivanov, Director of the Directorate of International Organizations and
Human Rights, Ministry of Foreign Affairs (Sofia, 16 November 1999).
[154] See, for instance, Koos Postma, *Changing Prejudice in Hungary: A Study on the Col-
lapse of State Socialism and Its Impact on Prejudice Against Gypsies and Jews* (Gronin-
gen: Rijksuniversiteit, 1996); and György Csepeli, Zoltán Fábián, and Endre Sík,
"Xenofóbia és a cigányságról alkotott vélemények," in Tamás Kolosi, György István
Tóth, and György Vukovich, eds., *Társadalmi Riport, 1998* (Budapest: TÁRKI, 1998),
458–89.

but I also want to note a few survey results that I find particularly telling. Polls in 1994 found that more than a third of Czechs aged between 15 and 29 agreed with skinhead attacks against the Roma, 30% of the population believed that they should be deported or isolated in ghettos, and 10 times more people could imagine a visit to Earth by extraterrestrials than could conceive of marrying a Rom.[155] A survey in 1999 revealed that 72% of Czechs do not feel the idea of building a wall to separate ethnic Czechs from the Roma is based on racial hatred, and 64% do not consider their society racist.[156] According to another recent Czech study, 40% of the students at a police academy were not sure if they would assist Romani children in an emergency, 10% were certain that they would not, and 90% thought that it was the Roma's fault that they were attacked by skinheads.[157] Similar polls yielded comparable results in both Bulgaria and Hungary.[158] Tragically, there is at least one Romani leader, Albert Daniel of Skalica, Slovakia, who agrees with the policemen by claiming that "The skinheads go after those Roma who are not good. The skinheads want to put things in order. I agree with what they do."[159]

In a Bulgarian survey, respondents were asked if they would vote for an "appropriate, competent, and honest" person if he were a Gypsy: only 12.5% of ethnic Bulgarians, 39.4% of ethnic Turks, and 70% of the Gypsies (!) answered in the affirmative.[160] A Romanian study probing interethnic relations found that 100% of ethnic Germans, 77% of Romanians, 50% of Hungarians, and 26% of the Roma (!) harbored unfavorable views of the Roma.[161] Researchers at the Slovak Academy of Sciences analyzing ethnic stereotypes asked respondents "What would be your first emotional reaction in terms of accepting or not accepting Gypsies?" Over 65% of them answered "I would expel the Roma from my country or I would only accept them as visitors."[162] As some of these surveys suggest, social relations between the Roma and other minority groups are fraught with similar animosity as with the dominant

[155] Jeremy Smith, "Right-Wing Groups on the Rise in Czech Republic," Reuter (Prague), 9 February 1994; Tom Gross, "A Blot on the Conscience," *Financial Times*, 19 December 1994; and Sabina Slonková and Roman Gallo, "Černo-bile soužiti," *Mladá Fronta Dneš*, 13 October 1994.

[156] CTK (Prague), 25 May 1999 quoted in RFE/RL II, 3:102 (26 May 1999).

[157] Hamberger, "A csehországi romák helyzete," 60.

[158] Kanev, "Dynamics of Inter-Ethnic Tensions," 229; and Ildikó Emese Nagy, "Minden tizedik rendőr rasszista," *Magyar Hírlap*, 28 March 1998.

[159] Cited in *Monitoring Minority Rights* (Bratislava), no. 2 (October–December 1998): 9.

[160] Mikhail Ivanov and Ilona Tomova, "Ethnic Groups and Inter-Ethnic Relations in Bulgaria," unpublished manuscript (Sofia, August 1993), 16.

[161] "77 la suta dintre romani ni ii sufera pe țigani," *Evenimentul zilei*, 19 October 1993.

[162] Vladimír Šedivý and Viktor Maroši, *Position of National Minorities and Ethnic Groups in the Slovak Republic* (Bratislava: Minority Rights Group, 1996), 16.

population. Notwithstanding recurrent interethnic tensions, non-Gypsy minority populations are far better integrated into East European societies than the Gypsies, even in the cases of Albanians in Macedonia or Turks in Bulgaria.[163] One of the rare cases of minority group solidarity occurred in March 1990 in Tîrgu Mureş, Romania, when a large number of Roma joined violent clashes between ethnic Romanians and Hungarians on the latter's side.[164]

Anti-Roma Violence

One of the most troubling developments in postcommunist Eastern Europe has been the large number of violent attacks on the Roma and their property. The emergence of nationalist parties allowed by the democratization process and the relative leniency of the new regimes toward expressions of nationalist views has been interpreted by some groups as permission to display openly racist sentiments. Given the lack of resources, states often cannot control extremist groups, many of whom have targeted their frustration at the Roma. In Romania, the virulently nationalist organization *Vatra Românească* ("Romanian Cradle") has openly called for a bloody war against the Roma.[165] In the early 1990s the Hungarian skinhead band, Gypsy Destroyer Regiment, played to packed houses its hit song "Gypsy Free Zone" (lyrics included: "exterminate the Gypsies, whether child, woman, or man").[166]

Physical violence against the Roma has occurred in every country of the region, although by far the most attacks took place in the Czech Republic. Throughout Eastern Europe, dozens of Roma have been killed, hundreds of their dwellings have been burned down, and thousands have become homeless as a result of interethnic violence.[167] In September 1993

---

[163] Interviews with Emilija Simoska and Mirjana Najcevska at the Center for Ethnic Relations at the Institute for Sociological, Political, and Juridical Research (Skopje, 9 March 1994); Gentchev (Sofia, 7 March 1995), and Tomova (Sofia, 8 March 1995).

[164] "Cigányúton Európába," *Reform*, 14 September 1990; and Tom Gallagher, *Romania After Ceausescu* (Edinburgh: University of Edinburgh Press, 1995), 88, 120.

[165] See Tom Gallagher, "Vatra Românească and Resurgent Nationalism in Romania," *Ethnic and Racial Studies*, 15:4 (1992): 570–99.

[166] Ferdinand Protzman, "Music of Hate Raises the Volume in Germany," *New York Times*, 2 November 1992.

[167] There is plenty of solid evidence, see for instance, *The Sunday Times*, 12 April 1990; *Reform*, 14 September 1990; *The Daily Telegraph*, 26 October 1990; "Poles Vent Their Economic Rage on Gypsies," *New York Times*, 25 July 1991; "Mlawa oder: Wenn Rassismus grassiert," *Die Presse* (Vienna), 2 September 1991; Ionescu, "Violence against Gypsies Escalates," 23–6; "Hates that Haunt," *The European*, 27–30 September 1991; Enache, "Die Minderheit der Roma," 21–2; "Mit dem Revolution vom Regen in die Traufe," *Frankfurter Allgemeine Zeitung*, 8 February 1992; "Czech 'Civilisation' Demands Gypsy Expulsions," *The Independent*, 13 January 1993; *The European*,

the Transylvanian village of Hadareni was the scene of the most serious attack on the Roma to date: 750 ethnic Romanians and Hungarians killed four Roma, destroyed 17 Romani dwellings, and forced 130 to flee.[168] Particularly in the early 1990s, police were often reluctant to interfere and provide sufficient protection to the victims given that members of the police force usually share the prejudices of the attackers. After 1993 the number of anti-Roma attacks declined everywhere except for the Czech Republic, owing to the growing effectiveness of police in arresting lawbreakers and the increasingly heavy penalties meted out by the legal system.[169]

The number of violent actions directed against the Gypsies across the region throughout the 1990s may well be in the thousands. As many as 1,250 attacks against the Roma may have occurred between 1990 and 1997 in the Czech Republic alone.[170] According to the Czech Ministry of Interior, between 1990 and 1993 16 Roma had been killed in racial attacks in the Czech lands.[171] By 1994, assaults – primarily against the Roma – had tripled to about 160; and, in 1996, skinheads or their sympathizers were thought to be responsible for twenty attacks per month.[172] The Romani Civic Initiative, a Czech Gypsy organization, claims that in 1989–98 29 Roma had been killed in racially motivated attacks in the Czech Republic.[173] The Romani Democratic Union tallied 18 serious

14–17 October 1993; Henry Kamm, "To the Gypsies Death is a Neighbor," *The New York Times*, 27 October 1993; Barbara Demick, "Anti-Gypsy Pogroms Rampant in Romania," *Philadelphia Inquirer*, 29 November 1993; "Increasing Violence Against Roma in Bulgaria," *Human Rights Watch/Helsinki*, 6:18 (1994): 1–33; Gyula Mihályka, "Mindenki fél mindenkitől," *Petőfi Népe* (Kecskemét), 2 May 1995; Donald Kenrick, "Attacks and Pogroms: A Selective Chronology," *Index on Censorship*, 27:4 (1998): 66–7; and "Rom in Slovakia Dies after Beating," RFE/RL Newsline II, 4:162 (23 August 2000). Publications of Amnesty International, Human Rights Watch, and the European Roma Rights Center provide extensive and detailed reports about attacks on the Roma across Europe.

[168] See *Magyar Nemzet*, 23 September 1993; *Frankfurter Rundschau*, 27 September 1993; and *The New York Times*, 27 October 1993.

[169] Interviews with Bițu (Bucharest, 23 May 1996); Florin Moisă, Program Coordinator, Open Society Foundation (Cluj, 25 October 1999); and Dan Oprescu, Head of the National Office for the Roma (Bucharest, 2 November 1999).

[170] Jane Perlez, "For Czechs, a Lecture on Gypsy Rights," *New York Times*, 9 November 1997.

[171] Tom Gross and James Hider, "Romanies Feel Law Is Unfair," *Prague Post*, 12–18 January 1994.

[172] Jane Perlez, "Czechs Use Laws to Exclude Gypsies From Gaining Citizenship and Voting," *New York Times*, 27 December 1995; and Jan Sliva, "Gypsies Plan to Emigrate for a Better Life in Canada," AP (Prague), 15 August 1997.

[173] "Czech Gypsies Call for Measures to Halt 'Racist' Attacks," AFP (Prague), 1 March 1998.

assaults on the Gypsies in Romania between January 1990 and July 1991; Dumitru Bidia, a Gypsy activist, claimed that 37 interethnic clashes occurred in the same country between 1989 and 1995.[174] In the first seven months of 1995, Slovak skinheads assaulted Roma on 30 different occasions.[175] Slovak authorities registered 19 racial attacks in 1996, stoking the Roma's resolve to set up a militia given that the state could not protect them.[176] Between 1991 and 1994, 21 to 26 skinhead attacks (primarily against Roma but also against Asians) were registered in Hungary annually, but by 1995 this number had dropped to about 10.[177] Obviously even one incident of ethnically or racially motivated assault is intolerable. At the same time, as Donald Horowitz has pointed out, in the global perspective anti-Roma violence has been relatively limited and has not been on the same scale as ethnic violence directed against the Tamils in Sri Lanka or the Bosnian Muslims and Kosovar Albanians in the former Yugoslavia.[178]

NGOs and international organizations have done an invaluable service by publicizing the attacks on the Roma, although they have not done an equally good job in providing balanced reporting. Their accounts are typically compiled by human rights activists who often do little more than collecting the "story" from the Gypsies without asking anyone else and then presenting it as reality.[179] The problems that may result was well-illustrated by *Los Angeles Times* reporter Carol J. Williams, who investigated an attack on the Roma in the Croatian village of Torjanci in 1991. Her account is worth quoting at length:

"The Ustasha (Croatia's World War II Fascists) attacked our village, and my husband is missing," declared Djulca Bogdan, a thin woman in a black lace kerchief who described herself and the 156 others given shelter in the community basketball court as "Catholic Croatian Gypsies." "They burned a horse alive," another woman added. "And they slit the throat of a dog and said, 'This is what

---

[174] Michel Conrath, "Gypsies Suffer Fall-out from the Romanian Revolution," AFP (Bucharest), 8 July 1991; and Vladimir Rodina, "Tension between Gypsies, Romanians," UPI (Bucharest), 17 January 1995.

[175] "Gypsy Groups Call for Banning of Skinheads," AFP (Bratislava), 1 August 1995.

[176] OMRI DD II, no. 14 (21 January 1997).

[177] "Öregszenek a börfejűek," *Népszabadság*, 28 July 1997.

[178] *The Romanies in Central and Eastern Europe: Illusions and Reality*, 11; and Horowitz's comments at the "Ethnic Conflict in Bulgaria and Romania Syposium," Duke University (Durham, NC; 21 September 1996).

[179] Interviews with Nora Costache, an activist with the Young Generation Society of the Roma (Bucharest, 14 March 1995); Ivan Ilchev, representative of the Project on Ethnic Relations and Professor of History at the University of Sofia (Sofia, 9 March 1995); Marushiakova and Popov (Sofia, 13 November 1999); David Murphy (Prague, 23 August 1999); Michal Vašečka (Bratislava, 10 September 1999); and Michelle Kelso, a researcher of the Romani Holocaust (Austin, 22 February and 4 May 2000).

we do to (Serbian) Chetniks!'" ... Reciting as if from a script, the Gypsies claimed that three of their fellow villagers had been killed, then gradually upped the death toll to 10. They said the attackers were Croatian fighters disguised in federal army uniforms who have slipped in through Hungary in a commandeered truck, although there is no road into Torjanci from Hungary. The chorus of witnesses claimed that the invaders had mined their houses, then said their houses had been burned, and that the attackers had stopped in the middle of the melee to inject themselves with drugs. "They killed my son," said Eva Ivanovic, as if suddenly remembering. "They shot him with dum-dum bullets when I wasn't more than 100 meters away." A Serbian journalist who had been taking notes of the reported atrocity smiled as he tucked away his notebook. "Gypsies!" he said, with both disgust and amusement. "They can be manipulated to say anything. Who knows what really happened?"[180]

Human rights organizations and Gypsy activists tend not to differentiate between attacks against the Roma and consider them all the manifestations of racism. This is not the most constructive way to approach the issue. One must not draw a parallel between violence committed as a result of some sort of provocation (a quarrel in the pub or reaction to perceived transgressions) and the attacks of skinheads and other extremist groups motivated by racism, pure and simple. The first category of violence may be alleviated by improvements in the Roma's socioeconomic conditions, easing interethnic tensions, growing societal recognition of the rule of law, and increasing state and societal condemnation of vigilante type violence as unacceptable. Though outcomes might be the same, the second category of violence, atrocities committed by extremist elements, is far more dangerous because it is entirely unprovoked and inherently racist. Let me illustrate this point with two examples.

(1) The anti-Gypsy assault in the tiny hamlet of Valeni la Posuluj, about 250 miles northwest of Bucharest, was touched off by a violent crime. In the summer of 1991 a Rom who had served a prison sentence for raping and killing a woman came to this village where his mother lived. He raped a popular local woman who was eight months pregnant, and then he fled. The villagers – who by now had been fed up with a series of Gypsy crimes and confounded by the inability of police to solve any of them – reacted by attacking the Roma at the end of the road, burning several of their houses and chasing their inhabitants away from the community.[181]

---

[180] Carol J. Williams, "E. Europe Upheaval Means Even Bleaker Times for Gypsies," *Los Angeles Times*, 20 December 1991.

[181] Based on a report by Judith Ingram, "Gypsy Nights: Mobs, Torches, Screaming Children," *New York Times*, 12 June 1992.

(2) In July 1995 approximately 30 skinheads in the central Slovakian town of Žiar nad Hronom went on a rampage against the town's Romani community. Mario Gorál, a 17-year-old Romani boy, could not hide quickly enough. The skinheads flung him to the ground, repeatedly hit him, with sticks on his head, poured gasoline on him, and set him on fire. He suffered burns to 60% of his body and was taken to hospital in serious condition. Gorál, by all accounts a peaceful youngster who shunned cigarettes and alcohol, died of his injuries 10 days later.[182]

There are also great disparities in societal reactions to the Roma in the region's countries. They seem to be the most hostile in the Czech Republic where, according to former presidential adviser Jiři Pehe, "racism is very extensive."[183] A 1999 survey of Opinion Window, an international polling organization, found that Czechs exhibit "substantially more widespread xenophobic opinions" than do many previously surveyed societies.[184] Konstanty Gebert, editor of the Jewish magazine *Midrasz* in Warsaw, agrees, noting that "Czech society is a classical West European case of hypocrisy and tolerated racism: It tolerates racism but lies about it and knows it."[185] Public attitudes toward the Roma tend to be more moderate elsewhere, in large part because they have been present in the region's other societies much longer. The political activist and liberal philosopher, G. M. Tamás, for instance, has contended that xenophobia and anti-Semitism was "astonishingly low" in Hungary (in fact, lower than in most European states).[186] Interethnic hostilities have been even rarer occurrences in Poland and Macedonia.

Generally speaking, the extremist political parties and organizations (such as the Republican Party in the Czech Republic, the Slovak National Party, *Vatra Românească*, and others) and skinhead gangs do not have a substantial support base and constitute marginal and isolated groups in these societies. The numerical strength of skinheads in the region is a debated issue. A 1999 article in the British weekly *The Economist* reported their numbers at 4,000 each in Hungary and the Czech Republic, 2,000

---

182 This account is taken from Ondrej Dostál, "Hot Summer for Romany Minority in Slovakia," unpublished report for the Project on Ethnic Relations (Bratislava, September 1995), 1.

183 See his article in *Lidové Noviny*, 29 October 1997; and "A rasszizmus gyökerei," *Új Magyarország*, 30 October 1997.

184 Cited in RFE/RL II, 4:20 (28 January 2000).

185 Interview with Gebert (Warsaw, 16 August 1999).

186 Tamás cited in János T. Turistvándy, " 'Teljességgel egyetértek'," *Heti Magyarország*, 4 February 1994, p. 5. See also G. M. Tamás, "Victory Defeated?" *Journal of Democracy*, 10:1 (January 1999): 64; and "Aggasztó méretű-e a romaellenesség?" *Népszabadság*, 23 April 1999.

in Poland (another source had the same estimate for Serbia), and 1,500 in Slovakia.[187] In April 2000, a German television commentator noted that there were 6,000 Czech skinheads.[188] As always, these figures should be viewed with a grain of salt. In Hungary, for instance, skinhead activity in 1998 was approximately 2–3% of what it was in the beginning of the 1990s and there were no more than a few hundred skinheads.[189] Officials explain this phenomenon with the aging of former skinheads, most of whom had joined mainstream society, and with the increasing ability of law enforcement agencies to monitor skinhead groups.[190]

Needless to say, the Roma have faced especially dire circumstances and major threats to their physical security during the wars in the former Yugoslavia, the country where their position was arguably the best in the region under communism. There is evidence that Gypsies were coerced into the military units of the warring parties; in some cases, family members found themselves on opposing sides of the war fighting against each other.[191] Roma often had to perform forced labor, digging ditches and defusing landmines. Like others caught up in the conflict, Roma, too, were forced from their homes at gunpoint, raped, and massacred because of their ethnicity.[192] In many cases they did not receive their fair share of relief packages for no other reason than being Gypsies. Tens of thousands of Roma from the former Yugoslavia fled to Western Europe, particularly to France, Germany, and Italy, in search of safety.

NATO's 1999 war against Yugoslavia exacerbated the difficulties of Roma living in Kosovo. The Kosovo Liberation Army and many displaced ethnic Albanians had charged that Gypsies collaborated with the Serbs and actively participated in atrocities against Albanians and looting

---

[187] "Nasty, Ubiquitous, and Unloved," *Economist*, 20 March 1999, 56–7, and Patrick Moore, "What Lies Behind Serbian Skinhead Violence against Roma," End Note to RFE/RL II, 1:149 (30 October 1997).

[188] RFE/RL II, 4:84 (28 April 2000).

[189] See the comments of Lipót Höltzl, Deputy Secretary of State at the Hungarian Ministry of Justice, in "Roma in Hungary: Views of Several Specialists," Research Directorate, Immigration and Refugee Board (Ottawa, February 1999), 6–7.

[190] "Öregszenek a börfejűek," *Népszabadság*, 28 July 1997.

[191] Judith Latham, "Roma of the Former Yugoslavia," paper presented at the National Convention of the American Association for the Advancement of Slavic Studies (Seattle, 20 November 1997), 16.

[192] See, for instance, Katrin Reemstma, "Report on the Fact-Finding Mission on the Situation of the Roma in Bosnia," *CPRSI (Contact Point for Roma and Sinti Issues) Newsletter* (OSCE), 2:6 (1996): 7–8, and her expanded report of the same title for the European Working Group for Roma in and Refugees from Bosnia (Berlin: Süd-Ost-Europa Kulturzentrum, 1996); Dragoljub Aćković, *Asunen Romalen: Slušajte Ljudi* (Belgrade: Rrominterpress, 1996); and Orhan Galjus, "Balkan Triptych," *Index on Censorship*, 27:4 (1998): 87–90.

the property of those who escaped to refugee camps. Although few Roma had done any serious fighting, many had been obliged to join with the Serb paramilitaries and the federal troops. Local Gypsy leaders and journalists had done the Roma a disservice by openly backing Yugoslav President Slobodan Milošević many times on radio and television.[193] After the war, thousands of Roma left Kosovo, primarily for Serbia, Montenegro, and Macedonia, though hundreds sailed to Italy and elsewhere in Western Europe where they applied for political asylum.[194]

CONCLUSION

The purpose of this chapter was to examine the impact of the postcommunist regime change on the social and economic marginality of the East European Roma. Their situation has deteriorated far below the societal average. The majority became unemployed, their average educational attainments have further regressed, and their social ills have become more acute. The longing for the "good times" of the socialist period of many ordinary Gypsies is not hard to understand. During that era many Roma got used to the guardianship of the paternalistic state and, in the new Eastern Europe, were unable to adapt to the merciless mechanisms of market forces. To make matters worse, extremist groups and some ordinary citizens exploited the passing of the socialist era's trepidations about racism and interethnic violence as democratization permitted nationalist and anti-Roma parties suppressed under communist rule. In sum, the regime change signified a disaster to most Gypsies only slightly mitigated by new opportunities for political mobilization and the helpful and supportive campaigns of NGOs and, with the passing of time, increasingly constructive state policies.

In Chapter 8 and 9 I will show that the appalling socioeconomic conditions and interethnic relations I examined in this chapter did make an impact on state policies toward the Roma. But, as I argued, Romani political mobilization and the activities of international organizations and NGOs also influenced state policies. The next two chapters will be devoted to the analyses of these factors.

---

[193] See "In the Conflict Over Kosovo, Gypsies Are Caught in the Middle," AFP (Belgrade), 10 July 1999; and "Gypsies Demand Safe Route from Kosovo as Fear Rises," AP (Pristina), 13 July 1999; and *Roma Rights: Newsletter of the European Roma Rights Center*, no. 2 (July 1999), special issue devoted to the Roma and the Kosovo war.
[194] RFE/RL II, 3:129 (2 July 1999).

6

Romani Mobilization

Political opportunity is one of the indispensable prerequisites of ethnic mobilization. The one significant gain that East European Gypsies made from the postcommunist transition was this chance to freely organize themselves. What were the major issues confronting the Roma at the outset of their mobilizational activities? What type of organizations have they created? What sort of organizational resources have they had, and how have they utilized them? How have Gypsy communities responded to their leaders' activities? How effective have been the Roma's mobilization efforts? The task of this chapter is to answer these questions.

PART I: THE WEAKNESS OF ROMANI IDENTITY

In order to put Romani activism in its proper context, we need to appreciate the extent to which the odds are stacked against it. Gypsy mobilization is still in its infancy: It is little more than a decade old. In Chapter 2 I outlined the prerequisites of successful ethnic mobilization. In the chapters that followed I explained that, in terms of mobilizational experience, the Gypsies have little to draw on. Nonetheless, even in imperial and authoritarian states a small number of Roma proved time and again that they understood the importance of organized political activism. For a variety of reasons, both endogenous and exogenous, they were unable to alleviate their problems. In the socialist period the state succeeded in keeping Romani activism down, though a small but important group of Gypsy intellectuals emerged that was prepared to take mobilization to a higher level.

As a general rule, the state no longer restrained Romani mobilization after 1989, although in some cases it divided and played off Gypsy organizations against one another. It is also important to note that external circumstances, more specifically the encouragement and practical help of foreign governments, international organizations, and NGOs, have motivated Romani activism. I will examine these factors in the next chapter.

What I am concerned with here is the endogenous causes for the Roma's lackluster performance in the political arena. Some of these, to be sure, lie in their socioeconomic problems (low educational level, poverty, and lacking ethnic solidarity) already discussed in Chapter 5. Others, such as organizations, leadership, and financial resources will be examined in the balance of this chapter. But now we need to explore the issue of Romani ethnic identity, perhaps the most important component of ethnic mobilization.

Non-Roma often presume that Gypsies possess a strong ethnic identity primarily because they seem to differ in so many ways from the majority population. This perception is quite erroneous: For a number of reasons I mentioned before, Romani identity tends to be very weak. In turn, the absence of a strong ethnic identity has been one of the key reasons for the deficiencies of Romani mobilization.[1] Many Gypsies refuse to identify themselves with their ethnic background. A 1990 research project on the Roma conducted by the Slovak Statistical Office revealed that 37% considered themselves Romani, 28% "Cigani" (Gypsies), 18% Slovaks, and 17% Hungarians. This study found that educated respondents were especially likely to deny their Romani identity.[2] My interviewees underscored this phenomenon. Ágnes Horváthová, a Slovak Romani activist and Helsinki Commission official, contended that most educated Roma want nothing more than to leave behind their Gypsiness. They try to marry non-Roma and hide their Romani identity from the children resulting from these mixed marriages. The next generation, laments Horváthová, is usually assimilated.[3] The difference that skin color makes must be acknowledged: It is much easier for lighter-colored Roma to assimilate and deny their identity.

In the opinion of Jiřina Šiklová, a sociology professor at Prague's Charles University, most Roma have lost their ethnic identity and "don't want to be Gypsies." Ironically, those who identify themselves as Roma, says Šiklová, tend to be either (a) Gypsies of very low social status who hope for higher social benefits or (b) Roma of the highest social status who possess political aspiration.[4] Voluntary assimilation has been the principal goal of several East European Romani organizations. Many Gypsy leaders are not aware of the paradox between their wish to follow majority lifestyles and the loss of their identity. Their programs often

---

[1] See Zoltan Barany, "Ethnic Mobilization and the State: The East European Roma," *Ethnic and Racial Studies*, 21:2 (March 1998): 312–13.
[2] Cited by Arne B. Mann, "The Formation of the Ethnic Identity of the Romany in Slovakia," in Jana Plichtová, ed., *Minorities in Politics* (Bratislava: Czechoslovak Committee of the European Cultural Foundation, 1992), 264.
[3] Interview with Horváthová (Bratislava, 8 September 1999).
[4] Interview with Šiklová (Prague, 31 August 1999).

point the way toward Romani assimilation and the reduction of their culture and traditions to folklore, thereby unintentionally replicating the Gypsy policies of socialist states.[5] Intellectuals typically play an essential role in ethnic mobilization. Because the Romani elite is extremely small, in many cases funded programs and projects cannot take off because no qualified Gypsies can be identified to lead them. Moreover, a large proportion of educated Roma choose not to be involved in Gypsy affairs. Many Roma who receive stipends or scholarships to help them earn university degrees and then to share their knowledge with their brethren are reluctant to return to their villages and turn away from them altogether.[6] Nicoleta Bițu, a Romanian Gypsy activist, points out that the more educated a Rom gets, the more questions are raised about her identity not just by the Gypsy community and members of the non-Gypsy population, but also by herself. In essence, Bițu says, education challenges Romani identity and contributes to the identity crisis of many Roma who eventually find themselves trying to assimilate.[7] Not surprisingly, there is an enormous cultural distance between the tiny Romani intelligentsia and the masses of undereducated and often apathetic ordinary Gypsies. This notion contributes to the poor political communication in the Romani community and to the fact that Gypsy politics is, more than anything, elite politics. It is dominated by a handful of Gypsy activists and leaders who desperately (but usually without success) try to prove that they do represent "their people" and that they do have a constituency.

Gypsy identity has evolved in a cultural context rather than in a historical one. Of course, "cultural" should not be taken to denote conventional works of literature or fine arts but, instead, the culture of *Romanipe* or Gypsyness, the notion of maintaining a way of life and, particularly, patterns of interaction with the *gadje*. There are few Roma, however, who are proud of this cultural identity, in large part because few of them continue to live by the old traditions. According to a recent Slovak survey, only 19% of the Gypsies asked think that Roma should preserve their culture and traditions.[8] Gypsy leaders like Jan Rušenko in the Czech Republic note that Roma, especially young Roma, must learn cultural pride to strengthen their identity.[9] Nonetheless, cultural identity

---

[5] See *Romové v České republice* (Prague: Socioklub, 1999), 542.

[6] Interview with Antal Heizer, chief councillor at the Prime Minister's Office (Budapest, 28 May 1998).

[7] Interview with Bițu (Bucharest, 13 March 1995).

[8] Michal Vašečka, "The Romanies in Slovakia," in Luboš Vagač, ed., *National Human Development Report for Slovakia 1998* (Bratislava: United Nations Development Program, 1998), 71.

[9] Cited in Linnet Myers, "Circling the Wagons: With Gypsies' New Freedom Comes More Persecution," *Chicago Tribune*, 28 December 1992.

can hardly provide the gist for political mobilization. For that, awareness of a shared historical tradition is necessary. But, as the Romani historian Bartolomej Daniel admits, "very few Roma know anything about their history and what they do know they learned from the *gadje*." Moreover, they "do not have any interest in their history" and some "do not believe even that the Holocaust had anything to do with their people."[10]

Slawomir Kapralski cogently argues that the creation of a Romani national identity necessarily involves the invention of tradition because the Roma – owing to the lack of their own written historical tradition – have little to draw on.[11] The centuries-long persecution of the Gypsies by states and societies in a variety of historical contexts *is* Romani history. Given the chronological proximity of *Porajmos*, it is especially important to make Roma cognizant of the indiscriminate slaughter of their forefathers during World War II, because this understanding can create a sense of belonging, a feeling of shared suffering. Gypsy communities of Eastern Europe are currently undergoing the process of ethnogenesis, a deliberate attempt to achieve the acknowledged status of a nonterritorial ethnonational group.[12] This process is particularly significant because, for the first time, the Roma themselves, rather than outsiders, are delineating their own ethnic and cultural identity. The common strands in Romani history and the Gypsies' presence in all European states have inspired some Romani activists to define Romani identity as a European identity, specific not to individual states but to the continent as a whole.

The fact that the Roma constitute a very diverse population has made the unfolding of the Romani movement all the more difficult. Intracommunity cleavages further split an already small potential constituency, impede political organization, and suggest the folly of expecting a single, united, Gypsy political party in any one country. These divisions partly explain the rapid proliferation of Romani organizations in the postsocialist era.

PART II: ROMANI ORGANIZATIONS

The fall of communism was still incomplete when Gypsy activists began to form their new independent organizations. The first such organization in Czechoslovakia, the Romani Civic Initiative (*Romská Občanská Iniciativa*, ROI) issued its first statement in November 1989. Gypsy leaders

---

[10] Interview with Bartolomej Daniel (Brno, 2 September 1999).
[11] See Kapralski, "Identity Building and the Holocaust: Roma Political Nationalism," *Nationalities Papers*, 25:2 (1997): 273.
[12] See Nicolae Gheorghe, "Roma-Gypsy Ethnicity in Eastern Europe," *Social Research*, 58:4 (Winter 1991): 830–1; and Kapralski, "Identity Building and the Holocaust," 269.

like Emil Sčuka and Jan Rušenko were among the first to join the Civic Forum and to take part in the discussions at Prague's Magic Lantern theater.[13] In Romania, the "Social-Cultural Federation of the Roma from Timiş County" was funded on 25 December 1989, on the day Elena and Nicolae Ceauşescu were executed.

At the end of 1989 there were no more than a few dozen Romani activists in Eastern Europe, but they left little doubt about their enthusiastic welcome of the *ancien régime*'s fall. Their infectious excitement about the new opportunities for mobilization was responsible for bringing hundreds of budding activists and politicians to the Romani movement. Many of these individuals saw the creation of organizations as the most appropriate vehicle for Gypsy mobilization. Depending on their interests and what they considered important, they set up associations focusing on gaining political representation, publicizing human rights abuses, and alleviating socioeconomic problems. One of the most conspicuous things about the Romani mobilization has been the large number of organizations created throughout the last decade. Table 6.1 provides a sense of this phenomenon. The obvious question, Why are there so many Romani groups?, has several answers. First, after decades of prohibition, the chance to start up independent organizations was tempting for many Gypsy and non-Gypsy activists. Second, the region's new association laws made it easy to register formal groups. According to the Hungarian association law, for instance, the signatures of eleven individuals are sufficent to register an organization. Third, the increasing availability of public and private financial support for Roma-related associations motivated more and more activists to set up formal organizations. Fourth, like others, many Romani activists wanted to be in leadership positions, and this was only possible if they established their own organizations. József Raduly, a Hungarian Romani activist, has noted that many formalized Gypsy groups came to life because this was the only way to receive money from the authorities and because having the title of "president" or "executive director" is far too luring for many Roma to resist.[14]

Dozens of Romani organizations have been formed around leaders who attract or appeal to a specific constituency, none of whom is willing to share power.[15] Therefore, a rift usually occurs in the leadership, result-

---

[13] Interview with Milena Hübschmannová, Professor of Romistics at Charles University (Prague, 27 August 1999).

[14] Zsolt Mester, "A cigány misszionárius: Beszélgetés Raduly Józseffel," *Pesti Hírlap*, 17 March 1994.

[15] Zoltan Barany, "Living on the Edge: The East European Roma in Postcommunist Politics and Societies," *Slavic Review*, 53:2 (Summer 1994): 334.

Table 6.1. Number of Romani Organizations in Eastern Europe (Includes All Organized Groups)

Country	Romani Organizations in Eastern Europe in Selected Years				
Bulgaria[a]				1997: 50	1999: 75+
Czechoslovakia[b]	1989: 44				
Czech Republic[c]			1994: 30+		1999: 75
Hungary[d]	1990: 18	1992: 96	1994: 210	1996: 240	1999: 250
Macedonia[e]		1993: 2			1999: 36
Poland[f]			1995: 5		1999: 7
Romania[g]			1994: 25	1995: 42	1999: 58
Slovakia[h]			1995: 36		1999: 92
Slovenia[i]					1999: 7

[a] 1997: O. Lipovski, ed., *Directory of Nongovernmental Organisations in Bulgaria* (Sofia: UBFA, 1997), list 30 registered organizations. An estimated 20 additional ones chose not to register. 1999: Interview with Savelina Danova (Sofia, 11 November 1999).

[b] Folkeryd and Svanberg, p. 37.

[c] 1994: Romana Vyšatová, "Romani Politics in the Czech Republic and Slovakia," unpublished manuscript, 1994. 1999: Interview with Jiřina Siklová (Prague, 31 August 1999).

[d] 1990, 1992, 1994: Erzsébet Ágoston, "A cigány munkanélküli réteg válságkezelésének helyzete (Budapest: Nemzeti és Etnikai Kisebbségi Hivatal, Cigányügyi Főosztály, 1994), p. 13. 1996: Interview with András Bíró (Budapest, 26 July 1996). 1999: Interview with Edit Rauh, Head of Roma Department, NEMO (Budapest, 9 December 1999). This last figure does not include the approximately 600 branch organizations of Lungo Drom.

[e] 1993: Only political organizations. "List of Political Parties and Associations on the Territory of Republic of Macedonia" (Skopje, September 1993). 1999: Interview with Slavica Indzevska, Program Coordinator, OSI (Skopje, 23 November 1999); and Neždet Mustafa, Mayor of Shuto Orizari (Skopje, 24 November 1999).

[f] 1995: Zoltan Barany, "Roma: Grim Realities in Eastern Europe," *Transition*, 1:4 (29 March 1995): 7. 1999: Interview with Adam Bartosz (Tarnów, 9 August 1999).

[g] 1994: Council of National Minorities (Bucharest, March 1995); 1995: interview with Catalina Ani and Klaus Fabrizius, members of the National Council for Minorities (Bucharest, 14 March 1995). 1999: National Office for Roma (Bucharest, 1999).

[h] 1995: Ondrej Dostál, "Hot Summer for Romany Minority in Slovakia," Analytical Report for PER (Bratislava, September 1995), p. 4. 1999: interview with Vincent Danihel, government commissioner for Roma issues (Bratislava, 10 September 1999). Includes 74 NGOs and 18 political parties.

[i] Interview with Vera Klopčič, Institute for Ethnic Studies (Ljubljana, 2 December 1999).

ing in splinter groups and parties that do their best to undermine each other. Many Romani parties have been created amidst great fanfare only to fade into oblivion a few months later, so that tracking them is very difficult. Hungarian Romani leaders have argued that many of the organizations that claim "national" status actually consist of single families, are founded purely for financial gain, or are essentially phantom groups.[16] It is important to notice, however, that with the maturation of Romani activism and the increasingly rigorous fiscal monitoring of funding agencies, the number of new organizations has begun to taper off and more of them have become active in pursuing projects useful for the Roma.

Are there too many Gypsy organizations in Eastern Europe, as many observers and Romani activists claim? Not necessarily. A growing number of organizations do a lot of good for the Roma and they have also served as practical training grounds for thousands of Gypsies across the region, thereby directly contributing to Romani mobilization. The fact that the majority of East European settlements with substantial Romani communities now are home to some sort of independent Gypsy organizations or their branches (whether a political party, dance club, soccer team, or self-help group) is an important accomplishment of Romani activism.

The majority of Gypsy organizations are loosely structured and are elite driven. Most of them are strictly local, but there is also a growing number of regional and national ones with branches in communities. For instance, *Partida Romilor* (Roma Party, PR), the most important Romanian Gypsy political organization, has established actively functioning branch offices in nearly every *judet* (county) of the country and *Lungo Drom*, a Hungarian sociopolitical organization, claims to have as many as 600 local groups. Their expanding responsibility and authority as well as uncooperative leaders at head offices at times drive local leaders to refuse to recognize the central bodies and register as independent associations. A good example of this phenomenon is the splitting off of the Independent Roma Union in Varna, Bulgaria from its parent organization, the Democratic Roma Union of Bulgaria.[17]

The question of how many members these organizations have is an elementary one, but the answer seldom reveals much about their real strengths or support base. First, even though it would be useful to maintain membership rosters owing to the fact that state support in many cases is proportionate to membership, most Romani groups do not keep even approximate membership lists given the high turnover and small number of their actual members. Second, the membership figures that Roma leaders are wont to give often sound unfathomably high and thus lack credence. In 1990, for instance, the Democratic-Christian Party of the Romanian Roma claimed 280,000 members while Czechoslovakia's Romani Civic Initiative claimed 121,000, and in 1992 the Democratic

---

[16] Aladár Horváth in *Budapest Week*, 9–15 September 1993; and Béla Osztojkán, *Megkérdezem Önt is* (Budapest: Phralipe, 1994), 71.
[17] Interview with Krassimir Kanev of the Helsinki Watch Group (Sofia, 6 March 1995).

Federation of Hungarian Gypsies claimed 110,000 members; none of these claims were substantiated, however.[18] As the Bulgarian human rights activist Krassimir Kanev has noted, many Romani leaders insist that *all* Roma in their country belong to their organizations in order to be taken seriously by state officials, but, of course, they elicit the opposite effect.[19] The majority of Romani leaders I asked mentioned improbably high membership numbers, but few were willing to produce supporting evidence. One of the few exceptions was Karel Holomek, leader of the Brno-based Association of Roma in Moravia (ARM), who claimed a modest 1,000 documented members. ARM's membership fees are 10 crowns ($0.30) per month, though Holomek conceded that few actually paid.[20] Membership in the Union of Polish Roma (UPR) that claims 5,000 registered members costs a hefty $120 annually, but UPR chairman Roman Kwiatkowski told me that only those with sufficient means were asked to pay.[21]

Many Romani leaders and *gadje* experts remain skeptical about the impact of Gypsy mobilization. The majority of Gypsy associations remain poorly organized, they have serious difficulties getting along with each other, let alone working together – in large part because of their intense competition for scarce resources – and they remain ineffective. Hungarian sociologists have noted that in Romani organizations

Grants and subsidies are swallowed up at the upper levels, and the effect of the organizations' work remains unnoticeable in the communities living in the direst circumstances.[22]

Perhaps a quarter of the Czech Romani organizations have concrete programs and pursue activities that have some impact on their communities, according to Holomek. The Bulgarian sociologist Ilona Tomova argues that most Romani organizations merely pretend to represent their community and that ordinary Gypsies do not know them or tend to believe that "our leaders live on our problems."[23]

At the same time, it is important to look at Romani mobilization in evolutionary terms. With the passing of time, the number of Gypsy organizations that have positively affected the Roma has grown, many of

[18] Franz Remmel, *Die Roma Rumäniens: Volk ohne Hinterland* (Vienna: Picus, 1993), 90; "Europas erste Zigeuner-Partei," *Der Standard* (Vienna), 17 May 1990; and "Mégis, ki képviseli a romákat?" *Köztársaság*, no. 13, 3 July 1992.

[19] Interview with Kanev (Sofia, 6 March 1995).

[20] Interview with Holomek (Brno, 1 September 1999).

[21] Interview with Kwiatkowski (Oświęcim, 19 August 1999).

[22] Gábor Havas, Gábor Kertesi, and István Kemény. "The Statistics of Deprivation: The Roma in Hungary," *The Hungarian Quarterly*, 36:138 (Summer 1995): 80.

[23] Interview with Tomova (Sofia, 15 November 1999).

their projects now are actually making a difference in the lives of Gypsies, and a growing number of activists have matured, gained experience, and focused their efforts on practical, worthwhile endeavors. In other words, although the majority of Romani groups remain ineffective, the improvements should be recognized and underscored.

Gypsy organizations may be classified in several ways: by the type of leadership (traditional or intellectual), by their geographic reach (local, regional, or national), or by the sources of financial support (public or private). I will discuss them according to the focus of their activities, distinguishing between socioeconomic and political organizations and bearing in mind that in some cases these areas overlap.

Socioeconomic Organizations

In the last decade the Roma have established a wide variety of social, cultural, and economic organizations from militias to protect themselves from racial attacks in Slovakia through trade unions and Gypsy university student associations in Romania to artists' groups in the Czech Republic. After the many poorly conceived projects of the early 1990s, Romani NGOs have been engaged in more and more useful and valuable undertakings as the decade had progressed. Meetings and conferences that are often useless no longer dominate the agenda of those seeking funding. More Romani NGOs are proposing to set up kindergarten classes, summer camps, self-help programs, training courses in traditional crafts as well as modern skills, and the like. Ivan Veselý, a Gypsy leader in Prague, contends that by the late 1990s the problem was not so much the dearth of useful and feasible projects but the availability of funding for them.[24] Dora Petkova, a program coordinator for the Open Society Foundation (OSF) in Sofia, notes that as Gypsy activists and their NGOs have become more experienced, it has become easier to work with them, yet it is still very difficult. She says that Romani NGOs rarely understand that not all of their projects can be funded and that the OSF's resources are limited. OSF-Bulgaria's budget for Roma-related programs has increased from $50,000 in 1996 to $150,000 in 1999, but Petkova insists that at least $300,000 would be needed to fund all worthy projects.[25]

Organizations focusing on Romani culture have played a significant role in shaping and strengthening Gypsy identity. Across the region, there are now Romani theatres (Košice, Skopje), Gypsy museums (Tarnów and Brno), and numerous cultural centers that put on music festivals and art exhibitions. There are also art galleries, soccer tournaments, writers'

---

[24] Interview with Veselý (Prague, 24 August 1999).
[25] Interview with Petkova (Sofia, 17 November 1999).

circles, and beauty pageants catering specifically to the Roma. Gypsy activists have established a growing number of social and self-help organizations that are making a difference in the lives of Roma. In the early 1990s, antidiscrimination and human rights activism were the main activities of these organizations, but that is no longer the case. Many Gypsy NGOs now help the Roma in their dealings with state bureaucracies whether they are applying for citizenship or welfare payments, or launching complaints because of discrimination. Others organize programs for young mothers to assist them in caring for their babies; still others campaign for the Roma to receive title for the land on which their houses were illegally built. There are Romani NGOs in Romania and Slovakia that assist Gypsies returning from abroad. In Hungary and Bulgaria, Gypsy organizations have succeeded in organizing small-scale agricultural cooperatives that provide their members with desperately needed food and, just as importantly, rewarding employment. A recently established Macedonian Romani NGO distributes food and medical supplies, and it offers legal aid to Gypsy refugees from Kosovo. Another one in the Czech Republic organizes after-school activities for Romani youngsters that keep them off the streets and involved in educational and creative activities.

Because traditional Romani society is male-dominated, I was surprised by the thriving of Gypsy women's organizations. In the early 1990s the Society for Romani Women in Public Life came into being in Hungary, and one of its organizers, Blanka Kozma, set up a cooperative, *Bokréta* (bouquet), for Gypsy women market vendors.[26] In Bulgaria there are half a dozen Romani women's organizations active in women's health, family planning, and skill qualification and acquisition activities (training hairdressers, cooks, and seamstresses). The purchase and distribution of schoolbooks has been the core project of the Association of Roma Women in Macedonia. As I noted, there are literally hundreds of East European Gypsy organizations and examining even a small portion of them is beyond the scope of this study. Instead I will briefly introduce a handful of the most competent Romani NGOs.

The *Wassdas* (Help) Foundation based in Cluj, Romania, is a local organization whose broad objective is to provide social help to Transylvanian Roma.[27] Prior to establishing Wassdas, its director, Géza Ötvös, paid his dues working for the international NGO, *Médecins sans Frontières* (Doctors Without Borders) for several years in the early 1990s. As for many Romani NGOs across the region, the Open Society

[26] Nándor Fehervári, "A szegénységgel kellett mindig szembenéznem," *Új Magyarország*, 11 April 1996.
[27] Interview with Géza Ötvös, head of the Wassdas Foundation (Cluj, 26 October 1999).

Foundation has been the main source of financial support for *Wassdas* in addition to the Romanian government, Hungarian foundations, and others. Its projects have included organizing summer camps for Romani children, renovating a community house, taking garbage away from Gypsy settlements, organizing legal education courses, and explaining to the Roma how to properly fill out election ballots.

Mesecina (Moon), an all-male Romani organization headquartered in Gostivar, Macedonia, is a well-organized, tightly structured Romani NGO, established in 1993.[28] Its activists are now well-trained, well-prepared, and experienced. *Mesecina* first started as a group primarily concerned with humanitarian issues, but in the second half of the 1990s it became active in educational, self-help, and legal protection projects. It is one of the first Macedonian NGOs that began to address issues at the grass-roots level. *Mesecina*'s work is also noteworthy because it has been instrumental in helping to develop other NGOs in Macedonia, most importantly *Daya* (Mother), its sister organization. *Daya* is an all-female association based in Kumanovo, whose projects focus on education for women and improving the position of Gypsy women in their families.

The Union of Polish Roma is led by an affluent Romani businessman, Roman Kwiatkowski, and based in Oświęcim (Auschwitz). Andrzej Mirga, by far the best educated and most prepared Polish Gypsy – who has since made a name for himself in the international Romani movement – was UPR's co-leader until 1995 when he resigned following a leadership conflict.[29] The two were instrumental in publicizing the Romani Holocaust. They organized a well-attended Romani Memorial Day (2 August 1995), which has since become an annual event. UPR has published and distributed a variety of publications and organized exhibitions and concerts commemorating the Porajmos. Like most successful Gypsy leaders, Kwiatkowski has many detractors within the international and the Polish Romani communities who charge that funds earmarked for activities commemorating the *Porajmos* ended up contributing to his personal wealth.[30] No one can deny, however, that Kwiatkowski established a vibrant cultural center (Cultural Association of the Roma in Poland) practically single-handedly and has cleverly capitalized on his organization being situated a couple of miles from the

[28] Interviews with Emilija Simoska and Mirjana Najcevska, researchers at the Center for Ethnic Relations, Institute for Sociological, Political, and Juridical Research, and Slavica Indzevska, a Program Officer of the Open Society Institute (both in Skopje, 23 November 1999).

[29] Interview with Mirga (Kraków, 29 July 1996).

[30] In fact, Kwiatkowski and two of his aides went on trial in Kraków on 8 August 2000 for defrauding money from a Swiss fund for Holocaust survivors. See Radio Free Europe/Radio Liberty Newsline, Part II (henceforth: RFE/RL II), 4:152 (9 August 2000).

Auschwitz–Birkenau concentration camps.[31] The UPR has been keen on maintaining good relations with Polish state agencies as well as with international foundations. Kwiatkowski has told me that, unlike most Romani NGOs, UPR has worked hard to improve the quality of its grant proposals, drafting, redrafting, and polishing them until they were "just right."[32] As a result, it has been effective in securing funding from both private and public institutions.

Finally, the *Centrul Romilor Pentru Interventie Sociala și Studii* (Center for Social Intervention and Studies, CRISS) deserves mention as a well-run and successful group based in Bucharest whose programs have extended to all regions of Romania. CRISS, established in 1993 and until 1998 run by Nicolae Gheorghe, another key player in international Romani politics, has done a wide variety of practical work ranging from preparing Gypsy children for school, vaccination campaigns, violence prevention seminars, income generation projects, antiracism campaigns, and training programs for Romani activists.[33]

Political Organizations

Although the number of socioeconomic organizations is far larger than those focusing on political participation, Romani activists have organized a few dozen political parties and NGOs across the region. It is important to note that in countries like Romania the state allows minority organizations to participate in local and national elections even if they are not registered as regular political parties.[34] The reason for this is that electoral laws generally require regular parties to have a national presence (i.e., they must have branch organizations in at least half of the counties) in order to participate in national elections. In the case of geographically compact minorities, such stature could not be easily achieved. In Bulgaria, parties based on ethnic identity are constitutionally forbidden to register. Nonetheless, as the case of the Movement for Rights and Freedoms – a party with a predominantly Turkish membership – has shown, it is possible to register as a political party if the organization

---

[31] Interview with Slawomir Kapralski, a Professor of Sociology at the Central European University (Warsaw, 18 August 1999).

[32] Interview with Kwiatkowski (Oświęcim, 19 August 1999) and "Information about activity of Roma People Association in Poland" (Oświęcim, 1999).

[33] See Romani CRISS, *Presentation of Romani CRISS and Its On-Going Projects* (Bucharest, September 1994), mimeo; and interviews with CRISS representatives Nicoleta Bițu (Bucharest, 14 March 1995 and 23 May 1996), Nicolae Gheorghe (Bucharest, 10 March 1995); and Costel Bercus (Bucharest, 29 October 1999).

[34] See Law No. 68, article 4 (15 July 1992) in *The Legislative and Institutional Framework for the National Minorities of Romania* (Bucharest: Romanian Institute for Human Rights, 1994), 95.

does not explicitly disclose its ethnic focus. Bulgarian Roma, too, have set up political parties in the late 1990s, among them the *Svobodna Bulgariya* (Free Bulgaria) and the Democratic Congress Party. There are also a growing number of Romani NGOs in the region whose work has increasingly focused on political concerns.

Judging by the small number of Romani members of parliament (MPs), one can easily infer that the Roma's political mobilization has been unsuccessful. At the same time, one must take into consideration their meager mobilizational resources, the generally low Gypsy political participation, and the often unfavorable political environment. During the second part of the 1990s, many Romani groups across the region have improved their organizations and campaigns and have succeeded in getting a growing number of Gypsies in local elections. Let us briefly look at some of the more prominent politicially oriented East European Romani organizations.

Partida Romilor, founded in March 1990, is the strongest Gypsy organization in Romania and one of the most successful one regionwide. It has offices in nearly every Romanian county and has been instrumental in assisting local Romani social groups. It has participated in local and national elections since 1992 and has succeeded in getting a growing number of local representatives elected. By the mid-1990s PR had a roster of 12,000 active members across Romania, and its local meetings have been generally attended by 200–400 people.[35] At PR's October 1999 national meeting more than 1,000 delegates participated from across the country. Throughout its existence, PR has been active in its attempts to form umbrella organizations uniting the various Romani political groups and to enter into electoral alliances with mainstream parties.

PR's improving performance is in sharp contrast with the Czech and Slovak Romani Civic Initiative (ROI), the most promising Romani party in Eastern Europe in the early 1990s whose fortunes have declined. In 1990–2, 11 MPs represented ROI in the Czech, Slovak, and the Czechoslovak legislatures, but since 1992 it has had no such success. The Czech ROI, led by Emil Sčuka and Ivan Veselý, does little more than occasionally protesting skinhead attacks or discriminatory policies. It does not lead or represent the Romani community, it organizes no noteworthy demonstrations, and, as the eminent Prague political analyst Ivan Gabal has told me, it is not part of the solution but part of the problem.[36]

---

[35] Interview with Gheorghe Raducanu, a PR leader and at the time the MP representing the Roma in the Romanian legislature (Bucharest, 14 March 1995).

[36] Interview with Gabal (Prague, 24 August 1999).

Veselý laments that ROI has no allies and no reserved seat in parliament but is unclear about how to improve the organization.[37] While ROI is the only registered Romani political party in the Czech Republic, its Slovak counterpart is one of 18. It has been a supporter of Vladimír Mečiar's Movement for a Democratic Slovakia (HZDS) even though few East European politicians have been more averse to supporting Romani causes than Mečiar and his party.

Although Hungary's *Lungo Drom* (Long Road, LD) began in 1990 as a local NGO based in the city of Szolnok, it has become the most important Romani organization in the country owing to its extraordinary success in Gypsy self-government elections. LD's leader, Flórián Farkas, has little formal education, but he succeeded in building up and improving his organization. He has also proved himself a master manipulator of politicians, a skill that allowed him to make LD the clear favorite of all three Hungarian postcommunist governments. Though his rivals are loath to admit it, LD has flourished because of its tightly knit structure (already in 1993 it had 90 documented branch organizations in eight counties), the many useful project it was able to complete, and Farkas' ability and willingness to reach compromises with government officials.[38]

Finally, mention must be made of Bulgaria's Human Rights Project (HRP), a well-organized NGO whose work has been extremely useful and constructive. HRP started out in 1992 to provide legal aid and representation to Roma and aggressively confronting governmental agencies for their discriminatory behavior. In time, HRP has succesfully capitalized on its multifaceted contacts with political elites and its extensive involvement in Romani communities. HRP has also emphasized the training of Gypsy activists, and by the late 1990s Roma constituted the majority of its staff. In 1998–9 HRP brought together some 76 Romani organizations to endorse the "Framework Program for Equal Participation of Roma in Bulgarian Public Life," which it has initiated and shaped from the beginning.[39] The Sofia government's eventual acceptance of the program signifies one of the major political successes of a Romani NGO in Eastern Europe.

---

[37] Interview with Veselý (Prague, 24 August 1999).

[38] See, for instance, "Farkas Flórián hosszú útja," *Népszabadság*, 3 November 1993; "Nyerőviszonyok: Roma politikatörténet," *Beszélő*, 11 May 1995; interviews with Farkas (Budapest, 4 August 1999) and Edit Rauh, head of the Roma Department of the Office for National and Ethnic Minorities (Budapest, 9 December 1999).

[39] See *Roma Rights in Focus* (newsletter of the HRP), no. 10 (1998); and interviews with HRP executive director Savelina Danova (Sofia, 11 and 17 November 1999).

The Programs and Objectives of Romani Organizations

Few Gypsy organizations have been able to devise realistic, consistent, and pragmatic programs during the 1990s though in this respect, too, the situation has improved by the end of the decade.[40] The political programs of Romani parties are often determined by the aspirations of individuals; thus, there is frequently little cohesion at the elite level, and it is often unclear which of the many leaders represents which goal. Often there is little agreement on specific points. One of the most divisive issues has been education in Romani language. Some Romani leaders support it because they believe that it would strengthen the ethnic identity of Gypsy communities. Others are opposed to classes in Romani owing to their conviction that it would further increase the social distance between Gypsies and *gadje* and it would diminish the Roma's chances on the labor market.[41] Still, the general aims of these organizations are similar across the region and much like those of other marginalized ethnic minorities. They include full recognition and the rights befitting a distinctive nationality, civil rights enforced by effective legal instruments, the modification of existing minority laws, an end to ethnic discrimination and strict enforcement of antidiscrimination laws, affirmative action programs in the form of state-supported social and public employment programs, better educational opportunities, more effective social welfare policies, and broadcast time in the state-owned media proportionate to the size of the Romani population and its fair portrayal therein.

Gypsy organizations have ardently protested policies damaging to their communities such as police passivity during anti-Roma attacks, the discriminatory procedures of the judicial system, the lack of Romani-language instruction, and the governments' reluctance to earmark more resources to solving their problems. More specific objectives have been particularly important on the local level where individual Gypsy leaders and/or activists have campaigned for, among other things, the installation of water and sewage treatment plants, securing facilities for cultural activities, stopping construction on a wall between Romani and *gadje* dwellings, special music classes for talented Gypsy children, a mosque to cater to Romani believers, and preferential lease of municipal land for agricultural purposes.

The programs and demands of Gypsy groups have often been unreasonable – because they were unattainable or not warranted or both – and the inevitable failures have increased the political apathy of many

---

[40] See, for instance, Anna Jurová, "Cigányok-romák Szlovákiában 1945 után," *Regio*, 7:2 (1996): 50–1.

[41] Interviews with Raducanu (Bucharest, 14 March 1995) and Emilija Simoska, Minister of Education in Macedonia in 1994–6 (Skopje, 23 November 1999).

Roma and have eroded support for their organizations. For instance, Gypsy parties routinely promise their supporters that they will place a specific number of their politicians in the local, regional, and state legislatures and nearly always fall far short of their pledges. More sensible objectives have been crowned with some successes such as, for example, the Hungarian Gypsies' peaceful antiracist demonstrations, the translation of school books to the Romani language in Romania, Slovak Gypsy activists' demand that the government prepare Romani-language forms for the 2001 census, and securing state financial support for privately organized Romani-language schools in Poland.[42]

What makes goals "reasonable" and, to a large extent, then, whether or not they are achieved depend on specific local conditions: the power and authority of the Romani organization, but even more importantly the priorities, possibilities, and especially the attitudes and policies of the pertinent local, regional, or state authorities. For instance, increasing Romani-language radio and/or television broadcast time for Macedonian and Romanian Gypsy parties was a realistic goal; for their Bulgarian counterparts it was not realistic despite the fact that the objective conditions existed in all three states. The efforts of a few Gypsy organizations, such as the Romani Integration Party (RIP) in Slovakia, have actually undermined commonly held Gypsy interests. Point 13 of RIP's Action Program reads

In our work, we do not want to isolate ourselves and create a legal Romany nationality from part of the population of the Slovak Republic, but we want to assist the more rapid *assimilation* of the Romany ethnic group by our political and educational work.[43]

But it is more important to emphasize the positive aspects of Romani institutions and their programs. More and more Roma are turning to their own NGOs with their grievances. Although many Gypsies are still unaware of Romani organizations, I have been impressed by the positive changes in this respect through the 1990s. Many Roma who claimed never to have heard of Gypsy leaders and NGOs in the mid-1990s were

---

[42] Zsolt Zádori, "A párbaj elmaradt," *Beszélő*, 17 July 1993, 9–12; *The Legislative and Institutional Framework for the National Minorities of Romania* (Bucharest: Romanian Institute for Human Rights, 1994), 29; RFE/RL II, 5:2 (4 January 2001); RFE/RL II, 5:13 (19 January 2001) and interview with Adam Andrasz, President of the Tarnów Gypsy Cultural Association (Tarnów, 9 August 1999).

[43] My emphasis. Cited in Mann, "The Formation of the Ethnic Identity of the Romany in Slovakia," 264. See also Viliam Figusch, ed., *Roma People in Slovakia and in Europe* (Bratislava: Information and Documentation Centre on the Council of Europe, 1995), 47.

not only aware of, but even participants in, the activities of Romani organizations when I revisited them at the end of the decade.

PART III: LEADERSHIP

Inspired, committed, intelligent, and foresightful leadership can be a tremendous mobilizational resource, while its absence may doom the prospects of mobilizational success. Leadership is particularly important in the case of Gypsy organizations because Romani mobilization is elite-centered, elite-driven, and extremely paternalistic. Not surprisingly, the minuscule Gypsy intelligentsia and middle class has not generated a large and diverse pool of leaders. Consequently, Gypsy politics has become the bailiwick of a small group of intellectuals and activists who have been unable influence or draw the Romani masses into politics.

Shortcomings

Romani elites have been plagued by a number of problems that have cost the East European Gypsies dearly. András Bíró says that the history of Romani politics is best understood as a rapid succession of hard-to-follow quarrels between personalities and the corresponding birth and demise of their organizations.[44] The common responses of most Roma and *gadje* interviewees I asked to characterize Gypsy leaders were "fractious," "backstabbing," and "meddlesome." A few Gypsy politicians concede that the most important leadership problem that Roma have encountered has not been the lack of educated leaders but, rather, "our national disease, *hamishagos* (to meddle or to disturb)," that "makes us want to hinder, instead of help, our own who are getting ahead."[45] In many cases Gypsy leaders expend more energy fighting each other than working for their cause. Ironically, differences of opinion between feuding Romani activists are often negligible; their bone of contention lies mainly in their ambition to supplant the other. I interviewed many government officials working on Romani affairs across Eastern Europe who lamented that their most frustrating task was compiling the list of participants for meetings, not knowing which Gypsy leaders were on speaking terms with each other at any given moment. Jiří Pehe notes that the most important problem with Romani leaders is that "they cannot rally around even such a fundamental issue as anti-Roma discrimination, instead they bicker and fight against one another."[46]

Many Gypsy leaders are hypersensitive, taken to call well-intentioned colleagues, observers, and politicians "racists" if they should disagree

---

[44] Interview with Bíró (Budapest, 26 July 1996).
[45] Ian Hancock cited by Isabel Fonseca, *Bury Me Standing: The Gypsies and Their Journey* (New York: Knopf, 1995), 296.
[46] Interview with Pehe, a former adviser to President Havel (Prague, 27 August 1999).

with them.[47] As I mentioned earlier, a fair number of contemporary Romani leaders were educated by, joined, and became active in the communist party.[48] This may be one reason why many Gypsy leaders tend to exhibit authoritarian tendencies. Few of the dozens of Romani activists I talked with through the 1990s allowed that there could be legitimate approaches and views other than their own. Those who do not accept the position of the given leader are often ostracized or shut out from the organization.[49] According to Ágnes Horváthová, most Romani leaders are far too emotional, impatient, and disinclined to compromise to be credible and effective representatives of their communities.[50]

The fact that a number of Romani leaders have found themselves in trouble with the law has further reduced their credibility, especially among the general population. In Hungary, for instance, in a twelve-month period in 1998–9 Flórián Farkas, the president, and János Kozák, a former vice president of the National Gypsy Self-Government, were charged with embezzlement. Kozák was sentenced to a 22-month prison term while Farkas, subject to several other legal proceedings as well, received a rare presidential pardon.[51] The at times embarrassing behavior of Romani leaders of national stature also hurts the Gypsies' cause. In August 1998, for instance, the Convention of Cooperation of Romani Associations and the *Partida Romilor* called for an investigation of Senator Corneliu Vadim Tudor, leader of the extremist Greater Romania Party, who publicly declared that Roma who were reluctant to integrate should be "interned in settlements."[52] His well-publicized friendship with Tudor hardly did credit to Madalin Voicu, a PR leader and the lone Gypsy MP in the Bucharest legislature (in 1996–2000), or his party. When I asked PR's two top leaders, Nicolae Paun and Ivan Gheorghe, about the Voicu Tudor relationship, they preferred not to comment on it.[53]

One of the most important shortcomings of many Romani activists and leaders is their inability to work well with state authorities. They

---

[47] This personality trait was also noted in Michael Stewart, *The Time of the Gypsies* (Boulder, CO: Westview, 1997), 92–3.

[48] Interview with Kanev, who notes that virtually all contemporary Bulgarian Romani leaders who reached adulthood before 1989 were at one point members of the Bulgarian Communist Party (Sofia, 6 March 1995).

[49] See, for instance "Mégis, ki képviseli a romáakat?"

[50] Interview with Horváthová (Bratislava, 8 September 1999).

[51] "Farkas Flórián: kegyelem után, újabb perek elött," *Magyar Hírlap*, 6 March 1998; and "Feladatokat remélnek a romák," *Népszabadság*, 29 January 1999.

[52] RFE/RL II, 2:162 (24 August 1998); and AFP (Bucharest), 26 August 1998.

[53] Interview with Paun and Gheorghe, President and Secretary General of Partida Romilor, respectively. (Bucharest, 5 November 1999).

often dismiss the genuinely good intentions of government officials, insist that a given ministry deal exclusively with them and not other Romani leaders, or let personal innuendo dominate their dealings with the authorities. As the Slovak Gypsy leader Klára Orgovánová says, one of the major weaknesses of Romani mobilization has been the Roma's inability to harness the goodwill of the government.[54]

Elite Cleavages

Romani elites are split along two major lines. The most important division is between traditional and modern leaders. The former tend to be rooted in and having a keen understanding of their communities. Typically they have little formal education but have been successful in business or some other respected endeavor. Some traditional leaders are self-promoting "ethnic entrepreneurs" who can use family influence to create momentary political spectacles while others have actually worked hard for Gypsy causes. Although they often claim to represent the entire Romani community of their country, they seldom command respect or authority outside their immediate surroundings. Traditional leaders are also more likely to make outrageous demands and threats (Ion Cioabă, for instance, was fond of threatening Germany with "Two million Gypsies with Romanian passports will soon be standing at the German border, wanting in"[55]), which is one reason why they receive so much publicity. The grandiloquent proclamations and ostentatious display of wealth of some traditional leaders have detracted attention from the severity of the Roma's problems.

New-style activists, on the other hand, tend to be younger, more dynamic, and well-educated (most individuals in this category are college graduates), and they are often multilingual and generally more clearly focused on practical objectives. Modern leaders are also more at home in *gadje* society and can communicate with state officials with much greater ease than traditional leaders. Not surprisingly, government bureaucrats and foundation officials tend to prefer dealing with modern activists.

The other important split is between leaders of different temperament or approach. The division is between those activists who one might best describe as "radical" or "extremist" versus those who are more moderate. Both types have advanced the Roma's cause, though in different ways. Radical activists have been instrumental in keeping the Roma on the government's agenda and in public focus. They often wildly exag-

---

[54] Interview with Orgovánová (Bratislava, 7 September 1999).
[55] Cited in "The Next Great Trek of the Gypsies," *World Press Review*, November 1990, 44.

Table 6.2. A Typology of East European Romani Leaders with Examples

	Radical	Moderate
Traditional	Florin Cioabă (Romania)	Amdi Bajram (Macedonia)
		Roman Kwiatkowki (Poland)
		Kyril Rashkov (Bulgaria)
New Style	Aladár Horváth (Hungary)	Karel Holomek (Czech Republic)
	Ivan Veselý (Czech Republic)	Faik Abdi (Macedonia)
		Antónia Hága (Hungary)
		Tibor Loran (Slovakia)

gerate their points and unfairly accuse state organizations and others for ignoring the Gypsies' conditions. Objectivity and a balanced approach may be missing from their political tool boxes, but those are not the things they find helpful in their mission. Moderates are more prepared to seek compromise and view their own communities in a critical, if compassionate, manner. Moderate activists tend to be more successful in accomplishing pragmatic goals and completing tangible projects, but those who finance their programs might well have been motivated to give by extremist leaders. Let us get acquainted with representatives of these leadership styles.

Four Leaders

The four leaders featured here fit into a four-part typology along the traditional–new style and moderate–radical axes (Table 6.2).

Florin Cioabă, son and heir of Ion Cioabă, is the flamboyant and wealthy Gypsy king from Sibiu, Romania, who epitomizes the traditional and radical leadership type. Florin, whose color-printed business card features a photo of himself in full regalia – including crown and sceptre – and identifies him as the "International King of gipsies[sic]" in Roman ian and English, actually wears many hats. He is a Romani representative (elected on *Partida Romilor*'s list) on the Sibiu City Council, a successful businessman, leader of his own Christian Roma Party, and a Pentecostal preacher. Although he has become somewhat wiser in his public statements in recent years, Cioabă takes after his father in his occasionally irrational statements, delivered with great verve, that make him the laughing stock of ordinary Romanians. When I asked him in late 1999 about his party's electoral chances in 2000, he insisted that all of the "three million Roma will vote for my party" and "I will have no problem reaching the 5% electoral threshold."[56] In keeping with this

[56] Interview with Cioabă (Sibiu, 27 October 1999).

belief, he brushed aside my suggestion of an electoral coalition with PR, a party he now prefers not to talk about. Cioabă likes to show off his wealth. The high point of a recent Gypsy conference in Sibiu was the tour of the royal palace complete with throne room, treasury, and stables (housing nine cars, including three Mercedes-Benz and one Lincoln) conducted by the king himself.[57]

Amdi Bajram is similar to Cioabă insofar as he, too, is a poorly educated but ostentatiously wealthy businessman from a traditional background, who has also organized his own party, the Alliance of Roma in Macedonia (AROM). Bajram, however, is a moderate and successful politician who has been a popularly elected member of the Macedonian legislature since 1996. Actually he has been elected twice, first in a majority-Macedonian electoral district in central Skopje and, in 1998, in the primarily Romani district of Shuto Orizari. Bajram has been widely criticized by Roma and non-Roma alike for his lack of political princi-ples (he has publicly said that his party "does not want to be against any government!") and for his often less than serious demeanor in parlia-ment.[58] Nonetheless, even his detractors admit that his many projects have helped Macedonian Gypsies in a variety of ways. Jelica Savinova, who is Secretary of both the Council of Interethnic Relations and the Parliamentary Committee for Interethnic Relations, notes that Bajram has worked tirelessly for a number of Roma-related causes, including the local self-government law (1997) that made the autonomous municipal-ity status of Shuto Orizari possible.[59] Bajram told me that his reason for always wanting to be allied with the government was his belief that he could do more for the Roma in power than in opposition.[60] Incidentally, the late Ion Cioabă was of the same opinion and, perhaps, for the same reason.[61]

There are several commonalities between new-style leaders. They have strong political convictions and commitments and have achieved some success in politics. Both Aladár Horváth and Karel Holomek served as elected MPs in their countries' national legislatures. In general, radical leaders tend to be younger (Horváth is in his late thirties) – their relative youth might be a clue to their political temperament – while

[57] AP (Sibiu), 24 February, 1999; *Magyar Hírlap*, 2 March 1999.
[58] Interviews with Simoska and Najcevska (Skopje, 23 November 1999); Elizabeta Georgieva, Head of the Human Rights and Minorities Department, Ministry of Foreign Affairs (Skopje, 23 November 1999); and Neždet Mustafa, Mayor of the Municipality of Shuto Orizari (Skopje, 24 November 1999).
[59] Interview with Savinova (Skopje, 30 November 1999).
[60] Interview with Bajram (Skopje, 29 November 1999).
[61] Cited in Gábor Noszkai, "Romák dél-kelet-európában," *Amaro Drom*, March 1995, 13.

moderates come from all age-groups though many of them are older (Holomek is in his sixties). Radical leaders tend to be unable to look at the Roma in a critical fashion whereas moderate ones are usually marked by their willingness to consider the Gypsies' own responsibility for their predicament.

Aladár Horváth is easily both the most charismatic and controversial Romani leader in Hungary. His courageous stance and organizational skills energized Gypsy mobilization in the late 1980s. Horváth has been the founding member of a number of useful organizations (such as the Roma Parliament, Roma Press Center, and the Roma Foundation for Civil Rights) and has been an indefatigable organizer of demonstrations, protests, and meetings on behalf of his people. He was elected an MP in 1990 on the list of the Alliance of Free Democrats (AFD), a center–left party, which chose not to put him on its list for the 1994 elections. Horváth is most famous, however, for his extremist public statements, bombastic overkill, conflicts with fellow Romani leaders, and refusal to accept workable compromises and to recognize the government's efforts to improve the Gypsies' position. He has a fondness for threatening the government with ethnic explosion and armed Gypsy insurgency, rating the occasional police violence as state-supported anti-Romani "pogroms," calling the authorities "fascists," and aggravating conflicts that are about to be calmly resolved by more moderate activists.[62] Horváth's actions tend to infuriate not just the majority populations but also many Gypsies and their leaders, like Béla Osztojkán and Flórián Farkas, who contend that his extremism hurts the Roma's cause.[63]

Karel Holomek, a retired engineer, is one of the very few second-generation Gypsy intellectuals in Eastern Europe (his father, Tomáš, was the first known Czech Rom who graduated from university). He is the embodiment of that rare breed, the well-educated, dedicated, multilingual, moderate, consensus-seeking Gypsy leader. Holomek is widely respected by government officials, Romani and gadje politicians, and ordinary Roma in the Czech Republic and abroad.[64] He was active in

[62] "A cigány misszionárius," *Pesti Hírlap*, 17 March 1994; "Tüntetés a 'romakonténer' ellen," *Népszabadság*, 24 November 1997; "Irigylésre méltó gettó," *Új Magyarország*, 25 November 1997; "1999 a roma pogromok éve?" *Napi Magyarország*, 18 September 1999; and interview with Horváth (Austin, 31 March 1995).

[63] "Kilakoltatják a fehervári romákat," *Magyar Hírlap*, 25 May 1997; "Verbuválták a cigánytüntetőket," *Új Magyarország*, 26 November 1997; "1999 a roma pogromok éve?" *Napi Magyarország*, 18 September 1999; and interviews with György Rostás-Farkas (Budapest, 7 June 1994) and Flórián Farkas (Budapest, 4 August 1999).

[64] Interviews with Andrzej Mirga (Kraków, 11 August 1999); Roman Kwiatkowski (Oświęcim, 19 August 1999); Zdeněk Matějka and Jan Pecháček, Secretary General of and Adviser to the Deputy Minister at the Ministry of Foreign Affairs, respectively

the Prague Spring and lost his job afterwards, being assigned to manual labor for two decades. Holomek signed the Charter 77 and has suffered without complaint for his convictions. A quiet and unassuming man, Holomek has done more for his people than perhaps any other Gypsy activist in the region. He is the founder of the Helsinki Citizens' Assembly Roma Section, the Chairman of the Association of Roma in Moravia, the founding editor of *Romano Hangoš* (Romani voice), and the engine behind the Museum of Romany Culture in Brno. Holomek is also one of the original organizers of ROI and served in 1990–2 in the Czech National Assembly as its MP. Since 1992 mainstream parties have routinely courted him to join their campaigns. Holomek told me – echoing the words of Faik Abdi in Macedonia, another former MP and thoughtful Gypsy activist – that one of his biggest concerns was to find equally committed and well-prepared successors who could build on the foundations he has helped to create.[65]

PART IV: COMMUNICATION AND FINANCIAL RESOURCES

Providing information to mainstream society and the Romani community is an important part of Gypsy mobilization. The financial resources necessary not only for "getting the message out," but also for office space, telephones, projects, election campaigns, and a plethora of other purposes, are likewise indispensable for the success of the Romani movement.

Communication and Media

Although there has been a marked improvement in the way that East European mainstream media have covered Romani affairs, the underlying biases of these societies still often surface. More often than not, media messages tend to underscore already rampant prejudices by focusing on negative phenomena commonly associated with the Gypsies such as crime, scandals, or migration. At the same time, media often neglect events and personalities that could increase societies' appreciation of successful Roma, the Gypsy contribution to cultural diversity, or the centuries' long marginalization of Romani communities. In several countries, regulations no longer permit the identification of the ethnic

(Prague, 23 August 1999); Ivan Gabal (Prague, 24 August 1999); Ivan Veselý and Klára Veselá-Samková, Czech Gypsy activists (Prague, 24 August 1999); Marta Miklušáková, Head of the Secretariat of the Council for Human Rights (Prague, 26 August 1999); and Šiklová (Prague, 31 August 1999).

[65] Interviews with Holomek (Brno, 1–2 September 1999) and Abdi, a former MP and leader of the Party for the Total Emanicpation of the Roma (Skopje, 11 March 1994 and 29 November 1999).

Table 6.3. Romani Media in Eastern Europe (1999)

Country	Periodical	Radio Station	Radio Broadcast	TV Station	TV Broadcast
Albania	4				
Bulgaria	5		6		5
Croatia	3		1		
Czech Republic	6		1		2
Hungary	7		2		2
Macedonia	3	13	3	2	2
Poland	2				
Romania	3				
Slovakia	3		1		1
Slovenia	1		2		
Yugoslavia	3		1		3

Sources: The database provided in "Romani and Traveller Media in Europe," *Roma Rights*, no. 4 (December 1999): 72–80; and interviews.

background of criminals. Still, journalists and commentators find ways to tell their audiences if perpetrators happen to be Roma, referring to "our dark-skinned compatriots" or "disadvantaged minority." In Bulgaria, the national media tends to ignore the Gypsy community altogether, providing a true reflection of the Roma's marginal situation in society.[66]

The press, television, and radio are potentially important tools for Romani mobilization. Gypsy activists have long recognized the persisting biases of the mainstream media and have tried to build access to the mainstream media and have campaigned for the creation of independent Gypsy media outlets since 1989.[67] Many regarded independent Romani newspapers, radio stations, and television channels especially desirable because they would have allowed the Roma to control programming and enjoy freer access to broadcast time.[68]

As Table 6.3 shows, Gypsy activists have been successful in establishing and sustaining dozens of periodicals (the frequency and regularity of publication varies widely from biweekly to semiannual) in the

[66] Interviews with Savelina Danova (Sofia, 11 November 1999) and Slavica Indzevska (Skopje, 23 November 1999). For the Slovak media's attitudes toward the Gypsies see Boris Benkovič and Lucia Vakulová, *Image of the Roma in Selected Slovak Media (June 1998-May 1999)* (Bratislava: Slovak Helsinki Committee, 2000).

[67] See, for instance, "Vázlatpontok a Phralipe tárgyalásaihoz," Budapest, 1990, mimeo; and interview with Klára Veselá-Samková and Ivan Veselý (Prague, 16 June 1994).

[68] On this issue, see Donald R. Browne, Charles M. Firestone, and Ellen Mickiewicz. *Television/Radio News & Minorities* (Washington: The Aspen Institute, 1994), 22–4.

region. This is no mean feat considering the obstacles that Romani publications constantly face. First, funding, usually provided by the state and foundations, is scarce and there is vigorous competition between applicants. In addition, revenues from advertisements are extremely low because potential advertisers are put off by the small circulation of Gypsy magazines and the low purchasing power of most Roma. Second, Gypsy periodicals appeal to a limited readership given that many Roma are illiterate or read little. More importantly, the large majority of even those Roma who read comfortably either are disinterested in Gypsy periodicals or cannot afford them.[69] Third, typically, the distribution of Romani magazines is a difficult task. Subscribers are few (primarily relevant NGOs and government agencies, prisons, etc., but few ordinary Roma), and street vendors, owing to their prejudices or the anticipation of low sales, are in most cases unwilling to carry Romani papers.[70] Fourth, editors have encountered serious problems in recruiting and retaining qualified journalists. In spite of a number of recent NGO-designed training programs, there are few Gypsy journalists. One of the complaints I most often heard about Romani media was that as soon as promising Gypsy journalists attract the attention of the mainstream media – where jobs are more prestigious and better remunerated – they tend to leave behind Romani publications.[71] Finally, in many areas only a minority of Gypsies can speak or read Romani and thus it is not useful as a language of publication. This is another drawback because it robs Gypsy communities of the inherent intimacy, exclusivity, and pride that publications in their own language could provide.

Given the problems associated with Romani newspapers, their effectiveness as a communication instrument of Gypsy mobilization has been decidedly limited. Radio and television broadcasts for and about the Roma can have a much larger impact because the proportion of Gypsies who use these media outlets is much higher than those who read newspapers. Since 1989 most East European state radio and television companies have introduced programs for the Gypsies and, in some cases, continued those that originated in the socialist period. The time that states allocate for Roma-related broadcasts is nowhere more than one

---

[69] See a 1998 research project on the Romanian Roma directed by Cătălin and Elena Zamfir found that only 7.3% read newspapers "often" and 56% "never" (Unpublished manuscript, 1999). See also, *The Media and the Roma in Contemporary Europe* (Princeton: PER, 1996), 14–16, 23.

[70] Interview with Judit Horváth, Editor-in-Chief of *Amaro Drom* (Austin, 31 March 1995); and Ivan Veselý (Prague, 24 August 1999).

[71] See, for instance, Orhan Galjus, "A Media Guided by Our Own Hand," *Transitions*, 4:4 (September 1997): 98–100; and interview with Anna Csongor, head of the Autonómia Foundation (Budapest, 4 August 1999).

hour per week. Gypsy activists have frequently complained that programs tend to contain too much music and dance rather than treatments of substantive political and socioeconomic issues.[72] In addition, in many cases programs are aired in the early morning or late night when the number of potential listeners and viewers is limited.

In Macedonia, Romani businessmen and activists have been able to start a number of local commercial television and radio stations that are, by all accounts, doing quite well.[73] NGOs, such as the Human Rights Project in Bulgaria, have paid for broadcast time in commercial radio stations for Roma-related programs, but it is fairly expensive and HRP officials have been unable to gauge the impact – and thus the cost-effectiveness – of the programs they pay for.[74] In December 1995 a Roma Press Center (RPC) began operations in Budapest with the aim of providing objective news to mainstream media outlets about the Roma. Funded by the government and the Open Society Foundation, RPC has eight employees in its head office and one reporter in each of Hungary's nineteen counties.

Financial Affairs and Resources

Romani communities are generally poor but mobilization is costly. Thus, the question of where the financial resources crucial for mobilization come from is important to examine. Across Eastern Europe, the bulk of the financial support for Gypsy groups and activities has come from the state. Governments in Hungary, the Czech Republic, Poland, Romania, and Slovenia have fully or partially bankrolled many Romani organizations and NGOs, from the Gypsy Cultural Association in Poland, through the Museum of Romani Culture in the Czech Republic, to the Union of Roma Associations in Slovenia. Bulgarian, Macedonian, and Slovak governments have earmarked considerably less money for Romani activities, albeit for different reasons (to be discussed in Chapter 8). In some cases the state provides support in proportion to the membership of the given organization, in others only if the group can raise a certain percentage of the requested funding from other sources.

State monies are usually distributed by ministries (especially culture, education, and labor), governmental minority commissions, and local authorities. Frequently, however, the state has not been an impartial grantor of its favors and its political preferences rather than the

---

[72] Interview with Jarka Balážová, editor of the Romani radio program in Prague (Prague, 14 August 1996).
[73] Interview with Neždet Mustafa, founder of "Shutel" television station in Skopje (Skopje, 24 November 1999).
[74] Interview with Danova (Sofia, 17 November 1999).

comparative merits of Gypsy organizations have determined the amount of disbursed funds. Romani organizations that are loyal to the government generally fare considerably better than those that are not. Gypsy political organizations in favor have included *Lungo Drom* in Hungary, the *Partida Romilor* in Romania since 1990, and the *Romani Civic Initiative* in Slovakia during Mečiar's rule. In 1999, for instance, PR received 4.6 billion lei (about $300,000) from the government, a great deal of money in Romania, one of the region's poorest states.[75] But the distribution of funding is nowhere as skewed in Eastern Europe as in Hungary. *Lungo Drom* has received a growing share of the centrally allocated funds for Romani groups throughout the 1990s, and especially since the 1994 introduction of the minority self-government system that LD has dominated.[76]

Domestic and international foundations – and, in some cases, foreign governments and international organizations (to be discussed in the next chapter) – are another major source of financial support for Romani NGOs. In a few instances, Gypsy political organizations have received funding from mainstream parties in exchange for campaigning for them in Romani communities or if they entered into political alliances. In Slovakia, for instance, Mečiar's HZDS has provided financial support for ROI while in Bulgaria the Bulgarian Socialist Party has given money to a number of Romani associations.[77]

To a large extent, Romani mobilization has been paid for by non-Roma because the Gypsies' own contributions remain, on the whole, minimal. This can be explained by the exceedingly modest disposable income of most Roma and the already mentioned reluctance of many wealthy Gypsies to support Romani causes. To be sure, there are a handful of activists who have put their money where their mouths are, spending considerable sums on Roma-related events, activities, and programs. Klára Veselá-Samková, a human rights lawyer and activist, told me that she and her husband, Ivan Veselý, had spent more than 750,000 Czech crowns (roughly $20,000) of their own money on the Romani movement.[78] The real "big spenders" are the few wealthy businessmen with political aspirations, among them Amdi Bajram, Florin Cioabă, and Kyril Rashkov (Rashkov is the honorary president of

---

[75] Interview with Dan Oprescu, Head of the National Office for the Roma (Bucharest, 2 November 1999).

[76] See, for instance, "Bujócska nélkül," *Amaro Drom*, April 1995, p. 10; "Nyerővis-zonyok," *Beszélő*, 11 May 1995, 23; and interview with Éva Orsós (Budapest, 25 July 1996).

[77] Interview with Rumyana Kolarova, a Professor of Political Science at the University of Sofia (Sofia, 6 March 1995).

[78] Interview with Veselá-Samková (Prague, 24 August 1999).

Svobodna Bulgariya party which is presided by his son, Anghel), who bankroll not only their own parties but also a number of other Gypsy-related causes.[79]

Notwithstanding the various sources of financial support, most Romani organizations are poorly funded. There are simply too many organizations competing for the finite amount of money that is available. Some Gypsy activists admit that they have been ineffective lobbyists incapable of capitalizing on funding opportunities.[80] Another, more important problem has been what one might politely call the lackluster financial management practices of a large number of Romani organizations. According to Holomek, finding colleagues who are "reliable with money" is exceedingly difficult.[81] The mainstream and the Romani media are full of reports of missing millions, dubious accounting schemes, corruption, and bribery in Gypsy NGOs and parties.[82] Rival Romani leaders display a penchant for publicly accusing each other of mismanaging funds.[83] Jiřina Šiklová recently directed a project examining the financial affairs of 65 Romani NGOs in the Czech Republic. The conclusions she reached were that the vast majority of Gypsy organizations cannot account for the money they receive. Šiklová claims that monies that were supposed to be spent on self-help projects or education programs often end up supporting the leaders' families and, in some cases, financing their emigration to Western Europe and North America.[84] Well-respected Romani NGOs, like CRISS in Romania, have also been accused of financial improprieties. According to Dan Pavel, the Bucharest director of the U.S.-based Project on Ethnic Relations, "there is no accountability as to how they use resources" and "CRISS employees have distinguished themselves in stealing money."[85]

---

[79] Interviews with Bajram (Skopje, 29 November 1999) Cioabă (Sibiu, 27 October 1999), and Lyudmilla Atanassova and Kamelia Stancheva, program coordinators of the Creating Effective Grassroots Alternatives (CEGA) NGO (Sofia, 10 November 1999).

[80] Interviews with Costel Vasile, leader of the Young Generation Society of the Roma (Bucharest, 14 March 1995); and Klára Orgovánová, Program Director of the Open Society Fund (Bratislava, 7 September 1999).

[81] Interview with Holomek (Brno, 1 September 1999).

[82] Some examples from Hungary: "Mégis, ki képviseli a romákat?" *Köztársaság*, 3 July 1992; "Hiányosságot igen, visszaélést nem talált a számvevőszék," and "Az elnökség és a központi hivatal tevékenysége ellenőrizhetetlen," *Amaro Drom*, April 1996, 12–13; "Lelassult a romák szociális lakásprogramja," *Magyar Hírlap*, 14 April 1998; "Képviselők árulása," *Amaro Drom*, February 1999, 10–11; and interview with Andrzej Mirga (Kraków, 11 August 1999).

[83] Interview with Ingrid Baumannová of the NOS Foundation (Bratislava, 6 September 1999).

[84] Interview with Šiklová (Prague, 31 August 1999).

[85] Interview with Dan Pavel (Bucharest, 2 November 1999).

Many ordinary Gypsies I talked with had so little confidence in their leaders' integrity that they preferred state and other *gadje* organizations to distribute funds.[86] There is no doubt that a significant proportion of the money that Romani organizations have received through the years has not been spent on the projects they were earmarked for. Extravagant meals and entertainment for Romani leaders have used up a lot of the scarce funds that should have been spent on alleviating the poverty of ordinary Roma often in the same community.[87] Gypsy leaders have often preferred to spend hard-to-come-by funds on festivals and worthless conferences used to showcase themselves in order to demonstrate their national standing instead of devising simple practical projects for their brethren. Romani activists who have served on the boards of funding agencies have on many occasions looked out for themselves, rather than for those they were supposed to help.[88] The lack of proper financial oversight by many governments and funding institutions is partly responsible for this state of affairs. Especially until the mid-1990s, few NGOs funding Romani organizations audited them. Even a major national Gypsy organization like *Lungo Drom*, which receives substantial amounts of taxpayers' money annually, has been able to get away with financial improprieties because the rules governing its fiscal affairs are remarkably lax.[89]

Clearly, as a result of all of these factors, state agencies, NGOs, and international organizations that have underwritten Romani organizations in the hope of improving the Gypsies' conditions did not get the return for their money they had anticipated. Experts on the finances of Romani mobilization agree that funders have relatively little to show for the millions of dollars they spent.[90]

---

[86] Conversations with Roma throughout Eastern Europe and interview with Jiřina Šiklová (Prague, 31 August 1999).

[87] See, for instance, "Széthúzás a hevesi romák között," *Heves megyei hírlap*, 10 March 1997.

[88] Interview with Marta Miklušáková (Prague, 26 August 1999).

[89] See the articles in *Phralipe*, December 1996, 3–8; Timothy William Waters and Rachel Guglielmo, "'Two Souls to Struggle with . . .' The Failing Implementation of Hungary's New Minorities Law and Discrimination Against the Gypsies," in John S. Micgiel, ed., *State and Nation Building in East Central Europe* (New York: Institute on East Central Europe, Columbia University, 1996), 184–6; and interview with Antal Heizer, Chief Adviser, Prime Minister's Office (Budapest, 28 May 1998).

[90] Interviews with Peter Hunčik, president of the Máray Foundation (Bratislava, 15 August 1996); David Murphy of the Nova Škola Foundation (Prague, 23 August 1999); Šiklová (Prague, 31 August 1999); Baumannová (Bratislava, 6 September 1999); and Elena Marushiakova and Vesselin Popov (Sofia, 13 November 1999).

PART V: ELECTORAL POLITICS AND BEHAVIOR

After a decade of effort, the Roma remain grossly underrepresented in local and national political bodies. However, the relatively small number of elected Romani officials does not accurately reflect the substantial increase of Gypsy presence in East European politics.

Factors Hindering Electoral Success

Some of the reasons for the lackluster electoral performance of Roma are rooted in the East European states' occasional efforts to contain Gypsy mobilization. Especially in the early 1990s, when Romani activists were inexperienced and ordinary Roma were easily deceived, state authorities and mainstream party officials frequently intimidated would-be Gypsy voters. During the June 1990 Bulgarian parliamentary elections, for instance, the Bulgarian Socialist Party (BSP) successfully manipulated the Gypsy community by spreading rumors and influencing their voting.[91] More recently, reliable sources have noted that Slovak officials managed to deceive Romani candidates at the 1998 mayoral election in the Gypsy-majority district Lunik 9 in the city of Košice.[92] Another problem is that for Romani parties and coalitions, it is very difficult to obtain the minimum 3–5% of the votes, the electoral threshold necessary for a party to gain parliamentary representation. Romania is the only East European state where all ethnic minorities, including the Roma, have a guaranteed seat in the legislature.

As I noted earlier, it would be unreasonable to expect the diverse Romani communities to field a single party. At the same time, the fact that Gypsy political organizations routinely divide between themselves the Romani vote has reduced their parliamentary representation. For instance, at the September 1992 Romanian elections five different Romani organizations split the nearly 120,000 votes that could have translated into four representatives. As a result, Gypsies had to settle for the one seat guaranteed by the constitution.[93] No fewer than 13 Romani political parties registered prior to the 1998 Slovak national elections, but eventually no Gypsy party ran candidates for

---

[91] See, for instance, *Destroying Ethnic Identity: The Gypsies of Bulgaria* (New York: Helsinki Watch, 1991), 43; and interviews with Professors Rumyana Kolarova and Nikolay Gentchev (Sofia, 6 and 7 March 1995).

[92] Jakob Hurrle, "On the Outskirts of Kosice," *Newsletter of the HCAR*, no. 6 (1998), pp. 13–15.

[93] Interviews with Varujan Vosganian, member of the parliamentary group of ethnic minorities, and Raducanu (Bucharest, 13 and 14 March 1995).

parliament on its own.[94] They were unable to form effective electoral coalitions with each other or with mainstream parties. Notwithstanding the fact that the Roma constitute nearly one-tenth of Slovakia's population, they failed to place a single MP in the national legislature in Bratislava.

In order to combine their strength, Romani groups in every East European state, time and again, have formed or attempted to form electoral coalitions and umbrella organizations with other Gypsy organizations. There are literally dozens of examples. As early as in December 1990, diverse Romani groups in Hungary rallied together in the *Romaparlament*, with the explicit goal to gain parliamentary seats. In 1993, seventeen Slovak Gypsy parties and groups formed the Union of Slovak Roma. In 1996 a handful of Gypsy activists formed the Union of Roma Associations in Slovenia; in the same year, Stanisław Stankiewicz organized the Highest Council of Roma in Poland. The majority of these umbrella organizations and coalitions have come up against the very same problems as individual Gypsy associations: mutual disdain and suspicions, infighting, and a marked inability to reach compromises.

There are some counterexamples, however. *Partida Romilor* in Romania succeeded in forming an alliance with eleven other Romani groups prior to the 1996 local elections in which 132 Gypsies were elected. Although PR was unsuccessful in national competition, it still received by far the most Romani votes, approximately 80,000.[95] The most promising recent development has been the 1997 collaboration agreement between the PR, CRISS, and the *Fundaţia Aven Amentza* (Come with Us Foundation) "for the realization of the Roma's common objectives" for a five-year period.[96] PR, CRISS, and other Romani organizations have also succeeded in creating a Working Group of Romani Associations in 1999, to work together with the Romanian government's Department for the Protection of National Minorities in developing a strategy to improve the Gypsies' conditions.[97]

---

[94] Michal Vašečka, "Roma and the 1998 Parliamentary Elections," in Martin Bútora et al., eds., *The 1998 Parliamentary Elections and Democratic Rebirth in Slovakia* (Bratislava: Institute for Public Affairs), 262.

[95] Interview with Nora Costache of the Young Generation Society of Roma (Bucharest, 23 May 1996); and OMRI Digest, 2:69 (5 April 1996).

[96] *Conventie-Cadru* (Framework Convention) document between the three organizations (Bucharest, 1 August 1997); and interview with Paun and Gheorghe of the PR (Bucharest, 5 November 1999).

[97] See *Roundtable Discussion of Government Policies on the Roma in Romania* (Princeton: PER, 1999); and interviews with Nicolae Gheorghe (Warsaw, 16 August 1999); Costel Bercus of CRISS (Bucharest, 29 October 1999).

Relations Between Romani and Majority Political Organizations

Building relations with the political parties of the majority population has been an objective of several East European Romani organizations given their failures to gain political representation on their own. Mainstream parties have seldom formed electoral coalitions with Gypsy parties, primarily because appealing to the Romani community has generally not been an important consideration for them for two reasons. First, the proportion of the Gypsies in the general population is relatively small and their voting participation has been typically far below that of the majority. Second and more important, putting a Rom on a party's list has been widely recognized as a liability given widespread societal biases against Roma. Therefore, offering Gypsies, however well-known and admired, spots on electoral lists takes courage that few parties have. In many cases Gypsy politicians are put on mainstream party rosters, but they are placed so low on the list that they have little chance of winning. Parties have often shied away from disclosing that one of their fair-skinned candidates was a Rom lest they should scare away potential voters. When during the 1992 electoral campaign Veselá Samková, then spokesperson of ROI, tried to put her party under the wing of Václav Klaus' Civic Democratic Party, she was told that "they were sorry, but they simply didn't want to risk the white vote."[98] According to László Lengyel, a noted Hungarian political analyst, for mainstream parties one Romani vote means the loss of two others.[99]

In general, mainstream parties have found other ways of courting Gypsy voters. They have tried to appeal to Romani groups on the local level and have asked well-known Romani personalities to campaign for them in their communities. For instance, during the 1996 national elections Ion Iliescu's then ruling Party of Democratic Socialism in Romania (PDSR) used Ion Cioabă to garner the substantial Romani vote in Sibiu.[100] Several East European parties resorted to the more direct approach of buying the Romani vote. Many observers claim that parties of all political hues have paid for Gypsy votes with cash, food supplies, or bribing Roma with festivals and conferences. Given the nature of these acts they are difficult to prove, but reports are

---

[98] Veselá-Samková cited in Paul Hockenos, *Free To Hate* (New York: Routledge, 1993), 231.

[99] "Ki bazsevál jövőre a cigányoknak?" *Népszava*, 24 August 1993. In conversations Zdeněk Matějka, Secretary General of the Czech Ministry of Foreign Affairs (Prague, 23 August 1999); and Yonko Grozev of the Bulgarian Helsinki Committee voiced the same opinion (Sofia, 11 November 1999).

[100] Open Media Research Institute Daily Digest, Part II (henceforth: OMRI DD II), 2:6 (9 January 1996) citing a Reuter report.

especially widespread concerning the HZDS in Slovakia and the BSP in Bulgaria.[101]

In general, mainstream parties seek to coopt the Roma through short-term political calculations rather than a prospective electoral program. According to Yonko Grozev, an official of the Bulgarian Helsinki Commission, the average politician's view is that he cannot rely on Gypsy votes because the Roma are so easy to manipulate. Thus, it does not make sense to devise a long-term electoral strategy with the Roma in mind, because two days before the election the rival party's representative can show up in the Romani community to distribute some money, food, or promise a festival and the Roma will vote for his party.[102] At times these electoral machinations have actually backfired. For instance, prior to the 1998 national and the 1999 presidential elections, campaign workers of two major parties distributed food in the Romani suburb Shuto Orizari in Macedonia, but the Gypsies voted for another party, the social democrats, that totally ignored them in their campaign.[103]

Perhaps the first serious electoral agreement between a major mainstream political party and an important Romani organization is the "protocol" targeting the 2000 national elections between the Ion Iliescu's PDSR and the *Partida Romilor*, concluded at the PR's October 1999 national congress.[104] According to the PDSR-PR concord, the PR would support the PDSR's campaign and encourage Roma to vote for Iliescu's party. In return, the PDSR offered to extend social help to the Roma and involve some of its members in policy making. Participants told me that the ambience at the congress was similar to Ceauşescu-era functions: lots of thunderous applause during Iliescu's speech at the end of which the Roma chanted "I-li-es-cu, I-li-es-cu" for minutes. Critics of the "PDSR-PR protocol," like Dan Pavel, are quick to point out that the Roma's conditions under Iliescu's six-year reign (1990–6) were far worse than since then.[105]

---

[101] See, for instance, Kate Dourian's report for Reuter (Sofia, 18 June 1990); interviews with Kolarova (Sofia, 6 March 1995); Kanev (Sofia, 6 March 1995); Marushiakova (Sofia, 9 March 1995); Grozev (Sofia, 11 November 1999); Orgovánová (Prešov, 13 June 1994 and Bratislava, 7 September 1999); Hunčik (Bratislava, 15 August 1996); Vašečka (Bratislava, 15 August 1996); and Baumannová (Bratislava, 6 September 1999).

[102] Interview with Grozev (Sofia, 11 November 1999).

[103] Interview with Simoska and Najcevska (Skopje, 23 November 1999).

[104] See "Iliescut támogatják a romák," *Szabadság* (Cluj), 25 October 1999; the protocol's text published in the PR's newspaper, *Asul de trefla*, no. 80 (1999), pp. 17–19; and Zoltan Barany, "Romani Marginality and Politics in Postsocialist Romania," in Henry F. Carey, ed., *Politics and Society in Post-Communist Romania* (Boulder, CO: Westview Press, forthcoming).

[105] Interview with Dan Pavel (Bucharest, 2 November 1999).

In contrast, PR president Nicolae Paun says that the PDSR-PR protocol is beneficial for the Roma for three reasons. First, for the first time in their history, an important political party was willing to engage the Romanian Gypsies in substantive discussions and to sign a policy agreement with them. Second, the PDSR committed itself to try to solve the Roma's social problems through a national strategy to be elaborated by the PR. Finally, the PDSR agreed to co-opt the PR into the governing process and promised two important places in the government: a state councillor at the President's Office for Roma affairs and a governmental minister responsible for dealing with the Roma.[106] Within weeks after its December 2000 electoral victory, PDSR delivered. It appointed PR leaders Gheorghe Raducanu to the former and Ivan Gheorghe (with the rank of deputy state secretary) to the latter post. Moreover, Madalin Voicu became an MP in the PDSR's colors. Paun became Voicu's successor as the MP for the Roma in the constitutionally allocated seat in parliament.

Perhaps inspired by the PR's success, eighteen Bulgarian Gypsy organizations joined forces in December 2000 to call on political parties to pledge to improve the Roma's conditions. Rumian Sechkov, head of the recently created National Council of the Roma, vowed that Gypsies would support only those parties in the April 2001 elections that agreed to put Roma on their lists and promised to increase Gypsy employment and Support Romani-language television programs.[107]

Gypsy Voting Behavior and Electoral Results

Some aspects of the electoral campaigns of Romani parties have been fairly similar to those of mainstream parties. Gypsy activists visit Romani communities, organize meetings and speak with constituents, put up electoral posters, and advertise themselves and their organizations in the Gypsy media. In exceptional cases wealthy Romani candidates, like Amdi Bajram in Macedonia in 1997, might distribute food or money among their constituents.[108] The majority of campaigns have been fairly disorganized, however, suffering from the lack of focus, cohesive leadership, and money. In recent years, as Romani mobilization has matured in some states, like Romania, campaigns have become more sophisticated and attracted more volunteer campaign workers.[109] In the case of those

---

[106] Interview with Nicolae Paun (Bucharest, 5 November 1999).
[107] RFE/RL II, 4:236 (7 December 2000).
[108] Telephone interview with Natasha Gaber, Center for Ethnic Studies (Skopje, 5 June 1997).
[109] Interviews with Nora Costache (Bucharest, 23 May 1996); and Ivan Gheorghe, Secretary General of PR (Bucharest, 5 November 1999).

Romani political organizations affiliated with mainstream parties, campaigning for that party – or against a particularly objectionable rival party – has been at the center of preelection activities.[110] Some mainstream NGOs (such as the Slovak NOS Foundation for Civic Society) have helped Gypsy candidates with training programs and workshops.[111]

Traditionally the Roma have kept their distance from politics, which many conceive of as a *gadje* concern and endeavor. Gypsy leaders often complain of the difficulty they face in persuading Roma to cast their ballots because most of them have no confidence in the electoral system. Another problem that is partly the fault of Romani leaders is that a large percentage of ordinary Gypsies are unaware of their organizations (90% in 1994 in Hungary).[112] Yet another difficulty is that many Roma simply do not know how to cast their ballots properly. Activists have documented numerous cases in Romania when the *bulibasha* or local Gypsy leader went to vote for the entire Gypsy community.[113] There have also been many instances when the Roma's votes were invalid because they voted for all, rather than for one, Gypsy organizations on the ballot. In addition, Roma who are illiterate or do not possess registration cards attesting to their permanent residency are not allowed to vote. Exogenous factors, like the restrictions of the Czech citizenship law, mainstream party manipulation, and the intimidating behavior of the authorities have also prevented thousands of potential Romani voters from exercising their rights.[114]

Several patterns of Romani voting behavior can be identified. First, the majority of Gypsies have tended to cast their votes for the party in power at the time of the election or for the party that is expected to win.[115] Second, a disproportionately large number of Roma have voted for the successors of former communist parties.[116] This is a logical manifestation of many Gypsies' nostalgia for the relative security and

---

[110] See, for instance, interview with Kanev (Sofia, 6 March 1995); and Eva Kekes, "Gypsy Leader Urges Roma to Vote Against Extreme Right," AP (Budapest), 19 May 1998.

[111] Interview with Baumannová (Bratislava, 6 September 1999).

[112] Havas, Kertesi, and Kemény, "The Statistics of Deprivation," 80; and interview with Thomas Keil, a sociologist at the University of Louisville (Bucharest, 2 June 1996).

[113] Interviews with Biţu (Bucharest, 23 May 1996); and Ötvös (Cluj, 26 October 1999).

[114] See Dan Ionescu, "The Gypsies Organize," *Report on Eastern Europe*, 1:29 (26 June 1990): 40; OMRI DD 2:9 (12 January 1996).

[115] "Gypsies Miss out as Eastern Europe's Democratic Caravan Hits the Road," *The Guardian*, 21 June 1990; "A Parlamentbe készül a Magyarországi Cigánypárt," *Népszabadság*, 15 June 1992; "Cigányvoksok," *Magyar Narancs*, 23 September 1993; and interview with Trajko Petrovski of Skopje's Marko Tsepenkov Institute (Arlington, TX, 27 March 1998).

[116] See, for instance, Dan Pavel, "Wanderers," *The New Republic*, 4 March 1991, 13; and interviews with Kolarova (Sofia, 6 March 1995) and Gentchev (Sofia, 7 March 1995).

prosperity they associate with the socialist era. Third, though other large ethnic minorities like Hungarians in Romania and Slovakia tend to vote along ethnic lines, Gypsies often do not because they have little confidence in their own. According to a recent analysis, "a Romani candidate is likely to receive only about a third of the votes of Romani voters and is unlikely to gain many votes at all from the majority population."[117] Fourth, the voting participation rate of Gypsies – given the factors outlined above – is far below that of the majority population. According to reliable estimates, less than 15% of Roma participate in elections.[118] In the 1994 Gypsy self-government election in Hungary, for instance, 8% of the Roma cast their ballots.[119]

Considering their proportion in the general population, there should be dozens of Romani MPs across the region. Instead, in late 1999 there were six: Monika Horáková in the Czech Republic, Madalin Voicu and Nicolae Paun in Romania, Asen Hristov in Bulgaria, and Amdi Bajram and Djulistana Markovska in Macedonia. Of the six, Bajram was elected on his own, Horáková, Hristov, Markovska, and Voicu were on mainstream parties' lists, and Paun has held the seat guaranteed to the Romani minority. Voicu's predecessor in the Bucharest legislature was Gheorghe Raducanu (1992–6); his successor, as noted above, is Nicolae Paun (2000–). With the exceptions of ROI in Czechoslovakia in 1990 (it placed five MPs in the federal, five in the Czech, and one in the Slovak legislatures[120]) and the Party for the Total Emancipation of Roma (Faik Abdi) and AROM (Bajram) in Macedonia, at least one of which has had an MP since 1990, Romani parties have not succeeded in sending any candidates to national legislatures. It is important to note that in 1990 ROI ran in a coalition with the victorious Civic Forum in the Czech Lands and the Public against Violence in Slovakia. There are only a handful of other Romani MPs who have been elected on mainstream parties' tickets: Manush Romanov (Union of Democratic Forces, 1990–1); Petar Gheorgiev (BSP, 1994–6), and Tsvetelin Kanchev[121] (Euroleft, 1996–2000) in Bulgaria; Ladislav Body (Communist Party of

---

[117] *Political Participation and the Roma in Hungary and Slovakia* (Princeton: PER, 1999), 5.

[118] See, for instance, interviews with János Báthory, an official at the Office for National and Ethnic Minorities (Budapest, 9 June 1994); Gheorghe Raducanu (Bucharest, 14 May 1995); Bíró (Budapest, 26 July 1996); Hunčik (Bratislava, 15 August 1996); and Gabal (24 August 1999).

[119] "Minket ne válasszanak külön!" *Amaro Drom*, March 1995, 5.

[120] Interview with Holomek, a former MP in the Czech legislature (Brno, 1 September 1999).

[121] In February 2000 Kanchev was sentenced to six years of imprisonment for theft. Correspondence with Ulf Brunnbauer of the University of Graz (2 March 2000).

Bohemia and Moravia and Left Bloc, 1990–6) in the Czech Republic; Madalin Voicu (PDSR, 2000–) in Romania; and Antónia Hága (AFD, 1990–8), Aladár Horváth (AFD, 1990–4), and Tamás Péli (Hungarian Socialist Party, 1992–4) in Hungary. Only a fatal automobile accident (a month before the November 1998 elections) prevented a Rom, Jan Kompuš, the leader of ROI in Slovakia, from gaining a parliamentary seat on the HZDS' list. An often forgotten point is that there might actually be quite a few more Roma in East European legislatures who do not openly identify themselves with their ethnic heritage.

There has been progress in Gypsy mobilization, and this progress is most clearly measurable in the growing number of Romani elected local officials. On the local level – especially in areas where Gypsies make up a substantial proportion of voters – Romani activists have improved their electoral record with each successive local election. In Romania, for instance, voters elected 106 Gypsies as local council members in 1992, 136 in 1996, and 160 (and 4 county councilpersons) in 2000.[122] In Macedonia, their number had increased from 15 in the 1990 municipal elections to 23 in 1996.[123] In Slovakia, Roma elected 56 Gypsy council members and 6 mayors in the 1998 local elections.[124] In Bulgaria relatively few Romani local officials were elected until the October 1999 local elections. For the first time, two Romani parties (*Svobodna Bulgariya* and the Democratic Congress Party) – though not registered as ethnic parties – managed to get 92 of their candidates elected.[125] Again, in addition to these Roma, dozens of others have succeeded in local elections representing mainstream parties and, quite likely, dozens more who do not openly identify themselves as Roma. In sum, there are now hundreds of Gypsy local councilpeople and perhaps a dozen municipal mayors and submayors across Eastern Europe.

Poland, where there are no known Romani council members, and the Czech Republic – where according to Holomek there are at most five – add little to this total and the obvious question is why? In Poland the

---

[122] *The Legislative and Institutional Framework*, 100; e-mail correspondence with OMRI archivist Karolina Jakab (26 November 1996); interview with Dan Oprescu (Bucharest, 2 November 1999); and e-mail communication with Lena Cruceru of PER (13 June 2000).

[123] *Basic Statistical Data for the Republic of Macedonia* (Skopje: Statistical Office of Macedonia, 1992), 48; and *Basic Statistical Data for the Republic of Macedonia* (Skopje: Statistical Office of Macedonia, 1998), 66–9.

[124] Michal Vašečka, "The Roma," in Gregoríj Mešeznikov, Michal Ivantyšyn, and Tom Nicholson, eds., *Slovakia 1998–1999: A Global Report on the State of Society* (Bratislava: Institute of Public Affairs, 1999), 404.

[125] Interview with Petar Atanasov, Secretary of the National Council on Ethnic and Demographic Issues at the Council of Ministers (Sofia, 15 November 1999).

Roma are so widely dispersed that they only make up a tiny proportion of the electorate in most electoral districts. For instance, the population of Kraków is 600,000, of whom only 600 are Gypsies.[126] The deficiencies of Gypsy mobilization, combined with more acute anti-Romani prejudices and the low geographical concentration of Gypsies, are the most important reasons for the small number of elected Romani officials in the Czech Republic.

Hungary is a special case given its minority self-government system that provides opportunities for minorities to form their own administrative bodies locally and nationally (to be discussed in more detail in Chapter 9). In the three elections held for minority self-government since 1994, Hungarian Roma elected an increasing number of local assemblies: 416 in 1994 and an additional 61 in 1995 (supplemental elections had to be held because some localities were not prepared), and 765 in 1998.[127] In 1995 a Budapest-wide Gypsy self-government was elected; in the same year and again in 1998, national Gypsy self-government was also elected. Although many observers have criticized both the electoral rules and the elections themselves, the important point is that thousands of Hungarian Roma have not only been involved in the electoral process but have also served in different capacities their own self-governments.

CONCLUSION

The regime change from socialism to democracy afforded the Roma the opportunity to alleviate their political marginality. After a decade of mobilization, however, the Gypsies remain woefully underrepresented in Eastern Europe's polities. Their weak ethnic identity, infighting, poor leadership, the proliferation of organizations, the relative absence of ethnic solidarity and substantial resources, and low voter participation have thwarted their collective action and impeded their ability to affect state policies. It is important also to underscore the diversity of Romani communities and their minimal political experience. Thus, the initial failings of Romani politics should not be unexpected.

Institutions constitute the backbone of Gypsy mobilization. Romani political organizations receive a poor grade when evaluated by Samuel Huntington's criteria of institutionalization[128]: They tend to be rigid and

---

[126] Interview with Mirga (Kraków, 29 July 1996).

[127] After 1998 two self-governments ceased to exist; therefore, their number in 2000 was 763. See Csaba Tabajdi, *Látlelet a magyarországi cigányság helyzetéről* (Budapest: Miniszterelnöki Hivatal, 1996), 12; "Helyi nyerők," *Amaro Drom*, November 1998, 3; and correspondence with Edit Rauh, 12 April 2000.

[128] See the discussion on the criteria of political institutionalization in Huntington, *Political Order in Changing Societies* (New Haven: Yale University Press, 1968), 12–24.

unadaptable; have simple structure (usually few if any subunits) and few, often ill-defined, objectives; and are marked by disunity. On the other hand, most Romani political organizations tend to be highly indepen- dent. As Gypsy associations and their leaders mature by virtue of their protracted participation in political processes, they are likely to achieve a higher level of institutionalization and become more effective.

Notwithstanding the fact that Gypsy mobilization is still in its infancy, the past decade has brought some important successes. In the last few years the Romani movement has become more mature, better organized, and more assertive across Eastern Europe. There is less infighting and more willingness to compromise. An growing number of Gypsies are in positions of decision making on the local level and thousands have become involved in public life, whether as volunteers working for NGOs or as the representatives of their communities. In sum, in the past decade the Roma have gained a political presence that states and societies have had to accept as legitimate. Undoubtedly, this presence will continue to expand as the number and effectiveness of Romani NGOs and organization increase.

7

The International Dimension

Migration and Institutions

International factors have had an important effect on the status of East European Gypsies. My task here is to marshal empirical evidence in support of this contention by analyzing three complex issues. In Part I, I discuss Gypsy migration to Western Europe (and to a smaller degree, North America) after the collapse of East European state-socialism. I argue that migration relieves the Roma's marginal conditions only in the economic sense and only in relative terms. Their social exclusion may actually increase because West European governments and societies are often just as inhospitable toward them as are those they leave behind. In Part II, I briefly examine the international Romani movement that emerged prior to but intensified in the 1990s. I contend that the lack of focus, fractiousness, and poor leadership of the Roma's international organizations in many ways mirror the characteristics of their political mobilization in East European states. In Part III, I analyze the activities and track record of non-Gypsy international organizations (IOs) and nongovernmental organizations (NGOs) in their attempts to publicize the Roma's plight and to improve their conditions. The key argument is that by monitoring and criticizing state minority policies as well as pursuing some important projects, they have been worthy champions of the Gypsies' cause.

PART I: GYPSY INTERSTATE MIGRATION AFTER 1989

Socialist states restricted travel to the West and heavily guarded their borders, thereby effectively preventing most citizens from leaving. Large-scale emigration soon followed the postcommunist East European governments' decision to reestablish full freedom of movement. In November 1992 the European Community's polling organization, Eurobarometer, asked nearly 20,000 people in 18 Central and East European countries the likelihood of their moving to Western Europe to live and work. The response from 7.3% of those surveyed was "definitely" or "probably," a figure that translated to about 16.7 million people across the region. As it turned out, many stayed, but by 1992 hundreds of thousands of East Europeans (600,000 from the former Yugoslavia alone) migrated to Western Europe.[1] Myron Weiner has suggested that internal ethnic conflicts are often internationalized through migration and refugee flows.[2] This is precisely what occurred in the Roma's case. They constituted a large proportion of those leaving for Western Europe, thereby making the East European states' "Gypsy problem" into an international issue.

Migration

In the early 1990s tens of thousands of Roma left Eastern Europe, particularly Bulgaria, Romania, and Yugoslavia, to escape discrimination, persecution, and, especially, economic hardship. Many made their way through Hungary and Czechoslovakia to Poland, which, given its geographical proximity, became a major stopover for those trying to reach Germany and, to a lesser extent, other West European states. Of the approximately 450,000 asylum seekers who entered Germany in 1992, 100,000 came through Poland. The influx of tens of thousands of Roma from Romania and Bulgaria who began to arrive in Poland as early as late 1990 was, according to Adam Bartosz, comparable only in its scale to the migration of liberated Gypsy slaves from Moldavia and Wallachia in the 1850s.[3] In Warsaw and in numerous Polish towns close to the German border, thousands of Roma camped out under bridges, railway stations, and other public spaces. In 1995, after repeated warnings, Polish police destroyed a Romanian Gypsy settlement under Warsaw's Grota Bridge, forcing its inhabitants to leave. The border town of Zgorzelec had perhaps the largest concentration of Gypsies from the Balkans, waiting for the chance to cross over to Görlitz on the German side. Living conditions in the border areas were abysmal; in some cases

---

[1] "Public Opinion about the European Community," *Central and Eastern Eurobarometer* no. 3 (Brussels: European Community, February 1993), 37.

[2] Weiner, Myron. "Peoples and states in a new Ethnic Order?" *Third World Quarterly*, 13:2 (1992): 321–2. See also Aristide Zolberg, "The Next Waves: Migration Theory for a Changing World," *International Migration Review*, 23 (1989): 403–30; F. W. Carter, R. A. French, and J. Salt, "International Migration between East and West in Europe," *Ethnic and Racial Studies*, 16:3 (July 1993): 467–91; Marco Martinello and Marc Poncelet, eds., *Migrations et Minorités ethniques dans l'espace Européen* (Brussels: De Boeck-Wesmael, 1993); and John Wrench and John Solomos, eds., *Racism and Migration in Western Europe* (Oxford: Berg, 1993).

[3] Adam Bartosz, "The Social and Political Status of the Roma in Poland," *Roma*, no. 40 (January 1994): 22.

Romani women gave birth on the street.[4] Polish authorities did not know how to handle large numbers of refugees and, in any case, were ill-equipped to care for them. Given the dearth of private charities, the Polish Red Cross had a virtual monopoly on helping the Roma and other refugees. A Red Cross official lamented that the Gypsies were not easy to help because "They want only money, other forms of assistance does not interest them. We have offered them food and clothing which they don't want but we have nothing more to give."[5]

With its high living standards and Europe's most liberal refugee law, Germany acted as a veritable magnet for the vast majority of East European Romani migrants.[6] German authorities reported that over half of the 35,345 Romanian citizens who reached Germany in 1990 were Roma.[7] Between January and September 1991 about 91,000 Romanian citizens entered Germany; 81% of them, according to the Gypsy activist Nicolae Gheorghe, were Roma.[8] The following year 33,600 Romanian Gypsies entered Germany. In 1991 alone, thousands of Roma left Macedonia for the German state of Nord-Rhein-Westphalia.

The postcommunist migration wave affected Yugoslavia more than any other East European state. Large-scale migration had begun prior to the wars that accompanied the breakup of the federation and accelerated after 1991. Moreover, proportionately – and perhaps even in absolute numbers – more Roma left Yugoslavia than any other ethnic group. By late 1991, according to sources in Belgrade, Gypsies were leaving the country "by the thousands daily."[9] A 1996 fact-finding

---

[4] "Romanians, Bulgarians Camping on Polish Border to Cross into Germany," DPA (Warsaw), 20 July 1991; and "Volk ohne Land – Rostock war nur der Auftakt," *Profil* (Vienna), 7 September 1992.

[5] "In Polen bleibt das Rote Kreuz alleine," *Die Tageszeitung*, 4 December 1993.

[6] Until it was changed in 1993, the law meant that anyone claiming asylum had to be housed and fed at public expense until their claim was adjudicated. See Hartmut Esser and Hermann Korte, "Federal Republic of Germany," in Thomas Hammar, ed., *European Immigration Policy: A Comparative Study* (Cambridge, UK: Cambridge University Press, 1985), 165–206; and Kay Hailbronner, "Citizenship and Nationhood in Germany," in William Rogers Brubaker, ed., *Immigration and the Politics of Citizenship in Europe and North America* (Lanham, MD: University Press of America, 1989), 67–80.

[7] David M. Crowe, *A History of the Gypsies of Eastern Europe and Russia* (London: I. B. Tauris, 1995), 147.

[8] John Tagliabue, "Romanian Gypsies Search for Safety and Stability in Changing Europe," *New York Times*, 27 November 1991. Between 1990 and 1996 approximately 240,000 people emigrated from Romania, of whom 46.8 percent were 18–40 years old and 52 percent women. See "Nem lanyhul a kivándorlás," *Magyar Nemzet*, 31 January 1997.

[9] *Borba* (Belgrade), 19–20 October 1991; cited in Patrick Moore, "The Minorities' Plight amid Civil War," *Report on Eastern Europe* 2:50 (13 December 1991): 32.

mission of the Organization for Security and Cooperation in Europe (OSCE) concluded that few Roma remained in Bosnia-Herzegovina (for instance, 200 of the 5,000–7,000 in Banja Luka, 190 of the 8,000 in Bijeljina), most of them having fled to Western Europe.[10] In 1998–9 many thousands of Roma left the Yugoslav province of Kosovo because they were persecuted by both ethnic Serbs and Albanians.

Most East European Romani migrants preferred Germany as their destination but they attempted to find refuge in other West European states as well, albeit with less success. By the early 1990s there were approximately 15,000 Gypsy asylum seekers in Sweden, although with little chance of being declared bona fide refugees. After a mob attack on the wealthy Romani neighborhood in the central Polish city of Mława in the summer of 1991, more than 1,000 Roma sought refuge in Sweden. Immigration authorities turned them back because according to Swedish law, persons aspiring for political refugee status must prove persecution by the authorities, not by other citizens, in their home country.[11] The United Kingdom and Ireland became a destination for East European Roma in the late 1990s. In 1997 over 500 Romanian Gypsies left for Ireland, hoping to take advantage of the country's "good welfare system and stable economy."[12] In the first seven months of the same year almost 1,100 Slovak Roma applied for asylum to British authorities who feared that 3,000 more were on their way.[13] They were not far off the mark. In August and September 1998 alone, according to the British Home Office, 1,611 Slovak and 460 Czech Roma requested political asylum in the United Kingdom. After a flurry of diplomatic activity, personal pleas from President Václav Havel, and Czech promises to pay more attention to the Roma's conditions, Tony Blair's government agreed not to reimpose visa requirements for Czech citizens. Irish authorities were less understanding and began to require visas from Slovak citizens in October 1998.

Gypsy migration from the former Czechoslovakia shows few signs of tapering off, although destinations have changed. After Slovak Roma turned up in Belgian and Danish immigration offices in early 1999, in

---

[10] See Katrin Reemstma's report in the OSCE's *CPRSI (Contact Point for Roma and Sinti Issues) Newsletter*, 2:6 (December 1996): 7–9.

[11] AP (Stockholm), 28 July 1991; Reuter (Warsaw), 4 August 1991; and David McQuaid, "The Growing Assertiveness of Minorities," *Report on Eastern Europe*, 2:50 (13 December 1991): 23.

[12] Nicolae Gheorghe cited by Mediafax (Bucharest), 26 August 1997; and Radio Free Europe/Radio Liberty Newsline, Part II (henceforth: RFE/RL II), 1:105 (28 August 1997).

[13] *Transitions*, 4:5 (October 1997): 9; and "Gypsy Asylum-Seekers Flood into Britain," *Globe and Mail* (Toronto), 21 October 1997.

late June 1999 more than 300 of them arrived in Finland asking for political asylum.[14] In July 1999, after the arrival of 1,069 in the first six months of the year, the Helsinki government joined Denmark and Norway and suspended its visa-free agreement with Slovakia. In November, Finland abolished the visa requirement for Slovaks after the number of asylum seekers receded, only to reimpose it again in mid-January 2000 in response to another wave of Gypsies arriving from Slovakia.[15] In early August 2000, less than three weeks after Finland abolished visa requirements for Slovak nationals yet again, 50 Slovak citizens (assumed to be Roma) arrived in Helsinki in search of asylum.[16] Judging by the numbers, Britain continues to seem attractive to Czech Gypsies. In January–May 1999 1,000 Czech Roma sought asylum in Britain, while in December 1999 there were 200 attempts.[17] The saga continues. . . . In September 2000 Belgium reimposed visa requirements on Slovak citizens, lifted just one month earlier, after the renewed influx of asylum seekers.[18]

Narrowing opportunities to settle in Western Europe directed a growing number of East European Roma across the Atlantic. On 4 August 1997 the Czech tabloid-style TV station NOVA aired a documentary showing the Roma living what they described "the good life" in Canada – a country with a refugee-friendly reputation across Eastern Europe. Within days the Czech national airline sold all economy-class tickets to Canada through October. Hundreds of Czech Gypsies – who, as Czech citizens, did not need visas – took the trip to apply for political asylum in Montreal, Toronto, and elsewhere. By 21 August all of Toronto's 39 family shelters were full owing to the new arrivals.[19] Two months later, Canada reintroduced visa requirements for Czech citizens. In mid-1998 Donald Kenrick wrote that, owing to the rigorous work of self-help and civil liberties organizations and an unusually responsive government, "The Hungarian Gypsies alone have shown no desire to get up and leave the country."[20] Although proportionately and in absolute numbers far fewer Roma chose to emigrate from Hungary than from other East European states, in 1997 300 but in 1998 1,380 Hungarians

---

[14] FNB/STT News Agency (Helsinki), 28 June 1999; reported in RFE/RL II, 3:126 (29 June 1999).

[15] RFE/RL II, 4:10 (14 January 2000).

[16] Ibid., 4:149 (4 August 2000).

[17] *Pravo* (Prague), 18 May 1999; CTK (Prague), 25 May 1999; and RFE/RL II 4:9 (13 January 2000).

[18] See RFE/RL II, 4:170 (4 September 2000) and 5:10 (16 January 2001).

[19] See, for instance, Jan Sliva, "Gypsies Plan to Emigrate for a Better Life in Canada," AP (Prague), 15 August 1997; and RFE/RL II, 1:101 (22 August 1997).

[20] Donald Kenrick, "How Many Roads," *Index on Censorship*, 27:4 (July/August 1998): 59.

applied for political asylum in Canada, the vast majority of them Roma.[21] In the summer of 2000, a group of 50 Hungarian Gypsies arrived in France to seek political asylum. Their leader said they did not feel safe in Hungary because of their origins, but a number of Romani groups and leaders – including Flórián Farkas (of the National Gypsy Self-Government) and Aladár Kotai (the head of the local self-government in the city of Ózd) – strongly denied any political persecution of the Roma in Hungary and insisted that the 50 Roma left for economic reasons.[22]

Though there have been a few cases of Czech town officials (in Mariánské Hory and Ostrava) offering to help pay for airline tickets for Gypsies who wanted to leave, this was by no means not the norm.[23] In fact, high-ranking government officials in the Czech Republic, Hungary, Slovakia, and elsewhere have repeatedly appealed to the Roma to stay.[24] Thus one should not take Kenrick seriously when he writes (in 1998!) that "What we are now seeing in eastern Europe is not so much genocide as ethnic cleansing, an attempt in many countries to persuade Gypsies to emigrate *en masse.*"[25] He refers to a few extremist Romanian and Polish politicians and organizations; but these, like the skinheads, enjoy modest popular support and less political power. Moreover, Kenrick also neglects to mention that in numerous cases Gypsies have actually asked authorities to help them emigrate by subsidizing their airfare.[26] In 1998, for instance, 200 Czech Romani families demanded that Vladimír Mlynar, the Prague government's minister in charge of ethnic affairs, help them leave for the United States. Mlynar

---

[21] See "Kósáné: Nem lesz tömeges kivándorlás," *Népszabadság,* 9 January 1999; and "Nem kaptak menedékjogot a magyar romák Kanadában," *Népszabadság,* 22 January 1999; and "Bizonytalan helyzetben a Kanadában rekedt romák," *Népszabadság,* 22 March 1999.

[22] RFE/RL II, 1:141 (25 July 2000); 4:143 (27 July 2000); Pál Szarka, "Politikai akciót gyanít a Fidesz," *Magyar Nemzet,* 27 July 2000; RFE/RL II, 4:151 (8 August 2000), 4:165 (29 August 2000). More recently, Roma from Hungary tried their luck in the Netherlands, though Canada remains a favored destination. See REF/RL II, 4:244 (19 December 2000); and Éva Erdei, "A mohácsi romàk Kanadàba tartanak," *Magyar Hírlap,* 29 September 2000.

[23] "Gypsies Eyeing Canada as Haven," *Globe and Mail* (Toronto), 13 August 1997; and Jan Sliva, "Gypsies Plan to Emigrate for a Better Life in Canada," AP (Prague), 15 August 1997.

[24] See, for instance, CTK (Prague), 14 August 1997; RFE/RL II 1:96 (15 August 1997); 3:128 (1 July 1999).

[25] Donald Kenrick, "How Many Roads," *Index on Censorship,* 27:4 (July–August 1998): 60.

[26] See, for instance, "Helping Romanies Emigrate Is No Solution," CTK (New York), 24 February 1998.

refused, saying he could not assist Czech nationals in leaving their country.[27]

It is important to note that by the late 1990s there were few instances of institutionalized political persecution of the Roma in Eastern Europe. Most of them remain mired in poverty, there is widespread societal discrimination against them, and many local officials, the police, and aid administrators share anti-Gypsy prejudices. But, as Gheorghe Raducanu, a Romanian Gypsy leader and a former member of parliament, noted as early as 1993, "There are very few Roma who must flee from Romania because of political persecution. The majority only want to make money quickly and have no right to asylum."[28] Several Romani leaders from across the region have echoed Raducanu's words, noting that mass unemployment and economic marginality rather than fear of skinhead attacks or political reasons drive the Roma to apply for political asylum.[29] Further evidence supporting their argument is that since the spring of 2000, hundreds of Slovak Roma have also petitioned for asylum in the Czech Republic even though the latter is supposed to have the most anti-Gypsy climate in Europe (but, not coincidentally, higher living standards than Slovakia).[30]

An often neglected question is, Which Roma are leaving Eastern Europe? The politicians and Gypsy activists I interviewed agree that the majority of Roma migrants are relatively well-to-do, middle-class Gypsies who can afford the substantial costs of travel to Western Europe and North America.[31] Karel Holomek, perhaps the most respected Czech Gypsy leader, has written the following:

[27] "Romanies Demand Departure for USA," CTK (Prague), 21 February 1998.

[28] "Erst im Himmel sicher," *Der Spiegel*, 19 July 1993.

[29] See, for instance, János Kozák, vice president of the National Gypsy Self-Government in Hungary (*Népszabadság*, 9 January 1999); Gejza Adam, chairman of the Slovak Romany Civic Initiative (AP [Helsinki], 29 June 1999; RFE/RL II, 3:127 [30 June 1999]); and interview with Adam Andrasz, vice president of the Highest Council of Roma in Poland (Tarnów, 9 August 1999).

[30] See RFE/RL II, 4:124 (27 June 2000); 4:126 (29 June 2000); 4:127 (30 June 2000); and 4:207 (25 October 2000).

[31] See interviews with David Murphy of the Nova Škola Foundation (Prague, 23 August 1999); Marta Miklušáková, Head of the Secretariat of the Council for Human Rights (Prague, 26 August 1999); Milena Hübschmannová, Professor of Romistics at Charles University (Prague 27 August 1999); Karel Holomek (Brno, 1 September 1999); Agnes Horváthová, Head of Secretariat, Slovak Helsinki Commission (Bratislava, 8 September 1999); and ethnographers Elena Marushiakova and Vesselin Popov (Sofia, 13 November 1999). William Zimmerman has shown in a different context – that of Yugoslav guest-workers – that the best-positioned people tend to leave. See Zimmerman, *Open Borders, Nonalignment, and the Political Evolution of Yugoslavia* (Princeton: Princeton University Press, 1987).

The tragedy is that those most vulnerable and living in the worst conditions are not able to apply for a visa due to their financial position and the fact that they are ill-prepared to take such a giant step. Unfortunately these are the Roma who need asylum the most.[32]

In fact, Elena Marushiakova and Vesselin Popov claim that many Bulgarians seeking asylum in Canada and the United States are not Roma at all. They are ethnic Bulgarians who are often instructed by U.S. NGOs and immigration lawyers to pose as Roma and testify that the reason why they cannot speak Romani is because speaking the language was forbidden in the communist era.[33] The two Bulgarian scholars contend that the reason why they have been unable to convince foreign officials and NGOs about the "mistaken identity" of asylum seekers is because NGOs and immigration lawyers have a vested interest in this issue. I, too, have some experience in this matter. In 1998, the Princeton-based Political Asylum Research and Documentation Service (PARDS) asked for my opinion about the case of a supposedly Romani woman from Romania applying for asylum in the United States. PARDS' director suggested that if I supported the woman's claims of persecution, there might be many more such requests and for my assessments I would be handsomely remunerated. After I concluded, based on a review of the evidence provided by PARDS, that the claims were spurious, PARDS refused to pay me and never contacted me again.

Romani asylum seekers in Western Europe and North America are often intimately familiar with immigration procedures because they are helped by Gypsy publications, travel agencies, and NGOs. The March 1999 issue of a Budapest-based Romani magazine published an article entitled "Step by Step: From Asylum Application to Canadian Citizenship" to guide the prospective refugee through the maize of Canadian immigration bureaucracy and to provide practical advice, such as how to obtain welfare payments.[34] Pál Csáky, the Slovak Deputy Prime Minister in charge of ethnic affairs, who has been accused by opposition parties of "failing to stop the recent exodus" of Roma, and Czech Foreign Minister Jan Kavan have suggested that Romani migration from their countries is well-organized.[35] In February 2000 Csáky's office started to investigate several Slovak travel agencies that print instructions on how Roma should behave once they reached a country, where

---

[32] Karel Holomek, "The Mass Asylum of Romany in the Ostrava Area," *Newsletter of the Helsinki Citizens' Assembly – Roma Section*, no. 3 (May 1998): 12.

[33] Interview with Marushiakova and Popov (Sofia, 13 November 1999).

[34] "Lépésröl lépésre: A menedékjog kérelemtöl a kanadai állampolgárságig," *Amaro Drom*, 9:3 (March 1999): 10–11.

[35] "Ki áll a romák kivándorlása hátterében?" *Napi Magyarország*, 4 August 1999; interview with Miklušáková (Prague, 26 August 1999); and "SDL halts privatisation parade," *Slovak Spectator*, 6–12 September 1999.

they could seek asylum, and how to secure the financial help extended to asylum seekers.[36]

The Roma's Situation in Their New Countries

Gypsies arriving in West European states soon discover that while their living standards might improve even if social assistance is their only source of income, public attitudes and policies toward them are rarely more charitable than in Eastern Europe. The socioeconomic traumas of German reunification, the large number of foreigners (most of them guest workers or their descendants) already in the country, the massive influx of East European, Asian, and African asylum seekers, and the resettlement of ethnic Germans from the former communist states created a tense social situation in Germany in the early 1990s.

No other immigrant group attracted as much criticism as the Roma. Local politicians and citizens had charged that many of the newly arriving Roma were aggressively begging on the streets, often grabbing people and refusing to let go, while groups of Gypsies attacked and robbed pedestrians who were unwilling to part with their cash voluntarily.[37] According to residents of Rostock, a northeastern German harbor city where neo-Nazis torched a building housing Romani asylum seekers in August 1992, the Gypsies "left garbage on the streets, stole from stores, and threatened shopkeepers."[38] Others noted that though Rostock had long been home to a Vietnamese community, "they were no problem." "Our only problem was the Gypsies," said one middle-age man, adding "Go look around, then ask yourself, what would you do if you lived here?"[39] Hermann Heinemann, the social minister of Nord-Rhein-Westphalia, noted that the Roma were "poisoning the atmosphere through their misbehavior."[40] He expressed the frustration of many Germans who viewed the Gypsies as the antithesis of their most prized values like stability, order, and cleanliness.

In the early 1990s, tensions resulted in hundreds of atrocities against immigrants, which included several murders, the burning of buildings housing refugees, and many assaults and other crimes.[41] In 1992, perhaps

---

[36] RFE/RL II, 4:23 (2 February 2000); and "Slovak Deputy Premier Says He Has Evidence of Organized 'Asylum Tourism'," BBC Monitoring (Bratislava, 7 November 2000).

[37] See, for instance, Michael Wall, "Germans Trying to Cope with Gypsy Migrants," NCA (Bonn), 1 August 1991.

[38] Marc Fisher, "Germany to Deport Gypsies," Washington Post, 18 September 1992.

[39] Ibid.

[40] Patricia Hudson, "Gypsy Migration and the Problems of Integration," NCA (Munich), 11 September 1992.

[41] See Jürgen Fijalkowski, "Aggressive Nationalism and Immigration in Germany," in Richard Caplan and John Feffer, eds., Europe's New Nationalisms: States and Minorities in Conflict (Oxford: Oxford University Press, 1996): 138–50.

the worst year of violence, 2,285 extremist acts were committed in Germany, claiming 17 lives (9 Germans and 8 foreigners).[42] Tragic as these incidents were, they did not signify Germany's descent into the racist abyss as some academics, journalists, and human rights activists suggested.[43] Though the cover notes of a scholarly book published in 1995 even declared that "Neo-fascism, for so long confined to the political wilderness, appears to be moving into the political mainstream across Europe," such bombastic overkill has hardly added to the editors' reputation.[44] Clearly, neo-fascism has not entered mainstream politics anywhere in Europe. (Right-wingers, conservatives, and nationalists should not be confused with fascists.) It bears remembering that in the early 1990s – the period when right-wing radicalism was at its height in Germany – there were an estimated 6,400 militants prone to violence, most of them skinheads, in a population of 80 million people.[45] By 1999 their number had decreased to about 5,000.[46] Neo-nazis in Europe, as in the United States, constitute a peripheral social group and a marginal political force despised by mainstream society.

The German government did not sit idly by while skinheads and neo-Nazis terrorized marginal groups. Authorities had arrested and prosecuted many skinheads.[47] Aside from rigorous police response to extremist activities, the government instituted seven legal bans on right-wing extremist groups in 1993 alone. In addition, as a gesture of goodwill to the Roma the Bonn government opened a Gypsy cultural center in Heidelberg in 1997. The vast majority of Germans also abhorred the actions of extremists; numerous spontaneous pro-refugee demonstrations at times mobilized as many as 300,000 people.[48]

---

[42] "Rightwing Radicalism in Germany," *Focus on Germany*, March 1993, 1–2.

[43] In the 1990s a number of publications created the impression that nationalism, racism, and ultraright extremism was about to take over Eastern Europe and Germany. See, for instance, Joseph Held, ed., *Democracy and Right-Wing Politics in Eastern Europe in the 1990s* (Boulder: East European Monographs, 1993); Paul Hockenos, *Free to Hate: The Rise of the Right in Post-Communist Eastern Europe* (New York: Routledge, 1993); Paul Latawski, ed., *Contemporary Nationalism in Eastern Europe* (New York: St. Martin's Press, 1995); and Aleksandar Pavkovic, Halyna Koscharsky, and Adam Czarnota, eds., *Nationalism and Postcommunism* (Brookfield, VT: Dartmouth, 1995).

[44] Luciano Cheles, Ronnie Ferguson, and Michalina Vaughan, eds., *The Far Right in Western & Eastern Europe* (London: Longman, 1995, 2nd edition).

[45] "Rightwing Radicalism in Germany," 3–4.

[46] *The Economist*, 20 March 1999, 56. For more recent accounts of their activities, see Alan Cowell, "Neo-Nazis Carving Out Fiefs in Eastern Germany," *New York Times*, 8 February 1998; and "Fighting Racism," *The Economist*, 5 August 2000, 50.

[47] "Germany to Deport Gypsies," *Washington Post*, 18 September 1992.

[48] See, for instance, "And They Still Come," *The Economist*, 14 November 1992, 58.

German authorities and German society, owing to the all-too-fresh memories of the Holocaust, have received the lion's share of international criticism for their alleged anti-Roma policies and racist attitudes. Gypsy organizations in Germany maintained that the country had a "historical responsibility" to welcome the Roma; and one of their most radical leaders, Rudko Kawczynski, warned that East European Roma face *Kristallnacht in jedem kleinen Dorf* (approximately, "pogroms in every little village") and "we are one step before a new holocaust of Roma in Europe. All the signs are clear."[49] International organizations subjected other West European societies to far less censure even though their attitudes toward the Gypsies were as objectionable as those of the heavily criticized Germans and East Europeans. Romanian President Ion Iliescu noted in a 1995 interview that

none of them (the Roma) are expelled (from Germany) for being a Gypsy, or a Romanian citizen, but for having infringed the law. They come back to Romania and are likely to have the same attitude toward the law: Why is it that, for the same deeds, in Romania they are considered victims of ethnic persecution, and in France, Germany or elsewhere they are considered mere criminals?[50]

There are many examples of what international organizations consider anti-Gypsy discrimination across Western Europe where pedestrians are occasionally warned by signs in shop windows that read "Beware of the Thieving Gypsies."[51] The mayor's office in the Paris suburb of Nanterre announced plans in 1993 to "transfer" several hundred Gypsies – owing to their "antisocial behavior" – from its jurisdiction to Neuville-sur-Ain, 300 miles away. Neuville's residents, joined by their mayor, organized themselves into armed brigades and proclaimed themselves prepared to do anything to stop the Roma from coming to town.[52] In 1985 the French cabinet established the National Council for Regional Languages and Cultures whose 37 members include a Romani representative. By the late 1990s, however, the regional languages program had come under intensifying attacks from nationalists fearful of "France's Balkanization" and the "exorbitant rights" given to

---

[49] "Kristallnacht in jedem Dorf" (Dorothea Hahn's interview with Kawczynski), *Die Tageszeitung*, 29 August 1992; and Maura Griffin Solovar, "Against the Odds: The Politics of Disunity" (interview with Kawczynski), *Transition*, 1:4 (29 March 1995): 10.

[50] Cited in Justin Burke, "An Anti-Gypsy Fervor Sweeps East Europe," *The Christian Science Monitor*, 31 August 1995.

[51] Ibid.

[52] See Bernard Fromentin, "Un Voyage a la Campagne pour les Roumains de Nanterre," *Liberation*, 4 March 1993; *IRR: European Race Audit*, Bulletin 3, April 1993; and Betty Alts and Sylvia Folts, *Weeping Violin: The Gypsy Tragedy in Europe* (Kirksville, MO: Thomas Jefferson University Press, 1996), 90.

minorities.[53] The British parliament revoked the 1968 Caravan Sites Act pertaining to "persons of nomadic habit of life, whatever their race or origin," which had opened local council sites to caravans. The backers of the 1994 decision, justified by the Roma's unruly behavior, argued that Gypsies should pay for their own camping grounds. This ruling put the owners of some 4,000 Romani caravans in a precarious position.[54] In 1997 city officials in Florence, Italy, ordered hundreds of Roma from the Balkans to leave several unauthorized settlements because of unacceptable living conditions and violation of health standards.

For nearly 50 years (1926–72), Swiss authorities abducted hundreds of Romani children from their families and supplied them with new identities in order to provide them with "civilized" upbringing. Pro Juventate, the country's largest charity for children that ran the program, agreed to make compensatory payments to the victims after 1975.[55] In the north Italian province of South Tyrol a local councillor created an uproar in October 1993 when he said all Gypsies living there should be gassed.[56] In February 1995, a pipe bomb planted by unidentified perpetrators under a sign that read *Roma zurück nach Indien* (Roma back to India) killed four Gypsies intent on removing it in the Austrian province of Burgenland. But attacks on the Roma occurred in virtually every country where they sought to find refuge, including Denmark, Holland, and Sweden.

Social attitudes toward the Roma are hardly more charitable in the West than in the East. In 1991 59% of Germans and 50% of Spaniards admitted that of all ethnic groups, they liked the Roma the least.[57] A 1993 nationwide survey revealed that two-thirds of Britons do not want to live near Gypsies (again, by far the highest percentage of "dislikes"

---

[53] See William Safran, "The French State and Ethnic Minority Cultures: Policy Dimensions and Problems," in Joseph J. Rudolph, Jr. and Robert J. Thompson, eds., *Ethnoterritorial Politics, Policy, and the Western World* (Boulder, CO: Lynne Rienner, 1989), 115–58; and "Our Lingo By Jingo," *The Economist*, 3 July 1999, 40–1.

[54] "Casting Out the Outcasts," *Geographical Magazine* (London), March 1993, 14–18; and Thomas A. Acton, "Unity in Diversity," *Cigány Néprajzi Tanulmányok*, 2 (Budapest: Mikszáth Kiadó, 1994), 80.

[55] See Mariella Mehr, *Kinder der Landstrasse: Ein Hilfswerk, ein Theater, und die Folgen* (Bern: Zytglogge Verlag, 1987). For a brief account, see Caroline Moorehead, "The 'Stealing' of the Gypsy Children," *Times* (London), 17 March 1988. In the late 1980s a television documentary entitled *Kinder der Landstrasse* (Children of the Open Road) was made about this program which was widely broadcast in Europe and North America.

[56] R. Senthilnathan, "Persecution Dogs Gypsies in Europe," *India Abroad*, 17 March 1995, 43.

[57] "Who Hates Whom?" *The European*, 27–30 September 1991.

in the poll).[58] In the United States as well, the Roma fare worst in the eyes of their fellow citizens. A 1989 study gauging the social standing of 57 ethnic groups found the Gypsies dead last, far behind the "Wisians," a fictitious entity inserted in the poll as a control population.[59] Moreover, there is little solidarity even between various Romani groups on the sub-elite level. Gypsy immigrants received little sympathy from Roma long settled in Germany (called Sinti) who, according to a Romani leader, "want nothing to do with their poor brothers from the east."[60] In Britain, too, Thomas Acton discovered that "English Romanichal Gypsies still often find it difficult to empathize with those [Roma] from other countries."[61]

At the same time, the material conditions of most East European Roma seeking asylum in Western Europe and North America undoubtedly improve. The German government did not allow asylum seekers to work but extended them a monthly cash payment of DM 700 (in 1993). This amount was far higher than the average monthly income in most East European states, and much of it could be saved given that Germany also provided applicants with food and housing. Six years later, Slovak Roma waiting for asylum hearings in Finland received monthly stipends equal to 11,300 Slovak crowns – that is, over four times the Slovak minimal wage and about 2,000 crowns more than the average salary.[62] No wonder that the Roma do not want to return to Eastern Europe. A Gypsy woman whose four-year-old son was born in Hamburg expressed the sentiment of many: "I don't want to go back to Montenegro. Germany is nice. People are kind here."[63]

Repatriation

In 1992, having experienced the arrival of millions of migrants in the previous years, the German Minister of Interior, Rudolf Seiters, reached

---

[58] William E. Schmidt, "British Poll Says Gypsies Face the Most Bias," *New York Times*, 25 October 1993.

[59] See Tom W. Smith, "What Do Americans Think about Jews?" Working Papers on Contemporary Anti-Semitism (American Jewish Committee, 1991); and "Gypsies Most Discriminated-Against Ethnic Population in America," *New York Times*, 8 January 1992.

[60] See Karen Breslau, "The Romani Enigma," *Newsweek*, 1 March 1993.

[61] Acton, "Unity in Diversity," 86.

[62] See RFE/RL II, 3: 148 (2 August 1999); and "Csáky szélmalomharca," *Napi Magyarország*, 16 August 1999.

[63] AFP (Dachau), 1 July 1993. For analyses of the Roma's situation in post–World War II Germany see Tilman Zülch, ed., *In Auschwitz vergast, bis heute verfolgt: Zur Situation der Roma (Zigeuner) in Deutschland und Europa* (Hamburg: Rowohlt, 1979); Luise Rinser, *Wer wirft den Stein? Zigeuner sein in Deutschland* (Stuttgart: Weitbrecht, 1985); and Reimer Gronemeyer, *Eigensinn und Hilfe: Zigeuner und Sozialpolitik heutiger Leistunggesellschaften* (Giessen: Focus, 1993).

an agreement with his Romanian colleague for the repatriation of some 30,000 Romanian citizens staying illegally in Germany. The concord took effect on 1 November 1992. The Bonn government gave DM 30 million (about US$20 million) to Romania in order to build housing and start training and social programs for those repatriated, an estimated three-quarters of whom were Gypsies.[64] Germany's decision unleashed a barrage of criticism from the international media warning of the resurgence of (in some newspapers' view, state-supported) extremism and racism in Germany.[65] Three salient points were usually absent from these reports, however. First, Germany did not deport the Roma because of their ethnicity but because they were illegally there. In the 1990s Germany also deported Bosnians, Vietnamese, and others.[66] Second, since World War II and especially since 1989, Germany has been the destination of a disproportionately large number of refugees. Third, Germany was only one of the numerous countries that deported illegal residents along with Denmark, France, Italy, Sweden, Switzerland, and other West European states.[67]

"Germany has decided to deport Romanian Gypsies asking for asylum because the neo-Nazis don't want them," read the first sentence of a *New York Times* article by Andrei Codrescu, a Romanian-American commentator.[68] *Times* editors must have soon felt qualms about printing this attack on Germany. An editorial four days later disapproved of the deci-

---

[64] Fredrik Folkeryd and Ingvar Svanberg, *Gypsies (Roma) in the Post-Totalitarian States* (Stockholm: Olof Palme International Center, 1995), 27–8. Under this agreement approximately 115,000 Romanian citizens were returned to Germany between late 1992 and early 1999. Although neither German nor Romanian authorities maintained statistics pertaining to their ethnicity, it is widely assumed that the great majority of them were Gypsies.

[65] See, for instance the 28 September 1992 issues of *Die Welt*, *Express* (Cologne), *Leipziger Zeitung*, *Rhein-Neckar Zeitung* (Heidelberg), *Stuttgarter Zeitung*; as well as "Blaming the Victims in Germany," *The Washington Post*, 20 September 1993; *Süddeutsche Zeitung* (Munich), 25 September 1993; and *Il Giornale* (Milan), 27 September 1993.

[66] See, for instance, "Germany's Vietnamese Gangsters," *Jane's Foreign Report*, no. 2407, 11 July 1996; and "Germany Determined to Return Bosnian Refugees," AFP (Bonn), 4 September 1996 reported in Open Media Research Institute Daily Digest, Part II (henceforth: OMRI DD II), no. 171 (4 September 1996); and "Germany's Forced Return of Bosnians," *The Forced Migration Monitor*, no. 19 (September 1997): 1–2.

[67] See, for instance, "Gypsies Deported by Sweden," Reuter (Warsaw), 4 August 1991; Paul Webster, "France Kicks Out Romanian Gypsies," *The Guardian*, 30 December 1993; DPA (Munich), 8 July 1993; "Immigrant Hunger Strikers Weaken in Paris," *International Herald Tribune*, 10–11 August 1996; "Switzerland and Federal Yugoslavia Agree on Return of Kosovar Refugees," OMRI DD II, no. 193, 4 October 1996; and Moyette Marrett, "Gypsies Beg for an End to Centuries of Bigotry," *The European*, 14–17 October 1993.

[68] Codrescu, "Gypsy Tragedy, German Amnesia," *New York Times*, 23 September 1992.

sion to repatriate the Gypsies but noted the unfairness of accusing Germany of recidivist Nazi behavior. The editors pointed out that "No other European government shelters as many refugees, and none contributes as much to Eastern Europe's financial needs."[69] Between 1989 and 1992 Germany received 1 million newcomers annually in addition to the 5 million foreigners who were settled there by 1989. This number is at least ten times higher than the corresponding figure for any other state. In the early 1990s over 60% of Europe's asylum seekers chose Germany as their destination.[70] As an article in the British weekly *The Economist* noted, "Germany is now paying a price few other countries would have accepted for not providing itself with better citizenship and immigration laws in the calmer years before unification."[71] Even for a prosperous state, taking care of so many immigrants constituted a major economic burden, particularly because in the early 1990s Germany faced serious economic problems.

According to Germany's liberal guarantee of asylum to the politically persecuted, all applicants had a right to individual hearings. Although approximately 95% of asylum applications were eventually rejected, the heavy backlog ensured that many remained in the country for years and, until 1992, hardly anyone was deported. During this time, the constitution required the state to care for them. Amidst the vocal condemnation of human rights organizations, the German parliament adopted a new law in 1993 that made it more difficult for nonpolitical refugees to stay in the country for years.[72] According to the law, asylum seekers can be turned back at the border if they enter Germany from countries the government considers "safe" (such as Poland or the Czech Republic). In order to bring illegal immigration under control, in May 1993 Germany concluded an agreement with Poland to help Warsaw cope with immigrants after Germany's new asylum law was to take effect two months later. The treaty included a DM 120 million (US$76 million) payment from Bonn to Warsaw to help the latter care for refugees and improve border security.[73]

Although several commentators wrote about Germany's racist and discriminatory policies against Romani immigrants, they ordinarily neglected to mention that the Bonn government demanded the re-

---

[69] "Gypsies and Germans, Wronged," *New York Times*, 27 September 1992.

[70] Mark Simon, "Déjà Vu: The Rising Right in Germany," *Jewish Monthly*, 106:10 (June/July 1992): 11.

[71] "Blaming the Victims," *The Economist*, 5 June 1993, 47.

[72] Stephen Kinzer, "Right Groups Attack German Plan on Refugees," *New York Times*, 7 February 1993.

[73] "Poland Plans Negotiations on Refugees with Other Neighbors," NCA (Bonn), 8 May 1993.

patriation of other illegal residents as well. Germany absorbed 320,000 refugees from Bosnia in the early 1990s, nearly as many as the rest of Western Europe combined (the runner-up was Sweden with 122,000, but other large West European nations provided refuge for only a tiny fraction of Germany's intake: France 15,000, Britain 13,000, Italy 8,000, Spain 2,500).[74] After the war, the German government insisted that those who could safely return to Bosnia should do so. The city of Berlin alone spent an estimated DM 500 million (US$325 million) a year on housing and feeding the refugees.[75]

It should also be pointed out that German authorities provided repatriated Roma with a variety of cash payments and assistance programs. In 1990 Johannes Rau, the minister-president of Nord-Rhein-Westphalia, offered DM 8,000 for every Rom from the former Yugoslavia (especially Macedonia) who recently settled in the state and were willing to go back. There were few takers.[76] To sweeten the deal, in 1991 the German government began constructing 70 single-family homes for the Roma in Shuto Orizari, in order to lure them back home. Moreover, it has financed several social and economic programs designed to assist the Macedonian Gypsies, spending approximately DM 30–5 million.[77] The German government's DM 30 million payment to help returning citizens soon became controversial among the repatriated Romanian Gypsies who wanted control of the funds. In 1994 Roma in the city of Oradea took legal action against Bishop László Tőkés, accusing him of not handing out the DM 15,000 German aid allocated to the Free and Democratic Community of Gypsies there.[78] Tőkés said that Germany had asked for payment to be halted because Romani leaders used monies for entirely different purposes than they were intended for.

PART II: THE INTERNATIONAL ROMANI MOVEMENT

Romani migration and the situation of the Gypsies in their countries of destination have been major concerns to the international Romani movement. The Roma in Germany and in the Romanian principalities made several minor attempts to mobilize their communities as early as the nineteenth century. Although they were unsuccessful, they demonstrated the will of a number of Romani leaders to work toward uniting diverse

---

[74] *The Economist*, 28 September 1996, 63–4.
[75] Alan Freeman, "Germany Expelling 320,000," *Globe and Mail*, 2 October 1996.
[76] Helmut Breuer, "Rau will Roma heimschicken aber sie wollen nicht zurück, *Die Welt*, 28 November 1990.
[77] Interview with Faik Abdi (Skopje, 11 March 1994).
[78] Hungarian Radio (Budapest), 26 March 1994, 11 GMT. For the larger context, see *New York Times*, 26 September 1993.

Gypsy groups. Since World War II, international Romani mobilization efforts have intensified and have achieved several noteworthy successes.

A Romani Homeland?

The notion of establishing specific geographical realm for the Gypsies has been a recurring theme of Romani nationalism. Similarly to the Zionist demand of setting aside a territory where Jews could live in peace, Gypsy nationalists have time and again lobbied for a safe haven that could become "Romanestan," the Romani homeland. Members of the Kwiek dynasty, the "Romani royals" of Poland, declared their intentions of establishing a Gypsy state as early as the 1930s.[79] King Gregory suggested that the state would be located on the banks of the Ganges river in India, the original homeland. In the plans of another member of the family, Joseph Kwiek, Romanestan would have been located in southern Africa. Nearly three decades later Gypsy leaders in France, some of them descendants of the Kwieks, "drew up elaborate nationalistic plans for the Roma, including the creation of an autonomous territory within France and a homeland in Somalia."[80]

The most recent indication that the "Romanestan" idea is not dead dates from 1993. Emboldened by the slow reaction of the international community to the Roma's predicament in the Balkans, in March 1993 the leadership of the Party for the Total Emancipation of the Roma (PTEMR), then the most important Gypsy organization in Macedonia, sent a letter to the United Nations urging "the establishment of a Romani nation and a state, to be called 'Romanistan'."[81] When I asked him about it, PTEMR chairman Faik Abdi told me that the letter should be considered a desperate attempt to call international attention to the Roma's plight rather than a serious proposal.[82]

As Thomas Acton writes, "'Romanestan' – a Gypsy Israel – was never a genuine political possibility even had it attracted the support of more than a few intellectuals."[83] Given the international community's lack of political will, the resistance of individual states to giving up a part of their territory for the Roma, the lack of Gypsy political and economic resources, and divisions within the world Romani community

---

[79] See Ian F. Hancock, "The East European Roots of Romani Nationalism," in David Crowe and John Kolsti, eds., *The Gypsies of Eastern Europe* (Armonk, NY: M. E. Sharpe, 1991), 142, 144.

[80] Ibid., 144.

[81] Zoltan Barany, "The Roma in Macedonia: Ethnic Politics and the Marginal Condition in a Balkan State," *Ethnic and Racial Studies*, 18:3 (July 1995): 523.

[82] Interview with Abdi (Skopje, 11 March 1994).

[83] Acton, "Unity in Diversity," 85.

pertaining to the desirability of a separate homeland, the idea has never been seriously considered on either the national or the supranational level.

The IRU and Other International Gypsy Organizations

Although the Roma made a few attempts to establish a pan-European organization as early as the 1930s, they met with scant success until the founding of the International Romani Union (IRU). The emergence of the IRU signified a milestone in the evolution of Romani nationalism. A successor of the International Gypsy Committee that was established in 1965, the IRU, adopted its name in 1978. Over 70 Romani organizations in some 28 countries have been officially members of IRU. Gypsy leaders have convened five World Romani Congresses in London (1971), Geneva (1978), Göttingen (1981), Serock, near Warsaw (1990), and Prague (2000).[84] These gatherings accomplished a number of objectives; these included establishing the "national" emblem (a red, sixteen-spoked wagon wheel in a horizontally divided field of blue and green) and anthem of the Roma, condemning anti-Gypsy discrimination, and demanding reparation payments for Holocaust victims, as well as electing members of leadership bodies (such as the Secretariat and the standing commissions on social affairs, war crimes, education, language standardization, etc.).

These congresses have rarely been the serious affairs one might expect. Adam Bartosz, a Polish ethnographer and the founding director of the Gypsy Museum in the southern Polish city of Tarnów, was one of the key organizers of the 1990 meeting. He told me that there was a small group of activists (Marcel Courtiade, Sait Balić, Rajko Djurić, Ian Hancock) who worked hard on issues and to get people to sit in meetings and make decisions. Most of the approximately 200 participants, however, treated meetings as just another get-together and excuse to drink, dance, and have a good time. Those present represented no one (twenty different individuals claimed to lead "the biggest Romanian Gypsy organization"), but, Bartosz says, virtually all those who took part wanted to be elected to some position, which is why Courtiade had to create so many commissions.[85] Several observers and activists contended that, as a result of factional disputes and clashing personalities, the IRU came out of the 1990 gathering considerably enfeebled. Indeed, one of

---

[84] For a brief history of Romany international organizations, see Ian F. Hancock, "The East European Roots of Romani Nationalism," *Nationality Papers*, 19:3 (Fall 1991): 261–5; Franz Remmel, *Die Roma Rumaniens*, 131–6; and Liégeois, *Roma, Gypsies, Travellers*, 249–71. For reports on the Fourth World Romany Congress, see *The Chicago Tribune*, 13 April 1990; and *The Economist*, 21 April 1990.

[85] Interviews with Adam Bartosz (Tarnów, 9–10 August 1999).

the high-profile participants, Ion Cioabă, noted after the Warsaw meeting that "today the IRU functions weakly."[86] The 2000 IRU World Congress was convened in the Czech capital, after a decade of decline – marked by continuous infighting and frequent charges and countercharges of corruption and bribery by rival leaders. Of the hundreds of "delegates" gathering at the Congress, few were democratically elected. The fact that those present hardly represented "the World's Roma" is obvious when considering that no participant came from Hungary, for instance.[87] Participants approved a resolution that the Roma around the world must be recognized as a separate nation, demanded compensation for survivors of the *Porajmos*, and elected Emil Ščuka, a Czech Rom, as the new IRU Chairman.[88]

The IRU has some important achievements to its credit. In 1979 the United Nations Council for Social and Economic Questions extended observer status to the Roma.[89] Since then, the IRU has gained representation in several organizations of the United Nations (e.g., UNICEF, UNESCO), and has sent a representative to Conference of Security and Cooperation in Europe (CSCE, since 1995 OSCE) meetings dealing with minorities. The IRU has played a role as a pressure group monitoring the Roma's conditions and participating in international conferences and seminars pertaining to them. It has vocally protested Germany's decision to return Gypsy migrants, promoted the standardization of the Romani language, and appealed to the young generation of Roma to improve their education.[90] In recent years the IRU, like many other Romani organizations, has focused on obtaining compensation for the Gypsy Holocaust victims from Germany and from Swiss banks, an endeavor that has been frustrated by repeated charges of embezzlement.[91] Participants at a January 1999 IRU meeting proposed to establish a Gypsy university in Paris with this money. With Ščuka and General Secretary Kristo Kiucukov, a Bulgarian Rom, at the helm, the new IRU leadership

---

[86] Remmel, *Die Roma Rumaniens*, 135.

[87] "Are They a Nation?" *The Economist*, 25 November 2000, 61.

[88] See the reports in RFE/RL II, 4:141 (25 July 2000); and 4:144 (28 July 2000).

[89] The application was presented by the actor Yul Brynner, an Honorary President of the second World Romani Congress, whose mother was a Romanian Gypsy. See "Romanies Apply for U.N. Affiliation," Reuter (New York), 1 June 1978.

[90] See Rajko Djurić's speech at the May 1994 international conference in Smolenice, Slovakia in *Roma People in Slovakia and in Europe* (Bratislava: Information and Documentation Centre on the Council of Europe, 1995), 26–8; and Andrzej Mirga and Nicolae Gheorghe, *The Roma in the Twenty-First Century: A Policy Paper* (Princeton: PER, 1997), 18.

[91] See "Gypsies Not Getting Holocaust Funds," AP (Cornetu, Romania), 13 July 2000; RFE II, 4:152 (9 August 2000); and interviews with *Porajmos* researcher and activist, Michelle Kelso (Austin, 22 February and 4 May 2000).

has campaigned for international recognition of the Roma as "a nation without a state" and some, thus far undefined, position in the European Union to be used for more effective advocacy of the Gypsies' rights.[92]

Like most Romani organizations on the national level, the International Romani Union has failed to improve the lives of ordinary Roma. Although it has done some useful work with refugees in Germany, the IRU has been unable to propose and devise, let alone implement, programs to alleviate Romani marginality.[93] It has not succeeded in bringing together the plethora of Gypsy communities or engaging in any useful endeavor on the grass roots level. Nor has the IRU been immune to the problems besetting local Romani organizations. Infighting within the organization's elite – generally precipitated by petty jealousies and power struggles – has been a serious weakness. In 1994, for instance, then IRU President Rajko Djurić accused two senior IRU officials of embezzling US$1,000,000 of the organization's funds precipitating the IRU's organizational enfeeblement.[94]

In a 1999 public letter of resignation, Ian Hancock, a former vice president of the IRU and an individual who has spent his entire adult life working for the Romani cause, notes that

over the past nine years, individuals have been dismissed from the Union without proper procedure, sometimes in the face of unproved and unprovable charges of massive theft, and others have been appointed to leading positions on the whim of the President. . . .[95]

Hancock contends that an individual in New York "was sold the IRU presidency for several thousand dollars" in 1991, and a "staff member of the Voice of America was privately offered the position of UN Representative for the Romani Union!"[96] Furthermore, Hancock writes the following:

The fact that some of the current executive members allegedly have criminal associations and are involved in law suits against them, also does much to shake my confidence in the integrity and credibility of the leadership of the International Romani Union.[97]

---

[92] RFE/RL II, 4:205 (23 October 2000); and "Nemzetet alapítanának romàk," *Népszabadság*, 29 January 2001.
[93] Interview with Nicoleta Bițu (Bucharest, 23 May 1996).
[94] See Zoltan Barany, "Living on the Edge: The East European Roma in Postcommunist Politics and Societies," *Slavic Review*, 53:2 (Summer 1994): 341–2; and interview with Livia Plaks (Bucharest, 27 May 1996).
[95] Hancock's letter is available on the internet at
http://www.romnews.com/a/hancock.html. All citations are from this document.
[96] Ibid.   [97] Ibid.

The IRU was organized during the communist period, and many of its leaders resided in East European states (especially Yugoslavia). They were heavily influenced by the excessively centralized and intolerant politics in their countries. Some Gypsy activists therefore felt that the IRU's demise would have been a blessing in disguise for it had not adapted itself to the changes in the political climate and could not appropriately react to the Gypsies' deteriorating socioeconomic conditions and international migration after 1989. The IRU, in Hancock's words, "has become an anchronism, a dinosaur,"[98] and it seems ill-equipped to meet the challenges of the international political and socioeconomic environment of the new millennium.

To preempt the organizational vacuum that would have been created by the IRU's expected demise in the early 1990s, Gypsy activists in the United States established a breakaway organization, the International Roma Federation (IRF), in 1993. The IRF was registered with the UN and claimed to have representatives in 20 countries, but its international character is largely fiction. Furthermore, some IRF leaders' commitment to the Romani cause, their preparation for becoming constructive participants of the international Gypsy movement, and the motivation behind their endeavors are suspect. When in 1993 I suggested the name of a well-known and reputable Romani activist as prospective IRF treasurer, the IRF official at the other end of the line countered with "You should know that I cannot put a Gypsy near money!"[99]

Democratization in Eastern Europe encouraged Romani organizational activities on the supranational level. In August 1992, Gypsy leaders from 22 Romani organizations in 10 countries established the European Roma Parliament (EUROM) in Budapest to fight discrimination and to promote Romani culture. The planning for EUROM had begun in 1990 at a meeting organized by the Rom and Sinti Union in Germany.[100] "There are 15 million Roma in European countries and sticking together is the only answer to their problems," said Aladár Horváth, a Gypsy representative in the Hungarian legislature and one of the organizers of the meeting.[101] Thus far EUROM has not been able to break out of the mold of ever more organizations called to life with much enthusiasm that fail to deliver on their early promise. According to Romani leaders, one of the motivating forces behind EUROM was

---

[98] Ibid.   [99] Telephone interview – transcript in files (13 November 1993).

[100] Jean-Pierre Liégeois, *Roma, Gypsies, Travellers* (Strassbourg: Council of Europe Press, 1994), 260.

[101] *The Independent*, 29 August 1992; and "Roma als überzeugte Europäer," *Die Presse*, 7 September 1992.

Council of Europe Deputy Secretary General Peter Leuprecht's commitment to Gypsy representation in the Council if Roma could form a legitimate all-European organization.[102] In August 1997 Florin Cioabă – son and heir of Ion – announced at a meeting commemorating the Holocaust held in Auschwitz that Gypsy representatives from six European states decided to set up a Parliament of European Roma.[103] They were apparently unaware of EUROM's existence. The ineffectuality of these efforts suggests that although on the national level Romani interest representation has developed considerably, it is extremely difficult to generate a European representative body from the multicolored cavalcade of national organizations. According to Nicolae Gheorghe, a drastic change in this state of affairs should not be expected until East European states become members of the European Union (EU). In the meantime, he suggests, the main task is the legitimation of local Romani groups.[104]

Funding is another serious problem that international Romani organizations have faced. While national governments finance many Gypsy organizations in their countries, they rarely subsidize international Romani groups, which generally rely on money provided by foundations and international organizations. Although some Romani leaders have discussed proposals such as the establishment of self-sustaining microcommunities, the fact is that none of the existing Romani organizations, institutions, or programs could survive without outside subsidies.[105] Several NGO executives I interviewed – all on the condition of anonymity – noted that many Gypsy activists expect them to fund their proposed projects but are reluctant to acknowledge the _gadje_ as equals in the preparation and implementation of programs. More importantly, "The Roma don't like it when foundations give money for studies _about_ them; they want to control the funds themselves but will mismanage it and use it for unintended purposes," contended one of my interviewees.

Some national Gypsy organizations, particularly the Roma National Congress (RNC) based in Germany, have also acquired a more international profile in recent years. RNC has been especially active in monitoring the situation of Gypsy migrants in Germany, directing European organizations' attention to their plight, and calling for a specially protected minority status of the Roma in Europe. The RNC has been instru-

---

[102] OMRI DD II, no. 14 (19 January 1996).

[103] Mediafax (Auschwitz/Oświęcim), 6 August 1997; reported in RFE/RL II, 1:91 (8 August 1997).

[104] "A roma képviselet máshol is gond" (Interview with Gheorghe), _Népszabadság_, 18 April 1998.

[105] Interview with PER President Allen Kassof (Princeton, 16–17 April 1997).

mental in promoting Romani rights. It also successfully campaigned for the establishment of the European Roma Rights Center.

Leadership

Over the last 15 years a handful of highly educated and multilingual Romani leaders have emerged from Eastern Europe – among them Gheorghe (Romania), Andrzej Mirga (Poland), and Klára Orgovánová (Slovakia) – who have made names for themselves in the international Gypsy movement through their insights, knowledge, and dedication as well as their able leadership of NGOs and other organizations. Gheorghe, the best known among them, enjoys a well-deserved and long-standing reputation as an indefatigable and imaginative Gypsy leader with whom IO and NGO executives can "do business." In the contemporary world no international meeting on Romani issues is complete without "star performers" like them. Not everyone is pleased with the new type of Gypsy activists. Romani politicians frequently charge that people like Gheorghe and Mirga have become, in effect, diplomats who no longer understand the problems of Gypsy communities. Flórián Farkas, Roman Kwiatkowski, and Florin Cioabă, among others, whose criticism might well be rooted in envy, accuse "international" Gypsy leaders of distancing themselves from the reality of everyday Romani experience.[106]

The objectives of Romani leaders are fundamentally similar – increasing the Gypsies' political clout and alleviating their socioeconomic marginality – but their leadership styles can be very different. The constructive and more or less objective demeanor of scholar-activists like Mirga clashes strongly with the militant and aggressive deportment of someone like Rudko Kawczynski, the one-time head of the Roma National Congress and former director of the Budapest-based Regional Roma Participation Program. In other words, the Romani movement, too, has its Martin Luther Kings and Malcolm Xs.

Meetings, seminars, and lectures at times degenerate into personal attacks and nasty innuendo. In 1998 I gave an invited lecture on East European state–Roma relations at the Central European University in Budapest. I tried to explain why the region's governments did not do more for the Gypsies by pointing to their other priorities and limited resources, that policies assisting the Roma were often political liabilities owing to societal prejudices, the deficiencies of Gypsy organizations, and so on. In the question–answer period and during the reception that followed, different audience members suggested that (a) I represented right-wing extremism, (b) I was a bleeding-heart liberal who should live next

[106] Interviews with Farkas (Budapest, 4 August 1999); Kwiatkowski (Oświwęcim, 19 August 1999); and Cioabă (Sibiu, 27 October 1999).

door to the Roma for a while "to understand who they really are," and (c) after years of studying the Gypsies and ethnic politics I should know that assisting them was an entirely lost cause and thus unworthy of discussion.

But I got off relatively easily. The Project on Ethnic Relations, an American NGO active in Romani affairs, organized a conference on the East European Gypsies held in Stupava (near Bratislava) in the spring of 1992. In addition to many Gypsy and non-Gypsy activists and politicians from the region, the organizers invited some Western scholars, among them Jennifer Hochschild and Donald Horowitz, eminent American students of racial and ethnic politics, to share their perspectives with the participants. As Horowitz was about to expand on how other marginal ethnic groups in the world shared the negative societal image of the Roma, Kawczynski interrupted him:

Roma are sitting, *gadje* are speaking. They are telling us what to do, which language to speak. They want to teach us how to speak our own language. What are they *doing* here? . . . Ten miles from here Gypsies are starving. This is not a concern of the *gadje*, it is our problem. They don't want to help us. They want to quell us, or else expel us or maybe to kill us.[107]

More recently, Kawczynski directed his tirades against Jean-Pierre Liégeois, a French scholar who has been studying the Roma for decades and has served as an expert on them for various European organizations. Liégeois, Kawczynski wrote,

must share in the blame for the current situation of Roma and Sinti in Western Europe. Millions of ecu [Euros] has passed through the bank accounts of his organizations over the many years of his work "for the Roma." The question of who has profited most from his work, the Roma or Liégeois himself, may be answered by ascertaining how many Roma even know who Liégeois is. After 20 years, with the exception of a few experts and linguists, none![108]

In a published rebuttal, Liégeois flatly disproves Kawczynski's allegations. Liégeois' Gypsy Research Center has, for most of its existence, had an annual budget under 1,000 ecus.[109] Though he may not be well known among the Roma, says Liégeois, neither is Kawczynski, who should be well known because he is a politician, not a scholar. Actually, most ordinary Gypsies in Eastern Europe are unaware of the existence of their

---

[107] Cited from Isabel Fonseca, *Bury Me Standing: The Gypsies and Their Journey* (New York: Knopf, 1995), 298. For a carefully edited report on the conference see *Romanies in Central and Eastern Europe: Illusions and Reality* (Princeton: PER, 1992).

[108] Kawczynski, "The Politics of Romani Politics," *Transitions*, 4:4 (September 1997): 27–8.

[109] "Letters," *Transitions*, 4:6 (November 1997): 4.

own supranational organizations, let alone their leaders. Other than a few Romani intellectuals and activists, the hundreds of Gypsies throughout the region I asked about these organizations claimed never to have heard of them.

Building Romani Identity

Many Roma may well have been affected, albeit indirectly, by the efforts of Gypsy organizations to strengthen Romani identity. International Romani organizations publicized the Roma's plight and kept it on the agenda of a variety of IOs and NGOs and, through and with them, have had a positive impact on state policies toward the Roma. The IRU and other Romani IOs have also played an important role in the strengthening Gypsy identity in the last two decades. Aside from generally advancing the Roma's cause, they also promoted specific issues with some success. One of these has been raising the Gypsies' consciousness about Romani history in general and the *Porajmos* in particular. A variety of Romani organizations have arranged dozens of events in the last decade to commemorate the extermination of their forebears. In June 1993 some 300 Roma staged a protest at the Dachau concentration camp, where thousands of Gypsies perished to call attention to their plight.[110] On 3 August 1994 over 3,000 Roma from Central and Eastern Europe gathered at the site of the Auschwitz–Birkenau concentration camp marking the 50th anniversary of the Nazi slaughter of the camp's remaining Gypsies.[111] Romani leaders have successfully lobbied for a memorial for Gypsy Holocaust victims in Berlin, similar to that honoring Jewish victims.[112]

Romani organizations have relentlessly reproached Germany for not explicitly owning up to its culpability. This campaign has contributed to a growing awareness among Germans and others of the Roma and their predicament. In 1982 Helmut Schmidt's social democratic government officially recognized the Nazi annihilation of the Roma as genocide, a crime against humanity.[113] Ten years later President Richard von Weizsacker made a strong plea for tolerance in connection with the arriving Gypsy immigrants and, in the following year, held talks with the

---

[110] Valerie Leroux, "Gypsies Flock to Camp Where Nazis Murdered Their Forebears," AFP (Dachau, Germany), 1 July 1993.

[111] *o Drom: Magazine for and about the Roma and Sinti in Europe* (Special issue in English), September 1994, 34.

[112] "German Gypsies Demand Berlin Holocaust Memorial," *Austin-American Statesman*, 31 July 1999.

[113] Lutz R. Reuter, "Ethnic-Cultural Minorities in Germany," in Russell F. Farnen, *Nationalism, Ethnicity, and Identity: Cross National and Comparative Perspectives* (New Brunswick, NJ: Transaction, 1994), 227.

representatives of Holocaust survivors and Germany's Romani and Sinti communities.[114] In May 1994 the Bundestag (the German parliament) observed a minute of silence in memory of the Roma and Sinti murdered in Nazi death camps.[115] This was the first time an official commemoration ceremony in Germany was dedicated to the Roma. German sources – along with American foundations and the Polish Ministry of Culture – have also been funding a center for the study and documentation of the Roma during World War II, to be housed in the Bržezinka section of the Auschwitz concentration camp. In March 1997 German President Roman Herzog acknowledged Germany's responsibility for the mass extermination of the Roma when he opened an exhibition commemorating the Romani Holocaust in the new Gypsy cultural center in Heidelberg. Although many Roma have yet to receive the reparation payments offered to other Holocaust victims, the growing recognition by German politicians of this injustice perhaps will lead to rectifying the situation in the foreseeable future.

Romani leaders have long realized that through centuries of strong external influences, the Romani language has undergone extensive mutation into dialects so different from each other that they are no longer mutually comprehensible. Thus, Spanish Gypsies, for instance, can no longer communicate with their brethren in Macedonia. Since 1989 a small but growing number of Roma have been rediscovering their linguistic heritage and have become fluent in the language. This phenomenon has increasingly turned the attention of Gypsy leaders and linguists (some of them non-Roma) to the standardization of the Romani language in order to foster communication between Romani communities throughout the world. This process has proved extremely difficult, however, not only for technical reasons but also because activists have found it virtually impossible to get Gypsies to agree which dialect of the Romani language should be accepted as the dominant one.[116] The many conferences and meetings focusing on language issues have generated limited progress on standardization.[117]

---

[114] "And Still They Come," *The Economist*, 14 November 1992, 58; and "Gypsy Auschwitz Survivors Meet German President," Reuter (Bonn), 28 January 1993.

[115] "German Parliament Commemorates Romani Victims," *Kethano Drom*, 2:2 (June 1994): 37.

[116] Interview with Elena Marushiakova (Sofia, 9 March 1995). See also Fraser, *The Gypsies*, 319.

[117] See Ágnes Diósi, *Szűz Mária zsebkendője* (Budapest: Kozmosz, 1990), 19; *International Herald Tribune*, 28 August 1990; and Yaron Matras, ed., *Romani in Contact* (Amsterdam: John Benjamins, 1995). For an extensive report on the 1993 Budapest conference, see *Kethano Drom*, 1:2–3 (May–June 1993): 5–13.

There is an increasingly vibrant international Romani movement that has been quite effective in publicizing the Gypsies' situation in Eastern Europe and elsewhere. Considering that two decades ago the world's Romani community enjoyed neither worldwide attention nor any sort of representation, the accomplishments of Romani and other activists are indeed substantial.

PART III: INTERNATIONAL AND NON-GOVERNMENTAL ORGANIZATIONS

During the communist period, Western supranational bodies could not get credible information on the status of ethnic minorities in socialist states owing to the paucity of dependable data and limitations on information flow outside of the Soviet Bloc. Especially since 1989, IOs and NGOs have become important in influencing East European policies toward the Roma and other marginal groups. There are two reasons for this. First, after 1989, when reliable information began to surface about the region's minorities, IOs started to display more interest in them due to their international migration, their difficult situation, and unacceptable state policies toward them. Second, during the communist period there was little incentive for East European states to respond to international criticisms of their minority policies because the IOs and NGOs had minimal leverage vis-à-vis the region's states. After 1989, this state of affairs changed drastically. European Union and NATO membership is a key foreign policy goal of most East European states. These organizations have made it clear that only states whose minority policies equal or at least approach the standards of Western democracies will be admitted to membership. In other words, multinational institutions now can successfully pressure East European governments because they can grant or withhold membership and associate membership privileges as well as financing for a variety of projects and programs.

International Organizations

The Council of Europe (CE) and the OSCE (CSCE until 1995) have been the most active supranational organizations active in Romani affairs. The CE has adopted guidelines, conventions, and resolutions pertaining to the Roma since 1969. An important one is the CE Parliamentary Assembly's Recommendation 1203 of 1993, which proposed a broad program of measures needed to improve the situation of European Roma. In the 1990s, together with the OSCE and other international bodies, it has established standards for government policy, created a mechanism for increasing the political visibility of issues related to the

Gypsies, discussed the various facets of the Roma's predicament, and sponsored research into Romani issues.

In the last decade the Council of Europe and the OSCE have organized innumerable conferences, seminars, and hearings to examine and call attention to the Gypsies' problems and to urge member states to stop discriminatory practices against them and introduce equal opportunity programs for them. The CE's Framework Convention on the Protection of National Minorities, which is ratified by member states and requires them to submit annual reports on human rights and minority affairs, has played a major role in raising political awareness of the need for more progressive policies.[118] The final documents of several large-scale CSCE/OSCE meetings specifically recognized the problems of the Gypsies, designated them as a special and threatened minority, and committed the organization and its member states to encourage research and study of their difficulties and to take measures to remedy them.[119] Together with the OSCE, the CE has organized dozens of fact-finding missions to East Europe to study the Gypsies' conditions.[120]

In September 1994 the CE and the CSCE organized a joint four-day seminar on the problems of the European Roma in Warsaw. The objective of the 259 participants who represented 34 states and 71 NGOs and IOs was to come up with specific proposals and suggest workable programs to alleviate Gypsy marginality. This was the first time when government officials were publicly challenged to respond to allegations concerning the treatment of the Romani minority.[121] At the meeting the CSCE High Commissioner on National Minorities, Max van der Stoel, and the Council of Europe's Peter Leuprecht stressed their organizations' concern over anti-Roma violence. One of the offshoots of this meeting was the Contact Point for Roma and Sinti Issues (CPRSI), established by the CSCE and headquartered in Warsaw.

The CPRSI operates within the framework of the OSCE's Office of Democratic Institutions and Human Rights. It is one of the first organizational manifestations of the growing recognition of the Gypsy problem's magnitude by a major supranational organization. The CPRSI organizes conferences – often in collaboration with the CE – publishes a regular newsletter, and serves as a clearing house of information about

---

[118] See, for instance, Nicolae Gheorghe and Jennifer Tanaka, *Public Policies Concerning Roma and Sinti in the OSCE Region*, Background paper 4 (Warsaw: OSCE, 1998).

[119] See Document of the Copenhagen Meeting of the Conference on the Human Dimension of the CSCE (Copenhagen, 1990), Paragraph 40; and Report of the CSCE Meeting of Experts on National Minorities (Geneva, 1991), Article VI.

[120] See Liégeois, *Roma, Gypsies, Travellers*.

[121] Romnews (information service of the Roma National Congress) (Warsaw), no. 17, 27 September 1994.

the Gypsies' situation across Europe. In 1996, nearly two years after the CPRSI was established, I visited its offices in Warsaw. There were no Roma on staff, none of the people in the office had any background in Gypsy affairs, and they did not check or confirm the validity of any information they received and subsequently distributed.[122] Since 1998, when the OSCE established the office of Roma and Sinti Adviser and appointed Nicolae Gheorghe to the position, CPRSI has become more dynamic.

The Coordinator of Activities on Roma/Gypsies of the Council of Europe's Population and Migration Division has also become a fixture at Roma-related conferences. The CE also set up its own Specialist Group on Roma/Gypsies, which met for the first time in Strasbourg in March 1996.[123] The group has about a dozen members with two-year mandates, seven of whom are nominated by their governments but are supposedly independent of them. Additional members are financed by their organizations. Although the Specialist Group's role is not clearly defined, it is to concentrate on human rights violations, women's rights, the situation of Romani refugees, and aiding the Council's larger objective, which is to help develop policies pertaining to European Roma. The first project of this group was a mission to examine the conditions of the Roma in Bosnia.

Two contending positions have developed in the Specialist Group. The first, represented by András Bíró and Cătălin Zamfir, favors concentrating on concrete social and economic problems. The second, supported by Andrzej Mirga and Nicolae Gheorghe, considers it dangerous to tackle these long-term difficulties first because they might serve as an excuse for governments to do little about deficiencies in the political and human rights arenas. Romani members of the group have also focused on defining and institutionalizing a new official status for the Gypsies as a European nationality that would allow their unbridled movement across the Continent.[124] Although its intentions are admirable, some participants of the Specialist Group, like Zamfir, contend that its practical effect on the Roma has been minimal.[125]

Occasionally the CE and other IOs have praised new legal instruments or improved policies of East European member states. For instance, the CE has commended Hungary's Law on Minorities as a model for all of Europe, the OSCE applauded the Bulgarian government's efforts to

---

[122] Interview with Elizabeth Winship of CPRSI/OSCE (Warsaw, 30 July 1996).

[123] See *Newsletter: Activities on Roma/Gypsies* (Council of Europe), no. 5 (25 April 1996); and interviews with Nicoleta Bițu (Bucharest, 23 May 1996) and Livia Plaks (Bucharest, 27 May 1996).

[124] Interview with Cătălin Zamfir, the official Romanian expert of the Specialist Group (Bucharest, 1 June 1996).

[125] Interview with Zamfir (Bucharest, 8 November 1999).

integrate Romani communities and organizations, and both organizations welcomed the new Slovak minority language law.[126] The condemnation of member states has been far more frequent, however. The CE and the OSCE, for instance, have strongly criticized former Slovak Prime Minister Vladimír Mečiar for his tirades against the Roma; they have also denounced racism in Bulgaria, the Czech Republic, Romania, and Slovakia. These are but a few examples of the countless criticisms, denunciations, and censures of East European states for their discriminatory policies and practices by IOs.[127]

Perhaps no other issue received more international publicity than the Czech citizenship law (discussed in more detail in the next chapter) widely considered to discriminate against the Roma owing to its stipulations such as that an applicant have a five-year record free of criminal convictions, permanent residence, and knowledge of the Czech language.[128] From 1993 on, the Czech Republic received censure from the UN, the CE, the OSCE, and other supranational institutions and NGOs for its citizenship law. These organizations were especially concerned because they believed that the Czech legislation might set a precedent for other countries, like Croatia and Macedonia, preparing new citizenship laws.[129]

The European Parliament, the EU's legislative arm, has also put the East European Roma on its agenda on a number of occasions in the last decade, confirming that their situation was an important part of accession criteria.[130] In 1997 the European Commission (the EU's executive body) proposed a broad, long-term program, Agenda 2000, which stresses the need for improving the East European Roma's conditions. This program is based on a country-by-country approach, it requires annual government reports, and it emphasizes effective monitoring of the

---

[126] BTA (Sofia), 18 May 1999; RFE/RL II, 3:98 (20 May 1999); 3:134 (13 July 1999); CTK (Bratislava), 19 July 1999; and RFE/RL II, 3:139 (20 July 1999).

[127] See, for instance, "CSCE Report on Roma in Czech Republic," NCA (Prague), 27 April 1993; Henry Kamm, "In New Eastern Europe, and Old Anti-Gypsy Bias," *New York Times*, 17 November 1993; "Gypsy Seminar Recommends Rights Mediator," CTK (Warsaw), 23 September 1993; "Tényfeltárás a kisebbségekért," *Új Magyarország*, 17 February 1995; OMRI DD II, no. 237 (7 December 1995); RFE/RL II, no. 4 (4 April 1997); "Czech Republic: Update on Issues Affecting Roma," Research Directorate, Immigration and Refugee Board (Ottawa: 20 August 1998), 13; and RFE/RL II, 4:215 (6 November 2000).

[128] See, for instance, Jane Perlez, "Czechs Use Laws to Exclude Gypsies from Gaining Citizenship and Voting," *New York Times*, 27 December 1995.

[129] See, for instance, ibid.; OMRI DD II, no. 250 (28 December 1995); and RFE/RL II, 1:123 (23 September 1997).

[130] See, for instance, OMRI DD II, no. 134 (12 July 1996); and *State Policies Toward Romani Communities in Candidate Countries to the EU: Government and Romani Participation in Policy-Making* (Princeton: PER, 1999).

implementation of national strategies. Every state that wants to join the EU has to accept the basic principles of Agenda 2000. At the same time, this program also provides incentives to East European governments to change their policies by funding programs for minorities (until 1997 these EU funds went primarily to NGOs).

The United Nations Commission on Human Rights turned its attention to the Roma for the first time in 1977. In 1992 the same body adopted Resolution 1992/65 entitled "On the Protection of the Roma (Gypsies)" asserting that the UN could not remain indifferent to the fate of any people facing racial discrimination and urging member states to implement measures to improve the Roma's conditions and eliminate anti-Gypsy discrimination. Officials of the United Nations and especially the UN High Commissioner for Refugees have strongly criticized East European states for their Romani policies. Key UN agencies, such as the Committee on Economic, Social, and Cultural Rights (CESCR), have singled out Romania a number of times for the situation of the Roma there. A report released by the CESCR in May 1994 noted that Gypsies in Romania faced major obstacles in obtaining jobs, though it neglected to mention most Roma's lack of employment qualifications.[131] Similarly, in 1998 another UN committee criticized the Hungarian government because of the "disproportionately high number of Roma" in Hungarian prisons.[132] Other UN agencies, particularly the UNICEF and the UNESCO, have taken steps to encourage and at least partially finance pragmatic programs – such as business courses and university scholarships – for Roma in several East European states. In Bulgaria, for instance, UNESCO has funded a broad project called "Let's bring the children back to school," which has assisted hundreds of Gypsy children completing their basic education.[133]

The International Organizations' Effect on State Policy

The Council of Europe and other supranational bodies have reiterated time and again that acceptable minority policy was a condition of membership in the organization and that improvement in the Roma's situation was a precondition of accession to the European Union, the international organization East European states are most keen to join.[134] The EU has repeatedly informed governments applying for membership

---

[131] "UN Body Hits Romania over Gypsy Discrimination," NCA (Geneva), 25 May 1994.

[132] "Aránytalanul sok roma van a magyar börtönökben," *Népszabadság*, 21 November 1998.

[133] "Reaching Out to Minorities," *Transitions*, 1:13 (28 July 1995): 59; and interview with Kalina Bozeva (Sofia, 18 March 1995).

[134] See, for instance, *Új Magyarország*, 7 September 1993; *Cigány Hírlap-Romano Zhurnalo*, 28 May 1996; *Roundtable Discussion of Government Policies on the Roma in Romania* (Princeton: PER, 1999), 7.

that an important part of membership criteria is how they deal with minority affairs (and within that broader concept, with the Roma). In fact, the Roma are specifically mentioned in the EU's country-by-country criteria for Bulgaria, Czech Republic, Hungary, Romania, and Slovakia.

The EU itself has strongly condemned specific East European policies, such as recurring Romanian police abuses against and Czech handling of the Roma.[135] In the fall of 1998 Rals Dreyer, acting head of the EU mission in the Czech Republic, contended that "Romany rights have become one of the most important issues of EU accession negotiations."[136] Although NATO has not been directly concerned with minority issues, one reason Slovakia could not join the first wave of enlargement in 1999 was its undemocratic policies toward ethnic minorities, including the Roma. In addition, legislators of some Western states have also held hearings about and lamented the situation of the Roma in Eastern Europe.

The United States withheld the granting of Most Favored Nation status to Romania until 1992, partly owing to its objectionable minority policies. In April 1994 the Subcommittee on International Security, International Organizations, and Human Rights of the Committee on Foreign Affairs of the U.S. House of Representatives held a hearing concerning the human rights abuses of the Roma.[137] The U.S. State Department's annual reports on human rights have repeatedly criticized East European governments policies toward the Roma.[138] According to a confidential source, Bulgarian President Petar Stoyanov received a letter from the State Department warning him that President Bill Clinton's scheduled November 1999 visit to Sofia might be jeopardized should the government fail to reach an agreement concerning a broad package of pro-Roma measures with Gypsy organizations.

There is no doubt that the main reason behind the changes in the Czech citizenship law in 1996 and in 1999 was the extensive criticism of IOs. Zdeněk Matějka, the former head of the OSCE's Prague office, contended that until 1996 the Czech government's biggest problem in terms of international relations had been the situation of and its policies

---

[135] See, for instance, *Jurnalul national*, 15 July 1996; the joint statement of Roma Federation and Romani CRISS (Bucharest, 18 July 1996); Reuter (Prague), 27 May 1998; and RFE/RL II, 2:100 (27 May 1998).

[136] "Slovaks v Czechs on Gypsies," *The Economist*, 7 November 1998, 52.

[137] See *Human Rights Abuses of the Roma* (Washington, D.C.: U.S. Government Printing Office, 1994).

[138] See, for instance, OMRI DD, no. 28 (8 February 1996); no. 48 (7 March 1996); Paul Goble, "Post-Communist States Diverge on Human Rights," RFE/RL II End Note, 2:21 (2 February 1998).

toward the Roma.[139] Clearly, East European politicians are increasingly aware of the pressure from the EU and other organizations. Dozens of politicians and experts from Warsaw to Sofia have openly or implicitly admitted to me that they considered international pressures the most important motivating force behind the changes in their countries' policies toward the Roma.[140] As a high-ranking Hungarian government official told me, "we fully recognize that the EU will not accept Hungary as a full member when 5% of the country's population is not integrated and socioeconomically miles behind the rest of the population."[141]

Non-Romani Foundations and NGOs

I have already discussed the work of NGOs directed by the East European Gypsies in the previous chapter. The focus in this section, then, is on independent non-Romani foundations and NGOs.

Amnesty International (AI) has publicized the violations of the Roma's rights in Eastern Europe and elsewhere for decades, but its activities have intensified since 1989. Although no one debates the merits of and the motivation behind AI's undertakings, at times its reports have been one-sided, have neglected improvements in minority policies, and have made unfair generalizations. In 1993 AI officials said that "political torture and murder are officially tolerated in at least ten countries," including Romania and Bulgaria, a statement most people familiar with these states considered astonishing.[142] In 1998, eighteen months after the elections that brought President Emil Constantinescu and a coalition of

---

[139] Interviews with Zdeněk Matějka (Prague, 14 August 1996) and Jonathan Stein of the European Studies Center of the Institute of EastWest Studies (Prague, 14 August 1996).

[140] See, for instance, interviews with Gabriella Varjú, Vice-President of the Office for National and Ethnic Minorities (5 August 1999); Zdeněk Matějka, Secretary General of the Ministry of Foreign Affairs and Jan Pecháček, Adviser to the Deputy Minister of Foreign Affairs (Prague, 23 August 1999); Vasil Hudak, Director of the EastWest Institute's Prague Center (Prague, 25 August 1999); Vera Klopčič, Institute for Ethnic Studies (Ljubljana, 2 December 1999); Pál Csáky, Deputy Prime Minister in Charge of Human Rights, Minorities, and Regional Development (Bratislava, 9 September 1999); Dan Oprescu, Head of National Office for the Roma, Department for the Protection of National Minorities, and Péter Eckstein-Kovács, Minister for the Protection of National Minorities (Bucharest, 2 November 1999); Petar Atanasov, Secretary of the National Council on Ethnic and Demographic Issues at the Council of Ministers (Sofia, 15 November 1999); Ventzislav Ivanov, director of the Directorate of International Organizations and Human Rights at the Ministry of Foreign Affairs (Sofia, 16 November 1999).

[141] Interview with Antal Heizer, Office of the Prime Minister (Budapest, 28 May 1998). See also "Roma in Hungary: Views of Several Specialists," Research Directorate, Immigration and Refugee Board (Ottawa, February 1999), 30.

[142] Stephen Kinzer, "Rights Groups Attack German Plan on Refugees," *New York Times*, 7 February 1993.

opposition parties to power, AI issued a 32-page document on continuing human rights violations in Romania referring to reports it received alleging government discrimination, shootings, torture, and deaths in custody, even though a few months earlier the OSCE's van der Stoel described the Bucharest government's line on minority policy as "courageous."[143] In December 2000 AI was forced to apologize to the Hungarian government for having published an advertisement in the Netherlands depicting a three-year old Romani child with his teeth allegedly broken by Hungarian police. Anna Burley, AI's European Director, who went to Budapest in January 2001 to make amends in person, admitted that the credibility of the picture was not checked by AI's Dutch member organization.[144]

Starting in 1990 Helsinki Watch/Human Rights Watch expanded its coverage to produce a series of publications detailing the situation of and widespread discrimination against the Roma in Eastern Europe. Most of these do not even make a pretense of objectivity because they extensively rely on interviews with Gypsy victims of discrimination on the basis of which blanket generalizations are made.[145] Helsinki Watch has inspected the Roma's conditions in several states of the region, organized meetings with local and state officials, and offered recommendations based on international law and agreements for improving minority policies. Helsinki Watch and its regionwide branch offices have also been active in monitoring Romani interstate migration and criticizing the governments for not improving the Gypsies' conditions. The International Helsinki Federation for Human Rights has issued numerous press releases protesting anti-Romani incidents in the region.[146]

Since 1989 in every East European state numerous NGOs have been established to monitor human rights. These organizations usually focus on civil and political rights, but, especially since the mid-1990s, their attention has often extended to social and economic discrimination. Some of these NGOs have done a great deal of useful work mostly inves-

---

[143] "Romania: Amnesty Reports Further Human Rights Abuses," NCA (London), 21 April 1998; and RFE/RL II, 1:3 (3 April 1997).

[144] RFE/RL II, 4:249 (29 December 2000); and "Bocsánatot Kért az Amnesty International," *Népszabadság*, 23 January 2001.

[145] Interview with David Murphy of the Nova Škola Foundation (Prague, 23 August 1999). The objectionable methods of Human Rights Watch have also been criticized in other contexts. In 1998 Human Rights Watch produced a 200-plus-page report on Russian orphanages based on interviews with less than 25 people and visits to 15 orphanages in one small area. According to one expert on the subject, the HRW's "extensive report" was a "disgrace." See Juliette Engel of the MiraMed Institute in Johnson's Russia List, no. 3063, item 3 (20 February 1999).

[146] Dan Ionescu, "Violence against Gypsies Escalates," *Report on Eastern Europe*, 2:25 (21 June 1991): 23.

tigating incidents, criticizing and advising the authorities (usually the ministries of education interior, labor, and the police forces) responsible for eliminating discrimination, and organizing meetings discussing them. In many cases, such as those of the Human Rights Project in Bulgaria, the Citizens' Solidarity and Tolerance Movement in the Czech Republic, the Union for Peace and Human Rights in Slovakia, and the Office for the Protection of National and Ethnic Minority Rights in Hungary, their dogged determination has led to dismissals and criminal proceedings against corrupt or abusive policemen and other officials, prosecution of those responsible for attacks against the Roma, changes in departmental/ministerial policies, and the like.

Since its founding in 1996, the European Roma Rights Center (ERRC) has aggressively monitored anti-Roma discrimination and upheld Romani rights. In addition, it has provided stipends for dozens of Gypsy law students across the region and for the legal defense of many Roma accused. ERRC has also acquired a reputation of publishing unbalanced reports and pursuing its objectives with rather more zeal and less tact than would be optimal.[147] The following two examples should illustrate why this is so. Shortly after the 1995 Burgenland pipe bomb incident mentioned earlier, the ERRC conducted an investigation into Austria's political, social, and legal situation. The resultant report found the country's policies xenophobic and its laws discriminatory, both reflecting its "racist climate." Extensive citations taken from the extreme nationalist (i.e., nonmainstream) press buttressed this conclusion.[148] The 62-page report failed to mention, however, that President Thomas Klestil, several members of the Austrian cabinet, at least 50 other state officials, and religious leaders protested against the attack with their presence at the victims' funeral.[149]

---

[147] Interviews with Flórián Farkas, President of the National Gypsy Self-Government (4 August 1999); Roman Kristof, editor of *Romano Hangoš* and coordinator of HCA-Roma section (Brno, 2 September 1999); Michal Vašečka (Bratislava, 10 September 1999); Elena Marushiakova and Vesselin Popov (Sofia, 13 November 1999); Trajko Petrovski, a researcher at the Institute of Folklore (Skopje, 25 November 1999); Vera Klopčič, a researcher at the Institute for Ethnic Studies (Ljubljana, 2 December 1999); and others who wish to remain anonymous. One researcher who objected the ERRC's constant portrayal of Roma as victims was told by Claude Cahn, ERRC's director of publications and research, that ERRC's "is an ideological approach and we are fully aware of its artificiality." Cahn informed a prospective contributor to the ERRC's newsletter, *Roma Rights*, that according to editorial policy, photos should only depict "poverty, degradation, violence, destroyed houses, etc." The researchers wish to remain anonymous, the documents are in my possession.

[148] See *Divide and Deport: Roma & Sinti in Austria* (Budapest: ERRC, 1996).

[149] See, for instance, "Nyugodjunk békében?" *Amaro Drom*, 5:3 (March 1995): 6–7, a report of the funeral by Hungarian Gypsy activist Aladár Horváth.

In July 1999, after the Finnish government reestablished visa requirements for Slovaks in response to the arrival of hundreds of asylum-
seeking Slovak Roma in Helsinki within a few days, ERRC described the
decision as "discriminatory" and, in a letter to Foreign Minister Tarja
Halonen, expressed its disappointment that the Finnish government has
"apparently succumbed to the widespread racial stereotype and anti-
Roma sentiment in much of Europe."[150] In essence, ERRC criticized the
Finns for refusing political asylum to economic refugees and upholding
their immigration laws that satisfy all international norms.

Although the intentions of human rights organizations are nearly
always admirable, their efforts are often misguided. In general, their data
collection methods have been unsound to say the least. In many cases
Romani victims are interviewed about the events in question and their
testimonies are presented as a factual account of what happened. Human
rights organizations often do not concern themselves with the problems
and realities of the Gypsies' daily life but concentrate on the headline
grabbing stories without a critical, objective approach. It is also important to remember that these organizations have a stake in making
things appear as grim as possible. They are financed by various foundations and agencies who might well reduce their contributions if reports
suggested that the Roma's conditions or state policies toward them had
actually improved. After all, at any given moment there are a plethora
of worthy causes needing to be funded. There is no doubt that human
rights organizations have done an indispensable job in encouraging
governments to maintain fundamental rights standards. Nevertheless,
their reports should be viewed with the same measure of skepticism
with which one might appraise the assertions of government officials.
Both sides have an interest in bending the truth.

Then again, several of my interviewees agreed with Nicolae Gheorghe,
who told me that "human rights organizations are not supposed to
be objective."[151] Dan Oprescu, Head of the Romanian government's
National Office for the Roma, noted that without organizations like the
ERRC exaggerating problems and pressuring politicians and the public, there would be less motivation to address the Roma's concerns.[152]
Ventzislav Ivanov, Director of the International Organizations and
Human Rights Directorate at the Bulgarian Ministry of Foreign Affairs,
suggested that East European governments needed NGOs like Amnesty
International "because we need someone to kick us in the pants" and
force us to respond with positive measures toward the Roma.[153] At the

---

[150] CTK (Bratislava), 7 July 1999.
[151] Interview with Gheorghe (Warsaw, 16 August 1999).
[152] Interview with Oprescu (Bucharest, 2 November 1999).
[153] Interview with Ivanov (Sofia, 16 November 1999).

same time, Ivanov lamented that many NGOs do not see the big picture and are not realistic about the speed that governments – especially of poor countries – can take to implement new policies.

There are several hundred East European foundations – the vast majority financed by Western sponsors – working for Roma-related causes in the region. Given space limitations, it is impossible to do them justice here so I will briefly mention two. The Sofia-based International Center for Minority Studies and Intercultural Relations was established in 1993. It is an NGO that has given scholarships to Gypsy and other minority students, supported minority publications, and financed special educational programs. Funded by UNESCO, the EU, the Open Society Fund, and other sources, the Center has also worked to improve the educational standards of Bulgaria's other minorities – particularly Bulgarian Muslims (Pomaks) and Turks – and minority Bulgarians in Albania, Moldova, Ukraine, and elsewhere.[154] In terms of pragmatic, tangible programs, no East European NGO has done more for the Roma than the Budapest-based Autonómia Foundation, established in 1990 and financed primarily by U.S. charitable organizations. The brainchild of András Bíró, who has had a long experience working for the United Nations in the Third World, the credo of Autonómia is that lending small amounts of seed money, in essence startup capital for minor business and agricultural ventures, to needy Romani communities will make a great difference not only in their economic situation but also in their self-esteem and life perspectives. Similarly to the microfinancing programs that have been successful in other poverty-stricken environments, Autonómia has funded hundreds of small-scale projects that have assisted thousands of impoverished Roma.[155]

Although there are many Western foundations that have financed Roma-related projects in Eastern Europe, none has done more than the Open Society Fund and Institute established and bankrolled by George Soros, a Hungarian-American financier and philanthropist. Aside from innumerable minority scholarships, meetings, and self-help programs, Soros' organizations across the region have funded the Budapest-based

[154] "Reaching Out to Minorities" (interview with Center Director Antonina Zhelyazkova), *Transition*, 1:13 (28 July 1995): 58–60.

[155] "Cigánykerék," *Köztársaság*, 3 July 1992; "Túlélési stratégia a cigányoknak," *Magyar Hírlap*, 14 June 1993; Béla Osztojkán, *Megkérdezem Önt is* (Budapest: Phralipe, 1994), 46–55; Gábor Kereszty and György Simó, "Helping Self-Help: Interview with András Bíró," *The Hungarian Quarterly*, 36:140 (Winter 1995): 70–7; and interviews with Bíró (Budapest, 26 July 1996; and Washington, D.C., 19 September 1996); and Anna Csongor, Autonómia's Executive Director (Budapest, 5 August 1999). For microfinancing in the international context, see Hartmut Schneider, ed., *Microfinance for the Poor?* (Paris: OECD, 1997); and Muhammad Yunus, *Banker to the Poor: Micro-Lending and the Battle Against World Poverty* (New York: Public Affairs, 1999).

Romani News Agency since its creation in 1995 and have also funded several schools for Gypsy students. When I asked officials at dozens of NGOs and foundations dealing with the Gypsies and other minorities from Poland to Macedonia who paid the staff, who paid for the equipment, rent, and other necessities, and who financed the projects, the answers I heard most often were "Soros" or the "Open Society Foundation." It is interesting, therefore, that Soros and his organizations have many detractors, especially those, one supposes, who failed to secure funds from them. There are many who say, not without some justification, that Soros' organizations have tended to favor ex-communists and left-wing liberals.[156] Be that as it may, there is no doubt that George Soros and his dollars have done tremendous good for an awe-inspiring variety of causes and people – prominently included among them are the Roma – in Eastern Europe, the former Soviet Union, and elsewhere.

The most important of the several American NGOs that work with Romani issues is the Project on Ethnic Relations (PER), based in Princeton, New Jersey. Founded in 1991 and financed by the Carnegie Corporation of New York with additional support from several other foundations and the Council of Europe, one of the main focuses of PER's activities has been the Roma along with broader work on ethnic relations and state-minority affairs in Eastern Europe. PER has brought together activists, experts, and politicians to discuss and find solutions to a number of issues including the relations between the Roma on the one hand, and the media, law enforcement agencies, state officials, and so on. Like many NGOs, PER has organized dozens of conferences and meetings between government officials, bureaucrats representing international organizations and NGOs, experts, and Gypsy activists in attractive settings. It has also supported some worthwhile enterprises such as seminars for policemen and education officials to become more sensitive to the Roma's concerns. In 1993 PER set up a Roma Advisory Council in order to advise PER on Romani issues and to provide an authoritative voice for the Gypsies in addressing IOs and governments. In addition, PER has published and widely distributed numerous useful reports and policy papers.

---

[156] See for instance, Richard C. Morais, "Beware of Billionaires Bearing Gifts," *Forbes*, 7 April 1997, 82–7. When an interviewer asked Soros why he supported former communists who suddenly turned democrats in 1989, he responded by saying "They [as ex-Communists] know better what democracy is than perhaps those who were always opposed to [the regime]." This, of course, is an enormous insult to those who at times paid with their lives for their democratic convictions in communist dictatorships. Ibid., 87.

Churches have also played an increasingly active role in trying to assist East European Roma since the late 1980s.[157] Politicians and Gypsy activists suggest that churches could play an even more important role noting that a few impassioned priests can do an enormous amount of good on the local level.[158] Their point is underscored by individual priests, like Father Stanisław Opocki in Poland, who has single-handedly established several schools for young Gypsy dropouts. The Roman Catholic church in Slovakia has been particularly agile in promoting the Roma's cause. It consecrated a pastoral center for the Gypsies in 1998, has organized well-attended pilgrimages, and has issued statements calling attention to their plight.[159]

The "Gypsy Industry"

In the last decade the acute nature of Gypsy marginality has spurred the emergence of hundreds of NGOs and international bureaucracies employing thousands of people. Many Romani leaders and experts cynically refer to this phenomenon as the "Gypsy industry," which, they contend, enriched the participating individuals but left most Roma unaffected.

Several hundreds of international meetings have been held in the last decade discussing various aspects of the Romani predicament. Though some have been successful to the extent that they have spawned practical programs and have directed attention to human rights violations, most have done little to advance the cause and have merely served as another opportunity to travel, socialize, and regurgitate for the umpteenth time familiar elements of the Gypsies' plight without actually doing something about them. In many cases there is little coordination between researchers whose studies tend to be repetitive, superficial, and pointless; activists who look out for their own interests having lost sight of the original goals; and decision makers who look "for a prescription

---

[157] See, for instance, Zoltan Barany, "Hungary's Gypsies," *Report on Eastern Europe*, 1:29 (20 July 1990): 28; and Viliam Figusch, ed., *Roma People in Slovakia and in Europe* (Bratislava: Information and Documentation Centre on the Council of Europe, 1995), 46–7.

[158] Interviews with János Wolfart (Budapest, 9 June 1994); Vasile Burtea, a Gypsy analyst at the Ministry of Labor (Bucharest, 15 March 1995); and Adam Andrasz, President of the Tarnów Cultural Gypsy Association and Vice President of the Highest Council of Roma in Poland (9 August 1999).

[159] See Michal Vašečka, "The Roma," in Gregoríj Mešeznikov, Michal Ivantyšyn, and Tom Nicholson, eds., *Slovakia 1998–1999: A Global Report on the State of Society* (Bratislava: Institute of Public Affairs, 1999), 413; and interview with Ágnes Horváthová, Head of the Secretariat of the Slovak Helsinki Commission (Bratislava, 8 September 1999).

without diagnosis, a treatment without analysis."[160] Unfortunately, all too few IOs and NGOs have targeted the implementation of these pragmatic programs. At the same time, a great deal of their money has been expended unwisely: on hefty fees for incompetent and unsuited consultants; unnecessary, expensive, and redundant conventions and symposia; and costly pilot programs that lead nowhere. Moreover, as Kevin Quigley, a former director of public policy at the Pew Charitable Trusts, writes, many NGOs and "foundations have worked almost exclusively with elites" and "have had considerable difficulty breaking out of capital cities and widening the circle of participants in their programs."[161]

In an article notable for its objectivity, Dan Oprescu writes,

I am fed up with seminars, workshops, and roundtables. I want some output from 1990 until now. Theoretically, they [NGOs] were supposed to train some "activists" to act within their respective communities. Where are those "activists"? Where is all the money spent on their training?[162]

Many Gypsy politicians across the region echo Oprescu's views. Flórián Farkas, for instance, told me that "We don't need any more conferences, we know precisely what the problems are. What we need is action."[163]

Many NGOs thrive on projects that are supposed to help the Roma, but only a small proportion of them actually do. According to Neždet Mustafa, the Gypsy mayor of Shuto Orizari, the sole driving force behind a large number of NGOs dealing with Romani issues is to get funded and refunded. He mentions, for instance, several expensive "computer training courses" for barely literate Romani children designed by a West European NGO whose employees quickly left – together with the computers – once they took the obligatory glossy photos to be used in their next brochure.[164]

Though Kawczynsky and other Romani activists often overstate their case, they are justifiably angry about the millions of dollars of NGO and foundation monies that were spent on fancy and often useless seminars and conferences instead of providing practical and direct help for the Gypsy communities. As we were surveying a particularly poverty-stricken Romani ghetto in eastern Slovakia, my guide, a well-known Slovak Gypsy activist, asked me "How many of these undernourished children do you think could be fed for the price of one of those confer-

---

[160] See Liégeois, *Roma, Gypsies, Travellers*, 309–11, citation from 311.
[161] Kevin F. F. Quigley, "For Democracy's Sake: How Foundations Fail – and Succeed," *World Policy Journal*, 13:1 (Spring 1996): 116.
[162] Dan Oprescu, "Public Policies on National Minorities in Romania (1996–1998)," *Sfera Politica*, no. 6 (January 1999): 18.
[163] Interview with Farkas (Budapest, 4 August 1999).
[164] Interview with Mustafa (Shuto Orizari, 24 November 1999).

ences they hold to talk about us in Geneva or Strasbourg?"[165] The bottom line is that though an increasing number of NGOs work to reduce the Roma's plight, they need to be more focused on pragmatic programs, they should be more flexible to adjust their projects to the changing needs of Gypsy communities, and they should use their resources more effectively.

CONCLUSION

What sort of *direct* influence do international organizations like the Council of Europe, OSCE, UN and others have on the lives of East European Roma? Very limited. Their strength lies primarily in publicizing problems, criticizing governments, and influencing their policies. It is often difficult to firmly establish direct correlation between international pressures and changes in domestic policies because governments are rarely keen on admitting that they had to give in to such pressures. There can be no doubt, however, that the changes governments have implemented regarding minorities in general and the Roma in particular are motivated in large part by external factors, such as a desire to join the EU. The leverage that IOs enjoy vis-à-vis the East European states and the willingness and ability to use it has been an important reason behind policy changes because the nascent democracies of the region have become increasingly sensitive of their international image.

International organizations and NGOs have played a crucial role in influencing state policy and, generally indirectly, Romani marginality. Nonetheless, some foundations and NGOs have managed to directly contribute to the alleviation of Romani marginality by formulating and implementing practical programs. Given the preponderance of organizations dealing with human rights and ill-defined issues of "European citizenship" for the Gypsies, it is to be hoped that initiatives that provide pragmatic, tangible assistance for the Roma will multiply in the future. One expects that as East European civil societies continue to expand, more will be done more successfully.

As we have seen, the national and local Gypsy organizations and the international Romani movement have been fraught with difficulties. By and large, their influence on state policy, while growing, has been decidedly modest. In a very real sense, then, supranational institutions and NGOs have been able to make up for the deficiencies of Gypsy political mobilization in helping the Roma and improving their current conditions and future prospects.

---

[165] The activist asked to remain anonymous.

8

State Institutions and Policies toward the Gypsies

Romani political mobilization and the activities of international organizations have been chiefly directed at influencing state minority policies because in most cases remedies for the Romani community's grievances either come from or are originated and directed by the state.[1] The modern state may be thought of as the sum of different bureaucracies or institutions that often have varying perspectives on the issues they confront. This is certainly the case where minorities are concerned. The East European countries, which regained their full sovereignty only after the fall of communism, have faced the challenge of building democratic states. An important part of this task has been to establish institutions that are conducive to constructive relations with ethnic minorities.

The primary focus of this chapter is on the political institutions that represent or embody the state to minorities. I am especially interested in how these institutions – from the president to local authorities – differ in their views of the Roma from state to state because these variations go far in explaining the policies states pursue. Part I is a comparative analysis of these institutions. Part II explores the role and importance of state institutions – generally subordinated to the government or legislature – that directly deal with Gypsy issues. Part III examines the various policy areas of special concern to the Roma and the effect they have had on their lives. The East European states' specific programs and their impact on Gypsy communities will be examined in the next chapter.

Before beginning the comparative analysis of political institutions as they pertain to the Gypsies, it seems useful to briefly outline the different directions in which East European states developed in the 1990s.[2]

---

[1] See Paul R. Brass, "Ethnic Groups and the State," in Paul R. Brass, *Ethnic Groups and the State* (New York: Barnes & Noble Books, 1985), 1–56.

[2] For fine recent analyses of East European political developments see Sorin Antohi and Vladimir Tismaneanu, eds., *Between Past and Future: The Revolutions of 1989 and Their*

Notwithstanding the many disparities among them, in most respects the Czech Republic, Hungary, and Poland have already established consolidated democracies. Stable multiparty systems are in place, new institutional frameworks have been erected, and several regularly scheduled free and unfettered local and national elections have been held, the results of which have been calmly accepted by politicians and the electorate. These three states became members of NATO in 1999, and they are considered well-placed for early entry into the European Union. Though Czechoslovakia did break up to its constituent parts in January 1993, it did so peacefully and with remarkable civility. Slovakia has been the East-Central European exception to the extent that parties committed to substantive democracy did not succeed in forming a government there until late 1998. For most of the preceding period the country was ruled by populist–nationalist forces with Prime Minister Vladimír Mcčiar at the helm. Despite its authoritarian proclivities (until 1998), Slovakia, like the other East-Central European states, has nonetheless succeeded in creating a relatively well functioning market economy.

Compared with East-Central Europe, democratic transition has progressed more slowly in the Balkans. The foremost similarity between Romania and Bulgaria is that for a number of reasons, one of which was the absence of political will, both countries missed the opportunity to develop viable market economies in the 1990s. In Romania, in contrast to East-Central Europe, the presidency became a powerful political institution. Nationalism was one of the more prominent ideological influences on President Ion Iliescu's (1990–6) regime, which at times exploited the antiminority sentiments of some political parties and certain segments of society. The opposition Democratic Convention scored a victory at the 1996 elections, but a number of governments under President Emil Constantinescu were unable to drastically improve the economy. The December 2000 national elections reflected the widespread public discontent and returned Iliescu and his social democrats (PDSR) to power. Although Bulgaria, where presidential powers are far more limited, has been more democratic than Romania (politics in Sofia was marred more by corruption and incompetence than authoritarian tendencies), a government dedicated to profound economic reform and European integration took office only in 1997. The years of wasted opportunity produced large-scale poverty and apathy in both societies. The poorest of the former Yugoslav republics, Macedonia, was the only one that managed to secede from the federal state without violence. In the 1990s Macedonia was the victim of a remarkable series of unfavorable events (the wars in Bosnia and Kosovo, embargo by Greece) that exacerbated economic problems and sharpened interethnic conflicts (between Macedonians and Albanians). The country's one good fortune was that it had an extraordinary president, Kiro Gligorov (1990–9), whose wisdom and foresight saved it from yet more calamities.

One more point. It seems fairly obvious that a number of factors affect state policies everywhere yet those who charge (often for good reasons) that the Romani issue occupies low priority on the East European governments' agendas tend to disregard them.[3] Thus the following points bear repeating:

- The proportion of Gypsy communities to the overall populations of East European countries is small and their economic resources and political power are negligible.
- The Roma are the region's most unpopular social group widely regarded as a major burden on slender public resources, therefore, assisting them is seldom considered "smart politics."
- The postcommunist regime change has presented a cluster of profound political, economic, and social problems to the democratizing states; and the "Gypsy question" has been only one of many concerns of these governments, and a relatively minor one at that.
- In view of the demands of economic transition and the modesty of state budgets, governments have had very limited resources for relieving the Roma's social ills.

The upshot is that, until East European states became more sensitive to the condemnation of western international organizations, most of them did not regard the Gypsies' plight as a pressing issue. Considering these points places state policies toward the Roma in a more balanced perspective.

PART I: STATE INSTITUTIONS AND MINORITIES

A discussion of state policies toward ethnic minorities must distinguish between different political institutions because the attitudes of these institutions tend to differ, often according to how far they are removed from actual contact with the Roma. The most pertinent of these institutions are the president, the prime minister, the national government and its ministries, the governmental agency or agencies responsible for minority (and, especially, Romani) affairs, and local governments.

---

[3] See Zoltan Barany, "Orphans of Transition: Gypsies in Eastern Europe," *Journal of Democracy*, 9:3 (July 1998): 150.

Presidents

The question of whether presidential or parliamentary systems are more favorable for successful democratic consolidation has been widely debated in academic circles.[4] Although disagreements remain concerning the benefits and drawbacks of specific constitutional arrangements, the majority of scholars agree that parliamentary systems, rather than presidential ones, are better equipped to tackle the obstacles of democratic consolidation owing to the higher likelihood of majority governments, greater ability to rule, lower tolerance for authoritarian presidential behavior, and so on.[5] The political influence that presidents enjoy varies considerably in the seven East European states that this study focuses on. It ranges from a great deal of decision-making power in a presidential–parliamentary system like Romania to largely symbolic presidential functions in pure parliamentary systems such as the Czech Republic, Hungary, and Slovakia.[6]

Given the nature of the office, of all political institutions the presidency is the farthest removed from actual contact with ordinary Roma. Still, presidents can play a major role by calling on governments and local authorities to pay attention to the concerns of minorities, encouraging the majority population to empathize with the Roma's plight, castigating discriminatory behavior wherever and whenever it occurs, and supporting interethnic harmony in their public statements.

As far as Romani communities are concerned, the most admirable East European presidents have been Kiro Gligorov of Macedonia (1991–9), Árpád Göncz of Hungary (1990–2000), and Zhelyu Zhelev of Bulgaria (1990–7). These politicians went out of their way to actively and persistently support Gypsy rights and culture, and they did their best to publicize the Roma's plight even at the risk of jeopardizing their own popularity. Macedonian Gypsy leaders were grateful to Gligorov, who, in a speech to the United Nations' General Assembly, explicitly noted the Romani community's difficulties in his country and used other venues to emphasize that the Gypsies were equal citizens of the state along with everybody else.[7] In a public opinion poll, 100% of

---

[4] See, for instance, Matthew Soberg Shugart and John Carey, *Presidents and Assemblies* (Cambridge: Cambridge University Press, 1992); and Juan J. Linz and Arturo Valenzuela, eds., *The Failure of Presidential Democracy: Comparative Perspectives* (Baltimore: Johns Hopkins University Press, 1994).

[5] Alfred Stepan and Cindy Skach, "Constitutional Frameworks and Democratic Consolidation: Parliamentarism versus Presidentialism," *World Politics*, 46 (October 1993): 1–22.

[6] Ibid., 4.

[7] Interview with Faik Abdi, leader of the Party for the Total Emanicpation of the Macedonian Roma (Skopje, 11 March 1994) and Bekir Arif, President of the Progressive

the Roma asked were in favor of Gligorov.[8] The president sponsored several Romani cultural festivals, and to the end of his term he remained involved in Gypsy affairs.

Throughout his decade-long tenure, Árpád Göncz made a plethora of similar gestures toward the Gypsies. In parliament and in a number of public forums, Göncz called finding a solution to the Romani predicament "a matter of vital importance" for Hungary's future, talked openly of the tragedy of the forgotten Romani Holocaust, and did his best to mediate between squabbling Gypsy organizations.[9] Zhelev's pro-Gypsy attitudes are perhaps even more noteworthy because he openly supported the Roma at a time when a series of Bulgarian governments refused to acknowledge their problems. He not only visited impoverished Gypsy communities and met on many occasions with their leaders but insisted that Roma should actively participate in all programs designed to assist them.[10] Zhelev maintained close contacts with Romani and non-Romani NGOs, and through his office he employed a group of experts who advised him on Gypsy issues.

Václav Havel, the president of Czechoslovakia (1989–92) and the Czech Republic (1993–), is perhaps the best-known East European politician who has also been an impassioned advocate of Romani rights. On innumerable occasions he spoke out against racism and discrimination, chastised governments for their passivity regarding the Gypsies, and condemned local authorities for their discriminatory actions. From the beginning of his presidency he attended Romani festivals, participated in events commemorating the *Porajmos*, and publicly comforted the victims of anti-Romani crimes.[11] In an interview with the *New York Times* he

Democratic Party of the Roma (Skopje, 13 March 1994); and Hugh Poulton, *Who Are the Macedonians?* (London: Hurst & Co., 1995), 191.

[8] "Politicians' Dec 1993 Poll Ratings Reported," *Puls* (in Macedonian), 10 December 1993; translated in *Foreign Broadcast Information Service – Eastern Europe*, 15 December 1993, 52.

[9] Árpád Göncz, ". . . megoldása az ország létkérdése," *Közös út*, 20 September 1990; "Hungary: Update on Issues Affecting Roma," Immigration and Refugee Board, Canada (Ottawa, 21 August 1998), 3; and "Virrasztás a roma áldozatokért," *Népszabadság*, 2 August 1999.

[10] Hugh Poulton, "The Rest of the Balkans," in Hugh Miall, ed., *Minority Rights in Eastern Europe* (New York: Council of Foreign Relations Press, 1994), 84; and interviews with Nikolai Gentchev, a Professor of History at the University of Sofia (Sofia, 7 March 1995), and Mikhail Ivanov, Chief Presidential Advisor on Ethnic and Religious Issues (Sofia, 8 March 1995).

[11] See, for instance, "Havel to Commemorate Wartime Genocide of Gypsies," AFP (Prague), 13 May 1995; "Havel Wants Strict Punishment for Skinheads Who Drowned Romany," CTK (Prague), 19 February 1998; "Hável aggódik Szlovákiáért," *Népszabadság*, 10 March 1998.

called the "Gypsy problem" a "litmus test of civil society," whereby the maturity of the majority Czech population might be measured.[12] When in May 1998 two Romani men attacked the far-right politician Miroslav Sladek and his bodyguards after his speech full of racist remarks and insults against Havel and his wife, the president thanked them for defending his honor and promptly pardoned them.[13] The reason why I did not include Havel among the first group of three presidents is because he not only failed to call for an amendment to the Czech citizenship law of 1992, which clearly discriminated against the Roma, but publicly defended it.[14] Some analysts believe that Czechs do not take Havel's pro-Roma views seriously, partly because he has not facilitated a dialogue between the government and Romani organizations.[15]

Presidents who supported the Gypsies' cause but did not distinguish themselves in this regard form the next group. The two postcommunist Polish presidents, Lech Wałęsa (1990–5) and Aleksander Kwaśniewski (1995–), have done little for the Roma, which may in large part be explained by Poland's small Gypsy population. The presidential highlight of the 1990s was Wałęsa's June 1994 visit to a commemorative exhibition in Oświęcim (Auschwitz) organized by Roma and devoted to the victims of *Porajmos*.[16] Slovakia's Michal Kováč (1993–8) made few public statements about the Gypsies, though when he did he sharply criticized the Mečiar government's Romani policies and condemned skinhead attacks.[17] Gypsy leaders identified him as "the only constitutional official who has understanding for our problems and reacts to our letters."[18] In stark contrast with his predecessor,

[12] Henry Kamm, "Havel Sees Hatred of Gypsies as a Litmus Test for Czechs," *New York Times*, 10 December 1993.

[13] "Havel Appreciates Romanies' Defense of His Honour," and "Havel Pardons Attackers of Czech Far Right Leader," CTK (Prague), 11 May 1998.

[14] Jane Perlez, "Czechs Use Laws to Exclude Gypsies," *New York Times*, 27 December 1993; Tom Gross and James Hider, "Romanies Feel Law Is Unfair," *Prague Post*, 12–18 January 1994; Tom Gross, "A Blot on the Conscience," *Financial Times*, 19 December 1994; and interviews with Milena Hübschmannová, Professor of Romistics at Charles University (Prague, 12 June 1995) and Jonathan Stein, a researcher at the European Studies Center of the Institute for EastWest Studies (Prague, 14 August 1996).

[15] Interview with Vasil Hudak, Director of the EastWest Institute's Prague Center (Prague, 25 August 1999).

[16] Interview with Andrzej Mirga, President of the Roma Federation of Poland (Kraków, 14 June 1994).

[17] Sharon Fisher, "Romanies in Slovakia," *RFE/RL Research Report*, 2:42 (22 October 1993): 59; "Gypsy Groups Call for Banning Skinheads," AFP (Bratislava), 1 August 1995; and interview with Deputy Prime Minister Pál Csáky (Bratislava, 9 September 1999).

[18] Open Media Research Institute Daily Digest II (henceforth: OMRI DD II), 26 September 1995.

Bulgarian President Petar Stoyanov has said little about the Roma since taking office in January 1997, though he has supported the ratification of pro-minority legislation.[19] Under the watch of Romanian President Emil Constantinescu, institutional discrimination against the Roma has decreased and minority policies in general have improved. But the president could have done much more to speak out on the Gypsies' behalf. Moreover, his easily avoidable mistake of refusing to make good on his promise to appoint a Gypsy councillor at the President's Office antagonized many Roma.[20]

One can fairly consider only two presidents whose words and actions at times betrayed indifference toward the Roma and may have made their situation more difficult. Romania's Ion Iliescu, for most of his rule (1990–6), needed the support of nationalist parties for his government's survival, and he shied away from antagonizing them by championing the Gypsies' cause. Unlike virtually all other East European presidents, Iliescu did not condemn anti-Gypsy violence in the early 1990s. At the same time, he shrewdly supported international conferences on ethnic tolerance which he used as platforms to promote an image of interethnic harmony in his country. In spite of profound and enduring ethnic tensions, Iliescu confidently noted at a 1995 conference that

Tolerance and acceptance of diversity are specific to Romanians, who have lived for centuries in harmony with Hungarians, Gypsies, Germans, and other ethnic groups

even as members of these minorities were protesting outside.[21] Iliescu may have changed his policies, however. As noted in chapter 6, his PDSR entered into an electoral agreement with Romania's strongest Gypsy party in 1999 and he quickly delivered on his promises upon reclaiming the presidency in December 2000. Among the new appointees is a presidential advisor on Gypsy issues, Gheorghe Raducanu.

Rudolf Schuster, Slovakia's president since June 1999, is easily the most controversial among his East European colleagues as far as his stance toward the Roma is concerned. Schuster, a high-ranking

---

[19] Radio Free Europe/Radio Liberty Newsline, Part II (henceforth: RFE/RL II), 2:145 (30 July 1998); interviews with Emil R. Cohen, President, Tolerance Foundation (Sofia, 11 November 1999); Savelina Danova, Executive Director of the Human Rights Project (Sofia, 11 November 1999); and Ilona Tomova, a sociologist at the Bulgarian Academy of Science (Sofia, 15 November 1999).

[20] Interview with Nicolae Paun, President of *Partida Romilor* (Bucharest, 5 November 1999).

[21] Roxana Dascalu, "Gypsies Question Romanian Record on Minorities," Reuter (Bucharest), 23 May 1995; and "Romania Opens Euro-Conference on Tolerance," AFP (Bucharest), 23 May 1995.

official during the communist era (at an April 2000 meeting he claimed that "I am proud of what I did under the former regime"[22]), served as mayor of the eastern Slovak city of Košice in the 1990s. His mayoral deeds included the eviction of dozens of Romani families from the city center and concentrating them into a derelict former military housing estate (Lunik 9) beyond Košice's western suburbs in order to beautify the city's downtown in 1995–8.[23] During the electoral campaign in 1998, Schuster expressed his opposition to positive discrimination programs for the Roma together with Jan Slota, the extremist chairman of the Slovak National Party, and in contrast to several prominent liberal politicians like Mikuláš Dzurinda, leader of the coalition of democratic parties.[24] More recently, Schuster sought advice from Havel and Göncz about ways to solve the Roma's problems.[25]

Prime Ministers and Governments

As a general rule, prime ministers and national governments tend to adopt more pragmatic attitudes toward minorities than presidents, particularly that of the Gypsies. Ordinarily, top officers of national governments are in more regular contact with local authorities and are more intimately familiar with the problems that local officials face and thus with the everyday realities of dealing with ethnic issues. Unlike most East European presidents, prime ministers and their governments are respon sible for developing and implementing policies and interacting with minority representatives. It is important to note that the power of governments may be limited vis-à-vis other institutions. This is certainly true in the Czech Republic, for instance, where the separation of powers between national and local governments hinders Prague's ability to protect the Roma on the local level.[26]

---

[22] RFE/RL II, 4:69 (6 April 2000).

[23] See, for instance, Jakob Hurrle, "On the outskirts of Košice," *Newsletter of the HCA-Roma Section*, no. 6 (1998): 12–15; the chapter "Contrast Slovakia" in the British Helsinki Human Rights Group report *Czech Republic 1999: Gypsies in the Czech Republic* (1999); and interviews with Ingrid Baumannová, a consultant to the Foundation for Civic Society (Bratislava, 6 September 1999); Ingrid Antalová, Executive Director of the Milan Simečka Foundation (Bratislava, 7 September 1999); Klára Orgov-ánová, Program Director at the Open Society Foundation (Bratislava, 7 September 1999); and e-mail communication with Michal Vašečka, Roma specialist at the Institute for Public Affairs (14 June 2000).

[24] Michal Vašečka, "Roma and the 1998 Parliamentary Elections," in Martin Bútora et al., eds., *The 1998 Parliamentary Elections and Democratic Rebirth in Slovakia* (Bratislava: Institute for Public Affairs, 1999), 261.

[25] RFE/RL II, 3:133 (12 July 1999); and 4:58 (22 March 2000).

[26] See Romana Vyšatová, "Romani Politics in the Czech Republic and Slovakia," unpublished manuscript, 1994.

The governments of the seven states have compiled varying records as far as their Romani (and more broadly, minority) policies are concerned. Only Hungarian and Macedonian governments may be said to have taken the Gypsies' predicament seriously throughout the entire postcommunist period and have consistently kept it on their agendas. In Poland, governments have generally maintained a positive attitude toward minorities, including the Roma, but given the country's ethnic composition, the issue of ethnic minorities has not been a crucial one. Governments of the other four states began to make serious efforts to devise substantive policies toward the Gypsies only in the second part of the 1990s. There were two main reasons for their shifts in policy: (1) the constant criticism of international organizations that endangered the prospect of their European integration efforts and (2) domestic political changes rooted in the accession of minority-friendly governments in Bulgaria (1997), the Czech Republic (1997), Romania (1996), and Slovakia (1998). Looking at the entire decade of the 1990s, however, the trend of increasing state attention to the Roma in all seven states through the decade is hard to ignore.

As a young man, József Antall, Hungary's first postcommunist prime minister (1990–3), wrote historical studies on the Roma.[27] Once in government, he recognized their growing difficulties and included them among his government's priorities. His cabinet members often participated in the conferences of Romani organizations and created what Nicolae Gheorghe has called by far the best legal-institutional framework for Gypsies in Eastern Europe.[28] Gyula Horn's socialist-liberal government (1994–8) built on these foundations, although many of its ambitious programs failed to be realized. In 1996 it held a "Gypsy day" in parliament when, for the first time in history, an entire day was devoted to discussion and debate about the Roma's situation. Horn, while supporting positive discrimination programs for the Gypsies, also dared to touch some taboo subjects by, for instance, calling on the Romani community to cast out those who wanted to live by crime and refused to work. Radical Gypsy leaders like Aladár Horváth termed these suggestions "racist."[29] Viktor Orbán's government (1998–) has been even more concerned about the issue than its predecessors and has worked out and begun to implement an ambitious medium-range program

---

[27] See, for instance, József Antall, "Tanulmány-vázlat a cigányokról, (1957)," *Közös út-Kethano Drom*, 1:1 (January 1993): 41–4.
[28] Interview with Nicolae Gheorghe, director of Romani CRISS (Bucharest, 31 May 1996).
[29] See RFE/RL II, 1:168 (27 November 1997); "Vádolják Hornt," *Magyar Hírlap*, 31 January 1998; "Nem érti a romák vádjait a miniszterelnök," *Magyar Hírlap*, 2 February 1998.

broken down to annual action plans. Although Hungarian governments did more for the Roma than others in the region, until the late 1990s they, too, had lacked a conceptually coherent program supported by guaranteed financing.[30]

Macedonian governments and prime ministers have been consistent in their attention to the Roma, partly because they realized that they had better be able to point to positive steps in minority policy given their at times questionable treatment of the much larger and "troublesome" Albanian minority. Unlike their counterparts in the Balkans, governments in Skopje have genuinely viewed the Roma as an integral part of society and have even invited Gypsy parties to take part in electoral coalitions.[31] Nonetheless, it must be remembered that the Skopje governments' opportunities to implement programs for the Roma are limited by their grave financial constraints to a larger extent than elsewhere in Eastern Europe. Thus prime ministers, like Branko Črvenkovski, have repeatedly turned to private companies, investors, and NGOs to assist in alleviating the Gypsies' troubles in adjusting to the postcommunist period.[32] Governments in Warsaw have performed well in their minority policies by the standards of the Council of Europe as well as of most Polish intellectuals and Romani leaders.[33] Again, it is important to reiterate that their job was easier than that of other governments owing to the small proportion of ethnic minorities in the population.

Until 1997, Czech governments have been the least sympathetic toward the Gypsies in the region, which seems paradoxical because the country has been one of the leaders of the post-1989 democratization process. Prime Minister Václav Klaus (1992–7) deserves much of the blame for this. His key – and at times, it seemed, only – priority was to swiftly marketize the Czech economy. Klaus' strong support for the infamous Czech citizenship law may well have been motivated, as one journalist speculates, by his wish to remove from his country the Roma,

---

[30] Interviews with Éva Orsós, President of the Office for National and Ethnic Minorities (Budapest, 25 July 1996); and András Bíró, President of the Autonómia Foundation (Budapest, 26 July 1996).

[31] Poulton, *Who Are the Macedonians?*, 195; and interview with Georgi Spasov, a political sociologist at the Institute for Institute for Sociological, Political, and Juridical Research (Skopje, 8 March 1994).

[32] OMRI DD II, no. 52 (14 March 1997) citing *Nova Makedonija* (Skopje), 13 March 1997. See also, *The Situation of Roma in the Republic of Macedonia* (Skopje: Ministry of Foreign Affairs, 1999).

[33] See interviews with Adam Bartosz, Director of the Tarnów Regional Museum, and Adam Andrasz, President of the Tarnów Cultural Gypsy Association (Tarnów, 9 August 1999); Konstanty Gebert, the Editor-in-Chief of the Jewish magazine, *Midrasz* (Warsaw, 16 August 1999); and Roman Kwiatkowski, President of the Association of Polish Roma (Oświęcim, 19 August 1999).

whom he perceived as "an economic drain and an obstacle on the head-long path to prosperity" as well as to pander "to the widespread and often crudely stated racism of much of the electorate."[34] Klaus and his government did little to discourage skinhead attacks or to condemn the racist measures of some local authorities.[35] Only in 1997 did his cabinet start to consider the situation of the Roma seriously, after their large-scale emigration sharpened international attention on Prague's policies. At that point the government discussed a report it commissioned – the first two versions of which it did not accept owing to their alleged pro-Gypsy bias – and passed resolutions regarding the Roma's predicament, but this was hardly sufficient to change a five-year record of inaction.[36] According to Prague political analyst Ivan Gabal, Klaus "simply refused to acknowledge the Roma issue because it was something outside of his area of comprehension. He thought," Gabal says, "that the market would solve everything."[37] Josef Tošovsky's caretaker government (1997–8) and Miloš Zeman's social democratic cabinet (1998–) have been much more willing to give the Gypsies' situation serious consideration and to conduct an open dialogue with foreign critics of Czech minority policies. The Zeman government has proposed several comprehensive "Romani programs" and seems committed to implementing them.

Slovakia's Vladimír Mečiar, would certainly be the winner of the imaginary prize for the most overtly discriminatory public anti-Gypsy statements by a leading East European politician. In September 1993, for instance, Mečiar declared that the Roma constituted a "socially un-adaptable population" with a high birth rate of "children who are poorly adaptable mentally, poorly adaptable socially, children with serious health disorders, children, simply, who are a great burden on this society."[38] Mečiar, whose government included the extreme nationalist Slovak National Party, was defended by his cabinet members who noted

---

[34] Tom Gross, "A Blot on the Conscience," *Financial Times*, 19 December 1999. See also Zoltan Barany, "Roma: Grim Realities in Eastern Europe," *Transition*, 1:4 (29 March 1995): 5.

[35] Peter S. Green, "Czech Beauty Queen Hopes to Purge Hometown of Gypsies," UPI (Prague), 16 April 1993; interview with Karel Holomek (Brno, 1 September 1999).

[36] See Resolution no. 686 of the Government of the Czech Republic, 29 October 1997; *Report on Human Rights in the CR in 1998* (Prague: Council of Human Rights, 1999); and interview with Marta Miklušáková, Head of the Secretariat of the Council for Human Rights (Prague, 26 August 1999).

[37] Interview with Ivan Gabal of Gabal Analysis and Consulting (Prague, 24 August 1999).

[38] See Lázár Stefán, "Súlyos vádak Meciár ellen," *Új Magyarország*, 7 September 1993; Henry Kamm, "In New Eastern Europe, an Old Anti-Gypsy Bias," *The New York Times*, 17 November 1993.

that the prime minister only verbalized what the great majority of Slovaks thought.[39] Facing growing international criticisms, in 1997 Mečiar's government approved a workable plan to improve on the Roma's situation, but analysts agree that it had no plans to implement it. Most of them concur with Ingrid Baumannová, an official of a Bratislava civil rights NGO, that "essentially nothing of substance was done for or about the Roma during Mečiar's reign."[40] One of the first decisions of Mikuláš Dzurinda's government, keen to get Slovakia on the fast track to European Union membership, was to appoint a deputy prime minister (an ethnic Hungarian) in charge of national minorities and human rights.[41] These and other measures indicated the government's recognition that the Gypsies' problems required immediate and substantive intervention.

Romanian prime ministers and their governments were somewhat more active in dealing with the Roma's problems, but substantive improvement in actual policy began only in 1996. Prime ministers and their governments during Iliescu's presidency did not seem to or want to recognize the severity of the Gypsies' problems. Prime Minister Petre Roman's (1990–1) suggestion that "if we had more time and money, we could put together a program for this minority" was emblematic of a number of Romanian governments' preference for excuses to actions.[42] In a few instances the government actually tacitly supported anti-Romani violence, as in June 1990 when Jiu Valley miners went on a rampage in Bucharest targeting, among others, Gypsies and killing dozens of them.[43] By the mid-1990s the government showed more interest in the Roma, although its policies (like others in the region) suffered from a lack of coherence and the requisite financial commitments. When in May 1996 I interviewed Viorel Hrebenciuc, the Secretary-General of the Government and Coordinator of its Council for National Minorities, he

[39] "Kein Zufall mehr," *Frankfurter Allgemeine Zeitung*, 14 September 1993.
[40] Interview with Baumannová (Bratislava, 6 September 1999). See also interviews with Columbus Igboanusi, legal adviser to InfoRoma (Bratislava, 6 September 1999); Orgovánová (Bratislava, 7 September 1999); and Vašečka (Bratislava, 10 September 1999); and Vašečka, "The Roma," in Gregoríj Mešeznikov, Michal Ivantyšyn, and Tom Nicholson, eds., *Slovakia 1998–1999: A Global Report on the State of Society* (Bratislava: Institute of Public Affairs, 1999), 399–400.
[41] See RFE/RL II, 2:213 (4 November 1998); and "Slovaks v Czechs on Gypsies," *The Economist*, 7 November 1998, 52.
[42] Cited in Franz Remmel, *Die Roma Rumäniens: Volk ohne Hinterland* (Vienna: Picus, 1993), 105.
[43] See Michael Shafir, "Government Encourages Vigilante Violence in Bucharest," *Report on Eastern Europe*, 1:27 (6 July 1990): 32–8; and interview with Bucharest PER Director Dan Pavel (Bucharest, 2 November 1999). Pavel says that officially only six or seven Gypsies died, but coroners' reports indicate 60 to 70 related Romani casualties.

underscored the dissimilar problems of Roma in various Romanian regions and noted that "though we have tried many things, we could not create miracles."[44] Nor could the more liberal governments since 1996 though, as in Slovakia, they have been able to establish a more promising institutional framework (including the creation of a new ministry dealing with minority affairs) and attract funds from the EU and other international organizations to finance programs designed for the Gypsies.

The passivity of the numerous Bulgarian governments in 1990–7 rivaled only those of their Slovak counterpart. Although prime ministers and cabinet members did not make overtly racist or anti-Gypsy statements, this is about the best that can be said about them from the Roma's perspective. In two lengthy visits to the country prior to 1997, I was not able to discover any serious or even half-hearted governmental attempts to acknowledge the Gypsies' problems, let alone to do something about them. In essence, what little was done for the Roma originated from President Zhelev's office. Ivan Kostov's government (1997–) has professed earnest ambitions to integrate the Roma, has set up a new office to spearhead the process, and, ably assisted by some domestic NGOs, has made some progress working out a national program. Kostov has been the first Bulgarian prime minister who has regularly expressed concern for the Roma in public speeches.[45]

It is noteworthy that Bulgarian, Hungarian, Polish, Slovak, and Romanian governments have all had their favorite Romani organizations who received a disproportionate share of resources for no reasons other than their political loyalties. This did not occur in the Czech Republic owing to the lack of governmental interest in cooperating with Gypsy organizations and, in all fairness, due to the general ineptitude of the latter. In Macedonia relatively few Romani organizations exist and they have preferred to seek the support of NGOs from which they can reasonably expect more money.

Legislatures

Most of the substantive work pertaining to minorities takes place in the specialized committees of national legislatures. I shall discuss them in Part II, but I want to make three general points about parliaments at this juncture. First, it obviously makes an enormous difference whether

---

[44] Interview with Hrebenciuc (Bucharest, 24 May 1996).
[45] See Maria Koinova's report, "Courting Minorities," in *Transition*, 5:12 (1998): 12–13; and interviews with Dimitrina Petrova, Director of the Human Rights Project (Sofia, 8 March 1995 and Budapest, 5 August 1999); ethnographer Elena Marushiakova (Sofia, 9 March 1994); and Emil R. Cohen (Sofia, 11 November 1999).

openly antiminority parties are represented in the legislature and, if so, how influential they are. The extremist political organizations in the region tend to be on the political margin. Only in Romania and Slovakia have they achieved a strong parliamentary presence in the 1990s. When in parliament, the Republican Party of Miroslav Sladek in the Czech Republic was successful only in creating political spectacles. Sladek, who may be the most openly anti-Romani politician in the region, has a penchant for talking about the "final solution to the Gypsy problem." In his nationally televised opening speech to the new parliament in 1994 (the Republicans gained a surprising 8% of the vote which netted them 18 seats in the legislature), Sladek said that Gypsy children were criminals by committing the criminal act of being born.[46] The venom of Slovak and Romanian extremist parties in parliament has been usually directed against the Hungarian minority, which is perceived as better organized and more threatening.

Second, an equally important issue is the parliamentary representation of ethnic minorities, especially those that owing to their small number or unsuccessful electoral campaigns have no chance to attain it. Among the seven East European states this study focuses on, only Romania established minority parliamentary representation guaranteed by law. A number of Romani leaders, however, do not consider guaranteed minority parliamentary representation desirable. Nicolae Gheorghe contends that once the social differences between minorities and the majority disappear, minority representation will lose its significance. He believes that though a fully competitive electoral system might not favor Roma in the short run, it stimulates more effective mobilization and would be beneficial for them in the long run.[47] It is also true that the process that led to the nomination of the Gypsy MP has deeply divided Romani organizations in Romania. Another point is that by joining together, different ethnic minorities can potentially acquire parliamentary representation on their own. In any event, minority representation has been extensively discussed in several East European states, but it is yet to be implemented. The Hungarian Constitution, for instance, provides for a seat for each ethnic minority, but they have yet to get them. The amendment of the 1993 national minority law, which is to outline

[46] Interviews with Zdeněk Matějka, head of the OSCE's Prague office (Prague, 14 August 1996); and Jonathan Stein (Prague, 14 August 1996). See also Paul Hockenos, *Free To Hate: The Rise of the Right in Post-Communist Eastern Europe* (New York: Routledge, 1993), 224–30.

[47] See Lajos Puporka's interview with Gheorghe, "A roma képviselet máshol is gond," *Népszabadság*, 18 April 1998; and *Political Participation and the Roma in Hungary and Slovakia* (Princeton: PER, 1999), 6.

the procedures pertaining to minority representation, has been repeatedly delayed in parliament.[48]

Third, most East European parliaments spent the bulk of their ses-
sions in the first half of the 1990s discussing and legislating issues crucial
for democratization and economic transition. As more and more of the
pertinent laws were codified and as the criticisms of international organizations began to hit home, they increasingly turned their attention to
matters relating to ethnic minorities and other marginal groups. Even
earlier in the decade, there were instances when backbenchers in the legislature proved far more enlightened than governments. One such event
occurred during the debate over the Bulgarian constitution in 1991 when
parliamentary deputies, led by Dimitrina Petrova and Krassen Stanchev,
lobbied their colleagues (in vain) against approving Article 11.4 that prohibited the formation of ethnic-based parties.[49] By the late 1990s, laws
were beginning to be debated and enacted about racial incitement and
discrimination. In 1999, for instance, the Chamber of Deputies in Prague
revoked the Ústí nad Labem city council's decision to build a wall seg-
regating Czechs from Gypsies, though the legislature was later overruled
by the Constitutional Court.[50]

Local Authorities

Governments and their ministries might embrace progressive policies,
and legislatures may enact laws against discrimination, but it is up to
local authorities to implement them. Thus, local officials play a crucial
role because for ordinary Roma they personify the state on a daily basis
as council members, aid administrators, policemen, and social workers.
Of all state institutions, the attitudes of local authorities toward the
Gypsies are the most problematic. Local officials are generally less educated and harbor more prejudices than representatives of the central state
bureaucracy. They often contend that the empathy and enlightened views
of presidents and ministers are naive, idealistic, and rarely matched by
actual experience with the Roma. As one embattled Hungarian mayor
said, "from a distance of 270 kilometers, the minister sees many things
differently from how we see [them] on the spot."[51] Although many local
officials are genuinely concerned with improving the conditions of Gypsy

---

[48] See, for instance, Csaba Tabajdi, *Az önazonosság labirintusa: A magyar kül- és
kisebbségpolitika rendszerváltása* (Budapest: CP Stúdió, 1998), 663–73; and interview
with Antal Heizer, Chief Advisor, Prime Minister's Office (Budapest, 28 May 1999).

[49] Interviews with Stanchev of the Institute for Market Economics (Sofia, 7 March 1995)
and Petrova (Sofia, 8 March 1995).

[50] RFE/RL II, 3:119 (18 June 1999); 3:201 (14 October 1999); and 4:74 (13 April 2000).

[51] Ibid., 1:110 (4 September 1997).

communities in their bailiwick, praiseworthy original intentions are often overlooked in their daily routine usually characterized by poor working conditions, inadequate resources, and low material rewards. Most of the outrageous transgressions of Romani rights take place in local settings. Especially in the early 1990s, a number of startling discriminatory measures and stunning statements have been directed against the Gypsies by local authorities. Although such incidents happened in all East European states, they occurred the least frequently – even when factoring in the small size of Romani communities – in Poland and Macedonia.

In the Czech Republic, "No Roma Allowed" signs have been almost routinely placed on restaurant doors and windows. In a much publicized incident, Emil Ščuka, the chairman of the Romani Civic Initiative, and his party waited in vain for a waiter at a restaurant in Jičín, only to be told by a policeman that "blacks are not served here."[52] In 1996 in the town of Breclav a sign barring Gypsies was displayed on a hotel owned by Rudolf Baranek, chairman of the Czech Association of Entrepreneurs and a candidate for the legislature. As punishment, his party moved Baranek from second to fifth place, below Gypsy activist Karel Holomek, on its electoral list of candidates.[53] Town officials in Všetín and Kladno prohibited "dirty, ill, or lice-infested people" to enter the municipal swimming pools, a step Romani activists claimed was taken to keep Gypsy children away.[54]

The most infamous case of anti-Gypsy discrimination by local authorities is the aforementioned wall in Ústí nad Labem. The saga that began in 1997 – and included the construction, demolition, reconstruction, and re-demolition of the structure, death threats against the principals, and international outcry from as far away as South Africa – seems to have ended in April 2000, with the Czech Constitutional Court's decision.[55] Nonetheless, five months before the Court's ruling that parliament cannot overturn decisions by municipal councils, authorities in Ústí nad Labem agreed to pull down the wall and to subsidize the purchase of houses somewhere else for Czech residents.[56]

---

[52] Maria Tulejova, "Romani Rights and Wrongs," *The Prague Post*, 8–14 September 1993.

[53] OMRI DD II, no. 60 (25 March 1996) citing CTK (Prague), 22 March 1996. See also, "Za zakaz ob sluhy možna da vezeni," *Lidové Noviny*, 14 August 1996.

[54] OMRI DD II, no. 204 (19 October 1995); and "Regional Court Upholds Fine on Kladno Mayor for Racist Conduct," CTK (Prague), 19 February 1998.

[55] See RFE/RL II, 3:195 (6 October 1999); Jana Bauerova, "Tensions Heighten as Usti Wall Comes Down," *The Prague Post*, 13 October 1999; RFE/RL II, 3:200 (13 October 1999); interview with Marta Miklušáková (Prague, 26 August 1999); and RFE/RL II, 4:74 (13 April 2000).

[56] See "Czechs' Wall for Gypsies Stirs Protest Across Europe," *New York Times*, 17 October 1999; and Nadia Rybarova, "Czech Town Pulls Down Anti-Gypsy Barricade,"

In Slovakia, the mayor of the town of Špišske Podhradie imposed a night-time curfew on "Gypsies and other suspicious people," justified by his view that they "sleep during the day and steal at night."[57] The city council of Jelšava refused five Romani families permanent residence in the municipality, even though they owned real estate there. The mayor conceded that "We know we are breaking the law" but, he said, "we don't want Jelšava to become a Roma city."[58] The mayor of the Hungarian city of Sátoraljaújhely cited "genetic reasons" for the town council decision to force out about 40 Roma.[59] According to a 1999 study, 43% of Hungarian municipal governments would prohibit Gypsies, if they could legally do so, from settling in their towns.[60]

Some journalists and Gypsy activists portray municipal officials as racist thugs who relish the opportunity to discriminate against Roma. (Officials, like the mayor of the Czech city of Plzeň who was accused of planning to put Roma in a "concentration camp," at times threaten to or actually sue those who make unsubstantiated but sensational allegations, at which point such charges are usually quickly withdrawn.[61]) The fact is that the job of local authorities is anything but easy. Their constituents' anti-Gypsy prejudices effectively preclude support for projects helping the Roma. Local council members often complain that bureaucrats in the capital cannot fathom the trials of sharing a town with Roma. As the deputy mayor of the Czech city of Most noted, "If you never lived with Gypsies, you don't know the problems."[62] Municipal officials also face the same problem as central institutions, trying to figure out how and with which of the numerous rival local Romani NGOs to cooperate.[63]

Even in the region's more prosperous countries, like Hungary, local authorities have very limited financial resources. For instance, a 1997

AP (Prague), 27 November 1999. The epilogue of this story is that the infamous wall was moved to the local zoo to replace a fence in July 2000. Zoo officials placed an inscription on one segment of the reerected wall that reads "rare species, to be seen only in Ústí nad Labem zoo." RFE/RL II, 4:139 (21 July 2000).

[57] See "Ausgangssperre für Zigeuner in slowakischem Dorf," *Süddeutsche Zeitung*, 12 July 1993; and Philip Sherwell, "Gypsies Suffer Racist Fallout of Communism's Collapse," *Globe and Mail*, 3 August 1993.

[58] Cited by Vašečka in "The Roma," 405.

[59] George Jahn, "Gypsies Remain Outcasts Despite Vast Change in Eastern Europe," AP (Budapest), 27 March 1998.

[60] Ildikó Emese Nagy, "Minden második település távol tartaná a romákat," *Magyar Hírlap*, 8 April 1999.

[61] British Helsinki Human Rights Group, *Gypsies in the Czech Republic*, 7.

[62] Cited by Juan O. Tamayo, "Gypsies among Hardest Hit Victims of Europe's Rising Tide of Racism," *Miami Herald*, 4 May 1993.

[63] See Martin Jansen, "Gypsies at the Council of Europe," *o Drom*, September 1994, 30.

Hungarian law introduced so-called "child-protection" payments. The state allocated 70% of the funds and local governments must come up with the rest, but they received no guidance as to which source should provide the money.[64] In most cases when local authorities evict or try to evict Roma from their dwellings, they do so because tenants do not pay rent and utilities for months at a time or occupy condemned buildings.[65] Instead of the requisite resources, municipalities ordinarily receive the condemnation of unsympathetic national governments, which, in turn, are criticized by international organizations. And, it should be noted that the Roma are often not easy to help. As local officials frequently realize, the initial enthusiasm of Gypsies about adult education classes and other assistance projects paid for by the municipality quickly turns into indifference.[66]

The picture is not all bleak, however. Throughout the region an increasing – though still small – number of municipalities have devised and devoted scarce funds to projects in order to assist Romani integration. Andrzej Mirga told me, for instance, that whenever he approached authorities in the Polish city of Kraków on behalf of the Roma, he always encountered sympathetic and helpful officials.[67] Local police stations have hired Gypsies, and county employment offices have been opened in areas heavily populated by Roma in Bulgaria. In Lom, a town of 45,000, where 86% of the 12,000 Gypsy residents are unemployed, municipal authorities have provided agricultural land for them and free office space for the local Romani NGO.[68] Bulgarian municipalities have granted thousands of Roma title to the land on which they have illegally built their dwellings.[69] In the Romanian city of Sibiu, representatives of the police as well as the Gypsy and other ethnic communities have established a routine of regular meetings in order to prevent and solve problems.[70]

The Czech city of Brno – aided by financial support from the Council of Europe – has been especially creative in its approach to the problems

---

[64] Gábor Matúz and Ferenc Sinkovics, "Te is! Neked is!," *Demokrata*, 2:37 (17 September 1998), 20.
[65] See, for instance, Ákos Tóth, "Tüntetés a romáknak szánt konténer ellen," *Népszabadság*, 24 November 1997.
[66] See for instance, "A putrit végképp eltörölni," *Heves megyei Hírlap*, 3 March 1997.
[67] Interview with Mirga (Kraków, 29 July 1996).
[68] See *The Roma in Bulgaria: Collaborative Efforts Between Local Authorities and Nongovernmental Organizations* (Princeton: PER, 1998).
[69] Interviews with Stanchev (Sofia, 7 March 1994) and Ivan Ilchev, Professor of History at the University of Sofia (Sofia, 9 March 1994).
[70] Interview with Florin Cioabă, the "International King of the Gypsies" (Sibiu, 27 October 1999).

of the local Romani community. The city, together with Romani NGOs, has worked out "Strategic Plan 2000," a complex action program that has included a wide range of successful projects dealing with interethnic relations, education, employment, culture, and crime prevention.[71] Unfortunately the Brno program is exceptional not only in the Czech Republic but also in the region. Though a relatively prosperous city like Brno obviously enjoys broader room for action than do towns less fortunate, the will of local politicians along with a cohesive and actively cooperative local Romani elite are two crucial ingredients of success that are still absent in most East European towns.

PART II: INSTITUTIONS DIRECTLY DEALING WITH ROMA

The numerous minority commissions, committees, and councils created and overseen by governments and legislatures across the region constitute the primary institutional locus of Romani, and more broadly, minority policy. As the East European states became more serious about doing something about the Gypsies' problems, the number and significance of these bodies increased. Just mentioning all of them would take up most of this chapter, so I shall limit the discussion to the most important ones. Thus, I leave out, for instance, the individual ministries – particularly education, employment, interior, culture, and so on – that maintain departments or subdepartments whose work is devoted to the Roma. It is important to recognize also that parliamentary committees whose primary concern is not minority affairs – such as committees on education – often spend the bulk of their time discussing minority affairs.[72] The overall attitudes in governmental or state agencies concerned with minorities depend on their ministers or directors (and the person[s] who appointed them). Generally speaking, individuals in these institutions possess the most expertise in minority (and Romani) affairs; therefore, this is where most of those with realistic views of the Gypsies' problems and sound ideas concerning potential solutions for them can be found.

Throughout the region these institutions have similar functions, though their performance has varied considerably. Government bodies are usually charged with protecting the Roma's rights and interests by planning policies and programs and preparing draft laws designed to

---

[71] See "Strategic Plan for Solution of Inter-Ethnic Relations between the Majority Population and the Romany Minority in the City of Brno," City of Brno, May 1999, 53 pp; and interviews with Karel Holomek, President of the Association of Roma in Moravia (Brno, 1 September 1999); Vladimír Adam, Head of the Social and Cultural Section, City of Brno (Brno, 2 September 1999); and social workers at the Romani Cultural Center (Brno, 9 September 1999).

[72] Interview with Emilija Simoska, Director of the Center for Ethnic Relations at the Institute for Sociological, Political, and Juridical Research (Skopje, 23 November 1999).

help them. They are ordinarily also responsible for disbursing funds to Romani organizations and Gypsy-related projects and, as much as possible, working together with Romani groups and NGOs. By their very nature, parliamentary committees have been a far less influential institutional component of minority policy. They are supposed to oversee and evaluate governmental policies and debate the laws proposed by the cabinet. Again, it is worth noting that in the second half of the 1990s these institutions tended to be more active and effective than earlier in the decade.

Governmental Bodies

The one important and active governmental body dealing with minorities and the Roma in Poland is the Department for the Culture of National Minorities in the Ministry of Culture and Art, which supports many activities and organizations.[73] The Czech government maintains three bodies to guide its minority policy.[74] The Council for National Minorities dates from the state-socialist period and has three permanent members including one Rom, Vladislav Gorál. It is supposed to be an "advisory, initiating, and coordinating body of the government," though its significance has been largely limited to acting as the representative of the government at minority-related events.[75] After the departure of the Klaus administration, two institutions were created. The Inter-Ministerial Commission for Roma Community Affairs has 24 members: 12 deputy ministers from the dozen ministries (from education to employment) that deal with the Gypsies' situation and 12 Romani experts complementing them. It is supposed to advise the government on issues pertaining to the Gypsies. The Council for Human Rights has functioned only since February 1999, but it has been perhaps the most active of the three. It has established eight working groups paralleling the Geneva Covenants (children's rights, women's rights, etc.) plus one for the rights of foreigners and another for human rights education. The Council's membership is made up by ten deputy ministers and ten human rights activists. Petr Uhl, the head of all three of these organizations, and Deputy Prime Minister Pável Rychetsky have been instrumental in giving the Gypsies' predicament a higher profile in the government and drafting a "Roma integration concept" that the cabinet approved in June 2000. Five months later, the government approved draft legislation that

---

[73] Interview with Mirga (Kraków, 14 June 1994 and 29 July 1996).
[74] This discussion is much informed by my interview (Prague, 26 August 1999) and subsequent correspondence with Miklušáková.
[75] "Statute: Nationalities Council of the Czech Republic Government," Appendix to Government Edict no. 259, 11 May 1994, Article 1, 1.

would set up a new Council for Ethnic Minorities in order to satisfy a key element of the Council of Europe's framework convention on ethnic minority rights.

Until late 1998 the superficiality of Slovakia's institutional framework for minority affairs rivaled only that of Bulgaria's. Save for a few much ignored and frustrated minority advisers, in the Mečiar government there were no offices concerned with the Roma until the fall of 1995. Then, after years of lobbying by Gypsy organizations, a Commissioner for Citizens Requiring Special Assistance was appointed. Romani activists protested both the institution's name and the fact that Mečiar appointed an ethnic Slovak, Branislav Baláž, rather than a Rom. Three years later Baláž proposed a workable plan for integrating the Roma into Slovak society which was not implemented.[76] Things changed rapidly once the Dzurinda government took office.[77] In February 1999 it established a Council for Minorities with 16 voting members who represent all 11 ethnic minorities (with Hungarians having three and Roma two members), the minister of culture, and the also newly appointed Deputy Prime Minister in Charge of Human Rights, Minorities, and Regional Development, Pál Csáky. Officials from eight ministries are also on the Council, but they do not have voting rights. After contentious negotiations with dozens of Romani NGOs and parties, in March 1999 Csáky appointed Vincent Danihel, a Gypsy lawyer, as the government's Commissioner for Romani Issues. Danihel's job is to make recommendations to the cabinet, coordinate the work of state bodies as it pertains to the Roma, and take part in planning the government's reform concept for Gypsy policy.[78]

Hungary's Office for National and Ethnic Minorities (ONEM), supervised by the minister of justice, was established in 1990. A separate department is devoted within the Office to Romani issues. In 1995 the government created a Co-ordination Council for Gypsy Affairs (CCGA; its members were representatives of Romani organizations and of relevant ministries), which was connected to ONEM. In 1996 the cabinet set up a Roma Program Committee (RPC) to deal with political issues concerning the implementation of its Gypsy program.[79] The Horn government, which created the last two bodies, also appointed the seasoned socialist minority expert, Csaba Tabajdi, as a political state secretary. As

---

[76] Interview with Vašečka (Bratislava, 10 August 1999).
[77] Interview with Pál Csáky, Deputy Prime Minister in Charge of Human Rights, Minorities, and Regional Development (Bratislava, 9 September 1999).
[78] Interview with Commissioner Vincent Danihel (Bratislava, 10 September 1999).
[79] *Synthesis of the Replies to the Questionnaire on Participation of Minorities in Decision-Making Processes* (Strasbourg: Council of Europe, 1999), 48.

it turned out, there were too many institutions with similar responsibilities, and Tabajdi had time and again attempted to strong-arm ONEM's leadership.[80] The Orbán government has simplified this convoluted institutional structure. In 1999 it abolished both the CCGA and the RPC and replaced them with an Inter-Ministerial Committee for Gypsy Affairs (ICGA) supervised by Minister of Justice Ibolya Dávid and ONEM's President (Toso Doncsev [1998–2000], János Báthory [2000–]). The other permanent members of the new body are representatives of the Prime Minister's Office, nine ministries, and the National Gypsy Self-Government.[81] The main responsibility of the ICGA is to implement the government's package of medium-range Gypsy policies.

Unlike the other states with lackluster minority policies, Romania established a suitable institutional framework already in the early 1990s. The problem was that these bodies lacked substance. In 1993 the cabinet set up an advisory body, the Council for National Minorities (CNM), made up of minority representatives elected by their communities as well as ministry officials. Although the CNM has organized six working committees, when I visited its offices in 1995 I was unable to discern what if anything they were actually doing.[82] In any event, while the Council has issued warnings against xenophobia and tried to mediate among Romani organizations, it has not played a major part in minority politics.[83] Its role, in fact, has diminished since 1996. As in Slovakia, things changed rapidly after the new government took office. In November 1996 the cabinet established a separate ministry, the Department for the Protection of National Minorities (DPNM), headed by an ethnic Hungarian (György Tokay and, after his resignation, Péter Eckstein-Kovács). In the ministry there is a new National Office for Roma (NOR). This three-person office was first led by a Rom, Vasile Burtea, who was replaced a few months later by a noted Romanian human rights expert, Dan Oprescu. In 1998 the government set up an Inter-Ministerial Committee for National Minorities with a Roma Inter-Ministerial Subcommission. The latter is overseen by NOR, and it is composed of ministry representatives and members of the Working Group of the Roma

[80] Interviews with Orsós (Budapest, 25 July 1996) and Bíró (Budapest, 26 July 1996). Bíró was a member of RPC until he resigned due to his frustration over the lack of its conceptual clarity. See also Ildikó Emese Nagy, "Farkas Flórián: kegyelem után, újabb perek elött," *Magyar Hírlap*, 6 March 1998.

[81] See Gábor Czene, "Új cigányügyi bizottság alakul," *Népszabadság*, 31 March 1999; and "A kormány 1048/1999 határozata," *Magyar Közlöny*, no. 39 (1999), 2734.

[82] Interviews with members of the Council for Minorities (Bucharest, 14 March 1995). See also *The Legislative and Institutional Framework for the National Minorities of Romania* (Bucharest: Romanian Institute of Human Rights, 1994), 101–14.

[83] RFE/RL II, 3:123 (24 June 1999).

Associations. Together they are responsible for drawing up the government's "Strategy for the protection of the Roma minority."[84] After the December 2000 national elections, DPNM was reorganized. The chief of its Romani department, with the rank of deputy state secretary, is Ivan Gheorghe, one of the leaders of the Roma Party.

In Bulgaria the institutional framework for minority affairs was even more embryonic and hollow than in the other states where minority-friendly governments came to power only in the second part of the 1990s. For instance, the government established a Committee for the Socially Disadvantaged" (to assist women, the elderly, as well as Roma) in 1993, but it met only twice in four years.[85] Finally, in December 1997 the new Kostov government introduced the National Council on Ethnic and Demographic Issues (NCEDI) whose chairman is Deputy Prime Minister Vesselin Metodiev. NCEDI permanent members come from ministries, government agencies, and ethnic organizations.[86] The Council appointed Iosif Nunev, an ethnic Rom and the former director of a Romani school, as its chief expert on Gypsy issues. Unlike in Slovakia, however, the government did not consult with representatives of the Gypsy community prior to Nunev's appointment.[87] According to its Secretary, Petar Atanasov, the Roma's situation has been the main focus of NCEDI's work and it has worked hard to mediate between the government and Gypsy NGOs in order to elaborate a workable long-range plan for Romani integration.[88]

Of all East European states, ethnic minorities make up by far the largest proportion of the population in Macedonia. This is why nearly all political institutions in the country are engaged in dealing with the concerns of minorities. There is only one office in the executive sphere that deals specifically with minority affairs, the Human Rights and Minorities Department at the Ministry of Foreign Affairs.[89] There is also a Council for Inter-Ethnic Relations whose members, all unpaid volunteers, are nominated by ethnic minorities and appointed by the president. Essentially, it acts as an advisory body that suggests guidelines pertain-

---

[84] See the Romanian government's "Partnership Protocol Regarding the Drawing Up of the Strategy for the Protection of the Roma Minority in Romania," (Bucharest, 28 April 1999), 2 pp.

[85] Interview with Tomova (Sofia, 15 November 1999).

[86] See "Regulation of the structure and organisation of the work of the National Council on Ethnic and Demographic Issues at the Council of Ministers," (Sofia, NCEDI, n.d.), 2 pp.

[87] Interview with Danova (Sofia, 11 November 1999).

[88] Interview with Atanasov (Sofia, 15 November 1999).

[89] Interview with Elizabeta Georgieva, Head of the Human Rights and Minorities Department, Ministry of Foreign Affairs (Skopje, 23 November 1999).

ing to minority laws and resolutions to the government. Since its inception in 1991 the Council has met only eleven times. Macedonian and foreign experts have suggested that it could play "a greater role in giving minority populations an effective voice in government."[90]

Parliamentary Committees

The body dealing with minority affairs in the Polish Sejm is the Commission on National and Ethnic Minorities, whose chairman is Jacek Kurón. Kurón, a former dissident who is one of the country's most popular public figures, has a great deal of moral influence, and the fact that he has made gestures to all minorities has made an impression on the population.[91] The Commission has engaged numerous minority experts, among them Roma. After several years of preparation in 1998 the Commission completed the draft minority law, which the Sejm has yet to discuss because parties have not considered it a priority.[92] In the Czech Chamber of Deputies the Subcommittee for Nationalities and the Subcommittee for the Application of the List of Basic Rights and Freedoms deal with minority affairs. They have enjoyed only marginal influence. The Slovak parliament's Committee for Human Rights and Minorities (CHRM) came to life only after 1998. By all accounts it has lacked dynamism and influence though recently it established a Sub-Committee on the Roma.[93] Owing to the relatively well organized Hungarian minority whose size is similar to that of the Romani community, the situation of the Gypsies has only been one of CHRM's key concerns. The Hungarian legislature's Standing Committee on Human Rights, Minorities, and Religious Affairs has not distinguished itself in any way. It will presumably play an important role during the discussion which is to lead to the amendment of the national minority law.

Romania has been the only state among the seven where minority representation not only is constitutionally prescribed, but has functioned

---

[90] See Barnett R. Rubin and Steven L. Burg, "Recommendations," 23; and Steven L. Burg, "Stabilizing the South Balkans," 34–45 in Barnett R. Rubin, ed., *Toward Comprehensive Peace in Southeast Europe: Conflict Prevention in the South Balkans* (New York: The Twentieth Century Fund Press, 1996); and interviews with Simoska (Skopje, 23 November 1999) and Jelica Savinova, Secretary of both the Council and the Committee for Inter-Ethnic Relations (Skopje, 30 November 1999).

[91] Interview with Gebert (Warsaw, 16 August 1999).

[92] See Wolfgang Schlott, "Die nationalen Minderheiten und ihre Grenzlandkulturen in Polen nach 1989," Forschungsstelle Osteuropa an der Universität Bremen, July 1994, 6 pp.; and interview with Andrzej Mirga, chairman of the Project on Ethnic Relations Roma Advisory Committee (Kraków, 11 August 1999).

[93] Interview with Orgovánová (Bratislava, 7 September 1999); and Csáky (Bratislava, 9 September 1999).

successfully for nearly a decade. The organizations of national minorities that fail to obtain a seat in the elections but do get at least 5% of the vote necessary for one are guaranteed one mandate.[94] (The party of the approximately 1.6 million strong Hungarian minority tends to garner roughly 7% of the vote and thus has a sizable group in both houses of parliament.) The Roma and twelve other ethnic minorities have composed the Committee for National Minorities in the Chamber of Deputies (lower house). With its 13 votes the Committee has the possibility of truly making a difference.[95] The coalition parties of the ruling Democratic Convention (1996–2000) enjoyed only a small majority in parliament and thus could not afford to alienate minority representatives. This might be the reason that for 1999 the Committee received three times the amount of funds it asked for (for offices, travel, etc.) from the government.[96]

In the Bulgarian legislature there is a Committee on Human Rights to which, according to my interviewees, deputies with no apparent relevant expertise are ordinarily assigned. Its chairman, Ivan Sungarski, an auto mechanic by trade, has on numerous occasions publicly identified the state of Utah as an example to be emulated because it prohibits African-Americans from settling![97] The most important body explicitly dealing with minorities in the Skopje National Assembly is the Commission for Inter-Ethnic Relations whose members are ten MPs elected by their colleagues (current members are one Rom, six Macedonians, two Albanians, and one Bosnian) in addition to the President of the Assembly. All legal acts relating to minorities must pass through the Commission, which, unlike the Council discussed above, meets regularly.[98] This has been the most active parliamentary committee among those discussed in this section.

The Ombudsman

The creation of the office of the ombudsman, an independent institution that protects citizens from overbearing authorities, has been an important development in postcommunist Eastern Europe. Commissioners, as ombudsmen are often called, investigate complaints, write reports for parliament, request inquiries in specific cases from the relevant ministries

---

[94] See Article 4, Law No. 68/July 15, 1992 in *The Legislative and Institutional Framework*, 95.

[95] Interview with Varujan Vosganian, a member of the committee, (Bucharest, 13 March 1995).

[96] Interview with Dan Oprescu, Head of National Office for the Roma, Department for the Protection of National Minorities, (Bucharest, 2 November 1999).

[97] Interviews with Danova (Sofia, 11 November 1999) and Elena Marushiakova and Vesselin Popov, eminent Bulgarian ethnographers (Sofia, 13 November 1999).

[98] Interview with Georgieva, (Skopje, 23 November 1999).

(e.g., ask the Ministry of Internal Affairs to examine complaints), participate in the meetings of minority-related institutions, and so on. The government is not required to follow up the ombudsmen's recommendations; thus their success depends largely on the administration's goodwill and cooperation. Perhaps this is the reason why this institution has been most successful in Hungary and Macedonia.

The establishment of the Hungarian Office of the Parliamentary Commissioners was ordained by the Constitution's Ombudsman Act of 1993. The ombudsmen – two for human rights, one for national and ethnic minorities, and one for data protection and freedom of information – are appointed by parliament for a once-renewable six-year term. In their first four years in office the authorities approved 80% of the ombudsmen's recommendations and the legislature accepted 65% of their proposals for changes in the law.[99] The Parliamentary Commissioner for National and Ethnic Minority Rights, Jenő Kaltenbach, has become a well-known and respected public figure. He has been influential even by international standards, owing to his determined antidiscrimination campaign. Through the media and minority organizations, Kaltenbach's office has made a concerted effort to publicize its existence and activities and make the Roma aware of this opportunity to redress their grievances. According to government officials, the position of the minority ombudsman was created primarily to protect Romani rights, and most of the complaints (by some accounts 98%) that Kaltenbach and his staff have dealt with have been lodged by Gypsies.[100]

Although the ombudsman's office (called the Institution of the Public Attorney) in Macedonia was established only in 1997, Branko Naumoski, his four deputies, and staff have made it an important factor in the country's public life. Their objectives and activities are similar to those of their colleagues elsewhere. Just like its Hungarian counterpart, the ombudsman is entirely independent of the government, is elected by the legislature, and receives his funds from the central budget. Naumoski told me that though his office does not keep information on the percentage of complaints received from Gypsies, he is aware of about a dozen such cases mainly having to do with refusal of social welfare payments and police brutality.[101]

<hr>

[99] Interview with Péter Polt, Deputy General Parliamentary Commissioner for Human Rights (Budapest, 4 August 1999). In 2000 Polt became Hungary's Attorney General.

[100] Interview with Sándor Petróczi of the Secretariat for Minority Policy, Prime Minister's Office (Budapest, 26 July 1996); and Antal Heizer, Chief Governmental Councillor, Prime Minister's Office (Budapest, 28 May 1998).

[101] Interview with Branko Naumoski (Skopje, 29 November 1999). See also *Public Attorney (Ombudsman)* (Skopje: Republic of Macedonia, Government Printing Office, 1998); and *Ombudsman: Annual Report 1998* (Skopje: Republic of Macedonia, Government Printing Office, 1999).

Poland's ombudsman office was established already in 1987. Though Adam Zielinski has not gained the influential stature of his colleagues mentioned above, he reacted strongly against antiminority incidents, such as anti-Roma violence in Mława in 1990 and the dissemination of anti-Semitic leaflets during the presidential campaign of the same year.[102] The recently appointed Romanian "People's Advocate" for human rights, Paul Mitroi, also deals with minority issues and has a well-known Romani expert, Vasile Burtea, working in his office. Thus far the office has had a low profile in part owing to the little publicity it has received. According to some minority experts, many people in Romania believe that the ombudsman's office is essentially free legal service and have flooded it with inheritance cases and the like.[103] In 1996 the Czech government rejected a draft law on ombudsman submitted by a group of MPs. After a long and contentions process, the Chamber of Deputies (legislature) in Prague elected former Minister of Justice, Otakar Motejl, as the Czech Republic's first ombudsman in December 2000. In Bulgaria and Slovakia this institution has not been introduced. The Slovak government decided to appoint an ombudsman overseeing human and national minority rights in 1998, although one is yet to be appointed.[104]

PART III: POLICY AREAS

Notwithstanding some local, regional, and national differences, the fundamental markers of the Gypsies' predicament are comparable in all of Eastern Europe. Consequently, though there are disparities in the way the region's states have approached improving the Roma's conditions, they have had to solve similar if not identical problems. The most important differences are in the individual governments' willingness and ability to confront them.

Constitutional and Legal Issues

In the state-socialist system the Gypsy minorities' legal status was either inadequately determined or ignored altogether. Most of the emerging democracies extended to the Roma legal standing equal to that of other ethnic minorities. Constitutions may describe them as an "ethnic" or "national" minority, but the difference has little practical significance. In some cases Gypsy politicians or activists, like Gheorghe Raducanu in Romania, actually participated in writing paragraphs pertaining to

---

[102] See *Synthesis of the Replies*, 78; and interview with Konstanty Gebert (Warsaw, 16 August 1999).
[103] Interview with Oprescu (Bucharest, 2 November 1999).
[104] Csáky cited in RFE/RL II, 2:241 (16 December 1998); and interview with Baumannová (Bratislava, 6 September 1999).

minorities.[105] Not all basic laws are entirely progressive, however. As Katherine Verdery notes, in the constitutions of states that were formerly parts of federations, often "sovereignty resides in a majority ethno-nation, not in individual citizens."[106] Macedonia's Constitution, for instance, defines the country as a "Slavic state." The Slovenian Consti-tution extends generous rights – including a guaranteed seat in the leg-islature – to the Italian and Hungarian minorities but not to the Gypsies and other ethnic minorities (some of whom are actually larger than the two favored groups).[107] Croatia's basic law omits the Roma from the list of minorities and reserves no parliamentary seat for their representative in contrast to Serbs, Czechs, Slovaks, and others.[108]

In Romania, what terminology to use in reference to the Gypsies became an explosive issue in 1995 when the government decided, without asking them, to start calling them "ţigani" (or Gypsies) ostensi-bly because of the similarity between "Romania" and "Roma." After much international criticism, the government changed its mind and settled on "Rroma." Nonetheless, many Roma, in fact, prefer to be called "Gypsies," which is the terminology a number of international organi-zations favor.[109] A frequently noted constitutional defect is Article 11(4) of the 1991 Bulgarian Constitution, which prohibits the founding of ethnic-based political parties. Still, as we have seen in Chapter 6, both ethnic Turks and the Roma have been able to do just that by leaving out any reference of their ethnic identity from the party statutes.

No legislation received more criticism from a wide spectrum of sources than the Czech Republic's Citizenship Law of 1993. In essence,

---

[105] See interviews with Dan Ionescu, a researcher at the Radio Free Europe Research Insti-tute (Munich, 7 July 1993); and with Gheorghe Raducanu, a member of the Council of National Minorities and a leader of *Partida Romilor* (Bucharest, 14 March 1995). For a recent analysis of the important role constitutional courts have come to play in the region, see Herman Schwartz, *The Struggle for Constitutional Justice in Post-Communist Europe* (Chicago: University of Chicago Press, 2000).

[106] Katherine Verdery, "Nationalism and National Sentiment in Post-Socialist Romania," *Slavic Review*, 52:2 (Summer 1993): 187.

[107] See Vera Klopčič and Janez Stergar, eds., *Ethnic Minorities in Slovenia* (Ljubljana: Institute for Ethnic Studies, 1994).

[108] *Synthesis of the replies*, 13.

[109] See "Romania Changes Official Name for Gypsies," Reuter (Bucharest), 2 May 1995; "Romaprotest in Bucharest," *Frankfurter Allgemeine Zeitung*, 23 May 1995; "Inter-viu acordat de minisitri Teodor Melescanu," *Jurnalul National*, 6 June 1995; interviews with Nicoleta Biţu and Nora Costache (Bucharest, 23 May 1996); Ágnes Osztovits, "Ha az öshazából nem jön támogatás" (interview with György Rostás-Farkas), *Magyar Nemzet*, 1 February 1997; and "Éhséglázadás elött" (interview with Flórián Farkas), *Új Magyarország*, 24 March 1997. The importance of ethnic communities' names is discussed in Harold R. Isaacs, *Idols of the Tribe: Group Identity and Political Change* (Cambridge: Harvard University Press, 1989), 71–93.

the law classified the vast majority of the approximately 200,000 Roma residing in the country – whether born there or not – as Slovaks and set a number of complicated bureaucratic hurdles and criteria before they could acquire Czech citizenship.[110] Applicants had to prove that they had no criminal record for five years, that they possessed registered permanent residence for two years, and that they owed no taxes in Slovakia. The law did not mention the Roma by name, but it clearly targeted them. Defenders of the bill came from some unexpected quarters and included Ludvík Vaculík, a famous writer whose "Two Thousand Words" was the key document of the 1968 Prague Spring.[111] He argued that if not being caught for crimes for five years was too difficult a criterion for the Roma to satisfy, then it is they who depart from the norms of the society into which they want to integrate.[112]

Part of the reason for the law's severity was that in late 1992, when the Czechoslovak federation was about to break up, towns in northern Bohemia experienced (or officials there said they did) a large in-migration of Gypsies followed by a rise in crime and public disorder. In fact, the mayors of several towns like Most, Homutov, and Ústí nad Labem requested a citizenship law that would create the legal basis to the deportation of these people. As usual, numbers are suspect, but the law surely put the status of tens of thousands of Gypsies on a precarious legal footing. In the summer of 1994 the Constitutional Court rejected the appeal by 46 parliamentary deputies to amend the law. In 1996, after a lengthy political battle – led by Jiři Payne, the Chairman of parliament's Foreign Relations Committee, who was subjected to intense pressure from the Council of Europe and the UN High Commissioner for Refugees – the law was amended.[113] The amendment satisfied few, however, because it only reduced the criminal record requirement to three years. Finally, after three more years of criticism and a governmental change, the citizenship law was modified again in

---

[110] See "Roma sollen in die Slowakei zurück," *Süddeutsche Zeitung*, 19 January 1993; Tom Gross, "Gypsies Fall Victim to Czech Racism," *Sunday Telegraph*, 24 October 1993; Krista D. Lyons, "Citizenship in New States: The Case of the Czech Republic," M.A. Thesis, Department of Government, University of Texas at Austin, 1995; interview with Jarka Balážová, editor of the Roma radio program (Prague, 14 August 1996); and Jiřina Siklová and Marta Miklušáková, "Denying Citizenship to the Czech Roma," *East European Constitutional Review*, 7:2 (1998): 61–4.

[111] See Ludvík Vaculík, "Two Thousand Words to Workers, Farmers, Scientists, Artists, and Everyone" (Prague, 27 June 1968) reprinted in Gale Stokes, ed., *From Stalinism to Pluralism: A Documentary History of Eastern Europe Since 1945* (New York: Oxford University Press, 1991), 126–30.

[112] Vaculík, "Umítečist a myslet, pánové?" *Respekt*, no. 44 (1994), 14.

[113] Interviews with Matějka and Stein (both Prague, 14 August 1996).

1999. It is now based on the premise that those who were permanent residents in the country in 1993 have the right of citizenship.[114]

At the urging of international organizations, national minority laws have been enacted in some East European states (e.g., Hungary, Romania) and others have been preparing such legislation (Czech Republic, Poland). Generally speaking, these documents have been progressive, although they do not always meet with the unqualified approval of Gypsy and other minority activists. For instance, Hungary's 1993 minority law has been applauded by the Council of Europe "as a model for all Europe," but it was criticized by Flórián Farkas for not allowing the direct election of minority representatives to parliament.[115] The 1999 Slovak law on minority languages does not please many Roma, who contend that it is impossible to implement given the dearth of state officials with Romani language facility.[116]

Positive and Negative Discrimination

Especially in the early 1990s, East European governments often supported, perpetuated, or ignored anti-Gypsy discrimination in virtually all areas from housing to education. The state-owned media's role in changing societal attitudes has been particularly important because of their inherent potential to influence public opinion. In fact, with the partial exception of Poland, Hungary, and Macedonia, the mainstream media in the region have generally portrayed the Roma in an unflattering light, playing on and thereby magnifying the majority's prejudices. Even in Poland, *Gazeta Wyborcza*, the country's most liberal newspaper, until recently identified only Romani suspects and criminals by ethnicity.[117] Gypsies received the most negative press coverage in the Czech Republic, where some newspapers until the late 1990s featured a *Černa rubrik* (black column) to detail the Roma's misdeeds.[118] Although, in principle, government programs forbade discrimination of all sorts, in reality the authorities seldom did much to discourage it.

By the late 1990s overt anti-Romani discrimination has gradually decreased across the region, but it is still taking place with troubling

---

[114] RFE/RL II, 2:199 (14 October 1998) and 3:133 (12 July 1999); and interviews with Zdeněk Matějka, Secretary General of, and Jan Pecháček, Adviser to the Deputy Minister at the Ministry of Foreign Affairs (Prague, 23 August 1999).

[115] See for instance, OMRI DD II, no. 14, 19 January 1996.

[116] Interview with Maria Koliková, a lawyer for the Minority Rights Group – Slovakia (Bratislava, 7 September 1999).

[117] Interview with Gebert (Warsaw, 16 August 1999).

[118] Interview with Hübschmannová (Prague, 27 August 1999). See also Jiři Homoláč, *A ta černa kronika!* (Brno: Doplnek, 1998), a book that examines how the Czech media manipulated the population's anti-Roma prejudices.

frequency. In the armed forces, for instance, Gypsies are still often assigned to menial tasks for no other reason than their ethnicity.[119] In 1998 Slovak Red Cross officials offered cash for ethnic Slovak and Hungarian flood victims but not to the Gypsies because "they would only drink it away."[120] The Romanian press still routinely depicts Roma as criminals or, in humorous publications like *Catavencu*, as people to be ridiculed.[121] In the classified sections of national newspapers, companies no longer publish job advertisements with "Roma excluded" for fear of lawsuits from Gypsy and human rights organizations. But while perusing advertisements for apartments one still often reads, "no Gypsy on the block"; this is to make the property more attractive to potential buyers.[122] Anti-racist and anti-discrimination bills – including laws banning extremist publications – have been passed in a growing number of East European states by the end of the 1990s. As with other laws designed to help minority populations, the problem lies not so much in the deficiencies of the laws themselves but in the often absent will to consistently enforce them.

Calls for positive discrimination packages for the Roma are heard with increasing frequency across the region. In 1997 Hungarian Minister of Labor Péter Kiss contended that affirmative action was necessary to provide jobs for them.[123] In Romania the Minister of Education, Andrei Marga, had repeatedly expressed his preference for positive discrimination measures to strengthen the Gypsies' performance in schools.[124] The new comprehensive governmental concepts for the Roma (discussed in the next chapter) prominently feature both antidiscrimination measures and positive discrimination (in education, housing, employment, etc.) programs. These are courageous initiatives because positive discrimination policies for an unpopular minority in relatively poor and deprived societies usually elicit a great deal of resistance. To ward off such anticipated opposition in Hungary, for example, the recipients of special assistance in agricultural pilot programs included 80% Roma and 20% other poor peasants.[125]

---

[119] Interviews with senior Defense Ministry officials (Bratislava, 9 September 1999) and with Deputy Defense Minister Velizar Shalamanov (Sofia, 18 November 1999).

[120] Interview with Orgovánová (Bratislava, 7 September 1999).

[121] Interview with television editor Marius Tabacu (Cluj, 25 October 1999); Andor Horváth, Deputy Editor-in-Chief of *Korunk* (Cluj, 26 October 1999); and with Costel Bercus, Coordinator of Romani CRISS (Bucharest, 30 October 1999).

[122] Interview with Florin Moisă, a program coordinator of the Open Society Foundation (Cluj, 25 October 1999).

[123] RFE/RL II, 1:168 (27 November 1997).

[124] See "Romania Plans Added Schooling for Gypsies," *Austin American-Statesman*, 19 April 1998; and interview with Eckstein-Kovács (Bucharest, 2 November 1999).

[125] Interview with Heizer (Budapest, 28 May 1998).

Combatting Extremism

After the fall of communism, nationalist extremist politicians and their followers have managed to carve out a troubling, if mostly marginal, presence in several East European states. They are similar in their hostility to minorities, particularly to the Roma, and have supplied journalists and analysts with a slew of quotable outrageous statements. Jan Slota has been the source of more than his fair share of them. His suggested solution to "the Gypsy problem" has been a "small courtyard and a long whip"; he said he would eat Hungarian goulash soup if it was made of Duray and Bugár (two ethnic Hungarian politicians) rather than pork; he claimed that 70% of the Roma were criminals; and on George Soros he said that "we don't want to cooperate with that Hungarian Jew."[126] In August 2000, Vitazoslav Moric, an MP also of the Slovak National Party (SNS), said that if Slovaks do not place "unadaptable Roma" in "reservations" (in order to reduce the crime rate), "they will place us there 20 years from now."[127] Even more disturbing is the fact that SNS chairwoman Anna Maliková saw no need to apologize for Moric's statement, noting that

the SNS is interested in a thorough solution of the problem of the Romany ethnic group, because it is not the Gypsies, but the rest of Slovakia's population, that is discriminated against.[128]

It is important to note, however, that the Slovak legislature stripped Moric of the immunity from prosecution he enjoys as a member of parliament. He was subsequently charged with inciting racial hatred, though the charge was later dropped on appeal.[129] Ever unrepentant, Moric "fine-tuned" his plans for Gypsy reservations in January 2001, noting that "all necessary conditions for life except money would be made available in them."[130]

Although they may not be quite so colorful, or, indeed, so unabashedly extremist as SNS deputies, there are like-minded politicians especially in the Czech Republic, Hungary, and Romania. A 1997 letter published in

---

[126] "Slovaks v Czechs on the Gypsies," *The Economist*, 7 November 1998, 52; Šedivý and Maroši, "Position of National Minorities," 14; Miroslav Kusý, "Human Rights," in Martin Bútora and Thomas W. Skladony, eds., *Slovakia 1996–1997: A Global Report on the State of Society* (Bratislava: Institute for Public Affairs, 1998), 42; interview with Vašečka, (Bratislava, 15 August 1999).

[127] RFE/RL II, 4:150 (7 August 2000).

[128] RFE/RL II, 4:151 (8 August 2000).

[129] Martina Pisárová, "Moric Turned Over for Prosecution;" and Tom Nicholson, "MP Charged with Spreading Hate," in *The Slovak Spectator*, 2–8 October 2000 and 9–15. October 2000, respectively.

[130] RFE/RL II, 5:4 (8 January 2001).

Politica, the weekly of the extreme nationalist Greater Romania Party, identified Romania's main enemy as "international Jewry headed by the freemason Bill Clinton, whose foreign minister is the Jewess Iana [sic] Miriam Korbel, known under the pseudonym of Madeleine Albright."[131] Extremists in Hungary, Slovakia, and Romania have commemorated their countries' wartime fascist leaders (Ferenc Szálasi, Jozef Tišo, and Ion Antonescu, respectively) and, in some cases, called for their rehabilitation.[132] Jean-Marie Le Pen, president of France's far-right National Front, has been a favorite guest of honor of nationalist gatherings from Budapest to Prague. In Prague Le Pen told journalists that he considered the Czech Republican Party "an equal partner"; his host, Miroslav Sladek, replied that he wanted to be "Le Pen's good apprentice."[133] István Csurka, the leader of the ominously named Hungarian Justice and Health Party (HJHP), suggested that Roma were inferior to Hungarians and said that Hungary had declined because of "genetic causes."[134]

As disturbing as these statements are, they are by no means representative of the mainstream of East European politics. Though extremist parties may garner enough votes to enter parliament, they may not stay there for long. For instance, Sladek's Republicans got about 8% of the vote in 1996; but two years later, having discredited themselves with their openly racist and extremist behavior, they managed to attract less than 3% (i.e., short of the 5% threshold needed for entering parliament). A different case is that of Csurka's party, which after gaining 1.59% of the vote in 1994 (the threshold here, too, is 5%) did far better in 1998, garnering 5.51%.[135] Since entering the Budapest legislature, however, Csurka and his parliamentary group have acted with relative restraint and have become a more or less constructive part of it.

In the last several years, East European states have been more prepared to fight extremism than they were in the early 1990s. The Czech government, for instance, recently approved a plan to clamp down on and possibly outlaw organizations that act against human rights and disseminate propaganda against Jews, Roma, homosexuals, and foreigners.[136] Anti-racism laws are being more frequently and consistently applied against skinheads and others across the region than even a few

---

[131] RFE/RL II, 1:43 (2 June 1997).
[132] See OMRI DD II, no. 56 (19 March 1996); OMRI DD II, no. 4 (7 January 1997) no. 61 (27 March 1997); and RFE/RL II, 5:14 (22 January 2001).
[133] RFE/RL II, 3:202, 15 October 1999.
[134] Eva Kekes, "Gypsy Leader Urges Roma to Vote Against Extreme Right," AP (Budapest), 19 May 1998.
[135] See Zoltan Barany, "Mass–Elite Relations and the Resurgence of Nationalism in Eastern Europe," *European Security*, 3:1 (Spring 1994): 173–6.
[136] RFE/RL II, 3:146 (29 July 1999).

years ago. Legal action has been taken against leading extremist politicians – such as Miroslav Sladek and Corneliu Vadim Tudor of the Greater Romania Party – for making racist statements. In August 2000 the Slovak parliament held a minute of silence in memory of a Gypsy woman killed in her home a few days earlier.

Right- and left-wing extremists are generally united in their opposition to European integration, which is one of the reasons for their modest electoral support. Whatever influence extremists now enjoy is likely to further diminish as democracy in Eastern Europe continues to develop and as governments and legislatures become more committed to enacting, and especially enforcing, antidiscrimination laws.[137]

Law Enforcement and the Judicial System

The attitude of state authorities toward anti-Gypsy attacks has changed substantially during the 1990s. Until the mid-1990s, policemen seldom helped the Roma, often looked the other way, or even supported perpetrators as Gypsies were beaten up or worse. While arresting, interrogating, and incarcerating Gypsies, police routinely used excessive force (in a few cases Roma inexplicably died in police custody) and abused their rights with impunity. Also, the usually half-hearted actions that police took to suppress interethnic violence produced disproportionately more arrested and prosecuted Roma than members of the opposing ethnic group. In some cases, like the 1993 incident in Hadareni, Romania, the knee-jerk reaction of the government was to actually blame the Gypsies for the violence.[138] The authorities ordinarily displayed little concern as Roma were assaulted and, in some cases, killed.

In the courts, Gypsies have been usually subjected to yet more discriminatory treatment. Even in countries with relatively tolerant minority policies, the Roma tend to receive incompetent representation and harsher sentences for the same crime than others. In the Czech Republic and Slovakia, judges have often ruled that attacks against the Gypsies cannot possibly be motivated by racism – and thus, applying more severe antiracism sentencing guidelines is inappropriate – since Roma and their tormentors are members of the same (Indo-European) race.[139]

---

[137] On the prospects of nationalism in postcommunist lands, see Francis Fukuyama, *The End of History and the Last Man* (New York: Free Press, 1993), 266–75.

[138] "To the Gypsies, Death Is a Neighbor and So Is This Implacable Hatred," *New York Times*, 27 October 1993; and "Statement of the Romanian Government Regarding the Events in the Village of Hadareni-Chetani, County of Mures, September 20–21, 1993," (from the Embassy of Romania in Washington, DC, 24 September 1993).

[139] See, for instance, OMRI DD II, no. 242 (14 December 1995); OMRI DD II, no. 14 (21 January 1997); Vašečka, "The Roma," 406; and interview with Maria Koliková (Bratislava, 7 September 1999).

According to Klára Veselá-Samková, an activist and lawyer who has represented hundreds of Roma in the Czech Republic, the courts remain "totally biased" against Roma. She contends that in smaller towns, especially, the Gypsies have no chance of winning a lawsuit against a Czech.[140]

Since the early 1990s things have changed in every state but, to be sure, not to the same extent. It is fair to say that the Roma are still extensively discriminated against by police and the courts. Even in the relatively progressive states like Macedonia, many Roma are still beaten up and humiliated by local police because the police know Roma are unlikely complain.[141] And in Hungary, in June 1999 a policeman assaulted a Gypsy college student in Budapest for apparently no reason other than his ethnicity.[142] Still, it is instructive to view state reaction to anti-Roma discrimination from an evolutionary perspective lest one should think that "nothing has happened," as some Gypsy and human rights activists are wont to say. Just the fact that one reads about incidents of police abusing their power is an improvement compared to the early 1990s. But much more has changed. Romania, for instance, received much deserved criticism in the early 1990s for ignoring anti-Roma violence; but since the 1994 attack on Gypsies in the village of Racsa, the government's response has noticeably improved and has included not only the arrest and prosecution of perpetrators but also the condemnation of such incidents.[143]

Across the region, policemen have actually been dismissed from the force or prosecuted for their actions against the Roma and others. Community policing and the training and hiring of Gypsy policemen and a number of other promising initiatives are cropping up from the Czech Republic to Bulgaria.[144] Anti-racism laws are being applied more often and with more consistency, and prosecutors seem to seek and get tougher sentences.[145] In Hungary, where Romani leaders have publicly recognized

---

[140] Interview with Veselá-Samková (Prague, 24 August 1999).

[141] Interview Emilija Simoska and Mirjana Najcevska of the Center for Ethnic Relations (Skopje, 23 November 1999).

[142] "Roma főiskolást bántalmaztak a Népligetben a járőrök," *Magyar Hírlap*, 11 June 1999.

[143] *Countering Anti-Roma Violence in Eastern Europe: The Snagov Conference and Related Efforts* (Princeton: PER, 1994), 17; and interview with Vasile and Costache (Bucharest, 14 March 1995).

[144] See, for instance, *CPRSI Newsletter* (OSCE-Warsaw), 2:2 (1996): 2; "Ministry to Take on Two Roma to Recruit Romani Policemen," CTK (Prague), 6 March 1998; RFE/RL II, 2:226 (23 November 1998); and interviews with Holomek and Adam (Brno, 1–2 September 1999).

[145] See, for instance, OMRI DD II, no. 38 (22 February 1996); "Judge to Deliver Verdict on Skinhead Murder Case," CTK (Prague), 20 March 1998; "Skinhead Sentenced to 14.5 Years in Prison for Racial Murder," CTK (Prague), 23 March 1998; RFE/RL II, 2:189 (30 September 1998), 2:195 (8 October 1998), and 3:15 (22 January 1999).

the major improvements in the attitudes of the police and the judiciary, judges are even being sent on courses to make them more aware of and sensitive to racially motivated crimes.[146] Undoubtedly, a lot remains to be done, but it is important to recognize the serious efforts some governments of the region have made in this area during the past several years.

I want to mention the relative absence of interethnic violence and the determination of state authorities not to allow such incidents in one East European state: Poland. The only mob attack on the Roma in the country occurred in the city of Mława in 1991. The reason why it is the only one may very well be the immediate and decisive action of the Polish authorities. After the event, the government promptly dispatched a fact-finding commission to Mława to investigate the case and compile a report. The media extensively discussed what happened and depicted it as an outrageous act of intolerance. Within a year there was a trial, and the court sentenced 20 attackers to prison terms (ranging between 6 months to 2 years).[147] Because of the attack, Mława became synonymous with backwardness in Poland, an image that so disturbed local officials that they organized a conference for sociologists and invited journalists to change public opinion about the city. The quick and decisive reaction of the authorities, the civic pride of local leaders, and the responsible reporting of the media are all the more impressive because they occurred in 1991, before international pressures made an impact on government policies.

Education, Employment, and Social Welfare

Most of the Roma's contemporary problems are indubitably rooted in poor education and the resultant limitations on the job market. Governments only began to design and implement comprehensive and long-term programs in the late 1990s, and I will discuss these extensively in the next chapter. Until the second half of the 1990s the criticisms of international organizations often fell on deaf ears or were not taken seriously by East European governments. Not all of them were willing to recognize the magnitude of the Roma's difficulties, let alone to devote significant resources to combatting them. Again, this does not mean that they did nothing.

In the early 1990s authorities in a number of countries initiated experimental programs and financially supported many others. A Hungarian

---

[146] See "Nasty, Ubiquitous, and Unloved," *The Economist*, 20 March 1999, 57; and Flórián Farkas cited in "Csökkent a rendőri diszkrimináció," *Magyar Nemzet*, 21 April 2000.

[147] Interviews with Andrzej Mirga, member of the Council of Europe's Expert Group on the Roma (Kraków, 29 July 1996); and Gebert (Warsaw, 16 August 1999).

policy introduced in 1990–1 earmarked supplemental funds on a per-student basis for schools that adopted a special curriculum for minorities.[148] In Poland, Father Stanisław Opocki started two schools in 1991 for Gypsy dropouts financed by the Ministry of Culture.[149] In 1993 so-called "zero-grade" classes were introduced for Romani children in the Czech Republic and Slovakia where they could experience a structured environment, improve their knowledge of the majority language, and be tutored in "health, hygiene, and social skills" in order to ease their transition into first grade.[150] The Slovenian government promulgated a similar but two-year preschool program complemented by positive discrimination measures in 1995.[151] In the Czech Republic and Hungary, schools began to employ a growing number of Romani assistants – familiar with Gypsy culture and language – to help classroom work. An increasing number of school books – either in Romani or in the majority language for or about the Gypsies – were published in Bulgaria, Hungary, Macedonia, Romania, and Slovakia as the decade wore on.

Hungary was first to establish an elite Romani high school named after Mahatma Gandhi in Pécs as well as a couple of specialized vocational schools like Kalyi Jag in Budapest. These examples have been followed by the introduction of the High School for Arts, oriented toward Romani culture, in Košice, Slovakia, in 1995 and the Romani Secondary School for Social Work in Kolín, the Czech Republic, in 1998. Other initiatives included the creation of thousands of fellowships (especially in Hungary) to support Gypsy high school and college students. In the early 1990s a number of postsecondary programs began across the region with the objective of teaching Romani language and culture to teachers and training Gypsies to teach Romani children. The most notable among them is the five-year Romistics program at Prague's Charles University (founded and directed by Professor Milena Hübschmannová) that began in 1991. Other programs for and about the Roma in higher education started at teachers' colleges in Ňitra (Slovakia), Zsámbék, and Eger (Hungary); and many other universities, like the University of Bucharest, began to offer Romani language instruction.

At the Sts. Cyril and Methodius University in Skopje, 10% of the seats were set aside for minority students as early as 1993, although they were

---

[148] Béla Osztojkán, *Megkérdezem Önt is* (Budapest: Phralipe, 1994), 82–3.
[149] Adam Bartosz, "Social and Political Status of the Roma in Poland," *Roma*, no. 40 (January 1994): 20.
[150] Fisher, "Romanies in Slovakia," 58–9; interview with Orgovánová (Prešov, 13 June 1994); and Vladimír Šedivý and Viktor Maroši, *Position of National Minorities and Ethnic Groups in the Slovak Republic* (Bratislava: Minority Rights Group, 1996), 22.
[151] See *Program ukrepov za pomož Romom v Republiki Sloveniji* (Ljubljana: Government of Slovenia, 1995).

seldom filled owing to the dearth of qualified applicants. In 1996, Minister of Education Emilija Simoska changed the percentage of minority seats at the university according to their proportion in the population (based on the census). Partly as a result of these measures, the number of Romani university students who took advantage of this program increased from 10 in 1994–5 to 41 in 1998–9.[152] The School of Social Work at the University of Bucharest has reserved for and filled 10–15 places with Romani students for nearly a decade.[153]

The introduction of new educational programs have been delayed not only due to the absence of political commitment, but also because of conceptual ambiguity about how to approach the problem, modest financial resources, lacking coordination between ministries and school districts, and conflicting messages from the Romani community regarding education in Romani language. Some activists favor teaching Romani as a second language, others prefer Romani as the language of instruction, still others consider no education in Romani at all as the most desirable alternative. Among those who do endorse the teaching of Romani, the question of which dialect to use has been a divisive issue. An even more important debate has centered on the question of whether segregated or integrated schooling is better for Gypsy children.[154] Some Romani leaders insist that separate schools like Kalyi Jag and the Gandhi High School offer the best alternative since they can freely adapt their methodologies to Gypsy children's culture, background, and social skills. Others contend, however, that it is dangerous to separate Romani children from their peers in the majority population because they need to learn about each other's cultures and how to interact with one another as they will need these skills later in life.

Aside from a few exceptions, comprehensive employment programs for the Roma did not appear in the region until the late 1990s. In this respect, too, Hungarian governments have been the quickest to initiate new programs and implement some of them. But in Hungary, similarly to the other states, ambitious plans in the first half of the 1990s often remained just that for the usual reasons: lacking political commitment, money, and coordination between national and local authorities. Another often neglected problem that limited most states' elbow room was the crisis of agriculture and construction industry in the early 1990s

---

[152] *Facts About the National Minorities in the Republic of Macedonia* (Skopje: Ministry of Foreign Affairs, 1997), 20; and *The Situation of the Roma in the Republic of Macedonia* (Skopje: Ministry of Foreign Affairs, 1999), 5.

[153] Interview with Elena Zamfir, the director of the program (Bucharest, 13 March 1995, and 3 November 1999).

[154] See, for instance, Simon Evans, "Separate but Superior?" in Hungary Report (distributed through e-mail), 2:5 (1996).

in several states that in the past had employed a disproportionately large number of Roma.

Beginning with the early 1990s, Hungary introduced numerous extensive public works projects (road building, construction, etc.) that, according to government officials, affected a large number of Roma. The government made a serious although not always successful effort to coordinate its labor policy for the Gypsies between individual ministries.[155] The Ministry of Labor and local authorities in cooperation with Romani NGOs also began programs whose objective was the resuscitation of traditional skills and occupations among the Gypsies. Although Hungarian authorities financed many retraining programs to help newly unemployed workers, many Roma were unable to participate in these courses because they had no skills on which new training could build.[156] In Hungary as well as in the Czech Republic and Romania regional and local employment centers were created for the Gypsies although they failed to make a serious dent in the number of unemployed Roma.[157] In several states, especially in Hungary, regional development programs – designed for relatively poor counties where many Roma live – allocated supplementary funding for creating employment for the Gypsies. Local governments in rural areas in Bulgaria, Hungary, and Romania leased or granted the use of agricultural land for Gypsies, and some programs provided them with free seed. In 1993 the Bulgarian Ministry of Labor and Social Policy – in response to sustained pressure from President Zhelev's office – started a program of temporary employment for Roma which has provided limited earning opportunities to a few thousand Gypsies.

Social welfare ministries in Eastern Europe faced major challenges in the early 1990s stemming from the fact that they had to create anew a comprehensive social safety net for those left behind by the economic transition in a period of severe fiscal constraints. A sign displayed on the door of a Ministry of Social Welfare official in Prague only half-jokingly identified it as the "Department of Unsolvable Problems."[158] In Bulgaria, Macedonia, and Romania, the state has often been unable to make regular social welfare payments. Although some East European states

---

[155] See the parliamentary speech of Minister of Labor Péter Kiss (Budapest, 25 November 1997), mimeo, 7 pp.; and Gábor Havas, Gábor Kertesi, and István Kemény, "The Statistics of Deprivation: The Roma in Hungary," *The Hungarian Quarterly*, 36:138 (Summer 1995): 79.

[156] János Wolfart, President of the Office for National and Ethnic Minorities, underscored this point in our interview (Budapest, 9 June 1994). See also János Zolnay, "A közmunka nem elfogadható megoldás," *Amaro Drom*, March 1996, 15.

[157] Interview with Vasile Burtea, a Gypsy analyst at the Ministry of Labor (Bucharest, 15 March 1995).

[158] Tamayo, "Gypsies Among Hardest Hit."

have shifted the responsibility for the implementation of social policy to local authorities, the latter have been ill-equipped to alleviate the Roma's difficulties given their modest budgets. The inadequacy of housing initiatives for the poor may also be mainly attributed to financial limitations. In Slovakia the short-lived government of Jan Čarnogursky prepared a housing program for the Roma in 1992 which was vetoed by his successor, Vladimír Mečiar. Hungary's housing program for the Roma resulted in only 100 new houses in 1994–8.[159] In some cases – especially in Bulgaria and Romania – the best that one could say about social policy for the Roma in the early 1990s is that it succeeded in fending off starvation. Eevertheless, it should be emphasized that the Roma have been the main consumers of all kinds of social assistance in the region where poverty among non-Roma has also been widespread.

State Financial Support for the Roma

Even when one takes into account the East European states' limited resources and other priorities, most governments of the region should have spent more money on alleviating the Roma's predicament. From the beginning of the 1990s, Hungarian governments have allocated far more money for the Roma than any other in the region.[160] In the annual budget, substantial sums were earmarked for Romani programs (broken down to individual ministries) as early 1992. Public foundations for the Roma and other minorities to finance programs, scholarships, and cultural organizations were established already during the last months of Miklós Németh's socialist government in 1990.[161] The national budget has designated monies to support hundreds of Romani organizations, publications, programs, and activities beginning with 1991. Year after year, governments in Budapest devoted an increasing proportion of their budgets to the Roma. In 1990, for instance, 40 active programs – some of them funded by NGOs – provided assistance to the Roma. In 1996–7, however, more than 500 programs were started or continued. By 1997 fully one-tenth of the Roma living in rural areas received some form of agriculture-related aid.[162]

Although Hungary has been widely acknowledged by international organizations for its leadership in this area, other countries have also

---

[159] Interview with Heizer (Budapest, 28 May 1998).
[160] See Katalin Ljubka, "Több mint 200 cigány szervezet vár anyagi támogatást," *Pesti Hírlap*, 16 February 1994; and Nicolae Gheorghe interviewed in Lajos Puporka, "A roma képviselet máshol is gond," *Magyar Hírlap*, 18 April 1998.
[161] Tabajdi, *Az önazonosság labirintusa*, 644.
[162] Gábor Czene, "A vidéki romák tizede kap mezőgazdasági támogatást," *Népszabadság*, 2 April 1998.

devoted growing, if still insufficient, funds to the Roma. The one important exception in this regard was Slovakia under the Mečiar government where budgetary allocations for the Roma (and other minorities) were subjected to major annual reductions from 1993 to 1997.[163] Romania, even during Iliescu's first tenure, financed many Gypsy organizations and programs although, to be sure, political preferences – as in other states of the region – often influenced the amount allocated to specific groups or causes. The institutional sources of money may have been different – that is, the ministries of culture, education, labor, social affairs, interior, or governmental organizations dealing specifically with the Gypsies – but the vast majority of the funds for Romani newspapers, groups, radio and television programs, and cultural events in all of the region with the exception of Macedonia came from the state.

Given the differences between the economic performance of states in East-Central Europe versus the Balkans, it is not surprising that the amounts of money for supporting the Roma have been more modest in Romania, Bulgaria, and Macedonia. In all of Eastern Europe, for instance, Romania spent the lowest proportion of its GDP on education, health, and social assistance in the early 1990s, less than Bulgaria and Albania and far less than any East-Central European state.[164]

CONCLUSION

East European governments have received mostly criticism from Romani leaders and activists for doing nothing or not doing enough to alleviate the Gypsies' predicament. No wonder that one encounters a sense of institutional fatigue among bureaucrats and politicians who work on Romani-related issues. As I tried to show in this chapter, the region's states could have done much more, but their very real efforts on the Gypsies' behalf ought not be belittled. They have established new institutional structures to deal with minority affairs, designed and introduced a number of programs and policies, and generally devoted increasing attention to the Roma's predicament. The status and rights of the Gypsies and other ethnic minorities have become more or less strongly safeguarded by new laws in all of the region even if in practice these rights are not always protected effectively. These are major accomplishments.

---

[163] See *Second Slovakia Roundtable* (Princeton: PER, 1996), 30; *Platná právna úprava v oblasti práva menšin v Slovenskej republike* (Bratislava: Minority Rights Group – Slovakia, 1999), 8–10; interview with Maria Koliková, lawyer for Minority Rights Group – Slovakia (Bratislava, 7 September 1999); and Sharon Otterman, "2001 Census: Will Roma Stand Up to Be Counted?" *Slovak Spectator*, 27 September–3 October 1999.

[164] Cătălin Zamfir, Marius Augustin Pop, and Elena Zamfir, *Romania '89–'93: Dynamics of Welfare and Social Protection* (Bucharest: UNICEF-Romania, 1994), 81–3.

All enforcable rights have "opportunity costs" and require governmental action and expenditure.[165]

At the same time, it is important to note the profound differences in the record of East European governments in this regard. As it turns out, the reputation of individual states as leaders or laggards of the post-communist democratization and marketization process does not always correspond to their behavior vis-à-vis minorities. The most conspicuous example is the Czech Republic, one of the region's most advanced states, where policies toward the Roma have been marked by inattention and intolerance. The blame for this should be laid at the doorstep of Prime Minister Václav Klaus and his government that demonstrated little willingness to understand or appreciate the Gypsies' complex problems. On the other hand, a lesser developed state like Macedonia has consistently maintained an enlightened and progressive view of the Roma even if it lacked the financial resources to substantively improve their material well-being. The Czech and the Macedonian cases underscore the importance of both political leadership and the level of social tolerance.

One should also emphasize the enormous differences in state behavior toward the Roma between the early and the late 1990s. In the early 1990s East European states – with the exception of Hungary and Macedonia – paid little attention to the Roma. There are some special reasons why these two countries are unusual; their relatively foresightful political leadership is just one of these. The other, more important one is the broader minority issue. Hungary from the late 1960s on had conducted progressive ethnic minority policies – especially with regard to the relatively small Slovak and Romanian minorities – at least in part to be able to justify its growing concern about Hungarian minorities in Slovakia, Romania, and other neighboring countries. Independent Macedonia had also benefited from the enlightened minority policies of federal Yugoslavia (until the mid-1980s). And, as I mentioned above, treating the Roma "right" was also important in Skopje because policies toward the far larger and better organized ethnic Albanians have been less successful.

In spite of all the difficulties associated with helping the Roma, by the late 1990s there was a marked improvement in state policy almost everywhere in the region. There is much less discrimination on the national and regional levels, although in local settings the Gypsies are still often disadvantaged. I firmly believe that the most important reason why a number of East European governments – especially those of the Czech Republic, Romania, and Slovakia – have put the Roma's predicament as a priority on their agendas after 1997–8 is the well-nigh relentless

---

[165] See Stephen Holmes and Cass Sunstein, *The Cost of Rights* (New York: Norton, 1998).

pressure of international organizations, especially the European Union and its related agencies. Since 1998 Hungary, too, has stepped up its efforts to implement long-term and conceptually sound programs for the Roma. Although the government in Sofia has also been more active in this regard than in years past, the sense I got during my last visit there in late 1999 and from subsequent correspondence with government officials and independent experts is that in Bulgaria there is more smoke than fire. In Poland, quite simply there is not all that much that remains to be done, a notion that has been underscored by the consistently glowing reports that Warsaw receives for its minority policies from international organizations. The Macedonian government has had no shortage of goodwill toward the Roma; what it continues to lack are financial resources that would enable it to implement its progressive policies.

Finally, it should be noted that as important as the creation of new institutional structures and the implementation of a new policies and programs are, they have not brought a significant improvement in the Roma's conditions in the 1990s. The aim of the comprehensive programs most East European states designed and introduced in the late 1990s is precisely that: to reverse the trend of the Roma's deepening marginality.

9

Romani Marginality Revisited

As I explained in the previous chapter, East European governments did not ignore the Roma's predicament in the early 1990s, but they could have undoubtedly done much more. By the end of the decade the criticisms of international organizations and NGOs, the sharpening demands of Gypsy elites and their communities, and changing political dynamics in several East European states (Bulgaria, Czech Republic, Romania, and Slovakia) where more liberal governments came to power prepared the ground for comprehensive medium- and long-term programs for Romani integration. Part I of this chapter will critically examine them. The implementation of these programs, however, has been seldom rapid, complete, or intensive. There are many indications that East European governments and societies have yet to understand the magnitude of the Roma's predicament and the importance of substituting committed and quick action to nice words and political maneuvers. Part II will argue that for a number of pressing reasons there is no time to waste. Moreover, it is in the interest not only of the Roma, but also of these states and societies, to put these programs (and, if necessary, their augmented and/or improved versions) into practice as quickly as possible.

Finally, in Part III I present some recommendations for a comprehensive long-term program that might serve as a blueprint for East European governments. To be sure, these suggestions might be viewed as an optimistic wish list, an idealistic cluster of measures and recommendations. But I firmly believe the need for laying down ideal scenarios to compare actual policies and actions with.

PART I: GOVERNMENT PROGRAMS FOR THE ROMA AT THE MILLENIUM

In this section I examine the comprehensive programs East European governments have designed or are in the process of elaborating for the Roma. All of them target the general goal of the Gypsies' integration into mainstream societies, but they differ in their sophistication, detail, and planning stage. I will discuss them in a decreasing order of their promise. Given that some of these documents tend to be very detailed and quite similar, I shall limit the analysis to pointing out general trends and particularly interesting features. To date, the Macedonian and Polish governments have not elaborated comprehensive programs for the Gypsies for the reasons I mentioned earlier: In Poland there are very few Roma, and their situation does not constitute a serious problem; in Macedonia, owing to the large proportion of ethnic minorities, policies in nearly all areas are at least partially concerned with minorities and no need has been voiced to formulate a plan specifically for the Roma.

Hungary's 1999 Governmental Resolution and the Roma Self-Government

Before examining the Hungarian government's resolution 1047/1999, which serves as the basis of its medium-term policy package for the Roma, the minority self-government system that has operated in the country since 1994 needs to be discussed. The legal basis for the establishment of minority self-governments was created by the 1993 Law on the Rights of National and Ethnic Minorities. This law, the only one of its kind in Europe, made it possible for every one of the country's ethnic minorities to organize self-governments both on the local and on the national levels.[1] Although 11 of Hungary's 13 ethnic minorities have succeeded in forming their national self-governments (NSGs), the Roma created nearly two-thirds of the local bodies (their number in 1999 was 763). The self-governments, whose election is governed by a complicated process, receive funds from the central budget and are responsible for the design and implementation of programs for members of their ethnic community.

The local minority self-government (LMSG) system has been an overwhelmingly positive experience for the Hungarian Roma and other minorities – and has attracted a lot of positive attention by other East European governments, like that of the Czech Republic, and much praise by international organizations – but it has been imperfect to say the least. Its critics correctly point out that the legal status and responsibilities of elected Romani representatives have not been unambiguously regulated.[2]

---

[1] Erzsi Sándor, "Cigányút," *168 óra*, 18 April 1995.

[2] See, for instance, Timothy William Waters and Rachel Guglielmo, " 'Two Souls to Struggle With . . .' The Failing Implementation of Hungary's New Minorities Law and Discrimination Against the Gypsies," in John S. Micgiel, ed., *State and Nation Building in East Central Europe* (New York: Institute on East Central Europe, Columbia University, 1996), 177–97; István T. Kerékgyártó, "Kisebbségi önkormányzatiság és a kulturális

LMSG elections themselves have frequently been inadequately prepared, and several electoral rules (currently, for instance, all citizens are allowed to vote for minority representatives) need to be changed.[3] *Lungo Drom,* the Gypsy organization that all three postcommunist Hungarian governments have favored, has been the best organized Romani NGO in the country. Still, the fact that it has dominated NSG elections (it received the majority of votes and won all 53 mandates both in 1995 and in 1999) has been in large part due to the winner-take-all type electoral rules. As a result, the Roma's NSG has not reflected the diversity of Gypsy organizations and of Romani society at large.

The funding of LMSGs is not guaranteed by law, and many of them have been chronically short of funds. At the same time, in many cases both Romani LMSGs and the NSG have had trouble keeping track of their finances, and charges of fiscal mismanagement and theft have not been uncommon.[4] One source of this problem has been the state's insufficient monitoring and supervision of LMSGs and their financial affairs, which means that they are rarely held accountable. An even more important general weakness has been the lacking codification of the relationship between the state's local authorities and Romani LMSGs. Local administrators are often hostile to and prejudiced against the Gypsies and expect representatives of the Romani LMSGs in their bailiwicks to provide services (such as garbage removal and welfare payments) that are clearly their own responsibilities. As a high-ranking government official told me in 1998, Romani LMSGs had worked well only in areas where the mayor and local authorities had been positively predisposed toward them.[5] Moreover, there have also been widely publicized tensions among individual Romani LMSG officials on the one hand, and between LMSGs and Gypsy communities on the other.[6]

---

autonómia," in *Tanulmányok a cigányság társadalmi helyzetének javítását célzó hosszú távú stratégia alapkérdéseiről* (Budapest: NEKH, 1999), 144–9; and Kai Schafft and Tibor Farkas, "Észrevételek a cigány kisebbségi önkormányzatok működéséről," *A falu,* 14 (Spring 1999): 77–82.

[3] See, for instance, Károly Lencsés, "A roma szervezetek tiltakoznak az Országos Választási Bizottságnál," *Magyar Hírlap,* 5 August 1998.

[4] See, for instance, "Romavád a putnoki rendőrök ellen," *Új Magyarország,* 15 October 1996; Ildikó Emese Nagy, "Kilakoltatják a fehérvári romákat," *Magyar Hírlap,* 25 November 1997; Ernő Kadét and Ernő Klecska, "Lelassult a romák szociális lakásprogramja," *Magyar Hírlap,* 14 April 1998; and " 'Eltűnt' fővárosi roma vezető," *Népszabadság,* 17 July 1998.

[5] Interview with Antal Heizer, Chief Advisor at the Prime Minister's Office (Budapest, 28 May 1998).

[6] See, for instance, Levente Fazekas-Ruck, "Romavoksok magyarokra?" *Magyar Nemzet,* 19 November 1994; "Földművelő romák?" *Új Magyarország,* 9 February 1995; and "Széthúzás a hevesi romák között," *Heves megyei Hírlap,* 10 March 1997.

Despite these serious problems, on balance the minority self-government system has been a success. It created a legal framework for the representation of minority interests. There are actually many instances of active cooperation between LMSGs and local authorities. Gypsy LMSGs have developed and initiated a wide variety of programs, have created thousands of jobs, and have invested a growing proportion of their budgets in worthwhile projects (e.g., housing, education, and job training). The minority self-government system has provided the opportunity for thousands of ordinary Roma to participate in public life and strengthen their people's political representation. The basis of most Romani LMSGs has been Romani civil organizations and NGOs and the fact that they could play an actual role in trying to solve their communities' problems has energized Gypsy mobilization.[7] The self-government system for the Roma might work well in a state like the Czech Republic, where the Gypsies constitute the only large and deeply marginalized ethnic minority. It would probably face serious political opposition in Romania and Slovakia, both with large Hungarian minorities, where concepts such as "self-administration" and "autonomy" would be interpreted as a step toward secession rather than pluralism.[8] The Hungarian government's recently professed commitment to improve the minority self-government system's financing and legal status and to firmly implement the 1993 minority law on all levels holds out the promise of more effective Romani representation. Just as importantly, it also bodes well for the construction of a more pluralistic and democratic society.[9]

The Orbán government's 1999 Resolution, which builds on and supersedes the 1995 and 1997 decrees of its predecessor, is the result of careful preparation that involved governmental and Gypsy leaders as well as many independent experts. The governmental body responsible for the implementation of the program is the Inter-Ministerial Committee for Gypsy Affairs (IMCGA). Its members must report to the IMCGA annually regarding the resources from which the following year's tasks would be financed and to the government about the implementation of the previous year's objectives and the amount of money needed for the next year's undertakings. The resolution charges the IMCGA with the formulation of a long-term strategy for the Roma with the participation of the Gypsy National Self-Government.

---

[7] Interview with Edit Rauh, Head of the Gypsy Department of the Office for National and Ethnic Minorities (Budapest, 9 December 1999).
[8] Kai A. Schafft and David L. Brown. "Social Capital and Grassroots Development: The Case of Roma Self-Governance in Hungary," *Social Problems*, 47:2 (2000): 215.
[9] For a fine summation of the LMSG system, see ibid., 214–16.

The six chapters of the Resolution's supplement outline the specific objectives of the medium-term package in substantive areas: education; culture; employment and regional development; social, health, and housing; antidiscrimination; and media and communications.[10] The state officials responsible for the individual programs (nearly all of them are ministers or the head of the Office for National and Ethnic Minorities) and their deadlines are identified for every portion of each chapter. The prescriptions of the resolution are very specific. The chapter on education, for instance, deals with problems of regular kindergarten and primary school attendance, calls for the increase of dormitory places for Romani children of high school age, and decrees the preparation of conditions for the creation of secondary level educational centers in Budapest and northeast Hungary. It supports the obtaining of qualifications and employment of those Roma youngsters and young adults who dropped out of the educational system and promotes the secondary and tertiary studies of socially disadvantaged young Gypsies. To ensure the success of these initiatives, the Resolution asks universities and public foundations concerned with minorities to administer a growing number of scholarships for Romani students. The Resolution also identifies as priorities the development of educational institutions maintained by self-governments and support for education in Romani language and culture which could accelerate the training of teachers and scholars in this field.

The chapter on culture supports specialized institutions serving the preservation of Romani culture, the availability of educational and cultural services, books, and schoolbooks for the Roma in their mother tongue in accordance with real demand, and state assistance to specialists who work in community centers. In the fields of employment and regional development the Resolution encourages cooperation between Gypsy self-governments and county labor centers as well as more intensive interaction between counties and regions. It also requires IMCGA members to submit reports on the evaluation of proposed programs that promote solutions for the Roma's employment difficulties, primarily for those who are permanently unemployed. This chapter also mandates the introduction of positive discrimination measures for the socially disadvantaged through additional support, places special emphasis on helping the employment chances and developing the entrepreneurial skills of Roma, and orders the continuation of public works projects in concert with regional development programs. The document recommends many other measures, including the enlargement of employment counseling services, support for programs administered by Regional Labor Force

---

[10] See "A Kormány 1047/1999. (V.5.) Korm. határozata," *Magyar Közlöny*, no. 39 (1999): 2727–34.

Development and Training Centers, the promotion of programs that offer agricultural land free to the Roma for cultivation, and the setting up of separate funds for the development of regions where the proportion of socially disadvantaged people is particularly high.

The Resolution on social, public health, and housing programs focuses on preventive healthcare, averting the reemergence of slums and slum-like neighborhoods, and evaluating the housing programs of the Gypsy National Self-Government and the Welfare Service Foundation. It also calls for the formulation of programs that find solutions to the Roma's housing problems. The antidiscrimination section requires rigorous enforcement of existing antidiscrimination legislation and the preparation of additional laws. Finally, the chapter on communication calls for better cooperation between NGOs and public foundations that support Romani media in order to facilitate the development of a realistic image of the Gypsies in society. It also encourages the formulation of training programs that familiarize self-government representatives with Romani education, employment, and public life.

The Slovak Government's Strategy

The new liberal government that took office in Slovakia in 1998 did far more in a year for the Gypsies than its predecessors did in eight. Deputy Prime Minister Pál Csáky and Vincent Danihel, the Government's Commissioner for Roma Affairs, coordinated and supervised the conceptual design and preparation of the Bratislava government's Strategy for the Roma.[11] Nicolae Gheorghe, the OSCE's Roma adviser, has called Slovakia's program the most conceptually sound in all of the region.[12]

The first part of the document includes the governmental resolution (accepted in September 1999) that outlines the recommended tasks and responsibilities of individual institutions (ministers, the prosecutor general, heads of regional authorities, etc.) concerning the preparation of programs. The second part lays out a set of measures for implementation by policy areas like human rights, education, culture, unemployment, housing, and others. This section, just as the Hungarian governmental resolution, specifies the person accountable for the design and evaluation of the feasibility of projects and sets a deadline by which they should be accomplished. The most substantive section of the document is the third part, which consists of the explanation of the Roma's

[11] See "Strategy of the Government of the Slovak Republic for the Solution of the Problems of the Roma National Minority and the Set of Measures for Its Implementation" (Bratislava: Government Publications, 1999), from which all citations are made.

[12] E-mail correspondence with Ildikó Haraszti, Deputy Prime Minister's Office, Bratislava (8 August 2000).

contemporary conditions that justifies the specific measures devised to help them. It includes nine broad areas that largely correspond to the Hungarian document.

The section on human and minority rights concedes that in spite of constitutional guarantees in practice the protection the Roma's rights leaves a lot to be desired. It notes that in many cases, violations of minority rights are not reported owing to expectations of lackadaisical police response. The document praises NGOs that publicize rights violations and conduct social and education projects for the Roma and pledges to support them in the future. Significantly, the Strategy notes that the enhancement of legal awareness in human and minority rights must continue "so that it achieves not only a comparable level with the majority population but also a higher standard of legal awareness." The Strategy insists that a comprehensive educational program should be formulated in order to remove inequalities between Romani and majority children in 15–20 years. The general objective of the education program is "a peaceful coexistence of all citizens in a multi-cultural society." The Strategy, as the Hungarian document, underscores the importance of stimulating Romani children in the school system, stresses kindergarten-level education with the participation of Gypsy assistants, the replacement of "special schools" with "flexible equalizing basic school classes," and raising the proportion of Roma in secondary and in higher education.

The section on language and culture emphasizes the need for a positive governmental approach to Romani linguistic and cultural values. It criticizes the previous government's practice of narrowing down Gypsy culture to songs and dances and calls for a policy that supports theaters, publications, cultural clubs, and the like. The Strategy also invites projects by, for, and about the Roma in the media and indends to establish Romani editorial groups in public media to hasten changes in public attitudes about the Gypsies. The section on employment recognizes the role of societal prejudices but also notes that a part of the Romani population "lacks interest in working, suffers from bad work morale, poor reliability, low work endurance, and has unrealistic wage requirements." These factors, the document points out, contribute both to "the negative experience of employers" and to "the shocking unemployment rate of the Roma." The task of the state's employment policy is to create conditions that will give Gypsies equal access to the labor market and to support "publicly beneficial workplaces" in districts hit by high Romani unemployment.

The Gypsies' housing conditions are especially poor in Slovakia, and the government wants to improve them through relaxing some eligibility criteria for state housing grants, amending the mortgage law, and the "implementation of projects addressing the comprehensive resocialization of the Romani community" living in Gypsy settlements that will also include education and training, employment, counseling, and so on. A follow-up government resolution (no. 294/2000) of the strategy identifies specific goals (e.g., the construction of 920 new apartments for the Roma in the Košice region alone). In addition, the Strategy proposes measures for raising the Gypsy population's health status (such as education focusing on hygiene, health awareness, preventive care, and responsible parenting). The reform proposals hold out the possibility of setting up regional self-government units that could "perform those self-government functions that cannot be performed by individual municipalities on the grounds of availability, economy, and efficiency of administration." Finally, the document identifies the state budget, the European Union's (EU) PHARE program, and national and international foundations as sources of financing for the comprehensive program. In the 1999 state budget the government allocated 15 million crowns (approximately US$430,000) to addressing the Roma's predicament. For 2001–2 it will appropriate 4 million euros (currently about US$4 million) to fund measures outlined in the "Strategy."[13]

The Czech Government's Concept of Romani Integration

Since 1997 Czech governments have made serious attempts to improve the negative record compiled by the Klaus administration. The offices of Deputy Prime Minister Pável Rychetsky and his deputy, Petr Uhl, who heads several governmental bureaucracies dealing with minorities and human rights, elaborated the "Concept for the Integration of the Romani Community" and drafted a minority rights law.[14] After some tension between several ministries (e.g., education and social welfare) and the drafters and a number of revisions that stripped the Concept of some of its most ambitious proposals, the government approved both documents in June 2000.

The ten-chapter Concept not only deals with those concerns that are similar to the Hungarian Resolution (e.g., education, antidiscrimination), but also includes separate sections on "The Roma as ethnic minority" (which deals with questions of demography and integration), affirmative action, change in social policy, the improvement of the Roma's physical security, the coexistence of different ethnic groups, and civic counseling centers. Unlike the Hungarian and Slovak documents, the Czech Concept

---

[13] "Information Material," 3.

[14] "Concept of Government Policy Towards Roma Community Members Supporting Their Integration into Society," (Prague, January 2000), 35 pp. (e-mail dispatch from Marta Miklušáková, Head of the Secretariat of the Council for Human Rights, 2 May 2000). All quotations are made from this document.

designates neither firm deadlines nor officials who are responsible for developing and implementing programs. Each chapter includes a by-and-large fair description of the current situation and then proposes numerous solutions to resolve problems. For instance, the chapter on racial discrimination acknowledges the absence of concrete legal guarantees against racial discrimination and the ineffectiveness of existing laws in several areas (employment, business, etc.) and notes that it is difficult to redress such complaints.

Several chapters also discuss the institution of Romani advisors, which was established by Governmental Resolution No. 686 (1997), the one major government document dealing with the Roma under the premiership of Václav Klaus. Although Gypsy advisors are now active in all 73 district offices of the Czech Republic, the original intention was that they be assigned directly to the heads of district offices. Many ended up working in the offices' social departments, however, where they have had little impact on policy.[15] The Concept calls for a reversal of this practice and proposes that one Romani advisor should be hired for every 1,500 Gypsies in a district. A previous draft concept dating from April 1999 approved the establishment of an "Office for Ethnic Equality and Roma Integration." The opponents of this proposal have argued, however, that because Gypsy integration was not a special service for the Roma but for society as a whole, the office should be redesigned. As an administrative body of the central state, the creation of this institution would need the support of all parliamentary parties. Although in June 2000 the government decided that there was "no need" to establish a separate office for ethnic minorities, five months later, as noted in Chapter 8, it reversed this decision and approved legislation for the creation of the new institution.[16]

The chapter on affirmative action explains that owing to "different historical development" the Roma find themselves in a difficult situation that they are seldom able to change on their own. Therefore, long-term, coordinated affirmative actions are necessary whose objective should be the societal integration of the Roma which will increase their self-esteem and free them from their reliance on social assistance. The specific

[15] See "Resolution of the Government of the Czech Republic of 29 October 1997, No. 686 on the Report on the Situation of the Romani Community in the Czech Republic and on the Present Situation in the Romani Community," (Prague, 29 October 1997), 4. The credit for initiating the Romani advisors program should actually go to Emil Ščuka and the Romani Civic Initiative (ROI). ROI raised this issue already in 1990 but the government's response at that time was that there was no money for it. Interview with Milena Hübschmannová (Prague, 27 August 1999).

[16] Radio Free Europe/Radio Liberty Newsline, Part II (hereafter RFE/RL II), 4:116 (15 June 2000) and 4:213 (2 November 2000).

affirmative action programs mentioned by the Concept include support for higher education such as special tutoring and scholarships, retraining for suitable employment, courses for women focusing on household skills, providing inexpensive rental accommodations, and preferential treatment for companies that employ Gypsies from "socially disadvantaged environments."

The proposed solutions for the Roma's problems in education, employment, healthcare, and so on, are similar to the Hungarian government's program. There are some differences, however, one of which is that the Czech document is much more detailed. For instance, the Concept emphasizes the need for preparatory or "zero-grade" classes prior to elementary school (because a much larger proportion of Gypsy children do not speak the language of majority education in the Czech Republic than in Hungary) and the gradual dismantling of the system of "special schools." The Concept also suggests ways in which the state may "pay our debts to people who graduated only from special schools" through offering make-up classes for which entrance examinations should be "changed so as to accept any applicant." Given that children at school learn little about ethnic minorities, the Concept calls for multicultural and tolerance education in the school system, not as a special class but as an integral part of all relevant subjects.

Finally, mention must be made of the separate chapter on the improvement of the Roma's security situation which is justified by the highest number of violent anti-Roma incidents in the region. To eliminate racially motivated attacks, the Concept supports (a) training for members of the police and the courts to recognize and appropriately punish them and (b) the development of a public relations campaign against racism.

Romania's National Strategy for the Protection of the Roma

The Romanian government's program is based on Governmental Decision no. 459/1998. It is similar to the three others outlined above to the extent that it attempts to deal with essentially the same problem areas: discrimination, employment, education, and so on. It is different, however, to the extent that the final elaboration of the program is yet to be completed. There are several important points that emerge from the preparatory work already accomplished.

First, the Romanian government committed itself to actively involving the representatives of Gypsy organizations to a larger extent than its counterparts elsewhere in the region. An agreement reached in May 1999 between the Department for the Protection of National Minorities, represented by Péter Eckstein-Kovács, the Minister for National Minorities, and the Working Group of Romanian Romani Associations (WGRA) institutionalized the Gypsies' participation by declaring that the two are equal partners in the elaboration of a national strategy.[17] The WGRA's number of representatives on the Interministerial Sub-Committee for Roma is identical to that of the government. These institutional participants agreed to cooperate in devising specific programs and to mediate in good faith if disagreements should arise.

Second, although the other states have also keenly sought the approval of the EU (this was strongly emphasized in my interviews with high-ranking officials[18]), in Romania the policy makers viewed not only the EU's endorsement but its financial support and active participation as special priorities.[19] In fact, EU representatives took part in discussions on the program and concluded a contract with the government that included a grant of 2 million Euros to be spent on improving the Roma's situation.[20]

Third, in Romania the government's approach seems to be based on the specific concerns and responsibility of individual ministries rather than on a more centralized strategy supervised by deputy prime ministers (as in the Czech Republic and Slovakia). Partly for this reason, a lot depends on individual ministries' attitudes toward the Roma. As Eckstein-Kovács admits, while the ministries of education and culture have been very active in pursuing solutions for the Gypsies' problems, other governmental departments have not been equally enthusiastic or flexible in designing and implementing programs or accepting Roma as qualified participants of the project.[21]

Finally, even though there is now institutionalized Romani participation in the development of policy, according to Dan Oprescu, the (now former) director of the National Office for Roma, the government has sole responsibility for the success of the program.[22] Nevertheless, the

---

[17] "Protocol Concerning the Elaboration of National Strategy for Protection of Roma Minority in Romania," (Bucharest, Department for the Protection of National Minorities, May 1999), 3 pp.

[18] Interviews with Gabriella Varjú, Vice-President of the Office for National and Ethnic Minorities (Budapest, 5 August 1999), Zdeněk Matějka, Secretary General of the Ministry of Foreign Affairs (Prague, 23 August 1999); and Pál Csáky, Deputy Prime Minister in Charge of Human Rights, Minorities, and Regional Development (Bratislava, 9 September 1999).

[19] Interviews with Péter Eckstein-Kovács, Minister for the Protection of National Minorities, and Dan Oprescu, Head of National Office for the Roma (Bucharest, 2 November 1999).

[20] See *Roundtable Discussion of Government Policies on the Roma in Romania* (Princeton: Project on Ethnic Relations, 1999).

[21] Interview with Eckstein-Kovács (Bucharest, 2 November 1999).

[22] Interview with Oprescu (Bucharest, 2 November 1999), and see *Roundtable Discussion*, 10.

Gypsies' representatives (WGRA) should have some degree of accountability not to mention the fact that Roma working in governmental agencies ought to have the same responsibility as other governmental officials.[23] One reason why the Romanian program is not further along is precisely the fact that while the WGRA's active involvement is a requirement, Romani participants are not accountable. At the same time, this paradoxical situation plays into the hand of those governmental officials who are not overly concerned with speedy actions.

It is already clear that the Romanian program will prescribe some of the same measures as those of the East-Central European states. In the educational sphere, for instance, every county-level educational office will employ a Romani official in charge of special projects and monitoring the Gypsies' progress. An affirmative action program that spans the entire educational system from kindergarten to university has already been introduced. The number of preferential seats set aside at universities for the Gypsies will be expanded (in 1999–2000 already more than 150 Roma took advantage of this program).[24] Several recently enacted laws, if consistently enforced, are expected to improve the Roma's conditions. The 1999 Civil Service Law, for instance, stipulates that those who deal directly with the public in areas where an ethnic minority makes up 20% or more of the population must speak the minority's language.[25] There are many villages in Romania where the Gypsies comprise a significant proportion of the population; and, given the dearth of non-Roma who speak Romani, the only solution will be the hiring of a large number of Roma.

Bulgaria's Framework Program for Romani Integration

Perhaps the most important thing worth knowing about the Bulgarian government's "Framework Program for Equal Integration of Romas in Bulgarian Society" is that it probably would not have materialized were it not for a Romani NGO, the Human Rights Project (HRP). As I mentioned in Chapter 6, the HRP's success in elaborating a comprehensive program for the Roma with the participation and agreement of 76 other Gypsy NGOs constitutes an impressive accomplishment. After protracted negotiations the Bulgarian government accepted a heavily diluted version of the Framework Program in the spring of 1999.[26]

---

[23] See Andrzej Mirga's observations in *Rountable Discussion*, 10.

[24] Interview with Oprescu (Bucharest, 2 November 1999).

[25] RFE/RL II, 3:127 (30 June 1999).

[26] See *Roma Rights in Focus: Newsletter of the Human Rights Project*, no. 10 (1998): 34–7; and interviews with HRP executive director Savelina Danova (Sofia, 11 and 17 November 1999); and Petar Atanasov, the Secretary of the National Council on Ethnic and Demographic Issues at the Council of Ministers (Sofia, 15 November 1999).

The reasons why I find the Bulgarian government's program the least promising in the region are that it assigns no responsibilities to individuals or institutions for implementation, it lacks specifics, and it suggests no firm deadlines by which projects should be introduced let alone completed.[27] The Framework Program consists of eight brief chapters that largely correspond to those of the other programs already discussed. The one relatively long section on "Protection Against Discrimination," for instance, laments that "Bulgaria is one of the few countries that does not have special state institutions for protection against discrimination" and suggests that one should be established. The chapter on employment notes that "we are not talking about some 'saving operations'," that is, stopgap measures, but a comprehensive program. There are no particulars to indicate what that program might look like, however, except that a "special fund with Government participation must be formed in order to guarantee Romas employment."

In Bulgaria, as in Slovakia, the dwellings of many Gypsies are located on land to which they have no legal claim and which are often not connected to electricity, water, and sewer lines. The Framework Program calls for an amendment to the law on territorial and town planning to legitimize such housing and grant their occupants ownership titles, and it recommends a "targeted government subsidy for Roma residential improvement." The document also points out the necessity of desegregating schools but notes that this will be a long and difficult process, and in the meantime "we must work on improving the quality of education" in these schools. One wonders if this approach might not serve as an excuse for doing little. Other proposals on education include countering racism in classrooms, providing opportunities to study the Romani language, programs for adult literacy and continuing education, and increasing the number of Gypsy university students. It is a positive sign that the Framework Program devotes a separate section to improving the situation of Romani women through special grants for university study, vocational training, programs to ease access to employment, and encouraging entrepreneurship.

The Question of Implementation

The mere existence of these comprehensive programs suggests that East European governments have come to realize that piecemeal measures and short-term projects will not provide satisfactory solutions to the Roma's problems. It is important to underscore again the profound influence of international organizations, primarily that of the European Union, in motivating the region's governments to address the predicament of their

---

[27] See "Framework Program for Equal Integration of Romas in Bulgarian Society" (Sofia, 22 April 1999), from which all citations are made.

Gypsy citizens. The programs generally acknowledge the magnitude of the Roma's problems, and those of especially the three East-Central European states (Hungary, Slovakia, and the Czech Republic) demonstrate a more or less sophisticated understanding of the necessary steps. At the same time, the true test of these programs will be the extent to which they are implemented. After all, in the past several years ambitious plans were drawn up and announced with great fanfare only to fade into oblivion. As Slovakia's Deputy Prime Minister Pál Csáky recently noted, what his government needed to improve the Roma's situation were "the will, the money, and the time."[28] Indeed, these are three crucial ingredients needed for these programs to succeed.

Writing in early 2001, my sense is that the current Hungarian and Slovak governments are the most seriously committed to implement their programs. Hungary has done the most for the Roma in the region throughout the 1990s. The Orbán government is even more dedicated to substantive action than its predecessors and has pegged improving the Gypsies' conditions as one of its main priorities.[29] The Slovak government that took office in 1998 was shocked by the Roma's conditions, especially after some of its members completed fact-finding missions to eastern Slovakia where some of the region's most poverty-stricken Gypsies live.[30] Mikuláš Dzurinda's cabinet may be especially committed to action because it needs to make up for the time lost under its predecessor and catch up with the other East-Central European states that are considered likely early candidates for EU membership.

The situation is different in the Czech Republic to the extent that a similar package of measures that Hungarian and Slovak governments accepted without much contention faced considerable controversy in Prague. Several innovative programs were cut from the Concept, and the final document turned out to be not much different from the Klaus government's resolution no. 686 of 1997.[31] There is no doubt about the commitment of Romanian officials (Eckstein-Kovács, Oprescu, and their successors in the new government of Adrian Nastase) who are responsible for shaping policy toward the Gypsies. But the profound and ongoing economic problems and the shifting political alliances in the country have

---

[28] Csáky cited in Sharon Otterman, "2001 Census: Will the Roma Stand Up to Be Counted," *The Slovak Spectator*, 27 September–3 October 1999.

[29] RFE/RL II, 4:77 (18 April 2000).

[30] Interviews with Csáky (Bratislava, 9 September 1999); Vincent Danihel, Government Commissioner for Roma Issues (Bratislava, 10 September 1999); Klára Orgovánová, a Program Director at the Open Society Foundation (Bratislava, 7 September 1999); and Michal Vašečka, Romani affairs specialist at the Institute for Public Affairs (Bratislava, 10 September 1999).

[31] E-mail correspondence with Marta Miklušáková (15 June 2000).

signified an environment that is hardly conducive to planning long-term policies. This is especially so in the case of expensive governmental programs for the Roma that are ordinarily opposed by a number of parliamentary parties. Moreover, in Bucharest there has been a lack of political will not to help the Gypsies per se, but to think strategically about *how* to assist them, a notion that is demonstrated by the somewhat haphazard nature of the government's program.[32]

Finally, it is clear that the main reason the Sofia government eventually accepted the HRP's program in 1999 was because it felt obligated to do so, given international publicity and pressure from the EU and the Council of Europe. A recent report by the HRP on the implementation of the Framework Program laments that in the vast majority of specific areas no action has been taken and concludes that one year after the inauguration of the Program "the Bulgarian government did not demonstrate adequate responsibility."[33] Independent experts agree that "no progress has been made" and "nothing has been done."[34]

Even if one assumes that East European governments are firmly committed to implement their programs – and this assumption does require a substantial leap of faith at the moment – the question of how to finance them remains. It is obvious that the breadth of the projects proposed and the number of individuals who need the state's assistance require tremendous resources, easily tens of millions of dollars in every state. But, it is equally clear that these countries at present would be hard pressed to come up with the necessary funds. Hungary has spent by far the most on the Roma in the region (its "Gypsy budget" for 2000 is 4.7 billion forints [roughly US$17.4 million]), but even this amount will prove insufficient for implementing all of its ambitious programs.[35] Romania and Bulgaria, two of the poorest countries in Europe, will likely find it a formidable challenge to raise the money for their programs. The Balkan governments' political will to shift resources for the implementation of these programs will not be sufficient simply because there are not enough resources to shift around. There is no doubt that the long-term financial commitment of international organizations, and especially that of the European Union, is also necessary to alleviate the difficulties of the East European Roma, especially in the region's most impoverished states.

[32] Interview with Cătălin Zamfir, Professor of Social Work at the University of Bucharest (Bucharest, 3 November 1999).

[33] See the "Report on the Implementation of the Framework Program for Equal Integration of Roma in Bulgarian Society," (Sofia: Human Rights Project, 2000), 7 pp.

[34] Electronic mail correspondence with ethnographers Elena Marushiakova and Vesselin Popov (3 June 2000).

[35] RFE/RL II, 4:77 (18 April 2000).

PART II: THE CASE FOR QUICK ACTION

"Time" is the third ingredient that Deputy Prime Minister Pál Csáky said his government needed. Those who expect a radical improvement in the Gypsies' conditions in the foreseeable future are surely going to be disappointed. Given the magnitude of the Roma's problems, the size of their communities, and the resources needed, the best that one can reasonably hope for in the next 10–15 years is continued incremental change. The reason is that the education of a new generation of Gypsies and the subsequent development of a substantial Romani middle class, both of which are critical components of Gypsy integration, will take many years. Romani integration should be viewed as a continuous process that must be one of the priorities of these governments and societies. Because programs and policies are unlikely to succeed in the short run, the only way to deal with the Roma's problems is through long-term, patient, and committed action. Therefore, the continuity of programs is crucial and it requires visionary politicians who most likely will be associated with a number of successive governments to stay focused on the issue. The most time-consuming part of these comprehensive programs is attitudinal change. Genuine Romani integration will not take place without fundamental changes both in the East European societies' view of the Gypsies and in the way Roma themselves relate to their social, economic, and political environment. Even in an optimal scenario, such changes could easily take a generation or more.

For politicians responsible for overseeing the comprehensive programs for the Roma, it is important to set achievable goals. Several politicians I interviewed in the region demonstrated a keen appreciation of this point. Pál Csáky told me that, among other things, he wanted to establish a well-functioning Romani self-government, to get progressive antidiscrimination and national minority laws enacted, to establish a fund for Romani integration as a separate item in the budget, and to encourage Gypsy organizational and mobilizational activities by 2005.[36] In our interview Péter Eckstein-Kovács identified the political and societal acceptance of a national strategy for the Roma and the creation of a separate pool of money in the budget for this purpose as his short-term goals.[37] Edit Rauh, the head of the Gypsy Department of the Hungarian Office for National and Ethnic Minorities, noted that one important task she considered crucial to achieve in the next few years was that no Rom would be prevented from attending high schools or colleges owing to financial reasons.[38] The five-year to-do list of Petar Atanasov, the Secre-

---

[36] Interview with Csáky (Bratislava, 9 September 1999).
[37] Interview with Eckstein-Kovács (Bucharest, 2 November 1999).
[38] Interview with Rauh (Budapest, 9 December 1999).

tary of the National Council on Ethnic and Demographic Issues in Bulgaria, includes the desegregation of "Gypsy schools," the implementation of a public awareness program to diminish societal prejudices, and the hiring of a large number of Roma into state administration and the police force.[39]

The experiences of the 1990s show that governments and societies need to do more to halt the growing marginalization of the Roma. To be sure, some East European governments introduced promising programs, explored a number of new approaches, and enacted dozens of laws, but the gap between majority populations and the Gypsies did not diminish. Politicians can always find excuses for not introducing or for delaying difficult policies. A number of government officials in the region – who asked not to be named – told me that "we should wait till the economy turns around," that "there are plenty of impoverished people here other than the Roma," and even that "without the EU's money there is little we can do." I strongly disagree.

Those who cannot decide what approach to take to solving the Gypsies' problems often refer to the conceptual differences among politicians, experts, and Romani leaders regarding the type of problem the Roma's predicament signifies. Some consider the Gypsies' situation more of a social than an ethnic problem, noting that owing to their weak ethnic identity they should be considered first and foremost a disadvantaged social group.[40] Others tend to view it as primarily an ethnic problem pointing to the prevalence and impact of inter-ethnic tensions; still others regard it as a political problem owing to their belief that with strong and decisive action on national, regional, and local levels the Roma's difficulties would quickly diminish. I agree with those who contend that given the complexity and various dimensions of the East European Gypsies' predicament, it poses social, ethnic, economic, and political dilemmas to states and societies.[41]

Another valid but hardly constructive question that one often hears and reads about in Eastern Europe concerns who is responsible for the Gypsies' predicament. It is true that many Romani leaders – especially of the radical ilk like Aladár Horváth, Ivan Veselý, and Rudko

---

[39] Interview with Atanasov (Sofia, 15 November 1999).

[40] See, for instance, Peter Winkler, "Roma Ethnic Group in Slovenia," in Miran Komac, ed., *Protection of Ethnic Communities in the Republic of Slovenia* (Ljubljana: Institute for Ethnic Studies, 1999), 73; interviews with Jiřina Šiklová, Professor of Sociology, Charles University (Prague, 31 August 1999), Michal Vašečka (Bratislava, 10 September 1999), and television editor Marius Tabacu (Cluj, 25 October 1999); and Miklós Ugró, "Szociális ügy," *Magyar Nemzet*, 27 July 2000.

[41] Interviews with Florin Moisă, Program Coordinator at the Open Society Foundation (Cluj, 25 October 1999); and Géza Ötvös, head of the Wassdas Foundation (Cluj, 26 October 1999).

Kawczynski – refuse to admit that the Gypsies might have something to do with their predicament. But there is also a growing number of activists – like Faik Abdi, Karel Holomek, and György Rostás-Farkas, among others – who believe in the personal responsibility of Roma and the obligation of Gypsy leaders to improve their people's conditions. In a public letter, Ian Hancock notes that the fact of historical persecution "cannot serve [for the Gypsies] as an excuse for inaction, or victim mentality."[42] I tend also to agree with Mark Braham, who writes that

While the Roma have every reason to blame others for much of their situation, they must also accept responsibility for much of their present condition. If that responsibility in the past has been diminished by a history of living under authoritarian regimes, from monarchist through fascist and communist periods, it cannot be avoided now during what Europeans generally hope is to be a period of social as well as political democracy. If the Roma want to benefit from new conditions, then they must also help to create them.[43]

Some of the leaders of the international Romani movement understand the responsibility of Gypsy elites to fashion new ideas and work together with states and international institutions in finding and implementing solutions.[44] At the same time, it ought to be recognized that East European states and societies bear a moral responsibility to try and make up for the enormous injustices they subjected the Roma to for seven centuries. But most importantly, assigning blame is not going to alleviate the Gypsies contemporary predicament. Working actively together to eliminate it could.

It is necessary to act without delay because in some countries, like Romania, Bulgaria, and Slovakia, where the Romani population is large, growing poorer, and more desperate than ever, inaction could produce a catastrophe. Even though improving the Roma's condition will be a heavy burden on East European states and societies, if put off any longer, the social, economic, and political costs of this undertaking are likely to be a lot higher. The Gypsies and their problems are not going to go away. To the contrary, as their numbers (and proportion in the region's overall populations) continue to grow, so will the magnitude of their difficulties. Without decisive change the Roma will remain uneducated, they will have no qualifications but for a decreasing number of the most menial

---

[42] See Hancock's letter of resignation from the International Romani Union (n.d.) on the Internet at http://www.romnews.com/a/hancock.html. See also Robert Elias, *The Politics of Victimization* (New York: Oxford University Press, 1986).

[43] Mark Braham, *The Untouchables: A Survey of the Roma People of Central and Eastern Europe* (Geneva: United Nations High Commissioner for Refugees, 1993), 124.

[44] See, for instance, Mirga and Gheorghe, *The Roma in the Twenty-First Century: A Policy Paper* (Princeton: PER, 1997), 35–6.

jobs, an even larger proportion of the Roma will be dependent on social welfare systems and thus pose a growing burden on governments and societies, and interethnic tensions will inevitably increase.

Furthermore, the very real possibility of hundreds of thousands or even millions of young impoverished Roma with nothing to do and nothing to lose should be a sobering scenario for East European states and societies. J. F. Brown may have slightly overstated the case when he wrote in 1994 that

Gypsy violence, even terrorism, is by no means an impossibility; the Gypsies, indeed, could be the new Eastern Europe's time bomb. If that bomb is not defused in this century, it could go off early in the next.[45]

But Brown was certainly right to point out the dire security implications of ignoring the Roma's situation.[46]

Another major argument for rapid action is that European Union officials and documents have made it abundantly clear to East European governments that a substantial improvement in the Gypsies' situation is one of the key conditions of acquiring membership. Given that EU integration is their most fundamental foreign policy objective, the need for a quick implementation of their programs for the Roma should be obvious.

It may also be useful to consider the minority issue as an integral part of raising democratic standards. The Gypsies and their plight should trigger some thought processes in East Europeans concerning the type of societies they want to build and live in. Though it is highly likely that the vast majority of East Europeans will not come to "like" the Roma in the foreseeable future, it is their duty to offer them the same opportunities majorities enjoy. George Schöpflin has pointed out that

Policies toward minorities should be governed by two broad principles if the aim is to integrate the minority and preserve a democratic system: In all cases, the spirit as well as the letter of the law should be observed, and the provision should actually go beyond what the minority may demand at any one time. These principles clearly imply that the agendas of the majority and its particular moral and affective imperatives will have to be restrained in favor of the minority. . . .[47]

---

[45] J. F. Brown, *Hopes and Shadows: Eastern Europe after Communism* (Durham, NC: Duke University Press, 1994), 228.

[46] On this point, see Zoltan Barany, "Marginality, Ethnopolitics, and the Question of Security: The East European Roma," in Hans-Georg Erhart and Albrecht Schnabel, eds., *The Southeast European Challenge: Ethnic Conflict and the International Response* (Baden-Baden: Nomos, 1999), 43–65.

[47] George Schöpflin, "Nationalism and National Minorities in East and Central Europe," *Journal of International Affairs*, 45:1 (Summer 1991): 59.

A democratic state is, in fact, a self-limiting state even if "self-limitation is not at all easy to practice in the moral–cultural area, although this is as central to an open society as any."[48]

PART III: SUGGESTIONS FOR A LONG-TERM PROGRAM OF ROMANI INTEGRATION FOR EAST EUROPEAN GOVERNMENTS

As I mentioned in the introduction to this chapter, I believe in the usefulness of setting up ideal types or optimal scenarios because they promote the impartial evaluation of actual accomplishments. My recommendations admittedly belong to this kind of model. They might be considered unrealistic, but I believe that the realization of this type of long-term (say, 25-year) program not only would halt the further deterioration of the Gypsies' situation vis-à-vis the majority but would actually allow them to make substantial progress in catching up. This is in the common interest of the region's states and societies, not to mention the interest of the Roma.

Space does not permit an all-encompassing point-by-point list of specific tasks, many of which are already included in some of the East European governments' programs. Therefore, I will emphasize in six broad areas those specific issues that have not received sufficient attention in most of governmental approaches.

1. Rights, Discrimination, and Law Enforcement

East European governments need to enact and enforce a package of laws that includes the unambiguous protection of human, civil, and minority rights and a separate antidiscrimination and antiracism legislation. Among other things, they must guarantee that all Gypsies who qualify become citizens and should encourage their awareness of their rights and responsibilities. Establishing the institution of an independent ombudsman whose specific task is the protection of minority rights and whose recommendations are taken seriously by state authorities should also be a priority. In order to weed out the passivity in the judicial system that in many places is the source of anti-Romani discrimination, minority rights ought to be included as a separate subject of the curricula of law schools and police academies, and already serving officers of the law need to be provided with this type of education. The heavily bureaucratized legal system usually signifies an intimidating and foreign environment for the Gypsies. Therefore, governments would do well to sponsor legal

---

[48] Ibid., 60. See also Robert L. Simon, "Pluralism and Equality: The Status of Minority Values in a Democracy," in John W. Chapman and Alan Wertheimer, eds., *Majorities and Minorities* (New York: New York University Press, 1990), 207–25.

awareness programs for Romani activists to enhance their familiarity with their rights and to encourage them to seek redress for potential rights abuses.

The significance of governments and state officials taking a public stance against discrimination of any sort cannot be overstated. Governments should also make sure that full legal remedies for victims of discrimination are applied and those who discriminate or commit racist acts are punished consistently and severely. The activities of law enforcement agencies need to be closely monitored to expose antiminority discrimination. Training and hiring a growing number of Gypsy policemen should be a priority of ministries of interior because such measures are likely to improve the traditional animosity between the Romani communities and the police.

Although the issue of positive discrimination is still debated in the region, the enormous disadvantages of the Gypsies in education, employment, housing, and other areas justify the introduction of equal opportunity programs. To paraphrase Jennifer Hochschild, the problem of severe poverty and its attendant behaviors and emotions can be solved only when East European governments and societies choose actually, not merely rhetorically, to open the opportunity structure to all.[49] The anticipated popular disapproval of such programs might be deflected if they are extended to all people of profound social handicap – regardless of ethnicity – and if it is verified that only those benefit who qualify.

It is also important that governments carefully weigh the implications and effects of various types of positive discrimination programs. The goal should be to level the playing field, to enable the disadvantaged to compete on an equal footing. Instead of quotas, which often seem unfair when people with lower qualifications are favored, strong measures should be taken to make sure that the Gypsies do acquire the proper credentials. For instance, I am not in support of lowering university admission criteria for Roma and other socially disadvantaged groups because I believe that it generates additional adverse phenomena such as increases in interethnic tensions and the diminution of the beneficiaries' self-confidence. Instead, governments should introduce programs that assist socially disadvantaged Gypsies and others throughout their educational careers, by encouraging their attendance of kindergartens, providing need-based fellowships for high school and college students, and offering special tutoring for university entrance examinations.

[49] Jennifer L. Hochschild, "Equal Opportunity and the Estranged Poor," *Annals of the American Academy of Political Science*, 501 (January 1989): 144.

2. Education and Employment

There is no more important and pressing issue than improving the Roma's living standards. In the short run, job training is the single biggest need. In the longer run, their educational standards must be raised. Without a drastic improvement in the Roma's educational achievements there will be no substantial change in their socioeconomic marginality. It is crucial that discrimination of all sorts be weeded out from the educational system and especially that normal children should not be assigned to "special schools" under any circumstances. Therefore, governments should establish a rigorous monitoring procedure over the assignment of children to schools serving the learning disabled. Counselors and assistants who understand the Gypsies social circumstances should be employed at kindergartens and schools in order to help the Roma's transition to a structured learning environment. Curricula and textbooks for all students must contain information regarding the culture and history of ethnic minorities. Hungary's experience with the Gandhi High School demonstrates the benefits of elite education to talented Romani children.[50] The establishment of similar schools should be a priority because they provide first-class education not only in general subjects but also in Romani language and culture. Therefore, they are expected to produce individuals with strong ethnic identity who will increase the size of the Gypsy middle class and serve as role models for young Roma.

The state should extend financial support to those students who cannot afford the costs of education. Governments should actively support after-school programs that offer Gypsy children worthwhile organized activities. It is imperative that an adequate number of teachers – preferably Roma – are trained who know Romani and understand the challenges Gypsy children face in the educational system. These teachers should be provided with the incentives that ensure their long-term commitment to Romani education.

Perhaps no educational project is more critical than changing the negative or indifferent attitudes most Roma share toward formal education. Governments must find the proper method to convince Gypsies that education is an essential requirement of prosperity and social integration. Therefore, the merits of an extensive media campaign publicizing the indispensability of educational achievement targeting Gypsy communities should be examined. Romani activists should be encouraged to participate in and preferably lead this campaign, which must be

---

[50] György Balavány, "Szükség volna még sok Gandhi Gimnáziumra," *Magyar Nemzet*, 10 February 2000.

complemented by strong financial incentives (fellowships, grants, etc.) for those who are willing to study. As Andrzej Mirga says, the key is to include education as one of the main values of future Romani communities, to make Gypsy parents realize that the sacrifices they make for their children's education is well worth it.[51] Many Romani activists across the region recognize that "everything hinges on education" and that education will foster not only economic prosperity but also more effective Gypsy mobilization, reduced interethnic tensions, and, ultimately, Romani integration.[52] Governments should assist Gypsy opinion makers to hammer this message home.

An educated Romani work force will be able to compete in the labor market provided that anti-Gypsy discrimination is strictly prohibited and consistently punished by the state. But training a new generation of Roma will take 15–20 years, and improving their socioeconomic conditions is an immediate task. What should be done in the meantime? In order to halt and reverse the Gypsies' growing impoverishment, authorities should develop, expand, and finance practical programs for unskilled and unemployed Roma that provide practical training, agricultural land and seed for cultivation, and employment in public works and other areas. Social service offices, for instance, should be able to identify work opportunities for Roma that provide them with jobs that demand no specialized training, such as caretakers of public buildings and areas, social workers (visiting and supplying meals), and the like.[53] Experience shows that unemployed Gypsies and others are often hard to motivate for work, therefore proper incentives should be included in these programs (such as remuneration that is higher than social welfare payments or a reduction of the latter) to stimulate participation.

Governments need to introduce positive discrimination programs in public sector employment for qualified Gypsies. They should also provide incentives to private companies (such as tax breaks or preferential consideration in public tenders) that train and employ Gypsies and other socioeconomically disadvantaged people. Just as importantly, Romani entrepreneurship ought to receive strong state support in the form of low-interest loans, reduced rental fees for office or business space, and tax benefits. Finally, it would seem worthwhile to actively encourage the Roma and other disadvantaged minorities to consider professional service in the armed forces as their career choice. Some

---

[51] Interview with Mirga (Kraków, 11 August 1999).
[52] See, for instance, Gizella Ranner, "Minden az oktatáson múlik avagy az oktatás szétsugárzó hatása," *Közös Út – Kethano Drom*, 3:2 (1995): 40–1.
[53] See Gábor Havas, Gábor Kertesi, and István Kemény, "The Statistics of Deprivation: The Roma in Hungary," *The Hungarian Quarterly*, 36:138 (Summer 1995): 79.

militaries, particularly that of the United States, have been quite successful in integrating minorities; and East European armies might find
their experiences instructive, especially given their current recruitment
difficulties.[54]

3. Social Policy

Governments need to prevent new forms of exclusion. Involuntary segregation from the majority population has proved harmful in the past
and it should be discouraged in the future. States should financially
support local efforts to eliminate existing Gypsy ghettos and provide
Roma with affordable housing in integrated areas. Regional projects that
assist the Roma in the design and construction of new dwellings or the
renovation of old ones are likely to promote a sense of ownership and
the pride and satisfaction that usually go with it. In this respect the Israeli
experience with the Bedouin population in the Negev region might prove
useful to study.[55]

Governments need to redouble efforts to improve the Roma's health
standards. State and local authorities must accept their responsibility to
eliminate housing conditions that signify health hazards or promote the
development of diseases. The provision of easy access to safe water,
sewage disposal, and garbage removal services has to be a top priority.
Community education programs on hygiene, nutrition, women's health,
and prenatal care should be actively supported. Actions must be taken
to ensure that all Gypsy children are immunized. Obviously it is imperative that Roma enjoy the same access to doctors, ambulance services,
and hospitals as the rest of the population.

The dependence of many Gypsies on social welfare payments has been
a widely debated and contentious issue across Eastern Europe. Even a
number of moderate Romani politicians contend that this dependence
must be reduced because it decreases the motivation of many Roma –
especially in large families – to seek work and contributes to sharpening
interethnic animosities.[56] The fact that some Gypsies spend a substantial
proportion of their welfare checks on alcohol and drugs has been
extensively documented.[57] To counter this phenomenon and to stop the

[54] On this issue, see Charles C. Moskos and John Sibley Butler, *All that We Can Be: Black Leadership and Racial Integration the Army Way* (New York: Basic Books, 1996).
[55] See, for instance, Yehuda Gradus and Eliahu Stern, "From Pre-Conceived to Respon-sive Planning: Cases of Settlement Design in Arid Environments," in Yehuda Gradus, ed., *Desert Development: Man and Technology in Sparselands* (Boston: D Reidel, 1985), 41–59.
[56] Interview with Karel Holomek (Brno, 1 September 1999).
[57] See, for instance, Michal Vašečka, "The Romanies in Slovakia," in Luboš Vagač, ed., *National Human Development Report for Slovakia 1998* (Bratislava: United Nations Development Program, 1998), 64.

manipulation and exploitation of Roma by Gypsy money[58] usurers, the Slovak Ministry of Labor, Social Affairs, and Family introduced the policy of "extraordinary receiver" through its district offices in 1998. These offices have become the "extraordinary receivers" of the Gypsies' welfare checks, and they are responsible for administering social benefits to the Roma through food stamps and child allowances.[59] In effect, this policy insured that Gypsies could feed their children and purchase necessities rather than alcohol. According to independent experts the program has been successful, although, not surprisingly, Roma are divided in their opinion of it.[60]

Politicians in Slovakia have also proposed that per-child subsidies for Roma be paid by the state only if school-age children regularly attended schools.[61] This recommendation is discriminatory because it is directed specifically at the Gypsies and it is detrimental to the welfare of their children. Less controversial are the child-protection laws in Romania (1994) and Hungary (1997) that tie social welfare payments (for all recipients) to school attendance while guaranteeing that children's welfare is safeguarded.[62] Furthermore, in order to decrease dependency on social welfare provisions which signifies an enormous burden on state resources, states might want to withdraw or reduce payments to those who possess the ability to work but refuse the opportunity to do so as long as it does not compromise child welfare. Such welfare-to-work programs have had some success in the United States and elsewhere.

4. Fostering Romani Participation

The Gypsies' problems will not be solved without their own active participation. Thus, it is important to foster the development of a Romani community that can actively and constructively take part in planning, monitoring, and implementing programs. States should take measures to assist the development of Gypsy civil society. There cannot be too many Romani nongovernmental organizations (NGOs) that actively contribute to the alleviation to the Roma's predicament. Those NGOs that are useful in this respect (it is largely irrelevant whether they conduct

---

[58] In fact, Jana Gajarová, a Slovak official in charge of Romani affairs, has claimed that many Gypsies are fleeing Slovakia because they cannot repay money lenders within the Romani community. See RFE/RL II, 4:207 (25 October 2000).

[59] Michal Vašečka, "The Roma," in Gregoríj Mešeznikov, Michal Ivantyšyn, and Tom Nicholson, eds., *Slovakia 1998–1999: A Global Report on the State of Society* (Bratislava: Institute of Public Affairs, 1999), 412.

[60] Ibid.

[61] Lucia Nicholsonová, "MP Suggests Roma 'Solution'," *The Slovak Spectator*, 24–30 January 2000.

[62] Interviews with Cătălin and Elena Zamfir (Bucharest, 3 November 1999); and Edit Rauh (Budapest, 9 December 1999).

self-help programs, organize summer camps, or put on ethnic festivals) should get state support; those that are not, should not. Instead of dividing Gypsy parties and NGOs, states should play a mediating role to discourage fractiousness between them. Governments and policy makers ought to work with as many successful Romani organizations as feasible because collaborating with one or a few "chosen ones" is likely to divide the Romani community and antagonize those who are neglected.

The Hungarian minority self-government system has thus far offered the most promising model for the enhancement of Romani political participation and representation. The current system's shortcomings can be eliminated by unambiguous legal regulations concerning electoral rules and their relationship to local administrations, guaranteeing financing, and introducing strict but fair and consistent monitoring and evaluation. The (qualified) success of the Hungarian experiment suggests that other governments in the region ought to consider the creation of a suitable variant of this institution.

It is exceedingly important that an increasing number of qualified Roma take part in state, regional, and local governmental bodies because there is no one better to supervise and implement policy for the Gypsies and because programs without Romani participation are likely to lack legitimacy. All institutions – ministries, governmental and legislative committees, public foundations, and so on – that are concerned with Romani policy should have Gypsies on staff. Governments need to depart from the practice of having a "token Gypsy" in the boardroom. They should require actual Romani participation in and contribution to decision making on all levels.

5. Changing Societal and Romani Attitudes

Social attitudes and deeply rooted prejudices change slowly. Still, concerted efforts by the states can and should change them because Romani integration will be difficult to achieve in a society that lacks tolerance of and solidarity with a marginal minority.[63] Governments should conduct a long-term program that, in addition to antidiscrimination and antiracism measures, educates and informs society about the Roma and, more generally, about minority rights and democracy. A substantial part of this program will be a public media campaign that replaces the emphasis in broadcasts and reports on Gypsy criminality and other adverse phenomena while stressing the positive contributions that Roma have made to the region's societies. East Europeans should also be informed

---

[63] See, for instance, Charles F. Andrain and David E. Apter. *Political Protest and Social Change: Analyzing Politics* (New York: New York University Press, 1995), 151–2.

about the centuries-long marginalization and persecution to which states and societies have subjected the Gypsies to be able to understand and put into the proper context the Roma's contemporary predicament. This media and educational campaign needs to explain to the majority the factors that demand a comprehensive Romani policy and the reasons why the probable consequences of alternative actions – that is, ignoring their plight or not doing enough – are unacceptable. Citizens need also to understand the unavoidable costs and the long-term benefits of Romani integration.

To be sure, the development of East European societies that are comfortable with diversity will take time. Still, it is important to acknowledge successes, however small. In my conversations with experts and policy makers across the region in 1999, I often heard that overt discrimination was on the decrease but that latent discrimination was yet to be constrained.[64] But the diminution of overt racism and discrimination is a very important achievement in itself. Again, it is unrealistic to expect that the majority will suddenly come to "like" the Gypsies. What states should try to ensure, however, is that the Roma are treated fairly and receive the same opportunities as others.

Governments might find it useful to encourage some changes in traditional Romani attitudes, another task that promises to be difficult and time-consuming. This endeavor should be planned and led by Romani activists and politicians. They need to raise the awareness and appreciation of Gypsy communities concerning the importance and desirability of formal education, gainful employment, and the acceptance of some fundamental social norms and standards without which public policies – no matter how progressive – will not succeed and integration will not be feasible. The British scholar, Roger Scruton, suggests the following:

It is impossible to resolve this problem if we simply ignore the fact that Gypsies have a statistically established propensity to petty crime. Even if there are causes which partly exculpate the Gypsies, you will never achieve reconciliation between them and the surrounding population if spokesmen for the Gypsies either ignore the criminal record entirely or imply that somehow Gypsy crimes are excusable. Any group that seeks the right of residence and equal treatment in the country where it finds itself must purchase these benefits through loyalty to the state and obedience to the law of the land. It would surely help if the Gypsies were to make it plain that they accept this principle. . . .[65]

---

[64] Interviews with Gabriella Varjú (Budapest, 5 August 1999); Marta Miklušáková (Prague, 26 August 1999); and Michal Vašečka (Bratislava, 10 September 1999).
[65] Roger Scruton, "One-Sided Coverage of Roma" (a letter to the editor) *Transition*, 4:6 (November 1997): 4.

What governments ought to do is to support the public relations work of Gypsy activists through providing them with free broadcast time in state-owned television and radio.

6. Government Relations

Central governments would do well to improve communication and enhance collaboration with local authorities who are generally less enthusiastic about programs for the Roma. Through education, training, and better flow of information, local officials should come to share the government's objectives. At the same time, the state must be attentive to and supportive of the initiatives of local authorities who are best acquainted with local conditions.

East European governments ought to recognize the important contribution that nongovernmental organizations can make (and have already made) to achieving the objectives of state policies. Whenever practical, the state should recruit NGOs to design and implement governmental programs. The experience of the past decade confirms the need that governments monitor the NGOs' activities and the way they spend public funds. Only those that satisfy the dual criteria of fiscal prudence and doing good should receive state support.

Until recently there has been little evidence of cooperation between East European states as far as their policies toward the Gypsies are concerned. Viorel Hrebenciuc, the head of Romanian minority policy, told me in 1996 that working together with colleagues in the region made little sense because the problems of the Roma were entirely different in the region's states.[66] He could not have been more wrong. It is evident that the fundamental predicament of the Gypsies is quite similar across Eastern Europe. Therefore, governments have much to learn from sharing their experiences with one another. Although there was tangible improvement in this respect by the late 1990s, more intensive cooperation is in the common interest of all of these states.[67] The governments' acceptance of the guidance and recommendations of international organizations is not only advisable but also, in most cases, genuinely beneficial. Even if one puts aside the issue of European integration, the EU, the Organization for Security and Cooperation in Europe, and other organizations not only have a great deal of practical advice to

---

[66] Interview with Viorel Hrebenciuc, Secretary General of the Government and Coordinator for Council of National Minorities (Bucharest, 24 May 1996).

[67] Interviews with Éva Orsós (Budapest, 25 July 1996); Gabriella Varjú (Budapest, 5 August 1999); Pál Csáky (Bratislava, 9 September 1999); and Péter Eckstein-Kovács (Bucharest, 2 November 1999). See also RFE/RL II, 3:133 (12 July 1999) and 4:58 (22 March 2000).

dispense but, equally significant, have resources that can lighten the financial burden of Romani integration on East European states and societies.

CONCLUSION

A decade after the collapse of state-socialism the Gypsies still remain the pariahs of Eastern Europe. In spite of the absence of substantial improvement in their socioeconomic conditions, however, in the last few years states have done more for them than ever before. The growing recognition of East European political elites of the Roma's problems and their increasing willingness to do something about them are hopeful signs. Still, given the magnitude of the Gypsies difficulties and the differences between their value system and that of the majorities, the depth of societal prejudices, the divisions within political elites, and the dearth of available resources, it is hard to be optimistic about changes in the Roma's conditions in the short and medium term. Realistically, the complexity of the challenge that Gypsy integration poses should also temper one's confidence about fundamental long-term improvements.

At the same time, there is no acceptable alternative to long-term, carefully conceived, and patiently implemented comprehensive programs to assist the Roma simply because there is no acceptable alternative to the Gypsies' social, economic, and political integration. Among the many requirements necessary to come closer to the realization of this objective, the significance of courageous, committed, and wise political leadership cannot be overrated. It will be easy to lose momentum and to get discouraged because substantial change will not come soon. The temptation to emphasize the inevitable failures must be resisted because it is likely to lead to apathy or inaction. Those who care about Romani integration may take to heart the Gypsy proverb that "a child is not born with teeth," meaning that everything takes time. When considering the long and difficult process in front of the region's states and societies (including the Roma), the need to recognize and reward successes, however small, should be appreciated.

Conclusion

At the beginning of this book I posed two competing arguments and identified six research questions. The first argument proposed that the type of regime or political system determined individual state policies toward minorities. The alternative argument suggested that conditions specific to individual countries were responsible for deciding the kind of policies states pursued. The first two of the six research questions I set corresponded to these arguments while the other four pertained to the changes in Romani marginality over time and in response to different state policies, the extent to which the Gypsies have been able to alter their marginality and influence the state, and the ways in which Romani marginality might be alleviated. In this concluding chapter my task is to evaluate the merits of the two arguments and summarize the answers to the research questions in light of the empirical evidence I have marshaled.

REGIMES AND REGIME CHANGE

Regime types and regime change do make a difference but certainly do not determine the minority policies of individual states. As we have seen, there were some similarities in the minority policies of states belonging to the same regime type, but there were also significant differences. I found that the more flexible the parameters of an individual regime type, the larger the variation of specific policies that regime type allows. In other words, the type of political system is the more reliable determinant of minority policies the more constrictive it is and the less pluralism it permits.

Let us take the example of the imperial regime type. Although the organizing principles of empires are similar, empires display substantial disparities in their structures and policies. The Habsburg and Ottoman states were comparable in that for centuries they ruled over large territories populated by different nations of different religious persuasions and they strove to maintain political stability and conquer additional territories. These fundamental markers of the imperial regime type nonetheless allowed for significant variations in the minority policies of different empires. The sultans, who were not particularly concerned with the direct control of their subject peoples, found that relatively tolerant ethnic and religious policies served well their key purpose of preserving stability in their empire. The rulers of the Habsburg Empire, on the other hand, were more interested in closely controlling their populations because they were keener to undertake empire-wide projects (e.g., administrative, infrastructural, and economic) than their counterparts in Istanbul, and such projects necessitated more extensive and intensive control of the population. The Gypsies' historical experience in the two empires clearly reflected these different approaches.

As I showed, such differences in minority policies might also prevail between states belonging to the authoritarian, state-socialist, and democratic regime types. To be sure, the range and parameters of these policy variations are different in particular regime types. That is to say, state-sanctioned persecution of minorities may be pursued in authoritarian states but not in contemporary democracies. Moreover, there might also be some overlap between state policies in different regime types. For instance, both authoritarian states and democracies might choose to remain indifferent and simply ignore their ethnic minorities. Thus, although in theory there were some disparities between Polish policies toward the Roma in the 1930s (when Poland was an authoritarian state) and in the 1970s (when it was a socialist state), in practice they were quite similar given that Warsaw's basic inclination was simply to ignore them.

At the other end of the spectrum are totalitarian states. The totalitarian regime type tends to impose a measure of uniformity on the policies of states belonging to this category. In the East European context, I discussed totalitarianism as a subcategory of the authoritarian regime type during the early 1940s and the state-socialist regime type from the mid-1940s to the mid-1950s. In both cases, foreign powers (Nazi Germany and the Soviet Union) played a major role in the imposition of totalitarianism. Fascists did not come to power in all East European states; and even where they did, they tended to last a short time (e.g., in Hungary between October 1944 and April 1945). More illuminating is the totalitarian subcategory in the state-socialist case.

The fundamental common denominator between the East European countries in the first decade of state-socialism was the strict control a Stalinist (i.e., totalitarian) Soviet Union exercised over them. In

Table C.1. Changes in Romani Marginality

Regime Change	Social	Economic	Political
Imperial to Authoritarian	Negative	Negative	Negative
Authoritarian to State-Socialist	Positive	Positive	Negative
State-Socialist to Democratic[a]	Negative	Negative	Positive

[a] This refers to emerging democracies and, thus, short-term changes.

this period, Moscow in many ways ruled the East European states as if they had been parts of the USSR, and the region's elites were, in fact, compelled to emulate Soviet policies. Consequently, the communist states' key objective (to maximize their control over their populations) was identical across the region. Thus, the fact that they belonged to the totalitarian subcategory of the state-socialist regime type served as an accurate indicator of their minority policies. As we have seen, the rigid control of communist parties across Eastern Europe in this period did not allow for major policy disparities toward the Gypsies as the fundamental policy objective everywhere was to assimilate them. Unlike its East European neighbors, Yugoslavia was not a totalitarian state in the 1950s, which goes far in explaining its different Romani policies.

The state-socialist regime type also well illustrates the variety of policies that may develop once the totalitarian characteristics of the political system are left behind. As Soviet control began to wane over the region in the mid-1950s, the actual decision-making power (within the restrictive framework of the state-socialist regime type) of East European elites increased. Some of them chose to pursue more liberal policies, while others opted for more hardline ones. The disparities between them explain the evolution of different Gypsy policies in the region in the wake of the totalitarian period.

Regime change, as I demonstrated, does *tend to* make a difference in minority policies because states of different regime types *tend to* (but by no means necessarily) pursue different policies. As I showed, the period of regime transition is usually characterized by political instability and uncertainty because the emerging state has yet to consolidate its power, devise new political institutional structures, and decide on policies to follow. Regime changes have historically denoted mostly (in two-thirds of all cases) deteriorating conditions for the Gypsies because they led to successive regime types in which their situation (socioeconomic and/or political) tended to worsen (Table C.1). Positive changes took place in their social and economic conditions as a result of the regime change

from authoritarianism to state-socialism and the improvement in their
political status in emerging democracies. It bears underscoring that in
Table C.1, as in the book, I refer to "emerging" democracies. It is to be
hoped that as East European democracies become more mature, they will
create environments in which the Roma's socioeconomic circumstances
will improve as well.

As I noted in Chapter 1, episodes of regime change are conducive
to ethnic mobilization. This point is supported by rising Romani
political activism in the early 1920s, mid- to late 1940s, and 1990s.
In the first two periods their mobilization did not lead to significant
long-term gains because the type of regimes that did develop (authoritarian and state-socialist) thwarted or prohibited independent political
activities. Given that democracies do create the opportunity for ethnic
mobilization, the Gypsies' prospects under these regimes are far more
promising.

STATE-SPECIFIC VARIABLES: FIVE INFLUENCES
ON STATE POLICY

Although state policies toward minorities might be guided by particular regime types, they could scarcely be satisfactorily explained
or understood without the factors that are specific to the state. As I
tried to show throughout this study, the five variables I identified in
Chapter 1 have influenced state policy to varying degrees in different
regime types.

Table C.2 provides an assessment of the extent (weak, moderate,
strong) to which individual variables impacted upon state policy.

Table C.2. The Effect of State-Specific Factors on Gypsy Policy

Variables	Imperial	Authoritarian	State-Socialist	Democracy
1. Political-institutional attributes of the state	Strong	Moderate	Moderate	Strong
2. Societal attitudes	Weak	Weak	Weak	Strong
3. Minority's socioeconomic conditions	Weak	Weak	Strong	Moderate
4. Minority's political mobilization level	Weak	Weak	Weak	Moderate
5. International organizations and NGOs	Weak	Weak	Weak	Strong

The only factor that has had at least a moderate impact on Gypsy policy in every regime type is what I call the "political-institutional attributes" of the individual polity. This variable is especially influential in the cases of empires and democracies – that is, in regime types that permit a wide range of institutional variation. In the case of imperial states, other variables (2–5) have little impact on policy making. Thus, the political-institutional attributes of the state largely explain the different policies the Ottoman and Habsburg empires pursued toward the Gypsies. One might reasonably suggest that the Roma's socioeconomic conditions at least moderately influenced the assimilationist policies of Maria Theresa and Joseph II. Still, the two emperors ruled for a relatively short period (50 years) in the life of the Habsburg empire, and their concern with the Roma was clearly exceptional.

In authoritarian and state-socialist polities the political-institutional variable played only a moderate role in determining policy given the limitations inherent in these regime types. Although there were considerable differences between the Gypsy policies of Czechoslovakia and Hungary, the fundamental determinants (party control, social engineering, etc.) of policy were similar. This was especially so in totalitarian periods when the regime type allowed for a very narrow range of policy variation. Finally, in the emerging democracies the first variable has had a strong influence on policy. The different attitudes of political elites toward the Roma in, say, Poland and Bulgaria go far in explaining the differences in their Gypsy policies.

Societal attitudes matter little in nondemocratic polities because states do not have a compelling reason to be responsive to them. On the other hand, in democracies people are voters (or potential voters) who enjoy the power to hold their elected representatives responsible. As we have seen, in the emerging East European democracies state policies have been strongly influenced by negative societal attitudes toward the Roma.

With the exception noted above of the Habsburg Empire in the second half of the eighteenth century, the Roma's socioeconomic predicament did not make an impact on Gypsy policies under empires or authoritarian states. It affected state-socialist policies strongly, however, given socialist polities' professed desire to create a classless society that could not be realized in view of the abysmal socioeconomic marginality of the Roma.

In new democracies the Gypsies' situation has influenced state policies only moderately. Nevertheless, in democracies, unlike in the other three regime types, Romani mobilizational efforts and the activities of international organizations have also had an impact (moderate and strong, respectively) on state policies. From the perspective of the

Gypsies, the influence of these three variables (3, 4, and 5) has been beneficial; that is, they pushed state policies in a positive direction. Nonetheless, their positive effect has been to some extent mitigated by the negative attitudes of several East European states (especially until the late 1990s) and societies (variables 1 and 2). As I tried to explain in Chapters 6, 8, and 9, this picture is made all the more complex by notable differences between individual states in terms of variables 1 and 4. That is, some governments have evidenced more willingness to address the Roma's plight than others. Similarly, Gypsy mobilization has been more successful in some states than in others.

Table C.2 reveals another important conclusion, namely, that the making of Gypsy policy is far more difficult in democracies than in any other type of political system. Put more succinctly, Romani policies in imperial and authoritarian states were moderately or strongly influenced only by the political-institutional characteristics of the state. In addition to this variable, the Gypsy policies of state-socialist polities were also influenced by the Roma's socioeconomic marginality.

Only in democracies are Gypsy policies moderately or strongly affected by all five variables. The reason for this is that of all the regime types, only democracies allow real elections, party competition, or unchecked minority mobilization and only democracies are responsive to societal attitudes. So, while regime type does not effectively indicate the sort of minority policies democracies will follow – given the wide range of policy variation – it is still crucially important to the extent that it explains the reasons why so many sources and impulses contribute to the making of minority policies. In other words, in the case of democracies, regime type and state-specific variables are so tightly connected that they are difficult to separate.

In sum, an evaluation of the two arguments yields a mixed picture. Both regime types and country-specific conditions matter, but the latter seem to be more important determinants of state policy toward the Gypsies. Again, this is especially so in the case of regime types that permit a significant measure of pluralism.

Let us briefly return to the research questions posed at the beginning of this book. I have shown that different regime types to some extent denote disparities in minority policies and, as regimes change, policies also tend to change. Throughout this book I also demonstrated the often significant differences in the minority policies states of the same regime type pursue. I offered a detailed explanation of how and why the Roma's socioeconomic and political status has changed over time (see Table C.1) and the extent to which state policies have affected Gypsy marginality. We have seen that state policies have made major differences in the Roma's situation in different historical eras. They could be extremely destructive (e.g., physical persecution) and quite beneficial (e.g., providing employment, education, and healthcare). The analysis of the Gypsies' political mobilization efforts has shown that they have been largely unable to change their own conditions; and, even in the emerging democracies, the Roma have succeeded in influencing state policies only to a limited extent.

Finally, I explained that Romani marginality can be alleviated only through long-term, committed state policies, changes in societal and Romani attitudes, and the continued support of international organizations and NGOs. At the beginning of this book I identified the social, economic, and political integration of the Roma as the goal that East European states, societies, and the Gypsies themselves should aim for. At the end of this study I am even more convinced that without integration the Roma will continue to remain the pariahs of these societies. It is in the common interest of all East Europeans to prevent this from happening. There are those, like Nicolae Gheorghe, who contend that the Gypsies' problems and, more generally, Romani integration should be solved on the European level. I disagree because I believe that passing the problem on to European organizations will lead to a dilution of national programs; moreover, it might serve the interests of those East European officials who prefer to look for excuses for not addressing the problem head on. International organizations and NGOs can and should play (and, as I have shown, have already played) an important role in promoting the Gypsies' cause. Nonetheless, I am convinced that the responsibility for Romani integration should lie with the region's political *and* Gypsy elites.

Needless to say, I hope that Romani integration will take place, but it is difficult to be optimistic. In the twentieth century alone the seven countries that this book has focused on underwent enormous transformations. Imperial, authoritarian, fascist, and socialist states have come and gone with all the attendant radical political, social, and economic changes. Entirely new political systems, social classes, and modes of economic life came into being and disintegrated. In a very real sense, what changed the least was the situation of the Gypsies. They are still at the bottom of these societies in nearly every respect, and their social integration is still thwarted by numerous serious obstacles. As this book has clearly shown, the Roma's predicament has transcended fundamental changes in regime types.

Although I would prefer to end this book on an upbeat note, it would not be honest. I cannot help but recall the words of one of the first people I seriously discussed the Roma's situation with. This hardened Romanian human rights activist told me that the "Gypsy problem" would never be resolved to the satisfaction of both the Roma and the societies around them. I remember having a hard time responding to her because I was so appalled in the face of such plain cynicism. Ten years later, I wish I could confidently say that she was wrong. I am truly sorry that I cannot.

References

This list excludes newspaper and magazine articles. All references are included in the footnotes.

Abraham, Dorel, Ilie Bădescu, and Septimiu Chelcea. *Interethnic Relations in Romania* (Cluj-Napoca: Editura Carpatica, 1995).

Aćković, Dragoljub. *Asunen Romalen: Slušajte Ljudi* (Belgrade: Rrominterpress, 1996).

Acton, Thomas A. "Unity in Diversity," *Cigány Néprajzi Tanulmányok*, 2 (Budapest: Mikszáth Kiadó, 1994), 79–98.

"Using the Gypsies' Own Language: Two Contrasting Approaches in Hungarian Schools," in Diane Tong, ed., *Gypsies: An Interdisciplinary Reader* (New York: Garland, 1998), 135–41.

Ágoston, Erzsébet. *A cigány munkanélküli réteg válságkezelésének helyzete* (Budapest: Ministry of Labor, 1994).

Alts, Betty, and Sylvia Folts. *Weeping Violin: The Gypsy Tragedy in Europe* (Kirksville, MO: Thomas Jefferson University Press, 1996).

Anderson, Benedict. *Imagined Communities: Reflections on the Origin and Spread of Nationalism* (London: Verso, rev. ed., 1991).

Andrain, Charles F., and David E. Apter. *Political Protest and Social Change: Analyzing Politics* (New York: New York University Press, 1995).

Andrić, Ivo. *The Bridge on the Drina* (London: Allen & Unwin, 1959).

Antall, József. "Tanulmány-vázlat a cigányokról, (1957)," *Közös út-Kethano Drom*, 1:1 (January 1993): 41–4.

Antohi, Sorin, and Vladimir Tismaneanu, eds. *Between Past and Future: The Revolutions of 1989 and Their Aftermath* (Budapest: CEU Press, 2000).

Arany, János. "A bajusz," in *Arany János költeményei* (Budapest: Helikon, 1983), 242–7.

Armstrong, John A. "Mobilized and Proletarian Diasporas," *American Political Science Review*, 70:2 (1976): 393–408.

Atkinson, Paul, and Sara Delamont. "Professions and Powerlessness: Female Marginality in the Learned Occupations," *The Sociological Review*, 38:1 (February 1990): 90–110.

363

Bailly, Antoine, and Eric Weiss-Altaner. "Thinking about the Edge: The Concept of Marginality," in Costis Hadjimichalis and David Sadler, eds., *Europe at the Margins: New Mosaics of Inequality* (Chichester, England: John Wiley & Sons, Ltd., 1995), 219–36.

Balogh, Katalin. " 'Minek az iskola?'," *Kultúra és közösség*, no. 4 (August 1989): 58–77.

Barany, Zoltan. "Hungary's Gypsies," *Report on Eastern Europe*, 1:29 (20 July 1990): 26–31.

"Democratic Changes Bring Mixed Blessings for Gypsies," *RFE/RL Research Report*, 1:20 (15 May 1992): 40–7.

"Mass–Elite Relations and the Resurgence of Nationalism in Eastern Europe," *European Security*, 3:1 (Spring 1994): 162–81.

"Living on the Edge: The East European Roma in Postcommunist Politics and Societies," *Slavic Review*, 53:2 (Summer 1994): 321–44.

"Roma: Grim Realities in Eastern Europe," *Transition*, 1:4 (29 March 1995): 3–8.

"The Roma in Macedonia: Ethnic Politics and the Marginal Condition in a Balkan State," *Ethnic and Racial Studies*, 18:3 (July 1995): 515–31.

"Ethnic Mobilization and the State: The East European Roma," *Ethnic and Racial Studies*, 21:2 (March 1998): 308–27.

"Orphans of Transition: Gypsies in Eastern Europe," *Journal of Democracy*, 9:3 (July 1998): 142–56.

"Memory and Experience: Anti-Roma Prejudice in Eastern Europe," Woodrow Wilson Center for International Scholars, Occasional Paper No. 50 (Washington, DC: July 1998), 23 pp.

"Marginality, Ethnopolitics, and the Question of Security: The East European Roma," in Hans-Georg Erhart and Albrecht Schnabel, eds., *The Southeast European Challenge: Ethnic Conflict and the International Response* (Baden-Baden: Nomos, 1999): 43–65.

"The Regional Perspective," in Aurel Braun and Zoltan Barany, eds., *Dilemmas of Transition: The Hungarian Experience* (Lanham, MD: Rowman & Littlefield, 1999), 91–113.

"The Poverty of Gypsy Studies," *NewsNet: The Newsletter of the American Association for the Advancement of Slavic Studies*, 40:3 (May 2000): 1–4.

"In Defense of Disciplined Scholarship," *NewsNet: Newsletter of the American Association for the Advancement of Slavic Studies*, 40:5 (November 2000): 9–12.

"Romani Marginality and Politics in Postsocialist Romania," in Henry F. Carey, ed., *Politics and Society in Post-Communist Romania* (Boulder, CO: Westview Press, forthcoming).

Bársony, János. *Fővárosi cigány dolgozók az építőiparban* (Budapest: Népművelési Intézet, 1981).

"Der Zigeunerholocaust in Ungarn," unpublished manuscript, 1994.

Barth, Fredrik. "Introduction," in Fredrik Barth, ed., *Ethnic Groups and Boundaries* (Boston: Allen & Unwin, 1970), 9–38.

Bartosz, Adam. "Social and Political Status of the Roma in Poland," *Roma*, no. 40 (January 1994): 16–23.

Báthory, János. "A cigányság a politika tükrében," *Világosság*, 29 (August–September 1988): 613–23.

Bell, Daniel. *Ethnic Groups and Boundaries: The Social Organization of Cultural Differences* (Boston: Little, Brown, 1975).

Bell, Peter D. *Peasants in Socialist Transition: Life in a Collectivized Hungarian Village* (Berkeley: University of California Press, 1984).

Benkovič, Boris, and Lucia Vakulová. *Image of the Roma in Selected Slovak Media (June 1998–May 1999)* (Bratislava: Slovak Helsinki Committee, 2000).

Bercovici, Konrad. *The Story of the Gypsies* (London: Jonathan Cape, 1929).

Berger, John. *Pig Earth* (London: Writers and Readers Publishing Cooperative, 1979).

Block, Gay, and Malka Drucker. *Rescuers: Portraits of Moral Courage in the Holocaust* (New York: Holmes and Meier, 1992).

Borrow, George. *The Zincali: An Account of the Gypsies of Spain* (London: John Murray, 1893).

Bourdieu, Pierre. *Travail et travailleurs en Algérie* (Paris: Éditions Mouton, 1965).

Bourdieu, Pierre, and Jean Claude Passeron. *Reproduction of Education, Society, and Culture* (London: Sage, 1977).

Bozeva, Kalina, ed. *Minority Groups in Bulgaria in a Human Rights Context* (Sofia: Committee for the Defense of Minority Rights, 1994).

Braham, Mark. *The Untouchables: A Survey of the Roma People in Central and Eastern Europe* (Geneva: United Nations High Commissioner for Refugees, 1993).

Brass, Paul R. "Ethnic Groups and the State," in Paul R. Brass, ed., *Ethnic Groups and the State* (New York: Barnes & Noble Books, 1985), 1–56.

Ethnicity and Nationalism: Theory and Comparison (New Delhi: Sage, 1991).

Bratinka, Pável. *Report on the Situation of the Romani Community in the Czech Republic* (Prague, 1997, mimeo).

Braude, Benjamin, and Bernard Lewis. "Introduction," in Benjamin Braude and Bernard Lewis, eds., *Christians and Jews in the Ottoman Empire. The Functioning of a Plural Society* (New York: Holmes and Meier, 1982), 1–34.

Breuilly, John. *Nationalism and the State* (Chicago: University of Chicago Press, 1993).

Bridges, George S., and Martha A. Myers, eds. *Inequality, Crime, and Social Control* (Boulder, CO: Westview, 1994).

Bright, Richard. *Travels from Vienna through Lower Hungary with Some Remarks on the State of Vienna during the Congress in the Year 1814* (Edinburgh: Archibald Constable, 1818).

British Helsinki Human Rights Group. *Czech Republic 1999: Gypsies in the Czech Republic*; www.bhhrg.org/czechrepublic/czechrepublic1999.htm.

Brown, J. F. *Hopes and Shadows: Eastern Europe after Communism* (Durham, NC: Duke University Press, 1994).

Browne, Donald R., Charles M. Firestone, and Ellen Mickiewicz. *Television/ Radio News & Minorities* (Washington, DC: The Aspen Institute, 1994).

Brubaker, Rogers. *Nationalism Reframed: Nationhood and the National Question in the New Europe* (New York: Cambridge University Press, 1996).

Brunner, Georg. "Minority Problems and Policies in East-Central Europe," in John R. Lampe and Daniel N. Nelson, eds., *East European Security Reconsidered* (Washington, DC: Woodrow Wilson Center Press, 1993), 145–54.

Bubevski, Dusan. "Nekoi aspekti na natsionalniot sostav na naselenieto vo SR Makedonija vo periodot 1948–1981 godina," *Problemi na demografskiot razvoj vo SR Makedonija* (Skopje: Macedonian Academy of Sciences, 1985), 535–50.

Bunce, Valerie. "The Political Economy of Postsocialism," *Slavic Review*, 58:4 (Winter 1999): 756–93.

Bunkše, E. V. "God, Thine Earth is Burning: Nature Attitudes and the Latvian Drive for Independence," *GeoJournal*, 26:2 (1992): 203–9.

Burg, Steven L. "Stabilizing the South Balkans" in Barnett R. Rubin, ed., *Toward Comprehensive Peace in Southeast Europe: Conflict Prevention in the South Balkans* (New York: The Twentieth Century Fund Press, 1996), 34–45.

Burks, R. V. *East European History: An Ethnic Approach* (Washington, DC: American Historical Association, 1961).

Carter, F. W., R. A. French, and J. Salt. "International Migration between East and West in Europe," *Ethnic and Racial Studies* 16:3 (July 1993): 467–91.

Castile, George Pierre. "On the Tarascannes of the Tarascans and the Indianness of the Indians," in George Pierre Castile and Gilbert Kushner, eds., *Persistent Peoples: Cultural Enclaves in Perspective* (Tucson: University of Arizona Press, 1981), 171–91.

Castles, Stephen. *Here for Good: Western Europe's New Ethnic Minorities* (London: Pluto, 1984).

Chaliand, Gerard, and Jean-Pierre Rageau. *The Penguin Atlas of Diasporas* (New York: Penguin Books, 1997).

Chary, Frederick B. *The Bulgarian Jews and the Final Solution, 1940–1944* (Pittsburgh: University of Pittsburgh Press, 1972).

Cheles, Luciano, Ronnie Ferguson, and Michalina Vaughan, eds. *The Far Right in Western & Eastern Europe* (London: Longman, 1995).

Chirot, Daniel. "The Rise of the West," *American Sociological Review*, 50:2 (April 1985): 181–95.

   ed. *The Origins of Backwardness in Eastern Europe: Economics & Politics from the Middle Ages until the Early Twentieth Century* (Berkeley: University of California Press, 1989).

City of Brno. "Strategic Plan for Solution of Inter-Ethnic Relations between the Majority Population and the Romany Minority in the City of Brno" (City of Brno, May 1999), 53 pp.

Cohn, Norman. *The Pursuit of Millennium: Revolutionary Millenarians and Mystical Anarchists of the Middle Ages* (New York: Oxford University Press, 1970).

Cohn, Werner. *The Gypsies* (Reading, MA: Addison-Wesley, 1973).

Commission of the European Communities. "Public Opinion about the European Community," *Central and Eastern Eurobarometer* no. 3 (Brussels: European Community, February 1993).

Connor, Walker. "A Nation is a Nation, is a State, is an Ethnic Group, is a ...," *Ethnic and Racial Studies*, 1:4 (October 1978): 379–88.

The National Question in Marxist-Leninist Theory and Practice (Princeton, NJ: Princeton University Press, 1984).

Conway, Laura. *Report on the Status of Romani Education in the Czech Republic* (Prague: Citizens' Solidarity and Tolerance Movement – HOST, 1996).

Council of Europe. *Synthesis of the Replies to the Questionnaire on Participation of Minorities in Decision-Making Processes* (Strasbourg: Council of Europe, 1999).

Council on Human Rights. *Report on Human Rights in the CR in 1998* (Prague: Council on Human Rights, 1999), 52 pp.

Council for National Minorities. *The Legislative and Institutional Framework for the National Minorities of Romania* (Bucharest: Romanian Institute for Human Rights, 1994).

Crowe, David M. "The Gypsy Historical Experience in Romania," in David M. Crowe and John Kolsti, eds. *The Gypsies of Eastern Europe* (Armonk, NY: M. E. Sharpe, 1991), 61–80.

"The Gypsies in Hungary," in David M. Crowe and John Kolsti, eds. *The Gypsies of Eastern Europe* (Armonk, NY: M. E. Sharpe, 1991), 117–32.

A History of the Gypsies of Eastern Europe and Russia (London: I. B. Tauris, 1995).

"The Roma (Gypsies) of Bulgaria and Romania: An Historical Perspective," paper read at the conference on "Ethnic Conflict in Bulgaria and Romania," Duke University (Durham, NC, September 1996).

Csalog, Zsolt. "Jegyzetek a cigányság támogatásának kérdéséről," *Szociálpolitikai Értesítő*, 2 (1984): 32–46.

Fel a kezekkel! (Budapest: Maecenas, 1989).

Csepeli, György, Zoltán Fábián, and Endre Sík. "Xenofóbia és a cigányságról alkotott vélemények," in Tamás Kolosi, György István Tóth, and György Vukovich, eds. *Társadalmi Riport, 1998* (Budapest: TÁRKI, 1998), 458–89.

Dahl, Robert A. *Polyarchy: Participation and Opposition* (New Haven: Yale University Press, 1971).

Davidová, Eva. *Romano Drom: Česty Romu, 1945–1990* (Olomuc: Vydatelstvi Univerzity Palackého, 1995).

"K výstavní prezentaci romského tématu v Československu a v České republice (1962–1997)," *Bulletin Muzea Romské Kultury*, no. 6 (1997): 24–8.

Deák, István. *Beyond Nationalism: A Social and Political History of the Habsburg Officer Corps* (New York: Oxford University Press, 1993).

Deutsch, Karl W. *Nationalism and Its Alternatives* (New York: Knopf, 1969).

Diamond, Larry. *Developing Democracy: Toward Consolidation* (Baltimore, MD: Johns Hopkins University Press, 1999).

Diósi, Ágnes. *Szűz Mária zsebkendője* (Budapest: Kozmosz, 1990).

"Legyen világosság!" *Kritika*, no. 1 (1993), 3–5.

Djurić, Rajko, Jörg Becken, and A. Bertolt Bengsch. *Ohne Heim-Ohne Grab: Die Geschichte der Roma und Sinti* (Berlin: Aufbau-Verlag, 1996).

Donnelly, Jack. "Human Rights in a New World Order: Implications for a New Europe," in David P. Forsythe, ed., *Human Rights in the New Europe: Problems and Progress* (Lincoln: University of Nebraska Press, 1994), 7–32.

Dostál, Ondrej. "Hot Summer for Romany Minority in Slovakia," unpublished report for the Project on Ethnic Relations (Bratislava: September 1995).

Douglas, Mary. *Purity and Danger: An Analysis of the Concepts of Pollution and Taboo* (London: ARK, 1983).

Drury, Beatrice. "Ethnic Mobilization: Some Theoretical Considerations," in John Rex and Beatrice Drury, eds., *Ethnic Mobilization in a Multicultural Europe* (Aldershot, England: Avebury, 1994), 13–22.

Easterbrook, Gregg. "Forgotten Benefactor of Humanity," *The Atlantic Monthly*, 279:1 (January 1997): 74–84.

Edelman, Murray. *The Symbolic Uses of Politics* (Urbana: University of Illinois Press, 1985).

Eisenstadt, S. N. *The Political System of Empires* (New York: Free Press, 1963).

Elias, Robert. *The Politics of Victimization* (New York: Oxford University Press, 1986).

Emerson, Rupert. *From Empire to Nation: The Rise to Self-Assertion of Asian and African Peoples* (Boston: Beacon Press, 1962).

Enache, Smaranda. "Die Minderheit der Roma in Rumänien," *Glaube in der 2. Welt*, 20:4 (1992): 20–7.

Enloe, Cynthia. *Ethnic Conflict and Political Development* (Boston: Little, Brown, & Co., 1973).

"The Growth of the State and Ethnic Mobilization: The American Experience," *Ethnic and Racial Studies*, 4:2 (April 1981): 123–37.

European Roma Rights Center. *Divide and Deport: Roma & Sinti in Austria* (Budapest: ERRC, 1996).

Esman, Milton J. "Ethnic Politics and Economic Power," *Comparative Politics*, 19:4 (July 1987): 395–418.

"Political and Psychological Factors in Ethnic Conflict," in Joseph Monteville, ed., *Conflict, Peacemaking, in Multiethnic Societies* (Lexington, MA: D. C. Heath, 1990), 53–64.

Ethnic Politics (Ithaca, NY: Cornell University Press, 1994).

Esser, Hartmut, and Hermann Korte. "Federal Republic of Germany," in Thomas Hammar, ed., *European Immigration Policy: A Comparative Study* (Cambridge: Cambridge University Press, 1985), 165–206.

Evans, Peter B., Dietrich Rueschemeyer, and Theda Skocpol, eds. *Bringing the State Back In* (New York: Cambridge University Press, 1985).

Eyoh, Dickson. "From the Belly to the Ballot: Ethnicity and Politics in Africa," *Queen's Quarterly*, 102:1 (Spring 1995): 39–51.

Feagin, Joe R. *Subordinating the Poor: Welfare and American Beliefs* (Englewood Cliffs, NJ: Prentice-Hall, 1975).

Racial and Ethnic Relations (Englewood Cliffs, NJ: Prentice-Hall, 1984, 2nd edition).

Fentress, James, and Chris Wickham. *Social Memory* (Oxford: Blackwell, 1992).

Fenyo, Mario D. *Hitler, Horthy, and Hungary: German-Hungarian Relations, 1941–1944* (New Haven, CT: Yale University Press, 1972).

Ferguson, Russell, et al. *Out There: Marginalization and Contemporary Cultures* (Cambridge, MA: MIT Press, 1990).

Ficowski, Jerzy. "Polish Gypsies Today," *Journal of the Gypsy Lore Society*, (4) 29:3 (1950): 92–102.

　The Gypsies in Poland: History and Customs (Warsaw: Interpress, 1985).

　Wieviel Trauer und Wege: Zigeuner in Polen (Frankfurt am Main: Peter Lang, 1992).

Figusch, Viliam, ed. *Roma People in Slovakia and in Europe* (Bratislava: Information and Documentation Centre on the Council of Europe, 1995).

Fijalkowski, Jürgen. "Aggressive Nationalism and Immigration in Germany," in Richard Caplan and John Feffer, eds., *Europe's New Nationalisms: States and Minorities in Conflict* (Oxford: Oxford University Press, 1996): 138–50.

Fish, M. Steven. "Postcommunist Subversion: Social Science and Democratization in East Europe and Eurasia," *Slavic Review*, 58:4 (Winter 1999): 794–823.

Fisher, Sharon. "Romanies in Slovakia," *RFE/RL Research Report*, 2:42 (22 October 1993): 54–9.

Folkeryd, Fredrik, and Ingvar Svanberg. *Gypsies (Roma) in the Post-Totalitarian States* (Stockholm: Olof Palme International Center, 1995).

Fonseca, Isabel. *Bury Me Standing: The Gypsies and Their Journey* (New York: Knopf, 1995).

Fraser, Angus. *The Gypsies* (Oxford: Blackwell, 1995, 2nd edition).

Friedlander, Henry. *The Origins of Nazi Genocide: From Euthanasia to the Final Solution* (Chapel Hill: University of North Carolina Press, 1995).

Friedman, Edward. "Ethnic Identity and the De-nationalization and Democratization of Leninist States," in Crawford Young, ed., *The Rising Tide of Cultural Pluralism: The Nation-State at Bay?* (Madison: University of Wisconsin Press, 1993), 222–41.

Fukuyama, Francis. *The End of History and the Last Man* (New York: Free Press, 1993).

Galjus, Orhan. "A Media Guided by Our Own Hand," *Transitions*, 4:4 (September 1997): 98–100.

　"Balkan Triptych," *Index on Censorship*, 27:4 (July–August 1998): 87–90.

Gallagher, Tom. "Vatra Românească and Resurgent Nationalism in Romania," *Ethnic and Racial Studies*, 15:4 (October 1992): 570–99.

　Romania After Ceausescu (Edinburgh: University of Edinburgh Press, 1995).

Gecelovský, Vladimír. "Právne normy týkajúce sa Rómov a ich aplikácia v Gemeri (1918–1938)," in Arne B. Mann, ed., *Neznámi Rómovia: Zo života a kultúry Cigánov-Rómov na Slovensku* (Bratislava: Ister Science Press, 1992), 79–90.

Gellner, Ernest. *Encounters with Nationalism* (Oxford: Blackwell, 1994).

　"Nationalism in the Vacuum," in Alexander J. Motyl, ed., *Thinking Theoretically about Soviet Nationalities* (New York: Columbia University Press, 1992), 243–54.

Gheorghe, Nicolae. "Roma-Gypsy Ethnicity in Eastern Europe," *Social Research*, 58:4 (Winter 1991): 829–44.

Gheorghe, Nicolae, and Jennifer Tanaka, *Public Policies Concerning Roma and Sinti in the OSCE Region*, Background paper 4 (Warsaw: OSCE, 1998), 32 pp.

"Ethnic Minorities in Romania under Socialism," *East European Quarterly*, 7:4 (January 1974): 435–58.

Gilberg, Trond. "Influence of State Policy on Ethnic Persistence and Nationality Formation: The Case of Eastern Europe," in Peter F. Sugar, ed., *Ethnic Diversity and Conflict in Eastern Europe* (Santa Barbara, CA: ABC-Clio, 1980), 185–235.

Gilbert, Martin. *The Holocaust* (New York: Holt, Rinehart, and Winston, 1985).

Ginzel, Günther B. *Mut zur Menschlichkeit: Hilfe für Verfolgte während der NS-Zeit* (Cologne: Rheinland, 1993).

Glaser, Daniel. "Dynamics of Ethnic Identification," *American Sociological Review*, 23:1 (February 1958): 31–40.

Government of Bulgaria. "Framework Program for Equal Integration of Romas in Bulgarian Society," (Sofia, 22 April 1999), 13 pp.

Government of the Czech Republic. "Statute: Nationalities Council of the Czech Republic Government," Appendix to Government Edict no. 259 (Prague, 11 May 1994), 5 pp.

"Resolution of the Government of the Czech Republic of 29 October 1997, No. 686 on the Report on the Situation of the Romani Community in the Czech Republic and on the Present Situation in the Romani Community" (Prague, 29 October 1997), 5 pp.

"Concept of Government Policy Towards Roma Community Members Supporting Their Integration into Society" (Prague, January 2000), 35 pp.

Government of Hungary. "A Kormány 1047/1999. (V.5.) Korm. határozata," *Magyar Közlöny*, no. 39 (1999): 2727–34.

Government of Macedonia. *Public Attorney (Ombudsman)* (Skopje: Republic of Macedonia, Government Printing Office, 1998).

Ombudsman: Annual Report 1998 (Skopje: Republic of Macedonia, Government Printing Office, 1999).

Government of Slovenia. *Program ukrepov za pomož Romom v Republiki Sloveniji* (Ljubljana: Government of Slovenia, 1995).

Government of the Slovak Republic. "Information Material on the Activities of the Slovak Republic Relating to the Resolution of Problems of the Roma National Minority in the Slovak Republic." (Bratislava: Government Publications, 1999), 12 pp.

"Strategy of the Government of the Slovak Republic for the Solution of the Problems of the Roma National Minority and the Set of Measures for Its Implementation" (Bratislava: Government Publications, 1999), 23 pp.

Gradus, Yehuda, and Eliahu Stern. "From Pre-Conceived to Responsive Planning: Cases of Settlement Design in Arid Environments," in Yehuda Gradus, ed., *Desert Development: Man and Technology in Sparselands* (Dordrecht: D. Reidel, 1995), 41–59.

Grebenarov, Stojan. "Gypsy-Bashing," *The Insider* (Sofia), no. 1 (1992): 20–3.

Greenfeld, Liah. *Nationalism: Five Roads to Modernity* (Cambridge: Harvard University Press, 1992).

Grellmann, H. M. G. *Dissertation on the Gypsies* (London: Ballantine, 1807, 2nd ed.).

Gronemeyer, Reimer. *Zigeuner in Osteuropa: Eine Bibliographie zu den Ländern Polen, Tschechoslowakei und Ungarn* (München: K. G. Saur, 1983).

Eigensinn und Hilfe: Zigeuner und Sozialpolitik heutiger Leistungsgesellschaften (Giessen: Focus, 1993).

Gurr, Ted Robert. *Minorities at Risk: A Global View of Ethnopolitical Conflicts* (Washington, DC: US Institute of Peace, 1993).

Gurr, Ted Robert, and Barbara Harff. *Ethnic Conflict in World Politics* (Boulder, CO: Westview Press, 1994).

Gurr, Ted Robert, and James R. Scarritt. "Minorities at Risk: A Global Survey," *Human Rights Quarterly*, 11:3 (August 1989): 375–405.

Guy, Willy. "Ways of Looking at Roms: The Case of Czechoslovakia," in Farnham Rehfisch, ed., *Gypsies, Tinkers, and Other Travellers* (London: Academic Press, 1975), 201–29.

Gyenei, Márta. "A létminimum alatt – Jajhalom (I.)," *Statisztikai Szemle*, 71:1 (January 1993): 16–31.

"A létminimum alatt – Jajhalom (II.)," *Statisztikai Szemle*, 71:2 (February 1993): 130–45.

Gyönyör, József. *Államalkotó nemzetiségek* (Bratislava: Madách, 1989).

Habermas, Jürgen. *The Structural Transformation of the Public Sphere: An Inquiry into a Category of Bourgeois Society* (Cambridge, MA: MIT Press, 1989).

Hailbronner, Kay. "Citizenship and Nationhood in Germany," in William Rogers Brubaker, ed., *Immigration and the Politics of Citizenship in Europe and North America* (Lanham, MD: University Press of America, 1989), 67–80.

Hamberger, Judit. "A csehországi romák helyzete," *Regio*, 7:2 (1996): 57–80.

Hancock, Ian F. *The Pariah Syndrome: An Account of Gypsy Slavery and Persecution* (Ann Arbor, MI: Karoma, 1987).

" 'Uniqueness' of the Victims: Gypsies, Jews, and the Holocaust," *Without Prejudice*, 1:2 (1988): 45–67.

"The East European Roots of Romani Nationalism," in David Crowe and John Kolsti, eds., *The Gypsies of Eastern Europe* (Armonk, NY: M. E. Sharpe, 1991), 133–50.

Hannan, Michael T. "The Dynamics of Ethnic Boundaries in Modern States," in John W. Meyer and Michael T. Hannan, eds., *National Development and the World System: Educational, Economic, and Political Change, 1950–1970* (Chicago: University of Chicago Press, 1979), 253–75.

Harman, Lesley D. *The Modern Stranger: On Language and Membership* (Amsterdam: Mouton de Gruyter, 1988).

Havas, Gábor. "A cigány közösségek történeti típusairól," *Kultúra és közösség*, no. 4 (August 1989): 3–21.

Havas, Gábor, Gábor Kertesi, and István Kemény. "The Statistics of Deprivation: The Roma in Hungary," *The Hungarian Quarterly*, 36:138 (Summer 1995): 67–80.

Havas, Gábor, István Kemény, and Gábor Kertesi. "A relatív cigány a klasszifikációs küzdőtéren," *Kritika*, 27:3 (March 1998): 31–5.

Hechter, Michael. "Group Formation and the Cultural Division of Labor," *American Journal of Sociology*, 84:2 (September 1978): 293–318.

Hedetoft, Ulf, ed. *Political Symbols, Symbolic Politics: European Identities in Transformation* (Brookfield, VT: Ashgate, 1998).

Hegedüs, András T. "A cigány identitás változásának problémái," *Kultúra és közösség*, no. 4 (August 1989): 104–12.

Held, Joseph, ed. *Democracy and Right-Wing Politics in Eastern Europe in the 1990s* (Boulder: East European Monographs, 1993).

Herbst, Susan. *Politics at the Margin: Historical Studies of Public Expression Outside the Mainstream* (New York: Cambridge University Press, 1994).

Hobsbawm, E. J. *Nations and Nationalism Since 1780: Programme, Myth, Reality* (Cambridge: Cambridge University Press, 1982).

Hobsbawm, Eric, and Terence Ranger, eds., *The Invention of Tradition* (Cambridge: Cambridge University Press, 1983).

Hochschild, Jennifer L. "Equal Opportunity and the Estranged Poor," *Annals of the American Academy of Political Science*, 501 (January 1989): 143–55.

Hockenos, Paul. *Free To Hate: The Rise of the Right in Post-Communist Eastern Europe* (New York: Routledge, 1993).

Holmes, Stephen, and Cass Sunstein. *The Cost of Rights* (New York: Norton, 1998).

Homolač, Jiří. *A ta černa kronika!* (Brno: Doplnek, 1998).

Hooks, Bell. *Ain't I a Woman: Black Women and Feminism* (Boston: South End Press, 1981).

Horowitz, Donald L. "Three Dimensions of Ethnic Politics," *World Politics*, 23:2 (January 1971): 233–44.

   Ethnic Groups in Conflict (Berkeley: University of California Press, 1985).

Huber, Konrad. "The Roma: Group Identity, Political Activism, and Policy Response in Post-1989 Europe," *Helsinki Monitor: Quarterly on Security and Cooperation in Europe*, 4:3 (1993): 44–51.

Hübschmannová, Milena. "Economic Stratification and Interaction: Roma, an Ethnic Jati in East Slovakia," in Diane Tong, ed., *Gypsies: An Interdisciplinary Reader* (New York: Garland, 1998), 233–67.

Human Rights Project. "Report on the Implementation of the Framework Program for Equal Integration of Roma in Bulgarian Society" (Sofia: Human Rights Project, 2000), 7 pp.

Human Rights Watch. *Destroying Ethnic Identity: The Gypsies of Bulgaria* (New York: Human Rights Watch, 1991).

   Destroying Ethnic Identity: The Gypsies of Romania (New York: Human Rights Watch, 1991).

   Struggling for Ethnic Identity: Czechoslovakia's Endangered Gypsies (New York: Human Rights Watch, 1992).

Huntington, Samuel P. *Political Order in Changing Societies* (New Haven: Yale University Press, 1968).

Huttenbach, Henry. "The Romani Porajmos: The Nazi Genocide of Gypsies in Germany and Eastern Europe," in David Crowe and John Kolsti, eds. *The Gypsies of Eastern Europe* (Armonk, NY: M. E. Sharpe, 1991), 31–50.

Ionescu, Dan. "Migration from Romania," *Report on Eastern Europe*, Special issue (1 December 1989): 17–20.

"The Gypsies Organize," *Report on Eastern Europe*, 1:29 (26 June 1990): 39–44.

"Violence against Gypsies Escalates," *Report on Eastern Europe*, 2:25 (21 June 1991): 23–6.

Isaacs, Harold. *Idols of the Tribe: Group Identity and Political Change* (Cambridge, MA: Harvard University Press, 1989 [originally published in New York: Harper & Row, 1975]).

Ivanov, Ivan P. "Institutionalized Racism and Its Victims," *Ethno Reporter* (Sofia), no. 3 (September 1998): 30–4.

Ivanov, Mikhail, and Ilona Tomova. "Ethnic Groups and Inter-Ethnic Relations in Bulgaria," unpublished manuscript (Sofia, August 1993), 20 pp.

Jacquier, C. "Le développement social urbain," *Les Temps Modernes*, no. 545–6 (January 1992): 165–79.

Janos, Andrew C. *The Political Backwardness in Hungary, 1825–1945* (Princeton: Princeton University Press, 1982).

"The Politics of Backwardness in Continental Europe, 1780–1945," *World Politics*, 41:3 (April 1989): 325–59.

Jazouli, A. *Les années banlieues* (Paris: Seuil, 1992).

Jopson, N. B. "*Romano Lil (Tsiganske Novine)*," *Journal of the Gypsy Lore Society*, series 3, 15:2 (1936): 86–9.

József, Archduke, and Henrik Wlislocki. *A cigányokról* (Budapest: Pallas, 1895).

Juhász, László, ed. *Róm znamená človek* (Bratislava: Friedrich Ebert Stiftung, 1999).

Jurová, Anna. *Vývoj romskej problematiky na Slovensku po roku 1945* (Bratislava: Goldpress Publishers, 1993).

"Cigányok-romák Szlovákiában 1945 után," *Regio*, 7:2 (1996): 35–56.

Kalvoda, Josef. "The Gypsies of Czechoslovakia," in David Crowe and John Kolsti, eds., *The Gypsies of Eastern Europe* (Armonk, NY: M. E. Sharpe, 1991), 93–116.

Kaminski, Ignacy-Marek. *The State of Ambiguity: Studies of Gypsy Refugees* (Gothenburg: University of Gothenburg Press, 1980).

Kanev, Krassimir. "The Image of the 'Other' in the Relations of the Religious Communities in Bulgaria," in Antonina Zhelyazkova, ed. *Relations of Compatibility and Incompatibility between Christians and Muslims in Bulgaria* (Sofia: International Centre for Minority Studies and Intercultural Relations, 1995), 356–63.

"Dynamics of Inter-Ethnic Tensions in Bulgaria and the Balkans," *Balkan Forum*, 4:2 (June 1996): 213–52.

Kann, Robert A. *The Multinational Empire: Nationalism and National Reform in the Habsburg Monarchy, 1848–1918* (New York: Columbia University Press, 1950).

A History of the Habsburg Empire, 1526–1918 (Berkeley: University of California Press, 1974).

Kann, Robert A., and Zdenek V. David. *The Peoples of the Eastern Habsburg Lands, 1526–1918* (Seattle: University of Washington Press, 1984).

Kapralski, Slawomir. "The Roma and the Holocaust: Inventing Tradition as Identity Building Process," conference paper (University of Kent, April 1995).

"Identity Building and the Holocaust: Roma Political Nationalism," *Nationalities Papers*, 25:2 (1997): 269–83.

Karklins, Rasma. *Ethnopolitics and Transition to Democracy: The Collapse of the USSR and Latvia* (Baltimore: Johns Hopkins University Press, 1994).

"Ethnopolitics and Language Strategies in Latvia," paper presented at the 1997 Annual Meeting of the American Political Science Association (Washington, DC, 28–31 August 1997), 24 pp.

Karpat, Kemal. *An Inquiry into the Social Foundations of Nationalism in the Ottoman State* (Princeton, NJ: Research Monograph No. 39, Center for International Studies, Woodrow Wilson School, Princeton University, 1973).

Karsai, László. *A cigánykérdés Magyarországon, 1919–1945: Út a cigány Holocausthoz* (Budapest: Cserépfalvi, 1992).

Kasfir, Nelson. "Explaining Ethnic Political Participation," *World Politics*, 31:3 (April 1979): 365–88.

Kedourie, Elie. *Nationalism* (London: Hutchinson, 1961).

Kelso, Michelle. "Gypsy Deportations to Transnistria: Romania, 1942–1944," in Donald Kenrick, ed., *In the Shadow of the Swastika* (Hertfordshire: University of Hertfordshire Press, 1999), 95–129.

Kemény, István. "A magyarországi cigánylakosság," *Valóság*, 17:1 (January 1974): 63–72.

Beszámoló a magyarországi cigányok helyzetével foglalkozó 1971 – ben végzett kutatásról (Budapest: MTA Szociológiai Intézet, 1976).

Kemény, István, Gábor Havas, and Gábor Kertesi. *Beszámoló a magyarországi roma (cigány) népesség helyzetével foglalkozó 1993 októbere és 1994 februárja között végzett kutatásról* (Budapest: MTA Szociológiai Intézet, 1994).

Kenedi, János. "Why Is the Gypsy the Scapegoat and Not the Jew?" *East European Reporter*, 2:1 (1986): 11–14.

Kenrick, Donald. "Romanies in the Nazi Period," *Cigány Néprajzi Tanulmányok*, 2 (Budapest: Mikszáth Kiadó, 1994), 69–73.

"How Many Roads," *Index on Censorship*, 27:4 (July–August 1998): 55–63.

Kenrick, Donald, and Grattan Puxon. *The Destiny of Europe's Gypsies* (London: Chatto, 1972).

Kerékgyártó, István T. "Kisebbségi önkormányzatiság és a kultúrális autonómia," in *Tanulmányok a cigányság társadalmi helyzetének javítását célzó hosszú távú stratégia alapkérdéseiről* (Budapest: NEKH, 1999), 144–9.

Kereszty, Gábor, and György Simó. "Helping Self-Help: Interview with András Bíró," *The Hungarian Quarterly*, 36:140 (Winter 1995): 70–7.

Kertesi, Gábor. "Cigányok a munkaerőpiacon," *Közgazdasági Szemle*, 41:11 (1994): 991–1023.

"Cigány gyerekek az iskolában, cigány felnőttek a munkaerőpiacon," *Közgazdasági Szemle*, 42:1 (January 1995): 30–65.

Keyder, Caglar. "The Ottoman Empire," in Karen Barkey and Mark von Hagen, eds., *After Empire: Multiethnic Societies and Nation Building: The Soviet Union and Russian, Ottoman, and Habsburg Empires* (Boulder, CO: Westview Press, 1997), 30–44.

Kili, Suna. "The Jews in Turkey: A Question of National or International Identity," in Russell F. Farnen, ed., *Nationalism, Ethnicity, and Identity: Cross-National and Comparative Perspectives* (New Brunswick, NJ: Transaction Publishers, 1994), 299–317.

King, Robert R. *Minorities under Communism: Nationalities as a Source of Tension in Balkan Communist States* (Cambridge, MA: Harvard University Press, 1973).

Kitschelt, Herbert. "Political Opportunity Structures and Political Protest: Anti-Nuclear Movements in Four Democracies," *British Journal of Political Science*, 16:1 (January 1986): 57–85.

Kliot, N. "Mediterranean Potential for Ethnic Conflict: Some Generalizations," *Tijdschrift voor Econ. en Soc. Geografie*, 80:3 (1989): 147–63.

Klopčič, Vera and Janez Stergar, eds. *Ethnic Minorities in Slovenia* (Ljubljana: Institute for Ethnic Studies, 1994).

Kogon, Eugen. *The Theory and Practice of Hell: The German Concentration Camps and the System Behind Them* (New York: Farrar, Straus, & Co., 1949).

Kolev, Alexander. "Census Taking in a Bulgarian Gypsy Mahala," *Journal of the Gypsy Lore Society*, series 5, 4:1 (1994): 33–46.

Kolsti, John. "Albanian Gypsies: The Silent Survivors," in David Crowe and John Kolsti, eds., *The Gypsies of Eastern Europe* (Armonk, NY: M. E. Sharpe, 1991), 51–60.

Konrád, György, and Iván Szelényi. "Social Conflicts of Urbanization," in Michael Harloe, ed., *Captive Cities: Studies in the Political Economy of Cities and Regions* (London: John Wiley & Sons, 1977), 157–86.

Kostelancik, David J. "The Gypsies of Czechoslovakia: Political and Ideological Considerations in the Development of Policy," *Studies in Comparative Communism*, 22:4 (Winter 1989): 307–21.

Kozák, Istvánné. "A cigány lakosság beilleszkedése társadalmunkba," *Társadalmi Szemle*, 37:8–9 (August–September 1982): 62–70.

Krasteva, Anna. "Ethnocultural Panorama of Bulgaria," *Balkan Forum*, 3:3 (1995): 235–52.

Kriesi, Hanspeter, et al. *New Social Movements in Western Europe: A Comparative Perspective* (Minneapolis: University of Minnesota Press, 1995).

Kubik, Jan. *The Power of Symbols against the Symbols of Power: The Rise of Solidarity and the Fall of State Socialism in Poland* (University Park: Pennsylvania State University Press, 1994).

Kusý, Miroslav. "Human Rights," in Martin Bútora and Thomas W. Skladony, eds., *Slovakia 1996–1997: A Global Report on the State of Society* (Bratislava: Institute for Public Affairs, 1998), 35–45.

Kymlicka, Will. *Multicultural Citizenship* (New York: Oxford University Press, 1995).

Ladányi, János. "A lakásrendszer változásai és a cigány népesség térbeni elhelyezkedésének átalakulása Budapesten," *Valóság*, 32:8 (August 1989): 73–90.

"A miskolci gettóügy," *Valóság*, 34:4 (April 1991): 45–54.

"Patterns of Residential Segregation and the Gypsy Minority in Budapest," *International Journal of Urban and Regional Research*, 17:1 (March 1993): 30–41.

Ladányi, János, and Iván Szelényi. "Ki a cigány?" *Kritika*, 26:12 (December 1997): 3–6.

Latawski, Paul. ed. *Contemporary Nationalism in Eastern Europe* (New York: St. Martin's Press, 1995).

Latham, Judith. "Roma of the Former Yugoslavia," paper presented at the National Convention of the American Association for the Advancement of Slavic Studies (Seattle, 20 November 1997), 40 pp.

Lee, Jung Young. *Marginality: The Key to Multicultural Theology* (Minneapolis: Fortress Press, 1995).

Lemon, Alaina. "Roma (Gypsies) in the Soviet Union and the Moscow Teatr 'Romen'," *Nationalities Papers*, 19:3 (Winter 1991): 359–72.

Levendel, László. "A cigányság gondja – mindannyiunk gondja," *Valóság*, 31:12 (December 1988): 28–36.

Levine, David N. ed. *On Individuality and Social Forms* (Chicago: University of Chicago Press, 1971).

Lewy, Guenter. *The Nazi Persecution of the Gypsies* (New York: Oxford University Press, 2000).

Liebich, Andre. "Minorities in Eastern Europe: Obstacles to Reliable Count," *RFE/RL Research Report*, 1:20 (15 May 1992): 32–9.

"The Ethnic Mosaic," *Geopolitique*, 35 (August 1992): 37–40.

Liégeois, Jean-Pierre. *Roma, Gypsies, Travellers* (Strassbourg: Council of Europe Press, 1994).

Lijphart, Arend. "Multiethnic Democracy," in Seymour Martin Lipset et al., eds., *The Encyclopedia of Democracy* (Washington: Congressional Quarterly Press, 1995), 853–65.

Linz, Juan J. *Totalitarian and Authoritarian Regimes* (Boulder, CO: Lynne Rienner, 2000).

Linz, Juan J., and Alfred Stepan. *Problems of Democratic Transition and Consolidation: Southern Europe, South America, and Post-Communist Europe* (Baltimore: Johns Hopkins University Press, 1996).

Linz, Juan J., and Arturo Valenzuela, eds. *The Failure of Presidential Democracy: Comparative Perspectives* (Baltimore: Johns Hopkins University Press, 1994).

Lipsky, Michael. "Protest as Political Resource," *American Political Science Review*, 62:4 (December 1968): 1144–58.

Livizeanu, Irina. *Cultural Politics in Greater Romania: Regionalism, Nation Building, and Ethnic Struggle* (Ithaca, NY: Cornell University Press, 1995).

Lockwood, William G. Review of David Crowe and John Kolsti, eds. *The Gypsies of Eastern Europe* in *Contemporary Sociology*, 22:1 (January 1993): 49–50.

Lowenthal, David. *The Past is a Foreign Country* (New York: Cambridge University Press, 1985).

Lyons, Krista D. "Citizenship in New States: The Case of the Czech Republic," M.A. Report, Department of Government, University of Texas at Austin, 1995, 51 pp.

Macartney, C. A. *National States and National Minorities* (London: Oxford University Press, 1934).

Macfarlane, L. J. *Human Rights: Realities and Possibilities* (New York: St. Martin's Press, 1990).

Malcolm, Noel. *Bosnia: A Short History* (New York: New York University Press, 1994).

Mann, Arne B. "The Formation of the Ethnic Identity of the Romany in Slovakia," in Jana Plichtová, ed., *Minorities in Politics* (Bratislava: Czechoslovak Committee of the European Cultural Foundation, 1992), 261–5.

"Motivation: The Inevitable Condition of Successful Education of Romany Children," Training Course for Teachers, Council of Europe (Spišská Nová Veš, Slovakia, 14–17 September 1994).

"Rroma (Gypsies) in Municipalities," Council of Europe Hearing report (Košice, 9 December 1995).

ed. *Neznámi Rómovia: Zo života a kultúry Cigánov-Rómov na Slovensku* (Bratislava: Ister Science Press, 1992).

Martinello, Marco, and Marc Poncelet, eds. *Migrations et Minorités ethniques dans l'espace Européen* (Brussels: De Boeck-Wesmael, 1993).

Marushiakova, Elena, and Vesselin Popov. "Political Socialization of Gypsies in Bulgaria," presented at the "Ethnic Issues in Bulgaria" conference (Munich, 13 September 1992).

eds. *Studii Romani* (Sofia: Club '90 Publishers, 1994).

Gypsies (Roma) in Bulgaria (Frankfurt: Peter Lang Verlag, 1997).

"The Bulgarian Romanies During the Second World War," in Donald Kenrick, ed., *In the Shadow of the Swastika: The Gypsies During the Second World War* (Hertfordshire: University of Hertfordshire Press, 1999), 89–94.

Mastny, Vojtech. "Eastern Europe and the West in the Perspective of Time," in William E. Griffith, ed., *Central and Eastern Europe: The Opening Curtain?* (Boulder, CO: Westview Press, 1989), 12–36.

Matras, Yaron, ed. *Romani in Contact* (Amsterdam: John Benjamins, 1995).

Mayall, David. *Gypsy-Travellers in Nineteenth Century Society* (Cambridge: Cambridge University Press, 1988).

McAdam, Doug. *Political Process and the Development of Black Insurgency, 1930–1979* (Chicago: University of Chicago Press, 1982).

McAdam, Doug, John D. McCarthy, and Mayer N. Zald, eds. *Comparative Perspectives of Social Movements: Political Opportunities, Mobilizing Structures, and Cultural Framings* (New York: Cambridge University Press, 1996).

McCagg, William O. "Cigánypolitika Magyarországon és Csehszlovákiában, 1945–1989," *Világosság*, 32:7/8 (July–August 1991): 547–60.

McCaghy, Charles H., James K. Skipper, Jr., and Mark Lefton, eds. *In Their Own Behalf: Voices from the Margin* (New York: Meredith, 1974).

McCormick, Thomas. "Marginal Status and Marginal Personality," *Social Forces*, 34 (October 1977): 48–55.

McIntosh, James R. *Perspectives on Marginality* (Boston: Allyn & Bacon, 1974).

McIntosh, Mary E., Martha Abele MacIver, Daniel G. Abele, and David B. Nolle. "Minority Rights and Majority Rule: Ethnic Tolerance in Romania and Bulgaria," in Leokadia Drobizheva et al., eds., *Ethnic Conflict in the Post-Soviet World: Case Studies and Analysis* (Armonk, NY: M. E. Sharpe, 1996), 37–66.

McNeill, William H. *Polyethnicity and National Unity in World History* (Toronto: University of Toronto Press, 1986).

McQuaid, David. "The Growing Assertiveness of Minorities," *Report on Eastern Europe*, 2:50 (13 December 1991): 19–23.

Medrano, Juan Diez. "The Effects of Ethnic Segregation and Ethnic Competition on Political Mobilization in the Basque Country," *American Sociological Review*, 59:6 (December 1994): 873–89.

Mehr, Mariella. *Kinder der Landstrasse: Ein Hilfswerk, ein Theater, und die Folgen* (Bern: Zytglogge Verlag, 1987).

Mennell, Stephen. "The Formation of We-Images: A Process Theory," in Craig Calhoun, ed., *Social Theory and the Politics of Identity* (Cambridge: Blackwell, 1994), 175–97.

Mihailova, Dimitrina. "Socialization Problems of the Gypsy Child in the Bulgarian Society," in *The Ethnic Situation in Bulgaria* (Sofia: Club '90 Publishers, 1993), 27–31.

Mill, John Stewart. *Three Essays* (New York: Oxford University Press, 1975).

Miller, Marshall Lee. *Bulgaria during the Second World War* (Stanford, CA: Stanford University Press, 1975).

Ministry of Foreign Affairs. *The Situation of the Roma in the Republic of Macedonia* (Skopje: Ministry of Foreign Affairs, 1999).

Facts About the National Minorities in the Republic of Macedonia (Skopje: Ministry of Foreign Affairs, 1997).

Minogue, Kenneth, and Beryl Williams. "Ethnic Conflict in the Soviet Union: The Revenge of Particularism," in Alexander J. Motyl, ed., *Thinking Theoretically about Soviet Nationalities* (New York: Columbia University Press, 1992), 225–42.

Minority Rights Group – Slovakia. *Platná právna úprava v oblasti práva menšin v Slovenskej republike* (Bratislava: Minority Rights Group – Slovakia, 1999), 16 pp.

Mirga, Andrzej. "Roma Territorial Behaviour and State Policy: The Case of the Socialist Countries of East Europe," in Michael J. Casimir and Aparna Rao, eds., *Mobility and Territoriality: Social and Spatial Boundaries among Foragers, Fishers, Pastoralists, and Peripatetics* (Oxford: Berg, 1992), 259–78.

"The Effects of State Assimilation Policy on Polish Gypsies," *Journal of the Gypsy Lore Society*, series 5, 3:2 (1993): 69–76.

Mirga, Andrzej, and Nicolae Gheorghe. *The Roma in the Twenty-First Century: A Policy Paper* (Princeton: PER, 1997).

Mirga, Andrzej, and Lech Mróz. *Cyganie: Odmienności nietolerancja* (Warsaw: Wydawnictwo Naukowe PWN, 1994).

Moldova, György. *Szabadíts meg a gonosztól! Riport a börtönökröl* (Budapest: Pannon, 1990).

Molnár, Péter, and Szilvia Szegö. "Cigányok Magyarországon," *Társadalmi Szemle*, 50:6 (June 1995): 68–83.

Moore, Patrick. "The Minorities' Plight Amid Civil War," *Report on Eastern Europe*, 2:50 (13 December 1991): 30–6.

Moskos, Charles C., and John Sibley Butler. *All that We Can Be: Black Leadership and Racial Integration the Army Way* (New York: Basic Books, 1996).

Mostov, Julie. "Democracy and the Politics of National Identity," *Studies in East European Thought*, 46:1 (1994): 9–31.

Motyl, Alexander J. "From Imperial Decay to Imperial Collapse: The Fall of the Soviet Empire in Comparative Perspective," in Richard L. Rudolph and David F. Good, eds., *Nationalism and Empire: The Habsburg Monarchy and the Soviet Union* (New York: St. Martin's Press, 1992), 15–43.

Mróz, Lech. "The Cursed Nation: Daniłowicz's View of the Gypsies," a foreword to Ignacy Daniłowicz, ed., *O cyganach wiadomość historyczna* (Oświęcim: Biblioteczka Cyganologii Polskiej, 1993), xix–xxxi.

Mueller, John. "Minorities and the Democratic Image," *East European Politics and Societies*, 9:3 (Fall 1995): 513–22.

  Capitalism, Democracy, & Ralph's Pretty Good Grocery (Princeton, NJ: Princeton University Press, 1999).

Müller-Hill, Benno. *Murderous Science: Elimination by Scientific Methods of Jews, Gypsies, and Others – Germany 1933–1945* (Oxford: Oxford University Press, 1988).

Mutafchieva, Vera. "The Turk, the Jew, and the Gypsy," in Antonina Zhelyazkova, ed., *Relations of Compatibility and Incompatibility between Christians and Muslims in Bulgaria* (Sofia: International Centre for Minority Studies and Intercultural Relations, 1995), 5–63.

Nagi, Saad Z. "Ethnic Identification and Nationalist Movements," *Human Organization*, 51:4 (1992): 307–17.

Nagy-Talavera, Nicholas M. *The Green Shirts and the Others: A History of Fascism in Hungary and Rumania* (Stanford, CA: Hoover Institution Press, 1970).

Najcevska, Mirjana, and Natasha Gaber. *Survey Results and Legal Background Regarding Ethnic Issues in the Republic of Macedonia* (Skopje: Sts. Cyril and Methodius University, 1995).

Necas, Ctibor. "Osudy československých Cikanu za nemecke okupace a nadvlady," *Středny Evropa*, 7 (1992): 117–29.

Nemzeti és Etnikai Kisebbségi Hivatal. *A magyarországi cigányság helyzetének történeti áttekintése napjainkig* (Budapest: Nemzeti és Etnikai Kisebbségi Hivatal, Cigányügyi Föosztály, 1994).

Nettl, J. P. *Political Mobilization: A Sociological Analysis of Methods and Concepts* (New York: Basic Books, 1967).

Nielsen, Francois. "Toward a Theory of Ethnic Solidarity in Modern Societies," *American Sociological Review*, 50:2 (April 1985): 133–49.

Nolutshungu, Sam C. "International Security and Marginality," in Sam C. Nolutshungu, ed., *Margins of Insecurity: Minorities and International Security* (Rochester, NY: University of Rochester Press, 1996), 1–35.

Norton, Anne. *Reflections on Political Identity* (Baltimore: Johns Hopkins University Press, 1988).

Okeley, Judith. *The Traveller Gypsy* (Cambridge: Cambridge University Press, 1983).

Oláh, Sándor. "Szimbólikus elhatárolódás egy település cigány lakói között," in *Egy más mellett élés: A magyar-román, magyar-cigány kapcsolatokról* (Csikszereda: Pro-Print, 1996), 207–24.

Olszewski, B. *Obraz Polski dzisiejszej: Fakty, cyfry, i tablice* (Warsaw: Orbis, 1938).

Olzak, Susan. "Contemporary Ethnic Mobilization," *Annual Review of Sociology*, 9 (1983): 355–74.

Ondrušek, Dušan. "Scenare optimisticke a pesimisticke," in László Juhász, ed., *Rom známena človek: Diskusia v Cilistove o palcivom probléme* (Bratislava: Friedrich Ebert Stiftung, 1999), 19–21.

Oprescu, Dan. "Public Policies on National Minorities in Romania (1996–1998)," *Sfera Politica*, no. 6 (January 1999): 13–18.

Orgovánová, Klára. "The Roma in Slovakia," *The East & Central Europe Program Bulletin* (New School for Social Research), 4:4 (May 1994): 1, 3, 6.

Ortakovski, Vladimir. "The Posititon of the Minorities in the Balkans," *Balkan Forum*, 5:1 (March 1997): 109–47.

Osztojkán, Béla. *Megkérdezem Önt is* (Budapest: Phralipe, 1994).

Pape, Markus. *Nikdo vam nebude verit: Dokument o koncentracim tabore Lety u Pišku* (Prague: G + G, 1997).

Park, Robert E. "Human Migration and the Marginal Man," *American Journal of Sociology*, 33:6 (May 1928): 881–93.

Race and Culture (Glencoe, IL: The Free Press, 1950).

Pavkovic, Aleksandar, Halyna Koscharsky, and Adam Czarnota, eds. *Nationalism and Postcommunism* (Brookfield, VT: Dartmouth, 1995).

Pearson, Raymond. *National Minorities in Eastern Europe, 1848–1945* (London: Macmillan, 1983).

Pellar, Ruben. " 'Sterilization with Grant' of Gypsies in Czechoslovakia," unpublished manuscript (Prague, 28 August 1991), 9 pp.

Perlman, J. *The Myth of Marginality* (Berkeley: University of California Press, 1979).

Pickvance, C. G. "Where Have Urban Movements Gone?" in Costis Hadjimichalis and David Sadler, eds., *Europe at the Margins: New Mosaics of Inequality* (Chichester, England: John Wiley & Sons, Ltd., 1995), 197–218.

Pipes, Richard. *The Formation of the Soviet Union: Communism and Nationalism, 1917–1923* (Cambridge: Harvard University Press, 1964).

Plichtová, Jana, ed. *Minorities in Politics* (Bratislava: Czechoslovak Committee of the European Cultural Foundation, 1992).

Pomogyi, László. *Cigánykérdés és cigányügyi igazgatás a polgári Magyarországon* (Budapest: Osiris-Századvég, 1995).

Popov, Vesselin. "Gypsy Nomads in Bulgaria: Traditions and Contemporary Dimension," unpublished manuscript, 1994.

Postma, Koos. *Changing Prejudice in Hungary: A Study on the Collapse of State Socialism and Its Impact on Prejudice Against Gypsies and Jews* (Groningen: Rijksuniversiteit, 1996).

Poulton, Hugh. *The Balkans: Minorities and States in Conflict* (London: Minority Rights Group, 1993, 2nd edition).

"The Roma in Macedonia: A Balkan Success Story?" *RFE/RL Research Report*, 2:19 (7 May 1993): 42–5.

"The Rest of the Balkans," in Hugh Miall, ed., *Minority Rights in Europe: Prospects for a Transnational Regime* (New York: Council of Foreign Relations Press, 1994), 66–86.

Who Are the Macedonians? (London: Hurst & Co., 1995).

Project on Ethnic Relations. *The Romanies in Central and Eastern Europe: Illusions and Reality* (Princeton: PER, 1992).

Countering Anti-Roma Violence in Eastern Europe: The Snagov Conference and Related Efforts (Princeton: PER, 1994).

Second Slovakia Roundtable (Princeton: PER, 1996).

The Media and the Roma in Contemporary Europe (Princeton: PER, 1996).

The Roma in Bulgaria: Collaborative Efforts between Local Authorities and Nongovernmental Organizations (Princeton: PER, 1998).

Roundtable Discussion of Government Policies on the Roma in Romania (Princeton: PER, 1999).

Political Participation and the Roma in Hungary and Slovakia (Princeton: PER, 1999).

State Policies Toward Romani Communities in Candidate Countries to the EU: Government and Romani Participation in Policy-Making (Princeton: PER, 1999).

Pugliese, Enrico. "New International Migrations and the 'European Fortress'," in Costis Hadjimichalis and David Sadler, eds., *Europe at the Margins: New Mosaics of Inequality* (Chichester, England: John Wiley & Sons, Ltd., 1995), 51–68.

Putnam, Robert D. *Making Democracy Work: Civic Traditions in Modern Italy* (Princeton: Princeton University Press, 1993).

Puxon, Grattan. *Rom: Europe's Gypsies* (London: Report #14 of Minority Rights Group, 1973).

Pye, Lucian W. *Politics, Personality, and Nation Building: Burma's Search for Identity* (New Haven: Yale University Press, 1962).

Quigley, Kevin F. "For Democracy's Sake: How Foundations Fail – and Succeed," *World Policy Journal*, 13:1 (Spring 1996): 109–18.

Radio Free Europe. "Gypsies in Eastern Europe and the Soviet Union," *Radio Free Europe Research*, RAD Background Report no. 72 (12 April 1978), 7 pp.

Radó, Péter. *A kisebbségi oktatás fejlesztése* (Budapest: MKM, 1995).

Ragin, Charles C. "Ethnic Political Mobilization: The Welsh Case," *American Sociological Review*, 44:4 (August 1979): 619–35.

Ramaga, Philip Vuciri. "Relativity of the Minority Concept," *Human Rights Quarterly*, 14:3 (August 1992): 409–28.

Reemtsma, Katrin. "Report on the Fact-Finding Mission on the Situation of the Roma in Bosnia," Report for the European Working Group for Roma in and Refugees from Bosnia (Berlin: Süd-Ost-Europa Kulturzentrum, 1996).

"Report on the Fact-Finding Mission on the Situation of the Roma in Bosnia," *CPRSI (Contact Point for Roma and Sinti Issues) Newsletter*, 2:6 (December 1996): 7–9.

Remmel, Franz. *Die Roma Rumäniens: Volk ohne Hinterland* (Vienna: Picus, 1993).

Remnick, Ronald A. *Theory of Ethnicity* (Lanham, MD: University Press of America, 1983).

Research Directorate. "Roma in the Czech Republic: Selected Issues," Immigration and Refugee Board, Canada (Ottawa, December 1997), 23 pp. and appendices.

"Czech Republic: Update on Issues Affecting Roma," Immigration and Refugee Board, Canada (Ottawa, 20 August 1998), 31 pp.

"Hungary: Update on Issues Affecting Roma," Immigration and Refugee Board, Canada (Ottawa, 21 August 1998), 12 pp. and attachments.

"Roma in Hungary: Views of Several Specialists," Immigration and Refugee Board, Canada (Ottawa, February 1999), 32 pp.

Reuter, Lutz R. "Ethnic-Cultural Minorities in Germany," in Russell F. Farnen, ed., *Nationalism, Ethnicity, and Identity: Cross National and Comparative Perspectives* (New Brunswick, NJ: Transaction, 1994), 207–76.

Rex, John. "Ethnic Mobilisation in Multi-Cultural Societies," in John Rex and Beatrice Drury, eds., *Ethnic Mobilization in a Multicultural Europe* (Aldershot, England: Avebury, 1994), 3–12.

Rinser, Luise. *Wer wirft den Stein? Zigeuner sein in Deutschland* (Stuttgart: Weitbrecht, 1985).

Ritter, Carol, and Sondra Myers, eds. *The Courage to Care: Rescuers of Jews During the Holocaust* (New York: New York University Press, 1986).

Roberts, Henry L. *Rumania: Political Problems of an Agrarian State* (New Haven: Yale University Press, 1951).

n.a. *Romové v České republice* (Prague: Socioklub, 1999).

Rostás-Farkas, György, and Ervin Karsai. *Ősi cigány mesterségek és foglalkozások* (Budapest: OMIKK, 1991).

Rothschild, Joseph. *East-Central Europe Between the Two Wars* (Seattle: University of Washington Press, 1974).

Ethnopolitics: A Conceptual Framework (New York: Columbia University Press, 1981).

Return to Diversity: A Political History of East Central Europe Since World War II (New York: Oxford University Press, 1989).

Rubin, Barnett R., and Steven L. Burg. "Recommendations," in Barnett R. Rubin, ed., *Toward Comprehensive Peace in Southeast Europe: Conflict Pre-*

vention in the South Balkans (New York: The Twentieth Century Fund Press, 1996), 11–24.

Safran, William. "The French State and Ethnic Minority Cultures: Policy Dimensions and Problems," in Joseph J. Rudolph, Jr., and Robert J. Thompson, eds., *Ethnoterritorial Politics, Policy, and the Western World* (Boulder, CO: Lynne Rienner, 1989), 115–58.

Schafft, Kai A., and David L. Brown. "Social Capital and Grassroots Development: The Case of Roma Self-Governance in Hungary," *Social Problems*, 47:2 (2000): 201–19.

Schafft, Kai, and Tibor Farkas. "Észrevételek a cigány kisebbségi önkormányzatok működéséről," *A falu*, 14 (Spring 1999): 77–82.

Schlott, Wolfgang. "Die nationalen Minderheiten und ihre Grenzlandkulturen in Polen nach 1989," Forschungsstelle Osteuropa an der Universität Bremen, July 1994, 6 pp.

Schmuelevitz, A. *The Jews of the Ottoman Empire in the Late Fifteenth and Sixteenth Centuries* (Leiden, Netherlands: Brill, 1984).

Schneider, Hartmut. ed. *Microfinance for the Poor?* (Paris: OECD, 1997).

Schöpflin, George. "The Political Traditions of Eastern Europe," *Daedalus*, 119:1 (Winter 1990): 55–90.

"Nationalism and National Minorities in East and Central Europe," *Journal of International Affairs*, 45:1 (Summer 1991): 51–65.

Schwartz, Herman. *The Struggle for Constitutional Justice in Post-Communist Europe* (Chicago: University of Chicago Press, 2000).

Schwarz, John E., and Thomas J. Volgy. *The Forgotten Americans* (New York: W. W. Norton, 1992).

Šedivý, Vladimír, and Viktor Maroši. *Position of National Minorities and Ethnic Groups in the Slovak Republic* (Bratislava: Minority Rights Group, 1996).

Seewann, Gerhard. "Zigeuner in Ungarn," *Südost-Europa*, 36:1 (January 1987): 19–32.

Seton-Watson, Hugh. *Eastern Europe Between the Wars* (Hamden, CT: Archon Books, 1962).

Shafir, Michael. "Government Encourages Vigilante Violence in Bucharest," *Report on Eastern Europe*, 1:27 (6 July 1990): 32–8.

Shain, Yossi. *The Frontier of Loyalty: Political Exiles in the Age of the Nation State* (Middletown, CT: Wesleyan University Press, 1989).

Shashi, S. S. *Roma: The Gypsy World* (Delhi: Sundeep Prakashan, 1990).

Sheffer, Gabriel. "Ethno-National Diasporas and Security," *Survival*, 36:1 (Spring 1994): 60–79.

Shields, R. *Places on the Margin: Alternative Geographies of Modernity* (London: Routledge, 1991).

Shugart, Matthew Soberg, and John Carey. *Presidents and Assemblies* (Cambridge: Cambridge University Press, 1992).

Sibley, David. *Outsiders in Urban Societies* (Oxford: Blackwell, 1981).

Geographies of Exclusion: Society and Difference in the West (London: Routledge, 1995).

Šiklová, Jiřina, and Marta Miklušáková. "Denying Citizenship to the Czech Roma," *East European Constitutional Review*, 7:2 (1998): 58–64.

Silverman, Carol. "Negotiating 'Gypsiness': Strategy in Context," *Journal of American Folklore*, 101:401 (July–September 1988): 261–75.
    "Persecution and Politicization: Roma (Gypsies) of Eastern Europe," *Cultural Survival Quarterly*, 19:2 (Summer 1995): 43–8.
Simmel, Georg. *Soziologie: Untersuchen über die Formen der Vergesellschaftung* (Berlin: Duncker and Humbolt, 1908).
    "The Stranger," in David N. Levine, ed., *On Individuality and Social Forms* (Chicago: University of Chicago Press, 1971), 143–9.
Simon, Robert L. "Pluralism and Equality: The Status of Minority Values in a Democracy," in John W. Chapman and Alan Wertheimer, eds., *Majorities and Minorities* (New York: New York University Press, 1990), 207–25.
Šišková, Tatjana. "Report on 'Education towards Tolerance and against Racism' project in Prague Schools," Czech Center for Conflict Prevention and Resolution (Prague) February 1998, 17 pp.
Siu, Paul C. P. "The Sojourner," *American Journal of Sociology*, 58:1 (1952): 34–44.
Skilling, H. Gordon. *Charter 77 and Human Rights in Czechoslovakia* (London: Allen & Unwin, 1981).
Slezkine, Yuri. "The USSR as a Communal Apartment, or How a Socialist State Promoted Ethnic Particularism," *Slavic Review*, 53:2 (Summer 1994): 414–52.
Smith, Anthony D. *National Identity* (Reno: University of Nevada Press, 1991).
    Theories of Nationalism (New York: Harper & Row, 1971).
Smith, Anya Peterson. *Ethnic Identity: Strategies of Diversity* (Bloomington: Indiana University Press, 1982).
Smith, Tom W. "What Do Americans Think About Jews?" Working Papers on Contemporary Anti-Semitism (American Jewish Committee, 1991).
Srb, Vladimír. "Některé demografické, ekonomické a kulturní charakteristiky cikánského obyvatelstva v ČSSR 1980," *Demografie*, 26:2 (1984): 161–72.
    "Koncentráce a urbanizáce Cykánu v Československu," *Česky Lid*, 73:2 (1986): 82–92.
    "Zmeny v reprodukci československých Romu, 1970–1980," *Demografie*, 30:7 (1988): 305–8.
Stalin, I. V. *Marksizm i natsional'nyi vopros* (Moscow: Politizdat, 1950).
Stankovic, Slobodan. "Gypsies to Get Their Own Television Program," *Radio Free Europe Research*, Yugoslav Situation Report No. 2 (11 February 1986): 18–21.
Statistical Office of Macedonia. *Basic Statistical Data for the Republic of Macedonia* (Skopje: Statistical Office of Macedonia, 1992).
    Basic Statistical Data for the Republic of Macedonia (Skopje: Statistical Office of Macedonia, 1998).
Stepan, Alfred, and Cindy Skach. "Constitutional Frameworks and Democratic Consolidation: Parliamentarism versus Presidentialism," *World Politics*, 46:1 (October 1993): 1–22.
Stewart, Michael. "Játék a lovakkal avagy a cigány keresekedők és a szerencse," *Kultúra és közösség*, no. 4 (August 1989): 21–40.

"Gypsies, Work and Civil Society," *Journal of Communist Studies*, 6:2 (June 1990): 140–62.

The Time of the Gypsies (Boulder, CO: Westview, 1997).

Stonequist, Everett V. *The Marginal Man: A Study in Personality and Culture Conflict* (New York: Charles Scribner's Sons, 1937).

Sugar, Peter F. *Southeastern Europe under Ottoman Rule, 1354–1804* (Seattle: University of Washington Press, 1977).

Sus, Jaroslav. *Cikánská otázka v ČSSR* (Prague: SNPL, 1963).

Szilágyi, Imre. "A romák Szlovéniában," *Regio*, 7:2 (1996): 81–95.

"A horvátországi romák helyzete," *Regio*, 7:3 (1996): 69–80.

Szuhay, Péter. "Arson on Gypsy Row," *The Hungarian Quarterly*, 36:138 (Winter 1995): 81–91.

"A cigány bandáról," *Amaro Drom*, 5:2 (February 1995): 18–20.

Szuhay, Péter, and Antónia Baráti, eds. *Pictures of the History of Gypsies in Hungary in the 20th Century* (Budapest: Néprajzi Múzeum, 1993).

Tabajdi, Csaba. *Látlelet a magyarországi cigányság helyzetéről* (Budapest: Miniszterelnöki Hivatal, 1996).

Az önazonosság labirintusa: A magyar kül- és kisebbségpolitika rendszerváltása (Budapest: CP Stúdió, 1998).

Tamás, Ervin, and Tamás Révész. *Búcsú a cigányteleptől* (Budapest: Kossuth, 1977).

Tamás, G. M. "Victory Defeated?" *Journal of Democracy*, 10:1 (January 1999): 63–8.

Tarrow, Sidney. *Power in Movement: Social Movements, Collective Action, and Politics* (New York: Cambridge University Press, 1994).

"Social Movements and Contentious Politics: A Review Article," *American Political Science Review*, 90:4 (December 1996): 874–83.

Thomson, S. Harrison. *Czechoslovakia in European History* (Princeton: Princeton University Press, 1943).

Thornberry, Patrick. *International Law and the Rights of Minorities* (Oxford: Oxford University Press, 1991).

Tilly, Charles. *From Mobilization to Revolution* (New York: Random House, 1978).

"How Empires End," in Karen Barkey and Mark von Hagen, eds., *After Empire: Multiethnic Societies and Nation Building: The Soviet Union and Russian, Ottoman, and Habsburg Empires* (Boulder, CO: Westview Press, 1997), 1–11.

Timmer, Doug A., and D. Stanley Eitzen. "The Root Causes of Urban Homelessness in the United States," *Humanity and Society*, 16:2 (May 1992): 159–75.

Timmer, Doug A., D. Stanley Eitzen, and Kathryn D. Talley. *Paths to Homelessness: Extreme Poverty and the Urban Housing Crisis* (Boulder, CO: Westview Press, 1994).

Todorova, Maria. *Imagining the Balkans* (New York: Oxford University Press, 1997).

Tomašević, Nebojša Bato, and Rajko Djurić. *Gypsies of the World: A Journey Into the Hidden World of Gypsy Life and Culture* (New York: Henry Holt & Co., 1988).

Tomova, Ilona. *The Gypsies in the Transition Period* (Sofia: International Centre for Minority Studies and Intercultural Relations, 1995).
"Változások és gondok a bolgár cigányközösségben," *Regio*, 7:3 (1996): 53–68.
Tong, Diane, ed. *Gypsies: A Multidisciplinary Annotated Bibliography* (New York: Garland, 1995).
Túróczi, Károly. "A cigányság társadalmi beilleszkedéséröl," *Valóság*, 5:6 (June 1962): 72–81.
Ulč, Otto. "Gypsies in Czechoslovakia: A Case of Unfinished Integration," *Eastern European Politics and Societies*, 2:2 (Spring 1988): 306–32.
"Integration of the Gypsies in Czechoslovakia," *Ethnic Groups*, 9:2 (1991): 107–17.
US Census Bureau. "Poverty in the United States: 1991," *Current Population Reports*, Series P-60, No. 181 (Washington, DC: US Government Printing Office, 1992).
US Congress. *Human Rights Abuses of the Roma (Gypsies)*, Hearing before the Subcommittee on International Security, International Organizations and Human Rights of the Committee of Foreign Affairs, House of Representatives (103rd Congress, Second Session, 14 April 1994) (Washington, DC: US Government Printing Office, 1994).
Vaculík, Ludvík. "Two Thousand Words to Workers, Farmers, Scientists, Artists, and Everyone" (Prague, 27 June 1968) reprinted in Gale Stokes, ed., *From Stalinism to Pluralism: A Documentary History of Eastern Europe Since 1945* (New York: Oxford University Press, 1991), 126–30.
Vašečka, Michal. "The Romanies in Slovakia," in Luboš Vagač, ed., *National Human Development Report for Slovakia 1998* (Bratislava: United Nations Development Program, 1998), 63–75.
"Roma and the 1998 Parliamentary Elections," in Martin Bútora et al., eds., *The 1998 Parliamentary Elections and Democratic Rebirth in Slovakia* (Bratislava: Institute for Public Affairs), 255–63.
"The Roma," in Gregoríj Mešeznikov, Michal Ivantyšyn, and Tom Nicholson, eds., *Slovakia 1998–1999: A Global Report on the State of Society* (Bratislava: Institute of Public Affairs, 1999), 395–415.
Vekerdi, József. *A magyarországi cigány kutatások története* (Debrecen: Kossuth Lajos Tudományegyetem, 1982).
Verdery, Katherine. "Nationalism and National Sentiment in Post-socialist Romania," *Slavic Review*, 52:2 (Summer 1993): 179–203.
Vincze, Sándor. "A cigány gyermekek nevelése, oktatása Jász-Nagykun-Szolnok megyében," *Magyar Közigazgatási Szemle*, no. 7 (June 1993): 419–26.
Vohryžek, Jozef. "O postaveni cikánu-romu v Československu," *Charta 77, 1977–1989: Od moralni k demokratické revoluci* (Bratislava: Archa, 1990), 217–25.
Vossen, Rüdiger. *Zigeuner* (Frankfurt am Main: Ullstein, 1983).
Vyšatová, Romana. "Romani Politics in the Czech Republic and Slovakia," unpublished manuscript, 1994.
Wallman, Sandra. "Introduction: The Scope of Ethnicity," in Sandra Wallman, ed., *Ethnicity at Work* (London: Macmillan, 1979), 1–16.

Waters, Timothy William, and Rachel Guglielmo. "'Two Souls to Struggle with ...' The Failing Implementation of Hungary's New Minorities Law and Discrimination Against the Gypsies," in John S. Micgiel, ed., *State and Nation Building in East Central Europe* (New York: Institute on East Central Europe, Columbia University, 1996), 177–97.

Weber, Max. *Economy and Society: An Outline of Interpretive Sociology* (Berkeley: University of California Press, 1978).

Weiner, Myron. "Peoples and States in a New Ethnic Order?" *Third World Quarterly*, 13:2 (1992): 317–33.

Weyrauch, Walter Otto, and Maureen Anne Bell. "Autonomous Lawmaking: The Case of the Gypsies," *The Yale Law Journal*, 103:2 (November 1993): 323–99.

Willems, Wim. *In Search of the True Gypsy: From Enlightenment to Final Solution* (London: Frank Cass, 1997).

Wilson, William Julius. *When Work Disappears: The World of the New Urban Poor* (New York: Knopf, 1996).

Winkler, Peter. "Roma Ethnic Group in Slovenia," in Miran Komac, ed., *Protection of Ethnic Communities in the Republic of Slovenia* (Ljubljana: Institute for Ethnic Studies, 1999), 71–5.

Wolchik, Sharon L. *Czechoslovakia in Transition: Politics, Economics, & Society* (London: Pinter, 1991).

Wolff, H. Kurt, ed. *The Sociology of Georg Simmel* (Glencoe, IL: The Free Press, 1950).

Wrench, John, and John Solomos, eds. *Racism and Migration in Western Europe* (Oxford: Berg, 1993).

Yunus, Muhammad. *Banker to the Poor: Micro-Lending and the Battle Against World Poverty* (New York: Public Affairs Press, 1999).

Zamfir, Cătălin, Marius Augustin Pop, and Elena Zamfir. *Romania '89–'93: Dynamics of Welfare and Social Protection* (Bucharest: UNICEF – Romania, 1994).

Zamfir, Elena. *The Situation of Child and Family in Romania* (Bucharest: Romanian Government 1995).

Zamfir, Elena, and Cătălin Zamfir. *The Romany Population* (Bucharest: Centre of Economic Information ad Documentation, 1993).

Ţigani: Între ignorare şi îngrijorare (Bucharest: Editura Alternative, 1993).

Zaslavsky, Victor. "The Soviet Union," in Karen Barkey and Mark von Hagen, eds., *After Empire: Multiethnic Societies and Nation Building: The Soviet Union and Russian, Ottoman, and Habsburg Empires* (Boulder, CO: Westview Press, 1997), 73–96.

Zimmerman, William. *Open Borders, Nonalignment, and the Political Evolution of Yugoslavia* (Princeton: Princeton University Press, 1987).

Zimmermann, Michael. *Verfolgt, vertrieben, vernichtet: die nationalsozialistische Vernichtungspolitik gegen Sinti und Roma* (Essen: Klartext, 1989).

Zolberg, Aristide. "The Next Waves: Migration Theory for a Changing World," *International Migration Review*, 23 (1989): 403–30.

Žugel, Jasna. "Integracija romske skupnosti v slovensko družbo," in *Romi na Slovenskem* (Ljubljana: Institute of Ethnic Studies, 1991), 113–21.

Zülch, Tilman, ed. *In Auschwitz vergast, bis heute verfolgt: Zur Situation der Roma (Zigener) in Deutschland und Europa* (Hamburg: Rowohlt, 1979).

Zywert, Josefat. "Problemy mlodźeźy cyganskiek w szkole podstawowej," *Kwartalnik Pedagogiczny*, 1 (1968): 103–9.

Index